Business Research Methods
A practical approach

Sheila Cameron and Deborah Price

The Chartered Institute of Personnel and Development is the leading publisher of books and reports for personnel and training professionals, students, and all those concerned with the effective management and development of people at work. For details of all our titles, please contact the publishing department:

tel: 020-8612 6204
e-mail: publish@cipd.co.uk
The catalogue of all CIPD titles can be viewed on the CIPD website:
www.cipd.co.uk/bookstore

Business Research Methods
A practical approach

Sheila Cameron and Deborah Price

Chartered Institute of Personnel and Development.

Published by the Chartered Institute of Personnel and Development,
151, The Broadway, London, SW19 1JQ

This edition first published 2009

Typeset by Fakenham Photosetting Ltd, Norfolk
Printed in Spain

British Library Cataloguing in Publication Data
A catalogue of this publication is available from the British Library

ISBN 978 1 84398 228 9

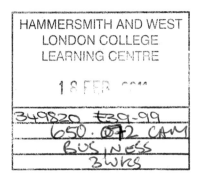

Chartered Institute of Personnel and Development, CIPD House,
151, The Broadway, London, SW19 1JQ

Tel: 020 8612 6200

E-mail: cipd@cipd.co.uk

Website: www.cipd.co.uk

Incorporated by Royal Charter.

Registered Charity No. 1079797

Contents

List of Figures and Tables

Acknowledgements

We should like to thank The Open University, both for giving us the space to write this book, and for the opportunity it has given us to work with, and learn from, many managers while they were researching issues of importance to themselves and their organisations. Thanks are also due to the many other universities with which we have been associated, whether as lecturers or as external examiners.

Especial thanks are due to those who have allowed us to draw on their experiences, in particular to Chris Rigby, Director of Ducamus, a consultancy specialising in Leadership Development and Change Management' for his generosity in sharing his own research story and for the many stimulating 'collaborative reflection' sessions we have shared during the production of this book. But also to the many students who remain anonymous, yet have shared their journey with us.

Sheila would like to thank Peter, James and Hester for their different but invaluable contributions to statistics and diagramming. Deborah would like to thank Colin, Andrew and Fiona, for not complaining too much about my not being there.

Glossary

Abduction A process of deriving explanatory hypotheses from data useful when there is no existing theory to draw upon.

Abstract A short piece of text at the beginning of a longer narrative (project report, academic paper or book) which succinctly outlines what is contained in the remainder of the piece.

Action Research The term originally coined by Lewin in 1946 for a process of 'learning by doing' – an approach in which the researcher is actively involved with participants seeking to make some sort of change, facilitating learning through cycles of action and **reflection**, and **dialogue** to develop shared meanings. The aim is to use **theory** to improve **practice** while developing theory further.

Action-oriented research Any research intended to inform and/or lead to action.

Analysis The process by which complex or multi-faceted issues, data or information is broken down into smaller aspects to obtain a better understanding.

Analysis of variance A statistical technique for determining whether mean differences exist between two or more samples.

ANOVA See **analysis of variance**.

Appendices Adjuncts to a proposal, report or dissertation which provide additional information or evidence to support arguments made in the main text.

Appendix The singular of appendices.

Applied research Research in which the aim is primarily to address issues of concern to practitioners.

Appreciative inquiry An approach to organisational change based upon exploring the positive aspects in a situation, looking for root causes of success rather than failure.

Argument A **claim**, together with a description of the **evidence** and its connection to the claim, that may convince the reader that the claim is justified.

Argument map A diagram showing **claim**, any sub-claims, **evidence** and links which together constitute your **argument**.

Arithmetic mean The arithmetical average of a set of observations – ie the total of all the observations divided by the number of observations. See also **median** and **mode** as other measures of **central tendency**.

Bar-chart A diagram showing **frequency distributions** as bars of different lengths.

Bias A tendency for results to come out one way rather than another, often because of conscious or unconscious influence by the researcher who, like everyone, is subject to **confirmatory bias**. See also **sampling bias**.

Bibliographical details The referencing information associated with a particular source of information.

Bibliography A list of everything you have read that has informed your research, thus a longer list than specific **references**, normally provided at the end of a proposal or dissertation, and typically using the **Harvard style**.

Boolean logic A system through which specific words or 'operators' are used to help to narrow or broaden a literature search.

Box plot A way of representing the distribution of a set of data, in which a box represents the middle 50% of values, and 'whiskers' show the wider range.

Brainstorming A technique in which a group or an individual generates a large number of ideas by noting as many of them as possible within a limited time-frame. The list of ideas is generated spontaneously from memory, insight, knowledge or intuition about the subject.

Case study An approach to research which uses multiple methods, gathers data from multiple levels or from multiple organisations. It is used where it is not possible to disaggregate the subject of the research from the organisation in which it is embedded.

Categorical data Data in which the 'values' represent categories rather than actual measures.

Category question A closed question from which the respondent selects one of a limited number of mutually exclusive categories.

Causal mapping A method of diagramming which enables the researcher to graphically represent the causal relationship between a number of **variables**, attributes or factors.

Causal relationship A relationship between one variable and another such that a change in one creates a change in the other.

Cause-and-effect diagram See **Ishikawa diagram**.

Census A 100% sample.

Central limit theorem A mathematical theorem stating that for a sample size of 30 or more, the distribution of all sample means of the same size will approximate to a **normal distribution** with the same mean as the **population** from which they are drawn.

Central tendency i) The propensity for respondents, when completing an odd-numbered **Likert scale**, to opt for the middle category. This requires minimal thought by the respondent and is usually the one which requires minimal commitment to a definite answer. ii) The 'middle' value of a set of sample values (see **arithmetic mean**).

Chi-squared test A popular non-**parametric statistical test** that can be used to test the significance of differences or associations between **variables**.

Claim Something you assert to be true – the end point of an **argument**.

Client The person who is hiring you for your professional expertise (or allowing you access to resources in order to do a research project as a student); someone who is a key **stakeholder** in any research you carry out for them, who may have power over the resources you will need and may have a strong vested interest in your findings. Building a good relationship with your client is an important research/consultancy skill.

Closed question A question that offers respondents a choice between a clearly defined and limited range of potential answers.

Cluster sampling also known as multi-stage An approach to sampling that involves more than one variable at a time – say, locations then individuals – and that allows for a relatively **representative** sample with less inconvenience than purely **random** sampling.

Code, coding A system by which a set of signifiers is selected to indicate meaning or frequency and enable the researcher to recognise themes emerging from a narrative or piece of text.

Code of ethics A set of rules that guide what is and what is not appropriate within the practice or research. Such a code normally also articulates the processes that the researcher has to go through in order to obtain ethical approval for the research.

Coding manual A journal or file in which the collected set of codes are stored so that they can be referred to as and when necessary.

Cognitive mapping A technique for representing cognitive structures/surfacing **tacit theory** and/or analysing **qualitative data**.

Collaborative reflection A process of reflection with others who have a shared interest in an issue and the thinking about it.

Compiled data Data that has been gathered and analysed or manipulated previously.

Concept A relatively abstract idea that has potentially practical meaning, such as 'hidden agenda' or 'marketing mix'.

Conclusion A position you reach on the basis of reliable evidence and sound argument that you have made explicit earlier on. If it lacks such underpinning, it is merely an opinion, which is unlikely to impress your client or your examiners. Your conclusion represents the sense you have made of your investigation and may form the basis for **recommendations**.

Confirmatory bias The tendency to be more sensitive to perceiving things that are consistent with your existing beliefs than those that challenge them.

Consent See **informed consent**.

Constructionism See **social constructionism**.

Content analysis A means of data analysis which codes narrative to enable the researcher to derive meaning from the key themes in the text.

Control group In an experimental design, a group selected as comparable to the group to which an experimental treatment is to be applied: any differences between groups post-treatment could be reasonably assumed to be attributable to the effects of the treatment.

Convenience sampling The non-random sampling of a group chosen for no reason other than that they are easy to contact. This may have value in very early stages when you are testing items or looking for ideas, but it is not recommended otherwise because it does not make for drawing trustworthy **conclusions**.

Conversation analysis A means of analysing narrative text which attempts to recognise the meaning, the structure and the sequences used in communicative language.

Correlation The degree of association between two sets of measures. There are different statistical techniques for calculating this, primarily **Pearson's rho** (or the **correlation coefficient**) and **Spearman's** rank correlation. If two things are correlated, even significantly, this does not mean that one necessarily *causes* the other. The reverse might be true, or both might be at least partly caused by some third factor you have not looked at.

Correlation coefficient A number between 0 and 1 representing the degree of **correlation** between two **variables**.

Covering letter A written front piece of text which introduces potential respondents to the focus of the research and outlines what the researcher would like them to do.

Credibility An important quality of **conclusions** and researcher, derived from the expertise and professionalism with which the research is approached and carried out, and in the case of conclusions, the competence with which they are presented. Credibility is linked to **trustworthiness**.

Critical evaluation Not being 'critical' in the everyday sense of fault-finding, but rather a process of carefully judging the value of something – thus if you were critically evaluating a research paper, you would look at the method used to collect evidence and therefore the likely validity of that evidence, the robustness of the logic used to argue from the evidence to conclusions, and both the 'added value' of those conclusions and their relevance to your own particular context and concerns.

Critical incident An event or occurrence that is of significance to the person or people involved.

Critical incident method A research method that requires the researcher to gather data pertaining to critical incidents.

Critical literature review A literature review which draws on both the strengths and limitations of the pieces considered.

Critical realism Realism with an emphasis on the role of power relations within the context of what is 'known'.

Data 'Facts': data is only useful if it provides **information** and/or can be used as **evidence**.

Deception The purposeful or accidental misleading of people with regard to the nature, the requirements or the consequences of research.

Deductive approach An approach to research in which **hypotheses** are deduced from **theory** and then **data** collected in order to test these hypotheses.

Deliberate distortion The purposeful manipulation of **data** such as to produce the results that the researcher 'requires' rather than those that are naturally forthcoming.

Delphi technique A technique for drawing upon a range of views normally from experts: these views are collated, circulated and then the experts express their views again. This often, though not always, results in a convergence of views.

Deontological view A view of **ethics** that asserts that some things are in absolute terms right or wrong, rather than justified in terms of their consequences.

Dependant variable A **variable** which changes as a result of changes to another variable.

Descriptive statistics A general term for techniques for summarising and presenting numerical data thus making them more easily understandable.

Diagnosis An incredibly important stage in any investigation, seeking underlying causes for the issue or problem which is of interest. It is a stage frequently ignored or given scant attention. Many issues in organisations are presented in terms that assume a particular set of causes for a problem. But causality is often improperly understood, particularly with **wicked problems** and **messes**. If action is taken in this case, it may make things worse rather than better.

Diagrams Representations of situations, systems or sequences (or part thereof) that rely on graphical elements as well as words. See **causal mapping**, **cognitive mapping**, **Ishikawa** (or fishbone) **diagram**, **multiple-cause diagram**, **relationship diagram**, **rich pictures**.

Dialogue A conversation intended to explore interpretations and assumptions and develop shared meanings. This conversation might be with oneself, or more productively with one or more other people.

Diary See **research diary**.

Discourse A somewhat archaic term for talking or holding forth on a topic, appropriated by sociologists to mean a sub-language which serves to unite a particular group of people and form barriers between them and the rest of humanity. Thus the language of academia is a 'discourse' with specific rules that preclude non-initiates from participating. Try reading 'serious' academic journals for first-hand experience of this.

Discourse analysis A technique that uses linguistic elements (especially those that represent links or that indicate connections or sequence) to analyse narrative or spoken text.

Discrete data Data in which values are discrete categories (eg the number of events) rather than continuously variable (eg heights).

Discussion A textual exploration of a particular focus. This might be of the literature, of a theory, of a method or of research findings.

Dispersion measure Any statistic (eg standard deviation) which provides an indication of the extent to which values in a sample are distributed around the 'centre'.

Dissertation A substantial piece of research used (usually finally) as a means of assessment for academic programmes of study.

Electronic interview The term used for an **interview** carried out by means of a series of e-mail exchanges.

Electronic questionnaire A **questionnaire** designed to be completed and distributed electronically. Often, limited versions (up to 15 questions) are available to download and use free of charge from the Internet – for example, Survey Monkey.

E-mail interview See **electronic interview**.

Empirical work The stages in the research process when the research gathers the necessary data from the people or the organisation.

Enquiry See **inquiry**.

Epistemology A word derived from the ancient Greek *epistēmē* 'embedded (information)', 'knowledge', and *logos* 'word', 'thought', 'study', thus together 'the study of knowledge' – the whole set of beliefs about what constitutes 'knowing' and how it impacts on finding things out. This sounds really sophisticated – and to a philosopher it is. But it is important to bring common sense to bear on issues of meaningfulness, and if 'epistemology' distracts you from this, stick with the common sense!

Ethics Strictly, the field of 'moral science' or a particular set of moral principles. In a research context, acting ethically means taking care to do no harm to the client or other participants in the project, acting openly and honestly in your dealings with them, observing confidentiality, and reporting your results accurately, without selectivity or bias, and fulfilling any commitments made such as making results available to those who asked for them. Most universities will require research proposals to have the approval of an ethics committee, because student (or academic) research done without taking ethical principles into account can damage the university's reputation. (Similarly, consultants are normally concerned to preserve their reputations by acting ethically, and most professional institutions have ethical codes.)

Evaluation A process through which the researcher considers the strengths and the limitations of an issue before drawing their own well-reasoned **conclusion**.

Evaluation research Research aimed at deriving a balanced assessment of a situation or of the impact of an initiative.

Evidence 'Information tending to establish fact' – thus information that can be used as a basis for **arguments** and **conclusions**. But see the complications under **post-modern**. Much of management 'evidence' is slippery and capable of multiple interpretations. The way you go about finding it may influence what you find, hence the concern with **methodology**.

Experiment A means of carrying out research in which a controlled change is made to a **variable** for an **experimental group**, with all other potential variables kept constant, and the effect observed. This effect is then assumed to be the result of the change. The experiment is often designed to test a **hypothesis**.

Experimental group The sample upon which an experiment is carried out – often contrasted with a **control group**.

Explanatory study Research carried out with the aim of explaining a situation of interest, either in terms of relationships between observed **variables** or in terms of the sense that participants make of the situation.

Exploratory study Research carried out to find out more about a situation of interest, perhaps as a basis for diagnosis and/or design of a subsequent **explanatory study**.

External researcher A researcher who does not ordinarily belong to the area in which the research takes place.

Face validity The appearance of validity in data because of the 'obviously relevant' nature of a question or measurement scale.

Facilitator A group member/leader with the role of helping the group to maintain a productive discussion without in any way himself or herself influencing the views expressed.

Factor analysis An approach which analyses the complex interactions between a large number of **variables**, seeking to find clusters of variables which are more highly inter-correlated. These clusters are the 'factors', and each variable in the cluster's contribution to that factor, or loading, is calculated.

Field notes Documented observations of the researcher recorded at the time of the interaction.

Filter question A question on a **questionnaire** which enables the researcher or the respondent to decide whether or not they continue with the questionnaire.

Fishbone diagram See **Ishikawa diagram**.

Fixed research design An approach to research in which everything is specified before data collection commences. It is associated with a **positivist** and **deductive**, **hypothesis**-testing approach, **quantitative** data and **statistical analysis**.

Flexible research design An approach to research that develops as information is collected. It is associated with a **constructionist** approach and **qualitative** data. See, for example, **Action Research, Grounded Theory**.

Focus groups Groups of people gathered to discuss an issue of common concern. The researcher will act as **facilitator** for the discussion, and record it in some way for later analysis. Such groups are useful in the early stages of research, when trying to clarify the nature of the issue and formulate a research question. A focus group is considered by some to be a group **interview**.

Forced-choice question A questions that offers respondents a limited range of possible choices.

Frequency distribution The distribution of the number of times each value or class of values occurs within a sample.

Functionalist paradigm A frame of reference that draws on objectivity and regulation and that upholds **positivist** traditions.

Gantt chart A process map that (for example) helps timetable research activities.

Gatekeeper A stakeholder who can permit or deny access to data, to information or to other stakeholders.

Generalisation A process of making **claims** about a wider category based upon findings from a single case or a smaller set of findings or sub-category.

Generalisability The extent to which **generalisation** is justified.

Grounded Theory A term often used loosely (and incorrectly) to indicate reliance on **interview** records with little recourse to **theory**. Although the joint originators (Glazer and Strauss) went on to develop their own differing definitions, the term is more correctly applied to a complex, rigorous and iterative approach to categorising elements in text (often, indeed, interview transcripts) with a view to deriving – without preconceptions – relevant concepts out of which theory may be constructed. Despite being widely claimed by students as their chosen 'methodology', we have yet to see a dissertation for which the claim is justified.

Group interview An interview process through which questions are directed to group members in turn for them to respond to as an individual in a group setting.

Harvard style An approach to referencing that in text references cites author and date of publication, whereas the full reference, listed alphabetically – author, date, title of article, *title of journal or book* in which it appears, Volume number, Issue number, location, publisher – is presented at the end of the report or dissertation.

Histogram A (normally vertical) bar chart in which the bars represent mutually exclusive categories into which observations can be placed. The height of the (normally adjacent) bars shows the frequency of observations falling into each category.

Hypothesis From a **positivist** perspective, a clear statement of an implication of a **theory**, which can be tested by means of research, normally expressed in terms as an 'alternative' hypothesis and a null hypothesis. The null hypothesis states that the implication is *not* apparent in the data collected. From a **pragmatist** perspective a hypothesis is a trial **concept**, being tested for its usefulness.

Idealism A school of thought which believes that abstractions (such as 'tree', 'quad') exist only in the mind. See also **social constructionism**.

Independent groups *t*-test See *t*-test.

Independent variable A **variable** that is deliberately being altered in order to see the effect of this alteration upon another, **dependant variable**.

In-depth interview An **interview** in which the respondent's views and opinions are explored at length and in detail.

Index number (plural, indices): small numbers to the right of something, and aligned with the top of the text, representing the power of a number, eg in X^2, the index number 2 indicates X to the power 2, ie X squared.

Indicator Something that gives an indication of something you are interested in because it is associated with it (eg days' absence and 'absenteeism') but which is susceptible to other influences and so less reliable than a **measure**.

Inductive reasoning A process of deriving **theory** from observations.

Inference, statistical See **statistical inference**.

Inferential statistics A branch of mathematics directed towards allowing you to decide how likely it is that observed relationships in your data are due to chance, or to estimate from a sample with a range within which there is a specified probability that a population value will lie.

Information Hard data (or something softer) which reduces your uncertainty about an issue or a question that concerns you.

Informed consent The prior agreement of a person or people to participate in research premised on a complete and accurate understanding of the implications in doing so.

Inquiry (also enquiry) A term used by pragmatists, constructionists and others to indicate flexible research with an emphasis on learning or finding out, rather than testing. Dewey used the term 'productive inquiry' for an inquiry prompted by a problem, concern or insight, generating solutions and/or new ideas. See also **appreciative inquiry**.

Integer A 'whole' number – ie not a fraction.

Internal researcher A researcher who is part of the organisation in which the research is undertaken.

Internet forum An online discussion group.

Interpretative paradigm A set of (**post-modern**) assumptions about reality and how to research it which are based upon a belief in a subjective reality that is created out of our language, itself developed in a social context. This paradigm is opposed to **logical positivism's** belief in an objective and unambiguous reality, and suggests very different approaches to research in organisations (eg **Action Research**).

Interpretivism One of the schools of thought that believes in a 'reality' constructed by an individual.

Inter-quartile range The distance between the first and third **quartile** of a set of data ordered according to size.

Interval data Data in which the intervals between numbers are equal so subtraction is a valid operation.

Interview A structured conversation intended to elicit useful information: a popular approach in student projects, but it requires a high level of skill in order to generate information of any value – students often pay too little attention to the basics of good interviewing practice.

Introduction The first substantial section of a project report, which takes the reader briefly through the whole research project.

Introductory letter A **covering letter** which introduces the researcher and the nature of the research to potential respondents or **gatekeepers**.

Investigate 'To examine or enquire into' – hence 'investigation', a term preferred to 'research' for many management projects, because it is closer to the purpose of the exercise, and has less academic baggage, although the definition of research above is actually more demanding, and closer to what is required in **dissertation** modules.

Ishikawa diagram also known as a fishbone or cause-and-effect diagram A form of graphic representation frequently used in quality-oriented research to identify possible causes of faults or errors. The main 'bones' show types of fault, and the smaller bones the different possible causes of each type.

Iteration (iterative) Moving forwards by going round in circles – a spiral of progress: you need to find out what you don't know before you can start to find it out. This is a key term in systems thinking, where trying to make sense of a messy situation proceeds by a slow process of trying to describe the situation in systems terms, realising that there are questions you cannot answer, trying to find parts of an answer, reframing the question, etc.

Journal See **research journal**.
Judgemental sampling See **non-probability sampling**.

Kolmogorov-Smirnov test A statistical test for determining whether an obtained distribution differs significantly from a **normal distribution**. (If it does, non-parametric tests will be needed.)

Level of significance See **statistical significance**.
Likert scale A closed-response scale

created by the US educational psychologist Rensis Likert that is usually measured on a scale of 1 to 5 or 1 to 7. The scale enables people to rate the extent to which they agree or disagree with a particular statement.

Linear regression A process of producing a **regression** line which fits a set of **data** allowing further points to be predicted.

Linear relationship A relationship between two variables that when plotted as a graph one against the other, results in a straight line.

Literature review A process of looking critically at what others have already written about topics relevant to that in which you are interested, discarding that which is of little value and/or relevance, and selecting from the remainder information, ideas and approaches to benefit your investigation.

Logical positivism The widespread set of ideas about research and how to do it, based on the belief that there is a 'reality' which an impartial observer can find out about by collecting **data** that can be objectively verified by other observers. It relies heavily upon **quantitative** measures and statistical techniques. The antithesis of **post-modernism**, **constructionism** and **Action Research**.

Longitudinal research Focused research that is carried out over time, either continuously or intermittently.

Looping See **messy looping**.

Lower quartile The value in a sample ordered by size which has 25% of values smaller than it, and 75% of values larger.

Management report A report produced specifically for managers of an organisation that usually follows a particular structure, and has clear headings and subheadings. These may be numbered, or in some organisations, paragraphs may be numbered in addition or instead.

Mean See **arithmetic mean**.

Measure A quantifiable or dimensional aspect of the thing measured (eg temperature in relation to heat), generally with reference to continuous variables rather than discrete ones such as counts. Contrasted with **indicator**.

Measurement validity The extent to which a **measure** indicates what it purports to measure.

Median When a set of values are ordered according to size, the median occurs in the middle – ie half the observations are smaller, half larger.

Mess Term used by Ackoff to describe a system of problems which because of their interrelatedness are not suited to an analytical solution-focused approach.

Messy looping A research process in which increasing understanding makes clear the need for back-tracking and redirection in order best to achieve the research process. (See also **spiral (learning)** and **iteration**.)

Methodology Strictly, this term means 'the study of, or knowledge about, methods', but it is often used in academic papers and dissertations as the heading for the section which describes and justifies the chosen research approach. In the academic sense an understanding of methodology is crucial – if you do not understand the strengths and weaknesses of possible research approaches, you are unlikely to choose an appropriate one, nor indeed to appreciate the way in which your chosen method will influence the information you collect, and should influence your conclusions. These issues will be clearly addressed in a good report

Mixed methods approach A research strategy through which different means of data-gathering for analysis are used.

Mixed methods research See **mixed methods approach**.

Mode In a set of observations or values, the mode is the most frequently-occurring value.

Moderator An alternative term for **facilitator**, used particularly in online discussions.

Mono method research An approach in which a single method of data-gathering and analysis is used as the basis for the researcher.

Multiple-cause diagram A visual way of exploring factors contributing to a particular event, and then moving back to explore the factors causing the causes, and so on. It is useful as a diagnostic tool to help identify factors that contribute to the issue being explored.

Multivariate analysis of variance A **hypothesis**-testing procedure used to determine whether differences exist between two or more samples.

Negative correlation An association or **correlation** between two variables in which larger values of one correspond with smaller values of the other.

Negative skew A distribution in which the majority of the data is to the right of the distribution.

Netiquette A system of common conventions used in electronic communications.

Nominal data Data in which numbers are used as nothing more than labels for categories, so mathematical operations cannot be carried out with them.

Non-parametric statistical test A test that can be used with data which do not meet the requirements for a **parametric test**.

Non-probability sample A sample in which the probability of each case being selected for the sample is not known.

Non-random sampling Sampling in which all the members of a **population** do not have an equal probability of being sampled.

Non-response rate The proportion of those who could have been interviewed or have completed questionnaires but who have 'chosen' not to participate.

Normal curve Bell-shaped curve showing distributions of a value in a

population, used as the foundation for many tests of statistical significance. It is defined by two parameters: its **mean** and its **standard deviation**.

Normal distribution The commonly-found distribution of values within a **population** giving rise to the **normal curve**.

Null hypothesis See **hypothesis**.

Objectivity The ability to understand things in a factual, rational and detached way.

Observation Gathering data and information through watching and interacting with people rather than posing direct scheduled questions.

Observer bias The tendency for observers to see what they intend to see or interpret what they see in ways that favour their objectives.

Observer effect , also known as the Hawthorne effectThe idea that people behave differently simply because they are being observed. As a consequence, the behaviours observed are not typical.

Official statistics Data and information produced by governments or official bodies.

One-way analysis of variance An **analysis of variance** in which there is only one **independent variable**.

Ontology An area of philosophy closely related to **epistemology**, but concerned with *being* rather than *knowing*.

Open question A question worded to allow respondents to determine how they wish to respond.

Operational definition A definition of a **concept** in terms of things that can be observed and/or measured.

Optical mark reader An electronic system which scans and reads response marks on a questionnaire and produces statistical analyses and visual representations of them (perhaps in the form of bar-charts or scatterplots).

Ordinal data Numerical data in which the numbers indicate size order, but nothing more.

Outlier An extreme value in a set of data.

Paired *t*-test A statistical test for difference between samples used when each member of one sample is associated with one member of the other sample.

Paradigm A mindset or a frame of reference that guides the ways in which people think, and the knowledge they have and can acquire.

Parametric statistic A statistical technique used with equal-interval or ratio data which are normally or near-normally distributed, variance in each group is equivalent, and samples are randomly drawn.

Parametric statistical test A test that can be used with large samples of **interval** or **ratio data** which can be assumed to be drawn from a **normal distribution**. Contrasted with **non-parametric test**.

Participant An individual who contributes to the research, usually by providing data or information.

Participant observation A process through which the researcher becomes part of the researched group and gathers data from the interactions which take place.

Pearson's *rho* Pearson's product moment correlation coefficient is a **parametric statistic** indicating the degree of **correlation** between two **variables**.

Peer review The process by which academic journals seek second opinions on papers before publishing them. It is not a total guarantee that what is published is good and/or error-free because the chosen 'expert reviewers' are themselves fallible/biased/driven by their own set of assumptions, but it serves as a useful filter. Journals that use this process can therefore be referred to with reasonable confidence.

Phenomenalism The belief that we can only know that which we can directly observe.

Phenomenology An approach to research which tries to create or produce objective knowledge.

Philosophical preferences Your own set of beliefs about the nature of reality and of knowledge. (See mainly **epistemology, social constructionism, positivism, realism, pragmatism**.)

Pie chart Circular diagram showing proportions of different categories within a whole as different-sized 'slices' of the pie.

Pilot test A small-scale preview of an interview/questionnaire to check feasibility, logistics and suitability.

Population The entire body of people, things or instances from whom a researcher may select a sample.

Positive correlation A **correlation** between two **variables** such that larger values in one correspond with larger values in the other.

Positivist Someone who has adopted the perspective of **logical positivism**.

Postal questionnaire A **questionnaire** delivered to the respondents in hard copy via the post.

Post-modern Describing the view that nothing is as it appears, and nothing can be 'known' in any general sense. This view is derived (by some impossibly learned French thinkers) from the maddening but horribly compelling idea that we are social animals living in a world that is constructed out of what we choose to notice and how we choose to think about it (and, to complicate matters further, that that choice is usually unconscious). Thus my world is not your world. And the whole 'scientific' endeavour for which I was trained is doomed to failure.

Power (of a statistical test) The probability that the test will reject a false null **hypothesis** (will not make a **Type II error**). As power increases, this probability (denoted by β) decreases. The power may thus be represented by $1 - \beta$.

PowerPoint A software package specifically designed for making presentations.

Practical business research Any systematic attempt at collecting and interpreting data and evidence in order to inform thinking, decisions and/or actions in relation to an issue of interest to an organisation or its stakeholders.

Practice What practitioners undertake: 'skilled activity leading to desired outcomes'. The word can also have other meanings – eg practice as a 'unit of sociological inquiry', something that is not simply what individuals do but the result of the interaction between this and the social context in which they do it. Ideas of 'best practice' are problematic in the light of the need to choose what is best for a particular context, and of current discussions of practice as the product of 'actor and context' rather than the actor alone.

Practitioner research Research carried out by those working in an organisation on topics relevant to their own professional practice.

Practitioner-researcher A researcher carrying out research into an organisation or practice, while working ('practising') his or her normal role within it.

Pragmatism A school of thought which states that meaning lies in the consequences of an idea, and that knowledge and action cannot be divorced one from the other.

Praxis A term used by Aristotle to describe the process of acting on conditions in order to change them (contrasted with theoria, the activities associated with knowing for its own sake). The term is now used to describe the iterative process of knowledge informing practice which in its turn informs knowledge – see **Action Research**.

Premise An assumption which when supported by evidence leads to a conclusion.

Primary data Data that you have

specifically collected or arranged to have collected (contrasted with **secondary data**).

Probability sampling Any sampling technique in which each member of the **population** sampled has a specific probability of being selected for the sample.

Probing question A question aimed at eliciting a person's views or opinions on a specific issue.

Professional journal A journal produced by a professional body for members of that specific body.

Project report A written report that presents the substance of a business research project to the relevant stakeholders.

Purposive sampling Any (non-**probability sampling**) sampling technique in which the sample is selected according to the judgement of the researcher.

QSR NVivo A software package that is useful in the analysis of narrative or textual content.

Qualitative Describing data in non-numerical form, whether cited in existing text or generated in interviews or via questionnaires. Such data tends to be richer than **quantitative** data, and enables a researcher to address 'real' issues not suited to quantitative measures, but presents challenges in terms of analysis and drawing trustworthy and credible conclusions. As with 'quantitative', the term is also used for methods for collecting and anlysing such data.

Quantitative Describing data in the form of numbers (or other comparable unit quantities). By extension, a 'quantitive method' means a method for generating or analysing such data, but many methods can generate both quantitative and **qualitative** data. Quantitive data has the advantage of looking impressive and credible and above all, comparable – but may mislead the unwary, for a good deal of interesting information is not suited to capture in numerical form.

Quartile A value that divides one quarter of a set of values from the next or other quarters according to size. The first quartile is the value that has ¼ of the values smaller than it, and the third quartile is the value which has ¾ of the values smaller than it.

Questionnaire A set of questions used to elicit useful information, and that can be used as the basis for a face-to-face or phone **interview**, or distributed electronically or in paper form for independent completion. It is a very popular approach, but its value depends upon the questionnaire being very carefully designed. A poorly designed questionnaire may have a very low response rate and/or generate 'information' that is irrelevant or impossible to interpret.

Quota sampling A **non-probability sampling** approach in which the intention is to represent the population by choosing specified 'quotas' to represent different characteristics of the population.

Radical humanist paradigm A sociological position which implies that people are complicit in using power to confine themselves to a subordinate position within an organisation.

Random probability sample A sample of a **population** in which each member has an equal chance of being sampled. Statistical tests/estimates may assume this form of sampling.

Randomised control group An experimental design in which subjects are allocated to either an experimental or a control group by chance, and then the same observations/measures made of both. Because the 'treatment' is applied only to the experimental group, any statistically significant differences between the measures for the two groups are assumed to be attributable to the 'treatment'.

Range (of a set of data) The difference between the largest and the smallest value. (See also **inter-quartile range**.)

Ranking question A question that requires the respondent to rate the relative importance of a range of issues.

Rating question A question that requires the respondent to rate the importance of an issue.

Ratio data Data on which the scale has equal intervals and a known zero so that you can multiply and divide data as well as add and subtract.

Raw data Data which has not been subject to manipulation or analysis.

Realism Originally a school of thought which believed that an objective reality existed and could be known about. Nowadays, a less extreme form of realism holds that there is an external reality, but not all of it can be objectively observed/measured. See also **critical realism**.

Recommendations A set of specific suggestions for action, which should flow sequentially from your conclusions.

Refereed academic journal An academic journal which requires that all publications be **peer reviewed** before publication is permitted.

References Sources that have informed your thinking and that you specifically mention (refer to) in something you write. These are normally listed at the end of your report. The **Harvard style** or convention of presentation is frequently adopted in academic writing.

Reflective writing Textual presentation required by many universities of dissertation students who must 'reflect' in writing on their research experience. This sort of writing at its best demonstrates a high level of thinking and writing skills. The process can aid learning throughout a professional career. See also **reflection**.

Reflection A process of thinking about what has happened or what you have done, and seeking to understand and evaluate it, drawing upon feedback, other people's thoughts and concepts to aid this evaluation. The goal is to learn from the process – reflection is seen by many as crucial to improving practice and a key component in **Action Research**. Simple reflection considers the extent to which action produced the desired results and the learning from this that might improve results next time. More sophisticated reflection considers how assumptions and unconscious theories have contributed to actions, and challenges the validity of these in the light of experience. This level of reflection is best carried out with others.

Regression analysis A technique for estimating further values from a **data** set: simple **linear regression** produces a line which best fits the data, which is then used to predict new values of y for values of x for which data does not exist.

Regression coefficient An indication of how well a **regression equation** fits the **data** – ie how much of the variation in the **dependant variable** can be attributed to variation in the **independent variable**.

Regression equation The equation that generates a **regression line** for a set of data, and/or is used to predict the value of the **dependant variable** from the value of the **independent variable**.

Regression line The line calculated to provide the best fit to a set of data points for which there is reason to believe a degree of linear correlation exists. It can be used to predict additional data points.

Relationship diagram A simple method of representing elements in a problem situation (using words) and the key relationships between them (in the form of connecting lines).

Relevance (of data) The extent to which the data helps you answer your research question.

Reliability (of data) The statistical likelihood that repeating the data-collection exercise will produce similar, if not identical, results.

Replication, replicability The ability to repeat a research process and produce results consistent with those produced previously.

Representative In relation to data, or more normally, to a sample, the extent to which it is typical of some larger group about which you wish to learn.

Research A systematic process of seeking information and interpreting it with the hope of advancing knowledge (but see **post-modernism** for the possible futility of this exercise) and/or improving **practice**.

Research design The overall plan for the research, showing what will be done and/or observed, in order to answer the overall research question or achieve the research purpose. It should specify whether the research is to be of a **fixed research design** or a **flexible research design**, follow **inductive reasoning** or a **deductive approach**, and/or will be heavily influenced by **philosophical preferences**.

Research ethics A code of practice that determines what is and what is not acceptable research practice.

Research ethics committee An approvals committee, usually mandated by an academic institution or organisation, which has the authority to approve or reject proposals for research based on the ethical implications of that research.

Research idea The initial basic thoughts and interests of the research which can be built, through engagement with the literature, into a **research purpose** or question.

Research journal A document within which you log all activity, information and thought related to your research.

Research method A technique for collecting **data**.

Research objective An objective that is to be achieved by means of research. The implication is that the research will result in either the revelation of new, useful information, the answer to a **research question**, or the affirmation of what was hitherto a mere **hypothesis**.

Research population The entire body of potential respondents (or items or instances) from which the researcher may draw a sample.

Research proposal A clear statement of what you intend to achieve and why, and how you intend to achieve it. Your proposal should detail resources needed (including any access to information) and time-scales. Your proposal allows your supervisor and your client to check that they are happy with what you intend to do (and to discuss and resolve any unhappiness), and the finally agreed proposal acts as a useful reference point against which you can repeatedly check your progress. Should your client subsequently change his/her mind, the agreed proposal may be useful in ensuring that you are given the facilities you need to complete the research.

Research purpose The over-arching aim of a research project, usually achieved by means of several more specific **research objectives** or **research questions**.

Research question(s) A statement of the question that your investigation is designed to address. The question acts to define and frame your research and should be as clearly defined as possible, given the nature of your concern. Research directed towards a less specific 'finding out' is hard to design and control – and to be avoided in a student project. The question may be a higher-level question equivalent to a **research purpose**, or one of a series of lower-level questions equivalent to a **research objective**.

Research strategy The proactive and planned approach to research.

Respondent An individual who divulges information in order to assist the research process – who 'responds'.

Response rate Especially for a **questionnaire**, the proportion of those requested to respond who actually did so.

Review article An article that presents a synopsis of a range of articles available with wider information in the area/field.

Rich picture A cartoon-like representation of factors possibly relevant to a situation or issue, 'invented' by Checkland (1981) as part of soft systems methodology. They are a useful way for a group to start working together to explore a complex issue.

Sample The people (or other data source) you have selected to investigate instead of seeking information on everyone/thing you are interested in. *Sampling* is usually a practical necessity, but the value of any conclusions about the wider population will depend on the representativeness of your sample of the wider **population** from which it is drawn. A stratified sample, selected according to a **sampling frame**, can help you to increase this representativeness. See also **convenience sampling**, **snowball sampling** and **random probability sample**.

Sampling bias A tendency to favour the selection of certain sample elements over others, leading to a sample that is not representative of the **population**.

Sampling error The difference between the (unknown) **population** value that you are estimating and the (known) **sample** statistic that you are using as the basis for your estimate.

Sampling fraction The proportion of the total **population** selected for a **sample**.

Sampling frame A complete list of all members of the **population** from which a **sample** is to be drawn.

Scatter graph A way of representing observations by placing a dot on a graph to represent the *x* and *y* values for each observation. Also known as a *scatterplot*.

Scientific research A term used to describe research (often from a **positivist** perspective) which proceeds by means of systematic experiment and/or observation and analysis.

Search engine A device which searches the World-Wide Web for data, for information and for other available sources of data and information.

Search string The set of words used to guide the search engine towards the data and information required.

Secondary data Data collected for purposes other than and incidental to your research.

Secondary sources Sources of data and information that are useful in your research but that have been gathered either by other people or for other purposes, or both.

Self-administered questionnaire A **questionnaire** that the respondent completes on his or her own without interactive recourse to the researcher.

Self-completion questionnaire See **self-administered questionnaire**.

Semi-structured interview A term frequently misapplied to a vague conversation. A semi-structured interview is one for which you have a clear framework of issues which you want your interviewee to address, but in which you allow some freedom as to how he or she addresses them. The advantage over a fully structured interview is that you might have designed your questions according to your own preconceptions, and would therefore 'discover' pretty much what you already thought. The disadvantages are that 'steering' a semi-structured interview requires a high level of skill, and analysing results can be a significant challenge.

Sensitive personal data Data that individuals may be reluctant to disclose for personal reasons.

Simple random sample Sample in which each member of the **population** being sampled has an equal chance of being included in the sample.

Skewness The degree of asymmetry in a distribution.

Snowball sampling A non-random

approach to deriving a **sample** by which initial respondents suggest others. It may be valuable in a **qualitative** approach where it is hard to identify relevant informants, but it is of limited value otherwise.

Social constructionism A school of thought which believes that 'reality' is constructed by individuals in a social setting.

Sociology A longstanding academic discipline (elsewhere defined as 'the science of the development and nature and laws of human society') that has given rise to an amazing vocabulary including 'post-modernism', and that has had a significant impact on how research on and in organisations is conducted.

Spearman's rho (ρ) a non-parametric statistic indicating the degree of **correlation** between two **variables**.

Spiral (learning) The idea – originally by Bruner – that learning proceeds in a circular fashion, as learning something about a topic enables you to learn more about it at a subsequent turn of the spiral. A curriculum should therefore revisit topics throughout the learning experience, rather than dealing with them sequentially and once only.

SPSS Statistical Package for the Social Sciences, widely-used software for statistical analysis.

Stakeholder Anyone with an interest in and/or influence on your project, including your client, your tutor and yourself. It is important to think carefully about who *their* stakeholders are, what they want from your project, what they do not want, and the extent to which they can help and hinder you. Managing your relationship with key stakeholders is an important part of doing successful management research.

Standard deviation An indication of the variability of values about a **mean**, the square root of the **variance**.

Standard error of the mean The **standard deviation** of the distribution of means of a number of samples about the **population** mean.

Statistical inference A process of inferring or predicting **population** parameters from sample data.

Statistical significance The odds against an observed result being due to chance. A cut-off is often set at 5%, although this still means that you have a 1 in 20 chance of a false positive result.

Statistical significance, level of The probability against getting results purely by chance.

Statistics The branch of mathematics that has developed a range of techniques for assessing the degree of reliance to place upon **evidence** generated in experiments or inquiries. Knowledge of statistics can inform the design of such experiments or inquiries so that the results are more likely to be meaningful.

Stratified random sampling An approach in which a **population** is divided into relevant categories or strata (eg by age or income group) and a random sample drawn from each of these categories.

Structured interview An interview which comprises a series of **closed questions** presented to the respondent, either as **a self-assessment questionnaire** or one delivered face to face.

Structured observation A planned and systematic means of watching people or events in order to gather research data or information.

Subjective Describing a view of the world based on what the individual feels and perceives rather than based on objective realities.

Supervisor The person who (usually) really wants you to succeed in your dissertation, and is prepared to put considerable effort, and often considerable expertise, at your disposal should you choose to make use of it.

Survey Any mechanism intended to gather **primary data** from a **population** or **sample**.

Symmetric distribution A distribution in which values are equally distributed about the most frequently-occurring value.

Symmetry of potential outcomes A situation in which the results of a research project will be of equal interest whichever way they turn out.

Synthesis The drawing together of different perspectives and arguments to produce a coherent discussion.

Tacit theory A set of beliefs or assumptions which unconsciously shape perception and thinking.

Telephone questionnaire A questionnaire presented to the respondent via the telephone.

Text Written or printed words which convey data, information or meaning to another person or people.

Theoretical sampling An emergent approach to defining and selecting a sample, most often associated with **Grounded Theory**.

Theoretical saturation The point at which in the analysis of data gathered using a **Grounded Theory** approach the findings reveal no new information.

Theory An organised set of assumptions which help to make sense of experience and which therefore influence how we act. A good deal of academic research is directed at developing explicit theory. However, we all operate on the basis of unconscious or **tacit theory**, the assumptions and logic of which may remain untested. One of the functions of explicit theory is to challenge the validity of unconscious theories.

'Theory' A loose term used by academics to refer to a whole raft of ideas, frameworks, guidelines for good practice, etc – and some **theory** – which they teach and which is intended to inform professional practice, including the conduct of a dissertation. If you fail to draw upon 'theory' for this purpose, you are unlikely to pass.

Thesis A research project report usually produced for the award of a Doctorate.

Transcription, transcript Written notes produced from the **field notes** or a recording of an interview or an observation.

Triangulation The use of multiple methods of data-gathering, data types or data analysis, or the use of multiple researchers to produce varied and rich research data.

Trustworthiness (of conclusions) The extent to which **conclusions** are to be trusted not to mislead, derived from the **relevance**, **representativeness** and **validity** of data and the logical rigour of analysis and/or arguments used to draw conclusions from the data.

***t*-Test** A **parametric statistical test** for determining whether the difference between two samples is statistically significant.

Type I error Rejecting the null **hypothesis** when it is true.

Type II error Accepting the null **hypothesis** when it is false.

Unstructured interview A conversation in which the interviewee takes the lead after you have defined your area of interest. It is very hard to draw meaningful conclusions from such interviews although they may be of value in the early stages of an investigation while you are still trying to explore the nature of concerns about an issue.

Upper quartile The value in a sample ordered by size which has 75% of values smaller, and 25% of values larger.

Validity Of a **measure** or **indicator**, the extent to which it measures what it purports to measure.

Variable Something that can vary in value, and for which values have been obtained.

Variance The average of the squares of the differences between each number in a sample and the **mean** value, sometimes used to indicate the spread of values in a sample about the mean. More usually its square root (the **standard deviation**) is used.

Web survey A survey – usually a questionnaire – which is produced, delivered and returned online. Completion can sometimes be directly on screen or may require respondents to download the file, complete the questionnaire, and then upload it again.

Wicked problem A term coined by Rittel to describe complex problems where both problem and solution are undefined, and progress has to be via reactive induction rather than deduction. (See also **mess**.)

Wikipedia *Wiki-wiki* is Hawaiian for 'very quick', indicating that this is a 'very quick' source of reference. It is an online collaboratively-authored free 'encyclopaedia', with entries on just about anything you might be interested in – a wonderful source of information, but because anyone can write in it, entries are not necessarily correct and must be taken as a starting point rather than as definitive data. Most academic institutions do not recognise Wikipedia as a *bona fide* academic source.

Preface

Welcome to *Business Research Methods*. You may be wondering why you should get hold of and use this textbook rather than any other. The answer is that our experience indicates that you need:

- a more concise, less daunting (but still rigorous) book that demystifies the research process
- an inspirational text that you can really engage with and that allows you to see the practical applicability of your work
- a book that enables you to gain insight into what researchers actually do.

Business Research Methods has been written to meet these requirements fully. It takes a real-world practical approach, making the research process more relevant, meaningful and effective.

PERSONAL APPROACH

Each chapter is written primarily by one of us two authors (although subjected to rigorous criticism by the other). When you see 'I' in the text, it refers to whichever of us was the main author for that particular chapter, as annotated by our names in the contents list. Any 'we' refers to a joint stance on the book as a whole or something relating to both author and reader. We hope that this personal approach will make it easier to read, easier for you to judge, and even perhaps easier for you at times to challenge the validity of what is said. You should be as critical of this book as of the other literature you read in the course of your research.

SPIRAL APPROACH

Research is a complex topic, and your understanding is likely to grow over time. The book therefore takes a spiral approach to topics, revisiting them in greater depth and sometimes in slightly different ways in subsequent chapters. This should help you develop a richer understanding of the importance of key issues. Moreover, where information in other chapters is particularly relevant, clear cross-references are located in the text margin.

SELECTIVE DEPTH RATHER THAN BREADTH

We are aiming at relevant depth rather than comprehensiveness, and at meeting the needs of a future *practitioner* rather than of an academic researcher.

RESEARCH STORIES

The book contains a number of stories told by or about researchers and their research in order to give a richer understanding of the issues involved.

GUIDANCE ON KEY PROBLEM AREAS

The book places research firmly in the real world, exploring why research is done and how to ensure that projects are meaningful for organisations. It also addresses the transferable skills of project management, communication and working with clients.

Introduction

Research is often seen as the domain of academics. This book argues that the ability to carry out worthwhile practical research is a key management and consultancy skill. Decisions and actions taken by managers can have far-reaching effects on their organisation, their colleagues' lives and their own careers. Good practical research would often have led to a different decision or action. Being able to carry out, commission and/or use others' research will contribute to your success as a manager or consultant.

This book aims to develop your understanding of the research process as it applies to practical organisational issues. It will enable you to judge the strengths and limitations of different research projects in different contexts, so that you can draw upon them appropriately, and will help you to develop your ability to carry out worthwhile practical business research.

Both of us are practising managers and management academics, and carry out and use research in both these roles. We regularly encounter a great deal of research that does not deliver what it promises. Some is truly dreadful, some even highly dangerous. It has the potential to mislead organisations into taking decisions that may threaten their profitability or viability and have a major impact on the lives of their employees. A proportion of this dangerous research is done by highly experienced managers and consultants. Another serious concern is the number of important decisions that are taken without adequate exploration of the issues involved, and based on little relevant information. Failure to carry out necessary research can be just as dangerous as doing bad research.

Because practical business research is potentially so important to organisations, we wanted to write a book that would help managers and intending managers to make better use of research within their organisations. To do this we had to understand why there was a problem. It seemed that one potential cause might be a growing gap between the concerns of practitioners and those of the people teaching them. Such a gap has been noted in several professions, including management. A number of universities have recognised this and now allow or require students to carry out a research project with a practical focus. Some offer a consultancy module.

The book is designed for practising managers and for students who intend eventually to put their research skills to practical rather than academic use. It focuses on the purposes of research and what you have to understand and be able to do in order to achieve your own research purpose. It uses a range of stories told by practising managers to help 'translate' general points into specific organisational contexts.

The basic format of most dissertations is derived from an academic model. You may find that neither this format nor the more academically-oriented research methods seem to meet your own research concerns. This 'misfit' may create unnecessary anxiety and make it difficult to think clearly about what you are trying to achieve. Such anxiety may stop you from developing the research skills that you will need in your career, and the quality of your research will suffer. The book aims to reduce this anxiety and improve the quality of your practical research and the enjoyment and learning you get from it.

The focus throughout is on what you have to consider and do when seeking to find out something useful about an issue of immediate concern to your own management practice or to your own or a client's organisation. If you are already a manager, it will help you think about how to gather and analyse information in order to understand a difficult issue and perhaps do something about it. If you are not yet a manager, the book will help you to carry out a useful and successful undergraduate or Master's-level dissertation. More importantly, it will help you develop skills that will be valuable in your subsequent career as a manager or consultant. If you are doing research for a PhD, or have a mainly academic interest in research, this book would be a useful starting point, but you would have to use more academic and specialist research texts as well.

The challenge in practical business research stems not from the relatively clear logic of the underlying research process but from the necessary complexities of business research issues and their contexts. Because complexity is hard to grasp, the book adopts a spiral approach. Topics are introduced in broad terms in the early part of the book, with a strong emphasis on understanding the research process as a whole, and revisited in more detail in later chapters. Looking at the big picture first, and then going into more detail, should make ideas easier to absorb. A similar spiral or looping approach is suggested for your own research. Again, an understanding of the underlying logic is essential if looping is to be systematic rather than random.

The many 'Research stories' in the book highlight different issues that practitioner-researchers have to address, and demonstrate some of the complexity. They should help you recognise similar issues in your own context and appreciate their significance. If you are already a practising manager, you will easily see connections with your own situation. If you are a full-time student and intending manager, the stories will show the importance of research skills for your future career, and make the issues covered far more meaningful.

Used thoughtfully, the book will develop your understanding of the basic research process, and the different assumptions upon which it may be based. It will equip you to select and then use one or more of the methods typically adopted by practitioner-researchers. The aim is to help you think constructively and flexibly about your own research, and you will have to engage with the questions posed throughout the book, and consider their implications for your own research.

If you use the book as a tool in this way, you should become justifiably confident about selecting an issue to address, refining it into a research question and proposal, selecting appropriate methods for collecting relevant information, and drawing useful and trustworthy conclusions from it all. You should have developed your skills in managing research projects, working constructively with clients, writing compelling accounts of your research, and maximising the professional development opportunities that research can offer. As a result you should *enjoy* your research experience, develop key professional skills, and produce results of value to an organisational client and possibly to a wider audience.

KEY POINTS

- Organisations need research, and managers have to be able to commission, judge and use others' research as well as doing research themselves to inform decisions.
- Practical research presents different challenges from academic research, and may have different priorities.
- This book will help you understand the challenges of carrying out worthwhile research into significant issues.
- It will help you develop a wide range of research-related professional skills.
- It will guide you through the processes of selecting, carrying out and reporting on a successful research project.

Walkthrough of textbook features

Students, consultants and managers are often time poor. And some of the ideas in the book can be difficult to grasp, even if you have some research experience. The following features are intended to overcome some of these difficulties.

CHAPTER-OPENING FEATURES

INTRODUCTION

The chapter introduction clearly explains the topics to follow.

LEARNING OUTCOMES

Each introduction is followed by a bulleted list that signposts what you can expect to learn from each chapter.

IN-TEXT FEATURES

KEY POINTS

At intervals in the text you will find 'Key Points' boxes. These are intended to alert you to areas that are particularly important and to help you to find your way around the book when reading other chapters.

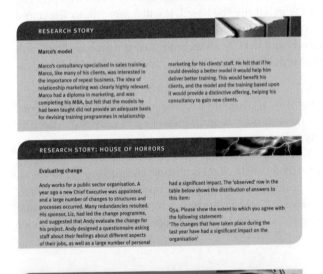

RESEARCH STORIES AND ILLUSTRATIONS

The book contains a number of 'Research Stories' told by or about researchers and their research to give a richer understanding of the issues involved. Most individual and organisation names and the stories about them have been modified slightly so that sources cannot be identified. However some researchers agreed to write their stories specifically for this book, and we have also drawn on published reports of relevant research.

Watch out for the lightening icon warning of particularly bad research.

Where we want to illustrate a specific point rather than tell a story you will find a 'Research Illustration'.

CONSIDER...

Research tends to be only as good as the thinking that went into its selection, design and planning. The book is designed to stimulate some of this thinking. At relevant points 'Consider...' boxes will prompt you to think about the issues raised in the text.

ACTIVITY

Take the skills you have just listed and ask yourself what evidence you have for the skills assessments you just made. Is this an intuition, a guess, or have you actively drawn upon evidence of your strengths and weaknesses in your current role? How might these skills relate to your future aspirations? Seek further evidence to support your assessments. Possible sources are colleagues (who may be prepared to give you feedback if asked), past performance appraisal reviews, your boss (who again may give informal feedback if you explain why you want it) and any mentor who may be able to advise you on what skills are important at higher levels.

Keep such evidence on your existing strengths and weaknesses, and about future requirements, in your journal. Add to this evidence by actively brainstorming a list of additional skills that might be worth developing.

ACTIVITIES

Sometimes you will need to do more than think in order to progress your research project. 'Activity' boxes will suggest tasks that will help you move forward.

Academic complexity
Chapters 6, 7 and 24

CROSS REFERENCES

Marginal cross references support the spiral approach of the text. Use them to develop your understanding of key issues.

END-OF-CHAPTER FEATURES

SUMMARY

End of chapter summaries bring together the main themes of a chapter.

REVIEW QUESTIONS

1. What is meant by 'practical business research' in this book?
2. How might this be distinguished from more academic research?
3. What can theory contribute to a practical research project?
4. What is the distinction between 'theory' as used in management teaching and 'a theory' as used more widely? Why might there be a need to make this distinction?
5. Why is it helpful to distinguish between tacit and formal theory?
6. What impact can theory have upon practical business research?
7. What distinguishes good business research from bad? Why is it important to be able to tell the difference?
8. Why is it better to see practical business research in terms of messy loops rather than a neat linear staircase?

REVIEW QUESTIONS

At the end of every chapter, 'Review Questions' have been provided to help you assess your understanding of central themes.

EXPLORE FURTHER

Bryman, A. and Bell, E. (2007) *Business Research Methods*, 2nd edition. Oxford: Oxford University Press. This is particularly strong on qualitative approaches

Robson, C. (2002) *Real World Research*, 2nd edition. Oxford: Blackwell. This is directed towards practitioner-researchers and provides a complementary and accessible discussion of issues connected with doing practical research

Saunders, M., Lewis, P. and Thornhill, A. (2007) *Research Methods for Business Students*, 4th edition. Harlow: FT/Prentice Hall. This takes a more academic approach and will again complement this chapter, and indeed the whole book, if you have a more academic interest in business research

Smith. M. (2001) at http://www.infed.org/thinkers/et-lewin.htm for an excellent overview of Lewin's work (also relevant to Chapter 14 on Action Research)

http://www.accel-team.com/techniques/force_field_analysis.html for a brief article on force-field analysis which you may find interesting

British Journal of Management (2001) Vol.12, December, Supplement 1. This contains a range of responses by academics to a report on 'The nature, social organisation and promotion of management research: towards policy' (Starkey and Tranfield, 1998), including one by Starkey and Madan on the 'relevance gap' between academics and practitioners, and an interesting critique in terms of different 'real worlds' by Karl Weick

EXPLORE FURTHER

To take your learning further, consider reading the books or visiting the web sites in the 'Explore Further' list.

END-OF-BOOK FEATURES

Methodology

GLOSSARY

Definitions are highlighted when they first appear in the text. The dictionary icon in the margin indicates that the key term and its definition can be found in a glossary at the end of the book.

REFERENCES

In the interests of clarity, we have avoided using a heavily referenced academic style. Other authors are referenced only where a key idea needs recognition, where something has been particularly well put and you might want to quote it, or if the text is something you might wish to read for yourself.

Walkthrough of the student and tutor support sites

Visit www.cipd.co.uk/brm to access the following online resources, designed to further enhance the learning and teaching experience.

ONLINE STUDENT RESOURCES

Look out for the mouse icon in the margin within the text, indicating where related student resources are available online.

WEB LINKS

A series of annotated web links organised by chapter have been provided to point you in the direction of important articles, reviews and research guides. These include web links from the book as well as any additional references.

Activity	Jan	Feb	Mar	Apr	May	Jun	Jul	Aug	Sep
Research proposal approved									
Review literature									
Finalise aim and objectives									
Draft literature review section									
Devise research approach									
Draft research approach section									
Review secondary data									
Organise interviews									
Develop interview questions									
Analyse data									
Administer questionnaire									

TEMPLATES AND FORMS

Electronic versions of all of the templates, forms and checklists within the text have been supplied to save you precious time recreating them. Use these to support your business research project.

CONSIDER...

What assumptions about 'knowledge' and its creation underpin the approach adopted by Mitroff and Emshoff in their research story?

....
....
....
....

ACTIVITY

Note your career, learning and other objectives for the research you will be undertaking.

Note any potential conflicts between these and other objectives (yours or those of other key stakeholders).

Consider how these conflicts might be reduced or otherwise dealt with.

Note your ideas in your research journal.

....
....
....
....

CONSIDER AND ACTIVITY PROMPTS

These are electronic versions of selected Consider... and Activity boxes from the book, marked with the mouse icon, with space provided for your notes. Use them as the basis for entries in your learning journal, print them and use them in class or add them to your notes.

Question 1

Put a Y (for 'Yes') against each of the following statements that you believe to be true:

- [ ] a) In practical business research the sole objective is to address an issue of importance to practising managers
- [ ] b) Practical business research is about collecting and interpreting information to inform decisions
- [ ] c) If it isn't systematic, it isn't research
- [ ] d) The only difference between academic and practical research is whether the research is carried out in a real organisation.

Question 2

SELF-TEST QUIZZES

Where appropriate, chapters have a self-test quiz to help you check your understanding of the text. Guidance answers are supplied.

ADDITIONAL STUDENT RESOURCES

These might be activities, asking you to review a piece of work or to identify and solve problems. Or they might be examples of practice, showing you a specific type of analysis or what constitutes good or bad practice.

SAMPLE QUESTIONNAIRE RESULTS

A simple data set derived from the analysis of a questionnaire is provided. Qualitative data is collated, whilst the quantitative data has been used to produce a range of data presentations (charts and graphs).The spreadsheet is structured so that changes in the data produce changes in the graphs and charts produced from that data.

ONLINE TUTOR RESOURCES

All of the tutor resources for this book are also available as a Zip file which can be easily downloaded into your Virtual Learning Environment.

Business Research Methods

CHAPTER 2
The Complexities of Business Research

Lecturer's Guide

This chapter explores some of the complexities which make practical business research necessarily messy, and diagnosis so crucial. Any or all of these could potentially form the substance of a lecture. Because stakeholders are dealt with in more detail in Chapter 4, and epistemology is developed further in Chapter 3, the suggested emphasis here is on understanding the implications of messiness, developing confidence in diagramming, becoming aware of the ease with which an involved researcher can bias results, and ending with a positive view of how the undoubted challenges provide scope for developing valuable transferable skills.

Unless students are familiar with the diagramming techniques covered in the book, it would be helpful to give at least two diagramming exercises as part of this lecture to make students more familiar with 'drawing' in a fairly loose way. Rich pictures are ideal for group drawing, and multiple-cause diagrams can usefully be 'read' by others to test the logic, so the suggested focus is on these. If ideas of reflective learning and the role of a reflective research journal were not introduced in conjunction with Chapter 1, unless students are already familiar with them from earlier courses they will need to be introduced here.

CHAPTER LEARNING OUTCOMES
The chapter should enable students to:.
* identify the main dimensions of complexity commonly found in business issues, and the additional complexities associated with researching them
* discuss the challenges these complexities pose for the business researcher

LECTURER'S GUIDE

Each chapter is accompanied by a set of lecturer's notes which will assist both new and experienced tutors in their teaching. The notes include an overview of the chapter, chapter and lecture learning outcomes, lecture aims and additional activities with guidance.

STUDENT HANDOUTS

At the end of each set of lecturer's notes you are prompted to distribute the accompanying student handout/s. These contain the additional activities provided in the lecturer's notes, briefs to help students complete those activities, answer sheets, as well as more specific information on areas such as diagramming.

LECTURE SLIDES

A set of customisable lecture slides in Microsoft PowerPoint is available for each chapter and can be used as the basis of a lecture presentation. The slides provide a succinct and visual presentation of the central themes in the book.

Rich picture of Beth's leaving rate situation

FIGURES AND TABLES FROM THE TEXT

All figures and tables from the book have been provided in high resolution format for downloading into presentation software.

PART 1

FROM FIRST IDEAS
TO POSSIBLE TOPICS

CHAPTER 1

Practical Business Research: An Overview

INTRODUCTION

Practical business research is carried out in a wide range of contexts, for different purposes, and in many different ways. It can have a substantial influence, for good or ill, upon organisations and upon the working lives of their employees. This book is intended to develop the skills you will need to carry out or draw on such research. Those skills will be of value to your career as a manager or consultant. Although the book will help you to do a good dissertation on a business-related topic, it is not designed to prepare you for a PhD.

The first part of the book covers the research process and the complexities of doing research in organisational contexts on topics of relevance to their managers. This chapter provides an introduction to most of the issues that you will have to consider when planning or evaluating such research. It aims to give you a clear overall picture of what business research means, what it can achieve, and how you can usefully draw upon theory to help with this. Some of the inevitable complexities involved in researching 'real' issues are highlighted and some of the hazards that they present are explored. It is important to avoid such hazards if your research is to be useful rather than misleading. (Many of these issues are developed further in subsequent chapters.)

The complexity of organisational issues makes it hard to grasp them fully at first. Research seldom therefore proceeds neatly by means of separate and self-contained stages. The process is necessarily both more integrated and messier. You are likely to develop your understanding of a complex issue through a series of insights, any of which may suggest profitable redirections in your investigation. To avoid chaos, and other hazards, you must work within a systematic framework, based upon a sound understanding of the business research process as a whole.

The book's structure reflects this belief in the need to understand the whole picture before focusing on specific parts. The last part of this chapter explains the structure we have adopted for the book, the style we have chosen, and the features that we have incorporated to help you use it to best effect. It explores the implications of these aspects for your own reading and thinking about research.

LEARNING OUTCOMES

This chapter should enable you to:

- define 'business research' and identify its potential benefits

- distinguish between 'business research methods' and the business research process

- identify the different forms that practical business research can take, and outline the range of outcomes that may be achieved

- draw upon theory to help make sense of organisational issues, and identify scope for further theory development during the research process

- give appropriate priority to seeking evidence to inform decisions and actions within organisations

- compare and contrast the academic and the practitioner research process

- plan how best to use the book to meet your specific learning aims

- start to identify ways in which your research might develop your management potential, as well as provide useful information about a real issue

WHAT IS PRACTICAL BUSINESS RESEARCH?

Managers have to make sense of what is going on both within their organisation and in its environment in order to take effective decisions and actions. Business research is about the process of collecting and interpreting the information needed for this.

Practical business research refers to any systematic attempt at collecting and interpreting data and evidence in order to inform thinking, decisions and/or actions in relation to an issue of interest to an organisation and/or its stakeholders.

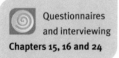

Questionnaires and interviewing
Chapters 15, 16 and 24

Definitions are important: communication depends upon your readers (or listeners) knowing what you mean by the words you use. You will have to pay attention to this in designing any questionnaires and in interviewing, and in writing up any research you do. You can see that the definition has a very practical orientation: the issue addressed is *of interest to an organisation and/or its stakeholders*.

Contrast this with the more academic perspective on research reflected by Buchanan *et al* (1988, p67) who stated that

> "the ultimate goal of the research enterprise is to gather empirical evidence upon which theories concerning aspects of behaviour in organisations can be based."

Theory and practitioner-researchers

Our definition is wider – it includes more than Buchanan's. Theory-building is not necessarily the ultimate goal of practical research, although theory can be a rich resource for practitioner-researchers. By our definition business research *may* lead to theory development, but it may not. Much valuable research is primarily driven by a need to address a particular organisational issue: this is why the book title emphasises that we have adopted *a practical approach*.

It is worth also looking at what is meant by 'research methods'. This often has a fairly restricted meaning. For example, Bryman and Bell (2007) say that

> "A research method is simply a technique for collecting data."

As you will discover, practical business research is far from simple. It is therefore reassuring to note that research methods are 'simply' techniques. Such techniques are, however, essential if practical business research is to inform rather than *misinform* decisions and actions which may have significant consequences for an organisation and its employees. Research methods (and related analytical techniques) are designed

Conclusions

to help you generate data that is valid and reliable and draw sound conclusions from it.

There are many different approaches to data collection and analysis, some fairly straightforward, some extremely complicated. The book focuses on those in common use by practitioner-researchers, and their role in the wider research process. Unless you understand the strengths of a method and its limitations, you may choose unwisely. If you do not understand how to use the method, even a wise choice may produce misleading data.

> **Mastering a research method is not enough: the quality of your thinking about all aspects of your research is crucial.**

The value of the data you collect will depend upon the quality of your thinking about the purpose of your research, the context in which you are conducting it, how best to collect relevant information and how to analyse and interpret what you find. It is this *thinking* that will make the research useful or not.

To choose and use techniques to good effect you must understand that the wider research process of data collection is but a part. In practical research, the biggest challenge may be working out just what issue you are seeking to address. Until you have done this, you cannot decide what information would be useful. But until you have collected some information you may not be able to define the issue in any sensible way. Think of chickens and eggs: the information (egg) will help you reframe the issue and the questions you ask (chicken); these questions will produce more information, which will help you reframe ... etc.

The only way out of this seeming bind is to spend some of the early part of your research alternating between information-gathering and redefining the issue. This idea of *looping*, or *iteration*, is important. Moving fluidly back and forth between different stages of a research process requires a sound grasp of the process as a whole, and its logic. Understanding this logic will enable you to think more flexibly and effectively. The first part of the book addresses both the logic and how to move effectively between stages.

Most managers make sense of issues more easily if they can relate them to their own experience. So we shall draw heavily upon the stories of researchers and their research projects. Some are very practically oriented, some have a more theoretical emphasis. Some highlight the hazards researchers encounter, some demonstrate the benefits research can bring. Some appear once, to make a particular point, others will be revisited in later chapters. Together they will make you more aware of the complexities, uncertainties and tensions faced by the practical researcher, and of how these may be addressed. This will also help you appreciate the type of thinking you will have to do.

It is easy to read something in a text and think 'Yes, that sounds fine' and move on without fully grasping the significance of an issue. The stories, and your consideration of their implications, are intended to counteract this tendency. This may help you to avoid some of the unwise choices in the stories we tell, and therefore to plan more productive research.

DIFFERENT FORMS OF BUSINESS RESEARCH

Practical business research covers a wide field. It is worth exploring the distinction between *academic* and *practical* or *practitioner* research and its implications. The difference goes beyond the simple one of who is doing the research. 'Pure' and 'applied' are often considered separate categories. Figure 1.1 suggests a continuum instead. And it shows some of the possible related distinctions.

Figure 1.1 A research continuum

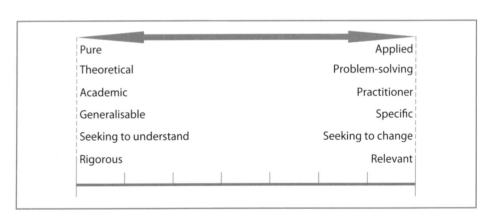

Pure	Applied
Theoretical	Problem-solving
Academic	Practitioner
Generalisable	Specific
Seeking to understand	Seeking to change
Rigorous	Relevant

There is increasing interest in both *practitioner research* – research carried out by practitioners into either their own practice or issues which affect it – and in the issues raised by doing research as an *insider*. The following illustration shows a representative sample of practical, and mostly also practitioner and insider, research projects I have encountered recently. At various points in the book we shall be looking at these (and other) projects in more detail to highlight issues of concern to researchers. Some we shall look at several times.

RESEARCH ILLUSTRATION

Typical practical and/or practitioner research projects

Justin's project was looking at whether to invest in one substantial development project or several smaller projects.

Beth was looking at labour turnover in her organisation because recent recruits seemed to be leaving not long after completing their initial training.

Jenny was exploring a possible 'green' policy for her organisation, aimed at reducing its carbon footprint.

Peter was aiming to develop a new business strategy for a small consultancy and to design promotional activity and materials in line with this.

Ben and **Emily** were each looking at knowledge

management in their organisations, and exploring how teams working on separate projects might learn from each other.

Marco was developing a new conceptual model of customer relationship management as the basis for a new training programme.

Chris wanted to explore the relationship between critical reflection and leadership development. (He subsequently established a consultancy business based on this.)

Andy evaluated a recent change initiative and made recommendations for further change in the light of the evaluation.

CONSIDER...

Where on the continuum would you place the illustration projects?

What are the possible advantages and limitations of using the continuum in Figure 1.1 as a framework for thinking about research?

I hope you *did* consider these questions – such exercises are an important part of getting value from the text. I expect that when you considered where the projects were placed on the continuum you had some difficulty, and started to question the adequacy of the continuum model. Although the labels at each end of Figure 1.1 often *tend* to be bundled together as shown, there may not be a single dimension. Most of the illustration projects fit comfortably towards the 'applied' end but Marco and

RESEARCH STORY

Marco's model

Marco's consultancy specialised in sales training. Marco, like many of his clients, was interested in the importance of repeat business. The idea of relationship marketing was clearly highly relevant. Marco had a diploma in marketing, and was completing his MBA, but felt that the models he had been taught did not provide an adequate basis for devising training programmes in relationship

marketing for his clients' staff. He felt that if he could develop a better model it would help him deliver better training. This would benefit his clients, and the model and the training based upon it would provide a distinctive offering, helping his consultancy to gain new clients.

Chris are more difficult to locate. Marco had a genuine theoretical interest in creating a new and generalisable theoretical model, but his goal was not merely to 'advance knowledge' – as looking at his story in more detail shows.

Marco's project was evidently seeking to be both theoretical and practical, yet it could not be simultaneously at both ends of the continuum. If the project was feasible (and it clearly was, because he achieved his purpose), it calls the model into question, since Figure 1.1 suggests that the further to the right you go, the less important theory becomes, and that rigour inevitably gives way to relevance. Neither is necessarily the case. Even for a practical project, thinking about how to conceptualise aspects of the issue is important. For Action Research (discussed in Chapter 14) much of the effort may go into exploring the tacit personal theories which unconsciously shape thinking (more of this later). Then again, 'theory' may be a product that can be put to very practical uses, as both Marco's and Chris's projects demonstrate. Theory may be of equal, albeit different, concern to academics and practitioners.

Action Research

An alternative, more complex model may work better. The model shown in Figure 1.2 uses relevance and rigour not as opposites but as independent dimensions. The 'blobs' show territory covered by different forms of what may be called research.

There are several reasons why Figure 1.1 was included despite its limitations:

- it represents fairly widespread assumptions about business research.
- it may help you to become aware of and evaluate your own assumptions.
- its simplicity made it a good starting point for thinking about an important aspect of research.
- it demonstrates how trying to fit 'reality' to a model can challenge the model and suggest how it might be improved.
- it is a good discipline to run with more than one model at any time because it saves you from believing that 'the model' is the reality. The ability to hold conflicting views at the same time is sometimes considered a mark of genius, and can lead to more flexible and creative thinking.

You will see that Figure 1.2 may be more helpful in some respects. I have placed the blobs to suggest some trade-off between relevance and rigour for cost and feasibility reasons, but to suggest too that both are important. Any concerns about rigour would have to be recognised, and conclusions framed accordingly.

But Figure 1.2 is still only a model, and still a gross oversimplification of the research territory, which has many more possible dimensions, as the list of projects suggested. These include:

- the research purpose
- the nature of the topic
- underlying philosophical assumptions about knowledge and research
- the nature of data deemed relevant.

All these are explored in later chapters. But first, because theory and practical research are so closely related it is important to explore this relationship further.

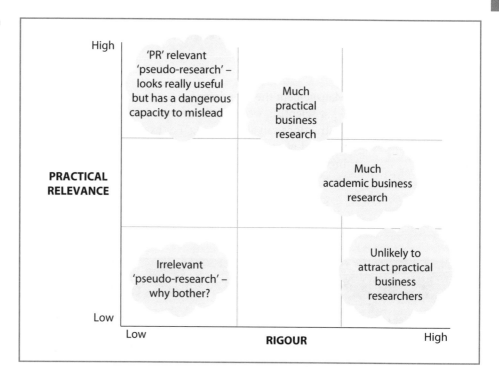

Figure 1.2 Possible research territories

WHAT DOES THEORY MEAN IN PRACTICAL BUSINESS RESEARCH?

Some research builds theory, some is designed to test theory, and some draws upon theory to frame an issue, pose relevant research questions and guide interpretation of the data collected. It is important to distinguish two very different uses of the term 'theory'.

To a scientist, a *theory* usually means an organised set of assumptions that generate testable – and tested – predictions. A theory *explains* an observed phenomenon, and the explanation will apply in a wide range of different contexts. The laws of physics allow you to make clear and testable and widely applicable predictions about speed, acceleration, temperature, etc, when other conditions are specified. You can reliably measure the variables concerned and thus test the predicted relationship between the variables.

 A theory: an organised set of assumptions that generate testable predictions of the relationship between variables.

Few *theories* about management or organisations fit this rigorous definition. There are too many variables involved, and few can be measured as easily or reliably as speed or temperature. Yet there is an extensive body of *formal management theory*. It is taught to management students and has a powerful influence on thinking about management issues. 'Theory' in management tends to be used primarily as a collective noun, encompassing a number of different, though related, abstractions, only some of which meet the definition for a *theory*. A useful definition of 'theory' in this broader sense, suitable for the purposes of business research, might be:

A theory: any concept, construct or conceptual framework that helps us think about and/or better understand some aspect of an issue of concern.

Management theory relates to issues of concern to managers. This definition includes what scientists would call a *theory*, but much more besides. Many different sorts of abstractions can aid thinking. For example, once I had heard the term 'hidden agenda' I looked at meetings in a totally different light. Other professions adopt a similarly broad definition. For example, Fook (2002, p83), writing of theory in social work, says that

> "Often just 'naming' or labelling a piece of behaviour can function to provide some explanation, or connect the behaviour with related ideas."

 CONSIDER...

List three or four of the management ideas that have had a significant impact upon you.

Try to note *how* your thinking shifted and the impact that this had on your perceptions and/or actions.

As an example of how you might have approached this, consider Lewin's (1951) idea of a force-field, with which you are almost certainly familiar. Lewin's idea of a force-field would fit into the broader collective definition of 'theory'. 'Force-field' is a *concept*: Lewin was using it to highlight his theoretical stance that individual motivation cannot be considered in isolation from its environment. His familiar 'opposing arrows' diagram is a *conceptual framework*, which allows you to think about a particular aspect of a situation in a structured way.

Thus when Jenny was looking at her 'green policy', she identified a number of forces favourable to change, and a number more that would oppose it. Figure 1.3 shows how she started to organise her thinking in these terms. Once she had identified these forces she could think about how she might plan to increase the 'drivers' or reduce the 'restrainers' in order to implement a new policy.

Figure 1.3 Force-field for a new 'green policy'

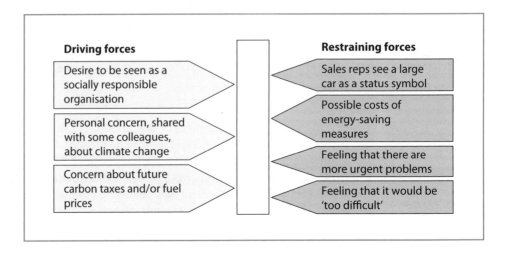

Diagnosis

If you were running a workshop during the early stages of a project, the force-field framework might provide a useful framework and language for shared diagnosis.

Here you can see that there is a very practical issue being addressed, but the idea of a force-field and the opposing forces framework allows an important aspect of the situation to be thought about and/or discussed in a structured way. Even inadequate theories can help. A colleague often says, 'All theory is wrong, but some theory is useful.' Provided, of course that you have the ability to *judge* its potential usefulness and use it appropriately. It is this *critical* ability that management programmes are intended to develop, and that the literature review section of a dissertation is intended to display.

Dissertation
literature review
Chapter 7

Incidentally, Lewin is frequently quoted as having asserted that there was nothing as practical as a good theory. Because when you are writing about research you will need to reference your quotes, you may be interested in the following 'aside'.

Research
Chapter 24

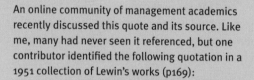

RESEARCH ILLUSTRATION

An online community of management academics recently discussed this quote and its source. Like me, many had never seen it referenced, but one contributor identified the following quotation in a 1951 collection of Lewin's works (p169):

Many psychologists working today in an applied field are keenly aware of the need for close co-operation between theoretical and applied psychology. This can be accomplished in psychology, as it has been accomplished in physics, if the

theorist does not look toward applied problems with highbrow aversion or with a fear of social problems, and if the applied psychologist realises that there is nothing so practical as a good theory.

Another contributor pointed out that the idea originally came from Dewey (discussed later in this chapter, and chapters 3 and 14), and that Kant, who died in 1804, apparently said, '*Es gibt nichts Praktischeres als eine gute Theorie*' (reference not provided).

TACIT THEORY

Thus far 'theory' has referred mainly to an explicit idea or framework. But much of our behaviour is guided by unarticulated concepts and frameworks of which we may be completely unaware. Phrases like 'Change is never ...' or 'A good leader always ...' or 'The only way to learn is ...' are often driven by *tacit* theory. Such unconscious frameworks sensitise us to some elements in a situation, blind us to others, and enable us to draw (potentially biased) conclusions about what we perceive.

Many have likened concepts to lenses. For example, Wittgenstein (1997; p450) said that an idea is 'like a pair of glasses on our nose through which we see whatever we look at', and suggested that these glasses are not always clear and can be difficult to take off. 'Tacit spectacles' can be particularly problematic because we may not know we are wearing them. Yet tacit theory, which is usually derived from *past* experience and teaching, may not be a reliable guide to understanding the situations we currently encounter.

Tacit theory
challenges
Chapters 2 and 14

The influence of tacit theory on both perception and interpretation presents real challenges for researchers seeking 'objective', unbiased observations. These will be addressed later. Part of the value of explicit theory in the broad sense is that it can be used to surface and challenge tacit theory.

- It is important to distinguish 'a theory' as scientists would use the term from 'theory' in management, which includes a wider range of ideas and frameworks.

- It is also important to distinguish formal theory (both in the singular and the general sense) from tacit theory which is not articulated, and of which you may not be aware.

- Formal theory can help you to surface, articulate and challenge previously tacit ideas and frameworks.

THE PURPOSES THEORY CAN SERVE

It was impossible to discuss what theory meant without some discussion of some aspects of its powerful role in shaping our thinking. But theory can serve a number of other less obvious purposes for the practitioner-researcher. Figure 1.4 shows a wider range of influences theory can have, and purposes it can serve. The additional ones are described below. Note that the figure includes one result of using theory uncritically that practitioners would want strenuously to avoid. In order to avoid it you need to judge the validity of the theory in question and its relevance for your context.

Figure 1.4 Possible roles of theory in practitioner research

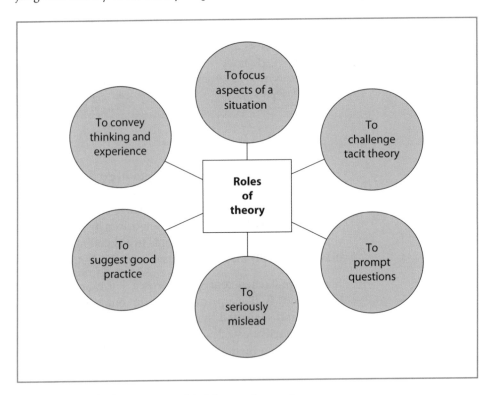

Theory as a vehicle to convey thinking and experience

Theory is an abstraction from a great deal of thought, experience and research in a wide range of contexts. It therefore encapsulates countless person-hours of 'thought-work' and can be a rich resource, serving to stimulate and extend your own thinking about issues, and spark insights into aspects of the issues confronting you.

Theory as a lens or knife to bring aspects of a situation into focus

Despite – or perhaps because of – the shortcomings of the notional continuum in Figure 1.1, it was a useful starting point for thinking about characteristics of different projects. Some of its value came from what it omitted: this can bring other aspects into sharper focus, while blurring yet others. Another helpful metaphor is to see a concept or framework as a dissecting knife. Each model allows you to cut a different 'slice' through the issue you are examining, and each slice will show the situation from a different angle. By looking at several different slices you can start to build some sort of picture of what is going on.

Theory to stimulate creative thought

A further important use of theory is to stimulate creative thought, whether individually or in groups. This use is analogous to a creativity technique called 'the force fit game' (Warfield *et al*, 1965). People faced with a problem split into two teams. Team A suggests an idea remote from the problem and the B Team have two minutes to come up with a practical solution based on that idea. Roles are then reversed. The process can stimulate some totally new ways of thinking. Even trying to locate the illustration projects on the single dimension shown in Figure 1.1 may have prompted thoughts or questions that would not otherwise have surfaced. If something 'didn't fit' you might have started to question both the model and your perception of the research.

Theory to suggest good (or bad) practice

Some theories purport to generate 'answers' to problems, or suggest prescriptions for action. Some organisations undertake massive changes and restructuring in the light of a talk or a book by a persuasive 'guru'. Sometimes this can be helpful, sometimes not. Consider the impact of ideas about branding, or product lifecycle, or lean manufacturing or Business Process Re-engineering (BPR). Experiences, particularly of BPR, have been mixed at best. This is why the diagram shows one possible use of theory as being to mislead. An uncritical approach to theory which suggests 'good practice' can be dangerous if it is based on weak evidence or logic, and/or applied to situations where it may not be appropriate.

ASSESSING THEORY'S VALUE

Evidence and arguments

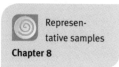

Evidence and arguments
Chapters 6 and 7

Represen-
tative samples
Chapter 8

When looking for useful theory to help you understand a practical issue, you will be considering the evidence and arguments upon which it is based, and what it adds to existing theory. These aspects will be explored later. Here I merely want to consider another influence on value: theory's relevance to context. One way to avoid being misled by inappropriate theory is to test its relevance in your own situation before adopting any 'good practice' it suggests. Such theory testing is one important purpose which practical business research can serve – as the following story shows. The idea of a representative sample will be discussed in more detail later.

The important point is to approach all theory as a potential tool that may serve a number of extremely useful purposes, but one that must be looked at critically, and used carefully as a source of ideas rather than solutions. Reflecting on the value of the ideas you used in the light of your research experience may contribute to further understanding of the theory and its potential. Indeed, it may help to develop the theory into something more useful and less potentially dangerous.

RESEARCH STORY

Theory testing

Decades ago, I was asked to do some research for the (then) Department of Employment (DE). This was at the time of the miners' strike, and consequent three-day week. The DE was considering a pay policy to control rampant wage inflation. Professor Elliot Jaques was urging them to adopt his theory of 'Time-span of discretion' (TSD) as a basis for determining pay levels for different jobs. TSD was determined by the length of time it would take for mildly substandard performance to be detected. Jaques had found that TSD was highly correlated with perceived fair pay.

The research from which this theory was derived had been done on 'white-collar workers' – those in office or supervisory jobs. Before basing a national pay policy upon TSD it seemed prudent to check whether the relationship also held for manual workers. I gathered data from a wide range of manual

employees, including some who killed, eviscerated or packed chickens, some electricity-generation workers, and some Welsh coal miners.

A team of us interviewed several hundred workers to find out their pay, and determine their satisfaction with it. We also obtained a 'measure' of TSD for each of them. Sadly, the predicted correlation was not found. This was a fairly academic exercise, carried out for a part-time MPhil degree, and with an academic supervisor. But you can see that there were very real practical implications. Without the research the DE might have been seriously misled by theory derived from a group of workers who were not representative of the working population as a whole. A national pay policy based upon this unrepresentative sample might have created serious problems for the government and the economy.

KEY POINTS

- *Management theory* includes ideas and frameworks that others have created as a result of experience, experiment and reflection, and is a potentially rich resource.

- It can be used to surface, challenge and extend your personal and often unconscious theories.

- This may help you approach complexity in a more structured fashion by looking at different 'slices' which you can then combine to create a richer understanding.

- Theory can aid thought and debate, suggest useful research questions and be modified in the light of your own thinking and research, allowing others to benefit from your research.

- You do, however, need the ability to assess the potential value of theory before using it as a guide.

THE IMPORTANCE OF EVIDENCE

Data

Whenever you construct an argument, you will need *data* and/or *evidence* to support your claims. It was suggested earlier that decisions were often taken without the benefit of research, and were the worse because of it. The following research story is offered to support this particular suggestion.

RESEARCH STORY

The police needed evidence ...

This story was told at a conference, and in a subsequent conversation, by Charles Phelps, the researcher concerned. The London Metropolitan Police was concerned with the diversity of its workforce, and since 2000 had been fairly successful in increasing recruitment from the Black and Minority Ethnic (BME) community. By 2007 22% of police staff were from BME communities (compared to 29% of the London population).

However, there were very few members of these communities at senior levels. The percentage of women in the police overall (59%) was actually greater than the percentage in the general population, but similarly there were few women at senior levels. (For example, for uniformed officers only 6% of chief superintendents were female, and only 3% were BME.)

Urgent action seemed to be called for. There was anecdotal evidence that women did poorly in the assessment centres that form part of the selection process. Some costly programmes were therefore introduced, aimed at preparing female and BME candidates for promotion panels, and thus increasing their chances of success.

These programmes had very little effect. It was therefore decided to carry out a more detailed 'diagnosis' of the issue, looking at the relevant evidence. (This is a good example of the sort of practical research that this book is designed to address.) The investigation showed that the problem was not 'differential success rates in promotion at senior levels' as had been assumed. Anecdotes are not always reliable evidence. In fact, success rates for women and BME candidates at the top level panels were *higher* than those for white males. The problem was that there were very few such candidates.

Further investigation of the statistics showed that the 'problem' seemed to stem from further down the organisation. For uniformed officers, the biggest change in proportionality happened at constable to sergeant level – for example, 22% of constables are female, but only 12% of police sergeants. The BME pattern was similar.

Additional data made it clear that some under-representation at that time was to be expected. Before 2000 very few BME staff had been recruited. So even though the figures showed that beyond sergeant level both female and BME officers were progressing faster than their white male counterparts (eg at inspector rank, white males had taken on average 55 months to gain promotion compared to 30 months for BME males), few BME officers had had time to work their way up to the senior ranks.

(Charles Phelps, personal communication, 2006)

This research did not, and was not intended to, address a more widespread issue of racial prejudice which led, in 2008, to the Black Police Association's campaign to prevent further recruitment of black police officers until a more equal situation was achieved. This was not an objective of the research. The research question was far more narrowly defined, and so must be judged against its reasonable and practical aims. There are several reasons why I think this simple case is a good example of business research and why it is important:

- there was an important issue of diversity and representation of minority groups at senior levels which had to be addressed.
- current expensive 'solutions' were failing to achieve their aim.
- relevant information was collected and systematically analysed.
- the research challenged existing assumptions about the nature of the problem and showed where the real problem lay.
- this allowed more appropriate action to be taken to address the issue.

This case is also helpful because the need for research seems so obvious in retrospect. Yet those commissioning the original training were convinced they 'knew' what the problem was, and were happy to take fairly major decisions on the basis of the spurious 'knowledge'. Later chapters will look at the complexities of knowing, and the distinctions between 'data', 'information' and 'evidence'. For the present, take this story as a lesson in how easy it is to 'know' something that is not true if you do not seek the relevant information.

WE ONLY THINK WE KNOW . . .

Why are managers comfortable with taking significant, potentially expensive, decisions on the basis of what they only *think* they know? Part of the reason may be our biology. The human brain has evolved to become very good at seeking and finding patterns, and ignoring anything which does not fit them – it is a necessary adaptation for rapid and (usually) effective decisions. It enables us to leap out of the way of the falling rock (or the oncoming bus) without wasting time on computing the significance of what we see. It is this drive to see patterns that drives our unconscious theorising.

But part of the price we pay for this adaptation may be the feeling that we 'know the answer' even – or perhaps particularly – when a problem is uncomfortably complex. 'Pattern matching' is an important part of expertise. We select aspects of the situation that are similar to past experience and assume that what worked then will work now. This presents consultant researchers with one of their biggest challenges: clients who are (prematurely and mistakenly) sure they know what 'the problem' is, and even its 'solution'. This why practitioner research, and the information and 'evidence' it produces is so important. Theory *may* challenge such assumptions. But more powerfully it may pose questions which prompt you to seek relevant and irrefutable evidence that both challenges assumptions and suggests more appropriate decisions and actions.

KEY POINTS

- Managers in organisations often take significant decisions without challenging their assumptions about problems and potential solutions.
- Because of the complexities, uncertainties and rates of change surrounding many management issues, these assumptions may not be justified.
- Decisions or actions based on faulty assumptions may fail to solve the perceived problem, and sometimes create additional problems.
- The chances of decisions or actions being appropriate can be greatly increased if they are informed by research to generate relevant and reliable data and evidence.
- Conceptual frameworks may help you decide what evidence you need to seek.

UNDERSTANDING THE RESEARCH PROCESS

Practical research is intended to achieve a specific purpose – namely, to inform thinking, decision-making and/or action. Its impact upon client organisations and their employees, as well as upon your own career, may be substantial. It is therefore vital that your research is trustworthy, your conclusions do not mislead. Understanding the research process will enable you both to assess the potential value of others' research and to conduct research yourself that is relevant, rigorous, and leads to trustworthy conclusions.

In principle, the research process is straightforward: you identify a possible issue, explore it to identify any underlying causes and clarify your thinking about what you might usefully achieve and relevant questions to ask. You then collect data and analyse it to provide answers to your questions and draw useful conclusions that will achieve your research purpose.

Recommen-
dations and
evaluation

Academic research usually stops at this point. Practical research frequently requires recommendations, and possibly action and evaluation of that action. Figure 1.5 shows the key stages, and Chapter 3 discusses the steps in more detail.

> **Good business research generates reliable and relevant data from which credible and trustworthy conclusions are drawn.**

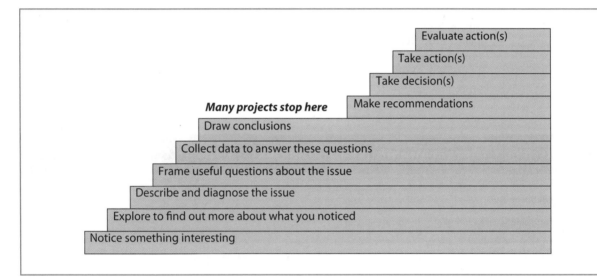

Figure 1.5 Basic logical steps in practical research

If the process is so straightforward, why is there so much flawed research? I would argue that there are several different sorts of complexity that make it difficult to do good practical business research, and almost impossible to do it in the simple linear fashion Figure 1.5 suggests. These are 'academic' complexity, issue complexity and contextual complexity. How you approach the challenges these complexities present will depend upon a fourth dimension: the philosophical complexities of what we believe about knowledge and knowing in such contexts.

Academic
complexity
Chapters 6, 7 and 24

Academic complexity relates to a point made earlier – the increasing gap between academics and practitioners. The academic literature on almost any management topic is now massive, and written according to conventions that are different from those for most other forms of writing. Some of this complexity will be explored later. Some you can usefully set aside for most practical research purposes: it can distract you from more important aspects of your research.

Issue complexity describes the way in which few issues in organisations are self-standing, or indeed quite what they first seem. An apparently simple problem may be part of a tangle of interrelated causes and effects. Unless these are understood, a 'solution' may create more problems than it solves. Chapter 2 explores this complexity in more detail, and suggests ways of dealing with it.

Stakeholders

Contextual complexity (also explored in Chapter 2) refers to the many different stakeholders involved in any organisational issue, and in any research project designed to address it. These stakeholders – who include you, the researcher – will often have conflicting aims. The uncertainties associated with any organisation operating in a turbulent environment create yet more complexity.

Because issues and their contexts are so complex, the neat sequence of logical steps shown in Figure 1.5 is unlikely to bear much resemblance to the way you will have to approach your research. Neither is the clear structure of headings required for a dissertation or academic paper much of a guide. It is more likely that the process will involve back-tracking and redirection at several points.

SOME OF THE REALITIES OF RESEARCH

Unless you are prepared for the complexities of research, the reality may come as a shock, and your research may start to go wrong almost from the start. Jamie's outline plan in the Research Illustration below is typical of those who fail to understand the complexities of research. (The heading indicates that it comes from our 'House of Horrors' archive – it warns you of the need to avoid the practices exemplified in the story.)

RESEARCH ILLUSTRATION: HOUSE OF HORRORS

Unreal planning

The following is an example of a dissertation plan

Activity in weeks	1–2	3–4	5–6	7–8	9–10	11–12	13–14	15–16	17–18
Topic identification	░								
Literature review		░	░						
Research question formulation				░					
Research method choice					░				
Data collection						░	░		
Data analysis and interpretation								░	
Write dissertation and submit									░

CONSIDER...

Look at the dissertation plan in the Research Illustration above. Why do you think Jamie drew up his plan in this way?

Jamie's approach is typical, rational and a recipe for disaster! He was probably uncertain about what was required, and in the absence of any other guidance took the recommended dissertation structure as the basis for his plan. But doing so offers a dangerous illusion of order. It allows you to reduce the 'dissertation problem' to a simple set of steps to be worked through systematically. Each can be 'checked off' when completed, and the next stage can then be undertaken. (Some courses reinforce this illusion by teaching parts of the process as separate modules.)

You may write your dissertation like this, although most dissertations would be better if redrafts allowed early drafts of later sections to influence subsequent drafts of earlier parts. But *doing* research is an entirely different process. One of the most dangerous mistakes you can make is to assume that these headings represent research activities, and therefore construct a research plan based upon them. Taking the structure of the final dissertation as representative of the research process is a dangerous misperception.

> **Doing research and writing up research are very different processes!**

Project management

Chapter 22

A plan like Jamie's creates a whole array of problems. There are some obvious practical issues. Very little time seems to have been allowed for dissertation-writing for example, or for data analysis and interpretation. And there seems to be no slack built into this plan. (Detailed guidance on project management is given later.)

Did you spot two more subtle shortcomings? Firstly, project planning normally needs, even at the outline stage, more detail. This plan would not help Jamie to manage the many activities needed to progress through the logical steps in the earlier diagram. But there is a far more important potential problem, and this lies in the linearity and discreteness of stages that the plan implies. Good practical research can almost never be approached in this fashion – as the next section argues.

ACTIVITY

If you are working towards a dissertation and do not yet have a copy of the requirements, obtain one now. You will find it useful shortly – though *not* as the sole basis for your plan.

PRACTICAL BUSINESS RESEARCH IS NOT LINEAR ...

The logical sequence of elements in the research process shown in Figure 1.5, dissertation structures, and the subheadings in academic research reports may *seem* to offer a 'route map' – a route map to *not* treat them as such. The logic may be clean, but the practice in real life is almost always much messier. As Buchanan *et al* (1988, p54) point out:

"It is now widely accepted that research accounts in academic journals depart considerably from the research practices of their authors."

They refer to Buchanan and Boddy's 1982 (pp54–5) paper, which

"implies that the research questions were based on a prior assessment of the literature and were selected as most appropriate in this context."

 Literature review

In fact, Buchanan admits to seizing an unexpected opportunity to gain access to an organisation where he had a contact. He had no time either to conduct a systematic literature review, or to design and pilot an interview schedule. His literature review came later – another necessary trade-off. A colleague told me the other day that she was still doing some of her literature search while writing up her PhD thesis.

Your report or dissertation will be constructed out of your research so as to represent your work clearly to your reader, and convey your conclusions convincingly. It will be a story – a *true* story, but one that is selective, and structured in order to communicate clearly. A blow-by-blow account of everything you actually did would normally tell a much more confused and confusing tale.

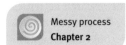 Messy process
Chapter 2

This is because useful research on complex issues tends to be a *messy* process. Elements overlap and recur. Early data may change your view of the problem, and of how to approach it. Deep insights may cause you to shift your whole topic or approach. If you treat your dissertation research as a tidy set of discrete stages, you may add up enough marks to pass. But there is a strong chance that your results will be of little use. Worse, whatever you 'learn' about research may make you *less* likely to do useful research in future.

 Lewin's work
Chapter 14

The idea of 'chicken and egg' iteration was suggested earlier – information refines questions which generate information which refines ideas, prompting new questions … and so on. Many researchers (see, for example, Lewin, 1948) have talked of research as a spiral with consecutive loops, in his case involving diagnostic investigation, planning and then taking action and evaluating it. Cope (2003) suggested a similar iterative model for consultancy. Bruner (1960) suggested a spiral curriculum as a model for education.

The underlying idea in each case is that what you currently understand limits what you can learn. At each loop you learn a little more, understand a little more, and are therefore ready to see something different and learn something different on the next circuit (as in Figure 1.6). I have been reminded of the spiral nature of learning while writing this book. It was necessary to read and reread a wide range of books and papers: I was amazed at how much more I found in them now that my own thinking has moved on. Even papers I read while preparing a first draft, then reread to check the final draft, seemed to contain far more than on first reading.

This is not because I had forgotten things from the first reading. I may well have forgotten, but I am comparing what seemed worth highlighting first time around with all the additional points screaming for the yellow pen at second reading. Reading and conversations in the interim had established questions and structures in my brain that enabled me to see far more meaning at the second pass.

But even a spiral may suggest too tidy a picture. Sometimes a tornado seems a better metaphor – you may feel you are in the grip of strong forces which shift you from one part of the research field to another almost against your will.

Figure 1.6 Research as a spiral

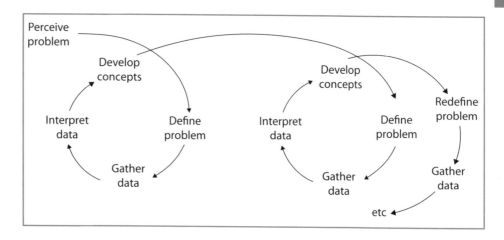

MESSY LOOPING

The tornado metaphor will certainly prepare you for the unexpected in research, but may be unnecessarily uncomfortable as a picture: more control is possible even if the control is far from perfect. It may be more helpful to see research as a process of 'messy looping'. The loops are less tidy and more organic and fluid than a spiral, but you have some influence over them.

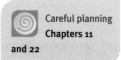

Careful planning
Chapters 11 and 22

Messy looping is far from a recipe for an unsystematic, unplanned approach. You need to plan carefully, but also to keep an open mind as you progress. You will probably need to work on several stages in parallel, to rethink, loop back and redirect your project if necessary without the loops getting tangled. Achieving this requires a clear understanding of the underlying research logic. With this as a firm foundation, looping can be a controlled and essential part of gaining insight and understanding.

A major problem with the dissertation plan in the Research Illustration is that it would discourage productive looping and redirection. The 'task and finish' approach it suggests would mean that any insights would be set aside. To revisit an earlier stage and redirect efforts would seem a serious and unwelcome setback.

> **Looping allows on-going learning and insights to improve the research.**

The first part of this book seeks to build your understanding of the research process, and of the complexities associated with it. This understanding will support a more flexible approach to your research, and help you identify a suitably broad topic to research. The second part will deepen your understanding of the constituent elements in the process, and their interrelationships. By the end of this part you should have gone through your first few loops and be confident in drawing up a research proposal (supported by a workable plan) for a worthwhile investigation.

You will still need to plan specific actions, and to chart them, but if you understand that looping is an essential part of the process you will keep your thinking flexible for longer. When redirection *is* required, you will be excited by the insights causing it, rather than frustrated by the need to revise your plan. Your loops will be purposeful, and based on a clear idea of all the stages in the process. Your planning will include slack to accommodate looping.

If you understand the research process as a whole, and think in terms of stages in your thinking, rather than the headings of a classic academic paper, you will be more likely to notice possible new questions or directions, and loop back to whichever earlier stage is appropriate. This will minimise the time and energy spent on unproductive investigation and maximise genuine progress.

OTHER BENEFITS FROM UNDERSTANDING THE RESEARCH PROCESS

Understanding the process is a prerequisite for doing good research. There are two further benefits. It will help you evaluate other people's research, and use that which is appropriate, and it will enable you to *learn* more from doing research. One reason so many professional courses include a research project is its learning potential. To realise that potential you need to focus on your own learning throughout the research. It is not enough to reflect on your learning only when the research is complete.

Maximising learning

Some dissertations ask you to include a section where you reflect on your experience of the research process. To gain maximum personal learning from your research experience, reflection has to be an on-going process, starting *now*, as Chapter 24 suggests. You must explore the reasons that lead you to 'loop', and to capture the insights they represent. You must reflect on all your experiences during a project if you are to learn from it effectively.

ACTIVITY

To maximise your learning, skim through Chapter 24 next, and plan to read it more carefully soon, certainly before starting Part 2. It is in Part 5 as the result of a logical grouping, but as with other chapters in that section, it is relevant from the start of your research.

Supervisor

Many professional organisations will require you to demonstrate continuing professional development, by reading, training, and perhaps by keeping a reflective log of your learning. A dissertation represents a transition from learning guided by lecturers to the self-directed learning you will continue to require as a professional. You will mainly be selecting and evaluating theoretical sources by yourself, as you will need to do after you qualify, and deciding what other data you need. Guidance from your supervisor will help you develop the necessary skills and understanding. Skills in reflective practice may significantly accelerate your career.

KEY POINTS

- Real-life research tends to be a messier process than logical steps and dissertation headings imply.
- Some stages may need to be revisited throughout the research, others only when your investigation suggests a rethinking or reframing of the issue.
- Researching complex issues thus requires a spiral or a messier looping process.
- Successful looping requires a sound understanding of the underlying research logic.
- Looping is often driven by an insight: such insights and other reflections are usefully captured in a written research journal.

DISTINGUISHING BAD RESEARCH FROM GOOD

If you understand what distinguishes good research from bad, you will be able to evaluate the research done by others as well as judge and improve your own research. Practical research can have a major impact on how people think about organisations, and the decisions and actions they take. Managers often need to draw upon published research and/or commission research from consultants.

If you understand the research process and the issues it presents, and know the characteristics of specific research methods, you will be able to recognise research that is badly carried out, and know when unsound conclusions are drawn from data. This will help you to commission and manage research done by consultants, and to give due weight to research commissioned by others. It is dangerous to accept consultants' claims simply because they are 'the expert'. Their findings may be just as misleading as other business research, and for similar reasons. You will develop your judgement skills by being critical of your own research.

So what makes research good? Good research is relevant, as rigorous as possible within the constraints of the situation, and *trustworthy* in that the conclusions drawn are firmly underpinned by the evidence collected. It is normally a plus if it produces results which are useful in a wider context. In contrast, 'bad' research is untrustworthy and can do substantial damage. Examples of obviously bad research may sensitise you to some of the potential flaws. Contrast the earlier story of evidence in the police diversity case with the following story. The title was promising – *'The evaluation of a recent change initiative and recommendations for further change in the light of the evaluation'*. As you read it, try to identify the problems with the account.

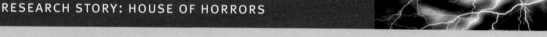

RESEARCH STORY: HOUSE OF HORRORS

Evaluating change

Andy works for a public sector organisation. A year ago a new Chief Executive was appointed, and a large number of changes to structures and processes occurred. Many redundancies resulted. His sponsor, Liz, had led the change programme, and suggested that Andy evaluate the change for his project. Andy designed a questionnaire asking staff about their feelings about different aspects of their jobs, as well as a large number of personal questions. He emailed this to 500 people (all those working in the three departments managed by his boss's boss); 40 questionnaires were returned.

Overall, it seemed that staff had fairly mixed feelings about their jobs. Some were happy, some less so. The only question on this lengthy questionnaire which specifically related to change was Question 54. I show Andy's 'results' below. You can see that most answers agreed that the changes had indeed

had a significant impact. The 'observed' row in the table below shows the distribution of answers to this item:

Q54. Please show the extent to which you agree with the following statement:
'The changes that have taken place during the last year have had a significant impact on the organisation'

Andy carried out a statistical analysis (using a chi-squared test) of the answers to this particular question. This test compares 'observed' responses with what you might 'expect' (normally, if your null hypothesis is true – more of this later).
The statistical analysis rated the difference between observed and expected as 'highly significant'.

Andy's report was thick and looked impressive. It included tables of responses to all 60 questionnaire items, graphs showing the same figures in the form of coloured bar-charts, and a verbal description of each table.

His main conclusion was that the change programme had been a tremendous success, having had a powerful impact throughout the organisation. He went on to recommend that the further changes currently under consideration should be implemented.

	Strongly agree	Agree	Neither agree nor disagree	Disagree	Strongly disagree
Observed	9	22	6	2	1
Expected	8	8	8	8	8

CONSIDER...

What might be problematic about the research?

What does this suggest about difficulties in carrying out business research, and the need to understand the process as a whole?

I hope you were worried by this story. As I read Andy's report I became more and more depressed. Indeed, he can claim some of the credit for our decision to write the book: clearly existing texts (which he had quoted extensively) had not helped him. The research was really important, with considerable potential to influence his organisation's future. Yet if the CEO followed his recommendations, the organisation would, at best, be no better than if the research had not been done. At worst, the impressive appearance of the graphs and statistical analysis might prevent the CEO and planning team from doing their own thinking about the advisability of further change, and perhaps commissioning a more reliable evaluation.

We shall return to the problems with Andy's research in more detail in subsequent chapters. Here, I shall merely highlight my main concerns, so that you can compare them with your own.

- *Size of sample*: I had a fairly serious worry about the very small proportion of people who sent back their questionnaires. It is possible that they were not representative of the organisation as a whole. (See chapters 9 and 20 for details.)

Significance levels **Chapter 20**

- *Statistical technique*: I was disturbed by Andy's statistical analysis, which seemed to me to be curious in the extreme and to have generated a 'significance level' that was meaningless.

Ethics and ethical considerations **Chapter 4**

- *Faulty logic*: By far my biggest worry was that Andy was making huge (il)logical leaps in interpreting the answers to his single question on the impact of changes. He has absolutely no justification for interpreting 'I agree that the changes ... have had a significant impact ...' because 'the change programme has been a tremendous success'. Nor was it clear what he could conclude about a future change from the impact of a previous one. His conclusions were totally untrustworthy. There are major ethical issues here.

Andy's research was *worse* than useless – it could have misinformed important decisions. He may not have been aware of some at least of its shortcomings. Others may have resulted from political pressures it would have been difficult to resist: such issues are an important aspect of many research contexts.

This story may be a fairly extreme case, but it highlights some fairly typical short-comings which later chapters will address. The key point to note here is that if Andy had *thought* about his research more carefully, he might have carried out his project very differently. Instead, as was clear from his report, he had treated his research as a series of discrete tasks rather than considering the process as a whole, or the purpose it was intended to achieve.

 Methodology

His literature search did not affect what he did in any way, nor did his discussion of 'methodology' map onto his eventual choice of approach. He had also seriously underestimated the amount of work required to carry out a worthwhile inves-tigation of a substantial topic. Had he understood the process better, he might have planned a less ambitious and less politically sensitive project, and been more successful.

KEY POINTS

- Although thinking, decisions and actions can be greatly helped by appropriate information, not all 'business research' is valuable.
- Good business research rests on clarity of purpose and a sound understanding of the business research process as a whole.
- Researching complex issues requires flexible and integrated thinking, and a willingness to iterate, rather than blindly carrying out a series of discrete tasks.
- The ability to evaluate your own research and that done by others is a key management skill.

Andy's research is at the 'bad' end of any research continuum. It lacked rigour, contributed little to his personal learning, and is unlikely to have done his career much good. Contrast this with Chris Rigby's dissertation story. Chris was studying full time for an MBA at Henley after working for many years as a school-teacher in New Zealand. He has kindly agreed to tell his story in some detail – it will be revisited in subsequent chapters, often in his own words. You will be able to see how approaching the research task with a range of purposes firmly in mind can make the experience radically different.

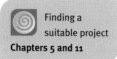 Finding a suitable project
Chapters 5 and 11

This story nicely illustrates a number of issues raised in the chapter. The first is that *you* are a key stakeholder in the research and can gain a lot from it if you plan a suitable project. Note too that the process has random elements, and that the literature search started early on and caused the direction to change during the research. Note also the hint that the final report was a post-hoc rationalisation, a 'convincing narrative' rather than an account of the actual process. Chris also provides a reassuring and encour-aging example of a researcher whose dissertation was the start of an on-going process of thinking, reflection and further research, and the basis for an interesting subsequent career as a researcher and consultant.

RESEARCH STORY

Reflection and leadership development

Chris started his studies with *'the vague idea that an MBA might provide a stepping-stone to a senior position in teaching. I was not entirely sure where the programme would lead at its conclusion. As it transpired, my dissertation research helped to reveal and clarify many of the issues that were contributing to this clouded, vague thinking.'*

Part of the course involved visits by a wide range of senior managers to talk about their organisations, and advise students.

'One presenter worked for Amec Oil & Gas and he made a comment that was pivotal. He suggested that if we were uncertain where our careers were heading beyond the MBA, and if a reason for being on the MBA was to open up new career avenues and opportunities, then the dissertation research was a good opportunity to begin that process by establishing contacts and a network to draw upon at a later stage. This clinched it for me. Some time later, Henley's Principal, Chris Bones, justified the requirement to undertake a dissertation –

something that for many felt like a very onerous and painful academic undertaking – in two ways. Firstly, the degree is a Master's-level qualification and therefore it is important to be able to demonstrate mastery in a particular field. Secondly, this mastery in a specialist field or niche could provide the distinguishing characteristic when re-entering the employment market. My strategy project had already taken me into the realms of leadership development and I felt a very strong urge that if I was to develop a career in leadership and leadership development, I had better get on with it and focus my research in this field. Leadership development it would be … Later, I was wandering in the library and picked up a new acquisition, Leadership Development in Balance: Made/Born, *by Bruce Avolio. … I decided to narrow my focus onto what I now claim was an investigation into the role of reflection in leadership development.'* [The original dissertation title addressed 'The importance of reflection and feedback'.]

THE STRUCTURE OF THIS BOOK, AND ITS OPTIMAL USE

The book's structure is influenced by a non-linear, spiral view both of the business research process itself and of the best way to learn about it. Thus this chapter has been a rapid pass through many of the issues you will encounter in more detail as you read the chapters indicated. Perhaps you have already briefly scanned one or two of those to explore particular points. This would be good looping!

You may now be both uneasy and a little excited about the potential difficulties and the potential rewards of a well-thought-through business research process. The stories may have alerted you to complications and potential benefits you have not previously considered. You may be unsure as yet about the idea of looping, and even less unsure about a 'messy' process. You may be starting to think about some aspects of research in a slightly different way.

The next three chapters offer a more detailed examination of the challenges of carrying out useful business research, an exploration of the investigative process itself, and of the things you need to be aware of about the context in which you are operating. Chapter 5 provides a framework for taking stock of the research opportunities currently available to you in the light of a deeper understanding of business research and its context. (If you cannot bear to wait until then to start thinking about possible topics, scan ahead. But your choice is likely to be better if you study Chapters 1 to 4 first.)

You will learn more from Part 2 if you think about what you read in the context of two or three possible research topics. It looks at stages in the standard academic research process, and will increase your understanding of the components of a dissertation or academic research paper. It will also help you 'translate' academic requirements into pointers to good practical research. You will get more out of Part 2 if you test the ideas against two or three potential project topics.

Because the stages in the business research process *cannot* be fully understood – or pursued – in isolation, there will be strong links made between these chapters. This means that by the end of Part 2 you will have a deeper understanding not only of the role of each element in research and its associated issues, but also of the entire process. By then you should have identified a specific research topic and have a clear idea of how to approach it. Chapter 11 will guide you through the process of turning your ideas into a formal research proposal for an academic supervisor; the thinking involved is relevant to other research proposals.

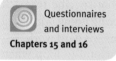

Questionnaires and interviews
Chapters 15 and 16

The third part of the book looks in some detail at the data collection methods most commonly used in small-scale practitioner business research. You may wish to look at all of these or only those that you are planning to use. However, there are some inter-dependencies: in particular, the chapters on questionnaires and interviews inform each other, and you should read both if you plan to use either.

Part 4 looks at how to analyse and interpret the data you collect. In a sense it is parallel to, rather than following on from, Part 3: you need to consider analytical methods at the same time as you think about your choice of data collection method. There is little point in choosing a method because it seems quick or easy, only to find later that analysing the kind of data your method generates is laborious and demands skills you do not possess.

Figure 1.7 The structure of this book

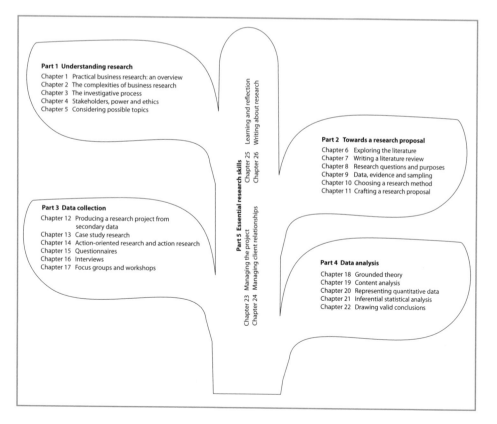

The final part of the book needs to be read in parallel with earlier parts, rather than afterwards. It addresses the on-going practicalities of managing a project, any clients, and your own learning. The final chapter addresses report or dissertation writing, and other forms of communication you may need during your research.

Figure 1.7 shows how the different chapters relate. You may find it helpful to spend some time using this figure as a guide to exploring links and getting a feel for how you will best be able to use the book. In particular, scan the chapters in Parts 4 and 5, so that you can allow suitable time for reading these and take note of points at which they will be useful.

USING THE BOOK

From Figure 1.7 you will see that the book is intended as a guide to doing your own research. It should help you to carry out a project that will meet the objectives of a range of stakeholders, including yourself. However, this will only happen if you *think* about the ideas put forward, both in the abstract and in terms of specific research projects you have encountered, have done yourself, or are considering doing. Thinking – particularly thinking which challenges your existing assumptions – is hard work. But this challenge is the ultimate goal of research. You may find it helpful to loop when using the book, skipping back and forth between chapters as the significance of points becomes clearer.

> It is essential to think as you read, to plan the order in which you address chapters, and to scan forwards and skip backwards as necessary.

Used in this way the book will develop your ability to judge the value of any research you are commissioning or reading about. Your own research is likely to be more useful to any client and other stakeholders. Your research experience should contribute substantially to your own professional development and future career. If the research is for a dissertation, you should gain high marks. If you are already qualified, the final chapter of the book may help you to impress a wider audience. Above all, you should approach your research with your brain fully and effectively active, feeling confident of your abilities to succeed, and to enjoy the process.

SUMMARY

This chapter has introduced the idea that practical business research is a topic of great importance to managers; it allows a more 'evidence-based' approach to key decisions and actions than is often observed. 'Evidence' may mean any sort of information relevant to the research question. 'Research methods' are ways of collecting such data as reliably as possible.

Practical business research may be directed towards theory-building or theory-testing, but typically its prime goal is to address a real organisational concern. In this case theory is an aid to effective research rather than its prime objective. 'Theory' here means any concept or framework of concepts which aids understanding and thinking about an issue of concern to managers.

Good business research almost never comprises the discrete, sequential stages of an eventual report. The 'stages' are better thought of as a repeating series of overlapping activities, a spiral or series of rather messier loops, driven by increasing insight. This process will enable you to develop a deeper understanding of complex issues.

Successful looping requires a clear understanding of the underlying logic of research, the formulation of objectives, translation of these into an answerable question, and the collection of evidence to enable you to answer this question and draw conclusions. You need to keep your research objectives firmly in mind throughout your research. Systematic looping will lead to credible and trustworthy conclusions.

To make best use of the book as a guide to doing good research, you will need to read Part 5 in parallel with the earlier parts, and to loop between chapters as your thinking progresses. It is important that you *think,* rather than merely read, using the *consider* prompts, and that you capture your reflections, preferably in writing. Some of this thinking is best done in the context of specific past or planned research.

If you follow this guidance, you should produce useful research and find the research process stimulating, developmental and even exciting.

REVIEW QUESTIONS

1. What is meant by 'practical business research' in this book?

2. How might this be distinguished from more academic research?

3. What can theory contribute to a practical research project?

4. What is the distinction between 'theory' as used in management teaching and 'a theory' as used more widely? Why might there be a need to make this distinction?

5. Why is it helpful to distinguish between tacit and formal theory?

6. What impact can theory have upon practical business research?

7. What distinguishes good business research from bad? Why is it important to be able to tell the difference?

8. Why is it better to see practical business research in terms of messy loops rather than a neat linear staircase?

9. Why is it important to use the book in a non-linear fashion?

10. Why is it important to 'consider' when instructed?

11. When do you need to start keeping a reflective journal?

12. When should you read Part 5 of the book?

EXPLORE FURTHER

Bryman, A. and Bell, E. (2007) *Business Research Methods*, 2nd edition. Oxford: Oxford University Press. This is particularly strong on qualitative approaches

Robson, C. (2002) *Real World Research*, 2nd edition. Oxford: Blackwell. This is directed towards practitioner-researchers and provides a complementary and accessible discussion of issues connected with doing practical research

Saunders, M., Lewis, P. and Thornhill, A. (2007) *Research Methods for Business Students*, 4th edition. Harlow: FT/Prentice Hall. This takes a more academic approach and will again complement this chapter, and indeed the whole book, if you have a more academic interest in business research

Smith. M. (2001) at http://www.infed.org/thinkers/et-lewin.htm for an excellent overview of Lewin's work (also relevant to Chapter 14 on Action Research)

http://www.accel-team.com/techniques/force_field_analysis.html for a brief article on force-field analysis which you may find interesting

British Journal of Management (2001) Vol.12, December, Supplement 1. This contains a range of responses by academics to a report on 'The nature, social organisation and promotion of management research: towards policy' (Starkey and Tranfield, 1998), including one by Starkey and Madan on the 'relevance gap' between academics and practitioners, and an interesting critique in terms of different 'real worlds' by Karl Weick

 Visit www.cipd.co.uk/brm for web links, templates, activities and other useful resources relating to this chapter.

CHAPTER 2

The Complexities of Business Research

INTRODUCTION

This chapter addresses one of the major difficulties facing the practitioner-researcher: the complexity of the issues addressed and their context. Most managers have a deep-rooted tendency to over-simplify, but if research is to be of value, complexity cannot be ignored. This chapter explores the complexities of business research on two levels. The first is the issue itself and its context; the second relates to what it means to 'know' about complex issues.

Issues are complex when they involve many interrelated causes, many possible consequences of actions, and a high degree of uncertainty. A number of stakeholders with different perspectives and potentially conflicting objectives are often involved. Issues exist within organisations that are themselves complex and often in a state of flux in response to changes in the wider environment. We find complexity difficult to handle – and this chapter offers some diagramming tools which may help.

Researching an issue or problem involves additional stakeholders and further tensions and conflicts. Clients, sponsors and academic supervisors are likely to have different goals for the research, and you will have your own development and career aims. You need to manage your relationship with all your stakeholders in the light of their potential to influence both the research and your future career. You will need to understand their agendas and their influence.

Changes beyond your control (or sometimes knowledge) present further complexities. You may be looking at an issue which has its origins in a situation that no longer exists, and making recommendations for an unknown future, while at the same time trying to cope with on-going change. There will be ample scope for your own perceptions to influence what you do, what you find, and what you interpret this to mean. It is important to appreciate the ease with which you may bias your results, and the need to minimise doing so.

This links to a deeper level of complexity, relating to what it means to add to *knowledge* in such complex contexts. What can we *know* about complex and uncertain business issues, and how can this knowledge be developed? There has been a lively debate on the nature of knowledge and knowing since the original Greek philosophers. Your own philosophical position on knowing contributes a further strand to the complexity of doing research, and will have a profound influence on the topic you choose and how you approach it.

These complexities mean that you need to put considerable effort into understanding a situation at a fairly deep level if you are to collect relevant data and interpret them reliably, and into understanding yourself, and your assumptions about the world and how to find out about it. This chapter suggests ways in which you can represent complexities and incorporate them into your thinking. Doing so will help you to carry out worthwhile research into complex issues and draw conclusions that deserve to be taken seriously.

LEARNING OUTCOMES

This chapter should enable you to:

- identify the main dimensions of complexity commonly found in business issues, and the additional complexities associated with researching them

- discuss the challenges these complexities pose for the business researcher

- use a range of techniques to map aspects of complexity

- identify your own perspective on what 'knowing' means in an organisational context and relate this to other perspectives

- evaluate the implications your perspective has for approaching your own research

- start recording your ideas and learning in a research journal.

COMPLEX ISSUES, WICKED PROBLEMS, AND MESSES

The first chapter suggested that research is a rather messy process of identifying an issue to address, finding reliable data relevant to that issue, and interpreting the data in order to reach conclusions. These might inform an argument for a new way of thinking and/or specific decisions or actions. The real challenge of practical research lies in finding ways of dealing with the complexities of the issue and its context. To do good business research you need to understand these complexities and how to deal with them.

It is easy to talk about complexity in the abstract, but harder to grasp the implications of it for research. Later in this section there is a research story which shows some of what complexity can mean in practice. But first I want to introduce the related ideas of 'wicked' and 'messy' problems: these provide a starting point for unpicking some of the complexities in the example.

The term 'wicked problem' was suggested by Rittel and Webber (1973). An approach called *systems thinking* was at this time challenging several aspects of conventional approaches to problem-solving and system design, and the idea of a 'wicked problem' is still in wide use today (see, for example, Camillus, 2008). Ackoff (1971), also thinking in systems terms, talked about 'mess management'.

Rittel invented the issue-based information system. He was working in the context of urban planning, and faced many of the problems that still plague business researchers. In trying to make sense of these difficulties, he decided that many problems had the following characteristics:

- the problem is not clearly structured: it is a constantly changing set of interlocking issues and constraints – indeed, what 'the problem' is depends upon whom you ask.
- the 'solution' is similarly ill-defined: the problem-solving process ends when you find something good enough or you run out of resources to look further. (You are probably familiar with Simon's (1969) concept of 'satisficing' – a term he coined to convey a combination of *satisfying* and *sufficing*, meaning doing enough to serve the purpose.)
- there are no 'right answers' – indeed, there are no objective measures of how good any solution is, although some solutions might be deemed better than others, and some deemed not good enough.
- solutions are usually impossible to undo: there will be costs to any solution, and because of the interrelatedness of issues, a wide range of consequences, some of which are likely to be unforeseen and may be undesirable.
- finding possible solutions is a creative rather than a deductive approach, although choosing between them will be a logical process.

You can see why he chose the term 'wicked'! Ackoff (1971) made a similar distinction between simple problems and what he called 'messes'. He suggests that in a management context *problem* is a conceptual construct, an abstraction akin to a still photo clipped from a movie. Problems, he says, satisfy three conditions:

- alternative courses of action are available to the problem owner(s);
- the choice made between them can have a significant effect;
- there is some doubt over the alternative to be selected.

Managers, he says, actually encounter not simple problems such as these, but large and complex sets of interacting problems – he calls these *dynamic systems of problems*, or *messes* (the term 'messy looping' is derived from this). Like Rittel and Webber, Ackoff emphasises the interrelatedness of the constituents of problematic situations.

It is this interrelatedness that explains why so many 'simple' solutions tend to make things worse rather than better. If your research is directed to bringing about improvements, you cannot afford to ignore elements that form part of the 'mess'.

> Conclusions drawn from information on only part of a wider system of problems will tend to be misleading.

DIFFERENT SORTS OF SOLUTION

Ackoff also made an interesting distinction between different sorts of solutions. He suggested that there are three things that can be done about problems: *resolve* them (find an outcome that *satisfices* – ie is good enough), *solve* them (find the best or optimal solution), or *dissolve* them. Dissolving problems is particularly interesting. Ackoff suggests that problem *dissolvers* seek to redesign the system or change its environment in such a way that the problem no longer – indeed, now cannot – arise. If you are carrying out research to address an issue that is viewed as problematic, this distinction may be important.

Problems can be resolved, solved or dissolved.

 Subjective and qualitative

Ackoff suggests that most managers, because of time pressures and lack of information are happy to *resolve* problems. They rely heavily on past experience and subjective judgement to inform their resolution, supplemented by primarily qualitative research. Tests, questionnaires and interviews are the main research methods they use, supplemented by a range of creativity and other techniques to involve participants, often facilitated by an external process consultant. (You will note that although Ackoff was writing some 40 years ago, this is still a dominant approach to bringing about change in response to some perceived issue.)

 Positivist

In contrast, Ackoff suggests some more technically inclined managers and 'Management Scientists' (we would probably call them 'positivist researchers' today – more of this later in the chapter) are problem-*solvers*. They would rather have an optimal solution than one that is 'good enough'. They may recognise that a *mess* exists, but they will approach this in an analytical fashion, identifying parts and interrelationships. Then – and this is the important part – they will seek to separate out aspect that *can* be treated as problems, and they are formulated as '*problems to which problem-solving methods can be applied*' (1971, p51). Such methods are likely to be highly analytical and quantitative. Remember this – it is an example of the adage that 'To a man with a hammer, everything is a nail', and is something that business researchers will encounter in many different aspects.

 Quantitative

In critiquing this approach, Ackoff starts from the definition of a 'mess' as a system of problems. The idea of 'system' has at its heart the belief that the whole is more than the sum of its parts, because the interrelationships between the parts are as important as the parts themselves. Parts of a system, if disconnected, lose their key properties and characteristics, and their removal alters the nature of the system. Cut off my hands, and they can no longer convey food to my mouth (and I will be significantly altered by their removal).

Dissecting out parts of a mess and 'solving' them in isolation is as meaningless as cutting off my hand in order to understand how I eat. Ackoff says (*ibid*) that the analytical solution-focused approach to problems that are part of a mess means that the researcher

> "loses their essential properties. As a consequence, what he perceives as the hard facts of the mess are really soft fictions of his imagination – abstractions only loosely related to reality."

You will have guessed that Ackoff advocates the 'design the problem away' or *dissolving* approach: I hope that by the end of the chapter you will agree with him. Chapter 14 on

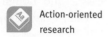

Action-oriented research

action-oriented research is consistent with this approach. For now it is worth looking at the implications of the ideas of 'wicked problems' and 'messes' in order to clarify some of the challenges you are likely to face as a researcher. The most important challenge is not to be seduced by the initial appearance of a problem.

THE COMPLEXITIES OF A SEEMINGLY STRAIGHTFORWARD PROJECT

See list in
Chapter 1

The projects listed earlier included a research project on the issue of labour turnover. This is a matter that is of concern to many organisations, in times of prosperity at least, and has featured in a number of MBA and MSc dissertations. It is also fairly typical of the sort of issue which managers might wish to address in their own organisations in order to improve performance.

CONSIDER...

In the story that follows, does Beth have a 'problem' in Ackoff's terms, or a 'mess'? Can you foresee difficulties with her recommended solution?

RESEARCH STORY

Looking at leaving

Beth managed a team of some 30 people. Over the last two years her life had become a constant treadmill of recruiting new staff to replace those who left, then training them, only to have them leave almost as soon as they were trained. The performance of her team was dropping steadily. Everyone was fed up with the overload caused by understaffing (it took some time to fill each vacancy) and by the difficulty of supporting inexperienced and inefficient recruits.

Beth decided that a project on labour turnover might enable her to solve the problem. She started to read about labour turnover, and then – since her reading suggested this – about induction and motivation as potentially relevant. (This gave her plenty of material for her literature review.)

Her reading, supplemented by Internet search and discussions with friends in other organisations, suggested the following possible approaches to

reducing labour turnover: increase pay in order to increase the likelihood that people would stay; raise pay generally; introduce some sort of bonus payable on completion of the first year of service; improve job design to increase job satisfaction; improve the induction of new staff; and/or improve the training programme.

Beth decided to carry out a comparison of these options. She interviewed a number of people to obtain estimates for the costs and likely impacts of each possible solution, and compared cost-effectiveness. She recommended that her organisation solved the problem by introducing an 'anniversary bonus', paid to staff on their first anniversary. This was relatively cheap and clearly targeted at those with the highest leaving rates. Her boss was impressed by her report, and the company subsequently introduced the recommended bonuses.

Clearly, Beth was treating this as a *problem* in Ackoff's terms. She identified a range of options and collected and analysed information in order to decide between them. But her conclusions were misleading because the situation was more complex than she had envisaged. She was thinking about 'solutions' from the outset, and did not spend enough time exploring the issue in order to understand it and diagnose the causes of the problem. As a result she drew far too narrow a frame around the issue, and thought only about the experience of people once they were in post. The problems caused by the 'solution' show why diagnosis is so important.

Tacit theory information

Chapter 1

Thinking about solutions without understanding the nature of the problem you are addressing is very common, but ill-advised. Each of Beth's potential solutions addressed a *different* problem: that people were unhappy with their pay or their jobs; or that they were inadequately inducted or trained; or that the pay was too low. Some, or all – or, indeed, none – of these may have been the case: without more information Beth did not know the cause of the leaving rates – although she probably had her own tacit theory relevant to the issue.

> **It is dangerous to consider a solution before understanding the problem.**

It is always important to check whether your perception of a problem is shared by other stakeholders. For example, it *might* have been that the problem was Beth's lack of interpersonal or other managerial skills!

It is also important to look at the wider context. In this case it would have been useful to compare Beth's team's retention rates with those of comparable teams in the organisation and elsewhere. This in itself might alter her perception of the problem. For example, it might be redefined as that of managing a team where most staff will always be fairly temporary.

More importantly, it is important to try to tease out all the strands in the mess. In Beth's case there were two major contributory factors. One was a new 'fairer' selection process; the other was the arrival of a major new employer in the area.

Previously employees had let family and friends know when a job was coming up, and recommended them to the relevant supervisor. This was now deemed to be potentially discriminatory, and all jobs were advertised. Applicants were selected on the basis of their qualifications and interview performance. Interview panels were particularly impressed by energy, enthusiasm and ambition, and painted a glowing picture of the job and organisation to 'sell' the job to such applicants. In reality these jobs presented few challenges to a bright and ambitious employee once their initial training was completed.

Once trained, however, these bright young employees were extremely attractive to the recently arrived multinational, which offered higher pay than Beth's company could ever afford and a clear career path for the ambitious employee. Those who did not move immediately were seriously under-challenged by their jobs, and often sought satisfaction in malicious gossip and undermining the work of others.

Given these facts, Beth's 'solution' had little chance of improving the situation. She was in part right that pay was non-competitive. But the 'affordable' solution of a one-off bonus did not address this – indeed, it made things very much worse.

 CONSIDER...

Before reading further, identify the stakeholders in this issue.

Think about the possible impacts on them of the introduction of a 12-month bonus.

RESEARCH STORY Continued

Looking at leaving

Stakeholders in the issue include Beth and her team, and all others upon whom the solution impacts. It was deemed unfair to target this bonus at just the job categories with the high labour turnover rates. So a one-year bonus was introduced across the organisation. Although this was still cheaper than a uniform pay rise, it was much more expensive than the more limited scheme originally envisaged. The bonus was being paid to many employees who would not be attractive to the multinational. Even in the targeted areas the impact was fairly minimal. The training lasted six months, and staff tended to work for a few months after this, because they could then claim 'substantial experience' on their CVs. So for this group of people the bonus moved the 'leaving peak' from 10 months to 12 months. During this additional two months dissatisfaction and disruption was, if anything, even higher.

Longer-serving employees were hugely resentful of this bonus. They had not had such a bonus, and why was it being paid to people who in their words were 'a complete waste of space', while they – who were working at high stress levels because of their junior colleagues' shortcomings – went unrewarded. The union started to argue for an annual bonus for all staff, as the 12-month bonus disproportionately rewarded younger staff and was therefore against age discrimination legislation. Overall staff satisfaction declined further. Other managers became increasingly resentful as the costs of the bonus scheme meant that their own bids for training and other initiatives were rejected.

While all this was going on, the approach to recruitment that had been a major causal factor in the case but that had never been questioned was extended to other areas of the organisation.

This is a small case, but I hope it has alerted you to the significance of some of the features of 'wicked problems' or 'messes', and to the implications for a potential researcher. Because wicked problems are so common, it is crucial to put substantial effort into understanding the full complexity of the immediate and wider context when researching an intricate issue. They may have substantial implications.

Table 2.1 endeavours to summarise some of these implications.

There may be a tremendous temptation (particularly if you have a background in science or engineering) to adopt a highly analytical 'problem-solving' approach, and define a manageable project to answer a clear and defined question. Indeed, this may be the way to protect your sanity. You will be drawing upon a skill that you already have. If you are doing a dissertation, you may produce an impressive report and will probably pass. If you are a consultant, your client may be impressed – in the short term.

But unless the issue is genuinely a simple problem rather than a wicked mess, the impact of your recommendations may not be what you intend. And there are substantial costs to this seductive approach.

- As a consultant you will risk offering a short-term solution that will rapidly generate as many problems as it created, making future business from that client unlikely.

- For a client the problems generated by an inappropriate solution may be costly, or even threaten the organisation's viability.

- As a researcher and learner you will be missing out on a huge opportunity to extend your capabilities.

Table 2.1 Elements and implications of complexity

Aspect of complexity	Implications for researcher
Issues are not simple problems but dynamic systems of *problems* or *messes,* which involve a range of people with different views of the problem, some of whom will have a powerful influence on your research.	Analysing the issue and treating the parts in isolation does not allow the problem to be understood. You must look at all the strands in the issue and its context, and identify stakeholder perspectives and influence.
Solutions are ill-defined, with no right answers, and no agreement as to what an answer might look like.	This means that it is not sensible to *look* for 'right' answers. Instead, think about *changes* and *possible consequences* from a variety of perspectives, not just your own.
There is often a lack of existing relevant information. Furthermore, it may not even be possible to generate reliable and relevant 'hard data'.	This is no real excuse for not trying to find some! 'Gut feelings' are not a good guide to action without supporting evidence. You may have to use a mix of research methods and draw your conclusions from different sorts of data.
Your own views are likely to influence how you define and approach the issue. You will tend towards a definition that is amenable to your preferred approach to problem-solving.	You need to be aware of this tendency, seek to minimise it, and recognise its existence when interpreting your findings.
A solution to an isolated problem within the mess is likely to be ineffective: any solution may have unforeseen and damaging consequences. Solutions are often costly and usually difficult to undo if they prove unhelpful.	You must recognise and resist any temptation or client pressure to offer such a solution. Before making recommendations you need to actively consider interrelationships and explore potential consequences for the wider system.
The idea of problem 'dissolving', or redesigning systems so that the problem no longer exists, offers the potential for longer-lasting improvements.	The resolve/solve/dissolve distinction may help you to address the issue on multiple levels and to consider the wider organisational system within which your 'system of problems' is nested and its environment.

For evidence see **Chapter 9**
For data see **Chapters 9 and 10**

Findings **Chapters 10, 19 and 22**

KEY POINTS

- Many business issues consist of a 'dynamic system of problems'; these are described as 'wicked' or 'messy'.
- The difference in perspective between key stakeholders adds to the complexity arising from the multiple interactions between the various aspects of the 'mess'.
- You need to explore as many aspects of the complexity as you can and act in the light of this, rather than trying to select parts of the mess and to treat them as stand-alone problems.
- Resist the temptation to oversimplify the issue or offer solutions before you fully understand the problem!

THE COMPLEXITIES OF DOING BUSINESS RESEARCH

In the previous chapter I suggested that although 'A research method is simply a technique for collecting data', the business research process is far from simple. I disagree with Thorpe and Moscarola's (1991, p127) claim that

> "research is in many ways simple and largely about being able to compromise, pose the right questions, and answer them in a way that satisfies the majority of the interested parties in the research."

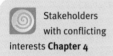

Stakeholders with conflicting interests **Chapter 4**

These are indeed the bare bones of research. But I can only assume they were being ironic, since they seem to be pointing to much of the source of the complexity involved. There is a real art in asking the right questions – as Chapter 8 will show – and when was it ever easy to compromise, or to satisfy stakeholders with conflicting interests?

CONSIDER...

Based upon what you have read thus far, jot down any additional complexities that might result from your needs as a researcher if you are also involved in the issue.

The 'interested parties' will include all those with an interest in your project and its results. Any or all of these interests may be in conflict. Your capacity to bias your results (often unconsciously) adds to the complexity and can be a particular problem if, like Beth, you are a part of the issue you are researching in addition to your interest as a researcher. The next chapter looks at complexities of the investigative process in more detail. Here I want to introduce some of the complexities stakeholders present.

STAKEHOLDERS IN YOUR RESEARCH

Stakeholders in the issue itself will depend upon the project concerned. Chapter 4 looks at ways in which you can analyse their likely influence, and plan to manage your relationships with them accordingly. *Researching* an issue involves additional stakeholders, and I shall address these here. This multiplicity of stakeholders adds substantially to the 'wickedness' of doing research. Any or all of these stakeholders may have conflicting objectives, leading to difficult decisions on your part. You may be unaware of some of their objectives. Indeed, the stakeholders may themselves be unaware of some of them at the outset.

The story continues from **Chapter 1**

Primary stakeholders in most projects, are the researcher, the organisational client or sponsor, and those whose co-operation will be required for the research. Secondary stakeholders are those who will be affected by your conclusions or by your research activities.

Your thinking about a possible project may still be at an early stage, so another instalment of Andy's (horror) story may help you realise the importance of stakeholders.

CONSIDER...

Read the first paragraph below – and before reading any further, quickly jot down likely stakeholders in Andy's research, and their possible objectives.

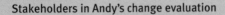

RESEARCH STORY Continued

Stakeholders in Andy's change evaluation

You will remember from the last chapter that Andy was evaluating the impact of a change programme, introduced a year ago by his sponsor Liz, at the request of the then newly arrived CEO. Although his recommendations were framed in terms of what the CEO should do next, it was Liz who was Andy's 'internal client'. At the start of the project there were a number of stakeholders in the project

Andy, whose objectives included passing his MBA, preferably with no more work than was absolutely necessary – he had recently become a father and his job was a demanding one. He also wanted to impress his superiors, particularly Liz, because he hoped to move into her team once he had his MBA.

Andy's sponsor, Liz, who had put a tremendous amount of effort into the change initiative, and wanted a report that would impress the CEO with what she had achieved. Although the economic savings were impressive, there were an increasing number of complaints from service users, and a legal case was threatened by an ex-staff-member. She felt that she needed evidence to safeguard her position.

The CEO, while not Andy's client, had been a protagonist of the change initiative and was interested in an evaluation of its effectiveness because further changes were in the pipeline. He was, however, slightly worried about potential sensitivities, given that the redundancies were still fairly recent, and had suggested that the departments which had suffered the most should be excluded from the study.

Andy's boss, Devendra, was uneasy about the project, because he was afraid that it would divert Andy's attention from his 'real' job. As someone who had narrowly survived the recent round of redundancies he also thought that it was time someone told the truth about the real costs of the change initiative (although not prepared to do so publicly himself because he still felt his job might be at threat if there were more changes).

Employees who received Andy's questionnaire were nervous about their jobs, resentful of the changes that had taken place and the increased workloads they were experiencing as a consequence. They were highly suspicious of this 'evaluation', and were not going to say anything that might put their jobs at risk. They did not trust the promise of confidentiality.

Andy's academic supervisor believed that anyone with an MBA should have mastered the important research skills he felt a dissertation should test. He emphasised the need for sound theoretical underpinnings derived from an extensive literature search, use of both quantitative and qualitative data, and rigorous analytical methods.

Andy's business school was concerned with its reputation and the maintenance of academic standards. Accrediting bodies take a considerable interest in dissertations, and they have to meet rigorous standards.

Andy's wife was exhausted with the baby and sleepless nights, and wanted him to come home from work as early as he could, not stay late working on his project.

Can you see some of the different conflicts at play here? At the most basic level there are competing demands on Andy's time from his boss, his client and his wife, and indeed, Andy himself, who was becoming increasingly stressed as the project progressed, and feeling he needed to be at home more.

Then there is a conflict between his supervisor's concern with the academic features of the work and his client's desire for a report to serve a specific purpose. Both Liz's desire to 'prove' that the changes had been successful and Andy's desire to impress Liz might together conflict with Andy's supervisor's concern for rigour and impartiality. Any desire to 'prove points' conflicts with a basic academic value of impartiality of research: this is one of the most worrying conflicts in this case. And when stakeholders limit access in order to limit what can be found out, as Liz did, the research is seriously compromised. The questions asked, and the sample allowed, were heavily influenced by Liz, on the grounds that what Andy had originally proposed was 'too sensitive'.

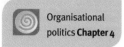
Organisational politics **Chapter 4**

Andy's experience shows that stakeholders can exert significant pressure on research. Like Liz, they may see the investigation as potentially threatening, and have strong views on what you may and may not do. Since they have the power to influence your future, or the futures of others involved in the research, it will be hard to resist complying with their views. Organisational politics is a key factor in the complexity faced by the business researcher, and will be addressed later.

KEY POINTS

- Business research is often made complex by the existence of a variety of stakeholders in the issue itself, and in the research project: these objectives may conflict.
- Potential stakeholders include your research supervisor, your client, those from whom you are seeking information, other employees in your target organisation(s), any co-researchers, work colleagues, your family and yourself.
- Your own learning, career, and 'time survival' objectives may themselves conflict.

You are a key stakeholder.

A research project will make significant demands on your time and energies, so those with competing demands on your time will be affected – work colleagues, family and friends are obvious stakeholders here. If your research is for a degree, your supervisor and your university are also stakeholders. You may also be seeking to use it to gain membership of a professional body such as the Chartered Management Institute (CMI) or the Chartered Institute of Personnel and Development (CIPD). If so, they will have objectives too, and your research will have to satisfy these, in addition to those of other stakeholders. Add any of these to your list if you need to.

RESEARCHER INFLUENCE

Perhaps the most important element in this web of complexity is the inevitable influence that as a researcher you will have on your results. You will affect your findings by the language you use to talk about an issue, how you frame the problem (what is in and what is out of the frame), the data you seek and the methods you use to collect and analyse it, and your reasoning in drawing conclusions and making recommendations. In any interview, the relationship you build with your informant will influence what they say. The influence may be greatest for 'soft', less objective data, but it is always there. If you want your findings to be more than merely a reflection of your view of the world, you need to be aware of this potential for influence – and guard against it.

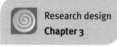
Research design **Chapter 3**

Whether or not you change your questions as you go (in flexible research designs, this is part of the design), the extent to which interviewees trust you, the personality they attribute to you, their assumptions about the sort of research you are doing and what it may bring about will all affect how they answer. (Chapter 16 suggests ways of minimising this influence in interviews.)

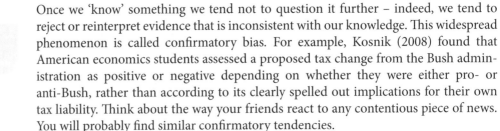

RESEARCH STORY

Silverman's first research

In his very personal account of doing qualitative research, David Silverman (2007) describes his first attempt at business-related research. He started with a project on white-collar workers' beliefs and values (similar in many ways to my 'Attitudes to pay' project described in the last chapter). He wanted to see whether where you worked and your future job prospects had any influence on how you saw yourself. (He was drawing on sociological theories about class and social status.) He designed a structured interview schedule, and was going to test his hypothesis by statistical analysis of the results.

However, as the interviews progressed, he found that he needed to go beyond the questions he had designed in order to obtain the sort of answers he wanted.

Silverman realised that although he could write up his results to appear suitably rigorous, what he was analysing was not 'raw data' at all. Instead, he had influenced it substantially. While Silverman was commendably aware of what he was doing, many interviewers are less self-aware.

Confirmatory bias

Confirmatory bias

Once we 'know' something we tend not to question it further – indeed, we tend to reject or reinterpret evidence that is inconsistent with our knowledge. This widespread phenomenon is called confirmatory bias. For example, Kosnik (2008) found that American economics students assessed a proposed tax change from the Bush administration as positive or negative depending on whether they were either pro- or anti-Bush, rather than according to its clearly spelled out implications for their own tax liability. Think about the way your friends react to any contentious piece of news. You will probably find similar confirmatory tendencies.

Coding answers
Chapters 18 and 19

If you happen to have strong views on the issue you are researching, this will increase the risk of bias. The influence starts even before you have observed (or failed to observe) something to interpret. You may not realise that you are choosing particular aspects to address because of your views, or designing a questionnaire in a certain way, or looking at some parts of an organisation or another, or selecting a specific sample within it to 'help you prove your point'. You may not realise that people who like you and want to help you may be giving you the answers they think you want to hear. If you are coding answers yourself, you may be doing it in a way that makes it more likely that you will get the result you want. But unless you are very careful you may well be doing this. Figure 2.1 shows some of the many ways in which you can influence your results, and some of the causes of such influence. Awareness, combined with a systematic approach and careful choice and use of methods can help minimise any such influence.

Sampling
Chapters 9

Some of your influence may be useful in practical terms. If you have good relationships with people around the organisation, they may be willing to take part themselves, and also to encourage people who work for them to return questionnaires or agree to be interviewed. You may have 'insider knowledge' into the non-obvious meanings of some of the statistics the organisation routinely keeps. Indeed, you may have to exercise some of your influence quite consciously to ensure that your client agrees to a project that is going to meet course or professional body requirements and satisfy your own learning and career objectives. Obviously it must be worthwhile for your client as well, but if it meets *only* their needs, it is probably not a project you should undertake.

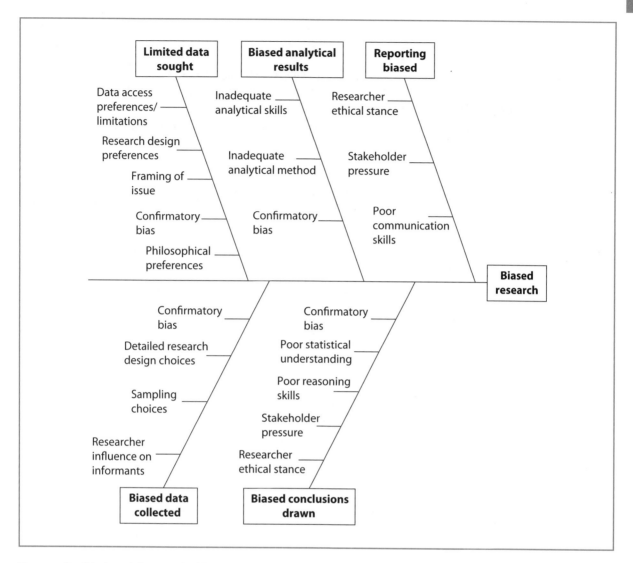

Figure 2.1 Possible channels for researcher bias

It is important to minimise bias caused by your own views about an issue.

The important thing is to be aware of your capacity to influence, and to use it to improve, rather than corrupt, the quantity and quality of evidence you collect. An important first step is to be as clear as possible about your own objectives in carrying out the research, and avoid any topics where the aim is to 'prove a point'. I shall come back to research objectives at the end of the chapter. A second step is to look carefully at the ways in which different research methods attempt to minimise this influence, to seek an appropriate one, and to take into account any inevitable bias when drawing conclusions and writing your report.

REPRESENTING COMPLEXITY

One of the reasons for feeling uncomfortable with complexity is the difficulty in grasping it – in 'getting your head around it'. We tend to use words when trying to note something, and prose is linear. What makes a mess so messy is the extent to which its different aspects are interrelated. This is made worse by the way in which different people's views of the parts and of the whole may differ widely.

Further information on diagramming is available at **www.cipd.co.uk/brm**

When you are dealing with a *mess* or a *wicked problem*, diagrams can be extremely useful. Diagrams can show non-linear sequences, and represent factors that are happening simultaneously. They can allow you to focus on a different aspect of the complexity in each diagram, eventually building a rich composite understanding of the situation. They can be drawn in a deliberately 'non-serious' way, reducing some of the anxieties associated with dealing with complexity. They can be drawn very quickly. They can be drawn by groups as well as individuals. The three previous points can combine to encourage a more creative approach to an issue. Diagrams can, if done well, communicate a lot of information 'at a glance', and so are useful for conveying information as well as generating it.

Useful diagram types for the early stages of issue exploration include Checkland's (1981) 'rich pictures', relationship diagrams, multiple-cause diagrams, Ishikawa fishbone diagrams, and basic cognitive mapping.

RICH PICTURES

A rich picture is a sort of cartoon. It is a way of capturing (normally on a very large piece of paper indeed) elements in a situation that *might* be relevant, and linking related elements by lines. Lines can be 'coded' – crossed swords often indicate conflict; £££s suggest financial relationships. No further structuring is included. Fig 2.2 gives an example.

You can see that this is not a piece of art – you don't need artistic talent to draw a rich picture. You merely need to allow yourself to 'doodle' without worrying about whether something is really important. The process is akin to a graphic brainstorm. You are seeking to *include* as much as possible.

Rich pictures were 'invented' by Peter Checkland (1981) as part of a specific 'soft systems methodology' – an approach to problem-solving and change based explicitly on systems ideas. It therefore stresses the need to look at the situation as a whole, and rich picturing is a first approach to this. Even if you do not intend to use systems ideas to inform your research, rich pictures have many advantages as an initial exploratory tool:

- because they look childish they can help you escape from your normal mindset and take a less limited, more creative view.

- they can be fun to draw as a group, and allow members to explore differences of view and come to a shared perspective.

- they allow you to absorb far more at a glance than can a verbal description.

- they can 'preserve' your initial view for future reference: this can be useful if you need to loop back. Thinking of the 'broad picture' becomes harder once you have started to draw boundaries around your thoughts.

- you can revisit the picture at regular intervals and add new elements or relationships.

Figure 2.2 Rich picture of Beth's leaving rate situation

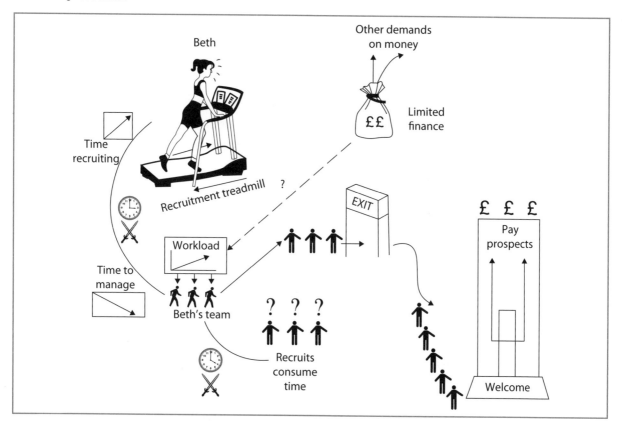

The *process* of drawing is perhaps the most valuable part of the exercise: both playfulness and spatial thinking are associated with creativity. But rich pictures really come into their own as part of a group exploration of an issue. The creative element will be stronger – drawing such pictures together can be good fun.

> **Rich pictures can capture initial ideas about a situation and make them visible.**

More importantly, the elements that others add to the picture will begin to make their thinking more visible to you. You can then question both their thinking and yours. You can 'interrogate' cartoons – in a constructive rather than critical way. Why is that there? Where might *I* have put it? Why did you draw it like this? Isn't there likely to be a relationship between this and that? Revisiting your own pictures after an interval may help you to become more aware of your own personal theories and assumptions. But such questions are more often prompted by differences between how you would represent something and how others do. Such differences may become far more apparent than if you had merely talked about the situation.

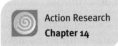

Action Research
Chapter 14

If you are seeking a shared understanding of a situation – and this will be a common requirement of any early diagnostic stage – rich pictures can both surface and capture some of the complexities caused by different perceptions and help to change these views. If the main thrust of your project is to advance shared thinking about practice, as in Action Research, rich pictures can be a useful aid to collective reflection.

Be careful how you use pictures, though. Rich pictures seldom impress those not involved in drawing them. For a report you will have to translate any useful information from your rich picture into a form more likely to be acceptable to your audience.

KEY POINTS

Rich pictures are used:

- **to stimulate the creative identification of as many potentially relevant factors as possible**
- **to build a shared understanding of a situation among stakeholders**
- **to capture and develop an 'unframed' picture for future reference**

They are *not* for communication in a formal report.

RELATIONSHIP DIAGRAMS

One of the advantages of a rich picture is that it enables you to convey key *relationships* in a situation: it has been argued that relationships between elements in a situation may be at least as important as the elements themselves. A relationship diagram is more sober – it lacks the exuberance and possible distraction of the cartoons. Instead, it shows elements and the relationships between them using words or short phrases connected by lines where they are related. You can see that if there are a lot of interconnections, things may rapidly become very messy: you might wish to focus on stronger relationships only, if this were the case. Figure 2.3 shows an example of a relationship diagram as it might appear in a final report.

It is possible to produce a working version using Post-Its on a whiteboard or flip sheets; you can then move the elements around and easily draw and redraw lines, or make temporary connections with string. One of the benefits of drawing a relationship diagram is that you may find that there are some sets of elements which are closely interrelated but which are also more loosely related to other aspects. Moving the elements around to create clusters of closely related elements will make the diagram far clearer.

KEY POINTS

Relationship diagrams are used:

- **to represent key relationships between elements in a situation**
- **to organise information from a rich picture for presentation to an uninitiated audience.**

Figure 2.3 A relationship diagram

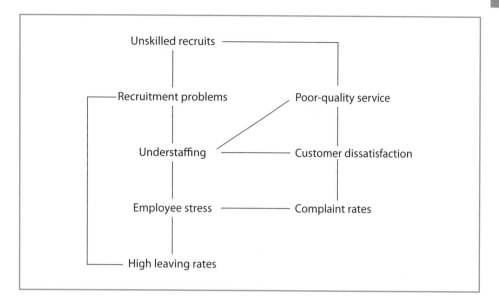

MULTIPLE-CAUSE DIAGRAMS

When you are exploring an issue that is problematic, key questions are 'Why?' and 'What?' Why does the problem exist? What is causing it? As part of our natural tendency to simplify, we often assume there is a single cause and stop looking when we have found it. But wicked problems or messes usually involve many causes. None of these would probably create the situation by itself, but together they bring it about. Furthermore, each of these causes has its own contributory factors. To understand a situation fully, and to dissolve (rather than merely solve) a problem, you might need to look a long way back along these causal chains. Multiple-cause diagramming is an extremely useful technique to counteract any 'single cause' tendencies. Drawing such diagrams can clarify and extend your thinking.

Multiple-cause diagrams help you explore levels of contributory factors.

The elements in a multiple-cause diagram are the event or situation you are investigating (this is often circled to distinguish it), phrases representing events or states that contribute to the causation of that situation or to other causal factors, and arrows. An arrow pointing from event A to event B means that event A causes or contributes to event B.

Figure 2.4 Examples of causal links

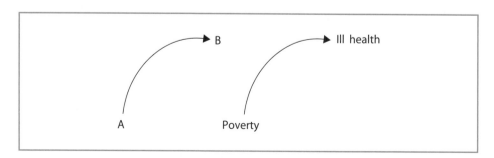

To draw a multiple-cause diagram, you think about what it is you want to explore. Suppose it was high rates of staff leaving. You would write this in a blob. You would then ask yourself why is this happening. You might ask supervisors why they thought it was, or ask recent recruits whether there was anything about the job that they did not like. This might produce a range of contributory factors: they didn't feel confident in their ability to do the job; the pressure was relentless; it wasn't what they had been led to expect. You would put these on to the diagram and draw an arrow from each to the 'leaving' blob. Then you would take each in turn and ask what might be causing *that*. You might go through this process of pushing back up the causal chain several times until you were satisfied that you had unravelled all the factors involved. Figure 2.5 shows how the diagram would start to build up from first thinking a) through the next layer of causal influences b).

Figure 2.5 Building a multiple-cause diagram

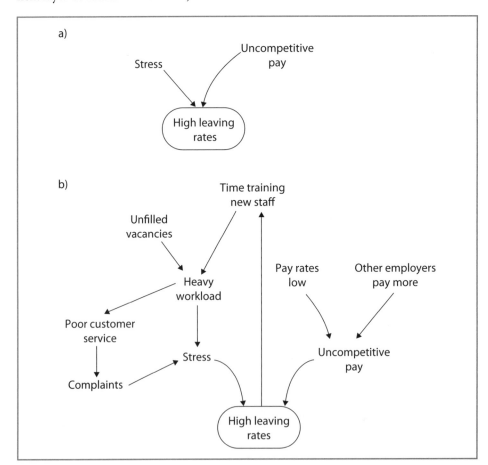

You can draw multiple-cause diagrams yourself to help you clarify your thinking and face up to the 'multi-causality' aspect of complexity. But equally, the technique is simple enough to be explained to a group and used for collaborative exploration of a situation, or as part of an interview with a key informant.

KEY POINTS

Multiple cause diagrams are used:

• to explore the factors causing or contributing to an issue

• to find root causes

• with individuals, in interviews, or with groups.

Note: the diagrams are always drawn backwards from the issue in question.

CAUSE-AND-EFFECT, OR ISHIKAWA FISHBONE DIAGRAMS

In contrast to a multiple-cause diagram which explores *existing* causes, an Ishikawa or fishbone diagram seeks to capture all *possible* causes. It is commonly used in quality management. Figure 2.6 shows an example. The manager was looking at reasons for payment problems within a Six Sigma framework. Each major 'bone' represents a type of error or quality fault, such as 'Does not match purchase order (PO)' or 'Does not match master agreement (MA)'. Many of the possible errors relate to the Accounts Payable (A/P) department and its system. You can see that having established all the possible categories of reason for a payment problem the manager looked at what might have caused these problems to be manifest. Possible causes such as 'Rate error' – appear on the smaller branches. Having established all the possible ways in which a payment problem might arise, the manager was able to collect data on the frequency of each type, and identify those which it was most important to address.

COGNITIVE MAPPING

Cognitive mapping refers to a variety of approaches towards attempting to represent cognitive structures, or people's tacit theory. Typically, cognitive maps seek to represent and link ideas that people are using, and often arrange them in a hierarchy. Multiple-cause diagrams are a very simple example of a cognitive map.

While the simplicity of a multiple-cause diagram is a virtue, you might wish to enrich your exploration of causality by extending your range of symbols and including possible effects as well as likely causes. For example, you might distinguish negative from positive effects, perhaps by circling positive effects and boxing negative ones, or by using different colours of Post-It if you are working on a board. The technique is useful with either individuals or groups

Because some effects can be an increase and some a decrease, it may be helpful to show this once you start to distinguish positive effects from negative. Increasing a bonus may increase team effort but decrease co-operation between teams, for example. Use a + or – sign beside an arrow to indicate this. The important thing would be for everyone to know and remember what the code is. Figure 2.7 shows an example of using a simple cognitive map to explore our thought processes when we were deciding whether or not to write this book.

Any more complexity than suggested above will probably make it difficult for you or your workshop participants or interviewees to use the diagram without training, practice, and probably supporting software. (Decision Explorer® is a widely used software tool that makes cognitive mapping and related diagrams relatively easy: see *Explore further* for trial details.)

Cognitive mapping can be used at all stages in a project – helping diagnosis, data collection in interviews or workshops, analysis and presentation of data, and exploring the potential unintended impact of solutions. It may be particularly helpful if part of your project involves surfacing and changing how people think. Bryson *et al* (2004) suggest that you although you cannot easily change people's minds directly, they may change their own minds if you help them articulate the set of constructs that constitute their personal, and often unconscious, theories. Action Research (see Chapter 14) is an obvious example, but in any action-oriented research you might find the tool useful.

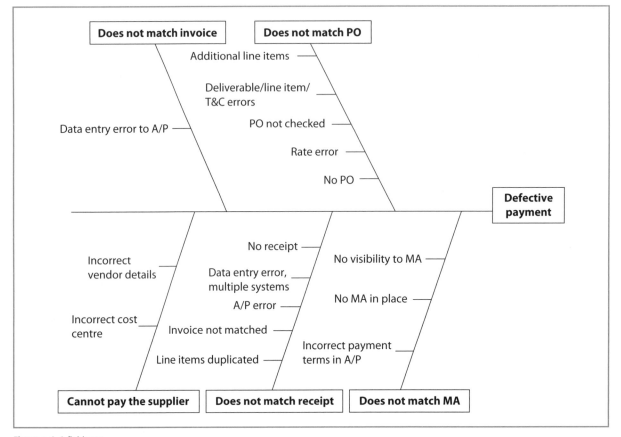

Figure 2.6 A fishbone
diagram, showing root
cause analysis of payment
defects

THE COMPLEXITIES OF KNOWING

Think back to the police 'evidence' case in the last chapter. The diversity experts 'knew' that the way to approach the under-representation of BME and female staff at senior levels was to coach candidates for promotion panels. But this was not in fact the case. Once upon a time people 'knew' that the world was flat (some still do!). That people 'know' something clearly does not make it true. For this reason it may help to think in terms of 'claims to knowledge', and examine these, rather than see knowledge as some indisputable entity.

Figure 2.7 Simple cognitive mapping of our thinking when deciding whether to write this book

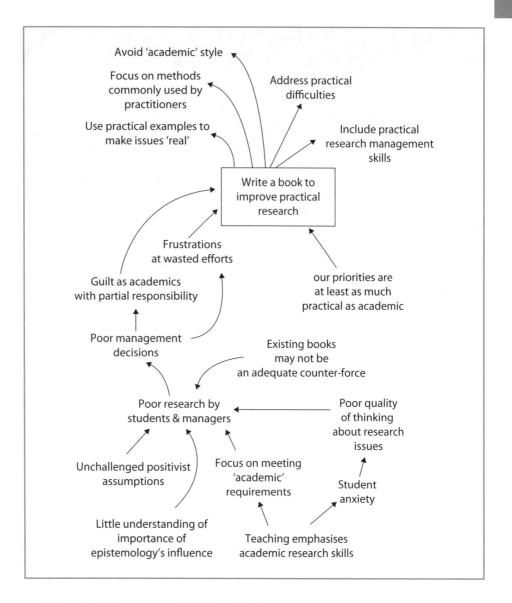

As Mitroff and Linstone put it (1993, p65), 'knowledge is inherently a very tricky, risky business'. Unless you understand some of the trickiness, and the risks, your research may do no more than reinforce what you already think you know. And even if this is not the case, your views about what is and is not knowledge will shape, and may seriously limit, your research. In this section I want to explore – albeit very briefly – some of the philosophical stances upon which thinking about research rests. First, though, consider the way in which our assumptions influence what we observe and how we interpret it.

Because a great deal of research involves observation and interpretation, it is important to be aware of the active nature of these endeavours, and of the influences upon them. Confirmatory bias, discussed earlier, is an example of the way in which perception and interpretation can be affected by your prior assumptions. This can happen even in respect of things you would not imagine to be subject to bias.

If all elements of knowledge are this 'tricky', even those that we might have considered relatively safe, such as simple observations of basic physical objects, how can we find

The Asch effect

You may be familiar with the so-called Asch effect. Asch (1963) carried out a fascinating experiment on the effects of social pressure. Subjects were asked to judge whether two lines were of equal length. The difference might be quite substantial; one might have been half as long again as the other. Before giving their judgement, subjects heard others give their answers. These others were accomplices of the researcher, and would say that the lines were the same. If six others had said the line was the same, 58% of subjects would also say they were the same. Subsequent interviews revealed that whereas some of these were just saying it, a small proportion had actually come to believe it. If even a simple observation – the relative lengths of two lines – is subject to distortion from minor social pressures, how 'objective' are observations and interpretations of more complex and ambiguous situations?

out anything useful about wicked problems and messes? This question lies at the root of most debate about research and research methods.

INQUIRY SYSTEMS

Around the time that Rittel and Ackoff were exploring the complexities of problems in organisations, some interesting work was being done on how we can find out, and develop knowledge, about such complex issues. Churchman (1971) wrote about 'inquiring systems', and Mason and Mitroff (1973; also Mitroff and Linstone, 1993) discussed 'inquiry systems (ISs)'. Mitroff was a student of Churchman, and drew directly on Ackoff's idea of a mess as a dynamic system of interrelated problems.

Thought of as a simple input–output system, an inquiry system takes some form of valid inputs, and an operator transforms them into outputs – 'valid knowledge for action'. Operating on all three parts of the system – inputs, transformation box, and outputs – is a guarantor which serves to 'guarantee' the inputs and the operator so that the outputs are valid. Figure 2.8 shows the basic framework.

Figure 2.8 An inquiry system (adapted from Mitroff and Linstone, 1993)

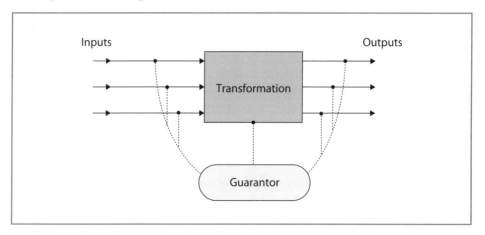

The guarantor is crucial. And this is where philosophy becomes important. What you count as valid inputs to an inquiry system will depend upon your philosophical beliefs about the nature of the world, and about what it means to 'know' something.

Such beliefs will influence the questions you ask, and what you will be prepared to accept as evidence. You need therefore to question what *you* think you 'know', and the evidence upon which you are basing this 'knowledge' very carefully when assessing your potential influence as a researcher.

But the problem goes deeper than that. The arguments about knowledge that have been raging for centuries go right down to the nature of the 'real' world. You cannot talk sensibly about what 'knowing' means without having some idea of the nature of 'the world' about which you are seeking to know. As Mitroff and Linstone put it (1993, p31):

> "The differences in the often heated battles between different ISs or philosophic systems, over what is truth, what is a proper way to decide important issues, is usually over the guarantor, although it is rarely put in this manner. Philosophic wars would be better termed 'guarantor wars.'"

I am obviously not going to do justice to millennia of philosophical debate in a page or two, and will do inevitable violence to some of the ideas: I hope you will find them interesting enough to read further. Some suggestions are given – the Internet can provide almost infinitely more if you have a lifetime or two to spare. Italicised words will provide a useful starting point for a search.

THE NATURE OF THE WORLD YOU 'KNOW' ABOUT ...

 Ontology and epistemology

Philosophers have long debated the question of what exists (ontology) and the question of what can be known and how (epistemology). If research is designed to add to knowledge, then both these questions seem highly relevant – the 'guarantor' of your system will depend upon the position you take on each. A version of the first question – does anything exist other than by our perception of it? – prompted the well-known limerick:

> "There was a young man who said 'God
>   Must think it exceedingly odd
>   If He finds that the tree
>   Continues to be,
>   When there's no one about in the Quad.'"

(For a discussion and an answering limerick, see Lucas, 2006.)

 Realism and idealism

Some schools of thought (eg realism, *objectivism*) believe that there *is* an objective reality out there. Things exist outside the human mind. The tree exists, no matter how empty the quad. Other schools (eg idealism) disagree with this position. I suspect only philosophers get particularly excited about the arboreal question. But the philosophical debate moved beyond the discussion of whether or not individuals exist to whether 'universal' qualities also really exist. As well as a quad full of individual trees, does 'tree' exist in the sense that both the mulberry and the magnolia are trees? *Realists* would say yes. *Idealists* disagree, claiming that these abstractions exist only in the mind.

This debate *is* of potential interest to business researchers. We might be happy to accept that individual human beings exist, just as we are happy with the unseen tree. But what about concepts that are not aligned to the particular? What about 'universals' like 'humankind'? We might not be investigating 'humankind', but many of the things business researchers investigate are even more abstract, and at least as open to debate. Is 'culture' real? Or 'dissatisfaction', or 'motivation', or 'the market', or 'customer loyalty', or 'leadership', or even 'knowledge' itself? You cannot touch, or smell, or see any of them. Crotty (1988) argues that our beliefs about the nature of such things are intricately entwined with our beliefs about the nature of knowledge, and together have a profound effect on how we approach research.

THE NATURE OF KNOWLEDGE AND KNOWING

The story continues from **Chapter 1**

The associated debate on what can be known and how (*epistemology*) has exercised philosophers for centuries. What is the philosophical underpinning that will act as guarantor of our inquiry system that will help us decide what knowledge actually is, what kinds of knowledge are possible, and how we can tell whether our knowledge is adequate and legitimate? The nature of what you are seeking to know about may well influence the meaning of 'knowing' about it, and both will influence how you approach research. In case this sounds a bit abstract, and perhaps irrelevant, let me continue my own early research story.

RESEARCH STORY Continued

Theory testing

At the time I chose to study psychology my parents tried to steer me towards a maths degree because 'only lunatics are interested in psychology'. To counteract this common view that psychology was not quite respectable, many psychologists at that time were trying very hard to make the subject more 'scientific' than even physics or chemistry.

Thus as an undergraduate I was trained to think of research as being solely concerned with things that you could measure objectively and analyse statistically. I studied two years of statistics, alongside the mathematicians. For my 'Attitudes to pay' project I therefore looked for objective, quantitative data. A standard pay satisfaction questionnaire was administered as a structured interview to 'measure' satisfaction with pay. A structured interview with the supervisor ascertained time-span of discretion (TSD) and pay records were used to determine actual pay rates.

After 10 or so interviews I started to wonder why some people on very low incomes seemed very

satisfied, while others on much higher salaries were dissatisfied. Halfway through my interviews it was becoming clear that any relationship between time-span of discretion and pay had little to do with their satisfaction level. So like Silverman (2007) I started adding in my own questions, along the lines of '*Why are you so satisfied (or dissatisfied) with your pay?*' One of the highest earners was really dissatisfied because he could afford only one car when his neighbour already had two. (This was before second cars were common.) One of those earning least was satisfied because she could afford a tin of salmon for her Sunday tea.

I became deeply discontented with the potential for what I considered to be 'proper research' to answer the questions I found interesting, and two years after starting my working life as a psychologist in a research unit, I abandoned any attempt at research for two decades, turning my attention instead to teaching and writing.

CONSIDER...

Why is this relevant to a discussion on ontology and epistemology? What philosophical stance was I adopting?

I was being a realist (in the philosophical sense) – I had been treating time-span of discretion and pay satisfaction as if they were *actual things*. I was being an *empiricist* in believing that the way of 'knowing' about them was to measure them with reliable instruments.

Phenomenalism and positivism

In my approach to measurement I was taking an epistemological position referred to as *positivism*, based in this case upon a *phenomenalist* view that we can only know what we can observe. This position is happy to attribute a reality not only to concrete objects but also to more abstract ideas such as 'satisfaction', provided they can be observed in some way and measured. Such observations form the basis for generalisable 'laws', thus increasing knowledge about the factors being researched. This position was also adopted by the *logical empiricists* during the 1930s to 1950s. The 'law' I was looking at was that TSD determines the level of pay the job-holder will deem to be fair.

> **The positivist view holds that knowledge can – and can only – be gained by objective observation and measurement.**

I was not unusual in being educated within a positivist frame. It is still widespread in many parts of the world. Yet it was shaping my thinking. Like other positivists I sought a fixed, predetermined research design, using objective measures which could be turned into numbers if they were not already numerical. I sought to formulate hypotheses and look for data which supported them, using statistics to determine the reliance to be placed on my findings. I saw my role as that of an objective and impartial observer and analyst. I was concerned with reliability and replicability of observations, and the rigour of my research in general. My findings related to an assumed objective reality, and I wanted to generalise to a wider population. Questionnaires and structured interviews appeal to positivists, together with 'hard' data that already exists in number form (such as error rates, costs, and absenteeism rates).

Reliability and replicability

Positivism can be a frustrating position for the business researcher, because it places severe limits on what can be researched. My 'rigorous' measurement of pay satisfaction via a well-established 'pay satisfaction' questionnaire was adding nothing to my understanding of what influenced satisfaction. No questionnaire or highly structured interview schedule was likely to cast light on the complex web of determinants of reactions to pay. I answered my particular research question, and in this case the answer informed an important government decision. It prevented other research from misleading my 'client'. But it did absolutely nothing to increase my – or the Department's – understanding about attitudes to pay.

I gave up on research because I did not realise that there was an alternative perspective. But within the social sciences there is a critique of positivism that hits it at the deepest level, challenging its underlying assumptions about both reality and knowing. I was assuming that 'satisfaction' existed whether or not I measured it. It was sitting somewhere inside my interviewees, waiting for me to uncover it; I did not realise that there were alternatives to this view. Indeed, Weick (2001, p571) suggests that the academic–practitioner gap identified earlier could be bridged by joint

> "academic–practitioner effort devoted to questions of how events come to be seen as 'real'."

Idealism, interpretivism and constructionism

If instead of *realism* you adopt an *idealist* position, the emphasis shifts from what is 'out there' to what is going on in your head. As a business researcher, much of what you are interested in may be a *social reality*, which from this perspective is considered the result of negotiations of meanings of and for situations. Knowledge about this will be derived from concepts and meanings. The job of the researcher is to capture this reality and re-present it in 'scientific' or academic language. You may find this sort of approach described as *Interpretivism* or *Social constructionism.*

Cause and effect Chapters 3 and 20

You can see now why an approach such as concept mapping is more than a tool for beginning to explore complexity. Where the positivist seeks to understand cause and effect and produce 'laws', the interpretivist looks for rules people use to make sense of social situations. Where the positivist seeks generalisable laws, interpretivists might argue that the underlying assumptions make it illogical to seek to generalise from one situation to another.

Social constructionists are particularly interested in the way in which views of reality result from social interactions, and the context in which these take place. (Remember the Asch effect even on perceptions of a simple pair of lines. How much stronger is the social influence likely to be on the construction of meaning in the work context?)

If you are of a constructionist turn, you will be attracted to methods that gather extremely rich and textured evidence which indicate ways of thinking, even if analysing this presents challenges. You will be drawn to focus groups, unstructured interviews and other textual sources. You may therefore be more comfortable working with qualitative data rather than quantitative, and may be more concerned with understanding a specific case than generalising your results more widely.

Quantitative/ qualitative distinction Chapter 9

(The quantitative/qualitative distinction in terms of data is discussed in more detail in chapter 9. Here it is enough to say that you may be able to mix methods to some extent, but may need to consciously consider both types in order to overcome your preferences.)

 CONSIDER...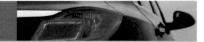

Decide whether positivism or constructionism is closer to your own view of the world, and of how you see the way to extend knowledge by research.

What does this imply for your own research project?

You may have had difficulty in coming down completely on one or other side of the epistemological fence. Academic researchers can become as heated as philosophers in arguing between these two extremes. Indeed, some of the most 'robust and energetic' discussions we have had while writing this book had their roots in our own rather different epistemological assumptions and preferences. But this is not the point of the exercise. It is more important to become aware of the assumptions you are making, and of their influence on what you consider to be valid methods and types of data in any research you do. Before thinking about this it is important to look at two other possible 'philosophical preferences'.

Updated realism

The distinction between positivism and constructionism may seem rather stark. Some practical researchers (see, for example, Robson, 2002) argue for an updated version of *realism* as a form of middle ground. There are many variants of this, but they tend to combine a belief in a reality external to ourselves with a rejection of the positivist position that this reality can, and should, be objectively measured.

Controlled experiments

Chapter 3

From this updated realist position, social phenomena may exist, but can be 'measured' only subjectively – observations will be subject to interpretation. No 'facts' are beyond dispute: 'knowledge' is a social and historical product. Today's realists share with positivists a belief in theory-building and testing as a way to advance knowledge, but recognise the complexity of social phenomena. They would doubt the possibility of the 'controlled experiment' which positivists see as a major tool. Instead, they would be more sensitive to the context of phenomena, and the 'constructed' nature of the interaction with the researcher. While positivists would see prediction as the test of a theory, realists might be happy with explanation. Realism with an emphasis on a questioning of context, and of power relations within this (including researcher power), is called *critical realism*.

Pragmatism

Pragmatism might be claimed to be an alternative middle position, although I would increasingly argue that it is of considerable relevance to most practical business research in its own right. It has elements in common with constructionism, although it predated it, but is happy too with an empirical stance. I should at this point declare that when I first started to read about pragmatism I discovered that without knowing it I had long abandoned my positivist assumptions for those of pragmatism, so despite my best efforts, what I write is inevitably slanted by this. If you now re-read Chapter 1 you will probably be able to see this.

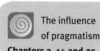

The influence of pragmatism

Chapters 3, 14 and 25

Pragmatism was founded in the aftermath of the American Civil War, possibly influenced by Nietzsche. Through Dewey, an early pragmatist, it has had, and continues to have a profound influence on education and ideas about learning and the role of reflection. It has influenced Action Research, and seems to be of increasing interest to those concerned with the development of professional practice (see, for example, Cook and Seely-Brown, 1999).

Pragmatists emphasise the socially constructed nature of sense and logic, and the role of dialogue in reconciling different views. It is amazing to think that Peirce, perhaps the first pragmatist, highlighted the role that 'conceptions' play in 'logic' as early as 1878, arguing that our very logic depends upon our past actions and the experiences they generated. As a consequence, different participants in an inquiry may have different logics, and different explanations may be needed to resolve their doubts.

You can see here that knowledge and action are closely related. Dewey (1910, 1916), for example, emphasised that concepts and meanings were generalisations of these actions and experiences, of the interactions the 'knower' had with their environment. Concepts (derived from action) had a very real practical function, serving as (or to inform) plans of further action. Pragmatic inquiry tends to use an array of different conceptual 'lenses' to look at an issue, and to consider the *usefulness* of a concept, rather than its *rightness*, and the *consequences* of both concepts and inquiry.

Thus a pragmatic inquiry tends to emphasise the role of concepts in making sense, and the social nature of this, finding the sense-making process as interesting as the thing being made sense of. The emphasis is less on possessing static knowledge and more on *knowing,* which Dewey saw as something that we *do* within a social context. The pragmatists suggested that truth is what works: the meaning of an idea rests in its practical consequences. It is therefore, inevitably, contextualised.

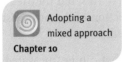

Adopting a
mixed approach
Chapter 10

It follows that it is reasonable to use whatever ways of thinking suit the question researched. (This is another example of the value of being able to think in terms of several conflicting models at any given time.) The positivist perspective might work *some* of the time. But pragmatists would consider it would be foolhardy to ignore the complexities of business situations in the interests of 'scientific rigour'. (This is part of the reason for the trade-off implied in Figure 1.2.) To tackle some of these complexities you may need to adopt a mixed approach, and run with two diametrically opposed sets of philosophical assumptions, two different ISs with different guarantors. (This would be a powerful exercise in developing flexible thinking!)

As with looping, a multiple-assumption, multiple-concept approach must be based upon an understanding of underlying principles. A flexible epistemology has to be underpinned by a clear understanding of the different possible ways of thinking and their strengths and limitations. You also need an awareness of the types of 'claims to knowledge' your approach allows, and clear thinking about what your findings mean and do not mean.

CREATING KNOWLEDGE?

You can see from the discussion above that your view on the nature of knowing will have a strong influence on the likely purpose of any research you choose to do, and on the methods you think it is appropriate to use to extend knowledge. Indeed, it can be seen as the foundation upon which everything you do will rest, as Figure 2.9 shows.

Figure 2.9 Research strata

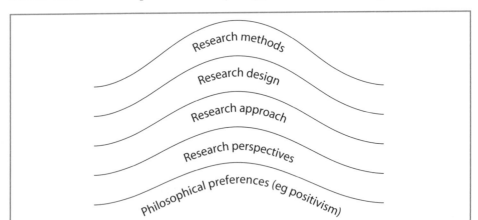

Your philosophical preferences concerning ontology and epistemology will form the guarantor of your inquiry system. They will determine what you choose to investigate, and what you deem valid inputs, valid operations, and valid knowledge outputs or your own inquiry system. Subsequent 'layers', as later chapters will show, will rest upon these philosophical foundations, which will serve as the 'quality control' for all elements of your inquiry system.

There will be much more about different methods in the middle parts of the book; at this stage you are only starting to think about your own view of knowledge creation, and its implications. The story of a classic piece of practical business research by

Mitroff and Emshoff (described in Mitroff and Linstone, 1993, or more fully in Mason and Mitroff, 1981) may help demonstrate a number of the points made thus far, and their significance.

 CONSIDER...

What assumptions about 'knowledge' and its creation underpin the approach adopted by Mitroff and Emshoff in their research story?

RESEARCH STORY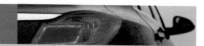

Disagreement in a drug company

The CEO of a pharmaceutical company was worried that generic substitutes were threatening profits from the company's leading prescription-only painkiller. The CEO tasked 12 key executives within the company to address this problem. These executives split into three groups, each arguing for a different solution. These were to lower the price, to raise the price, and to keep the price the same but cut costs. Each group argued from evidence (analyses of past sales, new information from trade magazines and field sales staff).

The more data they gathered, the *messier* the problem became. At this point Mitroff and Emshoff were called in. They observed a number of interesting things.

Each group was assuming different things about the nature of the problem, taking different things for granted, or judging them 'true' without being aware of it. As a result each group was selectively reinterpreting *existing* data to prove their case, although they were completely unaware that they were doing this.

Where there were no existing data, each group was collecting different data, from different sources, designed – again largely unconsciously – to prove the point. Thus the more data they collected, the more attached each group became to their preferred solution, and the further they were from a shared approach.

Mitroff and Emshoff 'unlocked' the situation by focusing on identifying stakeholders and their assumptions. They argued that 'an organisation is the entire set of relationships it has with itself and its stakeholders' (p142), and produced a stakeholder map [see Chapter 4]. They argued that 'assumptions are the properties of stakeholders' (p143), and so got each group to plot the assumptions they were making about key stakeholders (such as the physicians who might prescribe the drug, and the parent company of which they were a subsidiary) against two axes, the importance of the assumption and the degree of certainty they felt in its correctness.

One result of this approach was that instead of looking at parts of the problem, the executives started to think in terms of the system in which it was located, and its environment. Another result was that they decided to gather further data by raising the price in certain locations, and see how price-sensitive physicians were in their prescribing. (It is easier to reverse a price rise than a price cut.)

(Based on Mason & Mitroff, 1981)

This is a difficult question to answer. From the story it is possible to detect a mistrust in 'objective facts' and a recognition that perceptions of those involved are important. 'Facts' do not necessarily speak for themselves, but at the same time appropriate information (from the pilot price rise) can usefully inform decisions. This suggests that they are not positivists. There is also a 'systems' belief in the interconnectedness of things. This too will affect how an investigation is approached: emphasis on multiple perspectives is integral to such an approach, and apparent in the story. Metcalf (undated, p5) classifies Mason, Mitroff and Ackoff as 'systems-thinking pragmatists', which seems a fair description.

CRITIQUING YOUR OWN WORK

You will need to be *critical* of every aspect of your work, in the sense of questioning the validity or appropriateness of everything you do and how you do it, remembering also to question your choices of what *not* to consider. The first part of this chapter argued for the importance of considering a range of influences, some from outside the organisation, and it is important to be alert to these even if you do not have the resources to consider them fully. It helps to remember them even if you have to frame your 'problem' so as to exclude them altogether. You need to also be realistic about the extent to which it is appropriate to generalise your findings, and accept that sometimes this may be very limited.

KEY POINTS

- Philosophers have long debated whether reality 'exists' or is dependent upon our perception of it.
- *Positivists* believe that research demands impartial measurement of variables and analysis of these data.
- *Social constructionists* counter that if you are interested in a social reality, what matters is how this is constructed in a social context. This cannot be measured objectively.
- *Critical realists* seek a middle ground combining belief in an external reality with a recognition of the need for subjective measures.
- *Pragmatists* focus on the practical consequences of ideas and their inseparability from action.
- Identifying your own philosophical preferences may reduce the extent to which they limit your research.

THE COMPLEXITIES OF PERSONAL LEARNING AND DEVELOPMENT

You are a key stakeholder in your research, and must consider how to exploit its potential for personal development. Research projects draw on a wide range of conceptual, interpersonal and general management skills, and so offer huge scope for personal learning. Continuing professional development is essential for any professional practitioner, and your research can contribute to this.

> Research offers substantial potential for personal and career development.

Andy and Chris's Research Stories first featured in **Chapter 1**

If you are a student, the 'excuse' of needing a research project may enable you to take on work in an area, or at a level you have not yet experienced. Andy was hoping his project would enable him to move into change management, but had not thought more about learning potential. In contrast, Chris had put a lot of thought into choosing a project that would develop expertise and contacts relevant to his future career. I would argue that he got a great deal more out of his project as a result.

In talking about the personal learning he gained from his dissertation, Chris said:

"My understanding of the process of reflection – and in particular, critical reflection – as a key to the leadership development process deepened during the research, and as a result my understanding of myself, my experiences, how I had been influenced and shaped by these, developed almost in tandem. Daniel Goleman's *Vital Lies, Simple Truths*, Richard Boyatzis and Anne McKee's *Resonant Leadership* and Graham Lee's *Leadership Coaching* seemed to make such sense during the research – sense that I doubt I would have fathomed at the outset. This may sound a bit melodramatic but it was almost like a self-therapy process of peeling back layers of past experience, drawing back the curtains at the edges of the stage on which I lived and played out my life and exposing some of the props, wires and support structures that had held it together for most of my life. But that was a result of focusing on this particular theme. Whether such personal learning/development accompanies all business research is difficult to say."

Did you notice the suggestion of spiral learning in this quote? Chris mentions the ability to make sense of things differently because of prior learning and experience – in this case actually practising reflection. It may well be that he was already drawn to the topic because of a natural 'reflector' inclination. It is clear from what he says above that the specialist expertise he gained was not the only learning from the project. He really did 'think about his thinking', and as a result became able to think far more deeply and flexibly, and to continue to learn by reflection. Indeed, from the small beginnings of his dissertation he has become involved in several different types of consultancy, has been approached by a publishing house about a model he developed, and is doing further research.

This example should convince you that if you are contemplating doing research, this would be a good time to think more about your personal objectives for the research, and what a project might do for your learning and your career. Strictly, this is not necessarily adding to 'complexity', but it is an important additional dimension to doing research, and you must ensure that the other complexities do not prevent you from paying it the attention it deserves. Occasionally, your development needs may seem to conflict with time-saving and 'getting top marks' needs. If this happens, complexity will be increased.

 ACTIVITY

Note your career, learning and other objectives for the research you will be undertaking.

Note any potential conflicts between these and other objectives (yours or those of other key stakeholders).

Consider how these conflicts might be reduced or otherwise dealt with.

Note your ideas in your research journal.

CAPTURING YOUR LEARNING

I first met Chris because a mutual contact noted our shared interest in the role of reflection in leadership development. Reflection is both a way of capturing your learning and building upon it. You may need to include reflection on your research experience in your dissertation experience. If you get into the habit of reflecting at regular intervals as you carry out your research, you will learn far more from the experience, and find these marks easy to gain.

Proformas are available at
www.cipd.co.uk/brm

You may naturally reflect in writing, but it may be worth experimenting with some of the diagramming techniques introduced earlier as a supplement. You may already be a practised and habitual reflector: if so, that practice will really pay off during your research. If you are not, I strongly recommend that you read Chapter 24 before you start Chapter 3, and start to experiment with the formats suggested. Instructions to 'Note your ideas in your research journal' will then make more sense, and you will gain more from your subsequent reading and thinking. The following prompt for thought is also designed for you.

 CONSIDER...

What points have struck you while reading these first two chapters?

What implications do they have for your own research?

In the light of this, what should you start doing from now on to increase your chances of carrying out a successful research project?

SUMMARY

Most issues of interest to business researchers are not simple and isolated 'problems' but part of a more complex web of interrelated issues. There will also be a number of different stakeholder perspectives on the issue and the research project. These interrelationships and differing perspectives are important.

We have a tendency to over-simplify when faced with complexity. It may be tempting to analyse the problem and address parts in isolation, but this tends to create problems rather than solve or dissolve them. Various diagramming techniques can help overcome this tendency and can be a useful tool for individual, paired or group exploration and analysis.

Your approach to research will be strongly influenced by unconscious philosophical preferences. It is important to understand that there are different perspectives on knowledge and knowing, to identify your own, and start to think about the implications of this for your own research.

You are a key stakeholder in your own research, and you need to start thinking now about how you are going to take full advantage of the personal and career development opportunities a project can offer.

REVIEW QUESTIONS

1. What are the implications of considering an organisational issue as a simple problem rather than a wicked one or a mess?

2. Why might you want to dissolve a problem rather than solve it? Make clear the distinction between them.

3. What might it imply if you described your project as an inquiry rather than research?

4. Say whether your natural philosophical position is closest to positivism, constructionism, updated realism or pragmatism, and why.

5. What are the areas of overlap between pragmatism and constructionism, and what are the differences?

6. Why is it so important to be aware of your own philosophical preferences, and of your own assumptions and expectations about the issue you are looking at?

7. What are the main channels through which a researcher can influence the research findings, and what factors might contribute to the influence exerted?

8. When should you start keeping a research journal?

EXPLORE FURTHER

Bryson, J. M., Ackermann, F., Eden, C. and Finn, C. B. (2004) *Visible Thinking*. Chichester: Wiley. Provides detailed descriptions of how to use cognitive mapping

Lucas, J. R. (2006) 'The tree in the lonely quad', available online at http://users.ox.ac.uk/~jrlucas/reasreal/treechap.pdf. Provides a lucid if challenging discussion of phenomenology and related ideas, and an example of how philosophers argue

Metcalf, M. (undated but post-2006) 'Pragmatic inquiry', available online at http://unisa.edu.au/irg/papers/PRAGMATIC%20INQUIRY%20fin.doc [accessed 8 April 2009]

Mitroff, I. I. and Linstone, H. A. (1993) *The Unbounded Mind: Breaking the chains of traditional business thinking*. Oxford: Oxford University Press. A fascinating look at different ways of knowing that is soundly based on philosophy while keeping it well hidden!

Saunders, M., Lewis, P. and Thornhill, A. (2007) *Research Methods for Business Students*, 4th edition. Harlow: FT/Prentice Hall

Wattenberg, M. and Viégas, F. B. (2008) 'Emerging graphic tool gets people talking', *Harvard Business Review*, Vol.28, Issue 5: 30–2. Looks at uses of IBM software

http://www.ideasciences.com/products/decisionexplorer/trial.php to download a trial copy of Decision Explorer® for more complex cognitive mapping

http://www.iep.utm.edu/u/universa.htm for a discussion or realism and universals

http://uk.geocities.com/balihar_sanghera/carcinterpretivism.html for an accessible discussion of interpretivism and its research implications

http://www.cognexus.org/Rotman-interview_SharedUnderstanding.pdf for an interview with Jeff Conklin on 'Building shared understanding of wicked problems'

 Visit www.cipd.co.uk/brm for web links, templates, activities and other useful resources relating to this chapter.

CHAPTER 3

The Investigative Process

INTRODUCTION

This chapter looks at what the different complexities discussed in the last chapter mean in terms of thinking about the research process. If you are to use a looping approach (and even that implies a particular stance on 'knowing'), you need to understand both the underlying logic(s) of the research process, and how these are inevitably related to your philosophical preferences. This understanding is fundamental to the design of worthwhile research. For this reason your dissertation will need to establish your preferences, and show how your research is influenced by these, and logically consistent with them.

The very language you use to think and talk about your research will reflect your philosophical preferences (see Chapter 2), and influence the choices you make, often unconsciously. It will also influence your stakeholders. The discussion here aims to make you more aware of these influences, and help you appreciate the significance of the different schools of thought described in the previous chapter.

This chapter starts by examining the different words for research, and their implications, and the possible impact of talking in terms of 'research' or 'inquiry' aimed at generating 'data', 'information' or 'evidence'.

Research is purposeful. Your purpose should guide all the choices you make about your research, and so must be clear. The chapter explores possible research purposes, and their implications for approach and methods.

The chapter then looks at how theory and philosophical preferences impact upon the choices you make at different broad stages in the research process. These choices will determine your research design. Because practical projects tend to address 'wicked problems', and therefore present greater diagnostic challenges than more academic topics, there is a particular focus on the early stages in an investigation. Later stages are addressed in subsequent chapters.

Practical business research is very much the art of the possible – a range of conflicts and constraints may limit your choices. To make you more aware of how this may happen, evaluation research is taken as a typical 'case' of research and considered in some detail. It presents many of the challenges and choices you are likely to face when carrying out research in an organisation, whatever the issue you address.

LEARNING OUTCOMES

This chapter should enable you to:

- describe, and think about your work as 'inquiry', 'research' or 'investigation' as appropriate, in the light of their different associations

- choose and use the terms 'data', 'information' and 'evidence' advisedly, recognising their different associations and meanings

- follow the underlying logic of an investigation, even when looping, and anticipate the challenges most likely at each stage

- compare the logics of deductive, inductive, retroductive and abductive research

- identify differences between investigations designed for different purposes, and clarify possible purposes for your own research

- evaluate possible design choices for a research project with a specific purpose.

RESEARCH, INQUIRY OR INVESTIGATION?

The language we use tends to reflect and to reinforce our underlying philosophical preferences. Much of the process is unconscious, so it is worth surfacing and examining the issues involved. Understanding the significance of the terms may also help you to identify an author's epistemological perspective.

'Research', 'inquiry' and 'investigation' are all used to refer to forms of 'finding out', and these words have different associations for many people. These associations may unconsciously influence your thinking, your approach, and others' reactions.

 ACTIVITY

Take these pairs of words

> research : inquiry
>
> research : investigation
>
> inquiry : investigation

and try to note down two similarities and two differences in the meanings conveyed by the two words in each pair.

From this, derive a list of associations for each word.

Complete
definition
Chapter 1

Practical business research was defined earlier as a 'systematic attempt at collecting and interpreting data and evidence in order to inform thinking, decisions and/or actions …' and contrasted with a more academic definition of research as 'gather[ing] empirical evidence upon which theories concerning aspects of behaviour in organisations can be based'. By now you may be able to detect something of the philosophical preference behind each definition.

For many people 'research' has 'scientific' and 'academic' associations, and implies positivist assumptions. It shifts the 'guarantor' of the inquiry system towards concerns with precision, reliability and replicability of measures. Thus thinking of your project as *research* may predispose you towards a fixed, predetermined, often experimental research design, with a focus on precise objective measures. If so, you will try to isolate the variables in which you are interested, and to prevent all others from having an influence. Your priority will be theory-building and/or hypothesis-testing – you will seek a single definition of 'the problem', and *the* answer or solution to the problem you have defined.

If 'research' has the same associations for your stakeholders, the term may lead them to expect such an approach and/or to assume that your findings are derived from one. It is worth therefore considering other possible labels for what you are doing.

> Descriptive labels create expectations according to the associations such words have for those who use the labels.

INQUIRY

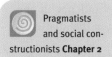

Pragmatists
and social con-
structionists **Chapter 2**

'Inquiry' was the term used by the pragmatists, and also by social constructionists. Scientific research underpinned by a positivist stance places a strong emphasis on the *rigour* of the method of collecting evidence: 'truth' might almost be deemed to rest upon method. It is important that results are independent of the observer and the audience. The pragmatists, in contrast, chose the term 'inquiry' to emphasise a number of differences in their approach. One of the differences was in the *contingent* nature of knowledge claims and their justification; these would depend upon the situation and the actors involved. The pragmatists believed that 'facts' were observed through filters of prior experience, and so would look different from different perspectives. These different perspectives were themselves worthy of investigation, and furthermore, any knowledge claims would have to be justified in different terms to different stakeholders. These features, they argued, meant that there was a need for a new epistemology, which had science at its core but drew its boundaries rather wider.

Epistemology

> Inquiry is associated with an open-ended and flexible approach to finding out.

This wider boundary would include different communities. These communities would use different concepts when thinking about problems and their nature, and would have different reasons for doubting any knowledge proposition. The aim of the inquiry would be both to identify and to take into account the concepts already being used, and to look for additional concepts that might help the community to bring about beneficial change. (Wenger's (1998) idea of communities of practice, currently influential in many professions, rests on this idea.)

For Action Research **Chapter 14**

You can see that this alters the position of the 'subjects' in the research process. Instead of being subordinate to the researcher, they become experts from their own perspective. The researcher becomes a fellow-learner in the research process (this is particularly apparent in Action Research). It is a far more flexible and open-minded process than conventional scientific research. Knowledge becomes community-based rather than universal, so the concern is less with methodological rigour, more with the 'doubters' in the community who force the inquirer to justify their knowledge claims in a way that is reasonable to that community.

I shall look at two variants of 'inquiry' to illustrate the different associations: Dewey's classic *productive inquiry*, and the more recent *appreciative inquiry* approach.

Productive inquiry

Pragmatists **Chapter 2**

Dewey (1910) was a leading pragmatist, and his idea of *productive inquiry* is still highly influential. Cook and Seely-Brown (1997) characterise productive inquiry as prompted by a problem, puzzle, provocative insight or something troublesome, and directed at addressing this. It is productive because it is directed towards some sort of answer, solution or resolution. And it is 'disciplined' by theory, concepts and rules of thumb (knowledge is a *tool for knowing* in Dewey's terms).

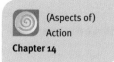
(Aspects of) Action **Chapter 14**

As the previous chapter discussed, in pragmatism the emphasis is shifted from abstract *knowledge* that we have, to *knowing* as an integral and social aspect of action. Churchman (1971), who did a lot of work on inquiry systems, put a similar point very clearly (p10):

> "To conceive of knowledge as a collection of information seems to rob the concept of all of its life. … Knowledge resides in the user and not in the collection. It is how the user reacts to a collection of information that matters."

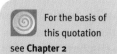
For the basis of this quotation see **Chapter 2**

From this perspective knowledge is a tool which serves the inquiry, potentially generating further knowing – another form of spiral. (You will remember how looping was necessary because when you discover something it prompts different questions.) The link between knowing and doing is particularly important for business research aimed at improving professional knowledge: this is tied up with practice. The pragmatist stance that 'knowing is part of something we do' is part of the reason why those concerned with professional development find pragmatism an attractive epistemology.

Although Dewey was writing a century ago, his ideas still seem highly relevant. The term 'productive inquiry' is favoured by my constructionist colleagues both because of its links to practice and because of its open-ended connotations.

Appreciative inquiry

Another argument for the term 'inquiry' is made by practitioners of *appreciative inquiry*. This approach originated in work by Cooperrider and Srivastva (1987), who were seeking to bring about organisational change. They found that when they stopped thinking in terms of an intervention, and instead talked of an inquiry, it shifted them into a learning mode. You can see that appreciative inquiry again is a highly action-oriented approach to 'finding out'. Note also the importance of descriptive labels. This move into the role of student caused a radical shift of emphasis away from looking for root causes of *problems* and towards seeking root causes of *success*. The focus on appreciating these successes explains the adjective 'appreciative'. Appreciative inquiry is now widely used as an effective approach to change. It can be summarised in terms of five core principles (see, for example, Reed, 2007, or Gordon, 2008):

Principles of appreciative inquiry

The constructionist principle: words create worlds, and human knowledge and organisational 'reality' are interwoven

The principle of simultaneity: inquiry and change proceed simultaneously

The poetic principle: we author our world and edit the plot – organisations are less like machines, more like a book in the process of being written

The anticipatory principle: how we think about the future shapes how we move towards it – images of the future thus guide the present

The positive principle: a focus on the positive will cause the negative to fall away; it will produce deeper engagement of those involved.

These principles are founded on some key assumptions: there is always something that works; our focus becomes our reality; reality is created moment to moment, and there are multiple realities; if we are to carry the past forward, it should be what is good about it; and the language we use creates our reality (Reed, 2007).

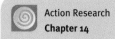 Action Research
Chapter 14

This serves to reinforce the importance of thinking about the impact of language on thought, akin to a constructionist epistemology. The interplay of questioning and action lies at the heart of Action Research. If you come to consider this research approach, you might revisit the ideas of appreciative inquiry – they could usefully influence aspects of your research.

The positive focus has several benefits. People are less defensive when thinking of positives, and can therefore think more flexibly. You can find solutions which 'play to the strengths' in the situation. These are all important when building relationships with stakeholders and informants. A negative focus creates defensiveness and you may lose sight of important *positive* elements in a mess, and risk destroying some of the factors that contribute to success.

INVESTIGATION

The third word commonly used to describe a research project is 'investigation'. This also describes a process of finding things out with a view to reaching a conclusion, and has fewer 'science lab' associations than 'research'. Investigation has associations of being systematic, purposeful, focused, rigorous, and leading to some form of decision and/or action. The emphasis is on the use of *evidence*, which itself shifts thinking in subtle ways, as will be discussed shortly.

It may be helpful to think in terms of the analogy of a police investigation, aimed at coming to a defensible view of what is going on (provided this analogy is not pushed too far). A police investigation seeks evidence in order to construct and sustain an argument, and this is a key element in most business research. (A frequent mistake of novice researchers is to concentrate on the need to get data rather than the need to answer a question or come to a position.) However, the analogy also highlights a potential disadvantage of the term: its association with finding a culprit. There is a need to be careful not to use the term with some stakeholders: it might cause them to fear that you were trying to apportion blame.

DATA, INFORMATION OR EVIDENCE?

Our original definition of business research talked of 'collecting and interpreting data and information …'. Is there a difference? Chapter 9 explores issues of data and evidence collection in much more detail. Here the focus is merely on how the words you use can influence your own and others' thinking. 'Data' (plural of *datum*, from the Latin for '[thing] given') tends to be used for 'hard facts', linked to a positivist perspective. A fact is a fact, but not all facts are information, and not all information is in the form of hard facts.

 Information is that which reduces your uncertainty in relation to an issue of interest.

 Andy's questionnaire featured in **Chapters 1 and 2**, and features again in **Chapter 4**

Some data may not do this. Think back to Andy's questionnaire, with its 50 demographic items, all carefully analysed and beautifully presented. Not one of these items contributed to his research question about the impact of organisational change. His report contained many pages of data but no information relevant to the question he was asking.

EVIDENCE

 The suggestion was in **Chapter 1**

It has already been suggested that *evidence* is more than data. It is *derived from* data through a process of combination and interpretation, and used to support an argument. In the sort of investigation we are talking about, 'the facts' rarely speak for themselves. They have to be interpreted. You may have to build a case from an array of information no one piece of which would be adequate alone. Items may be subjective (opinions, feelings, interpretations), and no more than indicative. But a number of such pieces of information may together provide strong support for an argument or conclusion. Presumably this is why there is interest in 'evidence-based' professional practice rather than fact- or information-based.

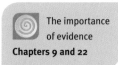 The importance of evidence **Chapters 9 and 22**

We believe that 'a fact is a fact', but neither information nor its interpretation as evidence is context-free. What counts as evidence, and how strongly it contributes to your case, will depend upon the case you are making. How you interpret information may depend upon the context from which it was derived, and your perspective in interpreting it. Your purpose and your frame of reference will influence your interpretation. Talking of 'data' when you mean something other than a hard fact may mislead an audience about the nature of your evidence, and the perceived strength of your conclusions.

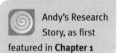 Andy's Research Story, as first featured in **Chapter 1**

Andy, in his change evaluation project, may have fallen into the trap of thinking that all data is equally worthwhile because he thought of 'data collection' as a discrete task. If he had thought and talked in terms of information and evidence, he might have come to think more about what data would be useful, and how he would use it.

> **Before collecting data, think about its informational value as evidence for your eventual conclusions.**

CHOOSING YOUR WORDS

In choosing to talk about words and their associations I am again reflecting my own philosophical (systems-thinking pragmatist?) perspective, and my view that concepts are tools which serve the *knowing* process. This implies a need to choose tools to suit your purpose. You can see how it is impossible to think about research without being influenced by that bedrock of your thinking, your philosophical preferences. These act as policemen, or guarantors in your inquiry system, making you see some things as 'obviously' important in the pursuit of knowledge, while blinding you to some other aspects.

Inquiry system guarantors
Chapter 2

The chapter title refers to the investigative process partly to emphasise the role of evidence and argument in the sort of 'finding out' that you will be doing. The other reason is the hope that 'investigative process' is relatively neutral in terms of epistemology – it has weaker positivist associations than 'research' and does not necessarily imply a pragmatist or constructionist approach as might 'inquiry'.

If language can have such a powerful influence (and I firmly believe it can), it is worth deliberately *thinking* in different terms to assess the effects of this. Also, choose your words carefully when interacting with stakeholders. Part of your aim is to be *credible* as a manager/researcher and different terms may impress different stakeholders. Note, though, that in any one context you need consistency. It would be potentially misleading to describe your project in fundamentally different ways to different stakeholders. You need to also avoid using language that creates unhelpful expectations which may affect how your conclusions are judged by others.

Being alert to the different connotations of these words will enable you to think more freely about your own project, and can alert you to the likely perspective taken in other investigations. Thinking of evidence rather than merely of data may similarly help you to think more effectively about what data/information will help answer your question. You might like to deliberately experiment with talking about your own research as an inquiry, an investigation *and* as research in order to broaden your perspective and increase the flexibility of your thinking. You could usefully reflect on the impact of the language you are using.

KEY POINTS

- 'Research', 'inquiry' and 'investigation' are used to describe similar activities, but have different associations and may indicate different philosophical preferences.
- Research has 'scientific' overtones, while inquiry emphasises the exploring and discovering nature of the activity.
- Similarly although 'data', 'information' and 'evidence' are sometimes used interchangeably, they have different associations.
- *Data* tends to convey 'hard facts' – *information* may be data or something softer, provided it helps reduce uncertainty.
- Both need interpretation, which will be context-dependent, if they are to become *evidence* to support a claim or argument. Your focus needs to be on evidence.

RESEARCH PURPOSES

 Project dimensions
Chapter 1

Earlier, you experimented with locating different projects on a single dimension and within a two-dimensional field with relevance and rigour as dimensions. Another important variable is the overall purpose of the investigation. Establishing a clear purpose is perhaps the most important thing you do: it will determine your subsequent choices because everything you do subsequently should be designed to achieve that purpose.

Robson (2002) suggests a useful broad framework for thinking about research purposes (note that different purposes may be more or less compatible with different philosophical preferences):

* exploratory research – aimed at finding out what is going on, seeking insights, generating ideas for future research

* descriptive research – based on extensive prior knowledge and aimed at providing an accurate portrayal of persons, events or situations

* explanatory research – aimed at identifying and explaining (often causal) relationships between aspects of the thing researched

* emancipatory research – creating opportunities and motivation to engage in social action.

 **CONSIDER...**

What might Robson's philosophical preferences be?

If you have a possible topic in mind, which of the above types of purpose might it serve?

Robson's book suggests that a new, *critical realism* is the most appropriate stance for practical research. You can perhaps detect the realist undertones in his categories: there is a suggestion of independently existing things to be researched, but talking of 'emancipation' (with its slave-trade associations) suggests the critical, (in the social science sense) recognition that social structures may act as 'chains' which must be broken. A pragmatist or constructionist set of categories might be very similar, but the labels might have emphasised understanding and finding interpretations and meanings rather than explaining relationships.

 Projects with more than one
purpose **Chapter 13**

It would be perfectly possible for a project to serve more than one of Robson's purposes. Indeed, unless others have explored and described it, it may need to. Description rests upon exploration, explanation upon description, and for me, emancipation rests upon understanding. On the other hand you might have found that these categories are not exhaustive. Does 'identify and explain relationships' cover all the aspects of business research which aim to go beyond describing but not so far as emancipating? Might the 'explanation', indeed, reinforce existing perspectives and 'enslave' people more firmly in prevailing mindsets?

RESEARCH PERSPECTIVES AND CHOICES

One of the problems with many dissertations is the almost total 'disconnect' between chapters on 'Methodology' and 'Data collection' and descriptions of methods actually used (assuming they are made clear at all). Yet the whole point of thinking about different epistemological positions is to help you decide what you really want to know, and what methods for collecting and analysing data will give you the best sort of answer, given your overall research aim. If this sequence is not absolutely clear in your research report, an essay on methodology and/or epistemology will contribute nothing to either your research planning or your dissertation. This section aims to 'join the dots' in this area and help you make considered choices about your research. It looks at how your research perspective is likely to be influenced by your philosophical preferences, and how this is likely to impact upon the research choices you make at later stages.

Before coming back to a more detailed exploration of the basic research steps, I want to look at some of the choices they will entail, and the logics that may influence them. I shall be operating mainly in the 'research perspective' layer of the strata suggested in the previous chapter and shown again in Figure 3.1.

Figure 3.1 Strata in thinking about research

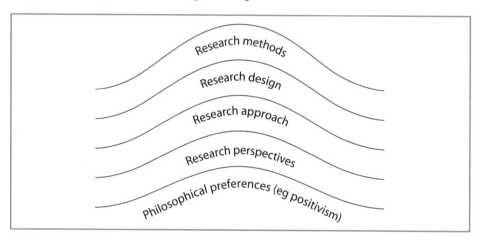

The previous chapter established some key differences in the philosophical preferences which act as *guarantors* of an inquiry system or IS (Mitroff and Linstone, 1993), influencing what are seen as appropriate inputs, appropriate operations on these inputs, and valid knowledge outputs. This chapter has already shown some of their influences. Before going further it might help to reiterate some of the most influential epistemologies. In very crude summary these could be split into four broad categories:

- **Positivism:** linked to a belief that phenomena exist independently of the observer, and can be known through direct observation. The role of the researcher is to develop generalisable theoretical statements about this independent reality, based on observation. Hypotheses can be derived from these theories and tested by means of further observation, and analysis of results. Method, and careful measurement and analysis, and reliability, replicability and validity of measures are the 'guarantors' of the knowledge generated. The output of a positivist IS might be confirmation of an existing theory or modifications to that theory which might allow more accurate or more generalisable predictions.

- **Updated realism:** linked to a belief that although phenomena (eg 'culture') may exist independently, we cannot necessarily observe them directly. Observations are tenuous, and subject to interpretation and reinterpretation. Nor can we predict as positivists might seek to do. The real world is complex, with many layers, and this makes isolating any specific variable very difficult. The output of a new realist IS might be an explanation showing how a particular event has occurred in a particular case, rather than prediction to other cases. It relates to mechanisms rather than laws, and these mechanisms are likely to be multiple, complex and contingent upon the situation.

- **Pragmatism:** similarly rooted in a belief in the complexity of situations, linked to a belief in multiple perspectives, 'theory-laden observation' and a belief that 'theory' and 'knowledge' serve as tools in 'knowing', something which is entangled in *doing*. The output of a pragmatic IS might be greater awareness of the concepts being used to perceive and make sense of a situation, new concepts to enhance perception and interpretation, and importantly, action to change the situation.

- **Constructionism:** linked to a belief that both social phenomena and the meanings attributed to them are constructed (and continually reconstructed) by those involved in a situation. This includes the researcher, so notions of objectivity and generalisability have little relevance. The role of the researcher is to understand the multiple and different 'realities' (and ways of making sense of these) of the actors in a situation. One challenge particularly highlighted by this perspective is the need to avoid imposing your own constructions upon your observations.

You can see that these philosophical positions have different logics, and powerful implications for the way in which you might choose to turn the basic logic of the 'research steps' into a specific research design. Consider first some of the most basic choices you are likely to make: these form your research perspective.

Sometimes these are termed 'design questions', and indeed they are a basic part of design. But I prefer to think of design as a process spanning a number of levels of choices, and culminating in a specific research design which (Bryman and Bell, 2007, p40):

> "provides a framework for the collection and analysis of data. A choice of research design reflects decisions about the priority given to a range of dimensions in the research process."

'Research perspective' is probably not an ideal title for the most basic choices needed, but it avoids some of the potential confusions of other labels. Key texts vary in their labelling of these strata: check which labels they are using for what.

By the 'perspective level', I am talking about the first level on which your philosophical preferences start obviously to influence the direction of your research. At this level both Bryman (2007) and Saunders *et al* (2007) identify a choice between inductive and deductive research. Bryman adds a choice between fixed and flexible designs. Since these two choices are not independent – inductive research suits a flexible design, while deductive research needs a more fixed one – I shall consider both as part of 'perspective'.

DEDUCTIVE OR INDUCTIVE RESEARCH?

The choice between a deductive or inductive approach concerns both the starting and end point of the research. It underpins all your other choices. At first glance the distinction is simple.

Deductive research starts with theory, and proceeds by testing hypotheses derived from the theory. **Inductive research** starts with the observations and derives theory from these.

If you are carrying out a research because you have to for a dissertation, deductive research has many attractions. You can conduct a tight experiment or other carefully controlled research design to do test your hypothesis, with careful measurement and sophisticated statistics. This will allow you to demonstrate your understanding of scientific method, and of data collection and analysis to your (positivist?) supervisor's satisfaction.

Even if, like me, you find it difficult to see organisational issues from this perspective, it is still worth understanding what a deductive approach entails. The principles of hypothesis-forming and testing that underpin the approach, and the research designs associated with this approach, are still the dominant view of research in much of the world.

Because deductive research starts with an existing theory, logically speaking inductive research comes first. Induction is the chicken that lays the theory egg. But it is deductive research that most people mean by 'scientific research': the researcher 'deduces' testable hypotheses from the theory and designs conditions to test these. Hypotheses normally relate to specific variables and the relationship between them.

 A hypothesis is a proposed relationship between two variables stated in a way that allows it to be tested.

Theory may be further developed in the light of the resulting observations. If you are doing deductive research, you need to know how to form a testable hypothesis.

HYPOTHESIS-FORMING AND TESTING

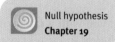 Null hypothesis
Chapter 19

A hypothesis is a clear statement of your deduction or prediction, often written as H_1. A key concept here is its converse, the *null hypothesis*, normally written H_0. Thus if your H_1 was that reducing price would result in increased sales, your H_0 would be that price reduction had no positive impact on sales. Null hypotheses are preferred when contradictory evidence might be more compelling than confirmatory. In my pay/time-span of discretion (TSD) research it was highly informative to find no association between TSD and perceived fair pay for a key category of workers. Had I found an association it might still have been necessary to check the relationship for remaining categories.

This is a version of the classic 'black swan' illustration of the power of disproof. Suppose your hypothesis was that all swans are white. You could observe a million white swans and still not have 'proved' your hypothesis. But the first black swan you encountered would disprove it.

 The null hypothesis, H_0, states that the hypothesised relationship does not exist.

Note that deductive research relates to *a* theory, or a limited number of theories, as earlier defined. For example, in my 'Attitudes to pay' research, my hypothesis was that

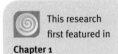

This research first featured in
Chapter 1

one variable – 'felt-fair pay' – would be correlated to another variable, time-span of discretion (TSD), because TSD theory asserted that the latter determined the former.

If you are drawing conclusions about specific variables, you need to make sure that any associations or differences you find relate to these variables rather than to something else entirely. This leads to a fixed, predetermined research design, discussed later. To control for extraneous effects you might look for a control group which matched your 'experimental' group and use this as a comparison, or take other steps to prevent influences.

Logical steps in the deductive approach

1 Identify a current theory relevant to your area of interest – identification is likely to be driven by gaps or inconsistencies in the literature.
2 Construct a hypothesis from the theory that was not contained in the original data from which the theory was derived. Test the theory by generating new observations that allow you to test the hypothesis.
3 'Operationalise' the hypothesis, by identifying factors that you can measure, and ways in which you might alter one or more of the variables. (The variables you alter are called independent variables, those that are affected are called dependent variables.)
4 Create the conditions for the observations which will allow you to put your hypotheses to the test, seeking reliable measures, and considering how to 'control' for impact or extraneous variables.
5 Generate data by observation/measurement, avoiding observer bias.
6 Analyse data to see whether observations are consistent with your hypotheses, ie are inconsistent with your null hypothesis (H_o).
7 Develop or modify the theory in the light of data if your hypothesis-testing suggests this to be necessary.

 CONSIDER...

What might be the main advantages and disadvantages of a deductive approach in practical business research?

Choosing a deductive approach for practical studies will present you with a range of challenges. Your first would be to find a relevant, interesting theory in current use that was sufficiently specific to allow the creation of testable hypotheses. You would then have to find feasible and reliable measures of key variables, and design adequate controls. You would also have to think about the inevitable limitations of this approach: it basically gives a yes/no answer. Unless you collect data that go beyond confirming a hypothesis, new insights or meanings are unlikely. From pragmatist or constructionist perspectives in particular, this may be a serious concern.

Advantages include tight definition – within a tight time-frame such as a dissertation this can be important. A deductive study is usually easier to plan. Observer bias may be minimised, although it is important to be aware of the potential the researcher still has to bias research findings through decisions over measures, and indeed over what to observe. It may be easier to 'sell' a deductive approach to some stakeholders (those who prefer 'scientific' research).

INDUCTIVE RESEARCH

Before you can have theory you need observations from which to derive it. Thus logically, induction precedes deduction. An inductive approach is perhaps most clearly exemplified by the approach called Grounded Theory, although it is based on assumptions far removed from a positivist frame. Indeed, when it was proposed, Grounded Theory represented a powerful challenge to the prevailing research orthodoxy. However, there is a real question about how to approach 'gathering knowledge' in complex social situations. The perceptions and meanings of those involved may be the key factor in the situation, so it is hard to think of generalisable theory which might prove a starting point for hypotheses. Alternatively, the phenomenon may be one about which relevant theory does not exist.

Grounded Theory **Chapters 10 and 18**

The following story describes an approach which the researchers, Rodon and Pastor (2007), describe as Grounded Theory. It relates to the introduction of an inter-organisational information system (IOIS) to 11 organisations in Barcelona.

RESEARCH STORY

Introducing an IOIS in Barcelona – an inductive approach

Introducing the system was proving problematic. The aim of the research was to gain understanding of the initial and on-going difficulties with implementation. The researchers wanted to describe and analyse the emerging implementation process, rather than 'explain it through cause–effect relations between a set of constructs' (*ibid*, p72) partly because their research problem had not been previously studied. They also wanted to generate new insights.

This guided their choice of an inductive approach. They chose interviewing as their main research method. Sampling was guided by emerging theory. Five general managers were interviewed first, using very open questions, then sampling became more focused on system users and personnel, who were asked to explain their experience with the IOIS, still using general questions. In parallel other sources were collected: minutes of meetings, internal documents, etc. Ideas were coded, and computer software was used to help manage the codes generated.

Data collection and analysis went on in parallel: insights emerging from the analysis allowed new questions to be incorporated into subsequent interviews, and checking that emerging concepts fitted reality. Action diagrams were used to structure ideas and to communicate these.

You can see the underlying social constructionist position here: the researchers are interested in finding how those involved in the situation make sense of it. Their choice of method was guided not only by the absence of relevant other research and therefore of theory from which hypotheses might be derived, but also by their underlying philosophical stance.

 ### CONSIDER...

How happy are you with the algorithm shown in Figure 3.2? (The figure assumes that the four 'philosophical preferences' listed earlier are exclusive and exhaustive.)

I would argue that the choice is more complicated. If there is *no* relevant theory, then indeed there is no choice. And if you are a constructionist you would be likely to describe your approach as inductive, since 'a theory' is to you a problematic idea. If meaning is the focus of your research, and meaning is constructed in an on-going way by those involved in the situation, then to use pre-existing theory (from which

Figure 3.2 Possible
algorithm for inductive/
deductive choice

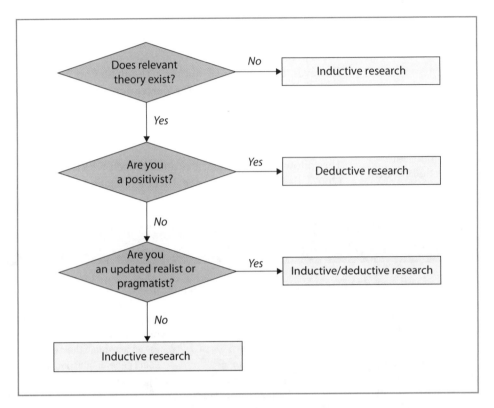

hypotheses are derived as described above) as your starting point does not make sense.

But where does this leave the realists and pragmatists? The realists would, I think, accept the idea of the deductive approach as a basic framework, but would broaden the range of factors which they felt had to be taken into consideration. This might mean that measurement and statistics had to be handled differently, even if they were the ultimate goal.

The pragmatists, however, have a slightly different and rather more complex take on the whole question. Two aspects of a simple deductive/inductive split are problematic for them. Firstly, they stress that while inductive research starts from observations, observations are neither theory-free nor theory-neutral. The researcher will bring their tacit theories to bear, these being based on both prior experience and familiarity with relevant formal theory and current debates. This tacit theory will act as a filter on information.

Secondly, 'hypothesis' has a very different meaning for pragmatists. If concepts are knowledge tools, then 'hypotheses' are tentative concepts, concepts 'on probation'. Such hypotheses are 'tested' in action, and 'observations' would relate to how well they helped make sense of something, rather than measures which could be statistically analysed. This suggests a very different approach to forming hypotheses, and a different role for the hypothesis in an inquiry system.

Pragmatic hypotheses are tentative concepts to be tested for their usefulness in action.

AN ABDUCTIVE APPROACH

Peirce (1955), the first pragmatist, questioned the adequacy of the 'way of knowing' implied by positivism, and the scientific approach. He regarded both inductive and deductive approaches as proceeding through a process of logical inference: induction proceeds by observation and classification in some way of what is observed – it proceeds from a similarity of facts. Hypotheses are derived by a process of deduction from a prior theory. No new evidence goes into forming the theory.

But between the classification that results from induction, and the production of a theory is a process of inference from something which cannot be directly observed – induction classifies, while hypothesis in this 'space' seeks to explain. Pierce calls this process of inference 'abduction' (Peirce, 1955, p151):

> "Abduction … is a process of drawing conclusions that includes preferring one hypothesis over others that could explain the facts when there is no basis in previous knowledge that could justify this preference …"

Abduction is based upon the *absence* of *a priori* hypotheses, presuppositions or existing theory. Abductive research applies where there may genuinely be no prior theory, and where explanation rather than theory-building is the goal. The following story shows how this approach was justified and used in a project in Israel. It is taken from Levin-Rozalis (2004). Although it is not a business issue, it presents many issues faced by business researchers.

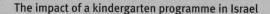

RESEARCH STORY

The impact of a kindergarten programme in Israel

The programme was designed to support children of Ethiopian origin and ran from 1988 to 1990. The research was carried out in 2000–2001 and intended to verify that there had been an impact of the programme on the children participating. You can see the challenges the researcher faced. He was sceptical that there had even been an effect. If there had been, how could he detect its influence 10 years on, in a specific cultural group, and when the aims of the programme had been very vague?

This meant that there was no *a priori* theory from which to deduce hypotheses to test, so a deductive approach was out. An inductive approach requires hypotheses to be formed through empirical generalisations, and this means that you do need to have some idea of what you are looking for and the conditions under which you will find it. But here it was not clear what the variables were. The conditions for abduction clearly applied, there were no presuppositions; the research was necessarily approached with an almost empty mind.

The researcher interviewed children who had been through the programme, and comparison groups of children who had not, also parents and teachers, and content-analysed the responses. Following an abductive process, a hypothesis was formed 'on probation' early in the research. This was then tested against subsequent data (a *retroductive* process) and a further probationary hypothesis formed. Two further abduction/retroduction cycles were carried out.

Rather contrary to expectations, the researcher found that the abductive approach gave a clear answer to the question: there was a detectable difference between those who had been through the programme and those who had not, and this seemed to stem from both the impact on the child's self-perception and the impact on the parent's perception of the child.

CONSIDER...

What are the key differences between the Grounded Theory inductive approach of the Barcelona story above, and the abductive approach in the Israel story?

I would argue that the similarities far outweigh any differences. The language used is different, and in the second case the concepts ('theory'?) are being sought for a purpose: to establish a difference between those who experienced the programme and those who did not. But in both cases the choice is justified in terms of the absence of prior theory, and there is a cycling between data and emerging concepts.

It is easy to spend longer agonising over labels than thinking about their meanings and implications. The important points to note here are that:

- Induction and deduction are seen as *complementary* within the positivist scientific method, and part of the same logic. Here the research goal is for the observations to establish patterns or generalities from which generalisable theory can be *induced*. Testable hypotheses or predictions are *deduced* from the theory.

- Induction is seen as the preferred approach from a constructionist perspective; generalisable theory is not compatible with a socially constructed reality which is continually being 'rewritten'. What is *induced* is the set of meanings or constructs used to make sense of the situation.

- Abduction is the label given to an approach which like induction starts from observation, but which sees hypotheses as 'concepts on probation' to be tested as the research develops. The test is the usefulness of the concepts for further 'knowing'.

KEY POINTS

- **An inductive approach starts with observations, then organises these with a view to developing understanding and/or theory.**
- **Inductive research benefits from a flexible research design.**
- **Deductive research involves deriving hypotheses from existing theory and testing these by means of experiment or systematic observation.**
- **Deductive research needs a fixed design, determined in advance, in order to allow rigorous controls. Scope for developing insight or understanding is limited.**
- **Both inductive and deductive research are consistent with a positivist approach, while constructionists may feel that only induction is appropriate.**
- **An abductive approach may be preferred by pragmatists, and can be used when you have no *a priori* theory. It allows you to cycle between observation and tentative hypothesis when you have no existing theory to test. The tentative hypotheses are tested in subsequent action.**

FIXED OR FLEXIBLE DESIGN?

You can see that choosing an inductive, abductive or deductive approach is linked to the choice between a fixed or flexible design. The deductive approach tends to be

Variables

associated with a positivist concern for methodological rigour, and the need to identify variables that can be varied, and measured, and others which can be controlled, so that relationships between the variables that concern you can be established. Thus it requires detailed pre-design of conditions and rigid adherence to them. With this approach there is no scope for looping. A flexible design, as in the two stories above, allows for findings to influence the research as it develops.

FLEXIBLE DESIGNS

Chris's project featured in both **Chapters 1 and 2**

If you are investigating a complex issue and seeking to understand the 'mess', or are interested in the sense that people make of a situation, a fixed design would be unhelpful. For a project where *understanding* an issue is important, you will learn far more with a flexible approach to data collection. The Barcelona story showed this sort of flexibility: on-going analysis informed subsequent choices of interviewees and questions. Chris's project found similar flexibility to be useful: note the hint that he might have initially seen dissertation headings as a route map, but rapidly learned that this was not the way to carry out productive research.

RESEARCH ILLUSTRATION continued

Reflection and leadership development

'During the course of my interviews, interviewees (and other parties interested in my progress) recommended additional readings which took my understanding to new depths and my interest to new heights ...

'This was not quite what was recommended in *The Dissertation Guidelines*, the Literature

Review culminating in a series of Research Questions which would then be investigated via a Research/ Questionnaire Schedule. Instead, my semi-structured interviews became richer in depth as I progressed through them because my understanding of the topic was being enriched by successive interviews and on-going recommended reading.'

FIXED DESIGNS

If you are seeking to test a hypothesis (in the positivist definition) you will typically have identified a causal relationship between variables suggested by a theory, and will be seeking evidence that such a relationship exists. To do this you will have to separate out the variable you are interested in from other possible effects. It is all very well to put people through a leadership training programme and measure performance before and after, but if at the same time major redundancies were being announced in some trainees' departments, while associated restructuring meant that some others received an unexpected upward regrading, you would be hard pushed to separate out the impact of the training from the impact of these other changes.

Most fixed designs are intended to help you test whether *only* the first variable in which you are interested is associated with changes in the second variable The classic fixed design is the *controlled experiment*. Two groups are selected at random. Both are 'measured' in some way. Then the experimental group receives the 'treatment' and both are measured after. If measurements are 'blind' – ie those doing the measuring do not know which group the research subject was assigned to – then you should end up with an objective measure of any impact of the experimental treatment.

Fully controlled experiments are rarely possible in practical business research. However, there may be situations which approximate to them, described as 'quasi-experiments' where some at least of the conditions for an experiment are arranged. 'Natural experiments', where changes are made for non-experimental reasons, are a particular case, although non-random allocation to groups may raise problems for the researcher, as you will see later in the chapter.

A MEETING OF LOGICS

What happens when these lower-level choices 'meet' the 'logical steps' suggested in Chapter 1? There is certainly a clear logic to the 'steps' that were shown in Figure 1.5. You need to have noticed something before you can explore, to have explored before you can describe, to describe before you can diagnose, to have at least some data before you can analyse it. That much is straightforward. But it was suggested that the steps were not a neat linear set of stages. They needed to be accomplished in an integrated fashion but probably by a series of loops. This section will describe the steps, considering how the integration is to be achieved, and how your chosen research perspective will affect choices at each step. Successful integration demands a clear understanding of the whole process, and how the parts contribute to each other and to the process as a whole. Otherwise, your loops will become very tangled, your evidence weak, and your conclusions untrustworthy. But it is also important to understand the influences on the different stages.

I shall focus on the part of the process in which you are interacting with data/information/evidence. Figure 3.3 shows a contracted version of the relevant part of the earlier diagram. (Chapter 22 looks in more detail at the process of drawing conclusions, and Part 5 deals with many of the practicalities of implementation.)

Figure 3.3 Logical research steps (contracted)

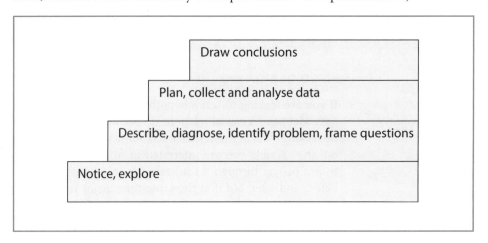

NOTICE, AND EXPLORE

Good managers are sensitive to signs that something is maybe not quite right, to potential opportunities, and to any confusion or lack of understanding about something important. Regular reflection will increase your ability to notice such things – noticing is an important management skill. You may notice an issue because it affects your own job, or you read something that resonates with your experience. Alternatively, your manager or organisational client may bring an issue to your attention.

Illustration projects **Chapter 1**

'Noticing' is usually prompted by surprise, discomfort or puzzlement, which suggests a dissonance with your tacit theory, or formal theories you believe in. As the pragmatists commented, observation is culture- and experience-laden. Concepts derived from your reading will sensitise you to a wider range of factors in a situation, and a habit of critical reflection will make you less likely to accept situations without question, and more likely to notice discrepancies or implications of what you observe.

Consider some of the illustration projects listed in chapter 1.

Because of the complexities of organisational life, issues are often not clear at the outset. But your subconscious operates with a great deal more information than your conscious mind, and generates unease for sound reasons, even if it takes some exploration to find out what these are. This is why the process of reflecting on something that 'strikes' you is potentially so valuable. 'Noticing' may not sound particularly challenging, but if you are immersed in a situation and the surrounding culture, it is easy to take for granted things that an outsider would instantly notice. It is here that reading can be helpful, providing theories etc to act as 'knowledge tools' and prompting questioning of aspects of the situation. Noticing potential topics in the literature will be much easier if you read critically, as discussed in Chapter 6.

New ideas, new information and new ways of making sense of situations can sensitise you to additional factors: you may find yourself back at the noticing stage at any point in your project. If so, before totally redirecting you must think carefully about how to balance the advantages of a richer or redirected project against time and resource constraints.

RESEARCH STORIES

Noticing

Emily was struck by the amount of duplication of effort there seemed to be around her. Many teams were working on similar projects, but there seemed to be no communication between them. She was fairly sure that other teams must have faced problems similar to those her team were currently struggling with, but could not access their experience. She felt that this meant that she was probably reinventing a lot of wheels, and the organisation would become much more effective if there were some way for learning from projects to be shared and captured.

When she read an announcement about her organisation's commitment to knowledge management she wondered whether this was actually a knowledge management issue. She thought that this might provide a context within which she could usefully investigate the potential for improving effectiveness – and saving money – by improving knowledge-sharing and management.

Ben had also settled on 'Knowledge management' as a topic, but instead of having noticed it as an issue of concern to his own role, his manager had 'noticed' and therefore suggested the issue, asking him to find out whether introducing a knowledge management system would save the organisation money. Both projects came out of the work situation.

Jenny had been reading about climate change and about corporate social responsibility. She started wondering about how she could 'make a difference' to her own organisation's carbon footprint.

Chris also was struck by something he read. This prompted him to start thinking more about the role of reflection and feedback. The literature is a great source of ideas, and may suggest questions that it would be helpful as well as interesting to try to answer.

Whenever you are struck by something, try to reflect in as much detail as you can on what struck you and why, and capture your thoughts in your research journal.

From noticing to exploring

Ben's boss was thinking in terms of a specific solution: a computer-based 'knowledge management system'. (You will remember that humans are prone to 'finding' premature solutions to misconceived problems.) Emily was taking a more 'open-ended' view of the situation. However, exploration is equally important in both cases.

> **Complex issues may not be what they seem: further exploration is important.**

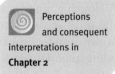

Perceptions and consequent interpretations in **Chapter 2**

Complex issues are seldom quite what they seem at first sight. What we *perceive* is filtered through our assumptions and expectations, and then interpreted in the light of these. This is why there has to be a process of exploration to find out more about the potential issue. Even when your sponsor or client has a clear solution in mind, it is important to do some exploration of your own before deciding how – indeed, whether – to proceed.

CONSIDER...

How might Emily go about exploring her potential knowledge management issue?

Perhaps the most important thing at the initial exploratory stage is to keep as open a mind as you can, and draw your 'frame' as wide as possible. Above all, resist predetermined solutions (such as 'We need a knowledge management system'). Clients with a solution in mind must be treated with caution. Emily would have to do some thinking and some finding out, seeking to gather and start to organise such information as is relatively easy to obtain. A 'rich picture' might be helpful in capturing ideas and keeping the frame as wide as possible: context is important

Rich pictures **Chapter 2**

She might read the new policy document, and speak to her sponsor about the 'knowledge' that has to be managed, current ways of sharing knowledge, and the possible impacts of improvements. She might talk to fellow team managers to see how they perceive the situation. She might look at what knowledge *is* shared, and how the existing information system is used. She might look at approaches in comparable organisations. She might look at one or two recent books or papers about knowledge management: these might suggest concepts to inform further discussions. Looping between reading and discussions allows each activity to inform the other. What she reads would make a different sort of sense because of earlier conversations and suggest ideas for further discussions.

Ben's boss is suggesting a knowledge management system as a potential solution, so can he skip this stage? Unless a similar exploration and deeper diagnosis has already been carried out, this would be dangerous. His boss's 'solution' may be premature. Perhaps existing systems could be used more effectively, rendering a new and expensive system unnecessary, or knowledge management may not be the problem.

A feature on this diagnosis is available at **www.cipd.co.uk/brm**

When does exploration stop? The first stage of exploration is fairly superficial, seeking breadth rather than depth, and staying at the level of appearance. The following questions may be helpful. Reading overviews of relevant topics would be more useful than in-depth explorations of specific theoretical aspects. There is a diagnostic element to this initial exploration, but initially your focus is likely to be more on the 'Whats' than on the 'Whys'.

Useful questions for exploration

What caused you to notice the issue – why are *you* interested in it?

What might you learn that is personally useful by addressing it?

What is the potential impact of the issue?

What would be the potential benefit of addressing it?

What is known about the issue already?

Who thinks it is a problem/issue that should be addressed?

Why do they think it is significant?

Who are the key stakeholders?

What are their objectives in relation to the issue?

Are there any strongly held views or sensitivities that might get in the way of your investigation?

Literature assessment

Chapters 6 and 10

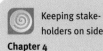

Keeping stakeholders on side

Chapter 4

Exploration lets you find out more about the topic that interests you, and form a tentative idea of possible directions an investigation might take. You need to reassure yourself that there is a relevant literature and that this has the potential to pose interesting questions. For an organisation-based project you might additionally need an initial assessment of the issue's significance to the organisation. And you need to check that there is no obvious risk of antagonism from powerful stakeholders. If you have a strong personal interest in your issue, you must also consider whether this presents a risk of bias, could restrict your perspective, or might be blinding you to dangers associated with the topic.

Initial exploration may suggest that an issue would be risky or unprofitable to investigate further.

Chris's project featured in both

Chapters 1 and 2

Because it may be easier to imagine exploring a real situation than an abstract topic, look at how Chris approached his initial theory-driven exploration.

A research brief may go no further than exploration (or in the more academic sense a detailed literature review). A fairly superficial investigation may be highly informative if there is widespread ignorance about the issue, or it might show the need for a more extensive exploration that would be a project in its own right.

If, however, exploration is the first stage in a more extended investigation, you would only stop exploring when you were convinced that there is an issue that is worth investigating. It is theoretically interesting and/or has the potential to benefit the organisation, offers scope for personal learning and poses no obvious risks. If you do not invest enough effort to establish this, you may waste a great deal of time and/ or encounter major problems later. Stop exploring only once you have done enough work to avoid obvious risks and limitations, and have settled on a broad area that looks worth investigating further.

When you move on to a deeper diagnosis or exploration you may still find that the apparent issue is not really suited to a research project. If you are planning a dissertation and *need* to do some research within a specific time-frame, it therefore makes sense to explore two or three different potential topics at this stage.

Reflection and leadership development

'Three not entirely unrelated topics were occupying my thinking at high level – reputation management, knowledge management and leadership development. I was fascinated by the themes of CSR, corporate ethics and how these related to and were manifested in corporate reputation and reputation management.

'Knowledge management was a topic that also interested me. The knowledge management forum had identified a number of potential research themes ('selling' KM into the organisation, integrating KM and the organsation's learning agenda) but this had a rather dull feel. I realise now, three years later, that the concept of the learning organisation was waiting to be explored and that I would have thoroughly enjoyed such work but at the time did not recognise its potential.

'During October–November ... I had undertaken an Integrated Strategy Project (ISP). The purpose of this exercise was to analyse the strategic direction of an organisation and to propose a business transformation plan [with the] International Baccalaureate Organisation (IBO), and its Strategic Director kindly steered my thinking towards proposing a leadership development programme for the IBO as a key element of its strategy to meet forthcoming challenges. This took me into the realms of leadership development and I felt a very strong urge that if I was to develop a career in leadership and leadership development, I had better get on with it and focus my research in this field.'

KEY POINTS

- Exploration must be broadly framed, and undertaken without preconceptions.
- You have to obtain information from a range of sources and do some initial reading.
- Diagrams may help you to explore and start to organise aspects of the complexity.
- It is helpful to explore two or three potential topics.
- Inadequate exploration costs more time later, and can threaten success.

DESCRIBE AND DIAGNOSE

The questions you asked while exploring will have enabled you to describe the situation, and say *what* is happening and *where*. You cannot diagnose until you have a clear *description* of the situation you are trying to diagnose.

In describing an issue you are seeking to provide a clear outline of what a situation or issue is, the ideas that are involved, why they are significant, the impact they are having, and the scope for further work. You are focusing at the level of *what* is involved. Sometimes this will be enough. Sometimes you will propose further research to allow a richer description. You will remember that description was one of Robson's (2002) four broad research purposes. When description is a step on the way to further research, it will have to be detailed enough to make clear why an investigation of the issue would be helpful, and give enough detail to act as a basis for starting to think how that investigation might be framed.

A clear description of a set of ideas or a situation can itself be a useful research output.

Note that although your exploration sought to keep an open mind, what you noticed, what you explored, and how you chose to describe what you saw will almost certainly be influenced by your preconceptions and tacit theory.

Diagnosis

In practical research addressing a problematic issue in an organisation you may need to understand some of the *why* before you can start to design an appropriate project. Research prompted by a problem needs to be directed at the root causes of the problem. 'Diagnosis' is the process of deeper investigation aimed at identifying these. The analogy is with a medical diagnosis. A calming cream might soothe a rash, but a doctor would want to be sure it was a heat rash or perhaps a mild allergy rather than measles or meningitis before offering it as a remedy.

Diagnosis is perhaps the most important stage in practical business research, because there is a high risk of misdiagnosing when issues are complex and 'messy', and treating symptoms rather than their causes. Such a 'solution' may make matters worse. In diagnosing a practical issue you are usually trying to deepen your understanding of a situation. This may involve a process of diverging and then narrowing, as Figure 3.4 shows. (A similar process of divergence and convergence can be useful at every choice point in your research.)

Figure 3.4 Divergence and convergence during the diagnostic process

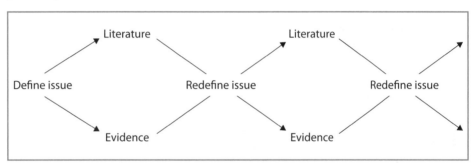

Whether or not your current research includes a diagnostic stage, you have to understand its importance if you plan to carry out practical research later in your career. This may be one of the 'gaps' between requirements for a dissertation and requirements for practical research contributing to some of the flawed research done by consultants.

To diagnose an issue you will have to start asking deeper questions, analysing relationships, and seeking more data and/or information. You need to understand the situation fully enough to avoid addressing the 'wrong' problem, even if your client has already 'diagnosed' the situation (although it may take tact to handle this situation).

You can see that although diagnosis is clearly a definite logical step, diagnostic activities frequently start during the exploratory stage, and may encompass extensive data collection if your main purpose is diagnostic. Diagnosis is a practical variant of Robson's 'explanatory' purpose. It is also quite likely that as your investigation progresses beyond the diagnostic stage you will identify further potential causal factors, the issue will start to look different, and you will need to loop back and seek more diagnostic information.

When considering how to proceed with diagnosis, Kipling's 'honest serving men' (from *The Elephant's Child*) are an excellent starting point.

> "I keep six honest serving men
> (They've taught me all I knew);

Their names are What, and Why, and When
And How, and Where and Who."

The box below shows how these might be incorporated into diagnostic questions. The questions are mainly aimed at diagnosing a problem issue, but many would be useful in other contexts.

 Useful questions for diagnosis
– for the issue defined at the end of exploration

Who are the key stakeholders?
Why do they think that this is an issue?
What do they feel about it?
What other relevant objectives do they have that might be influencing it?
How important do they think the issue is, and why?
What other evidence is there that this issue is significant?
When did it start to become an issue?
Why did it start to become an issue?
What factors contribute to the situation in question?
What data is available relevant to contributory factors?
What factors does it impact upon?
What data is available relevant to its impact?
What system(s) does this issue form a part of?
Who are the key personnel involved?
What other problems are related to this issue?
What constraints are there in the situation?
What opportunities might addressing the issue present?

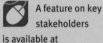 A feature on key stakeholders is available at **www.cipd.co.uk/brm**

Some of the questions may have featured at the exploratory stage – such as: Who are the key stakeholders? – but now you will probe more deeply or ask a wider range of people. You might incorporate workshops and focus groups into your diagnosis, capturing the outputs of group discussion and their analysis of the factors involved. Diagrams can usefully form part of this process and may subsequently provide evidence of how participants were thinking. You need to be aware of the evidential possibilities of everything you do at this stage. It is important to record and store these data carefully. Make sure that you keep careful records of even your diagnostic conversations, group discussions or other information collected (although you will have to remember the hazards confirmatory bias can present, and use them with caution).

 Workshops and focus groups
Chapter 17; diagrams
Chapter 2

Diagnosis presents several challenges, including:

- setting aside preconceptions – your own and others' – for otherwise they will limit what you perceive in the situation and how you interpret it

- drawing a sufficiently wide frame to include all the relevant influences, and looking for non-obvious relationships

- seeing the situation from different perspectives by exploring it with a wide range of stakeholders and by consciously adopting different perspectives yourself

- making sense of a large volume of seemingly chaotic information without resorting to your habitual filters and prejudices.

If the diagnosis is your entire investigation, a description of what you found and how you interpreted it will be your end point. If you plan further investigation, you may need to redefine your issue in the light of what you find during your diagnosis in order to formulate a realistic aim for your project, and agree this with your client.

Whichever your aim, at some point you will have to organise your findings, impose structure upon them and either draw conclusions or construct an argument as to what is required next. If diagnosis has been a preparatory stage for a dissertation, you must clarify your thinking about what it is that you can usefully propose, in order to make a convincing case for what you want to do.

Diagnosis makes sense from a realist or pragmatist problem-oriented perspective. For more theory-driven research projects such as Chris's interest in the role of reflection there is an equivalent 'deepening' stage after the initial exploration. He moved from an initial consideration of the role of reflection to a deeper exploration of the area he had decided was most interesting. The idea of diagnosis does not fit at all well with more scientific positivist research, which is not aimed at problem-solving. Within a constructionist frame the entire research endeavour might be deemed diagnosis, the goal being an in-depth understanding of a situation.

IDENTIFY A RESEARCH PROBLEM AND PURPOSE

If you are addressing a practical problem it is easy to confuse an organisational objective with your own research goal. It is an important distinction, and such confusion can lead to a lack of clarity in your investigation and in your report. Thinking in terms of a **research problem** may help. Figure 3.5 shows how these elements are connected.

Figure 3.5 Questions, purposes and organisational issues

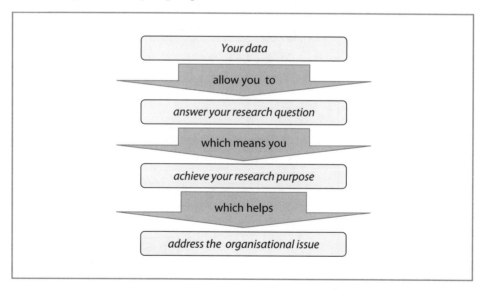

Your data

allow you to

answer your research question

which means you

achieve your research purpose

which helps

address the organisational issue

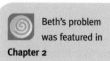

Beth's problem was featured in **Chapter 2**

Think back to Beth. There might be an *organisational* problem caused by high leaving rates. An *organisational* objective might be to reduce the costs of high leaving rates by improving retention. I suspect that part of her difficulties stemmed from not taking a mental step back, and thinking in terms of a relevant *research problem*. At its most basic, a research problem is something that you want to know and that research might be able to tell you.

Beth's research problem could usefully have been formulated in terms of gaining a better understanding of causes of high leaving rates. As it was, she leapt immediately to thinking about possible solutions to the organisational problem. Thinking in terms of a research problem enables you to move from thinking in terms of an organisational 'solution' towards thinking constructively about the objectives for your research, the question(s) your research might seek to answer, and the data and other information that would enable you to answer them.

Figure 3.6 is an expansion of Figure 3.5, showing alternatives depending on your approach. This reflects the logic of the 'steps': choices about a lower level can only be made when choices have been made at the level above. The branching signifies alternatives at that level, depending upon the nature of your issue and your philosophical preferences. A specific research question is another way of expressing an objective. A research question might be 'What do invoicing errors cost us?' The equivalent objective would be 'Determine the cost of invoicing errors'. Hypotheses serve at the same level. Whatever your approach, you have to ensure that if all your questions were answered (or objectives achieved, or hypotheses tested), this would achieve your research aim. (For simplicity's sake I shall now mainly use 'your question' to indicate question, objective or hypothesis as appropriate.)

Figure 3.6 A research hierarchy

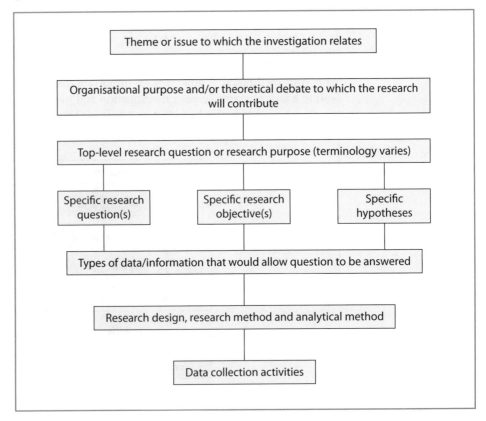

FRAME USEFUL QUESTIONS (OR CLEAR OBJECTIVES)

Question and answers are at the heart of any research. Until there is something you want to know (or know about) and you have framed your research question(s) and/or hypotheses, you cannot consider the data and/or evidence that would help you to answer them. Chapter 8 explores research questions in far more detail, so only brief examples are needed here.

As an example of student research questions consider the questions that Chris defined in his dissertation proposal (2005).

RESEARCH STORY continued

Reflection and leadership development

The initial title in the proposal was 'An investigation into the importance of reflection and feedback in leadership development' and the suggested research questions were:

- To what extent are current leadership development reflection and feedback practices in line with Avolio's model?

- Is there a significant relationship between overt/explicit reflection and feedback events and improved leadership behaviours?

- What are the perceived obstacles to effective feedback/reflection?

- Can a model of best practice be identified?

- Does the approach to reflection and feedback differ between in-house leadership development and that applied by executive coaches?

CONSIDER...

Can you think of the data or other information that would allow these questions to be answered?

How much light might answering the questions throw upon the importance of reflection and feedback?

All the questions are interesting, but only the second seems directly related to the research purpose implied by the title. Some could clearly be approached via the literature; some offered scope for finding out what trainers were actually doing and experiencing.

To see how the shape of research can change during a project, compare these questions with research questions listed for the subsequent paper based on the dissertation (Rigby and Dulewicz, 2007, pp14–15). These were:

'1 Is, and if so, in what form is, reflection incorporated into leadership development programmes?'

'2 Is reflection being undertaken for a specific purpose, and if so, is that purpose to develop particular leadership behaviours?'

'3 Is it an explicit outcome objective of the leadership development programme that participants will engage in reflection in the wake of the programme?'

'4 Is there any tracking of participants to identify if, in the wake of the programme, they reflect more and as a result are leading more effectively?'

The difference between the two sets of questions shows how during the research Chris's thinking progressed, and how the questions have shifted to ones which interviews with leadership trainers might help answer.

Challenges in framing questions or hypotheses stem from the need to balance what you would ideally like to know with what you can reasonably hope to find out. You may need to rephrase your research questions in the light of practical difficulties encountered, or insights gained as you progress. Which words you choose at this level will very much reflect your philosophical preferences and research perspective. Hypotheses will make most sense from a positivist perspective: you will prefer them if you believe that you can measure the relevant variables, you like the tight logic of the deductive approach, and you prefer quantitative methods. Working with tightly defined hypotheses can make it easier to decide what data you need, and allows you to choose and use inferential statistical techniques in order to draw reasonable conclusions about whether to accept or reject a hypothesis.

Philosophical preferences which lead you towards an inductive perspective will mean that you avoid this kind of hypothesis. If you are a pragmatist you will be more likely to think in terms of research objectives, since the value of any ideas rests in action. If you use the term 'hypothesis', it is more likely to be in the abductive sense of a tentative concept. Constructionists are more likely to think in terms of a higher-level research question, equating to research purpose, but may see subsidiary lower-level questions as helping to provide answers to the higher-level one.

PLAN, AND COLLECT DATA

Once you have a clear research purpose, and have specified questions, outcomes and/or hypotheses, you can start to think seriously about the observations and/or other information that would enable you to come up with relevant answers. Planning the data you need and designing a process for collecting it is the substance of much of the rest of this book. Chapters 9 and 10 and most of Part 3 are directed towards this, so the treatment here will be brief. However, there are some over-arching considerations connected with data planning and collection that must be understood in outline at least in order to understand the overall process.

What data would help answer your question?

Earlier it was suggested that your observations and other information collected must be *relevant*. Provided your diagnosis or deeper exploration has clarified the issue you are addressing, and you have therefore formulated a clear and relevant research aim, you are halfway to ensuring relevant data. You now have only to ensure that you seek data that are relevant to your question(s). They also need to be valid.

 CONSIDER...

If you are starting to think about a project, think of a possible question relevant to your topic and jot down the types of data/information that might contribute to an answer. Note your thoughts in your journal.

 Research proposal
Chapter 11

 Trustworthy conclusions
Chapters 9, 18 and 22

Until you have thought about the sort of information you need, you cannot think about how to collect it. Diagnosis and reading may have given you some ideas: by the time you draft a research proposal you need to be very clear about the data you need and why. If you cannot clearly see how to obtain reliable and relevant data, you should probably rewrite your research question. Similarly, if you lack the skills or resources to analyse the necessary data, you should rethink your research plans.

Collecting and analysing data always has associated costs (including your own time) so decisions will be needed about 'how much is enough'. (Note that data collection planning needs to include consideration of analysis.) The more (relevant and high-quality) data you have, the more confidence you will normally have in conclusions drawn from it. The important question is therefore how much data of the sort you plan to collect will enable you to draw sufficiently trustworthy conclusions. The decision is a difficult one and will depend upon the type of data, the distribution of any measures used, and the risks of drawing wrong conclusions. In data planning you need to allow a margin of error. Practical research seldom goes exactly to plan, and you want to be able to draw some useful conclusions at least even if there is some shortfall

What data collection method is appropriate?

Different methods make different demands in terms of how much data you need. Whatever data you are seeking, your data collection process also needs to be *rigorous*. Whether you are choosing to collect qualitative or quantitative data, you need to think extremely carefully about dealing with, accounting for and/or minimising bias, and ensuring that the information you collect will be adequate in the sense of allowing you to be reasonably confident in the conclusions they enable you to draw. Chapter 8 discusses what will be needed. At this point you need to think only in general terms how you might collect the sorts of data and information you need. It is impossible to think about data collection without thinking about research designs.

Chris's project featured in both **Chapters 1 and 2**

Let us go back to Chris, and how he decided first on the type of data he would seek and then how much. Note the flexibility of design and the interplay between reading and data collection. In his dissertation Chris chose interviewing as his method, and justified his choice of qualitative data thus:

RESEARCH STORY

Reflection and leadership development

'I was trying to explore how a particular process is undertaken in different organisations to interpret how local actors interpret a phenomenon. In addition to the justification in the above quotation, Miles and Huberman (1994) indicate that good qualitative data are more likely to lead to chance findings and new integrations. This was my experience as the interviews helped me to get beyond my initial conceptions and to generate and revise my conceptual framework. Almost every interviewee prompted me to explore books and readings that I had not previously considered.

This was particularly useful as one of my aims was to build expert knowledge in this field in order to develop my career. A purely quantitative approach would not have alerted me to these avenues for exploration.'

(Dissertation, p.41)

Because Chris was interviewing busy people in some depth, and had a tight deadline, the number of people providing information was limited to those who were willing to contribute their time and who could provide dates within the time-frame available for data collection. He conducted 17 interviews, three of these by phone.

Discussion in **Chapter 10 and Chapters 12 to 16**

Choice of research method and selected specific methods are discussed later, and you will need to read the relevant chapters before finalising your data plan. The third major related question, the research design to use, is discussed later in this chapter. For now, merely note the impact of philosophical preference on method chosen.

Data planning and collection present major challenges in practical research. There will be almost inevitable tensions between what you want and what it is feasible to obtain. You may not be able to directly 'measure' something that interests you, so you may have to rely on indicators. (For example, absence figures are a 'measure' of absence, being directly related to it. You might be interested in stress, and use absence figures as one possible *indicator* of stress. The link is much more tenuous, with implications for the strength of any conclusions you might want to draw.)

Indicators

DRAWING CONCLUSIONS AND MAKING RECOMMENDATIONS

The point of research is to enable you to reach conclusions in relation to your research question. Some may concern the adequacy or otherwise of theory: you might conclude that a theoretical framework needed revision or was of dubious value. Professionally oriented research might draw conclusions about the desirability or otherwise of professional practices, and/or their effectiveness (the executive coaching story later in the chapter is an example). The conclusions drawn from practical business research will often inform subsequent decision and action steps that have major financial implications.

An important distinction between practical and academic research was put succinctly by my colleague: in academic business research nobody dies. While this overstates the case somewhat, it is worth remembering that practical research can have wide-ranging effects on organisations and their employees. It is therefore vital that any conclusions are based on sound arguments and adequate data. It would be unprofessional, and unethical to draw firm conclusions that the data do not warrant. This is why Part 4 is devoted to analysing your data in ways that allow you to draw valid conclusions.

FROM CONCLUSIONS TO ACTION: FRAMING RECOMMENDATIONS

I want to go briefly beyond conclusions, because the points are so important that you must be aware of them from your first thoughts about possible topics. Practical research is often directed towards making recommendations for action. Recommendations should be in the form of concise actions suggested by the research. As when objective-setting, it may be helpful to think in SMART terms, and recommendations may also need to be costed. Recommendations must be firmly based upon your conclusions. Your statement of your research purpose will need to make clear that the research is directed towards recommendations: decisions about methods and data will then be taken with this in mind. Some highly practical projects may include implementing the recommendations, and evaluating them, while for Action Research repeated action and evaluation are essential components in the research process.

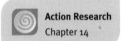
Action Research
Chapter 14

Serious caution is needed in framing recommendations: they can damage your reputations and others' lives if you get them wrong. A common flaw in practical research is to make unrealistic or ill-thought-out recommendations for action. Understanding the complexities of the issue and its context is as important here as during diagnosis. It is important that your recommendations do not go beyond your knowledge of the organisation and the issues involved. A recommendation for expensive action to address a minor issue in an organisation with cash-flow problems will damage your credibility. As will a recommendation for a policy change that is inconsistent with broader strategy or violates legal requirements. You may find it helpful to map possible effects to reduce the chance of unintended consequences.

If you are your own client, there is a serious risk that you will not be sufficiently critical of your conclusions. You should be at least as critical of recommendations that you have the power to implement as you would expect your board to be if you were presenting your case to them.

EVALUATION RESEARCH

To show what the above discussion of methods and design can mean in practice, this section looks at a common form of practical research: an evaluation exercise. An evaluation is a balanced assessment of an existing situation, or of the extent to which an initiative achieved its objectives. Evaluation is an area where business researchers often adopt a fixed design (though the Israel nursery evaluation research had very flexible elements).

Many research projects are designed to evaluate an initiative or a situation. Action-oriented projects may include a stage where the actions prompted by the research are evaluated. Understanding evaluation research is useful because:

- it is an important category of business research in its own right: evaluation skills are highly transferable;
- many expensive initiatives are not evaluated, and usefully could be, so it may be easy to find a useful project of this type;
- evaluating a past initiative avoids some of the risks of research dependent upon decisions or actions outside your control. A decision to postpone a promised work project can make it difficult to meet submission schedules.

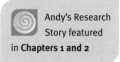 Andy's Research Story featured in **Chapters 1 and 2**

You will remember that Andy was offered 'Evaluating change' as a dissertation project. His experience highlighted some of the hazards which other types of research also present. Looking at these hazards in the context of evaluation may sensitise you to possible risks in your own project, whatever its purpose.

CONSIDER...

On the basis of what you have read thus far, and your experience of evaluation, what hazards or difficulties might an evaluation project present?

If you remembered Andy's difficulties you might have realised some of the difficulties with an evaluation project, particularly in the context of a dissertation. But there are others you may not have thought of.

Evaluations are a political minefield: Some stakeholders may have a strong vested interest in the outcome of the evaluation, or be extremely nervous about its impact upon their reputation. They may seek to block any attempt at an impartial and balanced assessment, restricting access to informants or other data, and censoring the questions you want to ask.

Evaluations are not as simple as they seem: There may be hidden complexities in addition to the political dimension. It may not be easy to decide upon criteria against which to evaluate, and find suitable measures. It may not be easy to separate the impact of an initiative from the effect of other changes in the context. Ethical issues may be involved.

Ethical issues
Chapter 4

Not all evaluations are suitable for a dissertation: Some clients may require a straightforward process of measurement which has little scope for being informed by theory, some may be seeking 'proof of success'. Both should be avoided.

 Questions to ask of a potential evaluation project

What is the purpose of the evaluation?
What is/was the objective of the situation or initiative being evaluated?
What information will help you assess the extent to which objectives are/were met?
Can you obtain data both before and after an initiative?
Do you have the skills to carry out the evaluation?

The following two cases illustrate the points above. The first concerns the evaluation of a leadership programme introduced two years previously by the CEO of a large public sector organisation. The client was the HR department who administered the programme and wanted to know whether continuing investment was justified by results. The story focuses on difficulties with identifying objectives, measuring their achievement, and ensuring that any change was not due to other factors, showing the tension between data you would like as a researcher, and that which it is feasible to collect.

RESEARCH STORY

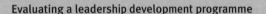

Evaluating a leadership development programme

The programme was designed to increase managers' effectiveness. There were three levels of possible measurement: impact on the organisation; impact on the team; impact on the individual. There were no existing data we could access on managers' effectiveness, either before or after the course. Appraisal information was confidential and it was deemed ethically unacceptable to ask people about their managers.

We decided to use a questionnaire, distributed electronically to managers who had gone through the programme to find out how effective they had found it in achieving its objectives – a much weaker indicator of actual effectiveness. Our first difficulty was establishing the objectives for the programme: nowhere were these clearly stated! Discussions with various stakeholders suggested that the programme was intended to increase participants' ability to take responsibility for their own objectives and decisions, set and communicate clear directions for their team, and motivate and develop team members to work effectively towards achieving these objectives. We

checked this articulation of objectives with our client and used these as the basis for designing a questionnaire asking past participants to assess the programme's impact on these aspects of their behaviour, as well as to give information on other factors which might affect impact. This part of the questionnaire was highly structured, allowing statistical analysis. We also asked open-ended questions to provide qualitative information that might cast light on the numbers.

Conclusions were cautious: self-assessments of performance are highly subjective, as are attributions of reasons. The most interesting finding was that there was a curious distribution of responses: people loved the programme or hated it. Some of the qualitative data hinted at reasons which might enable the programme to be offered more selectively. But the data provided only weak evidence of any actual effect. Further research would have been required to establish impact on effectiveness and find a 'fair' way of identifying those most likely to benefit.

The second story is drawn from an account of the difficulties associated with evaluating executive coaching (Ellam-Dyson and Palmer, 2008). Key points are extracted below, but it is a fascinating account and worth reading in its entirety. You will see interesting similarities with the case above in terms of difficulties faced, but a major difference in research design. There was a stronger focus on developing theory than in the previous case. Again a fixed design was used.

Coaching as a quasi-profession is fairly recent, so theory is relatively under-developed, and the evidence base for the practice is limited, despite its current popularity. 'Executive coaching' is normally taken to describe (expensive) coaching of top executives, although sometimes it means coaching of any managers.

The case that follows refers to a 'waiting list design'. Because this design may be a feasible approach to a control in practical research, Table 3.1 shows what it might mean in a study such as that described. 'M' denotes times when beliefs and behaviours were measured, while 'C' signifies that coaching was taking place.

Table 3.1 Example of 'waiting list' trial schedule

	Jan	Feb	Mar	Apr	May	Jun	Jul	Aug	Sep	Oct	Nov	Dec
Group A	MC	C	C	C	C	M						
Group B	M						MC	C	C	C	C	M

RESEARCH STORY

Evaluating the impact of executive coaching

The researchers' goal was to see whether core beliefs and behaviours of middle and senior managers changed as a result of coaching, and whether effects were influenced by the particular coaching techniques used. Beliefs were to be measured using standardised questionnaires, and behaviours were to be assessed by a 360-degree feedback tool. Their first challenge was to find an organisation willing to 'host' their research. While organisations might see value in evaluating such a costly intervention, they had concerns about confidentiality, resource implications and whether enough of their managers would take up the offer of coaching, or be prepared to complete questionnaires.

Eventually a voluntary organisation agreed to participate, and a group of 'high potential' managers were offered six hours' coaching in preparation for possible promotion to senior levels.

The researchers felt that a randomised controlled trial (RCT) would give the most reliable information. They wanted to split people into 'experimental group' and 'control group' on a random basis and apply the same measures to each, thus allowing the researchers to separate out the effects of coaching from other things going on at the same time (eg pay rises, redundancy threats and on-going learning from experience).

The organisation's reaction shows how real contexts raise issues not encountered in laboratory studies. 41 managers were selected for coaching from a pool of 100. The organisation suggested that the 59 rejected managers could form the control group. But selection had not been random – those likely to benefit had been chosen. The researchers suggested a common variant of the full RCT model as an alternative, the 'waiting list' approach. Selected managers would be randomly assigned to two groups, the first group starting coaching immediately, the second at a later point.

The organisation was worried that this was unfair. If coaching was a useful preparation for promotion, the 'waiting list' group might be disadvantaged during their wait. If any vacancies arose during this period, those receiving coaching first would have a better chance.

The researchers agreed there was a potential ethical issue and they abandoned the idea of using a rigorous design, deciding to rely instead on pre- and post-coaching measurement. This hit problems because of an unanticipated organisational decision to introduce a new 360-degree feedback tool: behaviour measures before and after the coaching were therefore not comparable.

(Story adapted from Ellam-Dyson and Palmer, 2008)

Can you see any other problems with the approach adopted in the coaching study?

The paper does not consider possible limitations of using predetermined quantitative measures of something as complex as 'behaviours' and 'beliefs'. You may have wondered whether what was 'measured' would be particularly enlightening, and whether interviews might have generated insights into what made coaching effective or ineffective and might usefully have supplemented the quantitative 'measures'.

KEY POINTS

- An evaluation is a seemingly simple process of assessing the extent to which the thing being evaluated meets the objectives set for it, and a popular project topic.
- As in other practical research, complexities include political and ethical issues, possible mixed purposes, and practical constraints on measurement and design.
- Because evaluation can be highly influential, it is important that the researcher has the necessary skills, or makes clear his or her limitations.

SUMMARY

Different words may lead you to think differently about your project. *Research* can encourage a more defined and limited approach than *inquiry*, and talking of *evidence* rather than data may help you to consider issues of interpretation and use of data.

Although it is possible to distinguish a logical series of steps in an investigative process, in which each step forms the basis for the next, although not all steps will feature in all projects. This series does not include searching the literature, an activity which may inform the whole process.

When researching complex issues, steps may have to overlap or be repeated. For research to remain systematic there must be a sound grasp of the underlying logic.

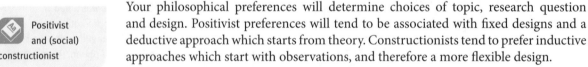

Positivist and (social) constructionist

Your philosophical preferences will determine choices of topic, research question and design. Positivist preferences will tend to be associated with fixed designs and a deductive approach which starts from theory. Constructionists tend to prefer inductive approaches which start with observations, and therefore a more flexible design.

In designing your own research you will have to consider how purpose, philosophical preference and context are interconnected, be critical of your own choices and their appropriateness for purpose, and justify your design choices to others.

Review questions

1. Distinguish between 'research', 'inquiry' and' investigation' in terms of their associations.

2. What are the strengths of an appreciative inquiry approach?

3. Distinguish between 'data', 'information' and 'evidence'.

4. What arguments would a pragmatist put forward in favour of choosing 'inquiry' over 'research'?

5. What different research purposes did Robson distinguish?

6. Why is it so important to be absolutely clear about your research purpose, and to distinguish it from any associated organisational purpose?

7. When might you prefer an inductive approach to a deductive one?

8. How is abductive research distinguished from inductive?

9. When formulating research hypotheses, what is the null hypothesis, and why is it so important?

10. What are the differences between this sort of research hypothesis and a hypothesis within a pragmatic inquiry?

11. What are the relative advantages and disadvantages of a fixed and a flexible research design?

12. When is it important to pay substantial attention to diagnosis, and why?

13. What features must you attend to when making recommendations based upon practical business research?

14. Why might it be difficult to use an experimental design in practical research?

15. What are the attractions of an evaluation dissertation project?

Explore further

Ellam-Dyson, V. and Palmer, C. (2008) 'The challenges of researching executive coaching', *The Coaching Psychologist*, Vol.4, No.2: 79–84 provide a longer version of the story

Reed, J. (2007) *Appreciative Inquiry*. London: Sage. Provides an excellent description of the approach

http://www.iep.utm.edu/d/dewey.htm for an extensive but accessible overview of Dewey's work

http://www.12manage.com/methods_cooperrider_appreciative_inquiry.html for a brief but informative overview of appreciative inquiry

http://www.wadsworth.com/psychology_d/templates/student_resources/workshops/res_methd/non_exper/non_exper_03.html for a brief discussion of different quasi-experimental designs used in psychology

http://209.85.229.132/search?q=cache:8NHbigw122QJ:www.unisa.edu.au/irg/papers/PRAGMATIC%2520INQUIRY%2520fin.doc+Churchman+productive+inquiry&cd=11&hl=en&ct=clnk for a discussion of the roots of pragmatic inquiry

http://uk.geocities.com/balihar_sanghera/ipsrretroductionandabduction.html for a discussion of retrodictive and abductive research

Visit www.cipd.co.uk/brm for web links, templates, activities and other useful resources relating to this chapter.

Stakeholders, Power and Ethics

INTRODUCTION

Your research is likely to have an impact on a number of different people. For example, people who help you to decide on your focus, people you need to gather data and information from, and the people who will read your project report. These are all stakeholders, and although the extent to which people are affected by your research will vary, it is important to pay attention to them – they can literally make or break your research. Stakeholders have the power to help or hinder your progress and in some cases the power to stop you doing something altogether. It is important to see who your powerful stakeholders are, and assess the extent to which they are likely to be a source of support or seek to block your research. This chapter therefore looks at stakeholders in more detail. Not all stakeholders are obvious: it is important to look at those whose influence may be indirect, or who have access to forms of power other than those stemming from authority.

Part of the complexity of research discussed earlier was the way in which different stakeholders can have *competing* needs and expectations. As a researcher, what you would like to do for your research might differ from what your manager would like you to do. Your supervisor may have different requirements again. Even your own objectives may not be totally compatible. It is important to identify these tensions, and seek compromises between them that do not undermine the quality of the research. This chapter looks at the most likely sources of tension, and how they may be handled.

If you identify influential stakeholders who are likely to support your research, you can consider how to enlist and use this support. If you identify those who are likely to be antagonistic and analyse the extent and likely sources of their power, you may be able to plan ways of engaging with them that may reduce their antagonism, or find ways of reducing their capacity to influence your work. It is important to remember that for some stakeholders *you* will be in a position of influence over *them*, and this power dynamic draws attention to the need to behave in ethical and appropriate ways.

This chapter will look at why it is important to think about the ethical implications of your research, and will indicate how you can take steps to ensure that your research is conducted in an ethical fashion.

LEARNING OUTCOMES

This chapter should enable you to:

- identify the major stakeholders in your research

- appreciate their different perspectives and interests and the potential tensions between these

- assess the extent of stakeholder power and its sources

- produce a stakeholder engagement plan to help you work with stakeholders in ways that may maximise support and minimise opposition to your work

- address any ethical implications of your research.

IDENTIFYING STAKEHOLDER INTERESTS

In order to manage the influence stakeholders can have upon your research you first need to recognise them and their motivations. Chapter 2 identified a range of fairly obvious stakeholders in Andy's change evaluation project – some influenced his work, some were influenced by it, some both. This section will help you to look at who can influence your research and will start to build a flowchart (from Figure 4.1 on) which will help you to create your own stakeholder engagement plan. The flowchart will build section by section and provide a map for you to refer to when thinking about the stakeholders in your own research. The first step towards your stakeholder engagement plan is to consider who your stakeholders are and assess the nature of their influence. It is often helpful to think of these people in terms of their being *direct* or *indirect* stakeholders.

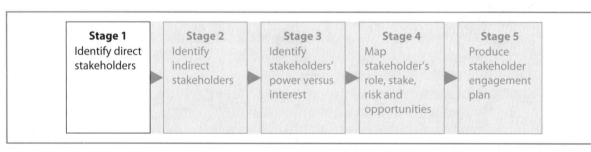

| **Stage 1**
Identify direct stakeholders | **Stage 2**
Identify indirect stakeholders | **Stage 3**
Identify stakeholders' power versus interest | **Stage 4**
Map stakeholder's role, stake, risk and opportunities | **Stage 5**
Produce stakeholder engagement plan |

Figure 4.1 Flowchart for stakeholder engagement plan – Stage 1

Using the example of Andy (from Chapter 2), the most obvious stakeholders are shown in Figure 4.2. These are the stakeholders who have direct contact with Andy and his project. Mapping stakeholder relationships in this way makes it easier to see who you have to consider, and it is a useful starting point for identifying some of the less obvious stakeholders.

Direct stakeholders then have personal contact with you as a researcher. These are likely to be the first people you think of when identifying your stakeholders. But there are also indirect stakeholders. These are people whose relationship with you is mediated through a direct stakeholder. They still have a vested interest in what is happening, but are not personally involved with you as researcher. When thinking about all of your stakeholders, it may be helpful to look at each of the direct stakeholders and consider whether they may themselves be subject to influence. By mapping all of Andy's stakeholders (Figure 4.3) it becomes apparent that each of them has a keen interest in the outcomes of Andy's research.

Figure 4.2 Direct stakeholders in Andy's research

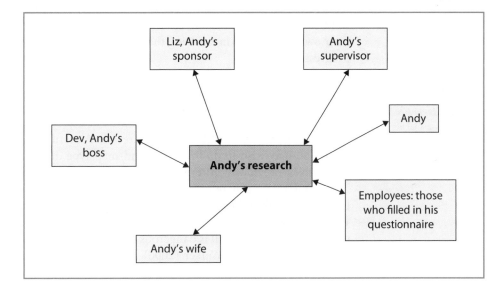

Figure 4.3 Direct and indirect stakeholders in Andy's research

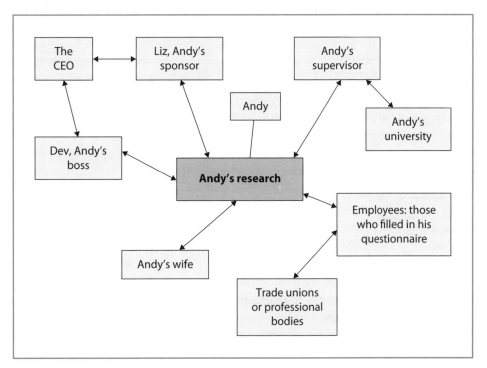

The trade unions wanted to ensure that there were no long-term repercussions for employees taking part in the research. Andy's university (and therefore his supervisor as well) cares about academic standards: because it is judged both by the completion rates of students and the quality of their work, it wants to see that Andy finishes his MBA and that the work he produces meets the required academic standards. The university also requires that all research is conducted ethically. Andy's CEO was genuinely interested in seeing what worked and what didn't work. The CEO was looking for constructive criticism, founded on an impartial evaluation: this would enable the company to identify best practice as well as learn from its mistakes. But this introduces a further complication. Andy had no direct contact with the CEO. Dev, Andy's boss understood the CEO's interest as being in the true *cost* of change whereas Liz, Andy's sponsor, had perceived the CEO as seeking evidence of success. (This may reflect her personal interest – confirmatory bias means that we tend to hear what we want to hear.) Both Dev and Liz were politically motivated: they were interested in their own careers and in ensuring that Andy's project did not interfere with their own progress.

Confirmatory bias **Chapter 2** or **Glossary**

IDENTIFYING YOUR STAKEHOLDERS

A feature on this is available at **www.cipd.co.uk/brm**

Before you can roll your sleeves up and look at how you manage your stakeholders, you must identify the stakeholders (Figure 4.4). A useful starting place is to brainstorm a list. You may wish to do this in a mind-map-type diagram used in the example of Andy given previously. Alternatively, you may wish to simply list the stakeholders. The important issue here is to generate as comprehensive a list as possible. Accurately listing your stakeholders allows you to be focused and specific in planning how you will deal with these people. However, it is vitally important that you do not throw your original list/map away – it is dangerous to assume that stakeholders and their interests are static. Bourne and Walker (2006) note that many of the difficulties that people encounter when trying to maintain good relationships with stakeholders are caused by people failing to 'recognise changes in the relative power or position of key stakeholders' (p.5). A consequence of this is that people then are unable to adapt or amend their research strategy to take account of the new relationship.

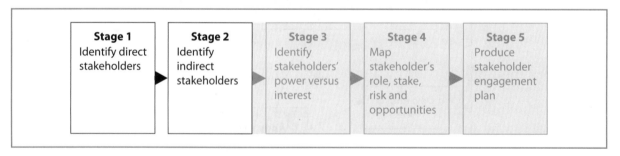

Figure 4.4 Flowchart for stakeholder engagement plan – Stage 2

A good rule of thumb is that if you are surprised by something that one of your stakeholders does or says, then you should return to your stakeholder analysis to see what could have happened to bring about that change.

It is important to identify stakeholders and to be aware that their relationship with you and your research may change.

CONSIDER...

Brainstorm a list of all the stakeholders for a research project that you are planning to do or are currently thinking about.

Identifying stakeholders and their interests, as Andy found out, is far from straight-forward! The influence of indirect stakeholders may be hard to assess because it can be distorted by genuine misperceptions and/or purposeful manipulation. And both of these may be consequences of tensions between the interests of the indirect stake-holder and the direct stakeholder(s) through whom they exert their interest.

STAKEHOLDER TENSIONS

We have discussed some of the specific tensions in Andy's case, and these are typical of the kinds of tensions you may find in your own research, but it is worth exploring some of the main generic sources of tension between stakeholders. I shall look at three broad categories of conflict: the tension between academic and organisational prior-ities in organisation-based dissertation research, the tension between researcher and colleagues for an internal consultancy project, and the tensions between client, those involved in the issue and an external consultant.

Organisational
stakeholders
Chapter 3

ACADEMIC—ORGANISATION TENSIONS

For many who undertake research as part of their studies, the biggest tension that exists between stakeholders exists between the academic stakeholders and their client and/or other organisational stakeholders. For those of you who are in this situation, the tension may be all too obvious. Tension between organisational and educational stakeholders exists because of the differences between what constitutes a good *business* project and what constitutes good *academic* research. These are linked to the discussion in Chapter 1 of possible theory–practice and relevance–rigour debates.

An organisational client is likely to care that the research provides a robust answer to a particular problem that is concerning them. As long as this is either the answer they want (if their interest in the research is to prove an existing point) or it generates useful information, or it makes acceptable recommendations that look as if they may solve a problem, they will be happy. Provided, that is, that the research is done in a way that does not upset people or disrupt their work, and does not make too many demands on other resources.

This is not to suggest that organisational clients are gullible. Starkey and Madan (2001, p55) suggest that researchers are dealing with 'increasingly critical and sophisticated stakeholders', who want to see strong justifications and well-reasoned arguments as the basis for accepting conclusions and recommendations. However, the level of *academic* rigour demanded by managers is likely to be significantly less than that demanded by the academic stakeholders. This can create tensions between the two. Your client may, for example, not understand why it is taking you quite so long to present him with a solution. He is not concerned with the 'literature review stuff' – he simply wants an answer.

Academics are more likely to want methodological rigour: a dissertation is designed to develop and test research skills. They will normally also want to see research that has some theoretical interest. The other thing a dissertation is designed to develop and test is academic competence. Students must therefore select a topic for which there is relevant theory. This will develop search skills, critical reading skills, the ability to relate ideas to an organisational context and perhaps to challenge or develop theory.

One area of negotiation will therefore concern the topic identified. Organisational clients frequently see a student project as a means of advancing a pet project which may have little potential theoretical interest or scope, or may allow scant exercise of research skills. Another negotiation may concern approach. Clients may have many reasons for wishing to constrain your sample, or may prefer a familiar method such as a questionnaire to an unfamiliar one such as a Grounded Theory approach. Again, negotiation may be necessary. Yet another compromise may be needed over resources. You might ideally want to interview a large sample or run a whole series of focus groups, but your client may not be prepared to invest so much staff time in the project.

 Grounded Theory

The third tension here comes from a possible conflict between organisational change and your needs for stability while you collect data. If an organisation decides to close the department while you are researching in it, that is unlikely to be negotiable! However, by engaging with stakeholders at the start you may be able to minimise the chance of choosing a sample that involves groups who are under threat.

TENSIONS IN INTERNAL CONSULTANCY

You have already seen that if, like Andy, you are carrying out a project within your own organisation, there can be a complex array of stakeholder tensions. Because many of the stakeholders will have power over your success within the organisation, they may have the power (discussed shortly) to ensure that it is their interests rather than yours which prevail. Tensions can exist between what you want to do, based on your initial understanding of a situation you know well, and what the different stakeholders demand. Perhaps viewing the problem from your level in the organisation gives you a different set of insights from those that your manager has. Because you have a job role as well as a researcher role the interests and influences are compounded. In Andy's case, Liz – as his sponsor – wanted one outcome from the project, Dev – his boss – wanted another, and the CEO, unbeknown to Andy, wanted a third. Andy could not do his project without both Dev and Liz's support, and so somehow these tensions had to be addressed.

TENSIONS IN EXTERNAL CONSULTANCY PROJECTS

As an external consultant you may be in an invidious position to start with! Consultants are often brought in to an organisation or department by one group of stakeholders but with a brief to look at a problem or an issue that is affecting another stakeholder group, with whom most of their work will be done. They may be suspicious of the consultants, feeling that you are on senior management's 'side', rather than theirs. If you work for a consultancy firm, there may be a further set of interests: those of your employer.

The idea of taking sides instantly creates a barrier between yourself as consultant and each of the stakeholder groups. (This can be a feature of internal consultancy roles too.) This is why a key skill of consultancy is managing the stakeholder relationships on which you are dependent. The following research story shows some of these interests.

RESEARCH STORY

Stakeholder tension at MiddletinX College

The Board of Governors of a local college of further education were unhappy about the senior management at the college. The Governors recognised that the college had no clear sense of direction, had no clear strategic plan, and was not preparing itself for impending changes to the government funding structure. It seemed that the Senior Management Team comprised the 'old boys network' – teachers (all male) who had been teaching in the college for at least ten years. Indeed, some of them had never taught anywhere else! Instead of being promoted for their expertise, they had been promoted based purely on length of service and on how well they got on with the headmaster.

The Board of Governors, sensing that they had to resolve the problems before the government funding structures changed, commissioned MiddletinX Consultancy to undertake a thorough review of the ways in which the college was run. The review included everything from the strategic planning processes at the top to the details of how the school was managed on a day-to-day basis.

Pietr was the senior consultant on this assignment. Before he could decide how to manage the stakeholder relationships he had to identify the direct stakeholders and establish what demands they placed upon him.

Pietr identified the following stakeholder perspectives:

The Board of Governors: They had written his brief and they were paying him. They wanted to know the truth about what was happening in the college.

His consultancy firm: They needed Pietr to produce a robust report which satisfied the Board of Governors and increased the likelihood of future assignments from them.

The Senior Management Team: They were somewhat aggrieved by the implication that they were not doing their jobs properly. They were also angry that an external consultancy had been contracted to 'investigate' them, implying that they were incapable of managing the situation by themselves.

The college staff: They wanted things to run better for their jobs depend on a secure future for the college. However, they did not want to be seen as telling tales on their managers.

The impact of stakeholder interests, and of tensions between them, will depend on the power that different stakeholders have, so it is important to understand sources of power, and how power can be exercised. Before Pietr could work effectively on the problems he recognised, he had to understand how powerful each of the groups were and their likely impact on his research.

STAKEHOLDER POWER

Power is normally defined in terms of the ability to influence, and often analysed in terms of its sources. For example, French and Raven (1959) suggested that power might be derived from position, control of resources, information, expertise, social connections and personal characteristics.

Political behaviour relates to activity directed towards gaining or exercising one of these forms of power. Looking at the MiddletinX story, the consultancy had position power over Pietr; the board might be deemed to have position power and resource power over the staff and over Pietr; staff had power derived from information and expertise. Their political behaviour can be categorised into three types, which are typical issues for many forms of research. They relate to control, access, and honesty.

THE POLITICS OF CONTROL

The politics of control determine what you can and what you cannot do. Stakeholders who are very powerful can insist on a particular topic, or change the overall direction of your research, or your specific research question. An organisation that is funding a researcher's studies may feel that it has the right to do this, and it certainly has the power. Being aware of these people and managing your relationship with them from the very beginning of your research proposal is important.

RESEARCH STORY

The evaluation that wasn't

Many years ago I was commissioned by the Head of Human Resources of a Metropolitan Borough Council to review a major organisational change. The Council had gone through a job evaluation exercise that seemed to have been successful. There had been some problems at the beginning of the change process, because the librarians 'strongly objected' to being on the same pay spine as the refuse collectors. However, once this issue was resolved, the rest of the change process seemed to have gone smoothly. Very few employees (2%) were worse off afterwards and very many (15%) were better off. Yet despite this, when the process of change was complete, sick absence rates increased significantly and the feeling amongst the managers was that morale and motivation were at rock bottom.

I worked for six months with the Director of HR devising a robust methodology to evaluate the organisation-wide change. The Director of HR presented our research proposal to the elected members, who promptly rejected the research completely.

Their only comment was that there was 'no point crying over spilt milk': whatever had happened was in the past and it was better left there. There was absolutely nothing that I or the Director of HR could do: six months' hard work had been rejected.

With hindsight this might have been prevented by a more proactive approach to the stakeholders. If we had discussed our ideas and the plans with the elected members, we might have understood their interests and presented a case which emphasised the value of the research, and the importance of learning lessons for the future. Hindsight is a great thing!

THE POLITICS OF ACCESS

As a researcher, you may need access to information, access to people, and/or access to resources. Although those in positions of authority can assist or block access (as Liz did, in limiting those to whom Andy's questionnaire could be sent), they are not the only people with this sort of power. It is important to be aware of those who have similar power for reasons other than seniority – it will be important to manage your relations with them as well. Senior management in Pietr's case might deny him access to members of staff whose opinions disagreed with theirs.

Those who are not in a position of rank or status yet who still have the power to grant or refuse access are often known as 'gatekeepers'. Examples of gatekeepers might be the Chief Executive's personal assistant, the doctor's receptionist or the personnel assistant who knows the social networks which exist within the organisation. Easterby-Smith *et al* (1991) describe the role of these people as a brokerage role – one in which the gatekeeper uses his or her contacts, information or networks to help (or hinder) access to the appropriate people.

In cases such as Pietr's consultancy, above, access to information was a key issue. The senior management team were unhappy with the consultants being brought in, and one way in which they might influence Pietr's assignment would be to deny access to the necessary data or information. This would have to be done with subtlety: if the Board of Governors suspected them of being obstructive, it could damage the board's trust in them.

RESEARCH STORY

Access and the 'volunteered' volunteers

A few years ago I was doing some research that involved running a series of focus groups at different levels of management within a large manufacturing sector organisation. The Senior Management Team allowed me access, but insisted that *they* chose the volunteers for the focus groups. The rationale they gave for this was that they knew what demands the organisation was making on the time of each of the managers and so were best placed to say which managers were able to attend which focus group. Fortunately in this particular instance, all the focus group members seemed willing to talk freely, but I was aware of the risk that this particular group of 'volunteers' might have been chosen because they knew the right things to say.

THE POLITICS OF HONESTY

Power may influence how open and honest any of the stakeholders are prepared to be. The politics of honesty can be most easily thought of in terms of the potential consequences of telling the truth (considering, of course, that the truth itself may only be a particular view of events). Informants who have been 'volunteered' by their manager might think twice about being critical of the manager. After all, he/she knows that they took part in the research and might be able to trace my comments back to them. In Pietr's situation, a junior teacher at the college might be reluctant to criticise the Senior Management Team to Pietr, fearing that negative comments might get back to them and that there might be consequences for their own future. They could refuse to answer, but it is more likely that they would choose to give only a partial truth, pretending that things are not quite as bad as they actually are. If really nervous, they might lie and pretend everything was fine. In either case, Pietr's results would not then give a fair reflection of the situation.

Members of the Senior Management Team might be fully aware of weaknesses at their level but be reluctant to implicate themselves, or friends and colleagues. Again they might choose to simply pretend that everything is fine.

YOUR RESEARCH AS A POLITICAL THREAT

Looking at the politics of control, the politics of access and the politics of honesty can highlight ways in which stakeholders can use their power to help or to hinder research. If you are starting to consider a project and have identified your stakeholders, consider this aspect of your research.

What are your likely stakeholders' sources of power and the means by which they might use them to influence your research?

You may have identified some or all of the following ways of exerting an influence, or indeed others. What follows is not an exhaustive list – rather, it is meant as an indication of the pervasive nature of control.

Influence may be exercised through instructions, or through policies, processes and systems. Things like policies tell people what they can and cannot do, and disciplinary systems are often in place to make sure that people conform to what is required. Information is often carefully controlled, and what people are able to do is often limited or enabled by the information that they have access to. Similarly, providing or withholding resources can help or hinder your research, and those with resource-based power over informants may influence the information they provide.

But power perceived as a threat can be reciprocal. Powerful stakeholders can curtail your research because your research has political repercussions for them. Often undertaking business research implies criticism of the current processes and systems. As Armstrong (2002) argues (and as demonstrated in the previous exercise), managers exert control in large part through the use of processes and systems. Even if they do not design the processes and systems themselves, they are often the ones who approve them. In such circumstances, any inquiry that seeks to criticise such processes and systems can be seen as offering a critique on the effectiveness of the manager. What is worse is that suggestions made to improve the processes or systems might in some way end up diluting the manager's power of control over that system. Armstrong argues that this is especially the case where management is 'abstracted' – by which he means situations in which managers are generalist managers who are managing professionals or technical experts. Here, the idea that a technical specialist is in a position to offer a criticism of a management practice when the manager cannot offer any reciprocal criticism of the technical aspects of the job is seen to undermine the kudos and the status of management.

Researchers must be aware of the sensitivities of management as well as being aware of the ways in which managers can enable or constrain the research project. There is a need to make sure that what is proposed to managers – a very powerful group of stakeholders – inclines them to be supportive rather than dismissive of the planned research. Indeed, Easterby-Smith *et al* (1994) cite the example of a Chinese emperor who had 400 scholars buried alive because he didn't like what they were saying! Although contemporary ways of exercising power are much less extreme, the fundamental issue remains that managers can enable or frustrate your business research.

Think about the ways in which your proposal for research could be seen to undermine the credibility of management.

In drawing these themes together it becomes apparent that it is important to consider the stakeholders in research. Having looked at the issue of direct and indirect stakeholders, having thought about the ways in which the research that we are planning can affect them, and having discussed why stakeholders are able to influence what we do by looking at the issues of power and control, it is now useful to think about how to recognise the stakeholders.

ANALYSING STAKEHOLDERS

Identifying stakeholders is crucial, but just being able to list the names of all those who have a vested interest in what you are doing is of little use. Indeed, Bryson (2003, p11) insists that 'Stakeholder analyses are undertaken for a purpose, and that purpose should be articulated before the analysis begins.' In short, if you are not going to use your stakeholder analysis to advise your plan for your research, there is little point in doing the analysis at all. Hopefully, however, your reading thus far will have highlighted the importance of identifying and managing the stakeholders – and will have highlighted some of the potential consequences of not doing so. The first question to ask yourself then is 'What do I want to/need to achieve from undertaking a stakeholder analysis?' Are you identifying the stakeholders to see who is supportive and who is unsupportive of your research? Are you identifying stakeholders so you can use them to access resources? Are you identifying stakeholders so you can circumvent problematic groups? Or even all of the above! It is important to clarify what you hope to achieve. Once you have done this, you are on the road to devising your stakeholder engagement plan. The next step is to identify the stakeholders. Bryson (*ibid*) presents a series of analyses which you may find it useful to consider. However, this section presents a hybrid approach.

STAKEHOLDERS' POWER VERSUS INTEREST

The next stage of your stakeholder analysis is to think about the relationship between the power that your stakeholders have and the level of vested interest they have in your research (Figure 4.5).

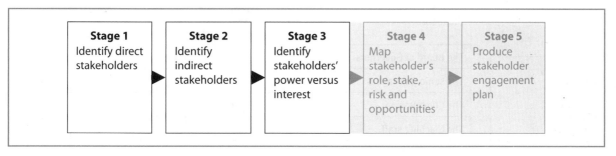

Figure 4.5 Flowchart for stakeholder engagement plan – Stage 3

It may be that the inquiry that you are planning has a whole range of very powerful stakeholders. However, if these people are not particularly interested in the focus of your research, there is probably little need for you to create complicated communication strategies to make sure that they are involved. You would be better instead focusing on those people who do have a keen interest. Likewise, it may be that a group of people are acutely interested in what happens in your inquiry but not very powerful. In the example of Andy used previously, doubtless the employees working in a different department from Andy would be very interested to see how well or otherwise the change was managed – after all, it might well happen to them next.

However, their distance from the research is likely to mean that they are powerless to intervene. Before you can start to work out who you ought to involve in your research plans, you must look at who is powerful and who is interested.

In this context, 'power' is considered to mean the extent to which stakeholders are able to intervene, interrupt or cause you to change your plans for research against your will. 'Interest' is taken to mean the extent to which stakeholders are actively concerned about what you are planning to do.

Table 4.1 below is provided as a framework in which you can map out the relative power versus interest of your stakeholders. The word 'relative' is important because in devising your stakeholder management plan you are likely to have to prioritise your efforts towards particular groups. You will simply not have time to consider every possible stakeholder in detail. To make this idea of relativity more meaningful it is suggested that the power and the influence of each stakeholder group be ranked on a scale of 1 to 5 in which 1 indicates very low and 5 indicates very high.

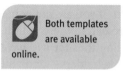
Both templates are available online.

Table 4.1 Stakeholders' power versus interest

Stakeholders	Power levels					Interest levels				
	1	2	3	4	5	1	2	3	4	5
Stakeholder A										
Stakeholder B										
Stakeholder C										
etc										

Key
1 Very low
2 Low
3 Average
4 High
5 Very high

To give you an indication of how this works, Table 4.2 below is an example based on Pietr's consultancy project in MiddletinX College. Underneath the table are some of the reasons which underpin the mapping.

Table 4.2 Stakeholders' power versus interest for Pietr

Stakeholders	Power levels					Interest levels				
	1	2	3	4	5	1	2	3	4	5
The Board of Governors					X					X
The senior managers				X						X
The Consultancy			X						X	
The teaching staff		X							X	

Key
1 Very low
2 Low
3 Average
4 High
5 Very high

The Board of Governors are extremely powerful. They have commissioned the research and they have set the brief. They can decide how, where and when the research is carried out. They are also the people who judge whether or not this research has achieved its goals.

The senior managers are less powerful than the Board of Governors but have still got the power to control what information Pietr has access to. They too have a high vested interest in the research findings because these are likely to have implications for the way in which they work in the future.

The Consultancy which employs Pietr has some power. It can direct Pietr in terms of what he should and should not be doing. However, it cannot control the issues within the organisation. It is also very interested in what happens – its reputation with this particular college depends on a successful result.

The teaching staff are (arguably) the least powerful of the stakeholders considered. They can withhold information or distort information but they cannot control access and the research is unlikely to be dependent solely on information gained from them. They are also interested in the outcomes of the research because these have implications for the ways in which they are managed. But essentially, the results are unlikely to have a significant impact on their teaching practice.

CONSIDER...

In respect of the stakeholders in your own (proposed) research, map their power and their interest. What insights does this mapping give you?

Identifying stakeholders' relative power and interest is the third stage in devising your stakeholder management plan.

STAKEHOLDERS' ROLE, STAKE, RISK AND OPPORTUNITY

Having identified the relative power and interest of your stakeholders, you must next think about the ways in which power may be used – that is, how your stakeholders might influence your research. To consider this, you need to think about a number of issues (Figure 4.6):

- What role does each of the stakeholders play in your research? What is their legitimate position?
- What does each of the stakeholders want to get out of your research? What is their stake?
- What risks do these demands present to you and your research?
- What opportunities do these demands present to you and your research?

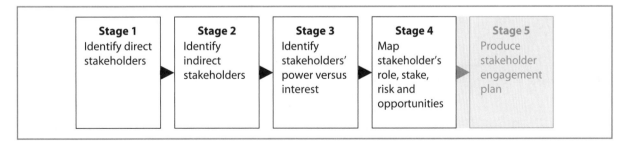

Figure 4.6 Flowchart for stakeholder engagement plan – Stage 4

| **Stage 1** Identify direct stakeholders | **Stage 2** Identify indirect stakeholders | **Stage 3** Identify stakeholders' power versus interest | **Stage 4** Map stakeholder's role, stake, risk and opportunities | **Stage 5** Produce stakeholder engagement plan |

Table 4.3 presents a convenient way of mapping these issues which you can then use to inform your stakeholder management plan. To give you some idea of how this

table might look when completed, the example of Pietr considered previously has been used as an illustration (Table 4.4).

Table 4.3 Stakeholders' role, stake, risk and opportunities

Stakeholder	Role	Stake	Risk	Opportunities
Stakeholder A				
Stakeholder B				
Stakeholder C				
etc				

This table is available at www.cipd.co.uk/brm

Table 4.4 Pietr's stakeholders' role, stake, risk and opportunities

Stakeholder	Role	Stake	Risk	Opportunities
Board of Governors	Commissioned the research	They want reliable and insightful research findings	Impending changes in government funding may mean they put pressure on to get the results quickly	Their legitimate power could be used to ensure that people co-operate with the research
Senior managers	The people whose effectiveness is being 'investigated' by this inquiry	They want the results to be as uncritical as possible	They may not give information, may give inaccurate information, or may mislead the inquiry to protect themselves	Some individuals may see this as an opportunity to air opinions that they have not been able to air previously
Consultancy	Pietr's bosses and the people responsible for managing him through the project	They want to see a research result that will please the Board of Governors	They may bow to demands by the Board to get the project finished more quickly	They may be willing to provide additional resources to help ensure a successful result
Teachers	People affected by the problems but not directly responsible for them	They want minimal disruption to their day-to-day job while the problems are put right	They may be afraid to tell the truth for fear of reprisals from their managers	They may be willing to speak openly because they are likely to have the backing of the Board of Governors

Identifying stakeholders' roles, stakes, risks and opportunities is the fourth stage leading up to a plan for how you will engage these people in your business research project.

Having completed the series of analyses, you are now in a position to produce your stakeholder engagement plan.

THE STAKEHOLDER ENGAGEMENT PLAN

In producing a stakeholder engagement plan (Figure 4.7) you are really producing a plan for communication. It sets out how you will use communication to inform and to persuade people.

A useful template to map out this plan is presented below (Table 4.5). This has been adapted from a document produced by the Prime Minster's Strategy Unit (http://interactive.cabinetoffice.gov.uk/strategy/survivalguide/downloads/stakeholder _engagement.pdf [accessed 15 October 2008]).

The stakeholder engagement plan uses the analyses you have done to help you to create a working document for stakeholder management. I use the term 'management' loosely here because unless you are in a very senior position within an organisation, you are unlikely to have direct control over your stakeholders. Instead, you should be trying to anticipate any problems, obstacles or arguments that might stand in the way of your producing a good piece of business research.

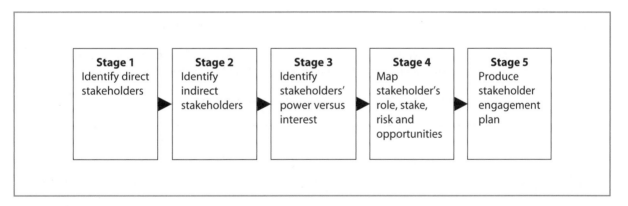

Figure 4.7 Flowchart for stakeholder engagement plan – Stage 5

By clearly mapping what each of the stakeholders wants from you and what you want from them, you are surfacing the very basis for this reciprocal relationship that you are trying to achieve.

Table 4.5 Stakeholder engagement plan template

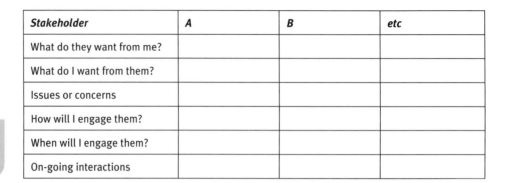

Stakeholder	A	B	etc
What do they want from me?			
What do I want from them?			
Issues or concerns			
How will I engage them?			
When will I engage them?			
On-going interactions			

This table is available at **www.cipd.co.uk/brm**

> A stakeholder engagement plan is a strategy for communication. It is important to revisit this throughout the research project and to make any changes as necessary depending on changes in stakeholder relationships.

Top tips for engaging stakeholders

1 Sell your research to people so that they can see the value of what you plan to do.
2 Find a high-level supportive sponsor.
3 Where possible consult with people or seek their advice when planning your research.
4 Let people know who else is involved.
5 Make sure you have the appropriate permissions and approvals.
6 Keep stakeholders up to date with how your research is developing.
7 Be open and willing to listen to their concerns and issues.
8 Think about and account for the demands that your research will place on other people.
9 Never be confrontational.
10 Try to adopt a neutral position such that you cannot be accused of siding with one party or another.
11 If people are trying to skew your research, be prepared to point out to them how this will produce unreliable research results.
12 Let people see the outline of any interview question before you interview them.

KEY POINTS

- Stakeholders are people who have a vested interest in your research.
- Stakeholders can direct the focus of your research or enable or constrain your actions.
- Before you can plan how you will manage the stakeholders, you must understand their power and the level of interest that they have in what you are proposing.
- You must be aware not only that the groups of stakeholders might change but that their level of interest and power may also change across the course of your research.
- A stakeholder engagement plan is a good way to factor in dealing with stakeholders – but you must review it across the course of your research.

In the previous section the politics of honesty were considered. Although the section noted the issues surrounding people's willingness to give you honest answers to your questions, there is also an issue regarding how fair it is of *you* to put people in a position whereby they feel vulnerable. Stakeholders in your research might feel vulnerable for a number of reasons. They may fear repercussions from powerful people if they do not participate; they may fear that whereas giving dishonest answers presents an unrealistic picture, giving honest answers points the figure of blame at someone; or they may feel that giving honest answers compromises their own position. As a researcher it is important to be aware of the ways in which your research creates moral and ethical dilemmas for those people you encounter.

THINKING ABOUT ETHICS

It hardly seems possible to pick up a newspaper these days without finding at least one headline containing the word 'ethics'. It is a word that everyone is familiar with. 'Ethical trading' and 'ethical standards' are terms often used in the media to describe the conduct of businesses or organisations. In common usage the word 'ethics' can mean generally 'doing the right things', and although at first glance this idea seems to be quite straightforward, the more you think about the implications of doing the right things, the more you appreciate just how complex the issue of ethics is.

CONSIDER...

What do you understand by the term 'ethics'? Make a few notes which summarise your understanding of it.

Are ethics important to you? If so, in what ways?

You will have come up with your own answers here but for me ethics is a set of values that guide what I do. They influence the ways in which I behave, the way I think and the attitudes I hold. Looking at the ways in which others define ethics can give some useful insights into what the term might imply for business research.

The definition offered by *Chamber's 20th-century Dictionary* (1993, p55) is:

 Ethics is 'that branch of philosophy which is concerned with human character and conduct; a system of morals or rules of behaviour'.

How does this definition help you to think about ethics in relation to your business research? The first thing to notice about ethics is that they relate to the ways in which human beings behave – they are within a person's control. If ethics are controlled by people, then it is safe to assume that it is people who make up the rules of behaviour. These ethical rules are formed when people make value-judgements about what is and what is not right, what is and what is not acceptable behaviour. Again, this seems very clear, very black and white – there are rules which tell people what is right and there are rules which tell people what is wrong. Is it really that easy?

CONSIDER...

What are your views on the following scenarios?

Should an ambulance that is breaking the speed limit to get a heart attack victim to hospital be given a speeding ticket?

Should a home-owner who, in trying to protect his property, injures a burglar be prosecuted?

If you found £5 in the street, would you hand it in to the police? What if you found £20 – would you hand this in? What if you found £100 – would you hand this in? What if you found £1,000 – would you hand that in?

For each of these scenarios, there is at least a day-long debate, and even then people may not agree! The aim here is to illustrate that the issue of ethics is not quite as simple as doing what is right and not doing what is wrong – there are areas of grey in between the black and the white, areas where it is sometimes difficult to tell what is right and what is wrong. Yet these issues are of huge importance when thinking about research. This section will start by looking at the ethical obligations of business research and will build on these to consider whom you have ethical responsibilities to. The section will then focus on the key considerations in discharging those responsibilities before discussing ethics approval processes.

WHY ARE ETHICS IMPORTANT IN RESEARCH?

Having previously asked you to consider why ethics may be important to you, the next exercise puts that consideration into a more specifically research-oriented context.

CONSIDER...

It is suggested that business researchers should think about ethics for a number of reasons. Make a note of what you think these reasons might be.

Refer back to your notes as each of the following themes is discussed, adding to your notes where the issues raised may be of particular relevance to your own research.

Researchers have to consider research ethics for a number of reasons relating to their legal, professional, cultural and personal obligations. Figure 4.8 (adapted from Daft, 2003, p139) demonstrates the relationship between these areas. What becomes apparent from this diagram is that a substantial amount of personal choice goes into decisions about what is right and what is wrong.

Legal obligations

Researchers are legally obliged to conform to the rules and laws which govern the society in which they are operating, and sanctions exist to oblige people to conform. If people break the law, they are punished by whatever means the society in which they live has chosen. There is little choice here, and this sometimes brings international disparities when thinking about business and research ethics on an international level.

Figure 4.8 Legal,
professional, cultural and
personal obligations

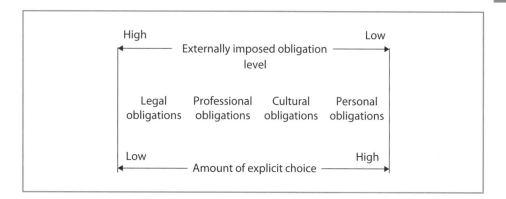

Professional obligations

Professional obligations are established to ensure the credibility of the profession and
to guide the conduct of all its members. Professions are governed by these regulatory
bodies, and in many cases people cannot practise within the profession without being
a member (eg the Royal Institute of British Architects, The Law Society or the British
Medical Association). With membership comes an obligation to abide by the code of
conduct, and when that code of conduct is breached, sanctions can include expulsion.
Professional obligations also extend to any organisation, company or university which
may be sponsoring your research. The case illustration of MidXmugton University
illustrates why.

RESEARCH STORY

Ethical research at MidXmugton University

Joe is a third-year undergraduate at MidXmugton
University. For his dissertation he has decided to see
if there is any relationship between the number of
microwave meals students eat and their academic
performance. To do this, Joe has asked a group of 50
of his fellow students to keep a diary over a period
of six months (January to June) in which they record
every microwave meal they have. He has also asked
them to provide him with a spreadsheet of their
academic results (assignment and examination
grades) for the previous 12 months. Joe was quite
confident that he knew what he was doing for his
research, so he didn't bother to seek the advice of
his supervisor.

Joe was delighted when the results of his research
showed clearly that those students who ate more
microwave meals had lower academic results, and
those students who ate fewer microwave meals
had higher academic results. Joe was even more
delighted when, following a conversation with a
journalist friend whom he played football with, his

research made the local and then the national press.
The headline read 'MICRO-WAVE GOODBYE TO YOUR
DEGREE: MIDXMUGTON UNIVERSITY PROVES THAT
MICROWAVE MEALS DAMAGE YOUR BRAIN'.

As a consequence of this publicity, the Head of
Department, the Vice Chancellor and the Pro-
Vice Chancellor for research were inundated
with complaints from major food manufacturing
companies as well as from the local and national
supermarkets who stocked such products. Joe's
research was fundamentally flawed. He cannot
assume that research results found from a group of
50 of his friends would be the same across an entire
population. However, the publicity that resulted
from the research not only instantly reduced sales
of microwave meals but became the cause for
legal action from some manufacturing companies
against the University. Joe's research threatened the
financial position of the University and undermined
the University's reputation as a credible academic
institution.

Cultural obligations

Cultural obligations are those informal rules which govern the ways in which people behave in the societies in which they live. Because these are informal rules, any wrongdoing will not meet with legal sanctions but may be frowned on by the local community. For example, in some cities in Europe it is perfectly acceptable to wear a coat made from animal fur. In others, where the wearing of such coats is entirely legal, people wearing such a coat are likely to have abuse or even paint hurled at them by animal rights protesters who object to the wearing of animal skins.

This example emphasises the ways in which the beliefs that some people hold can bring them into conflict with the domain of codified law. People who throw paint at those wearing fur coats are breaking the law. However, their personal belief that wearing such a coat is morally wrong is so strong that they are prepared to suffer the consequences of the law in order to make their views known.

Personal obligations

Personal obligations are the day-to-day choices that individuals make regarding their own behaviour, values and beliefs. These choices are not directly governed by the values of the society in which they live, or the laws by which they are governed – they are entirely at the behest of the individual.

If you think back to the ethical dilemmas you were presented with previously, your answers will have been based on your own values and your own beliefs. When I have posed Question 3 (about finding different amounts of money in the street) to groups of students, most of them have been prepared to keep and even enjoy spending the £5 they found on the pavement, yet nearly all of them would hand in the £1,000. The main argument given is that it would not be right to deprive someone of £1,000 which is, after all, their money. Nonetheless the £5 also belongs to someone else, and most are happy to keep it! Their responses are not necessarily right or wrong – they are simply reflections of the values to which people in these groups subscribed.

Although the Daft model represented in Figure 4.8 arranges ethical obligations along a continuum, they may be better thought of as interconnecting (Figure 4.9).

Ethical behaviours are guided by legal, professional, cultural and personal obligations.

 CONSIDER...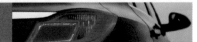

What do you think your obligations are, in relation to your business research?

Make a note of the key points and add this to your list as you read on.

By representing these obligations as interconnected it is easier to see that each of them interacts with the others, and most importantly how your research is located in the centre.

Figure 4.9 The interconnectedness of ethical obligations

Figure 4.9 The interconnectedness of ethical obligations

ETHICAL RESPONSIBILITIES IN RESEARCH

A useful way to think about the ethical responsibilities you have when planning your research is to use the headings set out by the British Educational Research Association at www.bera.ac.uk. These responsibilities are classified as:

- your responsibilities to the participants/respondents
- your responsibilities to those sponsoring or commissioning the research
- your responsibilities to the wider research community.

Responsibilities to participants/respondents

The participants/respondents are the people from whom you will obtain information or data. This includes everyone who contributes to the research process – for example:

- supervisors
- collaborators
- line managers and the organisation
- gatekeepers (people who control your access to others – eg a receptionist in a GP's surgery).

Your responsibilities to participants/respondents can be seen from three perspectives, namely *respect*, *informed consent* and *confidentiality*.

Respect

Treating people with respect requires you to think about the ways in which your research could be seen to undermine the values, the credibility or the roles and responsibilities of the people involved. Are you asking them to do things that are not normally part of their job? Are you asking them for information that they shouldn't be disclosing, or are you asking them to do something that they feel uncomfortable about? Respect means that you are careful not only about the ways in which you treat the person, but are careful about the ways in which you treat the information that they give to you. In planning your research you have to think about the people likely to be involved and what effect your research will have on them.

Treating people with respect means being aware of the power dynamic which exists between yourself as the researcher and the respondent. Where you are asking friends and colleagues to provide information, it is useful to consider the extent to which you are using the power of your relationship with them to persuade them to act in ways that make them feel compromised. Where you are gathering data or information from people junior to yourself, think about the extent to which your seniority or rank persuades them to behave in ways that they find uncomfortable or to give answers that they feel you want to hear.

 CONSIDER...

Referring back to the list of stakeholders in your own research, what would you have to do to ensure that you treated each of them with respect?

Informed consent

Getting informed consent requires you to have given people sufficient information about your research to allow them to make a reasoned judgement as to whether or not they want to be involved. In most circumstances this means that people need to know who you are, why you are doing this research, what the research entails (which includes what they actually have to do) and what will happen to the results. In most circumstances, the participants/respondents themselves make the decision whether or not they wish to take part in your research – however, there are circumstances where this is not the case. Particular care must be exercised when dealing with vulnerable groups. (For example, some research that I did many years ago investigated non-attendance rates at a psychiatric out-patient clinic.) Most institutions (both academic and organisational) will have a code of practice and an ethical approval process which you will have to go through before they will grant you permission to access such vulnerable groups. But even if organisational permission is given, you will still need permission from the respondents themselves and/or their representatives.

Under this umbrella of informed consent there are two issues that are worth thinking about separately – namely, the issues of *deception* and *coercion*. These words conjure up a range of dreadful images, and indeed in their most extreme forms can be very dangerous. But like everything else in research, there are levels or degrees to which these factors can creep in to otherwise *bona fide* research.

Deception

At worst, deception can be the purposeful misleading of the participants/respondents. This can be either by giving misleading information or by not giving people the information that they need. But at another level, deception also results from forgetting to tell people something that may be important to them, or by altering the emphasis of what you say to them to make them more inclined to participate.

Examples:

It may not be sufficient to tell your respondents that their identity will be protected because you have not asked specifically for their name if you know that other demographic data about age, gender, status, education and where they work etc, makes it highly likely that other people will be able to identify them and what they have said.

It is also interesting to note that some research is dependent on deception, which the following research case illustrates.

RESEARCH STORY

When the truth presents a problem

Porath and Erez (2007) devised a piece of research which looked at whether or not acts of rudeness had a detrimental impact on performance. To do this they sought a number of student volunteers who were told that the researchers were looking at the relationship between personality types and performance. This was obviously not the truth – however, had they told the volunteers that they were looking at the connection between rudeness and performance, it would have had an effect on the performance and therefore have skewed the results. Instead, the researchers recognised the need to deceive, they did it in a way that was not at all detrimental to the respondents, and they clearly explained what they had done in their paper.

Coercion

Coercion is the use of pressure or force to make people take part in your research. Again there are extreme examples of this where people feel that their job security is threatened if they do not take part in a particular piece of research. Robson (2002) notes the ways in which prisoners were offered the chance of early release if they took part in research to test potentially dangerous drugs. An alternative way of thinking about coercion is the use of 'inducements'. In the paper by Porath and Erez (2007) mentioned previously, the students who volunteered to take part in the research were rewarded with extra credit points – a practice deemed quite common in some areas of research in the USA.

Pressure, on the other hand, is creating in the mind of the participant/respondent a sense of duty or obligation to help you, even though, if given a choice, they would prefer to opt out. This can be done by creating a sense of vulnerability or a sense of neediness on the part of the researcher. An example of this would be persuading someone to take part in your research because if you don't get enough people, you won't be able to do the research and will therefore fail the course you have been studying for over the last four years. The respondent is likely to feel uncomfortable but may not want to be the cause of your failure. Pressure can also be brought to bear from the impact of social relationships seen earlier, from persuading people that helping you is the 'collegial' thing to do, or by convincing them that they will be the odd one out if they refuse to help.

Responsibilities to people sponsoring or commissioning the research

Mutual respect

Mutual respect requires that both parties are clear at the outset about what the research entails. Ideally, a written agreement will map out roles and responsibilities, time-frames and resources, and will clarify ownership of the final written report. Mutual respect also implies that no party will put pressure on the other to undertake practices that may be deemed illegal or unethical.

Integrity

You should make every effort to stick to the research plan and produce the desired results on time and within budget. Moreover, these results must be trustworthy and based on solid evidence derived from the research. You should deal genuinely and responsibly with any data given to you, and be aware of commercial sensitivities. You should use analysis methods which minimise distortion and which allow you to produce research findings that are trustworthy.

Loyalty

You should point out as soon as possible where unanticipated issues compromise your ability to produce the desired results or to produce them on time. Likewise, you should discuss with the sponsor as soon as possible where it has not been possible to stick to the brief. It is also important that you do not attempt to undertake any research for which you are not appropriately trained or skilled.

Responsibilities to the wider research community

Honesty

You are professionally obliged to produce results based on *bona fide* data in an accurate and unbiased way. It is important that these results fairly reflect the data and are not skewed by act (collecting only data likely to support the arguments that you wish to present) or omission (presenting only data which reinforces your views).

Respect

The issue of appropriate acknowledgement of the works of others could come in either category, that of honesty or respect. Whichever way, it is vital that all sources are appropriately referenced and due credit given to the original authors. Likewise, when presenting a critique of the work of others, this should be a balanced critique rather than one which sets out to discredit.

KEY POINTS

- In thinking about ethics, researchers are bound by legal, professional, cultural and personal obligations. Legal and professional obligations are governed by legislation, whereas cultural and personal obligations give the researcher the freedom to choose what they think to be good or bad practice.

- Researchers must show respect for people and for the information they give to the researcher. This involves making sure they give informed consent and respecting anonymity and confidentiality are respected.

- Respect for the sponsoring body requires a clear mutual understanding of what is expected, a balanced consideration of the data and the presentation of trustworthy results. Likewise, issues of confidentiality and anonymity must be respected.

● Respect for the research community obliges the researcher to produce genuine research results, to acknowledge the work of others by proper and complete referencing, and to critique without being destructive.

THE ETHICS APPROVAL PROCESS

Most academic institutions and public sector organisations will require you to submit an outline of your research for ethics approval *before* any primary data is gathered. Such approval systems are there to protect the interests of all parties involved. They protect you as a researcher by having people who have significant experience of the complexities of research read through your proposal to make sure there no potential ethical hazards. They protect your supervisor or mentor, allowing them to feel confident that you are aware of and prepared for the ethical issues you may encounter. They protect your respondents, making sure that your research does not place them in compromising positions or leave them vulnerable. Lastly, they protect the academic institution and/or the organisation in which the research is being undertaken. As you saw in the case of MidXmugton University presented previously, organisations can very easily be attributed with the blame when a researcher behaves in a way that is deemed inappropriate.

RESEARCH STORY

Making sure the survivors survive

An overseas student that I was supervising wanted to look at the impact of organisational downsizing on the morale and motivation of the survivors – those people left behind. Although the topic was really interesting, it did raise a number of ethical issues. First, would the managers of an organisation which had just gone through such a traumatic process (making over 100 people redundant) be willing for the student to do the research in this area? Without the managers' permission the research could not take place. To try to do it without the managers' permission would simply be deception. Second, there were concerns for the respondents themselves and the extent to which asking them to critique the recent downsizing exercise left them feeling vulnerable – ie 100 people had just been made redundant: what are the chances that if I am critical, I will be next?

I referred the case to the school's research ethics committee, and the solution proposed was that the student had to produce an informed consent form which outlined in detail what the research purpose was, what would be expected of the respondents, what control the respondents had over the process and what guarantees could and could not be made to them. Each respondent had to sign this form to agree that they had been fully informed and that they were still willing to participate. Only when these forms were signed would permission be given by the University for the research to go ahead.

An example form is available at **www.cipd.co.uk/brm**

Ethics approval processes usually have a number of levels of assessment. At one end is the 'automatic' or 'fast-track' approval process. This means that there are very few, if any, contentious issues in what you are proposing. The interim level is where your supervisor decides, on the basis of the information you have provided on the form, that 'additional' measures should be introduced. This is usually by means of an informed consent form.

The third level is where there are major concerns about the ethical implications of your research, in which case your supervisor may pass your proposal to the organisation's research ethics committee. At this stage you may be asked to expand on your intentions, providing more information than is collected on the standard form, or you may even be asked to present your proposal to the committee in person.

The basic form layout (Figure 4.10) allows you to outline the consequences of your research, and this form is usually submitted along with your research proposal. The first assessment is usually by your supervisor or line manager within an organisation.

Figure 4.10 Ethics approval form

ETHICS APPROVAL FORM
MidXmugton University

This ethics approval form must be submitted with your research proposal and *no primary data* should be gathered before ethics approval has been granted.

Please tick the box which most accurately reflects your planned research. If you are undertaking research using ONLY secondary sources of data, you only need complete Part A of the form.
If you complete only Part A of the form, ethics approval is automatically granted. If you are planning to undertake any empirical research which involves gathering data or information from people (for example, interviews, observations, questionnaires) you will have to complete both Parts A and B.

Part A
Put a tick against *either* Statement 1 *or* Statement 2.

Statement 1 My research does NOT involve the study of live human beings.		**Subsequent action** Ethics approval is automatic, but the form should still be sent with the research proposal
Statement 2 My research DOES involve the study of live human beings.		**Subsequent action** Complete Part B of the ethics approval form and send it with your research proposal

If you have ticked Statement 2, you must also complete Part B of the ethics approval form (below).

Part B
1 What is the purpose of this research?

....
....
....

2 What is the purpose of the primary data in this research?

....
....
....
....

3 Please tick the appropriate box against each of the questions in this table:

	Questions	Yes	No	n/a
i	Will you explain the purposes of your research to the participants?			
ii	Will participants be told that their participation is voluntary?			
iii	Will you assure respondents of confidentiality?			
iv	Will you be asking for written consent from participants?			
v	Will participants be told that they can withdraw at any time?			
vi	Will participants be given the option not to respond to certain questions?			
vii	Will participants be debriefed after their participation?			
viii	Will participants' contributions be anonymous/ anonymised?			

If you have answered No to any one of these questions, your supervisor may require you to have informed consent forms completed by the respondents.

4 Please tick the appropriate box against each of the questions in this table:

	Questions	Yes	No	n/a
i	Are you dealing with any vulnerable groups (eg children, people with learning disabilities)?			
ii	Are you focusing on sensitive issues (eg addiction, redundancy, sexuality)?			
iii	Are you planning to use recording equipment of any kind?			
iv	Will you be accessing confidential personal data?			
v	Is your research likely to cause stress or anxiety?			
vi	Will your research deliberately mislead participants in any way?			
vii	Are there any risks to the respondents (eg physical, reputational, personal)?			
viii	Are there any risks to the researcher (eg physical, reputational, personal)?			
ix	Are there any risks to the University?			
x	Are there any risks to the researched organisation?			
xi	Are you planning to use any inducements to participants?			

If you have answered Yes to any one of these questions, your approval may require a full ethics committee review. Your supervisor will advise you if you need to complete a further ethics approval form.

Does this research proposal have ethics approval?   Yes / No

If No, what action is required?

....

....

....

Signature of supervisor:

....

SUMMARY

This chapter has reconsidered the issue of stakeholders in some depth. The ability of stakeholders to control, direct or interrupt your research is simply one reason why these people have to be involved. The other reason relates to the issue of ethics. Stakeholders' power, their level of vested interest and their role will all have an impact on the stake they have in your research. And the stake that they have in your research will influence what they want you to prove or to disprove, to demonstrate or refute. As a researcher you must be guided by both the demands of the stakeholders and the need to ensure that the research that you produce is of the highest ethical standards.

For some of you this will create a dilemma. The demands of the stakeholders may be such that they require a particular set of evidence to be produced regardless. It is in order to prevent such situations arising that it is important to produce a stakeholder management plan. By considering ahead of time what people's demands are likely to be, by entering into honest discussion about what the research is and is not able to do, you stand a much better chance of being able to manage any unrealistic expectations.

A stakeholder management plan is important, but as with all plans, it is appropriate at one particular point in time. As you move through the different stages of the research, different stakeholders may take on greater significance, others become less important. It is therefore useful to revisit the plan throughout the course of your research, to anticipate any changes in stakeholder relationships and to plan how best to deal with these.

REVIEW QUESTIONS

1. What do you understand by the term 'stakeholder', and why is a consideration of stakeholders important when thinking about your business research project?

2. What tensions can exist between the different stakeholders in your research, and how can you most effectively deal with these tensions?

3. What do you understand by the terms 'politics of control', 'politics of access' and 'politics of honesty'? Why are each of these important considerations?

4. Why is it important to consider the ethical implications of your research?

5. Within the context of your research, to whom do you have ethical responsibilities? What are these responsibilities, and how can you ensure that you act ethically at all times?

EXPLORE FURTHER

British Psychological Society (2006) *Code of Ethics and Conduct*. http://www.bps.org.uk/downloadfile. cfm?file_uuid=5084a882-1143-dfd0-7e6c-f1938a65c242&ext=pdf for an excellent overview of a wide range of issues related to research ethics, both practical and theoretical

Chryssides, G. and Kaler, J. (1999) *An Introduction to Business Ethics*. London: Thomson Business Press. A good basic text on the subject of business ethics which helps frame rather than explore research ethics

ESRC (2009) *Research Ethics Framework*. Available online at http://www.esrc.ac.uk/ESRCInfoCentre/Images/ ESRC_Re_Ethics_Frame_tcm6-11291.pdf. An excellent set of guidelines and information about the ethical considerations of research in the social sciences.

Gregory, I. (2003) *Ethics in Research*. London: Continuum International Publishing Group. A very good and wide-ranging consideration of the importance of thinking about research ethics before, during, and after the research process

Hodgkinson, G. P., Herriot, P. and Anderson, N. (2001) 'Re-aligning the stakeholders in management research: lessons from industrial, work and organizational psychology', *British Journal of Management*, Vol.12 (Special Issue): S41–8. Although produced for an academic audience, the paper presents an accessible discussion on the problems faced by business researchers in making their work relevant to different stakeholder groups

Israel, M. and Hay, I. (2006) *Research Ethics for Social Scientists*. London: Sage. A useful book which looks at some of the theories behind research ethics as well as taking an international perspective

The Higher Education Academy (no date) http://www.ukcle.ac.uk/research/ethics/ resources.html. Provides access to the ethical guidelines produced by a range of professional bodies

 Visit www.cipd.co.uk/brm for web links, templates, activities and other useful resources relating to this chapter.

CHAPTER 5

Considering Possible Topics

INTRODUCTION

This (very short) chapter does not introduce new material, and is directed only at those choosing a topic for a dissertation. It provides a framework of questions that will allow you to structure the thinking you have done thus far and identify two or three possible topic areas. If you have been allocated a subject for your research or are doing research as part of a consultancy project, you can skip this chapter. Choosing a research topic for the first time can be a daunting prospect. Working through the questions in this chapter will help you to make a relatively painless start – by the end of it you may be surprised at how some 'obvious' potential areas appear.

At this stage you are merely exploring two or three *potential topic areas* within which a project might be developed. You will consider these in terms of your personal learning and career goals, academic requirements and the opportunities that may be available to you. The next part of the book will help you make an informed choice of a specific topic, and develop a proposal for research to investigate it.

The complex nature of business issues means that some potential project areas turn out to offer less than they initially seem to promise, some present unexpected barriers to progress or unacceptable risks, while others turn out to be far more interesting than they appeared at first sight. Because of this, it is advisable to start by developing ideas in two or three different areas if at all possible. This increases your chances of finding one that will be both feasible and exciting to progress. Progressing two or three possible topics at this stage means that you do not lose time if you hit a snag: you can step sideways rather than needing to loop back. Furthermore, you may find that unexpected insights in one area 'cross over' into another.

Once you have selected two or three possible broad areas you will be in a position to work through Part 2 of the book, testing what you read there against the ideas you have noted down. This will mean that by the end of Part 2 you will be in a position to craft a firm proposal for a specific investigation that will meet your learning and other needs, and the needs of other stakeholders in the research.

LEARNING OUTCOMES

This chapter should enable you to:

• reconsider your personal objectives in relation to possible research

• identify potential areas within which projects might be located

• identify likely stakeholders in each of these areas, and consider their aims

• frame possible research questions in relation to these areas

• assess potential types and sources of information relevant to possible research topics.

CLARIFYING YOUR OBJECTIVES

Research for a dissertation or similar is going to take a lot of your energies, but the potential for personal learning is probably far greater than for the rest of your MBA or other programme. One of the saddest things I read recently was the Reflections section of a substantial dissertation, which had involved a huge amount of work. The student reflected:

> "This was a tremendous learning experience for me: it was a really great opportunity for me to know how a dissertation must be written."

No other personal learning points were noted.

CONSIDER...

Why might this have disappointed an examiner.

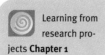
Learning from research projects **Chapter 1**

Writing well is certainly a valuable management skill, and the discipline and thinking required to write a dissertation will help to develop that skill. It may be excellent preparation for subsequent academic writing. But this student was seeking a career as a manager. If all he learned from hundreds of hours of work was how to write a dissertation, what had he really gained? Unless he failed he was unlikely to need this particular skill ever again. You should realise by now that a research project can generate far more learning than this, and can also offer other important career-related benefits.

CAREER AIMS

To get these benefits you must think about your wider aims and interests *before* you think seriously about possible research projects. Where would you like your career to go in the next five years? A dissertation can give you an 'excuse' to talk to people you might never otherwise have access to, thus developing useful contacts. It can offer you a chance to develop and practise particular skills, to become expert in a particular field, or to become a recognised organisational source of guidance on a key topic.

If you have a clear idea of your longer-term career objectives and other goals, you will be more likely to see how potential topics might contribute to achieving these goals. Note your thoughts in response to the following questions in your journal – you may find it useful to refer to them several times during the process of choosing a project.

Questions about your longer-term goals

Where would you like to be in your career at the end of the next five years?
What skills would help you achieve this kind of position?
What experience would help you follow the necessary path?
What knowledge and expertise would accelerate your progress?
What contacts might it be useful to develop?
What would help raise your profile in your organisation or more generally?
Can you think of any project areas that might contribute to any of the above?

Research journal
Chapter 25

You may not be able to answer all – even any – of these questions at present. It will depend upon where you are in your career, and upon whether you are adopting a rational and planned approach to your future. (Such an approach is far from being the only route to success: a more opportunistic emergent strategy can work just as well for some people.) But even if you cannot always answer, the process of thinking about the questions will sensitise you to possibilities in potential topic areas that you might not otherwise notice. Revisit these questions at intervals, and expand upon your answers in your journal as ideas come up.

PERSONAL INTEREST

Chris revealed
this primarily in
Chapter 1

A project can enable you to develop expertise in an area that interests you. A research project normally involves extensive reading, which will be far more enjoyable and less onerous if the topic is one in which you have a personal interest, perhaps because of connections with your experience.

You may remember Chris discussing how he came to settle upon leadership development. An earlier project on strategy had exposed him to the area of leadership development and this really interested him. This may have been because 'development' was related to his existing 'teaching' expertise. Whatever the reason, he picked a subject in which he was already really interested, and narrowed his focus to the role of reflection within leadership development because of a book he had read on leadership which he found fascinating.

Questions about your interests

If you were in the habit of reading about management before starting your current studies, what topics particularly interested you?
Have you found any topics particularly interesting during your course?
Were there any topics about which you read more than was strictly necessary, simply because you found the subject so fascinating?
Are there any management topics that you really enjoy discussing outside of classes?
Have you heard anyone discussing a potential project – or read a past project in the library – and wished you could do that project?

If you cannot identify areas of particular interest, do not worry unduly. (If *nothing* in your course has interested you, that itself might be a useful prompt to reflection.) If you are studying part-time, your choice may be largely driven by work or organisational priorities. But if you are a full-time student doing a more theoretical project, keep your need to find an interesting research topic in mind whenever you are reading. And devote some of your library browsing specifically to this.

> **A carefully chosen topic can create career opportunities, enable you to explore existing interests, and develop useful skills.**

Although there are many advantages to researching a topic in which you are already interested, as with everything in this area, requirements may conflict. Your interest must be considered in relation to organisational, academic and personal development needs, and you may find that you have to compromise.

PERSONAL DEVELOPMENT OBJECTIVES

There are many skills that a dissertation project can usefully develop. Some are fairly general, such as confidence and assertiveness, time management, listening or presentation skills. Some might relate to specific information-gathering skills with a wider application than research: interviewing is an example, or group facilitation, or searching databases. Some might relate to critical and or analytical skills, or technical skills such as using particular software.

 CONSIDER...

What skills would help your future career? (You may like to consider your current skills levels and the gap between them and the skills required in the sort of job you would like to have in the next few years.) Note your thoughts in your journal.

Part of the argument for a compulsory dissertation in MBAs and similar programmes is that managers frequently have to seek and evaluate evidence, so the ability to do this is crucial. You can start to practise this skill now.

ACTIVITY

Take the skills you have just listed and ask yourself what evidence you have for the skills assessments you just made. Is this an intuition, a guess, or have you actively drawn upon evidence of your strengths and weaknesses in your current role? How might these skills relate to your future aspirations? Seek further evidence to support your assessments. Possible sources are colleagues (who may be prepared to give you feedback if asked), past performance appraisal reviews, your boss (who again may give informal feedback if you explain why you want it) and any mentor who may be able to advise you on what skills are important at higher levels.

Keep such evidence on your existing strengths and weaknesses, and about future requirements, in your journal. Add to this evidence by actively brainstorming a list of additional skills that might be worth developing.

This activity will help you answer the next set of questions. (These build upon parts of the two earlier sets to enable you to identify shorter-term learning objectives that your project might serve.)

Questions about potential learning objectives

Is there a specific topic you would like to learn more about?

Do you have specific strengths you would like to develop? (What is your evidence?)

Do you have particular weaknesses you would like to address? (What is your evidence?)

Is there a specific role, or type of activity you would like to experience?

Are there specific skills (such as interviewing, facilitation, negotiation, strategy formulation) that you would like to develop?

Are there particular aspects of the organisation that you would like to learn more about?

Aim to list all the potential learning objectives that a dissertation project might conceivably relate to. You will be using them shortly.

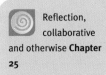

Reflection, collaborative and otherwise **Chapter 25**

It will be useful to revisit these questions at intervals and reflect on your answers. Try to identify any patterns or other indications of what is important to you. It can be helpful to find one or two friends or colleagues with whom to share your thoughts. A process of collaborative reflection might increase your awareness of your goals, and of how a project might serve these.

SETTING PRIORITIES

Once you have captured your objectives, it may help to organise them. Some may be more important than others. Some may be related. There may be some outcomes you would want to avoid at all costs. You can draw a simple *hierarchy of objectives* with your ultimate goal at the top, subordinate goals below, and goals subordinate to each of these in the next layer down. This produces something that looks like an organisational chart, but with goals instead of roles and their occupants! Figure 5.1 shows how you might start. You would then work further down the structure.

For example, to be recognised as a strategy expert you need have to have made a visible contribution to an aspect of strategy formulation in your own organisation, and at the level below this you might need to have carried out a strategy-related project and to have made your involvement highly visible, and perhaps have written an account of the project for your professional magazine ... You can see how this is starting to relate to a possible dissertation. You can see too that although the diagram may look very different, the process is logically similar to the process of multiple-cause mapping described in Chapter 2. You are starting with the end point, and pushing back, a level at a time, to find contributors to that end point. The difference is that in multiple-cause diagrams you are looking at past or present causes, whereas here you are looking at events that might be future contributory factors. It is akin to drawing a multiple-cause diagram for a situation that does not yet exist

Cognitive mapping **Chapter 2**

Alternatively, use a simple form of cognitive mapping as described earlier. You would have to use a similar 'laddering' principle to identify different levels of goal. For this, you could write all your objectives on Post-it™. Note that this approach enables you to look at negative goals – things you might want to avoid – as well as those you are seeking. It also starts not with your top goal but with all the goals you can think of. It might be useful to capture these by brainstorming all possible personal objectives (and things to be avoided at all costs) with fellow students to push you beyond the limits of your own mindset. If you do this, afterwards select those ideas that relate to your own goals before starting to structure them into levels.

To use cognitive mapping, take a large sheet of paper (or whiteboard) and start to arrange your goals so that the top-level ones are in the top third of the space. Then arrange your

Post-it™ using similar logic as in the hierarchy of objectives, seeking objectives which help achieve 'higher' objectives, and joining these with an arrow. You could also seek objectives that would hinder higher goals, and use a negative sign on their joining arrow.

Figure 5.1 Part of a hierarchy of objectives related to a main career goal

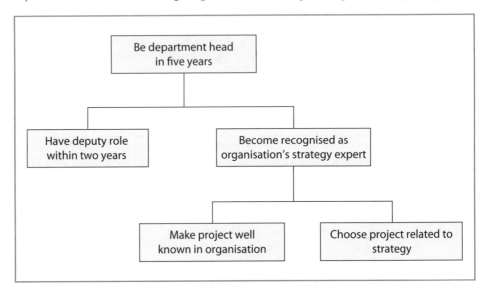

Figure 5.2 Part of a cognitive mapping of project-relevant goals

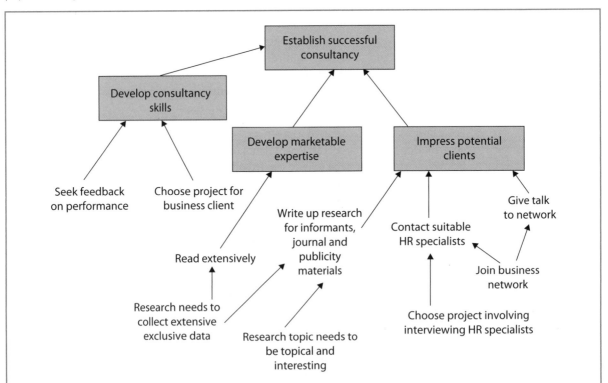

ACTIVITY

Think about your career objectives and map them as in Figure 5.2. Highlight any that might be relevant to your project. Save your notes, and revisit and revise the diagram at intervals.

The process of questioning and diagramming will clarify your sense of what you would like from a project (and from your career). Your requirements will need to be met within the constraints imposed by academic requirements. If you are doing a project with a client or sponsor within a real organisation, you will also have to ensure that your eventual project delivers something of value to the organisation as well.

EXPLORING ACADEMIC REQUIREMENTS

Obviously, you will want to meet academic requirements for your dissertation, and pass. Perhaps you would like a distinction. Chapters relating to dissertation sections offer writing suggestions, and Chapter 26 includes detailed overall guidance on writing dissertations and reports, but you will be limited by the quality of the research you have done. Here you must start thinking about the scope that possible topics offer for meeting academic requirements. The questions above were related to making a choice that would maximise your learning and enjoyment of your research. The next set of questions relates to academic requirements.

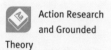
Action Research and Grounded Theory

Key variables here are the university's requirements for the dissertation, and your supervisor's preferences for research methods. It would probably not be a happy experience to undertake an Action Research or Grounded Theory project with a supervisor firmly wedded to a deductive strategy with rigorous fixed design and sophisticated statistical analysis.

Questions about academic requirements

Have you obtained, and carefully read, a copy of the dissertation requirements and marking scheme (if one is available)?

Have you also obtained a copy of any ethical approval form?

Do you understand how much 'theoretical' discussion is expected?

Is a critical review of relevant literature enough or are you expected to *use* and/or *develop* theory?

Are you expected to adopt any particular approach to research?

Is the project expected to inform/bring about action within an organisation?

Are you expected to generate 'primary' data (see Chapter 9) or will it be enough to draw upon secondary sources, collected by others?

Is your dissertation expected to include statistical analyses?

Of course you will want to look in greater detail at these requirements when you are drafting your formal proposal, but you need to have a feel for the sort of thing that will be required before you start to look at potential topic areas.

EXPLORING OPPORTUNITIES

Once you know what your requirements are for a project, and what those of your examiners are, you can start looking for opportunities. Whether you are looking for opportunities within your own organisation, you are a full-time student expected to find a willing organisation or informants, or you are planning a library-inspired project, start scouting for opportunities as soon as is feasible.

OPPORTUNITIES RELATED TO YOUR OWN JOB

If you are studying part-time, there may be things about your own job that you would like to address. Perhaps there are inefficiencies that bother you, or teamworking problems, or opportunities that you feel are being missed. If you are aware of issues that might usefully be addressed, now is the time to capture them. They may not all be suitable territory for a dissertation: you will be checking for that shortly. At this point simply list all the things you would love to *understand* better and/or *change* in the part of the organisation with which you are involved.

OPPORTUNITIES ELSEWHERE IN YOUR OWN ORGANISATION

It is also worth talking informally with colleagues to see what issues they perceive the organisation to be facing. Sound out possible sponsors – very gently at this stage – about any areas they might like to see addressed. It is important to keep these early conversations very general. A keen sponsor may seize on the chance of some free consultancy and offer you a very specific project that would not fit with either university or personal objectives. It is worth emphasising the fact that at this stage you are merely looking for possible issues to explore, or areas within which a project might eventually be located.

OPPORTUNITIES IN OTHER ORGANISATIONS

Some part-time programmes assume that your project will be carried out in your own organisation. But your organisation may be in too much flux for a project to be feasible. For example, a likely merger and/or major redundancies during the period of your research can create serious difficulties. Alternatively, you may not be working, or you may expect to leave your job during the dissertation period. In either case, if the expectation is that you will do a project in your own organisation, you should discuss your situation with your supervisor as soon as is possible. They may know of organisations that are willing to host student projects, or may suggest other possibilities.

For example, you may have contacts with other organisations who might be interested in some research. (One manager chose to carry out an excellent project in a local football club with which she was involved in a voluntary capacity, rather than in her own rather turbulent organisation. Another did a project for the local church.)

When approaching organisations other than your own, it is important to say very clearly what you are seeking from them, and what you can offer them in return, and be aware that they have no reason to trust you or offer you facilities. Students occasionally treat host organisations as if their 'almost MBA' status should make organisations overjoyed to host their research. This is a highly unrealistic assumption.

Unless your contacts are close and the organisation knows you well, they will be justifiably cautious about giving you access to information or providing staff time or other resources. You will have to establish your credibility as a potential researcher by appearing professional at all times, communicating very clearly what you are seeking and why, and not making unjustified or exaggerated claims to experience or expertise. Again, you will wish to keep early discussions very general: a 'ready-made' project here would be just as risky as in your own organisation. Note that finding a willing 'other' organisation may take longer than you expect. You need to start the process early.

PROJECTS WITHOUT AN ORGANISATIONAL CLIENT

 For projects using secondary sources read **chapter 12**

Thinking about projects not based in organisations has to be slightly different. You might want to do a library-based project, relying totally on secondary data. This might be an interesting opportunity to explore what is written on a topic of burning interest, and to develop search and critical thinking skills and expertise that might be attractive to a future employer. Or like Chris you might conduct an extended library-based investigation supplemented with some interviews with relevant practitioners. Or you might wish to consider a survey of some specified group (for example, a dissertation I recently read surveyed managers involved in business process outsourcing in a particular city in India).

This extension to making contact with practitioners or others has the advantage of helping you start networking. The disadvantage may be the time that it takes to negotiate access to your informants. However, this possibility shows that the field is wide open if you are not tied to a particular organisation and its issues. How you balance your own interests, career implications and academic aspects is up to you – but the following questions may be useful.

 Questions about a non-organisation-based project

What topics seem to be of current interest to relevant professionals?
What are the current debates?
Might a literature review from a novel perspective allow you to contribute to one of these debates?
Would expertise in this area help you achieve your career objectives above?
Have you read a paper that seems to be quoted by others, but which raises questions that no one has yet asked?
Are there inconsistencies between some of the most-quoted papers that no one has yet addressed?
Is there an area that you would like to work in that lacks a definitive treatment of an important issue?
Do you have (or could you get) access to informants who could provide relevant data?
Do you have particular opportunities to look at international aspects of an issue?

I have included the last question because many dissertation students are studying abroad, and are therefore exposed to 'theory' from a culture that may be significantly different from their own. If you are doing this, and if you are planning to work in your home culture after qualifying, a dissertation can offer an opportunity to test the relevance of the foreign theory in your own context, or to explore the implications of cultural differences. An international perspective might also be attractive if you work, or hope to work, in an international organisation.

CONSIDERATIONS OF DATA AND APPROACH

You will be starting to develop your thoughts about approaches, methods and data in the next part of the book. However, a quick check at this point might be helpful. The two or three topics you use as the basis for your work in Part 2 must be capable of being 'researched', in the sense of posing questions which data might enable you to answer. The following set of questions is more tentative, because there are many different approaches to most topics or themes: most issues have the potential to be usefully researched, unless they are very narrow. But in the interests of spiral learning it is worth spending a few minutes on the following questions.

Questions of data and approach

Can you identify any questions in the area of your possible issues that it would be useful for the organisation, or theoretically interesting to answer?

Can you think of possible data (quantitative or qualitative) or other information that might help answer these questions?

Can you think of a broad approach to collecting such information so that it would be unbiased and contribute to an answer to the questions?

ACTIVITY

It is now time to take stock of your answers. In the light of your thinking thus far, write down at least three – preferably more – possible issues, themes or topics that your research might address. Some might be slight variants of issues, some radically different from each other. The next section will enable you to evaluate the possibilities and refine them to two or three to work with during the next part of the book.

ASSESSING YOUR OPTIONS

Now that you have a number of thoughts, you may need to do a little looping. Look at one or two relatively recent books or general articles on topics you identified as being of interest. Have a few more discussions with people in your target organisation to see whether there are issues in the organisational area or of relevance to your theoretical interests. Discuss ideas with colleagues. Write down possible ideas in your journal.

If you feel that you do not have enough ideas yet, try brainstorming topics with fellow students or colleagues. Spend some time in the library looking at past dissertations. Look at the more practically oriented academic or professional journals in the areas that most interest you and see if there are any recent papers there that start you wondering about something.

Drafting a proposal

Chapter 11

Remember, all you are seeking at this stage are three broad issues or areas which you think it would be interesting and developmental for you, and/or useful for your organisation, to investigate in some way. You are not seeking the perfect topic. You are just seeking to establish that the areas or broad issues have sufficient potential complexity to offer scope for data collection and analysis of some sort, that there is theory which is relevant to the kinds of questions that you might be asking, and that it is interesting. Once you have explored the relevant literature some more, and thought more about a specific question to address, and about the evidence that would help you address it, and the methods for collecting the data you will use as evidence, then you will be able to draft a specific proposal – but not yet! All you are seeking at present is something as general as 'Do something about late order completion' or 'Something to do with leadership development'.

HAZARD-SPOTTING

For projects in real organisations you need to do some serious 'hazard-spotting' before going much further. Research for a dissertation presents a number of risks because of:

- the timescale over which it takes place – this means that changes in the context may prevent you from concluding your research

- the fact that you may be the initiator of the research rather than its notional client; the client might become dissatisfied at some point and withdraw support

- lengthy ethics approval processes in some organisations

- suspicion, rightly or wrongly, of your motives if you are doing insider research, particularly if you are involved in the issue you investigate.

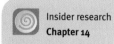
Insider research
Chapter 14

Even while you are still thinking in very general terms about potential broad topic areas it is worth asking a series of questions to reassure yourself that research in this area would have a reasonable chance of successful completion. As you develop your thinking towards a more specific project proposal you will need to revisit these questions at regular intervals.

Questions about the context

Would there be clear potential benefit for the organisation? Can you quantify this in any way?

Would there be any potential risks to the organisation from an investigation?

Is there any possibility that the part of the organisation within which your potential topic is located might be restructured or be threatened by redundancies?

Is there a risk of other changes that might make a project difficult?

If you have located a potential sponsor or client, are they reasonably open-minded about an investigation and what it might discover?

Are there other powerful stakeholders who might feel threatened by an investigation in this area?

Is any of the data you might want to collect likely to be sensitive in any way?

If so, might this make it hard to access that data?

If not, might there still be restrictions on using the data in a dissertation?

If so, would university provisions over confidentiality be enough to satisfy the client organisation?

Would your role as researcher be seen as threatening or otherwise inappropriate by any of the stakeholders?

Do you hold strong views about the issue that might threaten the impartiality of the research?

Is research in this broad area likely to require significant resources from the organisation?

If so, are the resources likely to be willingly provided?

Might there be ethical issues to consider?

Does the client organisation require ethical clearance, and if so, how long would this take?

Discard any contexts that look too risky, and note the possible risks against others. Look for other possibilities to replace any discards. Once you have done this, you can start to explore the possible areas in more depth. Some of the questions above may have prompted further questions about one or more areas. You may need to look for more information to answer these questions.

 ACTIVITY

Now that you have assessed your initial 'long list' of issues or topics, summarise your thinking on each in your research journal. It might be worth allowing two pages on each if your journal is in paper form – you will need to be able to add thoughts as you go along. Identify your two or three preferred issues or topics.

You will read the next seven chapters in a different way if you use your preferred potential issues or topics as a testing ground for the ideas and questions posed there. If you actively develop these ideas as you work through these chapters, you will have done the reading and thinking needed to produce a good research proposal, the end-point of the next part of the book.

SUMMARY

This chapter has not introduced any new material. Instead it has suggested a series of questions to help you organise your thinking thus far and prompt further exploration where necessary. This should have enabled you to identify two or three possible project areas. As you work through Part 2 these will act as a focus for thinking about the topics addressed, and that thinking will develop your understanding of the possible project areas. This will help you benefit from the next part of the book. And more importantly, it will let you devote as much time as possible to shaping your research ideas.

You are a key stakeholder in your dissertation, and must think about how a project might be used to serve personal learning and career objectives. The first set of questions related to identifying and structuring your own interests and development needs. Thinking clearly about these will make you more aware of the potential learning and other benefits offered by possible projects.

The next area to establish is the requirements of perhaps the other most important group of stakeholders in a dissertation – those who will be assessing it. You must ensure that the projects you consider are suitable for a dissertation.

Finally, you need to think about potential research contexts. Opportunities will depend upon whether or not you are working while studying. If you are planning to carry out your research in a specific organisation, you will have to consider the potential benefit to the organisation. Whatever context you choose, you will need to do a 'potential hazard check' and avoid unduly risky areas. Key risks will include potential restructuring and political sensitivities.

For areas that survive the check, you can start to think about what, within those areas, might be the basis for a research project, and how far such a project might be shaped to satisfy your purposes. If you are currently a manager, you will need to consider the potential for a dissertation to improve things for you at work. Your reading of subsequent chapters depends upon your having identified a small number of potential issues or themes.

CHAPTER 6

Exploring the Literature

INTRODUCTION

Exploring and engaging with the literature relevant to your particular focus must be a thread that runs through your entire research project. This is likely to start when your reading prompts possible ideas for research. If you plan to address an issue that is of concern to your organisation, then reading what others have said about the topic will be one of the first things you do – simply to help you to develop ideas about a project. Engaging with the literature will expose you to a range of discussions, helping you to focus in on the issues most relevant to you, and giving you access to accounts of methods for researching. The literature will provide you with a veritable treasure trove of historical ideas, and current debates on the topic will alert you to the questions thought to be important. As well as ideas you will find a lot of data and information relevant to your research. Because the search skills needed are common to finding both ideas and data, this chapter covers both forms of search.

I have used the terms 'search' and 'research' here because both are important. Although search is a necessary part of research, you have to go beyond merely looking for things. A vast array of material is available to you and the sheer volume can be problematic. You will need to make judgements about the value of what you find, and to relate and organise what seems to be important. In this you are moving into research. You will be drawing upon primary, secondary and tertiary sources of both ideas and data, and will have to treat each appropriately.

This chapter aims to help you understand the characteristics of different sources of information, to search these efficiently using appropriate search engines and gateways, and to evaluate what you find in terms of its usefulness for your own research. It suggests different ways of taking and organising notes on the material you deem potentially useful, so that it will be easier for you to refer to it when thinking about your research and writing a literature review for your project proposal and for your dissertation.

LEARNING OUTCOMES

This chapter should enable you to:

• appreciate the different types of information source and their specific characteristics

• recognise the different ways of accessing the literature via libraries or online, and the search skills needed to do it

• select literature appropriate to your research and assess its likely value

• read and take notes efficiently and effectively from your reading.

WHY IS LITERATURE RESEARCH IMPORTANT?

Literature is generally considered to be the body of knowledge available to you. It includes information and data from a range of sources and in a range of formats. It is for you to decide which elements of that literature are most helpful in informing your research. Exploring the literature helps you to shape your research project and provides a resource throughout. By searching the literature you can access resources that will

• help you to develop an understanding of the theories and concepts that you can use to make sense of what you do

• help you to gather evidence of what others have done, and

• help you to judge how well or otherwise this has worked.

If you are doing your research as part of an academic project, it is relatively easy to see the value of this: by including what you know and understand about the literature, you prove that you are able to produce an intellectually robust piece of work.

Familiarity with the literature is equally helpful in non-academic contexts. As a consultant, much of your credibility comes from your expertise. Both external consultancy assignments and internal problem-solving projects need credible frames of reference to support the methods being used. They must be informed by evidence that you can use to justify *your* answers to *your* audience, rather than simply presenting your personal opinion.

The academic literature and that produced by professional bodies gives you a feel for the process of business research. If you are new to research, familiarising yourself with the relevant literature can help you to see how different researchers word research questions, the terms they use, and what these terms mean. It shows how research questions use the literature to build the background to the investigation and then connect to a method for data-gathering. And it demonstrates how this process produces the conclusions which answer the question set. The literature and other sources of information can also provide contextual data which helps frame your focus, information about markets and the external environment, and insights into organisational policies and procedures.

> **A literature search is an integral part of practical business research.**

An appreciation of what others have done helps you to define and refine your research purpose or question. The iterative relationship between the literature and deriving the focus for your research question means that your reading gives you a better understanding of the nature and the amount of data and information available, as well as insights into how this is used. The following story is an example of this.

RESEARCH STORY

Constantinos and CSR

Constantinos, an MBA student, wanted to investigate how the culture of an organisation supported the organisation's Corporate Social Responsibility (CSR) programme. He started by undertaking desk research looking for books, articles and organisational information which discussed the relationship between organisational culture and CSR. To his surprise, he could actually find very few sources in which people made a clear connection between organisational culture and CSR.

Having realised that this made his original question problematic for an MBA dissertation (for a PhD it would have been an excellent opportunity to start to fill this gap), he decided to change his question to see how the literature on CSR implicitly rather than explicitly acknowledged culture. He changed his research question from one that investigated how the relationship worked in his organisation to one based only on secondary data on how culture implicitly appeared in the writings on CSR. Note that it was only by undertaking some thorough desk research that he realised the difficulties he would have in pursuing his first idea.

> **Literature research helps you to clarify your understanding of the core concepts you wish to look at, and to develop and refine your research question.**

The professional and academic literature not only gives you a good idea of how people frame their research questions but also gives you insights into the research methods they use to answer these questions, and an idea of the skills and the resources that you may need in order to replicate those methods. For example, it may be that something that you have read suggests a particularly good research method – but if this requires software you cannot obtain, or skills you cannot develop, it may not be a good choice for you.

> **Literature research helps you to identify research methods and evaluate their suitability for your own project.**

Considering what other people have done may mean that you can replicate methods, thus saving time and effort. If so, you may also be able to use their work to help you to anticipate any potential blocks or barriers that may prevent you from achieving your goals. Although learning from your own mistakes may be a powerful form of learning, you may not have the time for it.

In terms of contextualising your research in a wider academic debate, literature research helps you to see where arguments could be more balanced, where methodologies are weak or where the political slant of what is being written is skewed to meet the needs of a particular stakeholder group. If you are doing your research as part of an academic programme of study, desk research helps you to see where your work *contributes to* or *fits in with* the existing literature.

I have emphasised the word *contributes* here because this often causes problems for students who feel they have to produce something that is unique. This is not the case. The whole idea of a contribution can be seen as a continuum with unique and novel research at one end and the replication of previously tried and tested methods at the other. In the case of the latter, the uniqueness of the contribution may simply be that these methods have been applied in a different context.

KEY POINTS

- Literature research can familiarise you with the structure and the connectivities that exist with a research project.
- Literature research helps you to identify the key theories, the key sources of information and the key writers in the areas that you are considering for your research.
- Literature research can help you design and refine your research question.
- Literature research allows you to see which methods may be more or less useful to you.
- Literature research enables you to learn from the mistakes of others.
- Literature research enables you to see how your research contributes to the literature.

ACCESSING LITERATURE AND INFORMATION

To make effective use of the wealth of literature and information that is potentially available, you have to be able to access it efficiently. Although most of what you need may be available from traditional university libraries, most of that, and very much more besides, can be accessed via the Internet. The Internet is a great source of information and ideas. It gives access to the works of world-renowned business people, management gurus and scholars of international repute. It also allows you and me to put anything we like into the public domain. The Internet allows access to information and ideas, not all of which have academic, business or moral integrity.

The sheer volume of what is available, and the variable quality of some of it, means that if you want to draw upon the literature efficiently and effectively, you must understand the distinguishing characteristics of what you are looking for, where to look for it, and how to search efficiently. Later sections will deal with what to do with it once found. First let me consider different sorts of sources. Further detail on them will be given later.

PRIMARY AND SECONDARY SOURCES

Using data that other people have gathered and analysed can be an extremely efficient way of understanding the context for your research: such data is called secondary data, to distinguish it from primary data which you collect yourself. Chapter 9 explores the relative advantages and disadvantages of primary and secondary data. Here we consider primary, secondary and tertiary *sources* of secondary data (Figure 6.1).

Figure 6.1 Sources of data
and information

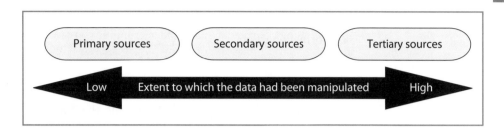

Primary sources

Primary sources are those where data, other findings or debates appear for the first time. They are normally written by the original researcher. Many papers in academic journals are of this kind. Other primary sources include reports, conference proceedings, theses and dissertations, some government publications and unpublished manuscripts. Some of these may be difficult to track down and/or difficult to read, but should include all the author's relevant data and arguments.

Secondary sources

Secondary sources represent some form of digest or gloss on the primary source. Thus a book on strategy might include descriptions of the key theories and key theorists in the area. Review articles in journals, newspaper reports, professional journals and many government publications are secondary sources. They tend to be more accessible, because they are often written for a wider audience, and they can save a lot of time because the author has done the work of searching out the relevant literature and selecting that which is best. The downside of this is that you are at the mercy of the author's selection and reporting, and reliant on their diligence and judgement. They may also be considering a topic from a perspective slightly different from your own, and therefore may not have included all the authors or issues who would be relevant to your research. Secondary sources in this way form a good starting point for familiarising yourself with the literature, but you may have to use them as a springboard for selecting appropriate primary sources.

Tertiary sources

Tertiary sources are designed to help you do this – they tend to be in the form of organised lists and/or brief summaries. Tertiary sources include indexes, abstracts and catalogues, and are likely to be where you first start. Citation indexes are a particularly useful way of using one interesting article as a starting point for finding other related and more recent papers. A citation index tells you all the articles that have subsequently referred to the original. Thus you can see how the ideas you liked in the first paper have influenced and been developed in later debates and research. Other useful lists can be found on the websites of publishers or booksellers. The other main tertiary sources tend to be associated with libraries or with online searches and so will be dealt with later. Indeed, online search tools now work as more efficient forms of what used to be indexes.

ACCESSING SOURCES

In order to gain access to the huge amount of available information, you have to know the different routes to get to it. They are:

- search engines

- gateways
- information sites
- Wikipedia
- library catalogues.

For online searches you have to understand the difference between search engines, gateways and information sites. This section discusses each of these, and gives you some of the 'clues' that can help you to judge the reliability of what you find. It also discusses how to use a library catalogue system, but because there are some slight variations in library processes and systems, you will have to learn how to use the specific resources available in your own university library (if you have access to one).

Search engines

A search engine is a device which searches the World-Wide Web for information. The most popular search engine in use today is Google, and you are probably already familiar with this or a similar engine. You may, however, not be using it as efficiently as you might, and there might be better engines for research purposes. The principles used in an effective Google search apply equally to those used on any other search engine.

Google is just one of many search engines available. The website of the University of California at Berkeley library offers a useful comparison between the functionality of different search engines, accessible at http:www.lib.berkeley.edu/TeachingLib/Guides/Internet/SearchEngines. html (Note: this type of address is known as a URL, a Unique Resource Locator. It is the equivalent to the name and address of the site you wish to visit. It contains clues about the likely reliability of the materials contained, as will be discussed shortly.)

ACTIVITY

To illustrate one of the main problems in using open-access search engines, do a quick Google search on the term 'corporate social responsibility' and see how many hits you come up with.

You may want to refine this. Do the same search on Google Scholar. (If you are not sure how to do this, read the instructions below.) How many hits this time?

Now try doing a Google search on the theme(s) that you are thinking about for your business research. How many hits now? What does this tell you about the focus for your research?

The activity above gives you an example of just how much information is available. I found 8,450,000 with Google, and 1,020,000 with Google Scholar. You may find you have even more because information is added every day – proof, if proof were needed, that search engines provide access to a massive resource – but it is important not to be overwhelmed. There are a number of techniques for selecting that which is most relevant for your research. The most important is to be careful about the terms or key words you use to search.

If you were to Google 'labour', you would find that the term is treated in a number of ways: to refer to the Labour Party, to labour as in work, and to labour as the process through which children are born. It is important therefore that the search terms used are as concise and as accurate as possible. The use of phrases or search strings, rather than single words, helps, and there is a range of options available on Google through which you can refine your search. By clicking on the 'Advanced Search' button, you can narrow down your focus, refining and/or excluding words from the search. Alternatively, you can search Google Scholar for academic texts – ie books and articles. Another means of refining your search is the 'Preference' option. By clicking on this you are given a range of features that can narrow your search by language, or by looking only for books as sources.

Google Scholar gives you references and in some cases access to information drawn from academic sources. This is useful in ensuring the credibility of the sources that you use to advise your business research. The majority of sources referenced here come from credible peer-reviewed journals or books. However, this may be problematic for researchers who do not have access to a university library, because many of the sources identified require payment for access to the full text article. Where the researcher does have access to a university library, this is rarely problematic. Most universities have well-stocked libraries with electronic access to both e-books and journals. You simply have to note the reference from your Google search and then access it through the library search systems.

URL clues

Another way of trying to determine the reliability of information sources identified through an Internet search is by considering the URL. As mentioned previously, this equates to the name and the address of the source of information and so a little detective work on the part of the researcher can help to ensure that only credible data is accessed. To do this it is important to understand what a URL comprises – below is an example of the URL for the Open University.

$$\text{h t t p :} / / \text{w w w .} \mathbf{o p e n} \text{. a c . u k}$$

| method | | name | domain | country

- *Method* – In this URL, the rules and systems by which data is transferred from one place to another is http (hypertext transfer protocol).

- *Name* – The name presented here is the name of the organisation to which the contents of the web pages relate.

- *Domain* – The domain is the type of organisation, what it does, what its function is. The domain is important in helping researchers to judge the reliability of the information they are presented with. Useful domains to look for are:

  .ac – an academic source (usually European)

  .edu – an academic source (usually US or Australian)

  .co – a company

  .com – a company

  .gov – a governmental source

  .nhs – the National Health Service, a public sector site

  .dwp – the Department for Work and Pensions, a public sector site

  .org – mostly associated with not-for-profit organisations, but care should be exercised because .org domain names can be sold to other organisations.

- *Country* – The country simply relates to the country within which the organisation is located. This is perhaps more complex than it first seems because many organisations have a global presence. In this case what often happens is that a general URL is given first. This leads to the home page from which it is possible to choose the country-specific location required. For an example see www.Ikea.com .

> Google searches can produce too many hits. Narrowing the search can help reduce the quantity of hits: checking the URL may help you select the more reliable data.

Gateways

Gateways are large Internet sites which enable you to access a selected range of information by navigating your way through. For example, the HMSO site www.hmso.gov.uk/information/pub-scheme.pdf offers a wide range of information. Other gateways would include the websites of professional bodies, universities or research funding bodies. Many of these gateways also grant access to further gateways. For instance, the University of Essex website allows access to the website of the Economic and Social Data Service. Most of these gateways can be accessed by logging directly on to them. Alternatively, access can be navigated through the use of a search engine.

The advantage of a relevant gateway site is that the resources have been preselected as being appropriate to a particular topic, and there will normally have been an element of quality control.

Information sites

These are websites which act as a repository for a wide range of information. Biz/ed is a good example of such a site. There is open access and the site (http://www.bized.co.uk) offers lots of information categorised by theme. A number of universities offer tutorial resources in a range of business topics: you will be referred to some of these in other chapters. Some further useful sites are suggested at the end of this chapter.

 ACTIVITY

If you have not done so before, log on to the Biz/ed website and see what categories of information they use. Search within a category relevant to your own research to see what information you might find useful. Keep a note of what you find so that you can use it when you start your research project.

Wikipedia

This is probably the most commonly used information site. Wikipedia is a 'web-based, free-content encyclopedia project' (http://en.wikipedia.org/ wiki/Wikipedia:About [accessed 14 February 2009]). Anybody can add or edit information on Wikipedia – they need not be experts in the field and there is no obligation for people to present robust arguments in support of any claims they make. Moreover, there is no professional body or academic community in place to ensure that what is posted on the site is valid, is accurate or is a true reflection of what the acknowledged experts in the field say. Although Wikipedia retains the right to remove any sub-standard information, what constitutes sub-standard information is open to debate. For this reason *most universities do not accept Wikipedia as a valid reference.*

However, Wikipedia can be a useful *starting point* for an information search. It is often good at explaining basic concepts in a very understandable way, one that would enable you then to explore them in more depth in the academic or professional literature. It is also extremely useful for accessing additional references, some of which are hyper-linked from the Wikipedia page.

> **Wikipedia presents a wide range of information but it is not 'quality controlled'. You must check the reliability of any ideas found there by verifying them with academically credible sources.**

Library catalogues

Most library catalogues allow you to search in different ways. Searches by author, searches by journal title or searches by area are all common. In addition to searching on these themes, searches can be at a basic or at an advanced level. A basic search allows you to enter the search theme in a text box and specify where the search engine should look for it. The text search theme can be a single word (eg budgeting) or can be a phrase (eg capital budgeting). Where phrases are used, it is usual to put them in quotation marks so that the system searches for the phrase rather than the individual words (eg "capital budgeting"). The advantage of searching on a single word is that it is more likely to generate a large number of identified sources of information. However, it can sometimes be too large – for example, a basic search on the word 'budgeting' through a university catalogue gave 114 sources of information which may or may not have been relevant. Phrases help to narrow that search. For example, by combining the words 'capital' and 'budgeting', the search now produces seven sources of information. If my business research was focusing on capital budgeting, I have already found a useful starting place.

A basic search can also be narrowed by directing the search to where it should look. A drop-down menu usually allows you to include specific fields – eg the title of a journal, the author, the subject or even the ISBN (the International Standard Book Number, a coding which identifies every edition of every book and its publisher, and is included on the copyright page).

Within the basic search function of most library search engines it is possible (and useful) to use what are known as Boolean operators. Boolean operators are a series of words ('AND', 'OR' and 'NOT') or symbols which help to refine the search in particular ways. For example, where items in the search words are vital to the search, then a + symbol or the word 'AND' can be added. We can see how this would work for our previous search. On the grounds that it was necessary to make sure that the data sources identified by the search did focus particularly on capital budgeting rather than on capital investment, it would be useful to search on capital + budgeting. The use of the + symbol, or the word 'AND', will automatically reduce the number of hits as the search engine only identifies items that correspond exactly to the search terms.

Sometimes it is necessary to broaden out the terms of the search. Taking the example above, if the researcher wished to focus on wider issues around, the use of the term 'OR' allows the search to be broadened. It enables the researcher to search for the themes even where the words may sometimes differ (for example, capital budgeting or capital investment). In some situations it may be necessary to specifically exclude particular words from the search. Going back to our example of budgeting, if the focus of the research changes and is no longer on capital budgeting, the terms used for the search might be 'budgeting NOT capital'.

Symbols are also used to refine and direct the search. In business research there is often a discrepancy between the UK and US way of spelling. Yet often, the search will have to consider both UK and US sources – and that becomes possible through the use of ? to miss out a letter where spellings differ. Take for example organi?ation. In this case, the search engine will look for both organisation and organization as part of the search. It is also possible to truncate words to allow the search engine to generate a large number of hits. In this case a * is put at the end of a truncated word. Thus our example becomes organis* . In this case, the search engine will search for anything that begins with organis- and may therefore generate hits on organisation, organise, organising, organiser, etc.

An 'advanced search' of a library search engine allows for the more meticulous use of search locations and Boolean operators. There are often at least three opportunities to insert text, each accompanied by a search direction (title, author, ISBN, etc) and each connected by the Boolean operators of 'AND', 'OR' and/or 'NOT'.

Possibly the most important feature of an electronic library search engine is the Help button! There is nearly always an icon from which you can email questions or ask for guidance from library staff. The simple rule is: *if in doubt, be prepared to ask for help*.

> **Library searches must be focused. Use Boolean operators where possible, and if in doubt click on the Help button and ask for help.**

THE ADVANTAGES AND DISADVANTAGES OF DIFFERENT FORMS OF LITERATURE

Having considered the *means* by which the literature and other information can be accessed, it is useful to consider the advantages and disadvantages of the different things you might find. This next section looks at the different forms of literature and how they can best be used to support your research. Those forms are:

- books
- academic journals
- professional journals
- organisational information (as printed or photocopied)
- government reports/White Papers
- theses and dissertations
- conference papers.

ACTIVITY

List the forms/sources of literature that you think you might find useful to draw upon in your research.

After you have read the next section on sources of literature, come back to this list and update it.

RESEARCH STORY

Reema's research

Reema works as a staff nurse in the Medrigal County Hospital. It is a small hospital with just nine long-stay wards. The unit specialises in long-term rehabilitation and many of its patients stay in hospital for very long periods of time (usually over 12 months). The staff work in care teams which comprise nursing, physiotherapy, occupational therapy, speech therapy, dietetics and medical staff, all of whom work closely with a small number of patients. Because the staff and patients work so closely together, it is good for patient progress and for staff morale if each of the care teams has a stable workforce. Reema senses that over the last two years the staff turnover rate has risen to a higher level than it ever has been previously. She wants to investigate this as part of her postgraduate Diploma in Management studies.

ACTIVITY

Based on the information you have, think about what Reema is trying to achieve and how she might use some of the different sources of secondary data to inform and advise her research.

Make brief notes, and refer to them as you read through the next section.

A walkthrough on Reema's research process is available at **www.cipd.co.uk/brm**

Books are the obvious starting point, but you should not confine your business research solely to the use of books.

BOOKS

Books are useful for communicating the classic theories, concepts and ideas within a subject area. They are good for presenting the reader with the views of a range of theorists and for giving an indication of the chronology of the ways in which thinking in the area has developed. Such classic theories are very often still useful today. However, most business research has to take on board current and contemporary thinking as well. It is important to remember that books tend to be secondary sources, and have the limitations of such sources. Some of the accounts of complex research or thinking may be very brief and fail to give the full flavour of the original work. Many books are written for teaching and learning purposes rather than for research, so accounts of both traditional and new schools of thought may not be backed up with a critical examination of the research methods used in the original sources. It is also common for there to be a time-lag of up to two years between writing and publication: if this is added to the time-lag for the original publication, you can see that they may not be as useful as other sources for communicating contemporary perspectives.

Reema has an intuition that staff turnover is increasing. By referring to books she can quickly get to understand how the literature characterises staff turnover, and this will enable her to distinguish between the different types of turnover and so refine her research focus. She will also be able to see what problems the academic literature says are caused by high turnover rates, and how they might be prevented. This will help her to think about the questions that she may have to ask people. She may also find descriptions of the types of things that organisations have done to try to reduce the rate of staff turnover.

RESEARCH ILLUSTRATION

Hofstede's national cultures

Many books discuss Geert Hofstede's notion of national culture, in which the cultures of different countries are classified by the extent to which they display a range of characteristics – eg power-distance and uncertainty avoidance. His classifications are still widely used. However, if you are planning to use them in your own research, it is wise to recognise that the research which underpins this model is based on employees of the same company (IBM) and all at the same level in the organisation. If your research is to be focused on people at the very bottom of a radically different type of organisation, you might well question the relevance of Hofstede's framework.

CONSIDER...

How do you think books might be of use to Reema in the initial stages of trying to consolidate her ideas about a project to do with staff turnover?

> Books offer a breadth of information which you can then explore in more depth from other sources.

ACADEMIC JOURNALS

Academic journals sometimes require a style of writing that makes them almost incomprehensible to anyone other than a 'hardened' academic. The key to using academic journals successfully is to pick those that are most understandable. Your mentor, your tutor or your supervisor may advise on which are most likely to help you.

Academic journals are useful for highlighting more contemporary thinking than appears in books ... sometimes. I say 'sometimes' because some of the most popular journals have a publication 'waiting list' which means that production can take up to two years. Despite this, journal articles are useful because, by their very nature, they have to bring something new to the research arena. They may present new ways of viewing the existing literature, challenging the things you have read about in text books. They may bring new research, new ways of interpreting old research or new ways of reading the results. Journal articles are also useful in that they demonstrate how to build arguments. Reading these articles gives you a picture of the main debates, highlights the main authors and provides references that you can draw on. Lastly, many journal articles are based on 'empirical' research rather than a purely theoretical debate, and because of this they can give you a good idea of the types of methods that have been used previously in the area that you are looking at.

> Academic journals give you an idea of how current writers in the field have reviewed the literature, how they have investigated their research issue, and what conclusions they have drawn.

CONSIDER...

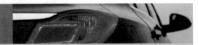

How might Reema use academic journals to inform her research?

It might be good for Reema to look at some journal articles and see how different people characterise turnover for the purpose of their own research. What do they say this includes or excludes, and who are the main authors whose work is used to support what the writer is saying? It would also be useful to see how the authors go about investigating the subject – do they use secondary data, and if so, how? Do they use primary data? If so, how, and how do they make connections between the two? Some insights into the specific research methods would be good also. Why did they choose a certain method? Did it work well – that is, did it help them to answer the research question that they set? What were the limitations of the methods used?

PROFESSIONAL JOURNALS/MAGAZINES

Journals from professional bodies give you a good idea of contemporary areas of interest and often from a practical perspective. Most professional bodies produce one or more journals – eg the Chartered Institute of Marketing produces *The Marketer*, the Chartered Management Institute produces *Management Today*, and the Chartered Institute of Personnel and Development produces *People Management*. Many also produce research reports. These publications give a useful practitioner orientation to the topic that you are looking at, and present a practical overview of the problems facing industry and business today. They can help you locate your ideas within a particular area and develop further insights into the issues relevant to your research.

However, professional journals do have some limitations. Where they include practical examples from organisations, there tends to be little consideration of how the data was gathered. And because they are written specifically for members of that profession, the political underpinnings of what is presented may be partisan. Lastly, authors of articles may be writing to promote themselves, their organisation or their ideas, so seeking to create a positive impression rather than a balanced consideration of the issue.

CONSIDER...

How might Reema use professional journals/magazines to inform her research?

By looking at what practical investigations had been done into the issue of turnover, Reema could gain insights into a number of things. First, the ways in which people framed their business research, what helped them to define the problem, and what data they had to gather to prove that the problem was actually a problem. Next she could see how they went about investigating the problem, what data was gathered, how it was analysed and whether this produced reliable results. Then she could look at the sources of literature used to inform the research. Reema would also have to be aware that professional journal articles are usually less thorough in their consideration of the weaknesses of their own approach than are some academic journal articles. She may therefore also benefit from trying to think through for herself what those weaknesses might be.

ACTIVITY

Find a copy of a relevant professional journal or magazine. Scan it to see how much of the content might be relevant to your own business research. Consider how the issues raised relate to your own work, and consider the strengths, the limitations and the practical relevance of using these to advise your own research. Note any key learning points.

ORGANISATIONAL INFORMATION

Organisation publications – via the website, end-of-year reports or internal and/or external communications – are often a useful source of information. An annual report will typically contain things like profit margins, share prices, number of employees or staff turnover rates. Such information is important if you are asserting that there is a problem within the organisation and you need evidence, facts and figures to back this up.

Reports by consultants who have looked at related issues in the not too distant past may be highly informative. You may also be able to use organisational information from other organisations (perhaps from their websites) to help contextualise information from your own. If you are trying to judge whether or not staff turnover is a problem for your organisation, you might want to compare these figures with the industry/sector average figures. A turnover rate of 15% might sound high to you, but if the industry average is 25% you might have to present your case as an opportunity for improvement rather than as a problem. There are many such indicators. Second, such information on its own is seldom sufficient. It is often not grounded in an academic literature and there is seldom any mention of research methods.

> Organisational information can help you frame your research question by providing evidence that a problem or opportunity exists.

 CONSIDER...

How might Reema use organisational information in her research?

At this stage in her thinking Reema is still working on her 'intuition' that there is a problem. Before she tries to investigate this, she must make sure that there is problem to investigate. By drawing on data collected from within the hospital by the HR team, Reema can find out what the turnover rate is – but she cannot make sense of this in isolation. To judge whether or not staff turnover is a problem, she must compare these figures with the previous years' turnover figures and with the figures for other hospitals.

GOVERNMENT REPORTS/WHITE PAPERS

Governments commission a huge amount of research which is available via government websites. Depending on the nature of the research, these can be used as a substantive part of the literature review (especially if undertaking a business research project based solely on secondary data) or as examples of contemporary research. In the UK and Europe there are many examples of government-sponsored research projects which may be described as academically robust and credible. Such reports are relevant far beyond the bounds of the public sector in which they are usually located.

Government reports can also be used to frame the political, economic or social context within which your business research is located. For example, if you are looking at workload planning, you will find it helpful to mention the EU Working Time Directive because it has implications for what people can and cannot do.

ACTIVITY

To find out what sorts of information are available and to familiarise yourself with the layout and navigation of the HMSO site, log on to www.hmso.gov.uk/information/pub-scheme.pdf .

See what reports and papers are available to you, and consider how you might be able to use them. Make a note of what may be useful (note the URL as well as the title) and keep these notes for future reference.

Government reports offer a wealth of information on a range of subjects, often derived from robust and credible research.

THESES AND DISSERTATIONS

If you are doing your research for a dissertation, past theses or dissertations on related topics may be a useful resource. They are useful as a source of ideas when planning your research or to see how other people have developed and structured their thinking when you have a reasonably clear idea of yours.

However, it is important to remember that theses and dissertations are written to answer their own particular research question, and because of this the literature review and the methodology will have been written with a very particular purpose in mind. To try to replicate either of these (no matter how well they worked originally) may mean that the focus of your research starts to drift. As you will see a little later, one of the skills in producing a literature review is the way in which you use it to navigate towards a certain point – ie the focus of your own business research.

Most theses and dissertations have done this in order to reach *their* goals, so the same structure or flow might not be appropriate for you. Be warned too that when you access a thesis or a dissertation, there is usually no indication in it whether it obtained a spectacular 'A' grade or a very minimal pass. You may be replicating a very poor approach.

Theses and dissertations give good examples of how others have conducted their research but they should be used for ideas, not as a template for your own work.

CONFERENCE PAPERS

Conference papers are also used for research produced as part of an academic programme of study because they illuminate contemporary perspectives. Conference papers can be traced in two ways. First, if you find an author who writes in a particular area, you may wish to see what conference papers they have also produced. Writers often reference their conference papers on their websites. Alternatively, you might have a good understanding of the sort of area that you want to look at but not much idea of who the main writers are. In this case it is useful to look through conference proceedings documents to see if there are special interest groups (sometimes called 'tracks' or 'streams') which relate to your subject or whether there are particular papers that might be of use. This does imply that you know which conferences to look at: your mentor, tutor or supervisor may be able to help you here. As with professional journals, conference papers are written for a particular audience and this will have an impact on the style of writing and the style of research that they represent.

GETTING STARTED

When starting to search the literature it is important to remember that you cannot read everything. This simply ends up with 'paralysis by analysis' – a situation in which you have so much information that you have no idea what you should be doing with it. Instead, you have to make educated choices over what you absolutely must include, what you could include if there is time or space, and what really should not be included. A good starting point is to have a focus that captures in general terms what you are trying to do.

- You might use key words
- You might map out a general sense of purpose, or
- You might pick two or three main constructs that you want to look at.

 Key steps in a literature search

Start with a broad topic, a working title, a draft research question.
Decide what type of literature you will start with.
Draw ideas and a sense of direction from this literature.
Use these ideas to refine your title/question and identify key words.
Search the wider literature using these key words.
Refine your research focus based on the ideas and themes that emerge from the literature.
Then you are ready to select the literature you want to review.

Start by devising a working title or just a topic that captures the key elements of what you are interested in (your client/mentor/tutor/supervisor may help). Do not spend hours trying to come up with a sexy, snazzy title for your research project – you can develop that when you have a clearer sense of what you actually want to do. Alternatively, you could pick some general themes, the types of problems you are considering looking at or the constructs themselves – eg mergers and acquisitions, or knowledge management. Try to focus this in on two, possibly three, main points; any more and you will simply be overwhelmed with information.

Remember that 'looping' is part of the process. As you become more familiar with the literature you will be able to refine your research focus. Likewise, as the focus for your research evolves, it should direct you towards new aspects of the literature.

Decide where in the literature you are going to start. If you have a good understanding of the area you are looking at, you may well want to start by looking at professional or academic journals. However, if you have only a vague understanding of the key themes, a good place to start might be reputable textbooks or review articles.

From your first encounter with the literature you may well find yourself in the same situation. You start off with a relatively clear idea about the focus of your research and then find yourself faced by eight or more themes all of which may be relevant. The thing to do is to try to categorise the literature into what you think may be more or less useful. Use your insights into the research context, pick themes that you feel resonate

RESEARCH ILLUSTRATION

Performance management

Mark has been asked to do some internal consultancy work in one of the administration departments of his organisation. He has some informal understanding of the department. However, over the past 12 months there have been rumours of an increasing number of problems. Deadlines are not being met, work often has to be redone, and the internal and external customers are becoming increasingly frustrated. The number of complaints has doubled – yet there is no obvious reason why performance should have dropped so dramatically. Mark decides that his research will focus on performance management, and so drafts a working title: *Performance Management in Dept Z: Problems and Solutions*.

Mark starts by looking for literature on performance management. He gathers background information from reputable textbooks in the area. The first thing he notices is that performance management is not just one single entity. Marchington and Wilkinson (2008, p264) describe it as a system which contains a whole range of issues such as induction and socialisation, performance appraisal, counselling and reinforcing performance standards. Not only that, but Mark begins to notice that performance is not just about managers 'doing' performance management – it is connected to job satisfaction, motivation, stress and bullying, and commitment to the organisation. Having started out with what he thought was a nice clear focus for his business research project, Mark now has at least eight different themes that he could follow up on.

with what other people have told you about the context, or seek guidance from your mentor, tutor or supervisor. Alternatively, you could simply review the themes that you have 'unearthed' in some priority order, reviewing those that you feel are most likely to help first.

Let's see how Mark deals with this. (In the interests of brevity, just six of the eight themes are reviewed.)

Having reduced the general literature to key themes, you can start to search against these themes. Again, you are looking for the key issues that relate to each of the themes and in particular the relevance of each of them to your business research. It may mean that you have to go back to the general textbooks again to get a broader understanding of some of the new themes, and again looking at review articles is good, but you will also have to draw out some of the ideas that are raised in those articles. At this stage you will have to widen the range of literature sources you use.

It is clear that Mark has gone through a number of loops between his research idea, the literature and an understanding of the context (Figure 6.2). This process is necessary if he is to reduce his research focus to something that is feasible as a project and about which he is able to draw on a specific literature.

CHOOSING WHAT TO READ

Having found some potentially relevant themes, you can now search to collect together the literature you wish to review. You will need to do this in stages because one piece of literature often directs you to another by mentioning a theme that you think might be useful for your research.

RESEARCH ILLUSTRATION continued

Performance management

Mark is faced with different themes, any of which may be crucial to his research – so how does he choose between them? He decides to use what he knows about the research context, and advice from his manager, to reduce the number of themes to three for the next stage of his literature search and review. This is how he dealt with each of the themes:

Induction and socialisation – Not sure that this is the cause of the problem. The staff have been here for many years and they all get on well. The only staff changes have been in the management, and the fact that two staff members have left and not been replaced. I think I will leave this to one side for now.

Reviewing and appraising performance – Not sure this is relevant. The problem is that performance has decreased significantly in between the annual performance appraisals. Again, I think I'll leave this to one side for now.

Reinforcing performance standards – This is being done: hence the consultancy. Managers have produced process and system guides, talked to people, shouted at people, monitored work and stopped overtime in case people were underperforming just so that they could do overtime. It would be useful to look at the effect that these systems have, not just at the systems themselves.

Motivation – Possibly a key issue. I am not sure whether people want to do a good job and can't or whether they don't want to do a good job. This might be a useful theme to look at in more detail, so I will use this as a key word in my next search.

Job satisfaction – Again, this might help to throw some light on the problem. If they don't like their job or are unhappy about the levels of responsibility or the ways in which they are managed, then they will underperform. This would be a good theme to look at.

Commitment – Commitment might also be a useful theme to look at. If people don't care about what they do or whether or not the organisation succeeds or fails, this might lead them to underperform.

OK, so the decision is made. I will now search for literature on the themes of *motivation*, *job satisfaction* and *commitment*. I will use these as key words in my search.

RESEARCH ILLUSTRATION continued

Performance management

Mark had narrowed his search down to motivation, job satisfaction and commitment. His first plan was to go back to the textbooks and see what they say about each of the themes. These are his notes:

Motivation – I thought of this in terms of just Maslow and Herzberg. However, from reading more, I think that the theories of Vroom or of Adams might be more useful to me. They give a different slant to the idea of motivation – one that might better suit my research.

Job satisfaction – This seems to be related to lots of specific criteria such as job scope, level of autonomy, etc, which might be really useful as questions to ask people, so I think it is worth expanding the search here to see what other ideas exist.

Commitment – This is a bit more daunting than I thought! I thought this was one neat theme – but from the reading, it seems that commitment isn't, that there are three different types of commitment. I am now not sure how a focus on these would help me to address the issue of underperformance.

I can now start to review the literature on *motivation* and *job satisfaction*.

RESEARCH STORY

Organisational identity

I recently did a literature review on the subject of organisational identity. However, it soon became apparent that I would be able to engage much better with what I was reading if I had a stronger understanding of the subject of social identities. I therefore got off the 'organisational identity' train and on to the 'social identity' train. I didn't explore every single aspect of social identity but just gleaned enough new knowledge to help me make better sense of the arguments and debates in the organisational identity literature.

Once you have a clearer understanding of the key themes, you must search for credible sources of information to support your research. You may wish to look at the main authors. These should include contemporary authors as well as those who wrote the classic texts in the area. General textbooks (the most recent edition) will give you the names of authors. Look for the most up-to-date references and follow them up. Alternatively, a Google and/or Google Scholar search on the subject area should throw up some ideas. If you are undertaking your research as part of an academic course, find out what the research interests of the faculty at your institution are. Academics are often willing to help by pointing you in the right general direction.

Having found the main authors, you may wish to look at the books, journals or conference proceedings in which these people write. This will often reveal other authors writing in that area. To illustrate, I will use the example of Alexandra and her literature review on the subject of organisational culture.

In choosing what to literature to read you can draw on particular authors, specific themes or different characteristics of the literature to help you navigate your way through.

SCANNING AND SKIMMING TECHNIQUES

Having used the key words to locate potentially useful pieces of literature, you now need to see just how useful these pieces are. Even when you have narrowed your search down to specific articles, it may be that despite containing your key words and being written by a renowned author, the contents or the context of the ideas are not actually what you are looking for. Because of this, scanning and then skimming are good techniques to narrow down your in-depth reading to those pieces most likely to be of use to you.

SCANNING

We use scanning when looking through a telephone directory. We know the words to look for (a name, a restaurant or a taxi company), we just have to find them in the text on the page. Often we use a finger or a pen as a place-marker. This marker keeps our focus and stops us from randomly searching, which is an inefficient way of trying to find specific text. Indicating your way logically through the text is more efficient – ie because you scan the whole document more quickly and more effectively, you are less likely to miss areas.

RESEARCH STORY

Alexandra's literature review on organisational culture

The first thing needed is the names of people writing in the area. By asking various people, people at work, people who have studied management courses, my supervisor at university, and by reading some of the general organisational behaviour textbooks, I have come across the following names:

Edgar Schein

Linda Smircich

Joanne Martin

Martin Parker

Paul Bate

Majken Schultz and Mary Jo Hatch.

Now I've got a list of names but I am also keen to make sure that I look at the different perspectives on culture. From my reading so far there seem to be a number of themes that keep coming up, so I might also look for words or phrases like 'corporate culture', 'homogeneity' or 'culture change' to identify those who see culture as being controlled by management. Likewise, I may look for words or phrases like 'organisational culture', 'heterogeneity' or 'emergent culture' to identify those who see culture as being something that naturally flows from a group of people.

Lastly, because much of the research on culture was done in the 1980s–1990s, I will want to make sure I have some contemporary perspectives in my literature. Accordingly, I may search on the authors to see what they are writing now or may just look for more contemporary research from 2000 onwards.

So what does my list of key words look like now? Something like this:

Based on these words I can now start to draw together a small batch of literature – possibly between 8 and 10 pieces. I may not actually read them all fully, but they will be the starting point for my selection process, a process which involves my scanning the work to see how useful or otherwise the piece might be.

Authors' names	Themes to read about	Miscellaneous
Edgar Schein	Organi?ational culture	Dates from 2000 onwards
Linda Smircich	Corporate culture	
Joanne Martin	Homogeneity	
Martin Parker	Heterogeneity	
Paul Bate	Culture change	
Mary Jo Hatch	Emergent culture	

Bibliographical
references
Chapter 26

Scanning the literature is the same. You quickly run your eyes over each page to find the particular words you are looking for. Papers in which you find plentiful references to these words, you will keep to one side for the next stage of the process. Those papers with none or very few references, you may wish to file away temporarily. *Don't* throw them away! 'Looping' means that you may want to go back to them. Store them electronically (if you can), retain the full bibliographical reference if you know you can access them later (for example, from an electronic journal), or file them away if you have them in hard copy. At this stage, even though most people prefer to read from hard copy paper versions, it is worth trying to scan things on the screen rather than printing everything out. There will be so much to print out and printing everything is not only not very environmentally friendly but it will also cost you in terms of paper, ink, electricity, etc.

Having scanned to help you identify what is useful, you must go through the pieces you have chosen in the next level of detail – ie skim-reading the work. Skim-reading is useful for getting a more in-depth feel for what the literature is saying. It gives you the overall sense of the messages being conveyed. Skim-reading is randomly systematic, if that makes any sense! It is *random* because you have to avoid trying to read the words from left to right (or right to left if you are reading in a language that writes right to left). If you do this, you will be drawn in to traditional reading, word by word, line by line. This takes much more time and at the moment you are still just checking whether this literature is worth reading in depth. Instead, you have to focus on the key areas and how they relate to your key words. It is *systematic* because you must adopt a logical approach that will help to ensure that you get the information you need to decide whether or not to read the literature fully.

Skim-reading is done in two stages: an initial skim (level 1 skimming) and a more detailed skim (level 2 skimming).

Level 1 skimming

At this level you do three things:

- Read the abstract.
- Read the headings of each subsection.
- Read the conclusions.

In some cases you will spot instantly that the piece does not cover the issues you want it to cover, and you can file it to one side. By reviewing the abstract, the headings and the conclusions it is quite easy to see whether the work is a theoretical piece or one based on practical research, whether the authors present a balanced debate or one skewed to what they want to say, whether the context of the work is relevant and whether the research methods used could be of use to you. These issues will help you to decide how useful the paper may be and which of your headings it covers.

Once you have skimmed a paper at this level, you can do one of three things:

- Discard it on the grounds of validity or relevance (although in the latter case file your notes in case a subsequent change of direction means that it becomes relevant).
- Remain unsure whether it is relevant enough to be included, since you have found a lot of papers.
- Decide it is relevant enough to read in full (Figure 6.2).

Level 2 skimming

For papers you are unsure about, level 2 skimming helps you to pay more attention to the piece. You should start by skimming the sections in the same way as previously but you should also either read the first paragraph of every subsection or read the first sentence of every paragraph. What you are trying to do is to get a better picture of how the arguments fit together and how they could inform your research.

Even at the early stages of your literature search, keeping notes and good housekeeping are vital. From the beginning you must set up a foolproof way of keeping notes and

Figure 6.2 Skimming the literature

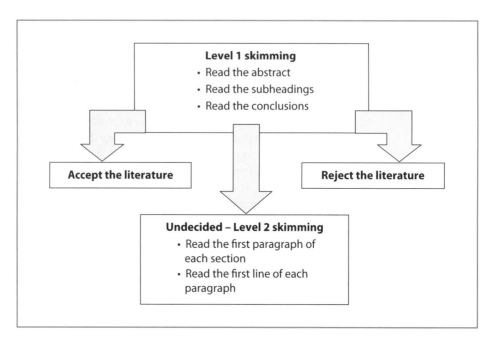

references. Always back up everything that is saved on your computer, and have a logical and memorable coding system for your files. Your university or your manager may not accept computer problems as an excuse for missing a deadline.

A good filing system is essential. It is not always easy to file by subject area, especially as many of the pieces that you look at will be of use to you for more than one reason. You need a system that will allow you to find relevant hard and electronic copies now but that will also be meaningful at some future point in time.

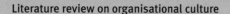

RESEARCH ILLUSTRATION continued

Literature review on organisational culture

As part of her literature review Alexandra has found *Organizational Culture and Identity*, a book by Martin Parker. It is useful to her because it presents a chronological review of the construct of culture. it is also helpful because it characterises culture in a particular way and it offers insights into a particular research methodology that may be useful to her in her own research.

Alexandra has to decide how to file this: as history of the construct, as contemporary characterisations of culture or as useful research methods? She also needs to know how to index or tag it so that she can readily find it again in future.

This is a simplified example – the book itself covers a much wider range of issues all of which would be relevant for Alexandra. In creating a filing system, a useful approach is to file by author, in alphabetical order. Once you have reviewed papers fully you should be able to remember what issues they cover, but only in the short term. If you need to access them in the long term, you must have a system of tagging to help you connect themes to sources. A parallel system on the computer is useful. Here you list the authors by name and bullet point the main themes of each of the pieces you have by them. That way if you are searching for a theme you can go to the computer system, which will direct you to your filing system. A foolproof approach, it is – alas – dependent on you putting things in the right place to start with.

NOTE-TAKING

Before you read the pieces that you have selected more thoroughly, it is worth thinking about how you will record both what the authors are saying and your own thoughts and ideas. There are a number of approaches to note-taking that you can use while reviewing the literature: the main ones are described below. Which one you choose is not important – what is important is that you choose one that works best for you.

However, whatever type of notes you choose, one thing is absolutely vital: you must ensure that you take your notes in a way that does not put you at risk of accidental plagiarism. Plagiarism can cause you to fail a dissertation. In other forms of writing it can put your career at risk. Read the following section extremely carefully.

PLAGIARISM

Plagiarism
Chapter 26

Whichever approach you choose, *you absolutely must be able to distinguish the words of the original authors from your own words*. A particularly easy way to find yourself accused of plagiarism is to take notes using some of your own words and occasionally the words of the authors, and then confuse the two. When you come to write up your literature review you may include chunks of text from the original author, in all honesty assuming them to be your own.

Text taken verbatim from external sources must be referenced as a quotation. If not, it is plagiarism. When taking notes you must be *meticulous* in noting any words you have written down that are not your own. Record page numbers as well as the full bibliographical reference because you will need both of these if you use a quotation, and it will save you hours of trying to track them down later.

STRUCTURAL NOTE-TAKING

Structural note-taking follows the basic structure that one would expect from a consultancy report, a business report or a piece of academic research. The easiest format for this is to produce a table with rows or columns listing the following headings against spaces to be filled in:

Your research question/problem/theme

The key themes/arguments/from the literature

The research methods used

The conclusions and the recommendations

The strengths of the piece

The weaknesses of the piece

Your own thoughts and ideas

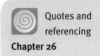

Quotes and referencing
Chapter 26

At the top of the table should be the full bibliographical reference of the piece of literature being reviewed. Include the name of the author(s), the year of publication, the title, the place the book was published and the publisher. Where appropriate in the table, note the page number of any quotes.

Structural note-taking allows you to develop a clear understanding of the ways in which each author addresses your key areas of interest. It is a system for categorising key themes and perspectives but must include your own views. It also enables you to make comparisons between the works of different authors to identify similarities and differences. It is important to record the strengths and weaknesses and your own ideas; otherwise, you will end up with simple descriptions, and that alone is not helpful when trying to critically review the literature.

> **Structural note-taking encourages you to pay attention to each of the component parts of the literature and note where each of these may be more or less useful to you.**

THEMATIC NOTE-TAKING

Thematic structuring
Chapter 7

Here the notes that you take relate to the main themes from the literature, which you use as headings. You can only do this when you have read enough to have a clear idea of which themes emerge and which ones are most important to you. In thematic note-taking, you read three or four pieces of literature and take from these pieces the ideas, the themes or the issues that are frequently raised. In thematic note-taking it is only by reading that you recognise these themes. Once you have recognised the themes and mapped them as headings, you revisit the texts and map the author's views, opinions or arguments under each of the headings. Although this 'retrospective' mapping process seems to be time-consuming, the advantage of this approach is that your notes are already grouped around the key themes. This is especially useful if you are structuring your literature review thematically. To give you an illustration of how this might look, below is a worked example.

> **Thematic note-taking is driven by the literature: it groups the contents under themes and encourages the reviewer to include his/her own comments.**

RESEARCH ILLUSTRATION continued

Literature review on organisational culture

From reviewing the literature on organisational culture, Alexandra found that a number of themes emerged:

Some authors define culture, others don't.

Some authors conflate corporate culture and organisational culture.

Some authors see culture as being something that an organisation has, some see it as being something that an organisation is (based on the seminal work of Smircich, 1983).

Some authors say that culture is controlled by the managers, others say it is controlled by the workgroup.

Based on the limited list above, Alexandra devised a table into which she could map each paper.

Author	Full bibliographical reference 1, plus tag to trace the source	Full bibliographical reference 2, plus tag to trace the source	Full bibliographical reference 3, plus tag to trace the source
Define?	No: says that culture is too complex	Yes: gives a clear definition of culture and the components of which it is made up	No, but says that culture is like a hologram, with the same core elements appearing in various subgroups in the organisation
Conflate?	No: says the two co-exist within an organisation	No: deals with one characterisation of culture which is 'corporate'	No: says that the culture is directed by management who convey values which in turn affect each of the 'holograms'
Has versus Is	Agrees with both – see co-exist comment made previously	Definitely *has*. Culture is like a structure: it is a movable commodity	Has. Managers decide how that culture should be in order to achieve business success, and then change the culture accordingly
Control	Depends on power. Control may shift between people/management	Culture is derived from leaders and then controlled by managers	Rests with managers. They must be aware that change to culture may be difficult but it is still do-able
Comments	Two cultures co-exist, which limits managers' ability to use culture	Presents this view because it allows her then to measure culture in the research part of the paper	Prescribes a way of assessing culture and then gives suggestions on how managers might move it from what it is to what they want

THREE-MINUTE ESSAYS

Three-minute essays are an extremely useful technique for capturing the essence of any learning experience. The process is simple. Once you have read something and taken notes, you spend three minutes writing down in a narrative free-flowing form what you have learned from the paper you have read. You then store these mini-essays (with full bibliographical reference, don't forget) with your notes.

Such mini-essays can capture all the nuances that you may have picked up from reviewing the paper but which do not naturally fit in to the framework for notes that you are using. They enable you to express opinions (which you may later need to justify by revisiting the paper), and they allow you to connect things in ways that are most natural to you. They also enable you to include references across and back to other pieces that you may have read, to lecture notes which may be of relevance or to themes from other areas of your studies.

> Three-minute essays allow you to harvest the issues that you think might be important from the papers you have read.

ANNOTATING PAPERS/BOOKS

Annotating papers and books (*never* annotate library books!) allows you to note down your immediate reaction to what you have read, to make connections between this and the work of other authors or to note the strengths, weaknesses or need for evidence. However, on its own this method of note-taking is not sufficient: you will eventually have to incorporate your annotations into some other note form.

This idea of revisiting themes is important. As you work through your literature review you will start by identifying a theme, and will then pull together the arguments presented around that theme. You have to be able to collect together all your notes on the theme in order to do this. Although you will often have to go back to the papers to seek clarification (and this is the point at which annotating them is particularly useful), annotated papers alone do not allow you to sort by themes as easily as do other methods.

> **Annotations are a useful adjunct to other methods.**

ORGANISING YOUR NOTES

You will have, fairly early on in the process, to decide how you will organise your notes. A sheaf of notes that made sense at the time but make none at all when you revisit them is not much help. Nor are notes in a variety of different places (physical or computer files) with no clear labelling or system to the heaps and files. There are several different possible approaches. You might find you want to use more than one, but if so, you must cross-reference carefully.

ANNOTATED BIBLIOGRAPHY

An annotated bibliography is simply a descriptive account of what is in each of the pieces of literature that you have reviewed. It is a useful means of organising your notes which requires you to read the text and your own notes, and then produce a summary. When you have done this for a number of sources of information, you have a document that gives you a précis of each text in turn, telling you what the author has said and done in the work and outlining your own evaluation of it. An annotated bibliography allows you to revisit each entry to see which texts you must revisit. It can form the basis from which you draw out the key debates, the arguments and counter-arguments and your own critique of the papers. An annotated review comprises a series of short (up to 200-word) summaries of each of the papers. Note that an annotated bibliography is *not* a literature review.

THEME DUMPS

Theme dumps are useful when you have to do an extensive literature review or are doing your thesis based purely on secondary data. Theme dumps, as you would expect, require you to draw themes from the literature and to use these themes as headings. A theme dump is a file which you head with the appropriate title and then drop in anything that you find that might be of use to you later. To give you an example, I will talk you through how I used this technique for deciding on which aspects of qualitative analysis I wanted to use as a part of my doctoral thesis.

A useful way to see a theme dump is as a warehouse in which references, contents and your own ideas under each theme are stored. You can then dip into and out of the theme dump to take out precisely what you want.

RESEARCH STORY

Use of language

For my PhD I had a general idea that I wanted to focus on the ways in which language was used, but I was quite unclear as to what this meant. What tools were there? What tools could I use? How could I make this decision?

To clarify my own thinking here, I started with a very broad review of the literature on qualitative analysis. The type of headings that emerged were

> Discourse analysis
>
> Conversation analysis
>
> Critical discourse analysis
>
> Content analysis
>
> Grounded Theory

These themes became my headings. I used a different notebook for each – you could equally use a computer-based system. Numerous papers were sorted by theme and the full bibliographical reference and a brief summary of what the authors said (as per the annotated bibliography) were noted in the relevant book. Importantly, I also noted what I (honestly) thought of both the paper and of the usefulness of the ideas for me and my research.

Noting the contents, the debates and the issues, the relative strengths and weaknesses and the usefulness to my research, I was able to decide that discourse analysis was likely to be the most effective method to use. But of course discourse analysis is a large area, so the process was repeated all over again, this time looking at the different types of analysis that could be used under the heading of Discourse analysis.

Guidelines for note-taking

Be systematic in your selection of literature to review.

Don't throw anything away – you may need it later.

Make sure you can tell which words are yours and which words have come from someone else. You *must* guard against accidental plagiarism.

Keep a full bibliographical reference of everything, even if you are not sure whether or not you will use it.

Note the page numbers of any quotations.

Decide on a system of note-taking sooner rather than later.

Organise and, if necessary, reorganise your notes at regular intervals.

Keep several back-ups of your work.

KEY POINTS

- You should consider how you will use primary, secondary and tertiary sources of information.
- Use only credible sources of information.
- Use a range of sources, but be aware of the strengths and limitations of each.
- Be selective about what you read.
- Use scanning and skimming techniques to help you focus.
- Use a logical system for note-taking.

SUMMARY

The literature is an invaluable resource, and searching it forms a key part of a research project. For research as part of a consultancy assignment or as a work-based project, the information gathered will help to frame the research question and give you insights into the ways in which others have investigated similar issues. For research as part of a programme of study, researching the literature will help you form your research question. It will give you the material for your literature review and show you how others have undertaken similar research.

While traditional sources of information continue to be useful, the Internet now offers opportunities to access a much wider range of information. Not all these resources are credible or trustworthy. Care must be taken in establishing the provenance of the information rather than risk undermining the credibility of your research.

'Literature' comes in many forms and you are advised to consider all of these to add depth and richness to your research. Planning your review of the literature is also important. A focused strategy for obtaining, scanning and skimming the literature helps you to control the quality and the quantity of the information you use to advise your research.

REVIEW QUESTIONS

1. Why is it important to search the literature as the basis for your business research?

2. What types of literature are available to you, and how can each of these be useful?

3. What are the strengths and the limitations of accessing data and information from the Internet?

4. What do you understand by the terms 'scanning' and 'skimming'? How can these be of use to you in your business research?

EXPLORE FURTHER

Baker, M. (2000) 'Writing a literature review', *Marketing Review*, Vol.1, No.2, Winter: 219–47. Aimed at the academic practitioner audience, this paper presents a useful discussion about the rationale for a literature review, how to go about reviewing the literature and how to produce a review

Cameron, S. (2005) *The MBA Handbook*, 5th edition. Harlow: FT/Prentice Hall. A concise consideration of the necessary search skills, reading skills and writing skills

Hart, C. (2003) *Doing a Literature Review: Releasing the social science imagination*. London: Sage. The most thorough and practical book on the subject

Bank of England: http:www.bankofengland.co.uk. Lots of information on monetary policy, financial statistics and information about money markets. Navigate to these from the home page

Biz/ed: http:www.bized.co.uk. News items and issues of current interest on the front page. Navigate through to 'Learning materials' for access to lots of information on everything from accounting and finance through to production and operations management

Brint: http:www.brint.com. Describes itself as a virtual gateway to information on business technology management and knowledge management. Gives full access to many published articles

Business Link: http:www.businesslink.gov.uk. Guidelines for new business start-ups but lots of useful insights into the processes and systems involved in start-ups many of which have relevance to established organisations

DirectGov: http:www.direct.gov.uk. A very impressive site which gives you access to a vast range of information. Navigate from the home page to the Central Government Index and you can access pretty well every government department and office that produces information

Database of Open-Access Journals: http:www.doaj.org. Free access to a number of journals. Click on Business and Economics and you will have the choice of business and management journals or economics journals

Economic and social data service: http:www.esds.ac.uk. National and international data ranging from UK labour force surveys to IMF (International Monetary Fund) trade and finance data. From United Nations reports to OEDC (Overseas Economic Development Council) data through to data from the World Bank

European Union: http://europa.eu. This is the Internet site of the European Union. From the home page you have access to EU statistics, legislation and reports

Visit www.cipd.co.uk/brm for web links, templates, activities and other useful resources relating to this chapter.

Writing a Literature Review

INTRODUCTION

The literature is a key resource throughout any practical business research project. If your research is aimed at an academic audience, you will usually be required to write one or more formal literature reviews. At the proposal stage (see Chapter 11) the review demonstrates that you have a clear understanding of relevant theories and concepts; these will form the basis for your project, suggesting your research question and ways of addressing it. Your review has to show that you have engaged critically with the work of both classic and contemporary writers in the area, and that you are able to assimilate what these writers are saying. It has to show how you will use the received wisdom from the literature to frame your own project, and any plans to challenge this received wisdom. Lastly, your literature review gives you the opportunity to navigate through the literature to produce a logical starting point for your own research.

By the time you write your final report, paper or dissertation (see Chapter 25), your perspective and focus may have changed, and you will have read more of the relevant literature in depth. Your final literature review will therefore have moved on from that which you wrote for your proposal and you will be placing as much emphasis on relating your findings to the existing literature as to justifying your starting point.

A literature review is much more – and much less – than your collected notes. It is an extensive and critical discussion which draws on the strengths and the limitations of a range of sources of information. This means that in reviewing the literature you have to *engage* with the ideas the literature contains. It is not sufficient to simply describe what authors have said: a literature review requires you to consider the context in which they are writing, and how this influences their views. It requires you to consider areas which are commonly discussed and those which are less well considered. And it requires you to draw your own well-reasoned conclusions from what you have read, rather than just presenting the views of the authors.

In order to produce a literature review you will need the ability to read *critically*. Reading critically requires you to think actively about what is written, how the arguments hang together, where there are strong points, where there are weak points, and how you might (or might not) be able to use the ideas presented. This chapter will consider the processes involved in producing a robust literature review. It will consider the different ways in which a literature review can be structured, and will consider the ways in which the conclusions to your literature review should segue into the next section of your project report.

If you are doing consultancy or a work-based research project, a literature review is unlikely to be a necessary chapter in your project report. However, an appreciation of the ways in which the literature can be used, the ability to evaluate its relevance and significance, and the ability to relate your work to key ideas will still help you to produce a credible report. Your reference to relevant theories and concepts will have to be carefully judged and phrased, though – some stakeholders may judge it to be no more than 'jargon' if it is not.

LEARNING OUTCOMES

This chapter should enable you to:

- distinguish a good literature review from a bad in terms of its relevance, its critical approach, and the extent to which it is used to frame proposed research

- extract and evaluate the significance of concepts or themes in your reading for the project you propose or have carried out

- organise what you have gained from your reading into a series of arguments which justify a particular research question or issue

- draw upon the literature to justify your proposed approach to the issue

- produce an outline literature review for your own project

- develop this outline into a review for inclusion in your proposal and/or final report.

THE CHARACTERISTICS OF A LITERATURE REVIEW

A literature review must present the reader(s) with a focused narrative that logically progresses through the different views and perspectives while drawing on the strengths and the limitations of them. It must flow seamlessly, to connect the different pieces of information and to build a solid argument. The characteristics that are the basis for achieving these things can be collectively known as 'the four Cs'. A literature review should be *coherent*, *critical*, *contemporary* and *conclusive* – although what this means will be slightly different in an academic context from purely practical research.

It should in any event be

- coherent – and flow logically from start to finish

- critical – and consider strengths and limitations
- contemporary – and balance new thinking with traditional thought
- conclusive – and produce some well-reasoned conclusions.

COHERENT

Notes and note-taking **Chapters 6, 9 and 11**

In producing a coherent literature review it is important to have a logical flow of argument which moves through the work you produce. Chapter 9 looks at argument-mapping and that approach is helpful here. The notes you have taken from your reading thus far, whether you have used structural note-taking or thematic note-taking, will have helped you to identify the core issues from the literature, and the different ways in which different authors deal with these issues. These notes should form the basis from which you can map out the arguments that you wish to present. The literature review should *build an argument* making sure that *clear connections* are made between each of the claims made, and that each claim is supported by *evidence*.

The 'coherence' in a consultancy project report will come from the coherence of your arguments, rather than by creating a logical path through the arguments of other writers. The extent to which to draw on the literature to do this will depend on the nature of your research and the demands of the stakeholders. Rather than compile a formal literature review section you may choose to allude to aspects from the literature in the introduction to your report, or in justifying your choice of method. It is important that in building these references in, you do so in a way that sustains the flow of the argument.

CRITICAL

Being critical in an academic literature review does not mean being destructive. Being critical means looking at both *strengths* and *limitations* of ideas and research while being aware of the *context* within which they were produced. It may be very easy to dismiss the idea of Scientific Management as being irrelevant in today's more people-focused organisations. Putting this into context means recognising that the theory was created over 100 years ago, at a time when manufacturing organisations wished to exercise more control over the workgroup. To dismiss the theory as irrelevant because it is old would be unjust. It would be more constructive to identify those contextual changes that might have influenced specific aspects of the theory, making it more or less relevant to the current context.

Part of being critical means seeing what one theory adds to another. For example, you might consider that part of a 'new' theory is merely a relabelling of an older framework. A critical assessment of this would consider how much is new, and what it contributes to the earlier model.

'Critical' within a purely practical context implies the ability to construct well-reasoned arguments. Although it is far less important to produce a literature review which documents the limitations of the work of others, it is equally important to recognise those limitations – not least because basing your research on weak or flawed theory will undermine the credibility of your project.

CONTEMPORARY

A literature review has to present a good *balance* between the classical theories which underpin what we presently understand as concepts or constructs, and more contemporary thinking. Although older theories give useful insights into how thinking in the field developed, on their own they are seldom sufficient. Your research project is likely to be addressing a present-day problem or issue that is influenced by the ways in which organisations operate today. Contemporary literature may give useful insights into the ways in which theories and concepts can be used to look at present-day issues.

The use of contemporary data is vital when presenting business research. The problems or opportunities that you are addressing are based in the here-and-now: the information you need to support your research should reflect an understanding of that context. The stakeholders of a work-based project are unlikely to be impressed by reference to 100-year-old theories, unless they can see that they have a direct relevance to the issues being investigated.

CONCLUSIVE

A literature review has to present a *logical argument*, to draw on a range of perspectives, and to reach a conclusion. The conclusions you draw must be *well-reasoned*. They may relate to areas that are under-represented in the literature, to the relative strengths of different arguments, or to the contemporary relevance of the theories and concepts considered. Whatever type of conclusions you draw, it is important that these then *lead on to* and help you to develop an argument for the research that you are proposing or are reporting on.

For consultancy projects where you are drawing on other ideas, you would similarly have to use logical arguments, from a range of perspectives, and use them to clearly justify what you propose. 'Conclusive' here means that you have to make a decision about what information is important for your research, recognising that only a limited amount of it will have been reviewed. The conclusions drawn should be cognisant of these limitations but still be able to offer a well-reasoned rationale for the forthcoming research.

REFERENCING IN YOUR LITERATURE REVIEW

Accurate and effective referencing is a key component of any research project. Even if you are producing a work-based or consultancy report in which you use the words or the ideas of other people, these *must* be appropriately referenced. Chapter 26 goes into much more detail about referencing and the format your referencing should take, but referencing is so vital in academic work that it is included briefly here.

Referencing is simply acknowledging that the work that you have produced uses or is based on the ideas of others. It might be that, from your reading, you come across a sentence or a short paragraph that so accurately reflects what you want to say that you would like to use it in your own work; you include the words *verbatim*. Alternatively, it might be the thoughts or the ideas of the author that you find most useful and you would like to present these, but in your own words in your report – you translate or *paraphrase* what they have written. Although, in practice, the ways in which each of these is referenced in the text differ, both must be referenced and be referenced properly.

AVOIDING PLAGIARISM

Failure to reference properly constitutes plagiarism, even where the referencing problems are accidental. You are responsible for everything that is contained within your report, including ensuring that all sources of data, of information and of narrative, are appropriately acknowledged. Problems with referencing can have dire consequences. If you are studying for an academic award, plagiarism may prevent you from obtaining it. If you are found to have included the unacknowledged work of others in a consultancy report, your own reputation and that of your organisation will be seriously damaged – and if your colleagues or managers find that work in a report you have presented to them is not, as you have implied, your own, your reputation and credibility will be compromised. You *must* reference properly.

In your work, where you use the exact words that another author has used, you have to distinguish these clearly from your own words: the reader must be able to spot instantly that you are using the words of others. To make these words distinct they should be presented in quotation marks and referenced to the author, the year and the page.

Examples

1 When thinking about the collective nature of organisational culture, 'it is important not to exaggerate the integration perspective' (Martin, 2002, p98).
2 When thinking about the collective nature of organisational culture, Martin (2002) notes that 'It is important not to exaggerate the integration perspective' (p98).

In the references section at the back of the report, the full bibliographical reference will appear as:

Martin, J. (2002) *Organizational Culture: Mapping the terrain*. Thousand Oaks, CA: Sage.

This referencing uses the Harvard system, the system that is most commonly used. However, there are other referencing systems, so you should check with your university or college to see what system they require.

Where you have taken the ideas of an author but have translated what they have said into your own words, this still has to be referenced, but this time you do not need to include the quotation marks or the page number.

Examples

1 The idea that organisational culture is 'collective' or 'integrated' emerges from much of the literature, although Martin (2002) argues that this should not be exaggerated.
2 Integrated or collective views of organisational culture should not, according to Martin (2002), be exaggerated.

A referencing exercise is also available at **www.cipd.co.uk/brm**

Again, in the back of the project report you would include the full bibliographical reference in the References section.

If you are unclear about how the reference should be expressed, go to Chapter 26 and use the examples there to guide you. Alternatively, speak to your tutor or supervisor. The most important message is that you have to reference all externally derived material in your report and you must reference it appropriately. Failure to do so could be deemed plagiarism and have dire consequences.

STRUCTURING YOUR LITERATURE REVIEW

Your literature review, like any other formal academic or business document, has to have a clear and logical structure. It has to guide the attention of the reader through from the first word to the last. It should therefore start with an introduction which frames what you are going to do, then have a main section (body) which synthesises rather than lists the literature, and lastly have a conclusion that enables you to draw on the literature review to present the case for your own research.

WRITING THE INTRODUCTION

The introduction to your literature review has to make the reader aware of what is coming next and why. The introduction should contain a number of key components – it should:

- introduce the general topics, themes or theories being considered
- define the boundaries of what is included and what is excluded
- explain why this literature has been chosen
- communicate the importance and/or significance of the topic.

The order in which the introduction covers each of these issues will depend on what you are trying to achieve. For example, if you are writing your literature review for an academic audience, you may wish to start by outlining how you have framed the research. They will know that the research could be framed in a wide range of ways, and by doing this at the beginning you are helping to manage their expectations about what is coming next. They already have an interest in the research you are doing and so there should be little need to try to attract their attention at the beginning. You can build up to the issues of importance and significance.

Example

Although culture has been a core theme in the management literature for many years (Deal and Kennedy, 1982; Peters and Waterman, 1982; Schein, 1984), there is a lack of clarity about what culture actually is (Smircich, 1983). Because culture is often touted as a means of exercising managerial control within an organisation, it is important to understand the construct and whether or not it can be used as a tool of management. In this literature review I will focus on the issues of corporate and organisational culture, from their first appearances in the management literature through to the ways in which contemporary authors characterise these constructs. I will conclude by demonstrating why culture is a key focus in my investigation of organisational control.

This introduction manages to frame quite nicely what the researcher is planning to do. The theme of culture has been introduced and it is supported by a clear understanding of why the literature has been chosen. The idea that culture can be used to 'manage' people is clearly of importance within an organisation, and the writer also makes clear that this idea of control is at the heart of their own research. The subject area also has clear boundaries, which are corporate culture and organisational culture. This is important because to simply use the word 'culture' could have implied national cultures, professional or occupational cultures or a wide range of other ways of interpreting the word.

If you are doing a work-based research project that is to be presented to a senior management team, you may have to convince your audience of the value of the research at the very beginning in order to engage them with your work. If you start by outlining how you have characterised a particular construct, you might lose their attention – they will not immediately be able to see 'what's in it for us'. Instead, if you start with the importance of the work and the significance of what you are doing, it will go some way to persuading the stakeholders of the value of reading the rest of your work.

THE MAIN BODY OF THE LITERATURE REVIEW

The main body of the literature review similarly has to follow a logical structure. Here you present the arguments that you have mapped out. The narrative must help you progress from the generic (the wider literature on the subject) to the specific (your research). It also must help guide your readers through this journey, and there are two main ways in which you can structure the main body of your literature review so that it provides this seamless flow.

A chronologically structured main body

A chronologically structured literature review charts the development of thinking in the field from its earliest times through to the present day. It develops coherent arguments for and against relevant texts and makes connections between the themes. For example, those looking at the issue of management control might start by looking at the classic School of Management, discuss why it was deemed appropriate at the time, consider the limitations of the approach and highlight how these limitations were thought by some to provoke the development of the next school of thinking, the Human Relations School, before moving to more recent schools of thought on the subject. The timeline provides a structure which allows the writer to discuss the relative merits of each of the schools of thought and use them to lead to the research that they have planned.

Just a word of warning. There is often a great temptation when undertaking a chronologically structured literature review to lapse into simply presenting sequential descriptions of what happened. This is not sufficient. You have to engage critically and discuss the strengths and limitations of ideas, and to position and counter-position debates using well-reasoned argument.

A thematically structured main body

A thematically structured literature review starts by outlining the main themes or debates that appear in the literature. It then develops discussions around each of these, demonstrating that you understand the themes/debates, are aware of the ways in which different authors treat them, and that you can recognise the strengths and limitations of each. It is important to demonstrate the connections that exist between the themes or debates because they will be used to create the flow through the main body of the literature review. For example, if you were presenting a literature review on the subject of 'organisational identity', you might wish to characterise the main debate as a division between those authors who hold fast to Albert and Whetton's (1985) original definition of organisational identity (as being the central, distinctive and enduring features of an organisation) and those authors who take a wider perspective by incorporating issues such as organisational image and social identities. From this point the literature review could construct a nice logical series of arguments which run through the main body, in which they discuss argument and counter-argument in an almost criss-cross fashion. Although this is a useful approach, you must also remember to include some of your own well-reasoned thoughts and ideas. This is evidence that you are thinking about what has been said rather than simply relaying it.

Whichever structure you adopt, there are some key points to note about the main body of a literature review.

Review guidelines

If you need to describe theory, do so briefly: your understanding of the theory will be apparent from the ways in which you use this to structure the debates.

Present a balanced debate. Try not to omit views that are not consistent with your own. This will simply skew the review.

Be critical but not destructive. It takes very little skill to say that something is rubbish, but a degree of intellectual engagement to recognise where work lacks academic rigour or makes unsubstantiated claims while still seeing what it may offer.

Develop coherent arguments for and against the texts and make connections between the themes. There should be a logical flow through the writing and obvious and explicit connections between the paragraphs. Don't assume the reader is a mind-reader!

Use quotations to support or refute a particular point, but use them sparingly. They are illustrating your point, not making it.

Present your own well-reasoned thoughts and ideas based on the texts you have reviewed and use evidence to support these. Demonstrate your own interpretation of the debates and show how this has led to the conclusions that you have drawn.

Strike a balance between discussion, quotations and your own opinions.

To help you envisage what a literature review should look like, a 'test yourself' exercise at the end of the chapter presents you with two good and two bad sample extracts.

Once you have constructed the main arguments from the literature and charted a path through the debates, you should close the literature review at the point at which the case for your own research emerges.

CONCLUDING YOUR LITERATURE REVIEW

The most important purpose of the conclusion to your review of the literature is to establish the purpose and set the direction for your research. The literature review should help produce and refine your research question and set the scene for your choice of method.

The conclusion to your literature review can be thought of as having three sections that are all effectively summaries.

The first is a very brief summary of the *main points* that have surfaced through the main body of the text. In putting this together you should consider:

- the main points of agreement (people often forget this one, choosing instead to focus on disagreement)

- the main points of disagreement (you can do this as well!)

- any problems, tensions or contradictions that exist within the literature

- any gaps in the literature.

The second summary corresponds to a summary of what you have drawn from the literature in relation to your research.

And the third is a summary of how your review of the literature has informed your own research. At this point you are demonstrating to the reader the ways in which your research builds on, adds to or consolidates the work that has been undertaken previously.

You may find the following checklist helpful when you have drafted your review.

Checklist for your literature review

Does your review
- ❏ draw *selectively* on what you have read?
- ❏ contribute to an understanding of the subject area relevant to your research question? (This might be the theories and the themes, it might be the methods, or it might be the philosophical positions which underpin the debates.)
- ❏ frame, define and refine your research question?
- ❏ locate your own research within the wider literature?
- ❏ integrate and synthesise the works of others in a logical and coherent fashion?
- ❏ review what works and what doesn't work in practice?
- ❏ include only what is relevant to your argument?

Have you ensured that your review does *not*
- ❏ summarise a book chapter on the subject?
- ❏ simply describe what each author has said?
- ❏ present each perspective in isolation?
- ❏ make unsubstantiated claims or draw conclusions that are not informed by the texts?
- ❏ summarise everything you ever read on the topic?

KEY POINTS

- A literature review helps you to frame your research purpose or question.
- It should be coherent, presenting a logical debate, and systematically structured.
- It should be critical, recognising strengths and limitations.
- It should be contemporary, drawing on recent literature.
- It should be conclusive – you should draw well-reasoned conclusions.

SUMMARY

The literature is a rich resource for helping you to develop your thinking, focus on a specific topic and formulate a clear research purpose or top-level research question. Searching and reading will form a strand throughout your research.

The process of organising your thoughts and notes into a critical literature review will be a key element in working out a firm dissertation proposal, with a clear purpose related to relevant concepts, and with methods informed by what others have done. (Research projects in non-academic contexts will be similarly informed but need not include a specific literature review.)

The purpose of this review is to support your *argument* that your proposed research project is worth doing, that the approach you propose is sensible, and that you are competent to do it. Your familiarity with the literature and your ability to engage with it critically support your claim to competence to carry out research.

Your initial review, developed in the light of further reading, will form a key part of your dissertation. This element will justify and contextualise your own research within the wider academic endeavour, and may in itself constitute research, adding to 'knowledge' about an area by bringing together, critiquing and building upon a body of existing literature.

A good review will be coherent, critical in a balanced way, contemporary and conclusive. It will be both much more and much less than a summary of all you have read. It will draw upon only those texts that are relevant, and will use them to construct an argument.

SAMPLE EXTRACTS OF LITERARY REVIEWS

ACTIVITY 1

Below are two extracts from literature reviews, one that may be characterised as good, another that may be characterised as poor. Read through them both and make your own notes regarding which is which, and the reasons why you think one is good and the other poor. The answers appear later in this chapter.

RESEARCH ILLUSTRATION

Transformational leadership and knowledge management

Review A

'Leadership is an influence relationship among leaders and followers who intend real changes that reflect their shared purposes' (Daft, 1999, p5). Leadership has been thought about in a number of ways. First the Traits school of thinking claimed that leadership was something that an individual was born with – that people either were or were not a leader (Daft, *ibid*) – and if you were not born with the correct attributes, you would simply never be a leader. Others (Blake and Mouton, cited in Daft, 1999) see leadership as being a balance between a focus on task and a focus on relationships. That in order to influence people to achieve the goals that you have set them, you need to balance a concern for the person with a concern for the job. Daft also notes a range of 'contingency approaches', in which features such as the nature of the follower group, the situation and the leader's style of decision-

making all have an influence on the leader's ability to lead. Lastly, Daft talks about visionary leadership and the ways in which a vision can inspire people and create commitment. This commitment may include the sharing of knowledge within the organisation.

Review B

Transformational leaders are often described as charismatic (Bass and Avolio, 2000), providing inspiration, motivation and a shared vision for those within the organisation. However, this vision is thought to do more than simply inspire and motivate the workgroup. It is seen by many as a means of creating a mechanism through which knowledge management (Nonaka and Takeuchi, 1995) can be introduced. Where people share in a vision, they share a vested interest in seeing that vision become a reality. Transformational leaders encourage people to share both their explicit and their tacit knowledge (Argyris and Schon, 1996), helping people to contribute more effectively to the organisation's goals. Although the human motivational aspects of this knowledge sharing are important, Garcia-Morales *et al* recognise a much more practical benefit, with their claim that 'Tacit knowledge enables the firm to obtain competitive advantage' (2008, p312). The benefits of knowledge management are therefore not simply altruistic; rather they are clearly intended to be of value to the success of the organisation as well as of value to the people who work within.

ACTIVITY 2

Below are two extracts from literature reviews, one that may be characterised as good, another that may be characterised as poor. Read through them both and make your own notes regarding which is which, and the reasons why you think one is good and the other poor.

RESEARCH ILLUSTRATION

The culture of the organisation

Review 1

Culture is something that everybody is familiar with. It is something that people talk about at work, something that we read about in the newspapers, and something that every organisation has. But culture has not always been a part of organisations. In the 1980s academics started writing about culture and suggesting that it might be used by managers as a means of controlling the workforce. Deal and Kennedy, Handy and Schein all produced models of culture which demonstrated how they characterised the concept. There was some criticism of these models, in particular Handy's model. Many academics thought that the model he produced was more a model of structure than a model of culture. As such this was not of use because managers wouldn't be clear which was which.

Review 2

Culture is thought to be a borrowed concept (Reichers and Schneider, 1990; Sackman, 1992), existing for many years only in the academic fields of anthropology and sociology. However, by the 1980s, many people studying organisations (Pettigrew, 1979; Deal and Kennedy, 1982) had suggested that culture might be of value to the practice of management. The concept was transferred into the realms of management (Price, 2006), and a number of debates emerged. First was the debate regarding definition. Authors such as Schein (1984) were quite happy to offer definitions of the concept and to defend the usefulness of definitions, while others such as Alvesson noted that 'definitions seldom succeed in giving such concepts any crystal-clear meaning' (1993, p2). The second debate related to the difference between organisational culture and corporate culture. Although some writers (Hofstede, 1986; Kotter and Heskett, 1992) use the terms interchangeably, others, such as Linstead and Grafton-Small (1992), are keen to make a distinction between the two. Corporate culture they see as being that directed by management, whereas organisational culture is that which emerges from the workgroups within the organisation. It is therefore beyond the control of management. The third debate is closely linked with the distinction between corporate and organisational culture. Where culture is to be a value to managers it has to be consistent across the organisation. The third debate highlights two schools of thought, one which sees culture as being homogenous and consistent across the organisation, and another which characterises culture as being fragmented or differentiated (Parker, 2000; Martin, 2002).

This feedback is available at www.cipd.co.uk/brm

FEEDBACK ON THE EXERCISES

Exercise 1

Review A would be classed as a poor literature review – and the reasons why this should be classed as poor are quite apparent. Although every effort has been made to present a clear view of what we understand by the term 'leadership', all that we have here is a series of descriptions. These only give us a very basic understanding of how leadership is characterised. Another problem is that the review seems to have been taken from just one textbook. Not only does this limit the range of issues covered but it also means that a rather uncritical view has been presented. What is presented does not indicate that the writer is aware of the limitations of any of these theories. Lastly, the review then just 'drops' the issue of knowledge management in at the end. There is a claim that this is connected to vision but no evidence to substantiate this claim.

The second extract, Review B, gives a far better feel for what a good literature review looks like. Rather than going backwards and describing the ways in which leadership has been characterised previously, it starts with a claim (supported by references which provide evidence) that transformational leaders are charismatic. It then goes on to build a connection between charisma and the use of vision to get people to be both inspired and to share knowledge. The writer then draws on some contemporary literature to recognise that this relationship allows two benefits – one to the people involved and the other to the organisation. Although this is not explicit, it implies that charismatic leadership is not simply about making people happy but is also about achieving practical organisational goals.

Exercise 2

The poor example here is Review 1, and this is fraught with difficulties. You have probably recognised many of the points yourself. The first problem is the lack of evidence for the huge number of claims that are being made. Can we be sure it is something that everybody reads about every day in a newspaper? Also, to state that culture is something that every organisation has means that the writer is adopting a very particular view of culture without really demonstrating how they have arrived at that view – or even that they have considered that there might be an alternative perspective. The flow of the narrative is also problematic: they have gone from talking about whether or not culture is useful to managers to models of culture. From an academic perspective there is 'underneath' this text a series of arguments which could quite easily connect the two – the writer has probably thought through these arguments in order to present this piece of work – but unless those arguments are made clear it is not fair to expect the reader to try to make those connections. Lastly, the referencing. Each of the names mentioned here should have the dates attached – and who *are* those many academics who have offered criticisms of Handy's model? They must be referenced so that the reader can follow up on their criticisms if they wish to.

The good example, Review 2, shows how a logical narrative flow allows the writer to present clearly to the reader some of the history of the concept, and can then lead them in to the ways in which this history has developed to the areas of contemporary debate. Claims are supported by references which act as evidence, and proper referencing has been used.

REVIEW QUESTIONS

1. What are the purposes of a literature review?

2. What should your introduction to the literature review do?

3. Your literature review should have four characteristics: what are they? What influence do they have on the way in which you write your literature review?

4. What should your conclusion contain?

EXPLORE FURTHER

Baker, M. (2000) 'Writing a literature review', *Marketing Review*, Vol.1, No.2, Winter: 219–47. Aimed at the academic practitioner audience, this paper presents a useful discussion about the rationale for a literature review, how to go about reviewing the literature, and how to produce a review

Hart, C. (2003) *Doing a Literature Review: Releasing the social science research imagination*. London: Sage. The most thorough and practical book on the subject

Knopf, J. (2006) 'Doing a literature review', *Political Science and Politics*, Vol.39: 127–32. Useful and accessible article which explains the importance of a literature review and then maps out the process

Maylor, H. and Blackmon, K. (2005) *Researching Business and Management*. Basingstoke: Palgrave Macmillan. A useful text which covers the range of activities from literature search through to referencing

McMillan, K. and Weyers, J. (2007) *How to Write Dissertations and Project Reports*. Harlow: Pearson/Prentice Hall. Good tools and techniques for searching, reading and presenting information

Wallace, M. and Wray, A. (2006) *Critical Reading and Writing for Postgraduates*. London: Sage. A useful book mainly focused on the process of reading and writing effectively. You simply need to think about these within the context of a literature review

 Visit www.cipd.co.uk/brm for web links, templates, activities and other useful resources relating to this chapter.

CHAPTER 8

Research Questions and Purposes

INTRODUCTION

It is essential to have a clear and specific focus for your research from the outset. Even if you choose to redirect your project slightly as a result of 'looping', you will have to ensure that your revised purpose is clear. There is some variation in how different universities refer to this purpose, as was indicated in Chapter 3. Some call it 'research problem', some 'research question', some 'research aim', some 'research purpose'. Because part of working out how to solve your problem/achieve your purpose often involves formulating a series of questions which are also called 'research questions' (although 'hypotheses' might also be used at this level), there is scope for confusion over the level of question that is intended. This chapter will try to avoid this confusion by talking of *research purpose* or *top-level research question* when the higher level is intended. For the sake of convenience *purpose/question* will sometimes be used as shorthand for this. The simpler term *research question* will be used to refer to the next level down, the sub-questions that together will help you to answer your top-level question.

Your dissertation title will have to reflect your research purpose or top-level question, and must be considered in parallel with purpose. All subsequent decisions about what you do must be guided by your purpose or top-level question. It is therefore crucial that you devote some time and effort to thinking about it. Your goal is to find a purpose that allows you to meet the competing demands of your different stakeholder groups. It has to be potentially achievable/answerable, and there must be a relevant literature upon which you can draw.

This chapter will explore the ways in which your purpose or top-level question is the starting point for everything that you do. It suggests ways of generating ideas about possible topics and the thought processes needed to turn these ideas into a clearly stated purpose or top-level question. Although the suggested process is presented as a logical set of steps for clarifying your purpose, in practice the process is of course not a linear one. Moving from early ideas to a clear question or purpose is likely to involve 'looping'.

Your general ideas will be refined into questions by the literature that you read, and at the same time the literature that you read will be refined by the questions that you define. This process of using the literature to advise the question to advise the literature to advise the question will enable you to distil your ideas into a robust and appropriate focus for your research project.

LEARNING OUTCOMES

This chapter should enable you to:

- appreciate what a top-level research question or clearly stated purpose is, and why it is so necessary

- consider the factors that you need to think about before devising a top-level research question or purpose

- identify the key elements that are necessary for a good top-level question or purpose

- distinguish clear and useful purposes or questions from those best avoided

- start defining and refining a clear purpose or top-level research question of your own

- produce testable hypotheses.

WHAT IS A TOP-LEVEL RESEARCH QUESTION OR PURPOSE?

A purpose or top-level research question provides the frame of reference for all you do (Figure 8.1). It communicates to your stakeholders exactly what your business research project is trying to achieve. It should be brief, yet still communicate clearly the focus of your research. Your purpose/question should provide a generic framework which leaves the reader in no doubt with regard to what is intended, but it should not explore the mechanics of what you are planning to do in any significant detail. The details of the business research project are communicated through the sub-questions or the research objectives that you will produce in support of your research question.

Figure 8.1 The hierarchy of research question structure

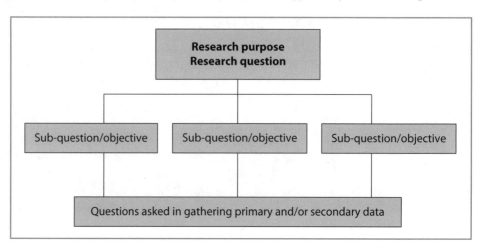

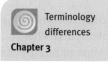

Terminology differences
Chapter 3

The different use of terminology parallels this difference between research questions and objectives at the next level down. Some purposes can be expressed as a top-level question that the research is directed at answering. Some cannot. Purists feel that 'question' should be used in the narrow sense of something that can be answered; others feel that it is fine to use it in the broader sense as in everyday usage, such as 'a question of logistics', where the term refers to an issue rather than to a specific question.

> **A top-level research question or purpose succinctly and clearly communicates to all stakeholders precisely what the research is intended to achieve.**

Your purpose/question has a dual role. Remember that you are a key stakeholder: your purpose/question helps you to focus on what you want or need to get out of your business research. This focus is necessary if you are to retain a sense of direction through the rest of the research. It is also a useful point of reference as you go through the research process, constantly drawing your attention to precisely what it is that you should be focusing on. This latter point is important in business research, where the eclectic nature of the subject makes it easy to drift away from your original theme. Your statement of purpose/question will also communicate the nature of your research to your other stakeholders, partly through the way it informs your title.

Your title and your purpose/question serve different purposes. The title is the headline of your research: it will influence people in deciding whether to read your report. Your purpose/question is the text which communicates clearly and succinctly exactly what you are planning to do. You must have thought carefully about this, first ensuring that it encapsulates exactly what you intend to achieve: resist the temptation to divert your energies into thinking about a title that is sexy, witty and snappy. Metaphorically, this is a little like putting new paint on a crumbling wall.

THE BACKGROUND TO YOUR PURPOSE/QUESTION

In order to devise your research question, you have to consider the background to your research – the fundamental objectives that form the basis for what you want to achieve. Major influences on your research purpose/question are:

- the context
- your intentions.

The impact of context

Ethics ethical approval **Chapter 4**

Considering the context draws your attention to the need to take account of the organisational background of your research. This is important in thinking about the political circumstances which may have an impact on what you can and cannot do. For example, you may be investigating a process of organisational change that has caused many people significant stress; you may have to plan well in advance because you foresee difficulties in negotiating access or obtaining permission or ethical approval; or you might have to spend time building contacts and networks or finding out what data and information is actually available and where.

Clarifying your intentions

It is important to recognise, ahead of time, exactly what you can achieve. This will be driven by an understanding of your motivations for the research. At this stage it is important to think about what you want to do in your own language. By that I mean do not try to phrase your intentions as a 'technical' research question or as a 'sexy' title. Be clear what you want to achieve, what you need to achieve, and what you *can* achieve. Doing this ahead of time is useful because once you start to build your research question, you can often get lost in the use of language – and regrettably this can result in communicating an inaccurate set of intentions to the stakeholders.

> **Your purpose/question needs to be built on a clear understanding of the context of your research and what you actually intend to do.**

DEVELOPING YOUR IDEAS

Before you can formulate a clear research purpose/question, you have to revisit the thinking you did in Chapter 5 and update it in the light of your reading and thinking since. Until now you have been working with three or more possible topics. Ideally, you will continue to think in terms of at least two of them – preferably all three. Before you finally construct a research proposal you must have thought about data and methods for collecting data, and these considerations may shift your final preference.

 ### ACTIVITY

Revisit your earlier work and for at least two topics devise a concise statement of:

- your personal objectives in relation to career and development, and your personal topic interests – these may have developed as a result of literature search since Chapter 5

- academic requirements – in particular the theoretical scope for exploring your topics in the light of your subsequent reading

- organisational opportunities – perhaps new issues have arisen or been suggested.

Consideration of these issues acts as a good starting point for developing the focus of your research. From here you can begin to consider the feasibility of your ideas. In order to do this it is useful to think about the following pragmatic issues:

Figure 8.2 Pragmatic issues in focusing on your research plan

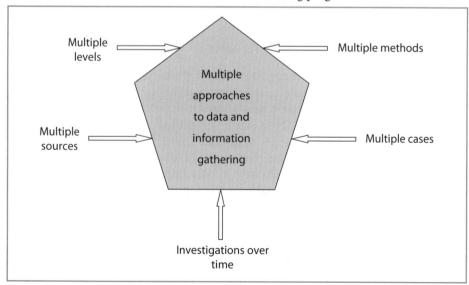

INTEREST

For business research to be effective you must engage critically with an academic literature to inform your thinking, and you have to understand research methods and how best to analyse the data gathered. You then need to use your research findings to draw some well-reasoned conclusions. This can be an incredibly time-consuming process, and one that will seem even longer if you have no (or very little) interest in the subject that you are investigating. Even if you are interested in the subject, there may be times when your interest wanes, and it is therefore important to pick a subject that will retain your attention, that matters to you and that you are enthusiastic about. This is sometimes not as easy as it sounds. Where organisational stakeholders have a vested interest in your research, where they are funding your studies or giving you permission to gather data in their organisation, they may put pressure on you to produce a particular piece of research – one that is driven by their needs or interests rather than yours. In such circumstances, careful negotiation is required to try to find some middle ground which accommodates the wishes of both parties.

SKILLS

Business research that requires you to take up new skills is fine as long as you can acquire those skills and you are confident that you can do so within the allocated time-frame you have. Saunders *et al* (2007) cite the example of trying to learn to speak a new language. No matter how much this new language may improve your research, it is highly unlikely that you will be able to acquire the level of linguistic skills you need within the time-frame. Alternatively, to acquire the skills of, for example, using a statistics package may be both feasible and be of use to you in the longer term.

RESOURCES

Here you should be thinking about the range of things that you may need to conduct your research. How much time do you need? Have you got access to the appropriate statistical package? Have you got access to the data you need or to the people you have to gather data from? Have you got the money you need to produce and distribute a sufficient number of questionnaires? All of these factors are important because no matter how good your research purpose/question is, if you cannot achieve what you set out to achieve, the exercise has been futile.

THE STAKEHOLDERS

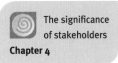

The significance of stakeholders
Chapter 4

Stakeholders have the power to enable or constrain your research. To engage stakeholders and enlist their support you must consider what is important to them. This requires some understanding of the politics of the research, the timeliness of what you are undertaking, the relevance of what you want to do, and how you frame this so that it appeals to their sense of 'what's in it for me'. In framing your research question, the roles these groups can play have to be considered. You should also remember that your relationship with stakeholders is a reciprocal one, and think about the impact that what you are proposing will have on others.

THE LITERATURE

The existing literature will give you a good idea about how other people have framed their research, and you can obtain a great deal from their insights. If you are undertaking your business research project as part of a work-based project or as a piece of internal consultancy, you may wish to focus your attentions on the 'established' ways of doing things. Using tried and tested methods associated with well-known practitioners or academics may help consolidate the credibility of your own research. If you are undertaking your business research project as part of an academic programme of study, you may wish to direct your own attention to areas that are less well served by the existing literature.

Engaging with the literature will give you a good sense of how people have addressed similar issues previously. Your relationship with the literature is an iterative one in which your ideas guide what you read and what you read then guides your ideas.

POTENTIAL METHODS AND FEASIBILITY

Your research purpose/question has to communicate what you are going to do. You must therefore have an understanding of what methods may be appropriate and whether or not you have the skills and resources to replicate those methods. You must also reflect on your methodological intentions – for example, if you propose an evaluation, then that has to be what you actually do.

At this stage it is necessary to seriously consider the *feasibility* of the potential research purpose or question that you are thinking about. Using the headings considered above is a good way of surfacing any potential obstacles as well as the potential enablers to your research. To do this, either you can construct a table (as in Table 8.1) or you may prefer to draw a mind map (Figure 8.2).

To help you to see how these practical methods might be used, Figure 8.3 presents a mind-map worked example based on the theme of investigating teamworking and why one team (Team A) performs well whereas another team (Team B) underperforms. To draw such a map, locate the theme at the centre of the map. Then start to 'populate' each of the branches with issues that will help you to make a decision for or against that particular theme. At this point you are still looking at generic areas rather than specific research questions: those will come out of this process. Include any factors that might sway your decision for or against a particular theme. These might include problems that you are anticipating, the advantages of focusing on this particular area, the actions or reactions of others, constraints and enablers, etc.

Table 8.1 Feasibility table template

This table is available as an e-document at **www.cipd.co.uk/brm**

Theme	Strengths	Limitations
Interest		
Literature		
Stakeholders		
Resources		
Methods and skills		

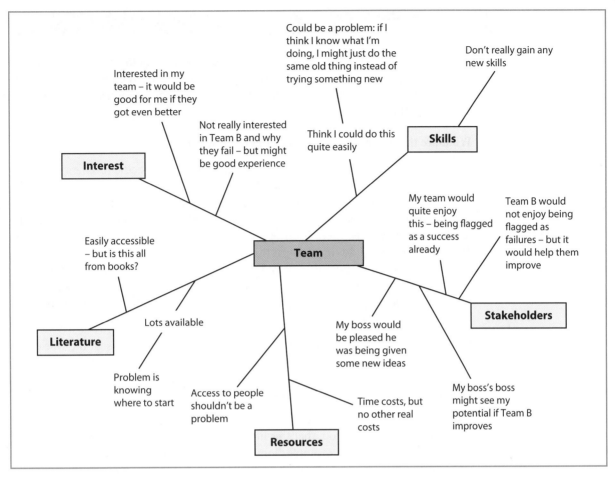

Figure 8.3 An example of a feasibility mind map

Having mapped out the issues for your theme, you can evaluate them. There is no one particular way to evaluate the results of your mind map – ultimately this process is a subjective one simply because many of the issues raised will be of personal value rather than being objectively 'calculable'. For example, in the map shown in Figure 8.2 the researcher notes the potential for this work to attract the attention of senior managers, and sees this as being an opportunity to show them his/her potential. If this is of key importance to the researcher, it is likely to sway the decision in favour of looking at improving the performance of Team B. If, on the other hand, the person is looking for something that presents more of a personal challenge, the decision might be in favour of looking for a research focus which requires the development of new skills.

> **The feasibility of each theme should be assessed and the assessment used to inform the research purpose/question.**

Once the general area has been defined, it is then important to start to work it up into a specific research purpose or top-level question.

DRAFTING YOUR RESEARCH PURPOSE/QUESTION

For most business research, at this stage two key issues should drive the creation of the research purpose/question. It must have a clear focus on the problems or opportunities you propose to address, and it must have a clear relationship to themes or concepts in the literature.

What are the potential problems or opportunities?

Here you are translating the issue you have chosen into a specific problem or opportunity. Using the mind map in Figure 8.2, there are a number of ways in which the problems or opportunities identified could be expressed. First, there are problems with Team B. The researcher may want to investigate these to see how they could be resolved. Alternatively, there is an opportunity to find out why Team A works well. The researcher could do this to see if their performance can be improved still further. Or, by taking both matters into consideration, he/she could view teamworking from a wider organisational perspective. By evaluating the strengths and the weaknesses of teamworking across the whole department, he/she could produce some organisation-wide recommendations.

Having surfaced the problems/opportunities that might be addressed, the researcher could then consider how they might be informed by the literature on teams.

What are the main themes from the literature?

The literature has to inform your research. You must therefore ensure that there is sufficient literature to guide you, that this literature is accessible and that you understand the literature. In the team example, 'looping' between research question and literature and research question and literature might have produced the following themes:

- Some argue for team roles as a means of making teams more effective.
- Some say a lack of diversity teams helps ease conflict but reduces creativity.
- Some say that teams have life-cycles and must work up to being effective.
- Some say that different types of teams should be constructed for specific purposes.
- Some debate whether team leaders should be allocated or allowed to emerge.

Do you think that the literature here would provide sufficient insights into how teams work? Sufficient for you to be able to start to investigate the problems/opportunities that you have identified? For most of you the answer is likely to be 'Probably'. Each of these themes is quite substantial, and they represent only a limited selection of what is available in the wider literature on teams.

 CONSIDER...

In respect of the themes you have identified for your own research, consider what problems confront you or what opportunities are available to you and whether there is sufficient literature available to inform your research.

Keep your notes to hand because you will be revisiting them at the end of the next section.

COMPONENTS OF A TOP-LEVEL RESEARCH QUESTION OR PURPOSE

As you begin to write your research purpose/question it is useful to consider the three component parts:

- the central theme
- the means of investigation
- the location of the research.

These help to ensure that you communicate your intentions accurately to your stake-holders. Your title will probably have to reflect these components, albeit in abbreviated form.

The central theme

Your research question must clearly indicate the problem, issue or focus of your research. You should be as clear as possible here and focus on one, possibly two, central themes. Any more than two and you risk compromising the feasibility of the research or, if it is a dissertation, sacrificing academic depth for breadth. The following Activity shows what can go wrong.

ACTIVITY

Toby is doing an MSc Marketing by distance learning. He currently works as a regional team leader for a company which sells pet foods to retail companies. The first draft of his top-level research question read as follows:

To what extent do the leaders or the managers of XYZ Company successfully communicate the vision of the company to motivate and inspire remotely based sales staff and help them to buy in to the strategic objectives?

Imagine first that you are Toby's line manager and he has just presented this to you to ask for your comments and for your permission to do the research. What do you think about the research question? What precisely do you think that Toby will be looking at? What are his objectives? And would you give him permission?

Next, imagine that you are a member of one of the sales teams that Toby wants to gather data from and you have been presented with this question to see if you would be willing to take part. What are your thoughts?

The manager's first thought might be that Toby is looking at effective communications – this is the central theme. Reading on, he or she might begin to think that perhaps the theme is how the vision of the company motivates staff. Then he or she might wonder what Toby is planning to do with this idea of inspiring people and how this fits with the other questions. Perhaps Toby is looking at whether sales staff buy in to the strategic objectives of the organisation? It would be very difficult indeed to cover all of these issues within the confines of one project. And if I were the manager I would be reluctant to give permission for Toby to do something that I am really not clear about.

His colleagues would have no better an idea of what Toby is trying to achieve. They would be unclear as to what was expected of them, and might be concerned that he could use anything they said to 'get at' management. Without more clarity they might be unwilling to take part in the research.

After further thinking, reading and guidance from his supervisor, Toby revised his statement.

Toby's new research purpose is:

An investigation into what the sales staff of XYZ Company understand by the vision of the company, and how well they think this vision motivates them to do a better job.

If you were Toby's line manager again, what would you think about this research purpose?

If you were a colleague what would you think?

Can you improve the statement further?

From both perspectives, this is much clearer. His manager would have a clearer sense of what Toby wants to do, and could see how the results of this research might be useful. His colleagues would also be able to see a purpose to the research and would no longer fear that it was being used to 'get at' management.

A third point worth making is that from an academic perspective this clarity is important. Toby can now see how he has to review the literature on corporate vision and in particular on the ways in which this impacts on motivation. For his primary data-gathering it is also clear that he will ask the sales staff what they think the vision of the company is, and about the extent to which they think this vision motivates them. This clarity will help him to map out the research objectives which will underpin the research question/purpose.

If you were seeking to improve Toby's statement further you might think about writing a title, and then deciding on describing what you propose in terms of a top-level research question *or* a research purpose. Toby's statement seems to be seeking to be all three.

- A succinct title might be something like *Vision and the Motivation of Sales Staff at XYZ Company*.

- The overall purpose might be: *To investigate the understanding of company vision among sales staff at XYZ Company and their perceptions of its impact upon their motivation*.

- A top-level research question might be: *What do sales staff at XYZ Company perceive the Company's vision to be, and what impact do they think this perceived vision has upon their motivation?*

The second key component of a research question is some description of what you are going to *do*.

The means of investigation

Whereas the central theme of your research purpose/question tells people what you will focus on, they also need to know what you are going to *do*. What you decide to do will frame your entire methodology and therefore have implications for the credibility of your research. Moreover, different stakeholders place different demands on your research. An academic piece of work based purely on qualitative data in which opinions and perceptions are sought may be frowned upon by managers commissioning the research as a piece of consultancy. Their needs may be better met by quantitative data or hypothesis-testing. Your research purpose/question should communicate the means of investigation in a way that stakeholders can understand.

The means of investigation usually includes words like 'investigate', 'analyse', 'assess', 'evaluate' or 'test'.

Thus far the research question has identified the theme of the research and given the reader some indication as to how this theme will be investigated. What the reader needs to know now is *where* it will be investigated.

The location of the research

The location of the research is important because it implies the level at which the analysis will take place, and this has relevance for the ways in which the results of the research are used. Research undertaken right across an organisation could quite reasonably advise managers of organisation-wide action that has to be taken. However, if the research has been confined to a single department, team or unit it would not be reasonable to assume that the results were representative of the organisation as a whole. Indeed, to do so would be at best naive, at worst dangerous. Toby is focusing on sales staff in his research. His results may suggest ways of improving the motivation levels of the sales staff but would be of little relevance in trying to improve the motivation of other workgroups within the organisation.

KEY POINTS

- A research purpose/question needs a central theme which locates your research within a particular body of academic literature.

- A research purpose/question should include a means of investigation which communicates to your stakeholders exactly what you intend to do.

- A research purpose/question has to specify a location which accurately reflects the level and boundaries of the subject of the analysis.

CONSIDER...

Using your notes from having identified the potential problems/opportunities and the literature, note the central theme, the means of investigation and the location for each of these and draft a top-level research question or purpose for each.

Keep these notes to hand because you will be reviewing them shortly.

Your research purpose/question should articulate clearly and specifically what you hope to achieve through your research. It should do this in as few words as possible and should be written in language that will be understood by your stakeholders. The ways in which you word your research purpose/question will depend on the motives for your research.

If your research is part of a programme of study, your question must demonstrate to the academic institution that this piece of work meets their standards of academic rigour; yet it also has to be written in such a way that it does not frighten off potential participants in your research. If your research is part of an internal consultancy assignment, it must demonstrate that you have understood the brief and considered the demands of those commissioning the research. The sponsors will want to see a research question that promises to do what they want it to. If your research is part of a work-based project, the research question must reflect accurately what you are planning to do while it also attracts the interest and support of stakeholders. Again you might have to sell the value of the research more if you are trying to engender support.

CHECKING YOUR RESEARCH PURPOSE/QUESTION

Your research purpose/question is the foundation on which your research is built. It must be solid. Before finalising your draft you can usefully make some final checks:

- Is your research purpose/question clear and comprehensible?
- Is the content of your research purpose/question accurate?

Is it clear and comprehensible?

A good exercise is to explain to yourself, in normal everyday language, what *exactly* you are trying to do and then to read your research purpose/question to see if what you have written reflects that. The great temptation is to try to word the question in 'research language' or 'business jargon', and people often get caught up in the semantics and lose the focus on the substance.

CONSIDER...

Compare the following paired alternative statements of purpose or top-level question. In each case, which of the pair communicates more clearly?

a)   Cultural efficacy in AbCCo: a phenomenological inquiry into the salience of culture in team effectiveness

   or

   How important is culture in AbCCo in producing an effective team? A qualitative investigation

b)   Hitting the ground running: How quickly can we get new people from 0 to 60 in Company ABC?

   or

   A critical evaluation of the effectiveness of induction processes in Company ABC

An alternative check is to imagine that you are trying to explain very briefly to someone who has no familiarity with business or research exactly what it is you are planning to do. (I always use my Mum as a model for this, not least because she is more than willing to tell me whether or not what I am saying is understandable!) You must communicate what you are planning to do clearly. Remember – you can fiddle around with the wording once you have got the substance right.

Is the content accurate?

The content of your research purpose/question should reflect exactly what you are intending to do. You should avoid grandiose promises (such as establishing causal relationships) unless you are going to be able to fulfil those promises. For example, it would be very difficult to prove the impact that a zero-based budgeting approach has on corporate success. So many other factors have an impact on corporate success that unless you could account for all of them, you would not know what the impact of zero-based budgeting was. You must also use language accurately in your research purpose/question. A term that often appears in students' research purpose/questions is 'corporate success'. What exactly does this mean? Everyone has his or her own understanding, but in research there has to be a particular focus. For corporate success this could be profitability, it could be the percentage of revenues invested in corporate social responsibility, it could mean market share, or it could mean new product development. Your research purpose/question must indicate *precisely* what you are looking at.

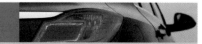

CONSIDER...

Check the purpose/question for each of your potential themes for comprehensibility and content.

RESEARCH OBJECTIVES

A top-level research question or purpose sets the specific framework within which your research will take place. But because this is the generic over-arching framework, it usually cannot communicate what you are intending to do in any depth or detail. This is why it is generally necessary to move to the next level of specificity and define a series of research objectives, research questions or hypotheses that will define further choices about how your research will be conducted.

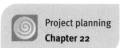
Project planning
Chapter 22

Research objectives can be written as short questions which together provide an answer to your top-level question, or as short objective statements which together achieve your purpose. For a deductive approach you might instead formulate a hypothesis or set of hypotheses to be tested. Whichever approach you adopt, this next level of specificity will indicate the sub-set of activities that are required to produce the research findings. When thinking about research objectives it is useful to think logically and sequentially through the processes necessary to gather the information that you need for your research. That way, they can be used as a baseline map which guides the project planning of your research.

You should try to limit your research objectives to between two and five, simply because this should be sufficient to guide you through the research process. To illustrate how these work the following illustration is based on the example given previously.

In both examples the ways in which the research objectives support the research question can be clearly seen. They provide a logical pathway which can then guide thinking about the research method and the project planning processes.

RESEARCH ILLUSTRATION

Introducing induction

Research purpose/question: *A critical evaluation of the effectiveness of induction processes in Company ABC*

In order to be able to achieve the goals of this research, a number of sub-questions must be answered:

- What are the current induction processes?

- What do they set out to achieve?

- Do people think that the processes achieves what they set out to achieve?

It would be quite reasonable for these to form the research objectives for this particular research question. However, if it was important to see what different groups of people thought of the induction processes, it might be necessary to add some more questions so that data is gathered from specific groups. For example:

- What are the current induction processes?

- What do managers think the induction processes set out to achieve?

- Do managers think that the process achieves what they set out to achieve?

- What do shopfloor workers think the induction processes set out to achieve?

- Do shopfloor workers think that the processes achieve what they set out to achieve?

WHAT CAN GO WRONG?

A poorly drafted top-level research question or purpose, or incomplete research questions or objectives, can make your subsequent research very difficult. Below is a list of what, in my experience, are the main problems encountered in producing a research question. Use this as a checklist to ensure that you do not make the same mistakes!

Lack of focus

This is a common problem. Terms like 'improved performance', 'increased effectiveness' or 'competitive advantage' are vague and mean different things to different people and to different organisations. For example, what does 'improved performance' mean? That better dividends are paid to shareholders? An increase in market share? More efficient systems and processes? It could mean any, or indeed all, of these things. Your focus has to be more specific.

Too broad a scope

This happens from a number of perspectives. Research may be located within too wide an area (eg an investigation into corporate social responsibility across *all* small to medium-sized enterprises across the UK). Likewise, the inclusion of too many themes is also problematic – for example, research that suggests investigating every single component of human resource management within an organisation. A third problem can arise in the range of analyses. Although mixed-method and multi-level research are laudable approaches, in situations where they produce 50 different data sets, all of which need individual analysis and some point at which the relationship between each is analysed, the analysis proposed is not likely to be feasible.

Too narrow a scope

The research question can be too narrow when it is focused on one very specific single element. In some cases this is apparent from the question itself. A research question that asks 'How effective was my performance appraisal in helping me to improve my performance?' may find that the data generated is very narrow indeed. Interestingly, in some cases the narrowness of the research question may not be apparent until you search the literature. You might remember my example of the student wishing to look at the relationship between CSR and organisational culture, using secondary data, only to find that there was very little literature indeed that drew attention to the relationship explicitly.

Tenuous connections

The links between your top-level research question or purpose and your next level of questions, objectives or hypotheses must be logically strong. Achievement at the lower level has to mean achievement of the higher purpose. It is easy to specify a higher question which you have no means of answering. To illustrate: a purpose 'To assess the effect of stress on error rates' would not be achieved via a research objective 'To find the correlation between stress and error rates'. Correlations do not establish a causal link.

Correlations
Chapter 19

The issue of demonstrating causal relationships is not a problem in itself, but may not be feasible in some practical contexts. If, for example, you were trying to demonstrate that a particular promotional strategy had had an impact on sales, the research could do two things. First it could calculate how many promotional vouchers were received as a proportion of total sales, and second it could measure (by asking consumers) the extent to which the campaign influenced their decision to purchase the product. Such business research could make some meaningful comments about the effectiveness of the promotional strategy.

If your purpose was to investigate how training and development improves corporate performance, this might be less straightforward. Even if you knew exactly what was meant by 'corporate performance', there are many organisational factors that affect it. How do you demonstrate that improvements in performance are attributable to training and development rather than to changes in the external environment? Or to the action of managers? Or to new operating systems? Measuring causal relationships requires a clear way of accounting for mediating variables – those that will always have an effect on the outcomes (in the example above, the operating processes would count as a mediating variable) – and moderating variables – those factors which may have an impact on the outcome that we are looking at (again, in our example of training and development, the issue of changes to the external environment may bring about an improvement in corporate performance).

WRITING HYPOTHESES

Where you are adopting a deductive approach, hypotheses are normally used instead of research questions. It is important therefore that you are confident in both selecting and using the appropriate statistical techniques before you decide to use hypotheses as the basis for your research. Hypotheses are statements which propose that there may be a relationship between two or more variables, which the research then goes on to test in some way. As with research questions, getting the focus of hypotheses correct is crucial, and in some respects you must be more sure of what you are doing when choosing hypothesis-testing simply because of the nature of the results that you produce.

In testing a hypothesis you are seeking to confirm a relationship – for example, I may suspect that an increase in sales may lead to an increase in profits – or refute the relationship – ie that an increase in sales will not lead to an increase in profits. In either case the results of your research will show that a particular relationship does or does not exist between those two variables.

THE PROCESS OF WRITING HYPOTHESES

The first stage is to form a general question. This might be from walking through the research question activities or it might be from your own observations. Make sure that there are two components or variables involved such that you can start to articulate the 'assumed' relationship between them.

The second stage requires you to write down what you anticipate this relationship to be. What impact does one variable have on the other variable? (Our example above was that an increase in sales may lead to an increase in profits.) This is the relationship that you will be testing. At this stage you must also identify the independent and the dependent variables because this relationship will have an impact on the statistical techniques used. The independent variable is the factor that is more fixed, and about which you are more certain. Its existence is not affected by the other variable. So, in our example, sales might be deemed the independent variable because they will exist regardless of the impact of profit. The independent variable is the one that is predicted to have an impact on the other. The dependent variable in our example would be profit. It is this that we anticipate will increase when there is an increase in sales. The dependent variable is affected by the independent variable.

The third stage is to write up this relationship as a hypothesis. The hypothesis advocates that there is a relationship, and is written as such:

H_1: An increase in sales leads to an increase in profits.

However, a hypothesis can also be used to demonstrate that there is no relationship – this is a null hypothesis. In this case, our example would read:

H_0: An increase in sales does not lead to an increase in profits.

Both of these examples are of one-tailed hypotheses – that is, the hypothesis has specified that there is or is not a particular relationship between the independent and dependent variable. However, in some circumstances it may not be possible to anticipate what that specific relationship might be – you may not know whether an increase in sales will increase or decrease profits. Where you are seeking to test just what the relationship is, a two-tailed hypothesis may be more appropriate. A two-tailed hypothesis exists where there is no prior understanding of what the relationship might be, just an understanding that there might be a relationship. To go to our example of the relationship between profits and sales, where we are not sure about the impact the independent variable (sales) will have on the dependent variable (profits), we may have to write the hypothesis as:

H_1: An increase in sales will have an impact on profits.

Or as a null hypothesis:

H_0: An increase in sales will not have an impact on profits.

In both of these cases the nature of the relationship has not been anticipated and the process of the analysis is what will reveal whether profits increase or decrease or whether there is no relationship between the two.

KEY POINTS

- A research question or purpose is the over-arching framework that will guide your business research.
- Research questions/purposes should be informed by the literature.
- Sub-questions or objectives can be used to map out how you will go about answering your research question.
- Considering your research question requires you to think about your stakeholders, your interests, the resources you have available and the methods that you are able to use.

SUMMARY

A clearly stated research purpose or top-level research question (terminology varies) is the foundation upon which all other decisions about your research rest, and has to be communicated to key stakeholders. It is important to invest sufficient time and effort in ensuring that your statement is clear, coherent and accurate.

Your top-level statement must convey the central theme of the research, the type of activity involved in achieving the purpose and the location for the research.

From your top-level question or purpose you must be able to draft a specific set of answerable questions, achievable objectives or testable hypotheses which together will answer your top-level question or achieve your research purpose.

Common faults include lack of focus or clarity, scope that is too broad or too narrow, or objectives that are not capable of achieving what your purpose states.

Review questions

1. What are the first things you must clarify before you start to write your research purpose/research question?

2. Why is it important to consider the literature before you produce your research purpose/question?

3. What impact do the stakeholders in your research have on your research purpose/research question?

4. What three components should a research purpose/question contain?

5. What factors must you consider when writing hypotheses?

Explore further

Blaxter, L., Hughes, C. and Tight, M. (2001) *How to Research*, revised 2nd edition. Buckingham: Open University Press. A good general text which makes apparent the links between the research purpose/question and the need for appropriate methods

Maylor, H. and Blackmon, K. (2005) *Researching Business and Management*. Basingstoke: Palgrave Macmillan. The section entitled 'What should I study?' gives a good process-oriented walkthrough of how to create a focus for your research project

Robson, C. (2002) *Real World Research*, 2nd edition. Oxford: Blackwell. A good breadth of consideration taken from a practical perspective

 Visit www.cipd.co.uk/brm for web links, templates, activities and other useful resources relating to this chapter.

CHAPTER 9

Data, Evidence and Sampling

INTRODUCTION

The collection of data and information and its interpretation and evaluation lies at the heart of business research. Later sections of the book cover specific methods for collecting and analysing data, but first you need to understand the distinctions between types of data, and their implications for analysis, interpretation, and the conclusions you draw.

In the previous chapter you thought about how to state the aims for your research/investigation in terms of a question or series of questions, or a set of objectives. Here you will start thinking about the types of data and/or information that might help provide answers to these questions or help you achieve the objectives. In order to draw justifiable conclusions you will have to analyse and/or interpret your data in an appropriate way that clearly relates to your question.

Some data may be invaluable in the context of one question but of little or no value in another. Part of the art of practical research is to collect enough useful data despite the constraints and tensions of the situation in which your issue is located. To do this you need to understand the different types of data available, and of their strengths and limitations both in general and in terms of how you choose to collect them.

The chapter looks at the different forms of data commonly used in business research. It discusses the relative advantages of using primary and secondary, and quantitative or qualitative, data and expands on the measure/indicator distinction made earlier. It looks at why data needs to be relevant, valid, reliable and representative, and at how to judge whether data meets these requirements.

If you are collecting primary data, you will usually be sampling from a wider population. The way you select your sample will limit the conclusions you can draw. You cannot draw broad conclusions if your research has a narrow and specific focus (a common, and dangerous flaw in research). The chapter explores the issues involved in sampling and the main ways in which business researchers can address them.

Your conclusions will be only as good as your data, and the arguments based upon the data. Good data does not, alas, guarantee good conclusions: failure to understand the data's characteristics and/or faulty logic can still lead to misleading conclusions. The chapter therefore introduces the general principles involved in drawing conclusions from evidence. This will enable you to ensure that your own conclusions are robust, and to evaluate the conclusions reached by other researchers.

LEARNING OUTCOMES

This chapter should enable you to:

- distinguish between data in general and evidence in relation to a particular investigation

- consider the data and information that is potentially relevant to your business research project

- distinguish primary data from secondary, qualitative from quantitative, and measures from indicators, and to understand the significance of these distinctions

- understand the basic influences on the significance of data, and to start thinking about how to collect data that is relevant, valid, reliable and representative

- appreciate the different ways in which a sample can be selected, and the advantages and disadvantages of each

- start to consider what evidence might be relevant to your own investigation.

TYPES OF DATA

Many types of data can be usefully distinguished. You will remember that it was suggested earlier that data could usefully be distinguished from information and evidence. *Data* means 'given [facts]' (from the Latin *dare*, 'to give'): note that it is plural, although it may be treated as singular in English. The word may sometimes suggest 'hard' objectively verifiable observations, or may be used less restrictively. *Information* technically refers to data that reduces uncertainty about something of interest. In everyday use it is applied to mean hard or soft data. *Evidence* means something similar to information in that it is relevant in reducing uncertainty, but has the added implication of contributing to building a 'case'. The distinctions and associations can have significant influence on your thinking and your communications with others.

This section takes two examples to show that the range of potential information is substantial. You will see that you may be able to draw on data from organisational records, government, professional or other sources, from the research literature, or from the experiences of other organisations facing similar issues. You may draw upon informal conversations, or more structured interviews, or the output of focus groups or workshops. Sources of potential evidence include:

- organisational records
- organisational publications
- benchmarking data
- surveys, past and recent
- workshops
- focus groups

- interviews
- observations
- conversations
- diaries
- professional body reports
- government statistics.

In this chapter I shall mainly refer to 'data', saying 'data and information' if it is important to remember that some of your data may be soft. 'Evidence' will highlight the role of data in reaching conclusions. Your aim will seldom be mere data collection, so moving from data to argument is important, and how you do it will depend partly on the nature of your data. The important distinctions normally made between types of data are primary or secondary, quantitative or qualitative, and measures or indicators.

PRIMARY OR SECONDARY DATA

One important distinction that most writers make is between primary and secondary data. This is akin to the distinction between primary and secondary sources you met in Chapters 6 and 7.

> **Primary data is data you gather for yourself. Secondary data has been gathered by others.**

Projects that rely on secondary data **Chapter 12**

Some projects rely entirely on secondary data. As a rough rule of thumb, it is cheaper (in financial and time/energy terms) to use secondary data. Someone else has made the investment in doing the work. The cloud to this silver lining is that they will have done this for their own purposes. As a result, data may not fully meet your own requirements, and it may be hard to judge how 'good' the data is. There may be little information about how it was collected, and it may not even be quite what it seems.

ACTIVITY

List the different sorts of data and information that might be relevant to one of the potential topics you identified in Chapter 5.

The illustration projects were introduced in **Chapter 1**

To show the sort of thing you might have considered lising, I shall look at two of the illustration projects described earlier and the data/information they considered collecting. I shall continue Chris's story, but I shall first consider Jenny's project that looked at reducing the carbon footprint of her organisation.

Reducing the carbon footprint

Jenny's research aim was to identify ways in which her organisation might save money (and help the planet) by reducing its carbon emissions. This aim generated a number of possible research objectives. She selected as most important:

- to determine the current level of emissions

- to identify the major contributors to this

- to identify changes that might reduce emissions

- to determine the costs and benefits of these changes

- to determine the likely acceptability of options.

Before reading more of Jenny's story, think of possible data she might collect, and classify it as either primary or secondary. Note any potential limitations in the data, and any difficulties she might encounter.

Some data already existed relevant to determining the current level of emissions. The organisation had records of gas and electricity used, and fuel for the distribution fleet. Expenses claims included mileage and other travel, the main other sources of direct emissions. She did not need to measure these factors herself. She could access the data from company records. They were secondary data.

It was possible to obtain emissions figures for different modes of transport, and analyse expenses claims to identify the breakdown for emissions due to travel and transport. It was much harder to break down fuel consumption within the factory, and distinguish between different uses to which the fuel was put. Jenny decided to use a fishbone diagram to identify the likely categories of energy consumption, to select those where change might in theory be possible, and to seek data on these. She therefore produced estimates of energy loss through uninsulated windows, and sampled energy use through lights and computers left on at night (she walked through the office at night a few times to obtain data). Her observations at night constituted primary data.

To help her think about ways of saving energy Jenny

looked outside the organisation. She found a wealth of information on government websites, and from other climate change organisations (secondary data). She also identified two local organisations who claimed to be leaders in this field and arranged to visit them to see what information (secondary data) they might be able to provide. She also ran focus groups within the company to identify both current attitudes to energy use and possible ways of saving energy (primary data).

When it came to her final objective there was no secondary data available. Having identified salesmen's mileage as a significant factor, and more fuel-efficient cars and more efficient routings as potential ways of reducing emissions, Jenny needed to know what their reactions would be to these ideas in order to assess the acceptability of these options. She therefore carried out in-depth interviews with a sample of the salesmen (primary data).

In addition to her technical reading about energy saving, Jenny was reading about attitudes and attitude change, because she felt that this would be an essential component in achieving the organisational goal of reducing energy use.

Now think about Chris's project on reflection and its relation to leadership development.

RESEARCH STORY

Reflection and leadership development

Chris was planning to devote a lot of time to understanding the literature on reflection and leadership development. But he also wanted to link this to existing practices. His dissertation proposal posed the following research questions:

'1 To what extent are current leadership development reflection and feedback practices in line with Avolio's model?

2 Is there a significant relationship between overt/

explicit reflection and feedback events and improved leadership behaviours?

3 What are the perceived obstacles to effective feedback/reflection?

4 Can a model of best practice be identified?

5 Does the approach to reflection and feedback differ between in-house leadership development and that applied by executive coaches?'

CONSIDER...

What primary and secondary data might Chris consider using in order to address each of these questions?

You can see the value of starting to think early on about what data would help you answer your research questions. Merely considering the question above probably made you realise that Chris's questions were quite ambitious for a dissertation. They were *interesting* questions, but could he realistically hope to obtain information that would enable him to answer them? This shows how great is the need for an *integrated* consideration of research questions and data. It would be foolhardy to finalise a research question without serious thought about what it would take to answer it.

RESEARCH STORY continued

Reflection and leadership development

It would have been far too big a project to answer the first question from primary data. There must be tens of thousands of different leadership development programmes and other forms of leadership development being offered, even within the UK. To provide a reliable answer to that question would require a far larger data sample than Chris had the resources to collect. He therefore searched the academic and professional literature for secondary accounts.

He supplemented these by carrying out a small number of semi-structured interviews with a selection of consultant trainers and sponsors designed to generate insights into current attitudes and practice, and to identify some of the barriers

they encountered (primary data). He also went back to a small number of his interviewees after he had completed his analysis to check that his conclusions seemed reasonable. This did not allow a definitive answer to the first question, but did provide useful information in relation to all of them.

The fourth question was accessible only through the literature, although subsequent thinking and research enabled Chris to identify a model of the connections between reflection and leadership performance that could be used to inform leadership development practice.

The fifth question proved difficult to answer within the constraints of the study.

QUANTITATIVE OR QUALITATIVE DATA

This is one of the most important distinctions to be made: your preference will be strongly linked to your philosophical preferences as well as to your research question. (Indeed, your preferences are likely to determine the question you choose to ask.) At its simplest, the distinction is that:

 Quantitative data is in the form of numbers and units; **qualitative data** is in the form of descriptions and opinions.

 Chris's interviews were described in **Chapter 3**

Looking back at the two Research stories above, you can identify both types. Jenny was using quantitative data on energy consumption. Some of the government information on potential energy savings was quantitative. But her interviews with salesmen generated qualitative data.

You will remember that Chris was interviewing to obtain qualitative data. However, one of the questions he asked was: 'Is reflection being undertaken within the programme, and if so, in what form?' He derived quantitative information from this by counting how often different forms of reflection were mentioned. For example, four respondents mentioned reflection in Action Learning sets, four mentioned reflective writing.

Influences on the choice

Your choice will be influenced by your philosophical preferences, the nature of your research question and practical considerations. Your preferences are likely to influence your question; there are some questions that are important from some perspectives, meaningless from others.

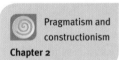 Pragmatism and constructionism **Chapter 2**

If you are a pragmatist or a constructionist, and interested in how meaning is constructed, qualitative data will be a fairly obvious choice for at least some of your research. It is richer and less shaped by your own preconceptions than most quantitative data. It can generate richer insights and understanding and form the basis for theory development where none exists. If you believe in a constructed reality, it is likely to be accessible primarily through qualitative data. However, it is time-consuming to collect, and may require sophisticated (and even more time-consuming) analysis if conclusions are to be robust, rather than mere reflections of your own thinking. Because of the time demands, you will normally be able to collect data from a very small sample, and your conclusions will be limited to what that sample will support.

The advantages of quantitative data

Positivism
Chapter 2

Quantitative data offers significant practical advantages. It is much less labour-intensive to collect and analyse, and allows you to draw conclusions which relate to a wider group because data can be drawn from a much larger sample. It may allow for statistical analysis which enables an estimation of the probability that chance might produce findings such as your own. If you are a positivist, this will be important to you. Many clients may find quantitative results more convincing: they seem more 'scientific' and appeal to the positivist (closet or overt) within most managers.

Some books distinguish between 'quantitative research' and 'qualitative research' with a similar divide between research methods. Some methods do indeed generate only quantitative data. But it may be possible to analyse qualitative data to produce numbers, which blurs the boundary somewhat. Furthermore, some data collection methods can produce either type of data. Interviews can produce quantitative or qualitative data, or indeed both. This makes it even harder to draw a firm line between quantitative and qualitative *methods*.

In choosing, you need to think first in terms of the data that will produce an answer to your question, then consider the preferences of your clients, and then decide on the best methods for collecting and analysing that data. Decisions will thus depend on the purpose of your research, and the preferences of your stakeholders, and resources available, as well as your own philosophical preferences. If your aim is to understand an issue and/or how people are considering it, seeking insights into either issue or thinking, you will need the richness of qualitative data. If your view of the world is a social constructionist one, you are more likely to ask such questions. However, you must remember the need to be *credible*. If your client does not believe your conclusions because they don't look 'scientific', you have wasted your time, no matter how sound those conclusions are.

Your choice will also depend upon your ability to analyse the data you collect. Some data is extremely time-consuming or requires a high level of skills in order to allow reliable conclusions to be drawn. It is important that before you choose your data and data collection method you think carefully about how you are going to analyse and use your data.

KEY POINTS

- Qualitative data may be richer than quantitative, but is more labour-intensive.
- Quantitative data allows a larger sample and may seem more scientific.
- Different data types suit different questions and require different analytical approaches.
- Using both may allow compensation for each type's limitations.
- Data is only useful if competently analysed: your choice must be informed by thoughts about how you are going to analyse your data.

MEASURE OR INDICATOR

This distinction is important when you come to consider what conclusions your data will support, and how strong is the evidence it can provide. A measure is fairly directly related to what is being measured. The measure may still be unreliable (see next section) but this will be a shortcoming of the instrument or measuring process. Thinking in terms of measures is associated with a realist assumption that there is something to be measured. For an indicator, the relationship with the thing being indicated is less direct. The instrument might measure perfectly accurately, but other things might be influencing what you are measuring. (If you are trying to explore an idea, the notion of 'measuring' it is problematic anyway.)

Take a physical example. Unless it develops a fault, the thermostat on my lounge wall 'measures' the temperature of the air in its vicinity fairly accurately. It also serves fairly well as a more general indicator of whether or not the house as a whole is getting a bit chilly, and therefore whether the boiler should switch on. However, other things can affect it. If I switch on an extra heater in the lounge because my feet are cold, the central heating may switch off, leaving my friend in the study shivering. If this thermostat was situated in the small room I never use, where the radiator is always switched off, it would still measure the room temperature correctly but be a poor indicator of whether or not the boiler ought to cut in.

RESEARCH STORY

Absenteeism in the Welsh valleys

The (then) Department of Employment was interested in understanding why absence seemed so high in some industries, and asked me to do some preliminary research into absenteeism (defined as voluntary absence, distinguished from 'involuntary' sick leave). I had to measure absenteeism. Companies keep absence records (more or less accurately) and this is a 'measure' of attendance. It is not, however, a measure of absenteeism: some absence will be due to illness.

I started by looking at Welsh coal mines, notorious for their high absence rates. I obtained official records on 'sickness' absence rates to look for patterns and interviewed a sample of employees about absence and its causes. It turned out that all sorts of factors were influencing the decision to come to work. Owen was always off on a Monday, I was told, ever since he fell in love with a woman old enough to be his mother, moved in with her, and had to stay home on Mondays to help her with her

laundry. All those in the next valley would be absent if the bus ran late, because the sanctions for lateness were more than those for absence. Then there were the hangovers after nights when the local team won. And so on. The interviews established that much of the absence was 'voluntary' and had many causes.

Soon after, I read a research paper reporting a comparison of the health (as assessed by medical records and an examination by a doctor) of a group of persistent absentees and a group with perfect attendance. There was no difference in the health of the two groups. Each contained the same proportion of those with serious illnesses, and of those with chronic complaints. This was supporting secondary evidence of an imperfect correlation between health and attendance records. Taken with my own research it led me to the conclusion that absence rates, although not a 'measure' of absenteeism, might be a reasonable indicator to use, particularly if long-term absences were excluded.

 Validity

It was still, however, important to remember that this was an indicator. A flu epidemic, for example, could have a major effect on the 'measure'. If even such an obvious 'measure' of health as sickness absence has such low validity, what about the other 'measures' often found in business research? What about 'management performance'? Or 'motivation', or 'job satisfaction' or 'client relationships'? How reliable are any 'measures' you might use for these, given that they are better thought of as indicators, even if you believe that things like motivation are 'real'?

CONSIDER...

Consider the data you might collect for your next investigation. How much of it would be 'measures', how much 'indicators', of what you were interested in?

Triangulation
Chapter 10

If you are to draw credible and trustworthy conclusions from your data, you have to be clear whether the data corresponds to measures or to indicators, or indeed, to neither. With indicators you must consider other influences on the indicator, and how likely, and how strong, they might be. You will almost certainly have to use several indicators to minimise the effect of external influences. If you 'triangulate' – ie use several different indicators for a single thing – each indicator will ideally be subject to *different* 'other influences'. If so, and the indicators point in the same direction, you can start to feel more confident in this shared indication.

KEY POINTS

- Measures are directly linked to the thing measured; indicators are more tenuously related.
- Indicators may be influenced by a range of other factors. Using several different indicators may help compensate for this.
- Many 'measures' in business research are in fact indicators. It is important to be aware of this when interpreting them.
- Research aimed at understanding how people create meaning may consider neither measures nor indicators.

TELLING GOOD DATA FROM BAD

Your eventual conclusions cannot be more reliable than the data or information upon which they are based. You can, alas, draw faulty conclusions from good evidence, if you lack the skills needed to build a sound argument, but the reverse is not true. You probably realise that if you are going to draw upon other people's (ie secondary) data you need to know how much trust to place in it. It may be less obvious to you that you need to be prepared to be equally critical of your own evidence.

'Good' data is relevant, valid, reliable and/or replicable and representative.

These are the traditional qualities that scientific quantitative data should meet. For qualitative data, particularly if used from a constructionist perspective, there will be slightly different requirements. The overall aim is the same: the data needs to provide firm and fair support for the conclusions drawn. However, because different sorts of questions are being addressed, and data is aimed at generating insights rather than testing predetermined hypotheses, the criteria have to be slightly different. The discussion that follows takes quantitative data as the starting point, before discussing the variations you may have to consider if your data is primarily qualitative.

RELEVANT

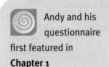

Andy and his questionnaire
first featured in **Chapter 1**

For any data to be valuable as evidence, first and foremost it must be *relevant*. Think back to poor Andy. The bulk of his questionnaire consisted of personal data about those replying. Were they male or female? How old were they? What section did they work in? How long had they worked there? What qualifications did they have? These personal data *might* have been relevant in a different study – for example, if Andy had been looking at whether personal characteristics influenced reactions to change. But his research question concerned only the impact of change on the organisation as a whole, so all these personal data were totally irrelevant. A large part of his report was made up of bar-charts showing gender, age, length of service and other breakdowns. But since these contributed nothing to answering his question about the impact of change, they were not relevant and added nothing to his report.

Irrelevant data is *worse* than useless. It wastes your time and energies in collecting and analysing it, leaving you no time to collect more useful data. It can also reduce the quantity or quality of the data you do obtain. As Chapter 15 points out, informants have limited supplies of time and patience. If a questionnaire gets too long, they may either stop answering it altogether or start answering at random.

> **Data is relevant when it has the potential to contribute to answering your research question.**

If you are seeking quantitative data within a fixed design, it may be relatively easy to define relevance. For a flexible study using qualitative data, some aspects of 'relevance' may emerge as the study progresses. Insights in early interviews can cause you to reshape your questions as the project progresses, and to seek data that is relevant to your emerging concerns.

Because of the complexity of some issues, a useful research objective might be simply to identify questions that subsequent research might usefully address. Relevance has to be defined in terms of your purpose at that particular stage in a research project (or programme). To rule out data prematurely as being irrelevant could limit the value of what you subsequently go on to do.

VALID

A measure (or indicator) is *valid* if it measures what it purports to measure. If it does not do 'what it says on the tin', conclusions based upon that data may be similarly invalid, and irrelevant and/or misleading. Sometimes this can be judged just by looking, as in Andy's case. If so, the measure has *face validity*. Face validity is important for your own satisfaction and for the credibility of your results with a client.

Questionnaire design
Chapter 15

Sometimes validity is more difficult to ensure. In the case of questionnaires, the science of questionnaire construction has advanced to a high level. If you are using a well-established instrument you should be able to find a lot of sophisticated evidence of its validity in relation to the constructs it purports to measure. Professional questionnaire designers use a range of complex statistical and other techniques to check the validity of their instruments. These are way beyond the scope of this book. Although many issues to do with simple questionnaire design are covered, there is no room for the detail you would need for a PhD or for developing a complex questionnaire to identify

Coal production figures

Some years ago a colleague was investigating factors influencing rates of coal production, again in Welsh mines. He planned to use the weekly production figures the mine sent to headquarters as his measure of production. It was only when he found that production seemed remarkably stable that he investigated. The manager of one colliery told him that although overall the mine produced what the figures said, production did not always occur in the week it was recorded. Conditions underground meant that there was substantial variability. But headquarters did not understand this. Therefore, if they had a bad week there would be visits from headquarters, and endless questions to answer. Since such visitations were time-consuming, coal was kept back in a good week in order to 'make up' production in a bad week.

new constructs with commercial potential. If you are using a simple questionnaire, it is probably enough to consider face validity, and to try to identify any ways in which answers could reflect something other than you intend. You need to be aware that validity is an issue.

This story shows that with secondary data it is very important to question its validity. 'Measures' made by others may serve a variety of purposes, and may not always be what they seem. Here, weekly production figures were an excellent indicator of average production but gave no indication at all of weekly variation. You need to check the validity of any data before using it.

> **It is important to check the validity of secondary data.**

 This study featured in **Chapter 3**

To take another example, as part of my evaluation of leadership development I was searching the literature for data on behavioural differences between leaders and non-leaders. I wanted to contrast leadership behaviour with management behaviour. I found a paper on 'leadership behaviours' which seemed to be highly relevant. Multivariate analysis of a wide range of behaviours had been carried out. Imagine my disappointment when I found that the researchers had defined 'leader' as anyone in a management position. This meant that their data was invalid in my context, because I was defining leadership as something different from management. Definitions may affect validity.

> **Different definitions may influence the validity of secondary data.**

Validity can also be influenced by the way something is measured. For example, anonymous self-reports might be a better guide to actual alcohol intake than answers given to an interviewer face to face. Both are indicators: measurement might require constant unobtrusive observation. The first might be a more valid indicator than the second. In extreme cases the 'results' might be a function of the method used, what is 'measured'. You may be familiar with Herzberg's (1966) two-factor theory of job satisfaction. He found a difference between factors people associated with feeling good at work and those associated with feeling bad. Critics of Herzberg's theory suggested that the difference he found between 'satisfiers' and 'dissatisfiers' might not reflect the real impact of the things mentioned, but rather indicate the widespread human tendency to take personal credit for good things that happen while putting the blame for bad experiences elsewhere.

> **Some data collection methods may lower the validity of the resulting data.**

Sometimes you may be using other researchers' conclusions as part of your evidence. If so, you have to judge not only the quality of their data but also the validity of their conclusions. In studies using quantitative data it is not uncommon for research reports to draw conclusions which overstate the findings, going beyond what the data justifies. One common reason is that researchers do not appreciate the limitations of their sample. Another common flaw is to assume that finding a correlation establishes a causal relationship, rather than accepting that a correlation is just that – a correlation!

It is equally important to think about the validity of qualitative findings. Much 'analysis' of, for example, informal and unstructured interviews consists of 'interpreting' what people say. It may be helpful to test constructs and conclusions in subsequent interviews. There is a real worry that when you start to place your own interpretations on data (and in social research you may find that such 'interpretations' are lengthier than the quotes that are being interpreted) the interpretation becomes primarily an indication of *your* way of thinking rather than that of the interviewee. If so, it has low validity as an indicator of the thought processes of the interviewee whose comments are being 'interpreted'. Sampling to 'prove a point' can similarly bias the conclusions.

KEY POINTS

- **For data to be valid measures (or indicators) must assess what they purport to.**
- **Data collection methods may influence validity.**
- **Different definitions and purposes may reduce the validity of secondary data in the context of your own study.**
- **Invalid data leads to misleading conclusions; so does faulty argument. When using others' conclusions as evidence you must check that both data and reasoning are valid.**

RELIABLE/REPLICABLE

A key requirement of a positivist approach is that data must to be *reliable* and *replicable*. Bryman (2001) suggests that it is worth considering three aspects of reliability:

- Is a measure stable over time?
- Is there internal consistency between items in a measuring scale?
- Is the 'measure' independent of the observer?

Single-case studies
Chapter 13

Reliable evidence is evidence you can trust. It does not depend upon who collects it or when it is collected. If a research instrument is reliable, another researcher using it on the same subject on a different day will get the same result. Thus reliable evidence will normally be *replicable*, if this makes sense for the type of research. In some practical business research the focus is a one-off event. For a single-case study, for example, replicability is irrelevant. Reliability may therefore be the more useful criterion for business research.

Both quantitative and qualitative data can be unreliable. A questionnaire may be designed in a way that makes it likely that people will lie. Or they may not understand the questions and be guessing their meaning. If the questionnaire is too long, they may answer later questions almost at random, without thinking. In such cases, if they filled in the same questionnaire again, they might answer quite differently. An interviewee may have been seeking to please an interviewer with whom they have developed a rapport. Different observers might record an interview differently, or code what is said in different ways.

The issue of reliability is more complex in research conducted from a pragmatist or constructionist perspective. If phenomenon and context are inextricably interrelated, and the researcher plays a part in constructing the 'reality' that is being investigated, the repeatability aspect of reliability means something different. Some of it will relate to recording and coding; reliability in this sense is hard to distinguish from validity as discussed above. Reliability of coding is an important issue, if you are using this approach.

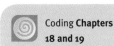
Coding **Chapters 18 and 19**

You need to think about all the potential sources of unreliability in your chosen method. Then when you are planning your data collection you can consider how to maximise the reliability of your data, and incorporate reliability checks.

REPRESENTATIVE

This idea is closely linked to those of validity and relevance, but it is such a major cause of problems that it is worth considering representativeness as a separate criterion for judging data. When collecting data there will be inevitable trade-offs between what is easy (or even possible) to collect and what is ideal.

You have probably heard the joke about the drunk crawling around under a lamp-post. A passing man stops and asks what he is doing. Looking for his keys, says the drunk. The man kindly starts to look too, but can find nothing. Eventually he asks if the drunk is sure he dropped them here. Oh no, says the drunk, it was further down the road. Why on earth, asks the kind passer-by, is he looking here, then? Because the light is better here, says the drunk. Consider the following story.

RESEARCH STORY: HOUSE OF HORRORS

Unrepresentative data

For his dissertation Logan interviewed six close colleagues within his own department (a classic example of the 'convenience sampling' method to be described shortly). If Logan had been exploring views within the department, his data might have been sufficiently representative. But on the strength of these interviews he drew conclusions about an entire industry. These six friends working in one small part of a smallish organisation were hardly representative of the industry as a whole!

If you seek your evidence only where it is easy to find, you are as likely to draw trust-worthy conclusions as the drunk to find his keys. Later in this chapter I shall look at the process of sampling, and the points you have to consider if your sample is to be representative of the wider group in which you are interested. Meanwhile, consider a better example.

RESEARCH STORY

Knowledge management

Emily was exploring potential for knowledge management. She wanted to know what projects were going on and what was involved. She did not have time to interview everyone. She obtained the list of on-going projects, classified these into four types, and interviewed three of the team leaders in each category to ensure that she had a sufficiently broad view of the sorts of knowledge involved. Later she developed a questionnaire which she sent to all team leaders. As a result she was reasonably confident that her conclusions on potential for better knowledge-sharing and capture were relevant to all projects.

If you are relying on secondary data, you may have to consider a number of aspects that affect representativeness. Do the data relate to a population sufficiently similar to your own? My TSD research was prompted by the fact that existing data related only to a subset of the working population. Factors like occupation, education, age, culture and geography may all be important.

The extent to which findings are current matters too. Findings that are 20 years old may be unrepresentative of today. Yet there may be a substantial time-lag in publishing research or statistics and some surveys are conducted only infrequently (say, every five or ten years). It may be difficult to find recent secondary data. You may have to draw on older data, and that may have been published some time after it was collected. In using such information as evidence you must judge how representative it is of the situation today, and weight it accordingly.

> **Representative data is derived from a sample that is representative of the population in which you are interested.**

Representativeness is a major issue for research designed to support generalisable conclusions from a small sample of observations, as a positivist or realist researcher might seek to do. Where the focus is more on how meaning is constructed in a situation, or on developing 'tools for knowing' about an issue which is inextricably entwined with its context, representativeness may not be an issue, because it is integral to the design.

SEEKING, FINDING AND DISCARDING DATA, INFORMATION AND/OR EVIDENCE

You now know that you will need to look for data that is relevant, valid, reliable, and representative. Validity and reliability may be properties of the data itself. Relevance and representativeness will depend upon its relation to uncertainties you are facing, upon your research question and/or upon the case that you wish to build for a decision or action.

You will remember that research was seldom (if ever) the neat, tidy staged process portrayed in most research reports, but over time you will still progress from exploration through shaping to gathering your main data to interpreting these data and using them as evidence for conclusions. You may have different uncertainties, and be trying to answer different questions, depending upon the stage you are at in the research process.

> **Different questions may serve different stages in the research process.**

Information that might be highly relevant to helping you focus your investigation might have little relevance to later research stages. There was a lot that Jenny needed to ask about early on to help her to decide on the best way to approach her 'carbon reduction' project. Once she had used this evidence to shape her direction, she could afford to discard most of it. It had helped her to feel confident that she could see a good way of approaching the issue. It helped her construct an excellent project proposal, which convinced her client that the project should go ahead along the lines she proposed. But once the proposal had been accepted, it had served its purpose. It did not contribute to the case she was building in her final report.

You need to constantly ask yourself a series of questions:

- What questions do I need to answer now?
- What data would help me answer these questions or otherwise reduce my uncertainty?
- How *much* will this data help?
- Who can help me get the data and/or evidence I need?

The answers will change as you progress: you must *keep* asking them.

One of the things a practical business researcher needs is an awareness of the potential information value of *everything that is observed* during an investigation, and the ability to exploit this – in the best possible sense – to help construct a robust case. If you are aware of the many different forms that evidence can take, you will find it easier to think constructively about what you might need, and to notice it when you unexpectedly find it. Capture such data, but reflect on the extent to which your perceptions may be shaped by your prior ways of thinking.

Consider how to gain sufficiently reliable and relevant evidence to provide an answer to your question. Finding relevant, reliable and convincing 'measures' for many factors of interest to business researchers is far from easy. Subjectivity and interpretation will often be inevitable. Many of the things that interest you are not easily measurable, and you may need to rely on a number of weaker indicators.

Obviously your answer is your own, but to start you thinking, consider Table 9.1 below. This relates to the early stages of Yiani's dissertation with an organisational client who had identified 'a problem with the car dealerships – sales figures are falling'. Yiani is concerned with outcomes for the client, but also – since this is a dissertation – with her own learning outcomes. The table shows how she organised some of her early thoughts about some of her potential evidence.

ACTIVITY

Revisit your earlier list of potential sources of data and evidence for a business researcher and add to it in the light of what you have read and thought since.

Consider which of them might be relevant to your own research, and note down issues of validity, reliability and representativeness that you ought to consider in relation to each.

Table 9.1 is not an example of how such a table *should* be constructed. Rather, it is meant to show some of the thinking that may be involved. This table was constructed early in the data planning process while Yiani was still unsure of the direction that the project would take. Thoughts about information to help shape the investigation were therefore clearer than thoughts about the eventual evidence that would be sought, but the researcher was already starting to think about this.

It is can be extremely helpful to start jotting down possible sources of evidence as early as possible, *provided* this does not 'lock' you into a premature pattern (remember the drunk and the lamp-post). Noting thoughts down is important because of the complexities of the situation and time pressures. It is easy to have a thought – and then to forget it. Keeping a notebook or BlackBerry handy can prevent this.

It is important to add to your table, and equally important to delete irrelevant data items, as your study becomes more defined or redirected. Move any data you have collected to a 'bottom drawer' file if necessary. It may hold back your thinking if you try to hang on to it. Shape your research to accommodate it. Don't discard it entirely: there is just a chance that a subsequent loop-back may make it relevant again.

> Avoid distorting your research by including data that is no longer relevant.

As soon as you start to think about potential data, start to think as well about how you might analyse it and represent it to a client, and how adequate it will be in terms of answering your question. Thinking about the end use may ensure that you collect enough data, and also prevent you from collecting data that will later have to be discarded.

Source	Type of data/evidence	Considerations of validity, etc
Client: re 'the problem'	Notes of initial meeting and subsequent discussions	Valid as indicators of client concern, but validity of the assessments of the causes of the problem cannot be assumed
Organisational records	For each dealership: Monthly sales figures Complaints from customers buying through that dealership Length of time dealer has been operating	Likely to be valid measures of what they say (though need to check if any 'massaging' of figures). Need to avoid assuming they are 'measures' of anything other than what they really are. Eg complaints may be related to the mix of products carried rather than the dealer *per se*

Key directors	Notes of informal discussions with each	May be hard to get them to be interviewed. The views of the marketing director and the director for product development would be particularly relevant, but the views of other directors about strategy as a whole might be informative so worth persisting. Client (CEO) may be able to influence them
	Records of board meetings	Assuming these are available (may be regarded as too confidential), there will still be the possibility that the record has been written for purposes other than as a full and accurate report of debate, so cannot assume fully valid
Competitors	Information on website Publicity materials sent on request for information by a potential buyer	Again this is written for a purpose. Can assume it is factually correct, but need to watch for what is *not* said
Customers	Probably should reserve these for the main stage: will be clearer what to ask once diagnosis is complete. Ideally conduct customer survey to assess views of product, dealer, and after-sales support. Might also ask about whether they used competitors' products and for their views on distinguishing factors	Think about this later . . .
Trade press	Information about size of market and trends	Should be relevant and reliable
Self: re 'potential for personal development'	Self-assessment of strengths and development areas. Own assessment of skills that would be useful	May well be biased: need to seek further evidence of strengths and weaknesses. However, I know I feel uneasy in meetings or conversations with colleagues I do not know well, so this is a reasonable indicator of one skills area I could usefully address
Others re same	Appraisal reports for last two years	Appraisal reports relate to past, not future, but the few 'could improve' areas are likley to be relevant to future career as well
	Commendation from boss	Commendation highlights a strength I need to remember and perhaps build upon
	Colleagues' assessment of areas for improvement	It will be difficult asking colleagues what they think of me, and they may not be prepared to be honest – what can I do to make it easier for them to say what they mean?

Table 9.1 An example of a first attempt at considering possible data in a car sales project

SAMPLING

Because so many researchers generalise from results derived from a sample, and do so in a flawed way, you need to understand the principles of sampling. Whether or not you intend to use a representative sample, understanding these principles may protect you from a major cause of untrustworthy conclusions in future research. Some of the non-representative sampling methods described are appropriate for some types of business research but hazardous in others.

Sometimes you can obtain data from all the situations or all the people who are relevant to your issue or question. For example, you might be investigating deliberate strategy formulation in an organisation where strategy is developed by the six members of the board. In this case it would be feasible to interview all six board members. Even with larger numbers you may be able to survey everyone. This '100% sample' is normally called a census. Sampling may not be an issue at all if, for example, your research is participative and involves all the 'actors' in the situation of interest.

 Andy and his questionnaire first featured in **Chapter 1**

From a constructionist perspective, sampling raises different issues. Take first the sort of sampling you might do when seeking quantitative data with a view to drawing conclusions about a larger group from which your sample is drawn. For example, in Andy's change evaluation project, the issue involved more people than he could possibly look at. If a census is not feasible, you will need to select a smaller number of people or objects for study.

Remember, if you want to draw wider conclusions, the data must be *representative*. It is important therefore that the sample from which you obtain your data is representative of the wider *population* in which you are interested. Note that in discussions of sampling, 'population' has a specialist meaning. It refers to the whole group from which the sample is drawn – that is, the group (people, items, instances, etc) to which you wish your conclusions to relate. Thus if you wanted to draw conclusions relevant to all of an organisation's 500 retail locations but had the resources to investigate only 25, unless all 500 were very similar indeed you would need to choose those 25 very carefully.

CONSTRUCTING A REPRESENTATIVE SAMPLE

There are several different approaches to sampling, and this section considers the main ones and their relative strengths and weaknesses. You will not be surprised that there is, as ever, a trade-off to be made between costs (in the broad sense) and the strength of the evidence generated – and therefore the potential value of the conclusions you will be able to draw.

These reservations were described in **Chapter 1**

Andy was collecting primarily quantitative data. Do you remember my reservations about Andy's sample? He was interested in the impact of change on a whole organisation, so he was sampling from a population which consisted of every employee in his organisation. He could not collect data from everyone, so he focused on what was feasible. Liz was supporting his project and agreed for Andy to email 500 people in three departments. Some 20 emails bounced because staff had left; only 40 of the questionnaires were returned.

Chris's project first featured in **Chapter 1**

Chris was collecting qualitative data. He was interested in leadership development in general, but there was no way he could interview everyone involved in delivering leadership training. For practical reasons he could only interview a relatively small number of people. He was working to a dissertation deadline. It was taking a lot of phone calls to get people to agree to be interviewed. By the time he had obtained agreement from 17 he reckoned that he had to start interviewing. It would simply have to be enough.

CONSIDER...

How adequate were Andy and Chris's samples, and why? What would that mean for the conclusions they might draw?

Randomness
Chapter 21

Both Andy and Chris were interested in an issue that went wider than the sample from which they collected data. Andy was 'allowed' a particular sample by a stakeholder with an interest in an answer which made the change look good. Perhaps things had gone relatively well in the departments offered for survey. Non-randomness is a major threat to representativeness. A further threat came from his low response rate – 40 out of 500 is a tiny proportion and again the choice to reply or not is non-random. As a proportion of the many thousands working for the organisation, 40 is invisibly small. I would argue that any conclusions drawn about the impact of the change on the organisation as a whole would be totally invalid because of the inadequacy of the sample.

Chris's questions similarly related to a very large population, and I would argue were unanswerable within the constraints of a dissertation. His selection was equally non-random. He 'selected' interviewees via contacts he had, which may already have been biased. Further 'selection' took place when they decided whether to be interviewed about reflection and leadership development: their decision may have been influenced by their interest in reflection. On that level his sample was as inadequate as Andy's.

But Chris had a personal purpose: to gain a deeper understanding of the role of leadership development. Although he may have failed to answer the research questions he posed, he did achieve this learning purpose, and gathered information that was of interest to a wider group, despite its limitations. As a study directed towards generating insight, carried out, as was noted earlier, in a flexible way, the sample had fewer limitations. This shows how you must always judge methods and design in terms of purpose, and may have to choose a purpose according to what is feasible, as well as what is interesting.

CONSIDER...

If it is necessary to work with a representative sample, how might you go about selecting it?

Listed below are the stages you would have to go through to define your sample for a study in which you are seeking to generalise your findings to a wider population. You will note that there are three key decisions: the population, the size you need, and the method you will apply.

Stage 1: Define the population

⌐► Stage 2: Decide on the sample size

⌐► Stage 3: Decide on the sampling method

⌐► Stage 4: Apply the method.

This investigation featured in **Chapter 2**

The first step is to identify the population in which you are interested. This will depend upon your research purpose and research questions. If your aim is to answer a question about organisations within a specific industry, then the population from which you sampled would include every organisation within that industry. If you wanted to know about the 11 organisations in Barcelona using the information system being investigated, those 11 organisations constitute your sample. You would then need to sample individuals within those organisations if you wanted data from individuals rather than from organisational records. Once you have established your aim, and therefore the relevant population, you can start to think about how to select a representative sample, and consider how big this sample needs to be.

SAMPLE SIZE

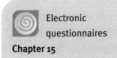
Electronic questionnaires **Chapter 15**

For quantitative research, bigger is usually better . . . up to a certain point. But for many methods there tend to be costs attached to a bigger sample. (Electronic questionnaires are something of an exception.) It would be wonderful to be able to give you a rule of thumb by which you could decide how big was big enough. Sadly, it is more complicated. The size of sample you require will depend upon the degree of variation in your population, the sort of analysis you intend to carry out, and the type and 'strength' of the conclusions you are seeking.

At an exploratory stage, you might be happy with a smallish sample. If you are sampling for your main research and aim to draw convincing conclusions to inform significant, possibly irreversible, action, you will be much more worried about the adequacy of your sample. If it is impossible to say what is 'big enough', can we say what we mean by 'big'?

Bryman (2001, p95), talking about social survey work, says that 'as the sample size climbs from low figures of 50, 100, 150 and so on', precision increases. This is the case until somewhere around 1,000, when the gains become very much less. It is absolute size that is important, not the proportion of the parent population that it represents. Thus you could be as happy about conclusions based on data from 1,000 Icelanders as from 1,000 Chinese.

This looks frightening: few practical researchers like the idea of analysing 1,000 questionnaires. Many novice researchers would regard 100 as a fairly *large* sample, even for a survey. But these numbers show that you may have to be somewhat circumspect in the conclusions you draw from smaller samples. If you plan to do statistical analyses, the significance of your findings will depend heavily upon your sample size. If you want to split your sample in order to make comparisons between subgroups, you may end up with some very small categories if your overall sample is not very large, and any differences you find will be less likely to be statistically significant as a result.

Statistical analyses and sample sizes **Chapter 21**

RESPONSE RATES

In deciding how big a sample you need it is important to allow for those who do not reply or refuse to take part. Interviewees may cancel at the last minute. Some of your research sites may close during the study. And you can almost guarantee that not everyone who receives an email questionnaire will return it. With a long-term study, people move away or otherwise lose contact. So your initial sample size has to allow for likely dropout: your conclusions will be based upon the data you actually get, not on what you hoped for. The response rate is the proportion of those whom you contact who actually take part.

The percentage response rate for a questionnaire is calculated as:

$$\frac{\text{Number of usable questionnaire responses you receive back}}{\text{Number of suitable people who received questionnaires}} \times 100$$

A low response rate reduces the size of your eventual sample, and it can threaten its representativeness. It is fairly easy to cope with the impact on size, provided you plan for this, by starting with a bigger sample than you need. For example, if you expect 50% of questionnaires to be returned, you would send out twice as many as you want to get back. If it is hard to estimate the likely response rate, send out as many questionnaires as you can afford. You do not have to analyse them all provided you sample carefully (normally randomly) from those you receive.

The influence of low response rates on representativeness is more subtle and harder to handle. The decision to respond may be non-random, and influenced by the factors you are interested in. The smaller the response rate, the more you should worry about this.

This is why the number you put in as the bottom line (the denominator) of the percentage fraction above will usually be slightly smaller than the size of the sample you selected. It must exclude those who had no choice (for example, questionnaires returned as undeliverable) and any responses that you excluded for some reason. (For example, if you were looking at the difference in pay before and after a part-time MBA, you might exclude those who said they had not worked before the course.)

Response rates for questionnaires are often around 30–50%, although many factors can influence this rate. Rates tend to be higher if the people know you or know of you, know why you want the data, share your goals, trust you to observe confidentiality, etc, and if they find the questionnaire interesting, not too long, and relatively easy to answer. You can do a lot to increase rates by contacting people in advance, by the quality of that contact, and by having the support of respected seniors in the organisation where appropriate.

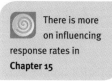 There is more on influencing response rates in **Chapter 15**

> **The way you approach your sample may strongly influence response rates.**

Other methods may have higher response rates, but you would still want to consider the impact of any dropout on the representativeness of your eventual sample. For example, of the 17 consultant/trainers who agreed to be interviewed by Chris, none dropped out. But he had to make a lot of phone calls to get those 17 people to agree to be interviewed. If those who refused were not interested in reflection, whereas those who accepted did so precisely because they *were*, any conclusions about the 'extent to which practices were in line with Avolio …' (tenuous at best with a sample this size) would be worthless.

If you deliberately chose a stratified sample (see below), it might be worth checking whether the make-up of respondents matches that which you intended. Thus if you chose a sample with 50 men and 50 women because the workforce as a whole had an even gender mix, you would be worried if 19 of the 20 replies you got were from women. Instead of drawing conclusions about the whole workforce, you might have to limit your conclusions to women employees. You would need to think carefully about the implications of any lack of representativeness in your respondents.

CONVENIENCE SAMPLING

Chris was using what is a widespread approach to sampling: selection according to convenience. For some purposes this is fine. You might use the people nearest to you to check whether the factors you are considering seem relevant to them, or use them as your first guinea-pigs in the early stages of designing a questionnaire. But a convenience sample is unlikely to be at all representative of a larger population: the characteristics that make people 'convenient' might also make them unrepresentative. If you intend to generalise to a larger population, using a convenience sample to generate data might be as productive as drunk's search for his keys under the lamp-post.

Consider Chris's interviews with 17 trainers and sponsors of training. When I asked him what, with hindsight, he would have done differently in his research, he replied that one of the things would be the way in which he sampled. What he actually said was:

RESEARCH STORY continued

Reflection and leadership development

'*My selection of interviewees was, in a sense, "opportunistic". Given that I had no guarantee of access to any organisations, however, and had set myself against the clock to meet the first deadline for submission, I felt I had little choice. Now [two* years later] I am aware of sources from which I could construct a much more representative sample (by industry sector, organisation size, turnover, employees, etc).'

Chris's key findings, drawn from his interviews with this 'opportunistic' sample, were carefully phrased. He found that varying degrees of reflection were built into all the programmes his interviewees were involved with, to some extent at least, but improved reflection was an explicit outcome for less than half of the programmes concerned. The ability to reflect was never assessed subsequent to the programme. He concluded that this suggested that there was scope to increase the effectiveness of leadership programmes by paying more attention to developing and supporting reflective skills during and after the programme.

 CONSIDER...

Do you think Chris would have had more confidence in his conclusions if he had sampled more systematically?

It might not have helped at all. Chris did not have time for more interviews. Interviewees were from a range of leading training providers, with some geographic spread in their UK location, and with worldwide coverage in terms of course participants. Any attempt at 'greater representativeness' would have increased the time (and cost) required to arrange interviews. A sample of 17 is so small in relation to the population he is interested in that it is hard to see how it could be much more representative than it was, nor allow stronger conclusions than he drew.

The research would be a useful starting point for further research, perhaps with a different method that allowed a larger sample, or with a narrower focus aiming for representativeness within a much smaller population. I would argue that it was the research questions that were the main problem: they were not appropriate to the resources available. The sample would have been fine for a more exploratory purpose, and this might have been more realistic.

SNOWBALL SAMPLING

A variant of convenience sampling is called 'snowball sampling' by analogy to the way in which a snowball picks up more and more snow as it rolls downhill. In this approach you ask each interviewee to suggest other informants. This allows you to identify relevant people previously unknown to you. And if your interviewee 'recommends' you, it may increase the new person's willingness to take part in your study. You can see that if each interviewee recommended several others, your 'snowball' could grow quite quickly.

Snowballing is fairly common in social research (see Bryman, 1999), and has a number of advantages for some studies. For example, there may be networks that researchers are not part of, and where trust is important. A researcher investigating aspects of drug abuse, say, might find this method extremely useful. It might also be appropriate in a study like the Barcelona IOIS project. As researchers developed their ideas about what they wanted to know, respondents might be able to suggest appropriate informants.

Snowballing is, however, *highly* unrepresentative. It will severely limit the conclusions you can draw about any wider population. But it has its uses in other types of business research. Suppose that Chris had been more interested in finding examples of *how* reflective skills were being successfully developed in some leadership programmes, rather than of *whether* they were. Most of the people he interviewed were paying very little attention to developing reflective skills. But for a few it was really important. They might have been able to put Chris in contact with others who shared their enthusiasm for reflection. I myself met Chris through my own interest in reflection. Networking is largely about finding common interests, and 'snowballing' can use this.

Like other forms of convenience sampling, snowballing has major limitations, particularly in terms of its representativeness. But like them it also has its uses. Rather than rejecting convenience sampling altogether, make sure that you are aware of its limitations, and use it only when the benefits outweigh the disadvantages. Remember, too, to be extremely careful not to make claims or draw conclusions that your data does not support.

RANDOM PROBABILITY SAMPLING

The most obvious way to go about obtaining a representative sample is to pick sample members at random from your population. This is the classic sampling strategy for scientific experimental design. By 'random' I mean that it is pure chance that determines which members are sampled: each member of the population has an equal probability of being selected. If this is done, there is no reason why the sample should be different from the population from which it is drawn. The challenge is to ensure that your sample *is* random.

CONSIDER...

An organisation has a list of its employees in alphabetical order. Would sampling everyone whose surname starts with one of two randomly-chosen letters be random?

If you have a list of employees ordered by staff number, would it be random to take the first 100?

What about using a list of random numbers to select from these staff numbers?

The problem with using random initial letters is that certain surnames are much more common in some parts of the world than others. Thus depending upon the letters you chose, you might obtain a disproportionate number of people from certain cultural backgrounds. If their background was likely to have some influence on the data you obtained from them, your sample would then not be representative of the employees as a whole.

Similarly, staff numbers are seldom allocated at random. Longer-serving staff might have lower numbers. If so, taking the first numbers on the list might mean that you ended up with a highly unrepresentative sample made up of all the longest-serving employees. Some sets of numbers might be allocated to specific categories of staff. Again, taking the first 10% could seriously skew your sample. These examples suggest that you must think carefully when you are sampling 'at random' to ensure that your sample is genuinely random.

Fortunately, random number tables are readily available in statistics books or on the Web to help you to select at random. Arm yourself with such a table. The procedure is then fairly simple (this method is often called simple random sampling).

 Guidelines for using random number tables
- Define the population. What is the set of people or other objects about whom/which you want to draw conclusions? List them. This constitutes your *sampling frame*.
- Allocate a number to every member of your target population. Random number tables tend to have five digits, but you can choose to use only the first or last two or three digits if that provides a large enough number to cover your population. Stick to whichever rule you decide on.
- Take your table and stick in a pin at random. Use the number you land on as your starting point and move systematically through the table. (You can go up, down, or sideways, but again, stick to whatever method you choose.)
- Pick the population member whose number corresponds to the random number you have landed on. If there is no match, move on to the next number until there is. Repeat until you have a sample of the size you want.

CONSIDER...

What reasons might there be to prefer a non-random approach to sampling?

You can see that although random sampling is an excellent approach, it can be fairly laborious in practice, particularly for a large population. It is not surprising that many researchers prefer the 'convenience' method precisely because it *is* so much more convenient.

The other problem is the very randomness of the process. Chance is a funny thing. Suppose you had a bag with 100 balls in it, 20 of them black, the rest white. You put your hand in the bag, and without being able to see what you are doing, pull out 10 balls. There is a high probability that you will get mostly white balls. But sometimes, simply by chance you would get 10 black balls.

This 'sample', resulting from a random probability approach, would be highly unrepresentative of the set of balls as a whole. Similarly, random probability sampling of employees could, even if you use random number tables, produce highly unrepresentative samples. You could still (*very* occasionally) end up with the 25 longest-serving employees in your sample. The possibility of such *sampling error* has to be taken into consideration when working out what your data means. It will be addressed in Chapter 20: inferential statistical techniques have been developed to cope with precisely this.

STRATIFIED RANDOM SAMPLING

One way around this is to use a *stratified* method. If you want your sample to 'represent' certain aspects of the population, you can pre-allocate the appropriate proportions of your sample to individual categories and then sample randomly within those categories. Suppose gender and length of service were important to you. If, say, 70% of employees were female and 50% had worked for two years or less, you might decide to sample randomly from each of the categories in the proportions shown in Table 9.2. The numbers show how many would sample in each category for a sample of 400.

Table 9.2 An example of a stratified sample

Female		Male	
up to two years' service: 35%		up to two years' service: 15%	
sample therefore 140 sample 140		sample therefore 60 sample 60	
more than two years' service: 35%		more than two years' service: 15%	
sample therefore 140 sample 140		sample therefore 60 sample 60	

This is a greatly simplified example, there only to give you a feel for how it works. If you sampled this way, your sample would better represent gender and length of service than a simple random sample. The downside is, of course, that it is more hassle, but in many cases it will be well worth it. Your findings will be more representative and your conclusions more credible as a result. However, you may have to remember that this is not a 'true' random sample when you are doing statistical analysis, because statistical tests tend to assume that your sample *is* random.

CLUSTER (OR MULTISTAGE) SAMPLING

Selecting from the whole population can be a laborious operation. Allocating numbers to thousands of people, or even working through existing numbered staff lists, may not be feasible. Even if you can do it, there may be logistical issues. If you are emailing or phoning, it may not matter where those you select for your sample are located. But if you need to travel to interview or observe, then the scattergun approach of either of the above methods may produce a widely dispersed sample that you cannot afford the time or money to visit. Cluster sampling addresses both these problems.

You select in a series of stages – how many will depend upon the nature of your investigation. At each stage the selection would be random. Thus to sample from a large organisation, you might select perhaps 10 of the 200 sites (if visiting were an issue, you might need to choose fewer). Within each site you might randomly select one department from the six. Within each department you might randomly select 20 staff. This would give you a sample of 200, and the laborious part of selecting from staff lists would be manageable. You would need 10 listings, and each might have no more than 100 staff listed. Furthermore, you would be dealing with only 10 locations if you had to visit to collect data.

Cluster sampling has more stages at which sampling error can creep in. But it is far more likely to produce a representative sample, and hence credible conclusions, than the convenience method.

THEORETICAL SAMPLING

If your aim is to use your sample to learn about a wider population, representativeness of the sample is important, and random probability sampling is frequently the best approach. However, if you are not a positivist, you may doubt the very possibility of such generalisations, and take a deliberately non-random approach to sampling. Theoretical sampling is one such approach, and lies at the core of the inductive Grounded Theory approach. Indeed, it is so central to that method that it is discussed in detail in Chapter 18 rather than here. I mention it here only to remind you that your

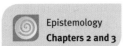
Epistemology
Chapters 2 and 3

epistemology may lead you to a very different approach to sampling: from a constructionist perspective you might choose sample members most likely to add information to what you already have, rather than at random. And you might stop when new informants are adding little new information, rather than because you have reached a specific and predetermined sample size. (Note: do not attempt theoretical sampling without reading Chapter 18 for the full method.)

DRAWING CONCLUSIONS FROM DATA

You collect data to help you answer your research question. If your data is reliable, valid and representative, or you are aware of its limitations, what more is required to enable you to draw valid conclusions? For practical research it is vital that conclusions do not mislead: they can inform major organisational decisions.

Analysis and conclusions
Chapters 18 to 22

Later chapters look at analysis and conclusions in more detail. Here I want to give only enough of an overview for planning purposes. You cannot think sensibly about what data you need unless you understand how you are going to use it to form an *argument* to support *conclusions*. 'Argument' is used here as understood by logicians rather than in its everyday domestic 'Yes you did!', 'No, I didn't!' sense.

A *conclusion* is a view that you come to on the strength of your data. You want others to agree with this view. You therefore need to construct an argument to persuade stake-holders to accept it. It is important that:

- It is clear where the conclusions come from.
- They are substantial – and substantiated.
- They are focused on the research question.
- They take into consideration all the relevant data.
- They make clear the degree of confidence that should be placed in them.

MAKING CLAIMS

An argument starts with a *claim* or *contention* – something you assert to be 'true'. An argument is made up of the *claim* and the reasons for making it. These reasons will be a combination of evidence and reasoning. The conclusion in the following story is an example of a claim: indeed, it actually contains a number of claims.

RESEARCH STORY

Student engagement

This is an on-going exploration of the issues of 'student engagement' on an MBA. We are interested in whether a change in approach to teaching might allow students to 'engage' better with what they learned and their own practice, and as a result do a better practical research project, and become more effective managers.

We have read many published reports in journals on management learning dealing with aspects of professional and practice-based learning including management teaching.

We conducted a number of focus groups with tutors, students and alumni, and discussed the significance of findings from these with key groups of relevant academics. Selected groups of tutors worked online to explore the issue from their perspective.

We looked at student reports on their final investigations and tutors' comments on these and the marks received, and at online discussions between tutors and students, and between students themselves. We also analysed assignment questions for all MBA courses.

As a result we concluded the following:

> We need to move the emphasis in teaching and assessment from teaching 'theory' as if its content is paramount towards an emphasis on helping managers select and use theory to improve their ways of thinking and their professional practice: this is our real goal.

Some academic colleagues are likely to be highly sceptical of this conclusion. Imagine that you were helping me to construct a case to convince them. A useful first step is to analyse the conclusion.

 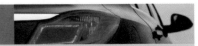
This conclusion is no more complicated than many of the 'claims' made in business research reports, but when you start to analyse it you can see that there are surprisingly many claims made in this single statement. Some are implicit, some explicit. I have listed eight, although you may see more.

- We currently teach theory as if content were paramount.
- The content of theory is not paramount.
- This is not how we should be teaching.
- The role of theory is to help managers think better.
- Theory-informed thinking leads to better management practice.
- We should be teaching managers to use theory to think better.
- We should be teaching managers to select appropriate theory.
- The real goal of management teaching is to improve management practice.

The following illustration shows how these claims might be refuted. The responses are a mix of *counter-claims*, claims to something different, and questioning of my right to claim. Some of the counter-claims include a supporting argument, some imply one. There are also some other responses. It might be tempting to dismiss some of the responses as 'rubbish', but these are all stakeholders and they can influence the success of subsequent action. Remember the pragmatist position, that different 'doubters' may require different evidence to be convinced.

RESEARCH STORY continued

Claims, counter-claims and other responses

The following shows some of the actual (and potential) responses to the claims above.

We currently teach theory as if content were paramount.

> – No, we don't: we insist that students apply theory.

The content of theory is not paramount.

> – But it is. If students don't know the theory, they don't deserve an MBA!

This is not how we should be teaching.

> – Who are you to tell me how I should be teaching?
> – Yes, it is how we should be teaching: it is what business schools do.
> – Yes, it is. I have always taught this way and I get really high pass rates.
> – Yes, it is. I have always taught this way and students are happy.

The role of theory is to help managers think better.

> – Come on! All the research shows that managers don't have time to think.
> – The role of theory is to help increase knowledge.

Theory-informed thinking leads to better management practice.

> – *How do you know this?*

We should be teaching managers to use theory to think better.

> – *We do already.*
> – *It isn't my job to teach managers to think. They are managers and graduates, and so should be able to do that already.*
> – *This isn't the role of theory.*

We should be teaching managers to select appropriate theory.

> – *If they know it properly, they'll know when to use it.*

> – *No, we shouldn't. See my earlier answers.*
> – *This isn't something you can teach.*

The real goal of management teaching is to improve management practice.

> – *No, it isn't. The real goal is education.*
> – *No, it isn't. I'm not here to prop up the capitalist system.*
> – *What do you mean 'improve'?*

You can see how a seemingly simple conclusion includes a great many claims, each of which offers scope for disagreement. Some of these 'refutations' may miss the point, from my perspective. Some may seem illogical. Some are important questions deserving an answer. I'll leave it to you to classify them, if you wish. But if you want to build an argument that will make your claims stick, you must go through a similar process of anticipating such reactions. This will help you to identify the data and arguments that will pre-empt such reactions. If you do this, your conclusions will be convincing and credible.

CHECKING CLAIMS

The above exercise should have shown the need for thinking carefully about the claims you make. The first thing to check is that a claim is *necessary*. All claims could be challenged, and by refuting one claim, your client is likely to think they have destroyed your entire argument. It therefore makes sense to exclude any claims that are *not* essential for your argument. For example, the final claim above did not have to be stated so strongly.

The claim that *anything* is 'the real goal' of teaching is almost impossible to justify. This point is particularly important because without some agreement about goals, agreement on the best way of achieving them is highly unlikely. There is little hope of gaining agreement to the 'real purpose', particularly as views are likely to be influenced by values, which are notoriously resistant to logic. However, a weaker claim along the lines that 'one purpose' or 'one potential valuable benefit' of management teaching is improved professional and/or organisational practice would be far less contentious.

Make only claims that are necessary to your conclusions.

Relevant potential evidence to support this weaker claim might include published research on management teaching (likely to be acceptable to an academic audience), primary and secondary data from our own past and current students about reasons for study, and surveys carried out elsewhere.

As well as claiming only what is necessary, and what you can justify, you must separate important but unrelated claims so that any doubts about one do not affect the others.

CONSTRUCTING AN ARGUMENT

Once you have thought carefully about the claims you wish to make, you can proceed to build an argument. To construct an argument to support a claim or contention you need evidence to support the claim, and reasoning to link the evidence to the claim. There are different sorts of logical links that you can use. Call your claim C and your evidence E. These links might then be in the form:

> E proves C.
>
> E suggests that C is likely.
>
> E is consistent with C.
>
> E is inconsistent with C.
>
> E suggests that C is unlikely.
>
> E disproves C.

These terms must be used with caution. 'Proof' and 'disproof' are fairly rare in practical business research. Very few things in business research can be 'proved' or 'disproved': you are far more likely to be using links related to consistency or suggestion. It is important that your conclusions do not claim more than the strength of the links warrants. Note that although consistency is a weaker link than suggestion, inconsistency may seem a stronger one than a suggestion to the contrary. However, when you are dealing with weak indicators, inconsistency is not uncommon.

Correlation does not imply causality

Correlation
Chapter 21

One particular hazard here relates to the difference between association and causality. Take a typical business research project quoted by Saunders *et al* (2003) on appraisal. Their student found that a poor performance appraisal rating was associated with negative feelings about the appraisal process. She could not tell from this finding alone whether a poor attitude to appraisal led to a poor rating, or a poor rating led to negative feelings about the process which generated it. Indeed, the appraisee might have felt negative about everything to do with the organisation, as a result of which he both performed poorly (generating a poor performance rating) and felt as negative about appraisal as he did about everything else at work. The association observed is *consistent* with a claim that poor attitude causes a poor appraisal, but does not by itself even *suggest* this causality.

You must also be particularly careful about the logical links you make when your evidence is derived from indicators rather than measures. Indicators may provide only weak evidence, consistency rather than suggestion, perhaps.

Mapping arguments

A simple argument consists of a single claim and supporting evidence. In a complex argument you may have evidence supporting a sub-claim which is itself evidence for a higher claim. (The claims identified above support the main conclusion.) You may need several layers of sub-claims.

When you are trying to sort out a complex argument it can therefore be helpful to map it. The thought processes are very similar to those used in a multiple-cause map: you start at the top and work back. But here the connectors are not arrows but lines. The vertical dimension indicates direction. The evidence is shown below the claim. You have to identify the claims you are making, the evidence that supports them, and the nature of links. Figure 9.1 shows part of an argument for the claim about management teaching.

The logical process is relatively straightforward: the difficulties arise when you have a mass of data consisting of indicators rather than measures. It can be extremely useful to start mapping your data as you collect it, seeing how arguments can be developed, and where evidence is weak and has to be supplemented. This is particularly important when using qualitative data but can be useful when you are using quantitiative data as evidence. If you leave thinking about conclusions and supporting evidence until after data collection is complete, you may not have time to fill any gaps that become apparent.

Figure 9.1 Part of an argument map in relation to management teaching

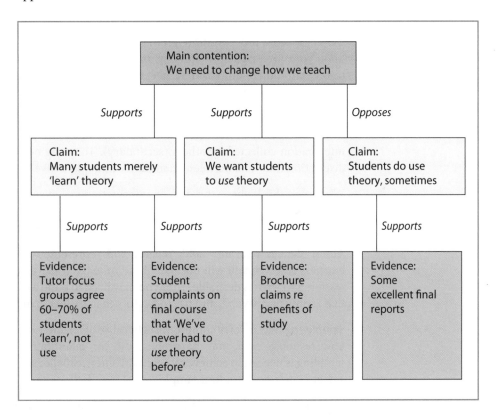

 ACTIVITY

Take one or two papers relevant to your project that you have already read carefully and map the claims, evidence and logical links involved.

Key points

- Conclusions are claims that you make, based on your data.

- You need to develop an argument in which you make clear the evidence upon which your claims are based, and the logical link between claim and evidence.

- Some evidence may itself be a supported claim.

- Argument mapping allows you to clarify your arguments and identify any weak links or unsupported claims.

- It can be useful when you are critically reviewing literature.

SUMMARY

Data consist of 'facts'. The collection of such 'facts' lies at the heart of any classic research process, although the nature of 'facts' is debated and depends upon your preferred epistemology. *Information* consists of data that helps to resolve your uncertainty with respect to something of interest to you. *Evidence* consists of information that will help you to draw conclusions that will inform decisions and/or action.

Information may be collected by yourself (primary) or you may draw upon information collected by others (secondary). This may be a more important distinction than that between quantitative and qualitative methods.

When you think about the data or information you need, it is important to think in parallel about how you will analyse the data or information in order to reach a conclusion in relation to your overall research question or purpose.

'Good' data is relevant, valid, reliable and representative. But in practical business research you will normally have to make trade-offs between what is feasible and what is desirable. Thus you may need to build a case upon evidence that is only partly valid, and use indicators that are less than perfectly reliable.

Sample size may involve compromises because of resource or other constraints. Low response rates may be problematic for quantitative studies. Careful sampling is needed to achieve representativeness. Smaller samples may require a deliberately non-random sample.

Conclusions must acknowledge limitations of sample size or the data used. Arguments to support your claims must be robust. Argument mapping can help you think clearly about your claims and how the evidence supports them.

REVIEW QUESTIONS

1. Why might it be unhelpful to classify methods as 'quantitative' or 'qualitative'?

2. What are the key criteria for good quantitative data?

3. How might the criteria for evaluating qualitative data differ from those for qualitative?

4. What must you avoid when drawing conclusions from qualitative interview data?

5. Why is it important to think about data analysis at the same time as you think about data collection?

6. When deciding on sample size, what factors must you take into account?

7. Why is response rate important, and what can you do to increase it?

8. What are the advantages and disadvantages of a 'snowball' approach to sampling, and when might it be most appropriate?

9. What might you be seeking to achieve in constructing your sample for a study with the purpose of increasing your understanding of the idea of 'leadership' within a specific organisation?

10. How might the required sample differ if your aim was to identify characteristics of successful leaders in a specific industry?

11. What is a claim, and why is it helpful to map the claims in any argument you are deriving from your data?

12. Why is it advisable to restrict your concluding claims to those which are essential to your argument and purpose?

EXPLORE FURTHER

Deming, W. E. (1960, reprinted 1990) *Sample Design in Business Research*. London: John Wiley. This is still well worth reading for sampling theory

Marshall, C. and Rossman, G. (2006) *Designing Qualitative Research*, 4th edition. London: Sage.

http://austhink.com/reason/tutorials/ . Provides an excellent series of short tutorials on mapping arguments

http://www.coventry.ac.uk/ec/~nhunt/meths/ss.html for a concise overview of sampling methods and selected spreadsheets which allow you to experiment with different samples

Visit www.cipd.co.uk/brm for web links, templates, activities and other useful resources relating to this chapter.

CHAPTER 10

Choosing a Research Method

INTRODUCTION

Once you have identified a topic, refined your research question and thought about the sort of data that would help you to answer it, you have to think seriously about your choice of data-collection method. Choosing appropriate research methods may present a substantial challenge if you are a new researcher. The literature on methods is full of unfamiliar language that you have to translate into practice, and the prospects of doing this can be daunting. Choosing an appropriate method depends on an understanding of what each method has to offer; what it can do and what it cannot do, and what type of research findings it will produce. These issues must be considered in the context of your specific project – alongside your research purpose, the demands of your stakeholders, the context of your research and the limitations of resources and skills.

This chapter explores how these factors must influence your choice of research method(s), and provides you with a brief overview of the main approaches and methods used in business research. The approaches considered are Case Studies, Grounded Theory and Action Research. The methods introduced are questionnaires, interviews, focus groups and observations. A series of questions is suggested: if you answer them in relation to your own research ideas, it will help you to identify the methods mostly likely to help you to produce the desired results. You can then find more detail in Part 3 of this book, where the most commonly used approaches and methods are explored in more depth.

LEARNING OUTCOMES

This chapter should enable you to:

• recognise the factors that must be considered before deciding on a research method

• judge the relative importance of each of these factors for your own research

• identify the strengths and the limitations of a range of research methods and select the most appropriate for your particular research.

Thus far in the research process you have thought about devising your research question and exploring the literature. You have also thought about different sorts of data and evidence, and some of the general issues relating to what makes data useful or less so. To make an informed decision on how best to gather and analyse your data, you will have to draw on the literature on research methods in order to identify the approach most likely to answer your research question. In selecting your research method, you must also consider a range of contextual issues:

- about your research
- about the literature
- about the context of your research
- about yourself.

First, and most important, is the nature and purpose of your research.

ABOUT YOUR RESEARCH

Your research is likely to be defined by three things: a central theme, a means of investigation, and a location (Figure 10.1). These would normally be reflected in the title of your project or dissertation. I shall start by considering the means of investigation and the location. The central theme is dealt with later, when considering the literature.

Figure 10.1 Considering your research

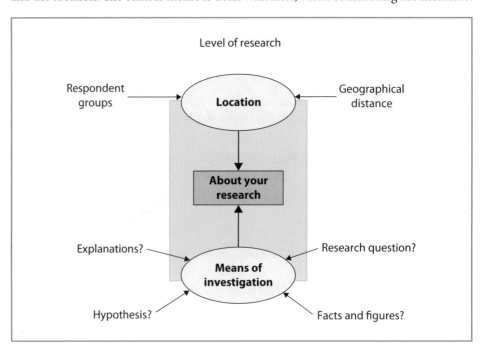

The means of investigation

By articulating the means of investigation in your research purpose, you set down exactly what it is that you want to do: this guides your choice of method. If you are trying to test a hypothesis or to identify the relationship that exists between two or more variables, the nature of your research will direct you towards quantitative/statistical methods. Alternatively, where you are seeking to explain rather than test, you may need a depth of description and discussion that cannot be gleaned from quantitative data. If so, you will have to consider methods that generate qualitative data.

Although this seems to indicate a clear divide between quantitative and qualitative data and approaches, in practice business research often requires elements of both – statistics to demonstrate the significance of a problem and narrative data to explain why it exists or what can be done about it. In such situations mixed methods (using both quantitative and qualitative methods) or a case study approach would enable you to gather the breadth and the depth of data required and help you to meet the needs of the different stakeholder groups.

The location

The next issue to consider is the location for your research. This has a range of implications for the approach needed and the feasibility of different methods. For example, research aimed at industry level might involve a huge population: you would simply not have the time or the resources to access a representative sample. So if you were planning to use a quantitative analysis, you would have to consider what impact the non-representative sample would have on your ability to generalise the results. If your research requires you to speak to the CEOs of major international corporations, you may find that they are willing to answer a short questionnaire but not willing to spend two hours being interviewed. If your research involves speaking to remotely based sales staff or people overseas, you might have to seek alternative methods to traditional face-to-face or focus group interviews.

ACTIVITY

Make notes about how the means of investigation and the location of your own research direct you towards or away from particular research methods. Keep these notes to hand, because you will revisit them as you become more familiar with the details of different methods.

ABOUT THE LITERATURE

The literature you have read thus far will have given you a useful indication of the nature of the research methods that you might use:

- the favoured approaches
- the choices from the range available
- the limitations of certain methods
- the resources required.

If your research is part of an academic programme of study, it is useful to try to identify the 'favoured' approaches in the literature. Favoured approaches are those that are deemed acceptable and appropriate within that particular discipline. Some disciplines tend towards quantitative approaches, others towards qualitative approaches. The approaches reflect the underlying philosophy of the discipline in question. This is important: if your research uses an approach that is deemed unacceptable to the discipline, it will be very difficult (and involve heated conceptual and philosophical debates) to demonstrate the credibility of your research.

> **A review of the literature should be used to inform the selection of your research method.**

If your research is part of a consultancy assignment or a work-based project, it may be worth replicating the methods used by renowned practitioners or academics because it may improve the credibility of your own research. However, there is a caveat here in that the methods must fit with your research. Where methods have been copied without proper consideration over whether they are appropriate or not, the result is bound to be poor research which lacks any credibility at all.

Reading the literature can give you a good idea of the range of methods available to you. Reading academic journals, professional journals and secondary data from within your own organisation will indicate the methods used to collect data, the sampling strategy used, the ways in which the data was analysed and the types of research findings that the data produced. These issues should frame your thinking – but you must also consider whether you have the time, the resources and the skills to do the same thing.

Reading the literature helps you to recognise the limitations of certain methods. Academic journal articles often discuss the limitations of their research, including the methods used. Professional journals are less inclined to do this, but the limitations can often be discerned from their suggestions for future research.

 CONSIDER...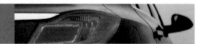

Think about your own research idea and jot down the ways in which your understanding of the literature encourages you to think about certain research methods.

ABOUT THE CONTEXT OF YOUR RESEARCH

Stakeholders, as we have seen, can frustrate or facilitate your research. They can also direct you to undertake your research in very particular ways. Where their demands are for verifiable facts and figures, for numbers that indicate trends, or for statistics that demonstrate relationships, your research will have to use quantitative methods that are able to produce these types of research findings. You will have to gather data in ways sympathetic to the need for quantitative analyses, and may have to learn new skills or use new software systems to help you in the analysis. Where stakeholders seek explanations, reasons why a problem exists and/or ideas about potential solutions, qualitative methods are more likely to generate the rich narrative data needed. Demands from stakeholders also create demands for resources.

Quantitative analyses may mean that you have to gain access to new technologies. Demands for generalisable results may mean that you have to access databases to get contact details or spend more on the production and distribution of hard-copy questionnaires. Time is also a resource that you must consider. Questionnaires may be less draining on your own time but can be accused of limiting the richness of the data gathered. Interviews allow for that richness but make significant demands on you in terms of organising, running and transcribing. The research methods chosen must reflect a balance between answering your research question in the best way possible and choosing a means of doing so that is feasible.

ABOUT YOURSELF

You too are a stakeholder in your research. You must therefore think about the ways in which *you* place demands or constraints on the research that you are planning to undertake – notably:

- your motives
- your skills, current and required
- your support networks
- the time available.

Thinking about your motives for the research is important. If you wish to develop new skills, you might be tempted to experiment with research methods that are new to you (recognising the risks associated with doing this); if you are trying to provide evidence of how to improve efficiency, you should consider how quantitative data could help you demonstrate this; if you are seeking to offer solutions to a problem, qualitative data might enable you to do it more effectively than pure numbers. Likewise, if you are trying to meet the demands of a range of stakeholders, mixed methods which allow you to speak to each of the groups may be a better choice for you.

These choices, however, are not made based simply on your motives. There is a need to consider the skills required, the time it would take you to acquire new skills, the support networks you have and how these could help and what actually interests you. All of these issues should be used to guide your choice of a research method.

> **It is important to think about the context of your research and your personal skills, abilities and resources when considering your approach to research.**

Rather than suggest the answers you might have come up with, the following research story is offered as a possible way of approaching the issues outlined above.

RESEARCH STORY

Enzo and the Internet

Enzo works for a small chain of electrical retailers and for his research project he and his boss have decided that it would be useful to assess the feasibility of introducing Internet sales to support the traditional retail outlets that they have at present. In starting to think about possible research methods, Enzo's thinking is as follows:

About the research question:

Am I trying to demonstrate something?

Yes – I need to know as accurately as possible whether or not it is feasible to introduce an Internet-based shopping service, so I will need solid data, facts and figures to support this.

Am I trying to explore something?

Yes. I must give my boss a well-reasoned argument that explains the reasons why people do or do not want to use this service. He will want a proper business case, not just a few figures.

What is my level of analysis?

My research is only looking at my organisation and so I should be able to get a reasonable sample size (once I have worked out what this is), and it should make access quite easy as well.

Who are my respondent group(s)?

I suppose the easiest answer is the company's customers, but the aim also is to see if new customers would use the Internet for purchases if this were available – so I suppose I am looking for some responses from people who are not our current customers.

About the literature:

What are the most common approaches?

People seem to use a market-research approach in which they use a semi-structured questionnaire which they talk through with people.

What methods of data collection are used?

Quite a few, really: Internet questionnaires, face-to-face interviews, self-assessment questionnaires and face-to-face surveys. Not many people use focus groups.

What methods of data analysis are used?

Lots of descriptive statistics, but very few people try to predict what the market take-up of a new service will be. Some qualitative data is analysed by content, some others just seem to move the odd quote across, which seems a bit odd.

What skills and resources do I have?

I should be able to design a semi-structured questionnaire which I can go through with people. I think I should have the interview skills necessary because the open sections will only be quite small – it is not as though I am directing a whole two-hour interview. Time might be a problem if I have to survey a lot of people – which I think I may need to.

Would the approaches from the literature be acceptable to my stakeholders?

Much of the information I need comes from the professional marketing literature, which has a very practical flavour to it. Because of this the approaches they adopt would meet the needs of my stakeholders.

About the context:

What are the stakeholders' demands?

The stakeholders are the managers within my organisation. They want me to produce a robust business case which argues for or against introducing the Internet shopping service. I must have a balance between facts and figures, and explanations of the reasons behind them.

What are the time limits?

The plan is that I present my preliminary findings in six months' time, and will then get some feedback on them before I present them to a board meeting in nine months' time.

What are the resource constraints?

Now I have gone through these questions I am becoming increasingly aware of the time it will take to go through the face-to-face semi-structured questionnaires with people. I might have to get some help from the sales staff.

About me:

What is the motive for my research?

My boss asked me to do this and I think it reflects his faith in me and the fact that he thinks I have the potential to be a manager myself. Accordingly, I want to do a really good job to show him that his faith in me is justified and to show other managers what I am capable of.

What are my strengths and limitations?

I have a clear idea of what I want to do and have read lots about the subject from both the professional journals and the marketing literature. I have the skills to design the data-gathering and the skills to do both quantitative and qualitative analyses as long as I don't try to produce predictive statistics (or even worse, pretend that my statistics are predictive). Time is a real limitation and I will have to get some help to gather the data.

What support/advice systems do I have?

My manager is really supportive and has asked the rest of the team to help me out where necessary. Because I am a member of the Chartered Institute of Marketing I can use their library and draw on resources from there as well.

KEY POINTS

When thinking about business research methods you should give clear consideration to:

- the nature of your research – you must be absolutely clear about what it is that you are trying to do
- the nature of the literature – learn from the examples presented by others undertaking research in the same areas
- the context of your research – which environmental factors will influence your choice, and how can you account for them?
- yourself – what skills, competences, resources and access to support do you have?

COMMON APPROACHES TO BUSINESS RESEARCH

Although the questions in the Research Story above give you a general sense of direction in terms of choosing a research method, you cannot choose a specific method unless you understand at least something about what that method allows you to do. You must also check that other methods would not do it better. To help you to think about this more clearly, the rest of this chapter has been structured to give you an understanding of some of the over-arching approaches to research. These are frameworks within which single or multiple methods of data-gathering can be used. Accordingly, the chapter then considers these methods of data-gathering. Lastly, it considers the different uses of multi-method research. To help you to visualise how all these things relate to each other, the checklist below summarises the three overlapping elements.

Approaches, data-gathering techniques and analysis methods

Approaches to research
- Case study approach
- Grounded Theory approach
- Action Research approach

Data-gathering techniques
- Questionnaires
- Interviews
- Focus groups
- Observations

Methods of analysis
- Descriptive statistics
- Inferential statistics
- Content coding analysis
- Discourse analysis

CASE STUDY RESEARCH

 Case study research
Chapter 13

Many issues in organisations cannot be disentangled from their context. For example, it is impossible to fully understand some aspects of budgetary control in isolation from issues of management style and control and the culture of the organisation. The term 'case study' is used to describe an approach that recognises and explores these interconnectivities within the context. This means something completely different from 'any project that happens to be conducted in a single organisation'. Case studies inevitably require the use of multiple methods for data collection:

- questionnaires
- interviews
- focus groups
- observations

or data collected in multiple areas of the organisation to allow them to draw on the relationship between research and context. Likewise, the use of multiple case studies offers a means of making wider comparisons of the relationship between the two.

What can it do?

A case study will allow you to understand the particular case in depth. This broader approach can give you a much better understanding of why issues have arisen, and of the connected aspects that you might need to consider when suggesting a course of action. It will help you to recognise the range of elements in a 'mess' (Ackoff, 1971) and will help prevent you from offering over-simplified solutions.

A case study is best used when the problems being considered are complex and an integral part of the wider organisation. It is useful where you are seeking to answer 'how?' or 'why?' questions rather than those phrased as 'what?' Where multiple case studies are used there is the opportunity for cross-organisational or inter-organisational comparisons.

What data will it produce?

A case study is an approach to research rather than a particular method of data collection. The data it will produce will depend on the methods chosen. However, within the frame of a case study it is important to think how the data gathered and the research findings generated from a range of different methods can be synthesised into one coherent commentary in the conclusions drawn.

What are the limitations of case study research?

A case study is not a useful approach where there is a single theme research question that can be answered by a unitary approach to research. It is not useful when the data required can better be gathered outside the context of the organisation (for example, market growth rates), and it is not useful where the demands of the stakeholders are for positivistic research to be delivered within a short time-frame.

Likewise, the integrative nature of a case study can make it quite difficult to know when the data-gathering should stop. As connections between themes emerge there can be a temptation to carry on gathering more and more data until any sense of what the researcher was looking at in the first place is lost.

GROUNDED THEORY

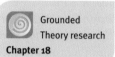

Grounded Theory research

Chapter 18

Although many business researchers claim to be using Grounded Theory, a failure to understand the complexities associated with the approach mean that what is produced is often a simple content coding approach rather than Grounded Theory in its purest form. Grounded Theory is based on the view that to understand something you have to start with observations, not literature: the observations should drive the theory rather than the reverse. Starting with the theory means that you start with a particular set of 'conceptual spectacles' that are liable to at best frame and at worst distort or obscure what is happening. A Grounded Theory approach avoids this framing of data by *not* reviewing the literature first, instead starting the research with just a vague and generic research question. The research question then presents people with a theme from which they develop the discussions in whichever direction they choose.

There is no predetermined list of questions in a grounded theory interview, no plan to raise specific themes and no list of things that the interview is intended to achieve. And it is not unusual to use a range of different methods of data-gathering:

- interviews
- focus groups
- observations

This 'emergent' approach to data-gathering is reflected in an emergent approach to sampling. Rather than deciding beforehand which people it would be useful to speak to, the researcher is guided by the results of the previous interview(s). This approach is known as theoretical sampling (Glaser and Strauss, 1967). Because the approach is so specific to Grounded Theory, it is considered in more depth in Chapter 18 rather than with other sampling strategies in Chapter 8.

The analysis of the data reflects this emergent approach. Rather than have a list of words/contents that the researcher searches for, and rather than collect all the data sets together and analyse these *en masse*, Grounded Theorists advocate that analysis be done by constant comparison. In this way, the analysis is taking place at the same time as the interview process, by recalling previous interviews while conducting the present one, and by revisiting the data previously collected. Research based on Grounded Theory concludes by reviewing the literature and seeing how the data derived can be seen as supporting or contradicting the views of other writers in the field.

What can it do?

A Grounded Theory approach can produce data that is genuinely driven by the views and opinions of the participants. It reflects *their* concerns, explanations and opinions, rather than those of the researcher or the literature. A Grounded Theory approach can provide a depth of rich information drawn from the feelings, the attitudes, the attributes and the behaviours of the participants – which can be seen as a more genuine reflection of what is happening within the organisation. It may surface issues not previously considered or suggest insights not provided by pre-existing theoretical frameworks.

What data will it produce?

Although it is possible to produce quantitative data, in practice this is highly unlikely, and would be dependent on a very particular type of organisation and research focus. A Grounded Theory approach can produce a wide range of qualitative data. Narrative data from interviews, open-text data from semi-structured questionnaires and observational data are frequently collected and used. Again, where many different types of data are produced the researcher must consider how to synthesise them to produce coherent research findings.

What are the limitations?

Grounded Theory is less useful where you want to answer a specific research question or where you need to provide evidence based on facts and figures. It can also be problematic if you are limited by time or by resources. Its non-traditional nature may also be problematic for stakeholders, both organisational and academic. Both groups often require a clear action plan in your research proposal – in addition, supervisors, managers and ethics committees will require a clear research question. Either is inconsistent with a Grounded Theory approach.

ACTION RESEARCH

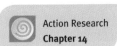 Action Research
Chapter 14

Action research is an approach which is centred on the idea that research should contribute to making a difference to practice. It should help to bring about change. This idea of bringing about change has a number of implications for the nature of the research and for the researchers themselves. A fundamental tenet which underpins Action Research is that change is not linear, that successful change is less about moving logically from point A to point Z and more about going around in a series of incremental loops. The stages in these loops advocate diagnosis which feeds into a plan of action, a plan of action which feeds the action itself, action taken which is then evaluated, and further diagnosis in the light of the evaluation. The process is iterative and integrated: each of these stages can be a part of one element of the research process, part of the literature review or part of the data-gathering processes.

The iterative process of Action Research is underpinned by the idea that the researcher is also part of the research. The multiple ways in which the researcher gathers the data:

- interviews
- questionnaires

- focus groups

- observations

and analyses it are reflections of the ways in which the researcher frames the problem. Moreover, the ways in which the researcher structures the research, the types of questions that they ask and of whom, will also have an impact on the ultimate success of the change. Here, Action Research draws attention to the ways in which researchers can create a sense of ownership and participation in the change on the part of the respondents, or can create a sense of isolation and of change being done to them. Action Research then argues that the researcher is not simply there to diagnose and suggest action but that the things that they do determine the success or failure of that action.

What can it do?

Action Research can help you to produce practical solutions to real-world business problems. Moreover, these solutions are based on the insights and ideas of people who are intimately involved in the situation. Action Research helps the researcher to appreciate multiple and possibly conflicting views of the situation, and it encourages you and your co-researchers to think how and why situations are viewed in a particular way. It also allows space for you as the researcher to consider your own role in bringing about any change, to reflect on why you have positioned your research in a particular way and to think about how it might presuppose a particular set of results.

What data will it produce?

Action Research does not prescribe any particular methods of data-gathering or analysis. In much the same way as a case study approach, Action Research provides a framework within which the research takes place. The framework here is premised on the need to achieve practical outcomes from an iterative process which involves reflection and insight. The data produced will depend on the ways in which the researcher chooses to gather what he or she needs. However, the nature of reflection, of insights and of an iterative process which seeks to suggest action means that qualitative data is favoured over quantitative in many academic reports of such research.

What are the limitations?

The limitations of Action Research are centred on the complexity of the process and the extent to which it normally involves a number of participants in the research. The iterative process is useful in that it helps you to feed new insights and new under-standings into the process, but it may be hard to know when to stop. And if you are writing a dissertation, you do need at some point to stop. The issue of reflection and gaining insights into why people adopt particular positions can also be problematic. There is the possibility that venturing into the realms of reflection could steer the research too far away from the original practical focus. The process of constantly reviewing and reflecting can be extremely time-consuming. This has implications for the time-frame within which you complete your research project and for those partici-pating in the research.

DATA-GATHERING TECHNIQUES

QUESTIONNAIRES

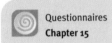
Questionnaires
Chapter 15

Questionnaires are a potentially cost-effective means of gathering large amounts of data. Electronic distribution reduces the financial and the environmental costs of producing and sending the questionnaires, and there are software packages available that can help the researcher to analyse the data. However, designing a good questionnaire is difficult, and even with a well-designed questionnaire, a researcher must have a good understanding of who the respondents are and of how to get these people to take time to complete the questionnaire.

What can they do?

A questionnaire can allow you to gather data relatively cheaply from a large group of people. It allows you to integrate the collection of quantitative and qualitative data through one means of data-gathering and can be given to people to complete on their own or can be used on a face-to-face basis.

What data will they produce?

The data gathered will depend on the content and structure of the questionnaires you use. Structured questionnaires gather quantitative data which can be used to produce descriptive and/or inferential statistical data. Semi-structured questionnaires gather a mix of qualitative and quantitative data, the proportions of which will depend on your research. At one extreme the questionnaire may present predominantly closed questions with a short open comments section at the end. At the other extreme the only quantitative data gathered may be demographic details. Open questionnaires gather free-form data. Because the respondent decides what he or she will and will not talk about, they are generally a high-risk strategy unless associated with a Grounded Theory approach. Depending on the nature of the data gathered, it can be analysed by using:

- descriptive statistics
- inferential statistics
- content coding analysis
- discourse analysis.

What are the limitations?

Questionnaires are quite difficult to design, so it is important to do a pilot study. Unless you have access to electronic distribution systems, the costs of postal questionnaires can be significant. Response rates are often unpredictable and may be very low, as a result of which you might not obtain enough data. In addition, analysing open answers may be extremely time-consuming.

INTERVIEWS

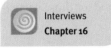
Interviews
Chapter 16

Because people are familiar with questionnaires, they are a very popular method of data-gathering, but beyond this, interviews can produce incredibly rich and illuminating data and can be used to gather both qualitative and quantitative data.

What can interviews do?

Interviews give you a degree of flexibility and adaptability that it is difficult to replicate using other methods. They allow you to re-word questions, to draw out discussions or to go through the questions out of sequence if that is the way in which the discussions develop. The whole process is more natural, akin to having a conversation.

The idea that you have selected someone to be interviewed demonstrates that you value what it is they have to say. This alongside the 'conversational' ambience makes people more willing to disclose things that they might be reluctant to put in writing on a questionnaire. Interviews also allow you to explore meanings rather than simply accept answers. The interactive nature means you can ask the respondent to elaborate, explain or clarify what they have said.

Lastly, interviews give the business researcher extracts of text that can be used to support or illustrate the research findings. A report presented to line managers is often richer if the researcher can include some actual quotations from the people who took part in the research.

What data will interviews produce?

Although often associated with qualitative data, interviews can be used to gather quantitative data. Structured questions which allow respondents to choose only between a limited range of answers can produce numerical data for statistical analysis. However, if using interviews to gather quantitative data as part of business research, it is important not to lose sight of the issues of the sample size. If you need data that is generalisable to the wider population or is of statistical significance, then interviews might be seen as an incredibly labour-intensive way of gathering such data. Depending on the nature of the data gathered, interview data can be analysed by using:

- descriptive statistics
- inferential statistics
- content coding analysis
- discourse analysis.

What are the limitations of interviews?

Interviews are really *very* time-consuming. You have to spend time devising the questions, negotiating access to people, arranging and travelling to the venue, running and recording the interview and allowing time for the transcription (as a general rule of thumb, transcribing an interview takes about four times as long as the interview itself). A brief calculation would mean that for every one-hour interview that you do, you should allow at least six hours plus travelling time!

Interviewing people requires a range of highly refined communication skills, from encouraging people to speak through to guiding them with regard to what they should be speaking about. Without these skills the interview runs the risk of drifting away from the key themes.

CONSIDER...

Imagine you are interviewing your boss. You have an hour to interview him/her but are aware of the fact that for the last 15 minutes he/she has spoken about nothing but his/her recent holiday. How would you politely say, 'I'm sure your holiday was very nice – but will you please answer my questions because I am running out of time'?

Directing an interview, particularly with someone senior to you, is not easy. Interviewees have no obligation to answer your questions – but your research does to a greater or lesser degree depend on them cooperating.

Interviews most commonly produce qualitative data in the form of a narrative. This then has to be carefully analysed, which again requires substantial skill and is highly time-consuming. The credibility of the data can be a limitation with some stakeholders. Where the pressure is to produce research findings that are essentially positivist – based on quantitative data – the use of interviews may be inappropriate. Even when interviews are used to gather quantitative data, there is still a need to consider the issues of sample size and ensuring statistical significance, as mentioned previously.

FOCUS GROUPS

Focus groups
Chapter 16

Many of the strengths and limitations considered in the previous section on interviews apply to using focus groups. Their strengths relate to the depth of data that can be gathered; their limitations crystallise the problems associated with qualitative data and are compounded by the need for a robust skill set. However, there are some unique points that relate to the use of focus groups.

What can focus groups do?

Focus groups allow for the collective exploration of themes and issues. The researcher prompts the group to discuss and explore, and discovers what is important to them in relation to the topic of interest to the researcher. This dialogue will expose differences in opinion and perspective that may be of interest to the researcher.

If competently run, focus groups can minimise the impact and influence of the researcher. Rather than interact on a one-to-one level, the researcher simply presents the issues to the group who then develop their discussions around the theme.

Focus groups also allow you to identify areas of agreement and of disagreement. The collective discussions often reveal areas of tension and conflict as well as areas of agreement and consensus.

Lastly, focus groups give the researcher the opportunity to observe the dynamics of the process. Being able to watch a group of people as they express their opinions and listen to those of others, as they argue for their own perspectives or withdraw from the discussions, allows the researcher to perceive the political and social interactions that take place.

What data can focus groups produce?

Focus groups can be used to gather both qualitative and quantitative data, but the gathering of quantitative data is slightly more problematic here. Getting consensus from the group may be difficult, and if the researcher divides the group into individual members and asks them each in turn, it changes the research method from a focus group to a group interview. The two are not the same – the latter is more akin to a set of individual interviews which happen to take place at the same time. A focus group is premised on integrative rather than individual discussions. Depending on the nature of the data gathered, focus group data can be analysed by using:

- descriptive statistics
- content coding analysis
- discourse analysis.

What are the limitations of focus groups?

Using focus groups is very time-consuming. The co-ordinating processes are complicated by the number of people involved and the work of transcription takes longer because of the number of different voices involved. The involvement of many people also increases the level of communication skills needed by the interviewer. Rather than controlling a single interaction, the interviewer has to control a complex social and political dynamic, to make sure that everyone has the chance to contribute, that specific individuals do not dominate and that the group discussions coalesce around the main themes – there is the potential for eight people to compare notes about their holidays!

Although perhaps more of a caveat than a limitation, the social and political structure of the group is also an important consideration. There must be a careful selection of focus group members – people who are able to speak about the issues being discussed but who are also able and willing to listen to other group members. It is important to know beforehand of any internal politics that might compromise the success of the focus group – but this knowledge is often implicit and therefore not readily accessible to outsiders such as consultants.

Lastly, when using focus groups you have to consider people's willingness to speak honestly and openly in front of a group of people. Where contentious issues, or issues related to personal opinion or commercial sensitivity, are to be discussed, it may be better to use individual interviews.

OBSERVATIONS

Observations, whether participant (so that the researcher is working alongside the people being observed) or non-participant (when the researcher is concentrating simply on the act of observing), are used infrequently in business research projects. This is largely because they tend to be even more unstructured than other means of gathering qualitative data. This lack of structure and the notion that much business research is driven by the need to produce some verifiable evidence for managers means that although they are popular in academic research, they have yet to prove themselves as a mainstream method for data-gathering in business research.

What can observations do?

Observations can give researchers the chance to locate themselves within an organisation or a situation and to see what really happens for themselves. They allow a researcher to appreciate the complexity of the researched situations, to note the interpersonal relations that exist and to see how individuals and/or groups work together to achieve the goals of the organisation. Observations enable the researcher to speak to people in a more natural, conversational way and to have the trajectory of that conversation driven by the people being observed.

What data can observations produce?

Observations can generate both quantitative and qualitative data. Quantitative data can be drawn from observing the number of times people perform specific tasks, the number of times specific people speak to other specific people, the number of products produced or the number of customers served. In this sense, observations can be linked back to the systems of Scientific Management and the issue of time-and-motion studies. From a qualitative perspective observations can gather a wealth of data.

Although the temptation is to focus just on narrative – ie the use of language, in particular what has actually been said – observations can be used to illuminate many other issues. In some of my own research, I have focused on the non-verbal aspects of communication as part of a non-participant observation. Instead of generating a 'transcript' of what had been said, my field notes instead produced a description of what I saw, including issues such as how one particular group of staff was particularly disrespectful towards another group of staff, and how mixed groups of people that worked together split into single-race or -gender groups as soon as they moved into a social space. Depending on the nature of the data gathered, it can be analysed by using:

- descriptive statistics
- content coding analysis
- discourse analysis.

What are the limitations of observations?

Observations are extremely time-consuming. They require prolonged periods of engagement and therefore long periods of concentration. Even with this investment, observations rarely produce the type of data that managers look for in business research projects, although there are exceptions. It might, for example be quite useful for a nurse manager to observe the ways in which staff interact with patients.

Likewise, taking field notes is not an easy skill to master and it takes substantial practice to be able to take coherent and relevant notes while being immersed in a situation. Even if good field notes are taken, it is then important to transcribe them as soon as possible – preferably on the same day that they have been gathered. This enables the researcher to explain and elaborate on any points from memory as necessary. It can mean that having spent eight hours observing people, the researcher then has to spend another three hours converting the field notes into a comprehensive transcript.

MIXING RESEARCH METHODS

By now it will be apparent that there are definite advantages and disadvantages to both qualitative and quantitative research. Used on its own, qualitative data gives you rich explanations but no verifiable evidence, whereas quantitative data gives you verifiable evidence but offers fewer explanations. Within organisations, the issues faced are often complex and multi-faceted. There is a need to encompass an array of different factors and use indicators and measures to highlight relationships and narratives to draw on aspects that cannot be reduced to numbers.

Because any single approach offers at best a partial picture, business researchers frequently opt for a mixed-methods approach. Doing this generates both qualitative and quantitative data. Using mixed methods allows you to meet the demands of a wider range of stakeholder groups than does single-method research. A combined approach also overcomes the shortcomings of using any individual method in isolation. Some academics argue against the use of mixed-methods research. They argue that research methods are more than just a practical means of data-gathering – they are reflections of the ontological and epistemological positions of the researcher. It is therefore disingenuous to try to move between approaches (Bryman and Bell, 2007). This position has some merit, but there is also an argument for a much more pragmatic approach, for using a mixture of qualitative and quantitative methods where research is undertaken as a practical means of resolving organisational problems.

Hammersley (1996, cited in Bryman and Bell, 2007) notes that there are three approaches to mixed methods research: triangulation, facilitation and complementarity.

TRIANGULATION

Ontology and epistemology

Originally, triangulation was used by those in the engineering professions to ensure the increased accuracy of the results they produced. By taking three measurements rather than two, engineers were more able to produce *accurate* and therefore *valid* results (Hassard and Cox, 1995). This motive of accuracy may seem somewhat at odds with the ontology and epistemology that underpin much qualitative research, yet triangulation is frequently used. The motives, however, are not to increase validity – indeed, Denzin and Lincoln go as far as to assert that triangulation is not a strategy for validation but is instead an 'alternative to validation' (1998, p4). The purpose of triangulation for qualitative research is to better illuminate the research – that is, 'to add depth and density to the data' (Price, 2006, p101). Triangulation allows you to view the core area of your research through a number of different lenses, so that this 'depth and density' (*ibid*) can be added in a number of ways (Denzin and Lincoln, 1998):

- methodological triangulation
- data triangulation
- investigator triangulation
- interdisciplinary triangulation

    – all brought to bear on the focus of the research.

Methodological triangulation

Methodological triangulation involves the use of multiple methods in that a range of different means of data-gathering are utilised. Common ways of doing this rely on the use of both questionnaires and interviews or focus groups or the use of interviews or questionnaires and observations. The focus of the research is the same – you are simply using different means of gathering data to see how the different forms of data illuminate similar or different perspectives.

Data triangulation

Data triangulation involves the use of multiple sources of data: the data that you gather comes from a range of different sources. These might be different groups of people within the organisation – they might be internal and external stakeholders – or the data might be gleaned from secondary sources such as intranet or Internet sites or published information.

Investigator triangulation

Investigator triangulation involves the use of multiple researchers. Although not common in practical business research, the use of more than one investigator is a really useful way of illustrating how the subjectivity of the researchers has an impact on the results that are produced, especially where interpretive research is undertaken.

Interdisciplinary triangulation

Interdisciplinary triangulation involves the use of multi-disciplinary research. Again, it is not common in some areas of business research but is extremely valuable where people from different professional or academic backgrounds can view the same research focus through their own disciplinary lenses. This may be of particular use to people working in collaborative or multi-disciplinary environments such as health and social care.

KEY POINTS

Triangulation allows you to create a greater depth and breadth of understanding of the research area.

There are four types of triangulation:

- methodological triangulation
- data triangulation
- investigator triangulation
- interdisciplinary triangulation.

Whichever mode of triangulation is used, you must consider – ahead of data collection – how you will synthesise the results.

FACILITATION

In facilitation there is a greater level of synergy between the research methods used. This is often demonstrated by the sequencing of data-gathering (Morgan, 1998, cited in Bryman, 2007), where one method is used first in order to facilitate the use of the second method. There is often a question as to whether qualitative research should precede or should follow quantitative research – the answer is: it depends! Below are two examples from my own dissertation students each of whom chose to sequence his or her research methods in very particular ways.

COMPLEMENTARITY

This is the most open of the approaches to mixed-methods research and is focused on addressing the issue of being able to see only a partial picture. In complementarity, two or more research methods are used to enable the researcher to see a more complete picture. For example, where a business research project is looking at the effectiveness of the budgeting process, it may be useful to undertake a quantitative analysis to see how accurately the budget predicts trends in expenditure. Likewise, it would also be useful to interview those involved in the budgeting process to find out their opinions.

ISSUES TO CONSIDER IN MIXED-METHODS RESEARCH

When thinking about mixed methods there is a need to consider the relationship between the questions asked and the sequencing or the order in which the different sets of data will be gathered. You should also think about how each will be analysed and the data synthesised to produce a coherent discussion of the results.

Producing coherent findings thus involves:

- aligning the questions
- sequencing the data-gathering
- synthesising the research findings.

Aligning the questions

Where mixed methods are used, there is ultimately going to be the need to draw together the results. This will be easier if you use the same key themes from the literature to inform those used to gather the quantitative data and the qualitative data. The questions must be constructed in such a way as to allow you to connect the responses and relate them back to the research question and the literature.

RESEARCH STORY

Sequencing of research methods

Eduardo's research question was based on seeing how he could improve internal communications in his company. Intuitively, he felt that communication could be better but also felt that if he simply asked people how to improve communication he would get such a broad-ranging and possibly random set of results that these would actually not help him to identify the key factors in need of improvement. He started his research with a quantitative survey of the effectiveness of internal communications. He produced a structured questionnaire from his review of the literature and sent it to a sample of people on the shop floor and a sample of middle managers. Once he had analysed his results he was able to clearly identify the main problem areas, and he used these as prompts in four focus groups, two made up of people from the shop floor and two drawn from middle managers. Clearly, he could not have directed the groups towards the key issues had he

not found them out from the quantitative survey he did first.

Michelle's research was looking at the effectiveness of the annual performance appraisal process. In order to judge the effectiveness of the process she first had to find out what the purpose of the appraisal process was. She started by interviewing two senior managers, two middle managers and the head of human resources. Having analysed the transcripts of these interviews using content analysis, she then devised a structured questionnaire which was sent to all the people who had an annual appraisal. Again, had Michelle not gathered the qualitative data which set out the intended purpose first, she would not have been able to create a questionnaire which assessed how effective the process was in meeting its own objectives.

Sequencing the data-gathering

We have seen, when we looked at the issue of facilitation (Hammersley, 1995), that the sequencing of data collection is very important. Where one means of data collection is clearly dependent on the research findings of another, the sequencing is less problematic. You simply cannot undertake the next investigation until you have those results. Where the approach is more akin to complementarity (*ibid*), you must think clearly of the potential impact that knowing one set of results could have on future data collection or analyses. For some business researchers this may not be a problem, but for a piece of my own research it was definitely an issue. Having gathered both quantitative (questionnaires) and qualitative (interviews) data, it was apparent to me that if I analysed the results of the questionnaires first, it would be very difficult for me not to allow this knowledge of the findings to influence (explicitly or implicitly) my qualitative (discourse analysis) analysis of the data. I therefore analysed the interviews before the questionnaires.

Synthesising the research findings

The skill in producing research findings that successfully synthesise the findings from different methods of data-gathering and analysis is not in the synthesis itself but is in the research design. If the research questions have been aligned, whether explicitly (asking almost the same question) or implicitly (using a more subtle thematic approach), then the process of connecting themes and presenting argument and counter-argument based on the different methodological positions is relatively straightforward: the themes flow logically and the contributions of each data source can be pulled together. Where little thought has gone into the design of the research it becomes almost impossible to create a coherent set of research findings from disparate themes and sources.

The notion of synthesising the research findings from mixed-methods research is crucial. I have referred previously to the problems encountered when text is simply taken verbatim from the qualitative analysis and used in a partisan way to support or refute the data derived from quantitative methods.

SUMMARY

The choice of research method depends upon a range of factors. Key among these will be your research purpose, stakeholder expectations, and your own skills and support networks. Your reading thus far will have given you a good idea of research methods used by others researching similar issues. Your chosen approach must be feasible and must, as a minimum, meet the demands of the most important stakeholders.

In order to think seriously about potential approaches and methods you have to understand what each can do and its limitations. The chapter described a number of these in brief, and further summary is not sensible.

Using several methods may help you meet the needs of a wider range of stakeholders, and create a richer and more complete set of findings. It may also help to overcome the limitations associated with single-method research and to draw on the differences and similarities between the findings.

Successful use of mixed methods requires you to plan carefully, and well in advance. You have to understand what each method can do and to decide which aspects of the research are best illuminated by which method.

Moreover, using multiple methods requires a wider skill base: you will probably need to be skilled in both quantitative and qualitative methods. Lastly, you will also have to synthesise the information generated to produce a set of coherent and trustworthy conclusions which answer your research question or otherwise meet your research purpose.

Review questions

1. Describe briefly what you understand about each of the following approaches to business research:

   Case Study approach
   Action Research approach
   Grounded Theory approach

2. Make brief notes for yourself on the strengths and the limitations of using questionnaires and using interviews.

3. What do you understand by the term 'triangulation'? What types of triangulation are you aware of, and how can these help you to more effectively answer your research question?

Explore further

Please note: further reading for Grounded Theory, Action Research, case study research, questionnaires, interviews and focus groups can be found at the end of each of the respective chapters devoted to them.

Research methodology and design:

Baker, M. (2001) 'Selecting a research methodology', *Marketing Review,* Vol.1, No,3, Spring; 373–97. Written for the academic practitioner, this paper gives a useful overview of the process of selecting an appropriate method for your research

Cresswell, J. W. (2007) *Qualitative Inquiry and Research Design: Choosing among five approaches.* Thousand Oaks, CA: Sage Publications. A good consideration of five qualitative methods, namely: biography, phenomenology, Grounded Theory, case study and ethnography. An excellent basis for comparison

Observations:

Atkinson, P. and Hammersley, M. (1998) 'Ethnography and participant observation', in Denzin, N. K. and Lincoln, Y. S. (eds) *Handbook of Qualitative Research.* London: Sage. Although written for academic researchers, this gives a clear understanding of the principles which underpin ethnography and observation

Delamont, S. (2004) 'Ethnography and participant observation', in Seale, C., Gobo, G., Gubrium, J. and Silverman, D. (eds) *Qualitative Research Practice.* London: Sage. Again written primarily for academic researchers, this is an accessible chapter which considers both theory and practice.

Robson, C. (1992) *Real World Research*, 2nd edition. Oxford: Blackwell: 309–45. The chapter entitled 'Observational methods' gives a good practically-oriented consideration

Multi-method research and triangulation:

Denzin, N. and Lincoln, Y. (1998) *Strategies of Qualitative Inquiry.* Thousand Oaks, CA: Sage Publications. One of the must-read texts when thinking about using multi-method research

Hassard, J. and Cox, J. W. (1995) 'Triangulation in organizational research: a re-presentation', *Organization,* Vol.21, No.1: 109–33. An interesting paper which throws a qualitative light on the subject of triangulation

Maylor, H. and Blackmon, K. (2005) *Researching Business and Management.* Basingstoke: Palgrave Macmillan. A useful categorisation of the types of triangulation

Teddlie, C. and Tashakkori, A. (2009) *Foundations of Mixed Method Research: Integrating quantitative and qualitative approaches in the social and behavioral sciences.* Thousand Oaks, CA: Sage Publications. A comprehensive text which gives a thorough consideration of mixed-methods research and how to ensure the integrity of it

 Visit www.cipd.co.uk/brm for web links, templates, activities and other useful resources relating to this chapter.

CHAPTER 11

Crafting a Research Proposal

INTRODUCTION

Once you have explored the context in which you intend to carry out your research, done some serious reading in relevant literatures, and decided on a specific topic, you are ready to write a proposal. A proposal for dissertation research serves as a framework for organising your thoughts, convinces your supervisor that you have a 'researchable' topic, have a realistic plan for carrying out worthwhile research, are competent to carry out this plan, and have considered any ethical implications of what you intend to do.

If you have an organisational client, the client's agreement to a proposal will similarly serve to establish your competence, and ensure that your client understands what you propose to do, knows what you intend to deliver, and is happy with the resources and other implications for the organisation. If you are doing research as a consultant rather than as a student, the equivalent document will be a jointly agreed consultancy brief serving similar purposes. The brief must clarify your expectations and your client's concerning the activities to be undertaken, the resources that will be required, and the outcomes to be expected.

Such clarity can prevent subsequent disagreements over what resources were to be provided, and what was expected at the end of the project. If disagreements arise over the brief, it is important to face up to them and resolve them, revising the brief accordingly. Similarly, your dissertation proposal may not satisfy your supervisor, and you will have to discuss the reasons for this and revise your proposal accordingly. In either case, the discussion will be invaluable: feedback and clarity at this stage can make for a far better piece of research.

I have called this 'crafting' a proposal because putting together a good proposal takes more than mere writing skill. You need to understand the perspectives of your supervisor and/or client, and their concerns, and ensure that these concerns are addressed. You will need to select carefully from the work you have already done in order to construct a clear and sound argument for what you propose. Only then will your writing skills be needed to communicate to supervisor and client.

This chapter enables you to check that you have done enough work on previous chapters to prepare you to draft your proposal. It explains in more detail the purpose of different possible elements of a proposal in both practical and academic contexts. This understanding will help you construct a proposal that will gain you useful feedback and eventual agreement. The skills you develop in the process will be relevant to future consultancy work or drafting funding proposals for more academic research.

LEARNING OUTCOMES

This chapter should enable you to:

- formulate a clear description of the issue you propose to address, and the overall purpose of your research

- justify that purpose in terms of its theoretical interest and/or practical importance, relating the issue to relevant current thinking and writing

- state clear specific research questions or objectives for the research, or hypotheses to test – answering/achieving/testing all of these must achieve your research purpose

- make clear how you propose to answer the questions (or achieve the outcomes or test the hypotheses) justifying your choice of approach

- specify the access and other resources you will need in order to carry out your plans and how you intend to achieve them, identifying any risks and continuing uncertainties

- demonstrate that your plan for carrying out these activities is realistic within the proposed time-scale, and that your planning has taken risks and uncertainties into account.

PREPARING YOUR ARGUMENTS

Your proposal will never be better than the thinking upon which it rests. Before drafting it you need to think about how you will convince your stakeholders to accept your proposal. This section will help you clarify the purpose of a proposal, and put together what is needed to achieve this purpose. It will enable you to establish whether your thinking and your evidence collection provides a sufficient basis for a proposal. If not, it will help you to see what else is needed. If it does, the next section will help you to craft a proposal that will convey your thinking.

A proposal must communicate clearly

- *what* you are interested in researching

- *why* you feel the research is worth doing, and

- *how* you propose to address the issue.

All three choices must be *justified*. Relevant stakeholders have to understand clearly your research purpose, be convinced that it is a worthwhile purpose, and feel that you have a good chance of achieving it.

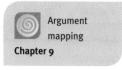
Argument
mapping
Chapter 9

It may help to think of the proposal as an argument for the action you propose. You can then map this argument, sorting out the evidence you need to support your claim. (Using argument mapping at this stage will also help you think clearly about your evidence when you come to write your dissertation.) Figure 11.1 shows in general terms how the main claim and the subordinate claims are related, and the evidence and arguments you might need to support these claims. This is not the only way of mapping a workable argument: if you find a better approach for your particular approach, use it. (Note that links are not labelled: all denote 'supports'.)

Figure 11.1 Mapping your argument

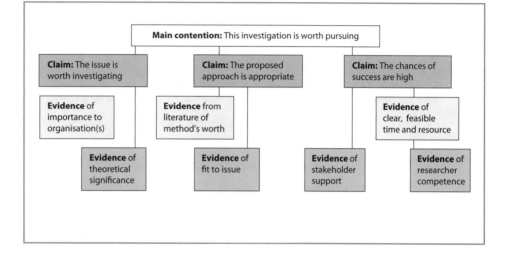

ACTIVITY

For each of these sub-claims, consider the types of evidence and argument you will need to present. Construct a map relevant to your own proposal and refer to it as you work through the chapter, modifying it in the light of your thinking. File it in your journal when it is complete.

In Chapter 5 you started the necessary thought processes for developing a proposal. Subsequent chapters should have advanced your thinking. Before organising your arguments answer the following questions to check that you are adequately prepared. They will show whether it would be helpful to revisit earlier chapters before going on. Once you have checked this, you can start to consider each of the sub-arguments you need to make and consider the sort of evidence that might support the claims you are trying to sustain.

A CLEAR PURPOSE

You need to be absolutely clear what the project is intended to achieve. Unless the purpose is clear to *you*, you cannot make it clear in your proposal. Unless they understand your purpose, your supervisor and/or client cannot assess your other claims. And they will need to assess them in order to be convinced. This clarity must be achieved on at least two levels.

The first level concerns the overall aim or purpose of the research. (Both terms are used for this 'top' level.) This will normally be indicated by the title of your project. The 'purposes' for research you have already encountered include.

ACTIVITY

Answer these questions before proceeding:

Have you identified an issue that is of interest to you, and to any client?

Have you revisited your answers to questions in Chapter 5, and updated them?

Have you read carefully your university's requirements for both proposal and dissertation?

Have you read enough about relevant topics to understand current concepts, frameworks and debates in relation to that issue?

Have you thought about what questions you could usefully ask related to the issue, and how the answers to those questions might achieve what you want to achieve in relation to the issue?

Have you thought about the ways in which you might obtain and analyse data in order to obtain those answers?

Have you considered whether you have the skills, time, and other resources to achieve what you propose?

- to explore the role of reflection in leadership development
- to evaluate the impact of change on the organisation
- to identify a cost-effective way to increase the retention of recruits
- to identify ways of saving money by reducing the carbon footprint of an organisation
- to test the relationship between 'time-span of discretion' and 'felt fair pay' for white-collar workers.

Note that these are purposes that the research project can reasonably be expected to achieve. There may also be an associated organisational purpose, but it is important to distinguish between the two. Jenny's carbon footprint title shows such an association: she is identifying ways of reducing costs. But her research aim is *to identify* ways of reducing costs. Her research aim is not *to reduce* costs. Others in the organisation will have to be involved in this. Unless you are doing an action-oriented project and you will be involved in implementation as part of this project, you need to claim as your research purpose only what the research project can, when complete, deliver. You may need to discuss the organisational purpose as part of your argument that the issue is worth addressing, but be absolutely clear about what the research project, *as a project*, can and cannot be expected to achieve. Do not include things that the *organisation* may later do with the project.

> It is important to specify a *research aim* that the *research project* can deliver.

CLEAR RESEARCH QUESTIONS/OBJECTIVES/HYPOTHESES

Research questions

Chapter 8

Once you have a clear overall purpose, you can think clearly about the research questions (I shall use 'etc' to indicate objectives or hypotheses) that will collectively allow this aim to be achieved. These research questions (etc) will be the basis against which your methods will be assessed.

- **Questions** must be sufficiently specific that they can be answered.
- **Objectives** must be achievable, and phrased in a way that lets you know when you have achieved them. You will be used to SMART (specific, measurable, achievable,

relevant and time-defined) objectives in other contexts. Research objectives cannot always be SMART, but it is always worth checking whether yours could usefully be SMARTer.

- **Hypotheses** must be clearly derived from your theory and sufficiently specific that it is clear to see how they can be tested.

I have emphasised specificity and clarity because they are an essential basis for a satisfying proposal. You will need to make it clear what information you will collect: there is no room for fuzziness or ambiguity. As Pajares (2007) says, 'Be excruciatingly consistent in your use of terms.' If part of your purpose is personal development, you will need the same clarity about your personal development objectives as about other objectives.

Two of the following stories remind you of earlier examples of writing research questions. The third (although the proposal received a comfortable pass grade) is slightly frightening. One specifies research questions, one specifies research outcomes, and one specifies objectives *and* hypotheses.

RESEARCH STORY

Reflection and leadership development

In his dissertation proposal Chris specified his research aim as: ' *To investigate the importance of reflection and feedback in leadership development'* . He translated this overall purpose into the following research questions:

To what extent are current leadership development reflection and feedback practices in line with Avolio's model?

Is there a significant relationship between overt/explicit reflection and feedback events and improved leadership behaviours?

What are the perceived obstacles to effective feedback/reflection?

Can a model of best practice be identified?

Does the approach to reflection and feedback differ between in-house leadership development and that applied by executive coaches?

RESEARCH STORY

Reducing the carbon footprint

Jenny deemed that the following research objectives would enable her to achieve her overall aim of identifying ways to reduce her organisation's carbon footprint:

- to determine the current level of emissions
- to identify the major contributors to this
- to identify changes that might reduce emissions
- to determine the costs and benefits of these changes
- to determine the likely acceptability of options.

RESEARCH STORY: HOUSE OF HORRORS

Marketing in India

Chander's proposed aim was '*To investigate how relationship marketing wins customer loyalty in India's automobile industry*'. He specified the following objectives:

- '*to understand the definition and importance of relationship marketing*
- *to understand the definition of 'customer loyalty' and the factors that affect it*
- *to investigate the relationship between relationship marketing and customer loyalty*
- *to investigate the relationship between relationship marketing and customer loyalty in India's automobile industry.*

H_0: There is no relationship between relationship marketing and customer loyalty

H_1: There is a relationship between relationship marketing and customer loyalty'

CONSIDER...

What do Chander's two hypotheses add to the research objectives?

What does the second hypothesis add to the first?

What information might enable the fourth objective to be achieved?

What sort of data would you need in order to test the null hypothesis?

Would achieving the objectives and testing the null hypothesis achieve the overall research aim?

It has to be doubted whether the hypotheses add anything to the third objective and therefore also to the fourth. Indeed, the objectives might be more useful without them; this is something that can be investigated, perhaps drawing on the literature. It remains even more doubtful whether Chander is in a position to test his hypotheses within the constraints of an MBA dissertation.

You might have considered that if the fourth objective had been worded as 'Investigate whether there is a relationship between the two variables', then testing the null hypothesis (H_0) would be an alternative way of saying the same thing. However, if the fourth objective implies investigating the nature of the relationship, testing the hypothesis would be too restricted – although it might be a useful preliminary filter: if no relationship was found, it would not be worth investigating it. Can you begin to see why extreme clarity is needed in the wording of aims and objectives?

Non-equivalence

Chapter 8

To test the null hypothesis H_0 you would need to be able to obtain measures of both 'relationship marketing' and 'customer loyalty' from a representative sample of 'the industry'. Finding both measures and an adequate sample might present challenges. Would the test achieve the overall aim? You will remember the earlier caution concerning the non-equivalence of correlation and causation. It is perhaps more likely that attention to customers creates loyalty than the reverse, but it is certainly perfectly possible that an organisation which cared about its customers also cared about its products, or that a profitable organisation had the resources to do both. (In one sense the H_0 is all you need because the H_1 is its converse, but most dissertations which test hypotheses specify both – I have never quite understood why.)

The 'evidence' your proposal offers of a clear purpose will be the clarity with which you express your aims and purposes and your questions or objectives, the clarity of the link between the two, and whether your questions or objectives are necessary and sufficient to meet the research purpose.

THE ISSUE IS SIGNIFICANT

Exploring the literature
Chapter 6

The evidence for significance will come from your initial explorations within your target organisation and/or your literature search. From the literature you would need to indicate the nature of the concepts you were interested in, and their relationships, and the questions that arose from your reading. You could usefully explain why a current debate on the topic is interesting or relevant or important in order to establish significance.

For an organisational issue useful evidence of significance might include indicative costs of an existing problem, or potential benefits of an opportunity or a description of the range of its impacts throughout the organisation. If the organisational issue is at all complex, you would also need to provide data and argument to establish that the issue was the appropriate issue to address. Any initial diagnostic work that either confirmed the presenting issue or identified a deeper one would be relevant here.

Personal development considerations **Chapter 5**

If you are choosing a topic because of its opportunities for personal development and your objectives reflect this, you might include evidence of existing strengths and weaknesses, and evidence of skills or experience needed for a future role.

THE APPROACH IS APPROPRIATE

In order to demonstrate that your approach is appropriate you would need to explain in sufficient detail *what* your approach will be and make clear *why* it is suitable. Without this clarity it will be impossible for your supervisor to judge whether your proposal should be accepted.

What is the approach?

You need to be specific here. What data to you intend to gather? How do you propose to gather your data? If you propose using a fixed experimental design with a control group, you must spell out clearly how control and experimental groups will be identified and treated. If you are proposing an evaluation, you must specify what aspects of the situation you would be evaluating. If you were evaluating a change, you would need to say how you would seek to distinguish the impact of the change from other impacts. If you intend to use a totally flexible design, you should say where you propose to start and at least the type of activity you propose to undertake to obtain data. If your study involves sampling, you must define your target population, say how big a sample you would be seeking, and state how you would select this sample.

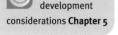

Sample selection
Chapter 10

You need to be as clear as possible about how you will collect data. If you propose to use a questionnaire, you must specify the type of questionnaire, and how you would design the questions. If possible you would append your draft questionnaire and say how you would pilot it. (A pilot stage is important.) If you intend interviewing, you must specify the type of interview and the areas covered. In either case, your methodology must include not merely how you propose to collect the data but how you propose to analyse it.

> An argument that an approach is appropriate must first make clear what the approach is!

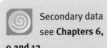

Secondary data
see **Chapters 6, 9 and 12**

If much of your research will involve exploring the literature, you need to be specific about what you will be looking for. If you are seeking secondary data, what data or information will you seek, and where will you look for it? Again, the more specific you can be, the stronger will be your other 'evidence' of competence, feasibility and appropriateness.

Why is this approach appropriate?

Here you are seeking to justify your approach. Part of your argument may relate to the nature of your topic. If you are primarily concerned with exploring, you will be arguing for a more open approach. If it is important to test a specific hypothesis, or you are wanting to evaluate the impact of a specific initiative, you will have to explain how your approach will isolate the variables in which you are interested and how you will choose valid measures.

If you are going to sample, you must explain why your proposed size of sample will be adequate, and how you will ensure that it is representative, or otherwise suitably informative. If you are seeking qualitative data, representativeness may be less of an issue. You must also justify your proposed analytical methods, showing why they are appropriate to the nature of the data, and how they will contribute to adequate conclusions in relation to your question

Above all, your argument needs to convince the reader that your approach will produce the data needed to answer your research question(s).

RESEARCH STORY: HOUSE OF HORRORS

Marketing in India

Chander's proposal addressed his proposed sampling approach thus:

'*The sample population will be India's automobile industry. There are two kinds of sampling method: probability sampling and non-probability sampling (Saunders, 2003). This study will use probability sampling. Obviously, the corporations which are sampled will be random ones.*

The larger the sample size, the lower the likely error. The author will determine an acceptable sample error (SE) using the statistical method (Saunders et al, 2003):

$SE = 1.96sqrt$ *(variability/n) at 95% confidence level.*'

CONSIDER...

How good an argument is this in support of a dissertation proposal? What might make it more convincing?

It is not 'obvious' from Chander's proposal that his sample must be random: it might be more important that it covered a range of *different* manufacturers. Or that he looked at distributors as well as manufacturers, or some other industry members. It depends on how he defines the 'industry': this was nowhere apparent in the proposal – and the population you are sampling from *must be clearly defined*. He really should have explained what population he was going to look at. Having established this, some sort of rationale for a random sample was needed. Then, since it would probably not be obvious how to sample at random from whatever the defined population, he should have said how he would arrive at his random sample. (How he would sample within his chosen organisations is not discussed, but probably should also have been.)

The sample error statement will have bothered you if you understand statistics. The problems should be clear to you once you have read Chapter 21. This suggests to me that he has copied something from his textbook without understanding what it means. In addition to not providing support for 'appropriate method', this part of the proposal provides evidence that is *inconsistent* with a claim of competence to carry out the research. So Chander's 'argument' about sampling fails to give me any idea of the size of sample he has in mind or how he proposes to select it *and* it diminishes my faith in his competence.

> **It is dangerous to include in your proposal anything that you do not understand.**

If he had instead defined his population (there might be as many as 80 major auto manufacturers and/or distributors, together with many suppliers, and various others whom he may or may not deem part of 'the industry') and said how many he proposed to approach, on what basis he proposed to select them, the type of employee he wanted to interview and/or send questionnaires (the introduction to the appended draft questionnaire suggests these to be marketing managers) and how within his selected manufacturers he would select marketing managers to approach, the proposal would have been far more convincing!

The literature that you *do* understand may be an excellent source of evidence on the appropriate methods to use for your project. Part of your reading will be directed towards methods used to address similar issues, and justifications of the method in the relevant part of the research papers in question. Some papers are specifically about methodology – some of these have already featured in Research Stories. Their conclusions may form part of your evidence.

ACHIEVING THE RESEARCH PURPOSE WILL SATISFY STAKEHOLDERS

If you have specified an organisational purpose to which your research is intended to contribute, you will have to include it in your 'argument'. It will strengthen your case that the project is required to establish the significance of the issue to the organisation and how the research will contribute to addressing that issue. This may be self-evident, as in Jenny's case: it is clear that if she seeks to reduce the carbon footprint by reducing energy consumption, this will reduce fuel bills. However, if she had justified the significance of her project in terms of *costs*, and then phrased her purpose in terms purely of *carbon footprint*, it would have been possible for her to go down a route of carbon offsetting and purchase of energy from a 'green' supplier that might actually have increased costs.

It is also possible that the link, although there, is not at all obvious and requires explaining: you might be taking a creative and unexpected approach to an established problem. So it is worth checking that if this line of argument is needed, your proposal includes it.

THE PROPOSAL IS REALISTIC

You need to establish that what you propose is likely to be successful in achieving your purpose. It is no good to have a worthwhile purpose, and an appropriate approach to achieving it, if it would take a miracle to achieve your purpose given the resources available. I once had a student whose purpose was to improve gender equality in Nigeria. This was certainly a worthwhile aim. Her sub-objectives of addressing educational, political and health inequalities seemed likely, if she met them, to achieve the overall purpose. The methods she proposed (involving the establishment of micro-credit, women's health centres, etc) were appropriate to the goals. But her chances of achieving these within the 12 months of her project (part of the requirement for the project was that the student should already have started to 'make a difference' as a result of his/her investigation) were vanishingly small.

You might well wonder whether Chander was likely to achieve his overall purpose by means of interviews and questionnaires (his only proposed data collection methods) and within a six-month period when he was working long hours and trying to fit his research into his non-working time.

> **It is easy to set over-ambitious aims – ensure that your research purpose is realistic.**

To build an argument that your proposal is feasible you must have thought about what it will involve and checked that you have, or can obtain, the resources, including time, that you will need. Your plan (more of this later) will therefore be a key part of your evidence of feasibility. You will have thought about your research objectives, and their sub- and sub-sub-objectives, and the activities that will be required to achieve them. You will have formed reasonable estimates of the time these activities will take (including any waiting time, such as waiting for questionnaires to be returned or permissions granted), have checked any dependencies between activities, and have devised a realistic plan.

You will have identified any potential risks to success and planned how to manage them so that you have a viable fall-back plan for even the worst scenario. (Chapter 22 looks at project management, including project planning and risk management, in more detail. You should have read the relevant parts of this chapter before you write your proposal.)

YOU ARE COMPETENT TO DO WHAT YOU PROPOSE

For a consultancy proposal a significant part of your aim will be to convince your client of your competence to do a good job. You will not get the assignment otherwise. Your supervisor may not approve your proposal if he or she thinks that you are destined to fail because you lack the necessary competence or expertise and have not planned to develop it. Competence will relate to many different aspects: understanding of topic(s) relevant to your issue; understanding of the research process as a whole and of specific methods; understanding of appropriate analytical techniques; ability to make sense of a complex issue; ability to reason clearly and communicate your reasoning; ability to appreciate the perspectives of other stakeholders and interact productively with them; ability to draw up a realistic plan; and ability to meet deadlines.

 ACTIVITY

If you have not already done so, list the competences your project will require, and note down ways in which your proposal might demonstrate them.

Some of your competence will be implicit in other aspects of your proposal, some will need to be addressed explicitly. You can demonstrate your understanding of the topic you are addressing through your discussion of the literature. By the time of your proposal you must have a reasonable grasp of relevant theory in order to frame a suitable project. Your ability to reason and communicate should be displayed throughout the proposal (argument mapping is really helpful for this). Your planning ability will be apparent from the plan that you include, and your discussion of how you propose to manage your stakeholders and acquire the necessary resources.

Some skills, however, may have to be explicitly addressed. These will include the technical ability to use specific data collection or analytical methods.

ETHICAL ISSUES HAVE BEEN ADDRESSED

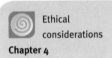
Ethical considerations
Chapter 4

It is always important to consider the ethical issues associated with any research. Most universities and some other institutions (notably the NHS) require all research to be approved by an ethics committee, but even if not, you must have thought about the ethical implications of what you propose. These would typically include some or all of the following:

- whether there are relevant published ethical guidelines (eg organisational and/or professional)
- where data will be collected, and whether you have all the necessary permissions
- the population from which you will be sampling, and how the sampling will be done
- how you will identify and approach potential participants
- how informed consent will be obtained, and how participants can withdraw consent, and what will happen to their data in such a case
- how data will be stored and disposed of to ensure data protection requirements are met
- whether participants will be recompensed, and whether anything beyond expenses might be deemed inducement
- whether any information will be withheld from participants, or misrepresented, and if so, whether it is fully justified
- whether participating might pose dilemmas for participants or make them feel under any pressure
- whether there might be any risk to participants, and if there is, how it will be minimised
- how participants will be debriefed.

ACTIVITY

Assess the evidence on the argument map you devised at the beginning of this section. Identify any gaps or weaknesses in your evidence and arguments. Note down what must be done to remedy these, and draw up an action plan for completing any necessary remaining reading, data collection or thinking.

KEY POINTS

- Your proposal can be seen as a claim that the project should go ahead in the way you propose.
- To support this claim you need evidence and arguments to demonstrate that the issue is worth addressing and that your proposed way of addressing it is appropriate and feasible.
- You need to demonstrate an understanding both of the context and of the relevant literature.
- You need to demonstrate, or plan to develop, the necessary competencies including clear reasoning and expression, realistic planning, and data collection and analysis skills.
- Avoid including ideas or words that you do not fully understand: these will probably suggest lack of competence.
- You must have carefully considered the ethical implications of what you propose.

CRAFTING YOUR PROPOSAL

If you have done the necessary thinking, actually writing your proposal should be relatively simple. You need to understand the constraints: word limits (typically 2,500 or so words) and deadlines have to be observed. You need to understand how to slot your thinking into the sections normally required in a dissertation: this section will explain how to do this. And you need to write clearly and reference your sources in the way your university requires. Chapter 26 addresses both these points. Finally, you need to keep the purpose of your proposal firmly in mind throughout your drafting.

The research proposal

- A research proposal makes clear the aim of the proposed research, and establishes its importance.
- It specifies how the research will be undertaken, and the time and other resources that will be needed to achieve it.
- It seeks to justify these choices and to establish your credibility and competence as a researcher and the feasibility of what you propose.
- It serves as a vehicle for feedback from client and/or sponsor.
- It prevents future disagreements over intended activities, outcomes and resources.

It is important to remember at all times that a research proposal is a vital document for three of the key stakeholders in the research process: your client, your supervisor and yourself. You will need to construct your arguments within the format(s) expected by your supervisor and/or client.

FORMAT

A dissertation proposal is typically expected to have most or all of the elements listed below. Different terms may be used. These are among the most common.

Elements in a proposal
- **Title:** This should clearly indicate the purpose and context of the study.
- **Summary/abstract:** This should be a brief précis of the proposal.
- **Introduction:** A brief orientation to the reader may be helpful.
- **Issue or problem/background:** This should establish the significance of the issue in its context.
- **Research purpose/aims:** These indicate the intended outcome of the research.
- **Literature review:** This includes an outline of the conceptual frameworks you will use.
- **Research question/objectives/hypotheses:** These should be as appropriate, clearly stated.
- **Research approach:** This describes the methods and procedures proposed for collecting and analysing data, and the reasons for their selection.
- **Scope and limitations:** As with any project planning it is important to make clear what is in scope and out of scope.
- **Resources:** You may be required to specify the resources needed (finance or other) and indicate how you will acquire any not already acquired.
- **Ethical considerations:** You may also have to append an ethics approval form.
- **A plan of work:** This should be sufficiently detailed to allow a feasibility check.
- **Reflections:** For a dissertation with a reflective chapter your proposal may need to describe how you propose to handle this element and/or express your evidence of reflection thus far.
- **References/Bibliography:** All references should be in the approved style.
- **Appendices:** These act to extend and support the proposal, providing additional evidence.

A proposal to a client might include a much shorter section on relevant concepts, and would normally exclude the critical literature review and the more philosophical elements of a discussion of intended approach. You would want to establish your credibility by displaying a quiet expertise in the area, and might have to justify a particular approach or the use of certain concepts, but would usually do no more than this required: most clients do not respond well to an excess of jargon. The language might be less abstract for an organisational client, and you might expect fewer references. But beneath the changes in style, the essence of the proposal would be the same.

It should be fairly clear to you by now how to use your argument map as the basis for writing a convincing proposal. However, brief commentary on some of the elements may be helpful.

Title, and title page

This is normally to be the proposed title for your eventual dissertation. It is the first thing that will be read, and the impression it creates is important. Remember – ideas are like spectacles. A professional title and nicely presented title page may create a lens through which everything else is interpreted slightly more favourably. (This applies to presentation in general.) Aim to be succinct but descriptive, including all key words without being too specific, to allow for subsequent shifts in direction. If a lengthy title is inevitable, put the more important words early in the title.

A title like 'Relationship Marketing and Customer Loyalty in the Indian Automobile Industry' or 'The Role of Reflection in Leadership Development' gives a clear idea of the topic while leaving room for subsequent alterations to detail. It conveys an impression of solidity rather than frivolity. What about 'An Investigation of Knowledge

Management Benchmarks for Operations Management with Process Outsourcing' or 'Fat Cats in Banking'? Attempts at 'catchy' or sensational titles are inconsistent with the credibility you are trying to establish. This is far from succinct and not very clear. 'An investigation of' or similar terms are fairly self-evident and therefore best omitted in the interests of succinctness.

As with a report, your title should appear on a title page which also shows who prepared the proposal, the date it was prepared, and the person(s) to whom it is addressed.

Summary

Not all proposals require that you include a summary, but if you are given the choice, do so. Although your proposal is far shorter than your final dissertation or client report, a summary can provide a useful overview. It should convey all the key points contained within the proposal, though without the detail or supporting arguments. The detail in the proposal itself will make more sense in the light of this overview. Aim to keep this short. Somewhere around 300 words might suffice.

Introduction

In your introduction you are aiming to create interest in the proposal that is to follow, and start to establish confidence in your ability to carry out the proposed research. You are also seeking to ease the reader into understanding what follows by setting down a foundation for subsequent sections. It helps briefly to cover the intended outcomes and their significance in a theoretical and/or practical context.

You can also usefully introduce yourself as a researcher, establishing your relationship to the topic and the perspective you will be taking. It can also be helpful to outline any relevant expertise you have. Because the role of the introduction is to prepare the reader, it is usually helpful to explain how the proposal is structured.

Your university may expect your introduction to have subsections addressing background and/or purpose, rather than devoting a whole section to each of these.

Issue or problem and overall research purpose

A key strand in your argument is that this project is worth doing. So you need to establish the rationale for what you propose. What are you addressing, what are you trying to achieve, and why is it important? This section should clearly answer these questions at the 'top level'. Pajares (2007) suggests, sensibly enough, that it will help you to keep this firmly in mind if your first words in this section are 'The purpose of this study ...' For example, in my own research on the relationship between perceived fair pay levels and time-span of discretion (TSD), the purpose was to assess the suitability of TSD as a predictor of fair pay levels for white-collar workers. The justification was that the government was being urged to use it, but so far all the evidence of such a relationship came from studies of manual workers.

Literature review

This section is intended to establish the theoretical context, key frameworks in current use, and your reasons for wanting to test or extend them. It might be a continuation or development or justification of an earlier conceptual justification of your proposed project (or might indeed replace it). It is important to establish your familiarity with the existing literature as evidence of an aspect of your competence and to convince your supervisor that you will make appropriate use of relevant theory. More detailed guidance is given in Chapters 6 and 7.

In a proposal to a client you would probably omit this section, but you would still need to draw upon your theoretical reading. For example, Kumar (1999) (who gives more detailed on proposal writing than many of the standard texts) suggests that your literature search should clearly inform all the other sections of your proposal rather than being segregated as a discrete section. I would argue strongly that it should do this even if you do have a specific literature review section! After all, you have reviewed the literature for a purpose, rather than as an activity in its own right. Part of that purpose is to inform all aspects of your approach to your research topic. You have already seen that you must draw upon your literature search even when writing your introduction and defining your purpose.

Research questions, research objectives and hypotheses

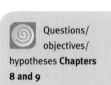

Questions/ objectives/ hypotheses **Chapters 8 and 9**

These have been dealt with earlier in the chapter, and in earlier chapters, so although it is essential to remember that they must be specific enough to allow a check that your proposed data will answer the question, and answering the question(s) will achieve the purpose, no more needs to be said here.

Proposed approach

This part of your proposal may be called 'Design', 'Methodology', 'Methods and procedures', or something similar. It is essential to make clear precisely what you plan to do and why. Whether you have translated your research aim into questions to be answered, objectives to be achieved, or hypotheses to be tested, having done it, you can describe and explain a sensible approach to obtaining the necessary information to achieve your aim.

You may be required to justify the philosophical assumptions which underlie your approach to information collection. A short essay on epistemology is not a substitute for a clear description of what you propose to do and an argument justifying the suitability of your chosen approach. Decisions about sampling, data collection and analysis and any experimental design must be clearly explained in terms of how they will provide a sound answer to your research question as well as justified in terms of your philosophical position on the nature of what it is important to know, and how you feel it is appropriate to find out about it.

Chapter 3 should have made clear how entwined your philosophy and your approach are likely to be, and indeed should be. This, and Chapter 9, should have shown the need for deliberate thought about the nature of an issue in relation to your natural philosophical preference. Ideally you will be able to move beyond it if necessary. You must be as clear as possible about what you propose at this stage. However, depending on the flexibility of your proposed design, your method may develop further as your investigation proceeds. A dissertation will need to include a fuller discussion of your approach, as described in Chapter 26.

Research plan

This will act as an important management tool for your project work, and so must be sufficiently detailed that following it will ensure that all necessary tasks are completed in an appropriate order and in time to meet deadlines. It will enable your supervisor to check that your plans are realistic and to check your progress, and your client to understand what is proposed. It is frighteningly easy to underestimate the time required for many (perhaps even most) of the activities involved in research. Suppress any optimistic tendencies when you are planning.

 CONSIDER...

Look at the action plan in Table 11.1 below and assess the student's research competence and degree of optimism from it. It refers to Chander's Marketing in India project. Note down any other points you might query.

Table 11.1 Illustrative project plan

Activity	Jan	Feb	Mar	Apr	May	Jun	Jul	Aug	Sep
Research proposal approved	■								
Review literature		■	■						
Finalise aim and objectives			■						
Draft literature review section				■					
Devise research approach				■	■	■			
Draft research approach section						■			
Review secondary data						■			
Organise interviews						■			
Develop interview questions						■			
Analyse data							■		
Administer questionnaire								■	
Enter data into computer								■	
Analyse data								■	
Draft findings chapter								■	
Update literature read								■	
Complete drafting thesis									■
Submit draft thesis for comment									■
Revise as per supervisor comment									■
Print and bind									■
Submit									■

This plan is better than many. Drafting starts early, and there are few obvious impossibilities such as analysing data before it is received. And it is sufficiently detailed to allow his supervisor to check that all the necessary activities have been allowed for and to check for feasibility of what is proposed. This highlights glaring omissions such as the actual interviews themselves! (Questionnaire design is not an omission: a draft was submitted with the proposal. But there is no mention of any pilot of the questionnaire, which is an essential stage.) Serious doubts remain about the feasibility of this plan.

I hope you thought that the student was being badly optimistic about what he could hope to achieve during June and again during September. To administer a question-naire, get it back, analyse it, and write up your findings on this and the interviews would be a real challenge. Obtaining a reasonable response rate normally involves one or more reminders.

But September looks worse. If most of the dissertation has been drafted, it might be possible to finalise it in a week or so, but will the supervisor be able to comment quickly? September tends to be a busy time anyway. If a lot of students want comments on drafts at that time, even a diligent supervisor might take a while to read and comment. And this appears to be the first submission of draft material. What if substantial revision is needed? Binding can take a while: you need to check local printers' lead times well in advance and allow for this.

I hope this helps you to be sceptical of your own plans. This is a genuine example of a reasonably competent-looking plan from a dissertation proposal!

Ethical considerations

Your proposal should normally include discussion of any ethical issues associated with your research, and how they will be addressed. For example, how will confidentiality and/or anonymity be preserved? How will you ensure free and informed participation? Do you have permission from any relevant ethics committee? If you are required to submit an ethics approval form with the proposal, complete it carefully.

Scope and limitations

It is important to outline both limits and limitations. Delimiting your project means making clear what is in scope and what is out of scope. This reassures your supervisor that you are not seeking to do too much (a common failing) and protects you from subsequent accusations from a client that you have failed to do something that they were expecting. It is important to have set down clearly in writing what is out of scope.

Limitations are inevitable weaknesses and shortcomings. Business research is never easy. There are lots of variables. Data may be expensive to obtain and your resources limited. There may be variables you cannot control, permissions that you need but cannot yet obtain. Recognising, detailing and discussing how you will deal with such limitations will make your proposal more convincing rather than less so. It will reduce confidence if there are clear weaknesses that you appear not to have recognised.

References

As with a report or dissertation, you will need to list everything you have referred to in the approved (normally Harvard) style, as explained in Chapter 26. Your reference list would be shorter than that for your eventual report. References should be chosen carefully for use in a proposal (very sparingly in a proposal for a client). Double-check that your references include all sources you have cited. Only include a wider bibliog-raphy (ie a list of everything you have read, even if not referred to in the proposal) if this is required by your university.

Appendices

As for a report, the appendices are an 'optional extra'. The proposal must be able to stand without them. They are used to supplement your proposal, giving detail that your audience *might* want and providing further evidence of your competence. Possible appendices might include detailed background of the context, fuller data collected as part of your initial diagnosis, sample letters and/or questionnaires or interview schedules. You may also have to append an ethics approval form.

Because it is easy to lose sight of the overall picture when drafting the details of your proposal, a final check before submission is advised: the following checklist may be useful.

Proposal pre-submission checklist

❏ Check that you have made your purpose crystal clear and justified its significance.
❏ Check that your objectives/questions/hypotheses are equally clear and would together achieve this purpose.
❏ Check that you have said what data will allow you to answer/achieve/test the above.
❏ Check that you have said how you will obtain and analyse the data, and why.
❏ Check that all claims are argued and evidenced, rather than being assertions.
❏ Check that your plan is sufficiently detailed and realistic.
❏ Check that your list of references (or bibliography if required) is complete and in the right format.
❏ Check that you have appended any useful evidence or additional information.
❏ Check that you have appended any necessary ethics form.
❏ Check that you are within the allowed word limit
❏ Check that the proposal is well presented.

SUMMARY

A project proposal can usefully be seen as an argument: you are seeking to convince your supervisor and/or client that the project you propose is worth doing, is being approached in a sensible fashion, and has a good chance of success.

Clarity throughout the proposal is essential. You need to be very clear about what you propose because it is difficult to make convincing arguments for something that is itself unclear. Argument mapping can help you to construct robust arguments based on sound logic and evidence.

Your proposal serves to generate useful feedback, and clear agreement on actions, deadlines and resources at the proposal stage can prevent later disagreements. It can build credibility with a client. The plan you include will act as a useful project management tool.

It is important to keep the purposes of the proposal firmly in mind while drafting. Your supervisor, your client and you may have different needs: you may have to 'version' the proposal to satisfy these. A client may require less theoretical content than a dissertation supervisor.

REVIEW QUESTIONS

1. What are the key things a proposal must communicate?

2. Why is argument mapping potentially useful when drafting a proposal?

3. Why is it important to distinguish between research aims and client aims?

4. Why is it important to make very clear what approach you intend to adopt?

5. Why must your proposal include a fairly detailed plan?

6. What are the key ethical issues that most proposals will have to address?

7. What are the main purposes that appendices can serve in your proposal, and what can they *not* do?

EXPLORE FURTHER

Kumar, R. (1999) *Research Methodology: A step-by-step guide for beginners.* London: Sage

Marshall, C. and Rossman, G. (2006) *Designing Qualitative Research*, 4th edition. London: Sage. (Obviously appropriate only for qualitative proposals)

Pajares, F. (2007) 'The elements of a proposal', available online from http://www.des.emory.edu/mfp/proposal. html [accessed 12 February 2009]. Provides excellent and extensive advice on proposal writing

http://www.nova.edu/ssss/QR/QR3-1/heath.html for advice on crafting proposals for qualitative research

 Visit www.cipd.co.uk/brm for web links, templates, activities and other useful resources relating to this chapter.

PART 3

DATA COLLECTION

CHAPTER 12

Producing a Research Project from Secondary Data

INTRODUCTION

Doing a successful business research project is not always dependent on doing empirical work within an organisation. Many people simply do not have access to an organisation, or they find that the organisation in which they work is somewhat unsupportive of their research. Where this is the case, business research based on secondary data is the only option available to them. For others, business research based on secondary data is the approach of choice.

Many people avoid doing research projects based on secondary data only, on the premise that they are fundamentally intellectual exercises rather than being of practical relevance. Although this may be true of a few 'theoretical' research projects, many secondary-data-based projects have real practical implications. Judging the success of a promotional campaign or showing where operational efficiencies can be gained can both be done from the use of secondary data only.

Although there are many features that make doing a project based on secondary data distinctive from primary-data-based research projects, there are also some marked similarities. The need for a clear research purpose/ research question, the need for an effective sampling strategy to ensure the reliability of the data gathered and the need to undertake robust analyses and produce trustworthy conclusions all still hold true. This chapter will help you to clarify what is required of a research project based on secondary data only, to see the strengths and weaknesses of this as an approach, and will set out a framework of considerations that will help guide you to produce a good piece of business research.

LEARNING OUTCOMES

This chapter should enable you to:

• appreciate the different types of secondary-data-based research project

• recognise the advantages and the disadvantages of doing your research project based purely on secondary data

• clarify how different types of secondary-data-based projects require different approaches to producing a robust piece of business research

• see from examples how research projects based only on secondary data can work well.

TYPES OF SECONDARY-DATA-BASED PROJECTS

The major types of secondary-data-based projects relate to:

• the researcher's own organisation

• multiple organisations

• contextual data and/or literature

• academic literature.

Secondary-data-based projects thus might or might not involve a focus on organisations. Some are focused on problem-solving within the researcher's own organisation, but in situations where access to primary data is difficult. A heavy workload may not allow time to interview people at work, or the organisation may not be supportive of the researcher's studies. However, it may be that perhaps the research is simply better done from just secondary data.

Secondary-data-based projects can also be conducted on a number of organisations. By using data put into the public domain by companies, it is possible to undertake some significant cross-company or even international comparisons. The data and information used here is often in the form of published financial or corporate reports, open-access materials placed on the Internet or intranet, or other publications such as marketing or recruitment literature.

Research that does not involve any specific organisations at all may simply draw on contextual data or literature. This is often in the form of market information, government publications or reports made by international bodies. Although this data and information frames the ways in which organisations are able to work, it presents a generic rather than organisationally specific perspective.

Lastly, some people choose to do their secondary-data-only research based just on the academic literature. These tend to be somewhat theoretical pieces of work, yet – as we will see later – they may still be of great practical relevance to organisations.

Regardless of the types of data and information being used for your research project, the basic need to plan the process effectively remains the same. There is a need to logically map out the process from your research purpose and data requirements, through to how you will convert your research findings into trustworthy conclusions. This plan helps to keep you focused and helps you to ensure that you achieve what you set out to achieve.

ORGANISATIONAL PROBLEM-SOLVING USING SECONDARY DATA

Using secondary data to solve an organisational problem means that you have to draw on a wide range of sources, mainly:

- academic literature
- professional literature
- contextual data and information
- research methods literature
- organisational data and information.

Research question

Chapter 8

Your research may start by drawing on academic texts to gain a better understanding of the constructs around which the problem is based, and to help you see how these constructs might inform your research question. You may draw on the professional literature to see what practices other people and organisations engage in, and how they are advised by empirical work. You may also want to look at the wider environmental, economic and market literature to see what other companies do and to better understand the accepted norms in the field. And you may also have to engage with the literature on research methods to determine a way to draw valid conclusions from a wide range of data often presented in different if not disparate ways. Lastly, you will have to draw data from the organisation such that you can both evidence the existence of the problem and use information as the basis for solving it.

CONSIDER...

Siobhan is planning to look at the effectiveness of budgetary controls within her organisation. This is a large manufacturing-sector organisation which produces sweets and other confectionery. The company operates in a highly competitive market. In the light of the issues mentioned previously, what types of secondary data do you think Siobhan will have to draw on, and why?

Your answers are likely to have identified many of the themes noted below, but it is useful to compare notes.

Academic texts

Siobhan has to understand what is meant by budgeting and why it is important. She must appreciate what mechanisms are available to guide the budgeting process and recognise the need for on-going control. She can use the academic texts to make sure that she has a clear understanding of all of these issues and to help her to frame her research purpose accordingly.

Professional texts

From these Siobhan can gather information on what actually works in practice, what are the strengths and the limitations of some of the approaches that people use, and how people actually use these systems within an organisation.

Contextual data and information

Wider market and economic literature will be useful to Siobhan in helping her to set the context for her research. It would be good to present information which shows just how competitive the market that the company operates in really is (for where the market is competitive, the organisation must keep firm control of costs to remain competitive), and this might give her a good justification for her research. She may also glean valuable information from the published financial reports of other companies, either to demonstrate what they do or to read from their balance sheet/profit and loss account how effective or ineffective others have been in controlling costs.

Research methods

Siobhan will have to read through the literature on research methods to decide how she is to make sense of all these different types of data, how she can analyse them to produce research findings, and how she can present them and evidence to support them in a convincing way.

Organisational data and information

Lastly, she will need some data which gives insights into what the organisation does. Perhaps she will have to look at the policy documents which outline the budget planning process. She is likely to want to look at the budgets produced, and will also certainly need to consider the end-of-year budgets and the extent to which targets have been met or variances exceeded.

MULTIPLE-ORGANISATION-BASED RESEARCH FROM SECONDARY DATA

Where the research looks at a number of organisations, the researcher will be seeking data that is already in the public domain. Here, things like published financial and end-of-year reports, information posted on the Internet and even literature on marketing campaigns or press releases can be used as sources. Wider market data and can also be used, and professional and academic literatures are usually used alongside these sources to bring in the academic context or framework which underpins the research.

RESEARCH BASED ON CONTEXTUAL DATA AND INFORMATION (NO ORGANISATION)

Business research projects based only on external and environmental data and information are able to draw on a wide range of different sources. Here, refining the focus of the research often requires an engagement with the academic literature to help to frame the research purpose/research question. The data then gathered as a means of answering that question may be economic information, market information or social and political information. Reports from Governments, international agencies or market research companies are all readily available.

RESEARCH BASED ON ACADEMIC LITERATURE (NO ORGANISATION)

Business research projects based only on academic literature are often thought of as theoretical rather than practical pieces of research. They require the researcher to draw on a depth of information and to review that literature to seek different perspectives, views or ways of understanding. Here the motives for the research are often to find out how people represent particular constructs, to explore how people characterise the relationship between constructs or to gain insights into the ways in which particular schools of thought have developed.

KEY POINTS

- Research based only on secondary data may or may not involve a focus on one or more organisations.
- Research based only on secondary data must be informed by academic and/or professional literature.
- Research based only on secondary data must give the same attention to methodological detail as does research involving active human participation.

FINDING A FOCUS

Business research projects are often driven by an understanding of the problems or opportunities that people face within their own organisation. In most cases primary data is necessary to enable the researcher to effectively answer the research question, and it is 'relatively' easy to see which data is going to be most useful in helping produce that answer.

However, where a business research project is based on secondary data only, that may not be the case, and even where a clear problem is identified, there is then a need to consider whether or not the appropriate data actually exists, and if it does, whether it is accessible. Where there is no clearly defined problem to focus on or where the only problems you can see cannot be answered using the data available, then creating a specific focus for the research can be difficult.

INVESTIGATIONS SPECIFIC TO AN ORGANISATION

When you are using only secondary data for your research, you must have an absolutely clear research focus. Achieving this focus can be quite difficult. In trying to decide what your focus could be, the process is similar to that considered in Chapter 7. You must think about a potential problem or opportunity to investigate, the stakeholders involved, your own levels of skills and interest, and how well the literature can inform your focus. Devise a list of three options or themes – that way, you stand a good chance of finding at least one that is do-able.

In addition to the feasibility assessment considered previously, you now have to think about the types of data and information you require in order to justify an argument that the problem or opportunity exists, and about what you need in order to try to solve the problem. It might be helpful here to think about the research purpose – ie what you are trying to do – and break that down to think about each of the things that you must do in order to fulfil that purpose. You will then have to identify what sorts of data and information you will require, and then to find out whether that data is available.

By recognising:

- data required
- data characteristics
- potential problems
- data availability

and thinking about these in line with the literature that has informed the ideas, you can now start to map out the research question.

The issue of 'looping' becomes apparent here. You are trying simultaneously to draw on the academic literature, your own areas of interest, the potential opportunities or problems within the organisation and the data and information that is available to you. You must also think how the ways in which the data and information that you can access have been analysed, and what influence this will have on your research question. For example, information produced specifically to promote a particular product may have been analysed in ways which presuppose particular results. You would have to consider what impact that potentially skewed analysis would have on your ability to produce reliable and trustworthy research findings.

You may now be able to produce your research question, or you may need to go through the looping process again. By the time you produce your research question you should have a thorough understanding of the ways in which the literature deals with the construct that will be your central theme, an understanding of the organisational context and the issues around the problem or the opportunity that you have identified, and a clear understanding of what data and information is available to you, and the characteristics of that data.

Although this is presented as a linear model in the box below, it is important to remember that at each stage the research may have to go back and revisit the stage before, as well as planning out the next stage ahead – it may well be 'messy'!

Clarifying the focus

Creating a clear focus for secondary-data-based research projects requires you to:
- identify potential problems or opportunities in your organisation
- try to connect these with your own areas of interest
- use the academic literature to inform your thinking
- jot down general ideas for possible research questions
- make a note of the research objectives needed to be able to answer the research questions
- identity the types of data you must obtain to meet the objectives/answer the questions
- find out if the relevant data is available and what the characteristics of that data are
- refine your research question based on your findings.

INVESTIGATIONS NOT SPECIFIC TO A SINGLE ORGANISATION

Devising the research questions when the research is not specific to an organisation is a very similar process to that above, except that there are two slightly different sub-approaches ('sub-approaches' in that they are derived from the same framework with some adaptations). The first is relevant where you are planning to look at a number of organisations but are doing so from the position of an outsider. Here you would have access only to information that is in the public domain. The first part of the process again requires you to identify the types of problems or the opportunities that could be investigated, connect these to your own areas of interest, and use the academic literature to inform the development of your ideas. The role of contextual data here is equally important – you still have to prove that the problem or opportunity exists by presenting evidence to justify your claim. The professional literature may be more or less helpful on this. It may offer useful insights into practices across companies. A key consideration at this point is the types of data and information that you can gather, not only from the perspectives of availability and the characteristics of that data, but also in terms of comparability. If your research is trying to compare issues across organisations, you have to make sure that the same types of data are available for each of the organisations in your study.

Once you are sure that appropriate data can be gathered from all the organisations involved, you can then start to refine your research question.

> **Where secondary-data-based research seeks to compare different organisations, it is vital to ensure that comparable data is available for all the organisations involved.**

INVESTIGATIONS NOT INVOLVING ORGANISATIONS

This type of research is often perceived as taking a 'theoretical' perspective – but this does not mean that the research is not going to be of any value to organisations. On the contrary, it is often theoretical research that identifies wider trends within markets, and shows how national and international factors may have an impact on businesses or start new trains of thought and new ideas which eventually translate into new practices or empirical research. The approach to creating a research focus may be somewhat different here, depending on your purpose. If your research is seeking to investigate a specific problem or opportunity located within markets or economies, this focus will drive you towards specific sources of data. You will have to consider what information is available, how this information has been produced, and whether or not you are able to make comparisons between the different data and information. You may have to base your research focus on an in-depth understanding of what is in the academic and/ or the professional literature. If your research is based on an intuitive idea that there may be a problem or an issue worthy of investigating, your initial engagement with the literature will be much broader as you trawl through it in an attempt to identify the areas for further investigation.

When doing a research project based on academic literature only, the specific focus is often an emergent one. You may start your review of the literature with little more than a general sense of direction, but find that there is a need to refine it as you become increasingly aware of the extent to which the literature addresses the issues being considered. Reading the literature allows you to test out the feasibility of a number of possible research questions. In this you need to be quite flexible in your approach, adapting your research ideas in the wake of what you find from the literature. However, you must also be aware that it is very difficult to make sure that your focus is not completely blown off course. As you review the literature, you are trying to create some sense of the theoretical landscape, a profile of what has been done and what has not been done. Understanding this landscape will help you to refine your research question and will also give you insights into the ways in which people investigate, analyse or characterise the constructs.

The process of 'looping', as described in the box below, requires you to look at the relationships between your areas of interest, the landscape of the literature, the availability of data and information, and the skills and abilities needed to address your research question.

Mapping the stages

Creating a clear focus for secondary-data-based research projects requires you to:

- generate general ideas for your focus from your own areas of interest, insights into the literature or an intuition that an area is less well considered
- review the literature to the extent that you understand the theoretical landscape
- use this understanding to refine and focus your research question
- use the research question to drive a further review of the literature
- use the review to further refine your research focus
- use the insights into research methods obtained from the literature to think about the skills and competences needed
- draw together the issues of interest, the theoretical landscape and the research skills needed to refine the research question.

You might think that a great deal of time has been spent here on describing how to refine a research question when undertaking secondary-data-only research. You would be right! The reason for it is simple. Research based on secondary data only is far more likely to drift off-beam than is research based on a combination of primary and secondary data, mainly because you are accessing a broader range of sources of data. Not only are these sources less focused on the particular data needed for your research but you will also find that connections are made across literatures and within literatures which distract you away from the core theme of your research.

However, there is another reason for needing a clear research question – and that is the potential to produce a simple descriptive text rather than any *bona fide* research project. Secondary-data-based research has to engage with many different sources of literature, from academic as well as professional perspectives, to review external market and economic data and to synthesise these to present a coherent case. But this on its own is not an investigation. If there is no research question, what is produced may be no more than a simple repackaging of the information that is freely available to anyone anyway. Without a clear research question, it is very easy indeed to simply produce a monograph about the market or the industry, rather than engage in proper business research.

It is of vital importance when undertaking research only from secondary data to make sure that a clear research purpose and/or research question guides the research process. This is true whether the research involves a focus on an organisation or not. Producing a descriptive story is problematic – if there is no research question, there is little need for a research method or means of analysis. If there is no analysis, any research findings will simply be a re-presentation of information that already exists. To illustrate how this drift can happen even with a research question, consider the case of Minette below.

CONSIDERING RESEARCH METHODS

This section looks briefly at the issues surrounding the use of methods when undertaking a secondary-data-only piece of research. Research methods themselves are

RESEARCH STORY: HOUSE OF HORRORS

Strategic planning

The research question that Minette set out to answer was 'What are the problems with the strategic planning process in ComplexcityXCo? An analysis of current practice'.

The research was to be based on secondary data only, but she did have access to internal documents from the company because she worked there. Minette started by looking at the literature on strategic planning, and she pulled together a good account of what strategy was, why it was important and the process that organisations go through in trying to produce a robust strategy. She then looked at the competitive market data so that she could make a case for how important the strategic planning process was to her company. She produced lots of figures on market share, market growth rate, and the gross and net profit for each of the main competitors in the market. She then gathered a whole range of internal documents – the process and policy documents which described the strategic

planning process in her organisation, information on the types of data each of the different contributors gathered to feed in to the process – and then included extracts from the strategy produced.

Although a copious quantity of work went into this, the main problem remained: there was no evaluation at all, and there was accordingly no way that she could answer the research question that she had set. Rather than identify the problems with the strategic planning process, she had simply described the process. A serious consequence of this was that although it showed that she was able to find and access data, it utterly failed to answer the research question. The report produced gave no indication of whether she even understood the data she had collected, let alone was able to evaluate it – and possibly worse still, gave her manager no idea of whether or not the strategic planning process was operating successfully.

discussed in overview in Chapter 10, and some are discussed in more depth in Part 3 of this book. However, their importance in secondary-data-only research must be emphasized. As the case of Minette demonstrated, it is not sufficient to simply re-present the information that has been gathered. There must be a formal way of examining and investigating that information, of synthesising the different sources, so that what is produced is a set of well-reasoned conclusions that are supported by evidence.

It is of crucial importance that you choose the research methods most likely to help you to answer your research question – methods that you have the skills and competences to use, and methods that are appropriate to the type of data that you have. Where data is gathered from various sources and in various formats, and when data has been produced for specific purposes and different stakeholders, you must consider *a priori* how you will deal with it. However, the fact that the data that you are planning to use has been gathered from secondary sources should not limit the types of analysis available to you – rather, you simply have to plan how you will deal with the issues mentioned.

Where you are thinking of using quantitative analysis it is useful to ask yourself the following questions:

- is the data 'raw' or compiled?
- how accurate is it?
- why was that data collected?
- how timely is it?

That is:

Are you dealing with data from a primary or a secondary source? Where the data has been compiled it may be necessary to find out what processes were involved in this operation, and how they have produced the results that they have.

How accurate is the data? You must check that there are no inconsistencies in the information gathered, because inconsistencies going into an analysis may well be magnified when they come out of further analysis.

What were the motives behind the data collection? Where data collection is seen as an arduous and unnecessary process that has been imposed on people, short cuts or even distortions may have taken place. Alternatively, where data has been collected to prove a specific point, the sources of data and the ways in which the data was collected may have been skewed.

How timely is the data? And is each set of data working to the same time-frames? These issues are especially important if dealing with financial reports. Consider how the nature of different 'year ends' may impact on the comparability of what otherwise might appear very similar data sets.

Where you are thinking of using qualitative analysis you may find it useful to ask the following questions:

- who was the intended 'audience'?
- how comparable is the data?
- why was that data collected?
- can you access soft copies?

That is:

Who was the information produced for? Narrative data is often written with a particular audience in mind. Indeed, you will be doing precisely this when writing up your project report. It is important to recognise the nature of this language, how it reflects the target audience, and how to take account of this in your analysis.

How comparable are the different sets of data? Data collected will reflect the motives for, and methods of, collection as well as the views and opinions of the respondent groups. When using this data you must be aware of how different methods of collection, different modes of analysis and the responses from different groups may undermine the comparability of the results.

What were the motives behind the collection of the data? Data is collected for a specific purpose. The purpose will be reflected in the ways in which questions are asked, in the method of data collection and in the means of analysis.

Can you can access soft copies of the data? If you can, it would be very useful in giving you the opportunity to run it through analysis software. Where data is only available as hard copy you will have to think about how this constrains you to specific types of analysis.

KEY POINTS

- Secondary-data-only research projects can be of practical use to an organisation.
- Secondary-data-only research must be based on a clear and unambiguous research question.
- There is a need to formally plan your research methodology.
- There is a need to consider the characteristics of the data you have access to.

USING FINDINGS AS EVIDENCE

The research findings drawn from secondary data should be as well reasoned and as justified as those drawn from primary data – the same processes of analysis should have been involved. Below is a simple set of guidelines presented more to act as a reminder of what constitutes evidence than to provide any new insights regarding the use of evidence in secondary-data research projects.

Guidelines for producing evidence

- Findings presented should relate directly to the data accessed and the ways in which it has been analysed. It is usual to introduce some of the researcher's own well-reasoned arguments, but these must still be grounded in the research that has gone before.
- Claims made have to be justified with well-reasoned argument and/or with reference to supporting figures, metrics or statistics. These help demonstrate the trustworthiness of the information being presented.
- Claims may also be supported by the use of narrative text from the research. The most powerful way of doing this is by quoting the results of any narrative analysis. The least effective way of doing it is to migrate quotations across. This latter approach should be used with caution because it can pave the way for accusations of selectivity and bias if the quotations are not supported by wider evidence or appear to be partisan.
- Counter-arguments should be considered and dismissed (or upheld as a caveat) using supporting information.
- The use of analogy is good, especially where the analogy is to a source that is deemed reliable. For example, although the research might be looking at a totally different topic, to draw analogies with research done previously by renowned academics or practitioners gives credibility to the new work.
- Comparisons are useful. These are often utilised to link the current research back to the academic literature that was used to inform it. They too give credibility to the new work.
- Research findings should be structured logically to allow the author to build his or her arguments and the reader to follow the ways in which the arguments have been built.

Research using only secondary data must comply with the same rules of evidence that research based on primary data does. If it cannot be justified, it doesn't go in.

DRAWING WELL-REASONED CONCLUSIONS

Again the issue of evidence is to the fore here, although it does not have to be presented in quite as much detail as in the research findings. It is important that no new information is contained in the conclusions: they should be clearly derived from the research processes that precede them. However, it is also useful here to note the ways in which the use of only secondary data may help to produce a particular set of conclusions. It is worth considering too how the sources of data may have exerted an influence, whether any prior analysis or manipulation of the data has enabled or constrained your own research, and whether the comparability of the data has had any impact.

In drawing well-reasoned conclusions it is not always possible to put forward the evidence that was presented previously. The conclusions become unwieldy and begin to lose their focus. Instead, you should refer back to the evidence already presented. Your conclusions should always be focused on answering the research question set. They should present a well-reasoned debate that recognises the limitations of your research even as it demonstrates what it has accomplished.

Conclusions should not introduce any new data and should recognise the limitations of the research process and the impact it has had on the conclusions drawn.

THE STRENGTHS AND WEAKNESSES OF USING ONLY SECONDARY DATA

Using only secondary data for your research gives you more control over the processes of data-gathering. Rather than having to negotiate access to people, arrange interviews or time to distribute questionnaires, and chase people for responses, you can schedule the data-collection processes to suit your own timetable. Secondary-data-only research also allows you to undertake research outside the confines of your own organisation. I have had a number of military students who have used secondary-data dissertations as a means of understanding more about different sectors and producing evidence of this understanding prior to finishing their commissions and moving to a new career. Secondary-data research enables you to expand your learning outside the confines of your own organisation. Anka, as you will see shortly, wanted to look at CSR from the perspective of organisations based in different countries, rather than stick to the single focus of her own organisation.

The limitations of secondary-data-only research relate fundamentally to the theme of reliability. Issues of finding out how timely the information is, how reliable the sources of information are, what has been done to the data to change it into information, and whether or not the data from different sources are comparable all must be taken into account.

Having considered the potential strengths and weaknesses of secondary-data-only research, it is useful to see some examples of where secondary-data-only research has been highly successful. Below are two examples of students who undertook secondary-data-only research.

RESEARCH STORY

Constantinos and CSR

Constantinos was undertaking his business research project as part of his MBA studies. He had come across the issue of corporate social responsibility (CSR) at various stages in the course but seldom had enough time to think about it in any substantial depth, despite its being topic in which he was extremely interested. When it came to thinking about a subject for his dissertation, the choice was easy: CSR. But what *about* CSR? Thinking through each of the areas he studied, Constantinos knew that he was also quite interested in the areas of organisational behaviour and HRM – so after some consideration he decided to look at the relationship between CSR and organisational culture. Because of the quite eclectic nature of this focus, it made sense to do this from the perspective of secondary data. With an outline idea of his research question which proposed to look at how organisational culture influenced the success of CSR, Constantinos took to the literature. After a lengthy search – and much

to his surprise – there was actually very little in the academic press that explicitly made the connection between the success of CSR and organisational culture.

Constantinos now found himself in a situation where the research question that he was keen to answer could not, it seemed, be answered in the way that he had planned. So he started to think through what it was that had made him decide on that research question. The answer was that from his experience in organisations and his understanding of both CSR and organisational culture, he intuitively felt that there had to be a relationship between the two – even if very few people had written about it. He decided therefore that if this relationship that he felt intuitively to be there really existed, it might be characterised implicitly rather than explicitly within the literature on CSR. Engaged in this process of 'looping', he returned back to the literature on CSR and to the literature on organisational culture to see how he could develop this idea.

Constantinos was aware that in the literature on culture, many writers characterise the construct as comprising a set of specific components. Accordingly, it became clear to him that if he were to search the literature on CSR for mention of or allusion to these components of culture, he could get a clearer picture of how the CSR literature perceives the relationship between CSR and culture. The research question subsequently changed – this time to focus on how the literature on CSR characterises the relationship between CSR and culture.

The next step was to think about how to go about this. A Google search on the term 'corporate social responsibility' returned over 4 million hits! Then there was the whole question of which research method to use. Reviewing the literature on research methods, Constantinos decided that some form of content analysis seemed to be an ideal way of examining the secondary data (literature on CSR) to identify the components of culture. He investigated a range of different ways of doing this and decided that using the Leximancer software would be the best. Leximancer the © to note that this is copyright trademark is a system that produces both frequency counts and conceptual maps showing how often specific words are used in the text and the relationships between these words. For example, if the word 'values' was used frequently in conjunction with the word 'organisational', the maps would

highlight this. Contantinos had to set up his own 'glossary' of terms which he extracted from the literature on organisational culture, so that the conceptual maps produced could draw out from the narrative where the words were used. He could then explore the context of each in more depth later.

This only left the issue of sampling. The work he was doing could never be based on a representative sample! Accordingly, he had to find a way of convenience sampling – a way of selecting a manageable number of articles which he could review. It was decided that a closed time-frame would be a good way of limiting the number of papers. Recognising that some papers take six months to get to press and others take two years to get to press, it was decided that the sample frame would be to look for the words 'corporate social responsibility' in the abstract of all papers published between 1 January 2008 and 1 July 2008 in the business-oriented academic press. From this perspective a spread of journals from the UK, Europe, the USA and Australia were selected to give the potential for an 'international' dimension to be added to the analysis. Again, the sample produced was too large, and so it was necessary to reduce the search to titles rather than abstracts.

At the time of writing this book, Constantinos has familiarised himself with the use of the software, is gathering in the papers and is using the academic literature on organisational culture to help him to derive the codes that the content analysis will search for.

RESEARCH STORY

Anka

Anka was taking a career break to look after her children and had taken the opportunity to use the time to do an MBA. She was a little concerned about being able to gain access to an organisation to do her research based on primary data, and so decided to focus on using secondary data instead. She, too, had an interest in the issue of corporate social responsibility (CSR), but from a different perspective. Living in Asia, she had noted from her studies that much of the literature that she read on the subject of CSR had a decidedly US slant. There

was very little that took an Asian view of CSR. Her intention was therefore to compare and contrast CSR practices between US and Asian businesses. There were a number of things that she had to do here. The first issue was to familarise herself with what was meant by CSR, why it was deemed to be a useful practice by some and as capitalist interference by others. She had to look at the ways in which CSR was characterised and to see if she could extract, from her review of the literature, some sort of framework that would act as a sort of measuring-stick, something that would give her the parameters against which she could compare the practices of US and Asian businesses.

This sounds like quite a simple process, but it turned out to be a large undertaking. Anka needed a solid understanding of a highly debatable issue, and had to obtain it from a huge expanse of available literature on CSR. She developed robust skills in selecting papers, and scanning and skimming before deciding which she would read thoroughly.

Running in parallel to this was a consideration of how she would access the data she needed. Anka could only use secondary data that was in the public domain. Also, because she was dealing with companies in Asia and companies in the USA, she had to make sure that the reports published and presented in the public domain contained comparable data. Lastly, it was important that the companies selected were seen to be comparable in terms of size (number of employees), age, revenues and markets. Although the research was never

intended to be representative, there was still a need to ensure that the research findings were as reliable and trustworthy as possible.

Anka selected Dahlsrud's model of CSR as the framework against which she would compare the companies' actions. She chose ten companies, five from each continent, and paired these across sectors, size, age, revenues and markets. This done, she then required a means of analysis, a means by which the comparisons could be made. Again using Dahlsrud's model of CSR she opted for content analysis, coding Dahlsrud's dimensions and searching for these manually through the published reports of the companies.

Her efforts were highly successful. She was able clearly to identify areas of similarity and of difference, to discuss these within the context of the wider CSR literature, to present well-justified conclusions grounded in evidence, and to make robust suggestions for future research. She also got an A!

SUMMARY

Using only secondary data for business research is often thought of as being too difficult for business researchers, or as lacking the ability to contribute anything practical to organisations. This chapter has demonstrated that neither of these is the case. Research from secondary data can be a reward process that has numerous benefits. It enables you to see things from different perspectives, to expand your experience of research to support your career development plans and to gain skills in accessing and navigating through the vast amounts of data that are currently available.

Using secondary data means that you are often more able to work to your own time-frames and at your own speed (deadlines permitting) than you are with primary-data-based research. However, this does not then mean that secondary-data-based research is the easy option.

Secondary-data-based research requires the same rigour and the same attention to detail that primary-data-based research does. You must consider the reliability of the data and information you use, how previous analyses have contributed to the characteristics of the information, and what impact this will have on your own research findings.

You need to consider the demands of your stakeholders, your own level of interest, and whether you have the skills of searching out and editing only that data and information which is of use to you. Doing so will help you to produce a valuable and trustworthy piece of business research.

REVIEW QUESTIONS

1. What are the four types of secondary-data-only research projects, and how do they differ?

2. Why is it important to have a clear and unambiguous research question when undertaking secondary-data-only research?

3. When gathering data from secondary sources, what characteristics or issues must you be aware of, and why?

4. What are the advantages of doing your business research project from secondary data only?

EXPLORE FURTHER

Dixon-Woods, M., Agarwal, S., Jones, D., Young, B. and Sutton, A. (2005) 'Synthesising qualitative and quantitative evidence: a review of possible methods', *Journal of Health Services Research and Policy*, Vol.10, No.1: 45–53. Provides a good overview of the processes and the practices of synthesising qualitative and quantitative data

Goodwin, J. and O'Connor, H. (2009) 'Contextualising the research process: using interviewer notes in the secondary analysis of qualitative data', *The Qualitative Report*, Vol.11, No.3: 374–93. Available online at http:// www.nova.edu.ssss/QR/QR11-2/goodwin.pdf [accessed 9 May 2009]

Heaton, J. (2008) 'Secondary analysis of qualitative data', in Alasuutari, P., Bickman, L. and Brannen, J. (eds) *The Handbook of Social Research Methods*. London: Sage. A good consideration of the processes and analyses of qualitative data

Hinds, P. S, Vogel, R. J. and Clarke-Steffen, L. (1997) 'The possibilities and pitfalls of doing a secondary analysis of a qualitative data set', *Qualitative Health Research*, Vol.7, No 3: 408–24. An interesting paper which looks at the methodological challenges presented when undertaking secondary analyses on qualitative data

Stewart, D. W. and Kamins, M. A. (1993) *Secondary Research: Information sources and methods*, 2nd edition. Newbury Park, CA: Sage Publications. A useful book written for academic researchers but which offers insights into a range of approaches to secondary research

 Visit www.cipd.co.uk/brm for web links, templates, activities and other useful resources relating to this chapter.

CHAPTER 13

Case Study Research

INTRODUCTION

A significant proportion of the research projects that we have both seen over the years is heralded as comprising case study research. However, on further investigation it becomes clear that there has actually been very little understanding of what a 'case study' actually entails. Case study research is directed towards understanding a 'case'. The 'case' essentially focuses on a key theme, but does this by accessing data from a range of different sources, and it is this idea of multiple perspectives that is one of the defining features of case study research.

Unfortunately, case study research is often regarded by business researchers as a 'one size fits all' approach to doing research, and because of this the term tends to be used in very vague and general ways, often to mean any research based in an organisation. What is described as 'case study research' frequently covers a multitude of sins, and all too frequently what is presented is a random collection of secondary organisational data, strung together with descriptive personal opinions. This produces little that is of any value. Likewise, case study research is often described as a research 'method'. This is not the case. A case study is a research *strategy* (Eisenhardt, 1991; Yin, 1995; Hartley, 2006), an *approach* to research which you have to *design,* and through which you use a range of research methods (secondary-data methods included) and analyses in an attempt to answer the research question.

Lastly, this 'one size fits all' perception means that many people assume that case study research is appropriate in all circumstances. Again this is not so. A case study approach is useful when the context within which the problem exists is a key consideration in the research. Where issues can be taken away from the context, a case study simply introduces levels of unnecessary complexity.

This chapter will discuss what a case study approach to research is and how it can be of value to your business research. It will then consider when a case study approach is most appropriate, before going on to outline a range of issues that you will have to think about if you are planning to use a case study approach for your business research.

LEARNING OUTCOMES

This chapter should enable you to:

• appreciate what a case study research strategy *does* and does *not* entail

• identify the research situations in which it is appropriate to use a case study approach

• design and implement a robust case study research strategy

• recognise the strengths and the limitations of a case study approach to business research.

WHAT IS A CASE STUDY APPROACH?

Yin suggests that a case study approach is a research tool (1992). It is an implement used to craft together a series of investigations which collectively produce a 'detailed investigation' (Hartley, 2006; p.323) of the research question. This series of investigations may use multiple methods, single methods at multiple levels or cross-case comparisons to give a rich picture of the focus of your research.

Robert Yin is credited with bringing the idea of case study research into prominence following his 1981 article entitled 'The case study crisis: some answers'. It is therefore useful to look to him to find our definition of what a case study is (Yin, 1984, p23; 1994, p13):

 'A **case study** is an empirical inquiry that investigates a contemporary phenomenon within its real-life context, especially when the boundaries between phenomenon and context are not clearly evident.'

What does this mean for you as you think about your undertaking business research? A distinctive feature of case study research is that the process of the research is *not detached* from the context within which that research is taking place. This makes this a particularly useful approach where the problem that you are addressing is enmeshed within the fabric of the organisation. In some cases it is quite easy to detach the focus of your research from the wider organisation. Where, for example, you are looking at the success of an IT project, the fact that this research has a definite beginning, a series of targets to hit en route and a clearly defined set of objectives at the end, makes this topic relatively easy to investigate in isolation. In other research situations, the ways in which you, as a researcher, construct your research or frame the research question will determine the extent to which your research can be detached from the wider organisation.

A case study approach is directed towards understanding a specific issue. This may mean that you are looking at an issue within a single organisation, or a specific issue across a number of organisations. (Sometimes research will look at two or three cases, but a single case study is highly labour-intensive so you are unlikely to be considering more than one case in your own research.) However, you are not looking to generalise beyond that case. You will note that Yin's definition does not prescribe any specific research method. The method you choose will have to be appropriate to the issue you are investigating and to its context. Indeed, because the issue you are seeking to understand is likely to be multi-faceted, you are likely to have to use a variety of methods in order to understand it. Such a *multi-method research strategy* is one of the distinguishing features of a case study approach. Each method might explore a different aspect of the case. You would create a coherent set of findings from these different methods by considering beforehand the way in which they work together to help you answer your research question.

For example, if you were planning to undertake a business research project to identify the effectiveness of the recruitment and selection processes in your organisation, there would be two approaches open to you: a simple quantitative analysis or a more multi-faceted approach which takes the wider implications of recruitment and selection into account. In the first you could look at the process of recruitment and selection in a very pragmatic way. The intention of any recruitment and selection process is to bring people into the organisation, and so your research may focus on the relationship between the number of adverts placed and the number of appointments made. There is no doubt that this is useful information – it will give you a very good indication of whether or not the adverts are attracting the right sort of people to apply.

However, if you are thinking about the effectiveness of recruitment and selection in wider organisational terms, you might want to know more than just the number of people that the recruitment process brings in. The impact of recruitment and selection processes goes much further than that. Beth in Chapters 1 and 2 was spending most of her time recruiting new people and then training them, only to have them leave shortly afterwards. A serious consequence of this was the demotivation of the remaining staff who were having to cover the work between appointments or support and advise new staff. Successful recruitment is about bringing the right people in, how long people stay, and whether they are able to do the job for which they have been appointed. And because this clearly has an effect on the day-to-day activities of the organisation, it means that assessing its 'effectiveness' is altogether more complicated than simply counting 'numbers in'.

The second approach takes this idea of the consequences of recruitment and selection to the heart of the research. The 'looping' process between the literature and your understanding of the organisation may indicate to you very early on that a simple metric will be of limited value (although not always – sometimes a case study can be an emergent process, and we will discuss this shortly). So you may decide to look at how new people recruited 'fit' within the organisation (Schneider, 1995, notes that where people do not fit, they leave). Things like job satisfaction and staff turnover may have to be considered. You may need to look at what image is created by your recruitment and selection processes – after all, job adverts and recruitment processes contribute to the organisation's image which is important in attracting staff as well as attracting customers and investors – or you may need to look at the costs versus benefits of the processes involved. In this second approach, the fact that recruitment and selection processes are seen as being more than just an 'upfront' operation means that your research is likely to have a number of sub-questions or research objectives. It may mean that multiple types of data are needed and that this data has to be gathered from many different sources.

So your choices are:

- to treat recruitment and selection as an isolated process and simply focus on the relationship between the number of adverts versus the number of appointments – a single research approach

or

- to treat recruitment and selection as a process that has consequences for, and therefore is an integrated part of, the fabric of the organisation – a case study approach.

As Hartley (2006, p323) notes, a case study allows the research to undertake

> "an analysis of the context and the processes which illuminate the theoretical issues being studied."

 ACTIVITY

Turn once more to the case of Beth, as discussed in Chapter 2. Imagine that Beth had been set each of the following tasks as the basis for her business research. Which of these research questions do you think could or should be considered by using a case study approach, and which do you think would be better not to use a case study approach? Note down the reasons behind your answers.

(a) Beth has been asked by her boss, Fiona, to look at the costs of staff turnover in the department.

(b) Beth has been asked by her boss, Fiona, to see if there has been any change in staff turnover following the implementation of a new shift rota.

(c) Beth has been asked by her boss, Fiona, to look at how staff turnover levels might be reduced in the department.

In the first example Fiona has asked Beth to look at something very specific – the costs of staff turnover. Whether or not this is suited to case study research depends on what Fiona means by the word 'costs'. If she is only interested in the financial costs, a simple set of calculations may well be sufficient and a case study approach would probably not be necessary. However, if by 'costs' she means the wider costs (for example, the costs of having to train up temporary staff to cover for people who have left), then a case study approach may be appropriate: multiple sources of information will be necessary.

In the second example Fiona has asked Beth to look at a simple comparison. She wants to know whether or not the new shift system has had an effect on the rates of staff turnover. In looking at this Beth need only look at what the rate was before the new rota system, and what the rate has been after the new rota system, and then she will have the answer. A case study approach is unlikely to be useful here – a statistical approach in which the relationship between the two is made clear may be more appropriate.

In the third approach Fiona does not simply want to know what is causing staff turnover but how to reduce it. Because turnover can have many different causes (in Chapter 2 we mentioned that the cause may be Beth herself!) it can also have many different solutions. Beth must make sure that she gathers lots of information from different sources and from people at different levels in the organisation. She must be able to get some idea of what the problems are, what potential solutions are available, and how these potential solutions may be more or less useful to her organisation. A case study approach would be very useful indeed here.

The examples above can give the impression that business researchers always know instantly when a case study approach is most appropriate, yet this is not always the case.

RESEARCH STORY

Not just the ticket

David works as a team leader in the IT department of a leisure centre. The centre's managers introduced a new electronic ticket and entry machine. The machines were part of a multi-faceted system. When people needed to book in advance – eg for the squash or badminton courts – they could do so online, pay electronically and print off an e-ticket. They then simply inserted the ticket into the machine to get into the leisure centre. When people didn't need to pre-book, they simply selected what facility they wanted to use and paid at the ticket machine. The ticket was produced and that allowed them to get into the leisure centre. The objective behind the project was to free up administration staff time so that they could spend more time on health promotion issues, in particular inspiring children vulnerable to future health problems to get involved in sport. David was asked to evaluate the project.

David's investigation involved producing a semi-structured questionnaire which asked staff to rank the extent to which the key performance indicators had been met. It seemed that the project had been pretty much a success. Apart from a few teething troubles, the machine and the electronic system of remote booking worked well. The project came in on time and only slightly over budget. However, as part of his questionnaire David included a section for open comments on what worked really well and what didn't work. To his surprise, although the introduction of the technology – the project plan – had worked well, the objective of getting the administration staff more involved in health promotion had not been met at all. The questionnaire suggested a number of reasons for this, ranging from failure to communicate to poor leadership and the unavailability of the appropriate training and development. So substantial were the issues raised in the open comments that David decided to revisit his research and undertake a more integrated and wide-ranging case study approach, one better able to evaluate the broader aspects of the project. By interviewing people and holding focus groups at different levels within the organisation he sought to identify how successful the project *really* was.

It is perhaps easy with hindsight to think that David should have appreciated the potential difficulties beforehand. However, the evaluation of an IT project, where there is a clear project plan and clear performance indicators, is often something that can be done with a single isolated piece of research. What David's case illustrates is first, that a case study approach to research might be an emergent one rather than one that is planned in advance. And second, that even when you have gathered your data you must be willing to be open and honest with yourself about whether or not it really does help you to answer your research question in the best way possible.

KEY POINTS

- A case study approach is an approach to research rather than a method.
- A case study approach focuses on a specific case from a number of different perspectives.
- A case study approach is appropriate when the focus of the research cannot be separated from the organisation within which it is embedded.

CHOOSING A CASE STUDY APPROACH

Although in many cases your own understanding of the nature of the problems you are investigating will lead you to opt for a case study approach, as you have seen it is not always possible to 'predict' when such an approach is most appropriate. Sometimes the need to use multiple methods or to gather data from multiple levels or sources becomes obvious only as you gather your data. In other cases the limitations of the data you have gathered may only become apparent as you analyse that data.

David, for example, suddenly realised that the limitations of the IT project lay not with 'project management' but with the idea that this can take place within but somehow detached from the organisational context. This insight then led to two key motivations behind his case study research. First was the recognition that the project had an impact on and was influenced by the wider organisational context. The aim was not simply to introduce a 'technology' but was to use this to allow staff to be redeployed to a more proactive health promotion role.

> A case study approach is useful when the focus of the study cannot be detached from the organisational context within which it exists.

The second revelation was that in order to produce any meaningful results, David had to gather data and information from a range of different sources and stakeholders. It was not sufficient to simply 'measure' the effectiveness of the technology – the success of the project was to be judged by the ways in which the staff, freed from administrative duties, undertook this new proactive health promotion role. David had therefore to gather data and information from people at many levels within the organisation in order to judge whether or not they were indeed changing the nature of the work they did.

> A case study approach is useful when your research requires that you gather data from different sources all of which contribute to a specific point in the context of that case.

A case study, then, uses data from a range of sources, levels or methods to help construct a more complete picture of the research focus. David could draw on secondary data and information about the costs and the project time-frames as well as primary data from the people whose roles and responsibilities were supposed to change in the wake of the introduction of the new technology. Using case study research in this way helps you to identify different aspects of complexity, to see where the problems are embedded in the wider organisational issues, and to draw on evidence to help explain what is happening.

DATA AND INFORMATION SOURCES

The divide between primary and secondary data is only one way in which different types of data can be used to create the holistic picture of an organisation that is so crucial to case study research. There are multiple approaches to data and information gathering, using different:

- methods
- levels within the organisation
- sources
- cases or organisations
- time periods.

Despite the potential complexity here, Robson (2002) notes the temptation to see case study research as a 'soft option' (p178) which lacks the credibility of the more 'hard-nosed' (*ibid*) scientific approaches. And doubtless where the term is used in a vague and generic way, this may well be the case. The counter to such an accusation is the richness and depth of data that is produced and used to inform case study research. This idea of seeking data from different sources, seeking the views and opinions of people at different levels within the organisation, or by using investigations over time offers rich insights into the different perceptions, the changing research landscape or the complexity of the situation and gives you scope to question, where there are differences, why they exist.

The use of multiple methods of data collection or of multiple sources of information implies that there is likely to be a difference in the types of data that might be used in case study research – that is, you are likely to have to draw upon both qualitative and quantitative data. Although it is argued that a case study approach can successfully use 'just' quantitative data and thus produce research that retains the integrity of a realist tradition (Robson, 2002), it is important to include a caveat here. The key advantage of case study research is the way in which the issues under investigation are embedded within the context of the case: they are part of the fabric of the organisation. Quantitative data necessarily requires some degree of separation from context. It requires the researcher to identify specific attributes or dependent/independent variables, which necessarily isolates the issues from the context within which they are embedded. If you are asking closed questions about the implementation of an IT project, your answers will relate only to the specific questions that you ask. Hartley (2006) adds to this debate by recognising that producing reliable and valid quantitative results will be frustrated because there will always be too many variables to disaggregate and 'test'. Quantitative data alone is problematic, therefore, because the wider emergent issues of context and the degree to which the problems are enmeshed with the day-to-day life of the organisation will not be revealed.

However, quantitative data offers useful insights as part of a portfolio of data gathered in a case study approach. It can help you to identify discrepancies in the ways in which different groups respond, it can indicate key areas worthy of further investigation, and it can help you frame the issues in ways that are important to your stakeholders.

> **A case study approach benefits most where the results draw on the synergies between qualitative and quantitative data.**

The examples of how to approach case study research used thus far have related to an investigation in a single organisation at one point in time, and for the vast majority of business researchers this approach will be the one adopted. However, it is useful to be aware that case studies are not necessarily confined to one particular organisation, nor to one particular point in time – rather, they can involve a number of organisations or multiple cases and be over a prolonged or intermittent period.

Multiple cases

Where multiple cases are used, the intention of the research is often to compare and contrast the findings, to look for similarities and for differences. For many first-time business researchers, this introduces an additional level of complexity in trying to gain access to a number of different organisations. However, for those people undertaking a business research project using secondary data only, it is often a particularly useful approach. You recall from Chapter 12 how Anka selected five US companies and five Indian companies and used the secondary data that they had published on their websites to enable her to draw inferences about and comparisons between the two. The embeddedness in Anka's research came from the use of Dahlsrud's model which looked at the integration of the issue of CSR with the contextual and organisational issues.

Single cases over time

The demands that stakeholders make of your business research often require you to have a clear start point and a clear end point to your research. You have a set of 'deliverables' and a date by which these are to be delivered. However, where business research is trying to look at the success or the effectiveness of more substantial organisational events, a 'one-off' approach may not be sufficient. Kurt Lewin was originally motivated to establish his 'unfreeze, move, refreeze' (1951) model for organisational change because his research demonstrated that the problem with change was not necessarily getting people to change in the first instance, but was to ensure that the changes made actually stuck. The problems facing those implementing change lay in making sure that people did not slip back into their old ways of working. In such a situation, then, business research which evaluates a process of change immediately after it has been introduced may demonstrate that it has been a complete success, whereas results of research undertaken 12 months later might tell a very different story!

The approach to research which involves a number of investigations over a prolonged period of time is known as longitudinal research, and it enables you to see how issues develop, how practices become established and how perceptions evolve. However, it is again worth emphasising that for longitudinal research to be considered a case study approach it must be focused on issues that cannot be separated from the context within which they exist.

UNDERTAKING CASE STUDY RESEARCH

A case study approach to research is one that must be carefully considered and planned for. It is not sufficient to simply drop the term 'case study approach' into your proposal or your research methodology without a clear understanding of what it implies or indeed why this approach is the most appropriate.

By now you will be aware that there are two key criteria to be used in judging whether or not a case study approach is the best research strategy for your business research. The first is the in-depth focus on a particular case. This might be a single organisation at one point in time, a single organisation over a period of time, or, less commonly, a number of organisations. The second key focus of case study research is its embeddedness within the organisational context. Where it is not helpful to try to separate the problems from the wider aspects of the organisation in which they are located, a case study approach is likely to be appropriate. However, both of these criteria have wider implications for the nature of your research. Case study research is useful for helping you to recognise those aspects of an issue or problem that are not codified – aspects such as perceptions, attitudes, behaviours and beliefs; aspects such as everyday ways of working and everyday ways of doing things, how people deal with things that are usual or different, and the ways in which people relate to the codified processes and systems within which they work. There is obviously within this some emphasis on the qualitative aspects of business research, but it is useful to note that quantitative methods also play an important part in case study research.

In order to appreciate the ways in which people work within and 'perceive' the structures of control throughout the organisation, there is a need to recognise what systems and processes actually exist, the policies that guide what people do, the metrics that measure the effectiveness of those policies, and the ways in which those structures and processes are communicated or enforced. Quantitative data and information is important in setting the framework and in helping you to describe the structures of the organisation within which the focus of your research is located.

A case study approach is a complex way of undertaking business research which should be undertaken only if it is the most effective approach for you. Despite small variations on the theme, most authors (cf Eisenhardt, 1989; Soy, 1997) who suggest the ways in which case study research should be approached, do so by elaborating on the framework mapped out by Yin (1994). Accordingly, the framework presented in the box below draws on the work of all of these authors to map out an approach that is more suited to people using a case study approach for practical business research.

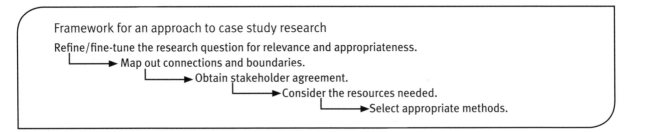

Framework for an approach to case study research

Refine/fine-tune the research question for relevance and appropriateness.
→ Map out connections and boundaries.
→ Obtain stakeholder agreement.
→ Consider the resources needed.
→ Select appropriate methods.

REFINE THE RESEARCH QUESTION

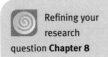

Refining your research question **Chapter 8**

Those of you who have read through the first Part of this book will have already given substantial consideration to refining your research question. For those of you who have just 'dropped in' at this particular section, I would recommend that you turn back to Chapter 8 to get a deeper insight into the key issues in producing a sound research question which forms a solid base for your research. Here we consider the ways in which your research question guides your decision for or against a case study approach.

When thinking about a case study approach to your research, you should assess whether or not what you are intending to achieve (the outcomes) is best served by using a case study. Yin (1994) points out that case study research is most appropriate when the research questions are asking *how* or *why* rather than questions that ask *what*. Research questions that ask how or why are often based on some exploration, some idea of eliciting different perspectives that can then be drawn together to help describe or explain. 'How' or 'why' questions both require a depth of information. Conversely, research questions that ask 'what' are often based on simply eliciting the facts of the matter; for this a breadth of information that can be seen as statistically valid may be more appropriate than qualitative depth.

 ACTIVITY

Compare the following two sets of questions and make notes about the appropriateness or otherwise of using a case study approach to investigate each.

What is the current cost of sales?
Why is our current cost of sales so high?
What performance benchmarks are used by our competitors?
How do our competitors use performance benchmarking?

What you should see from the examples in the Activity above is the way in which the use of the word 'what' seems to imply the need for measurement, for something that gives a definite answer, rather than something that requires rich description and explanation. Before considering a case study approach you must make sure that it is the most efficient and effective way of answering your research question.

MAP OUT THE CONNECTIONS AND SET BOUNDARIES

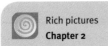
Rich pictures
Chapter 2

Because a case study approach is based on the embeddedness of the problem within the wider organisational context, it is useful to try to surface what this embeddedness actually means. For this it is beneficial to draw on some of the tools considered earlier – things like mind maps, relationship diagrams and rich pictures can help you recognise the potential connectivities and see how they might help to direct your data-gathering. Surfacing these connectivities enables you to draw together your understanding of the theories and concepts that have underpinned your research, to see how they inform your research question, and to determine what your research will include and exclude.

This issue of connectivity is also important when undertaking multiple-case research, because this is the point at which you should be considering which organisations you will involve in your research. The need, when using multiple cases, to ensure that you gather comparable data from each makes it useful to replicate this mapping process to help identify where you can and where you cannot access appropriate data.

OBTAIN STAKEHOLDER AGREEMENT

The stakeholders in your research will have a number of requirements. They will require your research findings to be presented in ways that are meaningful to them. They will require your research to be completed within a specific time-frame and possibly within a specific budget. They may also require that the research be confined to areas that they can realistically do something about. A case study approach takes time, it produces a range of different types of data and information, and by its very nature it is difficult to contain within a narrow frame of reference. Where you are considering a case study approach, you must ensure that it is going to be of value to at least some of your stake-holders and at the same time ensure that the time taken and the nature of the results are not going to be a problem for others.

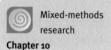

Mixed-methods research
Chapter 10

Despite the potential for problems, a case study approach may be the only means by which you can meet the demands of many or even all of the stakeholders. By using multiple sources of data you have more flexibility to be able to present the appropriate results to the appropriate people. For example, if you choose to use mixed methods, gathering qualitative and quantitative data as part of your research, you might manage to meet the needs of those who require quantitative or statistical evidence to 'prove' the existence of a problem, while at the same time producing the qualitative evidence that seeks to explore and explain the reasons for that problem. Mixed methods within a case study framework enable you to address the weaknesses of using one method in isolation. One of the criticisms often levelled at qualitative research is that it does not give managers the hard facts and figures that they need to base organisational decisions on. Although it could be argued that care must be exercised in accepting facts and figures as 'the truth', there is no doubting that they provide useful indicators and convey a certain degree of confidence to managers when making decisions. Having said that, although statistics can give your stakeholders a picture of what is happening and inferential statistics may even predict what will happen in the future, numbers and units cannot offer an explanation why. A case study approach enables you to use qualitative and quantitative to answer both the 'what' and the 'why' questions.

MAKE SURE THAT YOU HAVE CONSIDERED THE RESOURCES YOU WILL NEED

The nature of a case study approach to research is such that it requires you to think about the breadth of issues that have an impact or a potential impact on the focus of your inquiry. You will have to devise a research strategy that allows you to use a range of research methods in meaningful ways. The use of multiple means of data-gathering and analysis has practical implications. Have you got the skills needed to use a range of research methods? Have you got the time required to undertake a series of different data-gathering and analysing events? Have you got access to (and the time to access) the different groups of respondents? And have you got the abilities to synthesise such a breadth of data into trustworthy and reliable research findings?

SELECT METHODS APPROPRIATE TO YOUR RESEARCH AND YOUR ABILITIES

Selecting an appropriate research method is complicated enough when you are seeking to use just one. When using more than one approach, the complications are multiplied. You have to consider the nature of the data you wish to gather, the information that you want to produce from that data and then work out which approaches are most appropriate, *and* you have to consider the synergies between the methods used. The conclusions that you draw must pull together the research findings into a coherent and cohesive set of arguments, so you may have to pull together statistical data with the qualitative narrative gained from interviews. In selecting your research methods you should think about your skills, the time-frame available to you, and the ways in which the research produced by the different types of analyses can be drawn together in a reliable manner.

THE STRENGTHS AND LIMITATIONS OF A CASE STUDY APPROACH TO RESEARCH

Despite the popularity of a case study approach to research, it is important to be aware of the strengths and the limitations associated with it. It is only by being aware of these that business researchers can make an educated choice over whether or not a case study approach is the most appropriate approach for their specific research.

THE STRENGTHS OF A CASE STUDY APPROACH

A case study approach

- allows the researcher to investigate organisational issues within the context in which they exist
- encourages the researcher to access a range and a depth of information
- encourages the use of multiple sources of data or multiple means of data collection
- enables the researcher to potentially meet the needs of a wider range of stakeholders.

THE LIMITATIONS OF A CASE STUDY APPROACH

- the 'embeddedness' of the problem can make it difficult to clearly define what should and what should not be included.
- the use of multiple sources of data and multiple methods of data-gathering makes the process very time-consuming.
- the use of multiple methods requires a wider analytical skill set.
- the researcher has to be sure that he or she can synthesise the research findings to present a coherent set of conclusions.

KEY POINTS

Case study research draws on multiple sources of data through:

- **multiple levels of data collection**
- **the use of multiple methods**
- **the use of multiple sources of data**
- **the use of multiple cases**
- **using investigations over time.**

SUMMARY

The term 'case study' is overused and misused in business research. Much of what people present as case study research is nothing more than research that happens to be based within an organisation. A case study approach is far more complex than that, and it is this complexity which means that the approach can produce rich and insightful data. A case study approach is one which helps you to recognise the relationships that exist between the issues at the centre of your research and the context within which your research takes place. It draws on the connectivities and enables you to explore a much wider range of factors than would ordinarily be possible. But because of this, undertaking a case study approach to research is far from simple. You have to think about which connections to make, and where your research will start and finish. You have to think about the skills and the resources you will need to enable you to produce a thorough piece of work. You have to think about the time-frame and the nature of the results you will produce, and whether or not these will be acceptable to your stake-holders. And you have to choose methods of data-gathering and analysis effectively so that you can synthesise the research findings to produce trustworthy and reliable conclusions. If you manage to achieve all of these things, you will produce a valuable piece of business research and develop a whole new range of skills and competences in the process.

REVIEW QUESTIONS

1. What are the defining characteristics of a case study approach to research?

2. When is a case study approach most appropriate?

3. What approaches to data- and information-gathering can be used within a case study approach, and what are the advantages of these?

4. What are the strengths and the limitations of a case study approach?

EXPLORE FURTHER

Chad, P. (2001) 'Case research in marketing', *Marketing Review*, Spring: 303–23. Written for the academic practitioner, the paper demonstrates how structuring a case study approach can help overcome the idea that the information produced is 'too' qualitative

Hartley, J. (2006) 'Case study research', in Cassell, C. and Symmons, G. (eds) *Essential Guide to Qualitative Methods in Organizational Research*. London: Sage: 323–33. A short chapter which gives a useful consideration of when to choose case study research and how to approach it

Stake, R. (1998) 'Case studies', in Denzin, N. and Lincoln, Y. (eds) *Strategies of Qualitative Inquiry*. Thousand Oaks, CA: Sage Publications: 86–109. A good critical consideration which highlights the strengths and the limitations of using a case study approach

Tellis, W. (1997a) 'Introduction to case study', *The Qualitative Report*, Vol.3, No.2, July. Available online at *http://www.nova.edu/ssss/QR/QR3-2/tellis1.html* [accessed 20 March 2009]

Tellis, W. (1997b) 'Application of a case study methodology', *The Qualitative Report*, Vol.3, No.3, September. Available online at *http://www.nova.edu/ssss/QR/QR3-3/tellis2.html* [accessed 20 March 2009]. Both of Tellis's papers provide excellent coverage of all aspects of case study research, from the history of the approach through to the practicalities of doing case study research; also rich in references to other valuable sources of information

 Visit www.cipd.co.uk/brm for web links, templates, activities and other useful resources relating to this chapter.

CHAPTER 14

Action-Oriented Research and Action Research

INTRODUCTION

Practical business research is often directed towards action and change. If your research is intended to produce recommendations for change, or includes an implementation stage, you must plan for this. Such action-oriented research is often loosely and improperly called 'action research'. *Action Research* is a specific and highly complex approach to research, associated with a pragmatist belief (see Chapter 2) in the interdependence of *knowing* and *doing*. Most action-oriented research is not Action Research, as this chapter will show. But many of the ideas and issues associated with Action Research are potentially relevant to all action-oriented research, so this chapter is relevant to any action-oriented research.

Like the case study and Grounded Theory approaches, Action Research is an approach, not a research *method*. It is not a specific way of collecting data; indeed, many different data-collection methods may be used. It is more a set of beliefs about how best to go about change-oriented research, and the importance of both participation and critical reflection. Successful change can be helped or hindered by the research process adopted.

Action Research ideas are particularly relevant to research that addresses aspects of professional practice, and the way in which shared meanings influence action. Action Research tends to focus on the role of assumptions, the role of social context, and the role of researcher-involvement. Although Action Research stems from pragmatism, it is also compatible with constructionist assumptions.

There are many variants of 'Action Research', partly because the term is used in a wide variety of contexts. These include sociology and education, as well as business and management. Despite the variation there is a fairly clear common core. Action Research is distinguished by the involvement of the researcher, the collaboration of others, repeated cycles of action, observation and reflection, and a rigorous approach to the process as a whole. The research process aims to make explicit, and call into question, the impact of participants' assumptions about their roles, and assumptions reflected by the context within which they are working.

The researcher is often one of the participants, an 'insider' working – and intending to continue working – for the organisation in which the research takes place. Action Research brings the issues associated with insider researching into sharp focus, and they will be examined here. That section of the chapter will therefore be relevant to you if you are carrying out insider research using another approach.

This chapter will help you decide whether the approach is suitable and feasible for your project. The answer will probably be 'No' it is a demanding approach and requires an extended time period which few dissertation schedules allow. If you decide against Action Research, you will still find that the chapter helps you carry out successful action-oriented research, and the chapter concludes with lessons for any change-oriented project.

LEARNING OUTCOMES

This chapter should enable you to:

- identify features of research that would enable you to classify it as Action Research, and the challenges and opportunities posed by these features

- evaluate the suitability of Action Research as an approach to your own research

- incorporate elements of Action Research in your own investigation if appropriate

- design your research in a way that will make subsequent change easier, rather than creating resistance to it

- make appropriate action-oriented recommendations.

ACTION-ORIENTED RESEARCH

Business research

Chapter 1

You will remember our definition of business research in terms of having the purpose of informing 'thinking, decisions *and/or actions* in relation to an issue of organisational interest'. Academic business research often focuses on 'informing thinking' by developing new constructs or theories, or a critique of existing theories. More practical business research is often slanted towards action. It draws upon relevant ideas and research, and may develop some of these ideas further, but the main purpose is often to inform or bring about change in an organisation or part thereof.

Bringing about successful change is surprisingly difficult. Research can, fairly obviously, increase understanding of the situation and of what has to change. Less obviously, the process can, if carefully planned, also increase readiness for change. Conversely, it can create expectations or reactions that make subsequent change more difficult. Action Research has features that might help.

Student researchers may not be in a position to take, or even influence, action. Academic researchers may not be interested in doing so. Some professional bodies (for example, the CIPD) still follow the academic research model, and emphasise literature review and discussion of methodology rather than research outcomes for an organisation. But the current debate over a possible academic–practitioner divide has influenced a number of universities to place a greater emphasis on developing 'research' and 'change' skills; these are important for practitioners. My own institution, for example, requires its (part-time) MBA students to produce a report of a real *evidence-based initiative* they have done, rather than a dissertation. Students are required to 'make a difference' to their organisation. This enables managers to develop skills that will be of value throughout their professional careers.

CHANGE IS DIFFICULT

If you plan to bring about change in an organisation, you have to recognise that it is notoriously difficult. You may have personal experience of a change programme that failed to achieve its objectives. Glowing reports of change initiatives appear in the professional literature, but these are normally written by their initiators shortly after the programme is launched. If you talk to employees in those organisations a year or two later, you will often hear a very different story.

Beer *et al* (1990) wrote a paper entitled 'Why change programmes don't produce change' which still resonates with many managers. They studied six large corporations over a period of four years and concluded that large-scale change programmes are themselves the greatest obstacle to the organisational revitalisation that is their goal.

Many change programmes *are* large-scale. The CEO announces the new vision, strategy, and/or major restructuring, and assumes that the announcement will bring about any necessary changes in attitudes and therefore changes in behaviours. This assumption is faulty. Indeed, Beer *et al* suggest that the reverse is true. Successful change, they conclude, happens at the grass-roots level, through informal efforts to solve business problems. If you change behaviour, you will create a change in attitudes, rather than the reverse.

> **Changing behaviour is more likely to change attitudes than an attempt to change attitude in order to change behaviour.**

This is reassuring for many small-scale practitioner researchers – it is encouraging to realise that the grass-roots research that you are likely to be undertaking can itself be a powerful force for change.

MAKING CHANGE MORE SUCCESSFUL

Beer *et al* suggest that there are 'six steps to effective change', the first two of which are particularly relevant to the change-oriented practical business researcher:

- use joint diagnosis of business problems to mobilise commitment to change
- develop a shared vision of how to change roles and responsibilities.

Shared diagnosis (see Chapters 2 and 3 for ways of approaching diagnosis) has two advantages:

- the diagnosis is more likely to identify the important elements in the situation
- if people are involved, they are far more likely to 'own' any solution.

In the first Part of the book we highlighted the common tendency for clients or other key stakeholders to believe that they know what 'the problem' is, and the likelihood that it is much more complex than they realise. Most issues in organisations are likely to involve a complex and dynamic system of interrelated problems – a 'mess'. Those at the grass roots will be aware of aspects of the mess that their seniors may not have considered. If you have been involved in imposed change, you have probably heard despairing colleagues say, 'They just don't understand what's important', or 'What on earth made them think that this would work?' – 'they' being whoever specified the change.

Perceptions are part of the mess – and its solution

Part of the mess may involve the perceptions of those involved, and their interpretations of requirements, constraints and possibilities. These perceptions may be influenced by unconscious theories and assumptions. When this is the case, these ideas will need to be surfaced and challenged if change is to be effective.

'Shared vision' is also important. People are attached to their existing roles and responsibilities. They have learned how to survive and flourish in these roles, and their very identity may be partly determined by them. If people do not believe that the reason for change is important, and that a change in their roles will help to achieve the goals of the exercise, and have not themselves been involved in the necessary redesign, they are very likely to resist the necessary changes.

Beer *et al* go on to suggest that lasting change happens when a successful initiative spreads organically, even if this may 'look' less efficient than imposing it from on high. (This neatly parallels the tension between an 'efficient and scientific' positivist approach and a more organic, uncertain, but potentially more relevant constructionist one.)

RESEARCH STORY

Involvement for commitment

One of the organisations Beer *et al* researched, Navigation Devices, was working towards a structural change. Engineers were somewhat resistant, but in the light of changes happening elsewhere, started to re-examine their roles and rethink their ways of organising themselves. They spent nearly a year doing this, conducting two surveys and holding off-site meetings before coming to accept – after a hiccup – a matrix structure. This could have been imposed much more quickly: it was a fairly obvious solution. But the involvement in the investigation and decision meant that the engineers 'owned' the structure and were committed to making it work.

This Research Story illustrates just how much time may be needed for a participative approach to diagnosis and decisions. The exercise involved the extensive collection of evidence and reflection on existing ways of operating. But the research process itself made a major contribution to the ultimate acceptance of the conclusions. Action Research is an approach that recognises this need for involvement and rethinking. Even if you do not plan to adopt it for your own research, you might consider the lessons it has for the value of involving key stakeholders in thinking about issues, and in reaching decisions as part of the research process.

THE CHARACTERISTICS OF ACTION RESEARCH

Reason and Bradbury (2008, p4) define Action Research as

> "a participatory process concerned with developing practical knowing in the pursuit of worthwhile human purposes ... It seeks to bring together action and reflection, theory and practice."

It was Kurt Lewin (see, for example, 1957) who first used the term 'Action Research', suggesting that one way to learn about organisations was to try to change them. During World War II he had been involved in work aimed at changing householders' views of alternatives to meat, by involving them in group discussions. Action Research has continued to be the term applied to a participative approach in which practitioners work together in an experimental and reflective way in order to bring about change.

Action Research is frequently carried out by a practitioner who is an 'insider' to the organisation in which the issue is located, and one of the group which the issue primarily concerns. One of the criticisms sometimes made of the approach is that this threatens the objectivity of the researcher, and therefore the value of any conclusions. Since this criticism applies to any insider research, and because Action Researchers have thought about it in some depth, the issue will be dealt with in a later section of the chapter, together with other 'lessons' Action Research can teach.

The approach starts with an idea or issue and is characterised by personal and usually also collaborative reflection on existing thinking and practice relevant to it. An essential component is a willingness to question one's own beliefs and preconceptions, and to change them where appropriate. Concepts are not predetermined but develop as the research progresses. It is thus a highly flexible approach to research, which is both a strength and a challenge for some clients.

A CYCLIC PROCESS

Action Research is based on a cyclic process of action (normally collective), reflection on the results of action, and further action in the light of this reflection. It is thus highly participative, and incorporates an examination of the assumptions and personal theories that contribute to sustaining the situation being researched. It might be described as 'research from the inside out'.

Lewin (1957) suggested a spiral with four stages in each coil. These stages are: identifying an idea, doing some investigating, planning some action, acting, and evaluating the action. This would lead to rethinking, amending the plan, taking more action, and so on. Each loop can be seen as a small experiment or piece of research.

Stringer (1999) summarised the process as three repeated phases of 'look–think–act'. My favourite version of this consists of three questions: *'Wot? So wot? Wot next?'* (Reg Butterfield, personal communication.) Whatever the elements denominated in the spiral, unless you have a spiral with several coils, unless action is part of the loop, and observation and fairly critical reflection are also contained in each loop, the research is not Action Research. The approach is now widely used in educational and social research, and there are now many variants of the approach suited to different contexts reflecting different philosophical preferences.

> **Action Research describes a cyclic process of planning, action and evaluation directed towards improving both understanding and action.**

It is worth looking at these elements individually, but first let us consider the process as a whole. Lewin suggested a relatively tidy spiral, as shown in Figure 14.1.

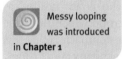
Dynamic organisation
Chapter 2

This cycle has marked similarities with many subsequent models for change which also emphasise the need to *iterate*, or go through a repeating cycle of evaluating the impact of an initiative and then either adjusting or building upon it to sustain momentum. Underlying such models is the belief that organisations are dynamic and that it is not useful to think of change in terms of problems that are 'solved'.

Thus far I have summarised the position as stated in many textbooks. You will already realise that for most dissertations and, indeed, for most consultancy assignments it will not be practical to spiral through many loops. But there are other reservations about the approach, including the issue of lack of objectivity, to which we shall return shortly.

Messy looping was introduced in Chapter 1

The tidiness of a repeating spiral is slightly at variance with the 'messy looping' idea that was suggested earlier as appropriate to practical business research. Classic Action Research has indeed been criticised for its 'apparent' straightforwardness in this

Figure 14.1 An Action Research spiral

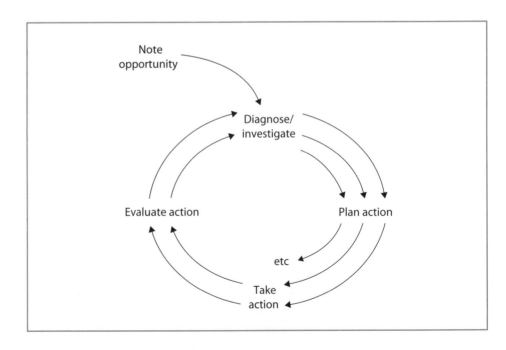

respect. In fact, Ladkin (2004) suggests something much closer to messy looping when she says (p143):

> "Inquiry cycles are 'messy', and are not necessarily discrete or linear. They can move much more fluidly, double back on themselves, and take unpredictable routes."

This looping is linked to another characteristic feature of the approach, namely, that ideas develop as you go along, rather than being predetermined at the time of planning.

THE ON-GOING DEVELOPMENT OF IDEAS

Academic research is often directed towards testing existing theories, whereas practical research often takes existing concepts and uses them to provide a framework for investigating a business issue. Action research is practical, in that it is rooted in action, but theoretical in that it develops ideas out of action. (You will find similarities here with the approach taken by Grounded Theorists.)

Grounded
Theory
Chapter 18

Lewin was concerned with developing theory as much as he was concerned with addressing real issues. His biographer (Marrow, 1969, p128) says that:

> "theory often evolved and became refined as the data unfolded, rather than being systematically detailed in advance. Lewin was led by both data and theory, each feeding the other, each guiding the research process."

This reciprocal relationship between theory and data-gathering means that each can influence the other. Rather than base research on preconceived theoretical ideas, the use of theory is emergent, based on a cycle of action, research and reflection. Instead of trying to see action through the lens of theory, the two work hand in hand, although the relative emphasis given to action and theory may vary. (The variant known as Action Science particularly emphasises theory creation and rigour of the research process.)

> **Action Research involves an on-going development of ideas through (often collaborative) reflection on actions.**

COLLABORATION

The collection and interpretation of data is a core feature of any research. Action Research is a highly participative approach, and reflection and interpretation is often done collaboratively. Indeed, since the pragmatist underpinnings of the approach see knowing as something which takes place in a social context, collaboration is perhaps *the* defining characteristic of most Action Research projects.

This integration of research, researcher(s) and change is very different from the positivist ideal of a detached and impartial researcher driving the investigation from a position of expertise according to a predetermined plan. It stems from the belief in 'knowing by doing' that underpins the approach. But Action Research *is* an experimental approach. The loops in the spiral are a series of experiments in that action is taken and evaluated. The aim is not only to produce knowledge that is of value to those who are collaborating, but also to develop more generalisable knowledge where possible.

KEY POINTS

- Action Research is a flexible approach to research within which a number of different methods may be used.
- It rests upon a pragmatic interest in knowledge as a tool for action and further knowing, and a belief that knowing takes place in a social context.
- It involves a series of cycles of investigation, planning, action and evaluation.
- Critical and usually collaborative reflection is a key feature.

THE ROLE OF REFLECTION IN ACTION RESEARCH

One of the basic beliefs underlying Action Research is that action is driven by ways of thinking and perceiving, and that thinking can be altered by action. The situation you are investigating will normally involve a number of people who will all have different ways of understanding the situation. Your – and their – observations will inevitably be biased by selective perception and differences in interpretation, and your research must embrace these multiple understandings. A major part of the research process will therefore involve surfacing and questioning these differing 'filters' through which the situation is perceived and interpreted by those involved.

It is these different perspectives and the reflection upon them which create the conditions for increasing understanding. It is action that puts this understanding to the test. If an altered way of perceiving or thinking leads to improved action, learning has taken place which means that 'change' is likely to be sustained. Observations on the results of the action can then initiate a further loop of the spiral to move both practice and understanding onwards a little further.

 CONSIDER...

Is the Action Research spiral merely a version of the familiar Kolb experiential learning cycle?

Kolb's cycle
Chapter 25

If you answered Yes here, you missed some significant differences. There are marked similarities with the Kolb experiential learning cycle's experience → reflect → interpret/ theorise → take action → experience, etc. But 'experience' has become 'evaluate' (data collection may well be needed), 'reflection' has become 'investigation and diagnosis' (further scope for data collection) and 'theorising' has morphed into 'action planning'.

Coghlan and Brannick (2001) suggest that *each* of the four main stages in Figure 14.1 should have superimposed upon it the experiential learning cycle. Thus at each stage of the action research cycle there is reflection on what is experienced at that stage. The researchers need to observe what is happening and their reactions to it. They need to interpret their observations by considering how their thinking may be influencing what has happened, and any implications of this for the 'theories' and assumptions that are shaping their thinking. In the light of discussion they may modify these theories and assumptions. This might suggest new actions to be monitored, evaluated and discussed. It is the rigour of this reflective process, just as much as the rigour of any data collection, that differentiates Action Research from experiential learning.

Chapter 1 suggested a relevance-rigour 'territory' in which business research projects could be located. Degree of theorising adds a third dimension. But thinking in terms of rigour or theory does not reflect the emphasis on *learning* by action and reflection that is central to Action Research. Coghlan and Brannick (2001) suggest another set of dimensions that may give a feel for how Action Research fits with other research. These relate to the learning intentions of the research, both for the individual and for the organisational system involved. Table 14.1 shows these. They suggest that the area you are most likely to be involved in if you are relatively new to research is **D** – this is therefore shaded.

Table 14.1 The Action Research space (adapted from Coghlan and Brannick, 2001)

	System: self-study in action not intended	*System:* self-study in action intended
Researcher: self-study in action intended	**A:** In-depth reflective practice directed towards personal development	**B:** Large-scale Action Research directed towards transformational organisational change
Researcher: **self-study in action not intended**	**C:** Most traditional research, whether qualitative or quantitative, where the emphasis is on the data and its message	**D:** Pragmatic Action Research, typical of internal consulting projects and MBA dissertations

Reason and McArdle (undated) suggest that you can locate your likely research slightly differently by attending to the level of inquiry, and state that there are three levels on which a 'bringing together' of action and reflection, theory and practice needs to take place. To be fully effective in bringing about change, they suggest, an Action Research project must stimulate action on all three of these levels, and strive for connections between them. Table 14.2 builds upon their suggestions, aiming to show how these levels interconnect. The shaded area is the normal focus of small-scale action-oriented practical business research.

Table 14.2 Levels of inquiry in Action Research

Level	*Domain*	*Importance*
First Person research (or practices)	Inquiry into one's own life, seeking to increase awareness of choices available and of the effects of these choices on the outside world	This personal awareness is essential for leadership in any social enterprise, and for effective Second Person inquiry
Second Person research (or practices)	Inquiry with others into issues of mutual concern through a cycle of action and reflection to develop both understanding and practice	This allows continued development of lasting change to practices at a given level. It depends upon the First Person level and can feed into Third Person inquiry
Third Person research (or practices)	Many people's views are brought together, creating a wider community of inquiry most of whom may never actually meet	This allows 'whole system' change, with widespread involvement in planning built upon lower-level inquiries

CONSIDER...

Can you equate any of these 'levels' with the areas in Table 14.1? If not, what is the difficulty, and what are the implications of the mismatch?

The 'First Person' domain seems to map onto **A** on Table 14.1, and the 'Third Person' seems close to **B**. But the shaded area on Table 14.2 does not seem to map exactly onto that in Table 14.1, despite the fact that these are the areas each model suggests as likely to be the focus of your own research. Because each model probably looked plausible to you, exploring the reasons for this apparent mismatch may be informative.

CONSIDER...

Why might there be this mismatch between the two shaded areas?

Three differences between the models seem to contribute to this. Firstly, although Coghlan and Brannick suggest that reflective learning should take place at *each* stage of the action research cycle, they describe area **D** as 'Action Research' – albeit qualified as pragmatic – when it seems to lack the core intention of individual learning from involvement in the process. This involvement is normally deemed essential to action research. It may be that this part of the territory would be better titled 'practical action-oriented business research'.

Another key difference making mapping difficult is that the mapping shown in Table 14.1 seems to omit the collaborative Second Person level of research altogether. Yet this is where many Action Research projects are located. Thirdly, the Coghlan and Brannick domains can easily appear to be mutually exclusive, while Reason and McArdle make the convincing point that each level is a prerequisite for the next. Unless a researcher is reflecting at the personal level, it will be difficult to take part in small group reflection – and unless small groups are effectively reflecting, there is nothing upon which the wider Third Person research can build.

So although Table 14.1 usefully highlights the learning intentions of researcher and client organisation, you may find the idea of 'levels' in Table 14.2 to be more useful. (I have included this comparison partly to remind you of the complexity of the issues addressed in this area, and to show how using different models 'slices' through different aspects of this complexity, often posing useful questions.)

THE LIMITATIONS OF SUCH A REFLECTIVE APPROACH

At the start of the chapter I suggested that Action Research was not an easy option. One reason is the time needed. Even remaining at the 'Second Person' level can be surprisingly time-consuming. As with other approaches to business research, it is important to recognise and plan for the time required. It does not make sense to talk of Action Research unless you go through several cycles of inquiry, because the cyclic nature of the approach is a defining feature. This means that willing co-practitioners have to be found to collaborate. The following story gives an idea of what may be involved.

RESEARCH STORY

Kate McArdle's young women managers (YoWiMs)

This is described in the short Reason and McArdle paper cited above. The YoWiM group met for half a day every four weeks to discuss their concerns, observations and experiences, and the outcomes of 'action experiments' which they had carried out since the last meeting (for example, experimenting with different ways of responding to patronising and bullying behaviour from male managers).

The collective reflection created a supportive space in which YoWiMs could explore not only their observations and feelings about the experiment, but aspects of the context that had created the original situation. They became 'critical' in the sociological sense of power structures in their contexts that were creating and sustaining the challenges they faced, and began to see them less as somehow 'their own fault'. A particularly valuable feature was that over the course of the meetings the YoWiMs learned to 'really listen' to each other, as opposed to 'waiting their turn to speak'. This was a hugely valuable skill in itself (see Chapter 16 for the importance of real listening in interviewing), but it also made the women aware of how little their voices were heard in their own organisations.

Kate was the initiating facilitator for the group, and was using the experience as part of her own research for a PhD. She was using 'co-operative inquiry', a highly participant variant of Action Research, as her underlying model She therefore paid particular attention to her own interventions and tried to make her choices transparent to the group, thus using her own inquiry practice to develop and support the inquiry practices of the YoWiMs. She also kept careful records of all this in her research journal, kept copies of emails and transcripts of group sessions as potential future 'evidence', and reflected on her own behaviour privately and with her research supervisor.

You can see that this approach is a long way from the scientific approach suggested by positivism, and in writing a convincing report of work like this great care would be needed in order to create a convincing narrative supported by evidence. But at the same time you can see that by the definition in Chapter 1, this counts as business research. Kate was systematically collecting information. In her personal reflections and discussions with supervisors she was interpreting it, and presumably testing her interpretations with the YoWiMs. You can also clearly see how this 'First Person' level was a necessary prerequisite for the second level.

KEY POINTS

- Reflection is an integral component of Action Research, because the approach is based upon developing ideas that work in action.
- Personal reflection is the foundation upon which collaborative reflection rests. It needs to be critical and disciplined.
- Collaborative reflection depends upon careful listening with an open and flexible mind.
- It allows you to address the perceptions and ways of thinking that typically form a substantial part of an organisational 'mess'.

EVALUATING AN ACTION RESEARCH APPROACH

Earlier it was suggested that from some perspectives 'good' research is characterised by the rigour of its methods. From most perspectives, relevance of data and the credibility and trustworthiness of its conclusions are important. Theoretical significance may be a criterion from some perspectives. The discussion thus far has stressed that *relevance* has to be interpreted in terms of relevance to the research purpose and to any organisational purpose to which the research is intended to contribute. And the chosen method must 'fit' the issue (and indeed, must fit with the researcher's preferred way of working) and be feasible within the constraints of the situation.

Action research has been criticised for lack of objectivity and lack of methodological rigour: a major perceived problem is the scope for bias by the often insider researcher. However, this critique is frequently based upon positivist assumptions, whereas Action Research comes from a pragmatist position. (Another example of just how fundamental your philosophical preferences are when thinking about research!)

RELEVANCE AND RIGOUR

Data collected in Action Research tends to score high on relevance. The approach starts from an emphasis on addressing practical issues and developing practical knowledge. The insider position of the researcher means that the broad area selected for attention is likely to be relevant to the Action Researchers. Whether it is of wider organisational relevance may or may not be a relevant question.

The collaborative nature of the process from the outset and the intensity of the reflection involved make it highly likely that the issue eventually settled upon, and actions chosen, will be relevant to the situation. The collaborators are both co-researchers and co-subjects in the research. The repeated evaluation and diagnostic phases in which they collaborate, and the on-going reflection at each stage, mean that this relevance is likely to be sustained and even increased as the process continues. The *level* of relevance may vary. A 'First Person' investigation may be of primary relevance to the individual concerned, but breadth of relevance will increase as and when the project moves up to Second Person and possibly Third Person levels.

From a pragmatist perspective, rigour in Action Research relates to care in monitoring and evaluating the results of actions (which a positivist would approve) and the quality of the reflection involved (which they would consider irrelevant). Kate's approach to her research in the story above makes clear just how rigorous such an approach has to be, even if the rigour is different from that which you would expect in, for example, a randomised controls experimental project.

RELIABILTY/REPLICABILITY

These criteria are important if you are seeking to express universal 'laws' based upon observation. If you believe that issues are so deeply contextualised that such 'laws' are a doubtful quest, the criteria are different. In Action Research, the nature of your data will depend upon the balance of research methods used within the Action Research framework. The more 'scientific' is the approach, the more likely that some of the data at least will meet these criteria. But Action Research tends to be a one-off, so the intervention as a whole is unlikely to be capable of replication. Much of the 'data' in a research project will consist of records of individual learning and reflective conversations. These will require interpretation and analysis. Chapter 9 discusses how to analyse such content in a systematic and structured way, but the 'raw material' may still fail to convince a sceptical positivist client.

An additional and major concern relates to the wider process, and has to do with the involvement of the researcher(s). Even if it is an 'outsider' project, the researcher is deeply involved in the project rather than a mere observer. And as noted, a great deal of Action Research is carried out by one of the practitioners involved. Far from being the impartial external observer of classic science, the Action Researcher is right in there, addressing an issue that is usually of personal concern, and 'leading' the collaborative reflection and planning that is central to the research. How can a researcher avoid bias under these conditions? This question can equally be asked of all the collaborators in their dual roles of researchers and subjects of research.

TRUSTWORTHINESS AND CREDIBILITY

If the qualitative nature of your data may threaten your credibility with some stake-holders, it is the potential for bias that may worry others and cause them to question its trustworthiness. By the normal criteria, these are serious flaws. Indeed, Reason and Bradbury (2001) suggest that different criteria should be applied. These concern the extent to which the research:

- produces enduring (and not initially anticipated) consequences
- deals with pragmatic issues to do with practice
- demonstrates democracy and collaboration
- addresses questions of significance
- takes into account a number of different ways of knowing.

These are the criteria an academic supervisor might apply (and supervising such projects requires a distinctive approach). A client might be more concerned with the over-arching question 'Is this likely to be useful?'

OTHER CONSIDERATIONS

Doing Action Research requires substantial openness on the part of the researcher and others involved, and a willingness to live with uncertainty, to reframe issues. Action Research projects can change direction with each cycle. You and your client, and any supervisor, need to be happy with this uncertainty. Even with a clear purpose, your research proposal may be far less precise in terms of objectives and action planning than most projects. You must be prepared to devote substantial time to reflecting both individually and collectively in order to change ways of understanding situations. You need to find others willing to commit quite a lot of time to working in this way: it is not a quick route to change.

In a sense, Action Research is a formal expression of what was being suggested in Part 1 as an appropriate approach to messy problems. It involves messy looping, pays repeated attention to diagnosis, involves reflective learning, and is participative.

 CONSIDER...

Why is Action Research not *the* recommended framework for all action-oriented research?

The issue may have its roots not in different perceptions but in more objectively observable factors. If so, research involving selective observations of these factors may be more relevant. Even where an Action Research approach would seem to fit, the full model may not be feasible. You may not be able to find collaborators willing to adopt this open and 'critically subjective' approach, and to devote to time to what they may see as 'your' project. Your client may not be prepared to invest staff time, even if the potential collaborators are willing. The project may have too short a time-scale for several iterations of the Action Research spiral. You may feel that you lack the skills needed to facilitate collaborative reflection and action planning. If you are doing the research for a dissertation, your supervisor may lack the skills to support this approach.

ACTIVITY

List the advantages and disadvantages of an Action Research project for your own research. Evaluate these, and decide whether a full approach is feasible and desirable. If it is not, which elements might you learn from for your research?

LESSONS FOR ACTION-ORIENTED RESEARCH

It is worth noting Ladkin's (2004) suggestion that *no one* ever actually does Action Research; it is an aspiration rather than a real possibility. It describes an orientation towards research characterised by

> "the intention of the researcher, coupled with a commitment to rigorous reflection and experimentation with new understandings or behaviours." (*ibid*, p479)

But it is not something that anyone ever fully achieves.

It would seem that for most messy issues where it is feasible Action Research offers a fairly robust and epistemologically justifiable framework, but acceptability is far from guaranteed, and the resources needed may not be available. Your client may be concerned about the potentially subversive nature of such a 'bottom-up' approach. Actions are taken from very early on, and by those involved. The thinking is usually being done – as Beer *et al* (1990) suggested it should be – from the bottom up.

The lessons that any action-oriented project can learn from Action Research include:

- the challenges of insider research have to be managed.
- it is important to consider the perceived ownership of the project: successful change may come from beneath.
- involving stakeholders throughout the project is important.
- you have to be able to live with uncertainty.
- you must be aware of the impact of your own preconceptions and your dual role if you are researching as an insider.
- successful change may be incremental.

THE CHALLENGES OF INSIDER RESEARCH

Not all insider research is Action Research, and not all Action Research is done by insiders. Nevertheless, there is a large overlap between the two categories, and it is

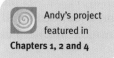

Andy's project featured in
Chapters 1, 2 and 4

worth looking in some detail at the issues you face if researching your own organisation. Many of these have been touched on earlier: you will remember that some of Andy's difficulties in evaluating change stemmed from the pressures he was subjected to by his superiors. This section brings together the range of issues and implications for insider research.

Coghlan (2001) explored the issues in some depth – what follows here is necessarily only an overview. He highlights three sets of differences between insiders and outsiders:

- pre-understanding – ie prior knowledge, preconceptions and assumptions
- the dual role
- political pressures.

As with most things in business there are advantages and disadvantages associated with each set of differences. They operate via perception, interpretation and choice of action. What you think you know, and the assumptions you make, will shape the way you see situations, what you notice, what you choose to focus upon, and the questions you ask. Your tacit theory will influence the way you interpret what you observe, and any answers you receive to your questions. The fact that your research can influence your career success may make you more susceptible to political pressures and less likely to challenge constraints placed upon your research than an outsider might be.

Prior knowledge can be useful in many ways – but if you share existing assumptions you may not challenge them, and you may think you 'know' some of the answers and so not ask the questions, as Table 14.3 suggests.

Table 14.3 The advantages and disadvantages of insider research

Advantages	*Disadvantages*
Prior knowledge and assumptions	
You start with contextual knowledge. You can draw upon informal networks. You can appreciate the significance of critical events. You can see behind 'the rhetoric'. Shared assumptions may make communication easier. Knowing the constraints may mean your recommendations are realistic.	You may assume things exist or are inevitable that are not. Data may be harder to perceive, and therefore challenge existing mindsets. You may fail to probe in an interview if you 'know' what the interviewee means. You may interpret answers to confirm what you already 'know'. You may be less likely to challenge constraints.
Dual role	
People are more willing to co-operate if they know you. You may have routine access to some relevant information. You may be in a better position to influence implementation.	People may be less open, or answer 'in role'. An outsider might find it easier to gain access to some information. An outsider's recommendations may be taken more seriously. Your own job and research objectives may be in conflict.
Political pressures	
Your knowledge of political structures may help you work with rather than against them. If only one contract is at stake, it may be easier to resist pressures.	You may be unaware of some political dimensions. Your job and promotion prospects are at stake, so pressures can be intense.

Coghlan (2001) draws some useful lessons from his analysis. Firstly, he stresses the need (already mentioned) to be aware of the potential impact of prior knowledge and use this awareness to reframe one's own understanding of the situation. The need to consider its potential to bias conclusions has already been noted.

The political dimension must also be considered from the outset: as an insider researcher you are in a position to consider both overt and covert political dimensions, and should do so when framing your project.

If your project is directed towards organisational learning, you will need a strategy for moving from personal and group learning to organisational learning. This might be thought of as the third level in Table 14.2, but is an important point for any action-oriented research.

OWNERSHIP AND INVOLVEMENT

In the conventional model, the researcher draws conclusions and makes recommendations but leaves the decision up to the client. This gives the client control over whether or not to implement the recommendations. With Action Research, if the client is not part of the research group they may feel they have lost control. Or perhaps they will feel that their authority is diminished if decisions they see as their domain become taken by others. Anxieties over this may be rationalised as concerns that the approach is 'unscientific'. Alternatively, the client may genuinely fail to recognise the different sort of rigour this approach demands. Ownership is entangled with political issues, and these need to be considered.

There is also an issue of personal ownership if you take on the role of 'first among equals' (and the equality is important). You will need a high level of facilitation skills, and the 'First Person' skills of openness to your own ways of thinking, and willingness to reflect on them and adapt in the light of reflection. And you need to maintain a sense of shared ownership in this, rather than creating the feeling that it is 'your' project.

Ownership and involvement are closely related. Here I have distinguished between the emotional implications of perception of ownership for reactions to subsequent change, and the impact of involvement on quality of change decisions. But they are two aspects of the same need to involve everyone, and both are related to the point about successful change starting from the bottom.

Stakeholder involvement

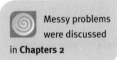

Messy problems were discussed in **Chapters 2**

For 'messy' problems there will be a range of interconnected difficulties, and a range of perspectives on them from your client and other stakeholders. Collaborative discussion on perceptions, interpretations and assumptions can be an invaluable part of investigating the underlying issues. Shared diagnosis from a range of perspectives is likely to be more effective. A problem collectively diagnosed is a problem owned. Shared planning and evaluation of actions taken in the light of diagnosis will further foster commitment and motivation, and a sense of shared ownership. Your project will also benefit from diversity of knowledge and perspectives so that plans are more likely to be realistic. Furthermore, working together on a research-based project can be an effective form of team development.

LIVING WITH UNCERTAINTY

You may personally find a flexible and open-ended approach such as Action Research makes you uncomfortable. If your research is for a qualification, you may find it very difficult to write a report on your research that will satisfy your supervisor or other assessors, or indeed to find a supervisor willing to agree such a project. The open-ended nature of the research may also make it difficult to complete a research ethics form, because you cannot specify the research question and proposed procedures as clearly as the committee will expect.

However, for issues that are genuinely messy, and where differing perceptions are part of the problem, it may take some time to explore all the relevant aspects of the issue and its context. Perceptions of 'the problem' may shift radically during this exploration. If you firm up a research design too soon, you risk addressing a trivial aspect of an issue, and indeed making it worse. Being willing to be flexible and to accept uncertainty well into a practical project is likely to substantially improve the value of your eventual research findings.

INDIVIDUAL AND COLLABORATIVE REFLECTION

Individual reflection is an important contributor to personal learning: you will gain far more from your research if reflection becomes a part of your professional practice. Because collaborative reflection is often more effective than individual reflection, it can be really useful to build in sessions with stakeholders during which you jointly think about how things are going, and about how thinking about the issue is shifting and might perhaps shift further. You might have to call them 'review sessions', if reflection is not part of organisational practice, but incorporating thinking about thinking, as well as thinking about progress, can make such sessions far more useful. It will help to consider aspects of the initial issue that now seem to be becoming relevant, and explore the reasons for shifts in perception. This will enhance the quality of your research and generate learning for your stakeholders – and through this, increase their readiness for any subsequent change.

AN INCREMENTAL APPROACH

Although many change projects are conceived of as one-off initiatives, there may be considerable value in an incremental approach, with on-going evaluation adjustment and further development. This will enable the necessary changes in thinking and behaviour to occur slowly and in ways that are more likely to persist. Each change will be welcomed as a slight and manageable improvement, rather than as a threat to long-established ways of operating.

SUMMARY

Action Research is normally characterised by the belief that knowing is rooted in the experience of doing. It has an emphasis on producing practical knowledge, and involves a cyclic experimental process of action and reflection with practitioners as co-researchers who generate and help interpret data. Such data may include accounts and recording of practice. This research group will discuss ways of experimenting with and evaluating actions suggested by the reflective process which will serve to generate further data.

As an approach it requires a substantial time investment, normally from colleagues as well as you, and an open and flexible mind, and willingness to reflect intensively and critically. You will need a high level of facilitation skills if you choose this approach.

Action Research may not be appropriate to all projects. It may also not be acceptable to some clients or supervisors. It may even be an ideal unattainable in reality. But many of the issues it addresses are relevant to all action-oriented research. There are lessons relating to the need for flexibility, the importance of involving stakeholders on all levels, and the importance of creating shared ownership of a project if subsequent changes are to be successfully implemented.

REVIEW QUESTIONS

1. What are the defining characteristics of an Action Research approach?

2. Where do 'experiments' feature within Action Research?

3. What features of a pragmatic epistemology are reflected in an Action Research approach?

4. What are the key differences between the experiential learning cycle and Lewin's Action Research cycle?

5. What is the role of reflection within each cycle?

6. Why might Action Research be an 'ideal' rather than a feasible approach for practical research?

7. What key lessons might a practical business researcher take from Action Research?

EXPLORE FURTHER

Action Research, a quarterly international refereed journal published by Sage, which contains papers relevant to Action Research theory and practice. In particular, Vol.7, Issue 1 (2009) is a special issue devoted to the role of theory in Action Research, and contains a number of interesting papers on this topic

Coghlan, D. (2001) 'Insider Action Research projects: implications for practicing managers', *Management Learning*, Vol.32, No.1: 49–60. Provides detailed and insightful discussion of a range of important issues from framing the project to contributing to organisational learning

Coghlan, D. and Brannick, T. (2001) *Doing Action Research in Your Own Organization*. London: Sage

Johnson, A. P. (2007) *A Short Guide to Action Research*, 3rd edition. Boston, MA: Allyn & Bacon

McNiff, J., Whitehead, J. and Lomax, P. (2003) *You and Your Action Research Project*. London: Routledge

Reason, P. and Bradbury, H. (eds) (2001) *Handbook of Action Research: Participative inquiry and practice*. London: Sage

Stringer, E. T. (2007) *Action Research: A handbook for practitioners*, 3rd edition. Newbury Park, CA: Sage Publications

 Visit www.cipd.co.uk/brm for web links, templates, activities and other useful resources relating to this chapter.

CHAPTER 15

Questionnaires

INTRODUCTION

Questionnaires are widely used in business research. They are a technique familiar to most people: you have probably been asked to complete at least one questionnaire recently yourself. This familiarity means that you are likely to feel more confident using questionnaires than using other methods, and your clients and informants are likely to be comfortable with this as a proposed approach too. This is a *big* plus.

Then there are 'economic' reasons for their popularity. It is relatively easy to draft something that looks like a questionnaire and to print multiple copies. And these days it is possible – for free, or very cheaply – to access websites that will enable you to distribute questionnaires and receive back an analysis of the results. Results can be presented in impressive tables or bar charts, and everyone will be happy.

Well, perhaps. There are as many pitfalls awaiting the questionnaire researcher as await those choosing any other method.

The first of the pitfalls is that your research question may simply not be suited to being answered via a questionnaire. Even if it is, unless you think carefully about your questionnaire and about how recipients are likely to react to it, you may get very few or no responses. (Have you ever started to fill in a questionnaire but given up because it was too long, too intrusive, or because you frankly couldn't see the point?) If people do reply, will you be able to interpret their responses?

However, if you avoid these pitfalls, a questionnaire can be a useful approach, enabling you to access useful information relatively cheaply from a large number of relevant informants. But the 'if' represents a minefield. Will people respond? Will they respond in time? Does the sample have to be representative? How will the data be analysed, and will you be able to draw valid conclusions from the results?

These seemingly innocent questions are hugely important. This chapter will help you understand the many challenges presented by questionnaire-based research, and help you design a questionnaire which people will be prepared to answer – in ways that will tell you what you want to know. It will also help you identify the issues that you will have to address if, despite your best efforts, fewer than you had hoped actually respond.

LEARNING OUTCOMES

This chapter should enable you to:

- recognise the strengths and limitations of using a questionnaire

- distinguish the types of data and information that a questionnaire allows you to gather

- determine whether a questionnaire would indeed be an appropriate approach to generating evidence that will help you answer your research question

- appreciate the requirements for a 'good' questionnaire item

- produce a first draft of a questionnaire for piloting.

QUESTIONNAIRES AND THEIR USES

Questionnaires are a means of asking large numbers of people about what they think, feel or do. A questionnaire is a standard set of predetermined questions presented to people in the same order. It is normally self-administered but can also be used over the phone or face to face, although that is normally more costly. Some questions may be about the respondents themselves (demographic information such as age, gender or other potentially relevant personal factor) rather than about the topic of direct interest. This allows the researcher to look at respondents as a whole, and to break them into sub-groups to compare answers on specific questions. For example: do men answer some questions differently from women? Do younger people answer differently from older ones? Do those working in marketing differ in their answers from those working in HR?

Questionnaires have obvious advantages – clients usually see them as an acceptable approach, and you can distribute them, usually without much expense, to a large number of people and their returns will give you lots of data to analyse and include in your final report. A questionnaire can help you gather a number of different pieces of information which cumulatively contribute to your inquiry, or help to refine the next stage of data-gathering. The disadvantages are less obvious but at least as important.

Think about the following ideas that some students had about a small-scale project they were required to do as part of a marketing course. All were considering using a questionnaire. What do you think about their plans? How likely are they to be able to address the issue that they are setting out to address?

ACTIVITY

In which of the following inquiries do you think a questionnaire would be appropriate? What issues might the researcher be taking into account when considering this approach? Note down your reasons for your opinion in each case. (It may help to think about the sorts of questions each might ask.)

Ellie works part-time at Chez Nous, a local restaurant. Her boss, the owner, is worried about the fact that fewer and fewer people are patronising the restaurant. He wonders whether the menu is the problem – in particular, whether there should there be more choice. Could Ellie use this as the basis for her research project? She was considering looking at customer satisfaction within the restaurant, to see whether this was related to the dishes that customers selected from the menu. Now she is thinking of designing a questionnaire for diners to rate their satisfaction with their visit, to rate presentation and taste of their selected main dish, and to indicate the likelihood that they would order it again if it were still on the menu.

Claude works with Ellie, and is addressing the same problem of falling customer numbers. However, he has noticed that almost no one orders fish, and is thinking about using a questionnaire to find out why.

Gary shares a flat with Claude and Ellie. He is a full-time student and so has not got a job, but still needs to find a topic for his own inquiry. He has heard Ellie and Claude talk about the problems of the restaurant and thinks that perhaps he will stop people on the street where the restaurant is and, using a short face-to-face questionnaire, ask why they are not eating at Chez Nous.

Nigella is also a student and wants to develop a website to advertise local restaurants when she graduates. She is thinking of testing the feasibility of the idea as part of her BSc project. That way, she can start to develop the business itself as soon as she graduates. She is planning to send all local restaurant owners a questionnaire about their marketing needs.

A draft questionnaire is available at **www.cipd.co.uk/brm**

Your responses may differ from those outlined below – and if they do, thinking about the reasons behind these responses may be informative.

Ellie could design a short and simple questionnaire to address satisfaction. She could ask for an overall satisfaction rating, include questions about general factors like décor and service, ask what people had selected from the menu, and then ask them to rate their food choice on a number of different aspects (perhaps derived from her own ideas about what makes a good restaurant meal, or from the sorts of things restaurant critics comment upon). Assuming that the menu does not change too often, she could split customers into categories according to choice of meal and compare satisfaction ratings between groups. She might also include demographic factors such as age and gender, and see whether ratings differed according to her chosen factors. Would people answer her questionnaire? She has a nicely defined and captive audience – offered a questionnaire over a free cup of coffee, many diners might be happy to oblige. Would this help her answer her client's question? Apparently not. She seems to be trying to address the quality of the overall dining experience rather than whether the menu offered attractive choices, which was her client's question. And she is giving the questionnaire only to those who have chosen to patronise the restaurant, not to those who have not. So although she might be able to find out if they would come back again (and if so, how often), she will not be addressing all those who might have come but never did.

It seems, therefore, that she has a nicely defined group of potential respondents (although probably not the right ones), could ask some specific and relevant questions of them and have a fair chance of getting most of them to answer. However, unless she asks rather different questions from those she is considering, she will probably not find out whether the menu ought to be changed.

Claude's approach is even more problematic. He might choose to ask customers open-ended questions such as 'Why didn't you order fish?' But such answers are often very hard to deal with. People might give a variety of different answers – eg 'I don't like fish,' 'I worry about sustainable cod stocks in the North Sea,' 'I always have steak,' 'I'm a vegetarian,' 'I love your fish pie, but it wasn't on tonight,' 'Mary was having lamb, so I wanted something that would go with red wine,' and of course 'I had fish last time and didn't think it was very good.' Making any sense of such a disparate set of answers is a nightmare. This is why such *open-ended* questions are used with caution in question-naires. *Closed* questions – those that offer a limited set of options – are much easier to analyse. The next section addresses the issues of question types in more detail.

Claude could choose to use closed questions for those who did choose fish, but since those customers are in a tiny minority, he might have very few people to ask. More problematic is the idea that what he seems to be investigating is tangential to the real problem. Even if he is right and proportionately very few people order fish, it will not answer the question 'Why are fewer and fewer people patronising the restaurant?' Diagnosis is vital, and Claude's questions have 'jumped' this crucial stage. Although it might be better to ask all customers about influences on choice – or even on factors which led them to choose the restaurant – this is not what he plans. And as with Ellie, this would still tell him nothing about those who are *not* eating there.

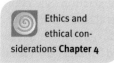

Diagnosis
Chapter 2

Gary may in some respects be better placed to gather the information which the owner is interested in. At least he is asking the right type of questions of a potentially large group of people – but they are still not necessarily an appropriate sample. Depending on the time of day he stands on the street, the people he stops might, for example, work in the area but live some way away and prefer to eat nearer home. Also, if you were accosted on the street, how likely would you be to answer a set of questions? Many of us have been stopped and offered 'inducements' to answer market research questions. (At various times I have been offered a bar of chocolate, shampoo, a chopping board and a gift voucher.) Gary is unlikely to be able to call on such resources, and even if he could, there are ethical issues related to the use of 'inducements' which need serious consideration. If only one person in 30 is prepared to answer, responses may be very unrepresentative of potential customers. Issues of maximising the likelihood that people will answer your questionnaire, and what to do if they don't, are addressed later in the chapter.

Ethics and
ethical con-
siderations **Chapter 4**

Another worry might be the reaction of the restaurant owner if he finds out that his restaurant's name is being used in this way without his permission. This relates to both the ethical issues and stakeholder perspectives discussed in Chapter 4.

Nigella clearly knows who her target respondents are, although she too may face issues of whether or not they are willing to spend time on a questionnaire. She may or may not have a clear enough idea of what to ask to make a questionnaire suitable for collecting the information she needs – it depends on how well researched her business plans are. But in her case there is an additional consideration. Part of her agenda may be to start to form links with potential clients of her new advertising website. If so, meeting the owners face to face, interviewing them and starting to develop a relationship with them would serve this purpose far better than a questionnaire.

> Questionnaires are useful in a range of circumstances, but success is dependent on having a focused and unambiguous research question.

WHEN TO CHOOSE A QUESTIONNAIRE

Questionnaires are particularly useful when

- your resources are limited
- you want to collect data from a lot of people
- these people can be accessed and are likely to be able and willing to respond to the questionnaire you send them
- you know the questions you want to ask
- you are sure that they are easily understood.

These requirements are examined in a little more detail below.

For gathering large amounts of data cost-effectively ...

Questionnaires are relatively cheap to produce and require much less time to administer than individual interviews or focus groups. Questionnaires sent by email or web page are cheaper than those sent through the post and you have the chance to forewarn people about your questionnaire, send reminders to those not replying, and use automated analyses of results.

When you have clear and specific research questions ...

Questionnaires must be based on a clear and specific research question/purpose and you must know *precisely* what information is required to answer that research question. Otherwise, the data you gather will be inappropriate. If you are still at the diagnostic stage and unsure quite what the issue is, a questionnaire – unless it is almost totally open-ended – will not be the best approach. Your questions will arise from, and therefore be limited by, *your* ideas (as was the case with Claude).

Where you have a clear and specific group of appropriate respondents ...

Identifying the right people to provide information relevant is crucial. Both Ellie and Claude had a clearly defined group of people but not one that would help them answer the owner's questions. They could find out what would make existing diners more or less likely to return, but if the owner is interested in attracting new customers, the target population is harder to define. Nigella was the only one with no problems in defining her appropriate respondents.

When appropriate respondents are able and willing to reply honestly ...

Ethics and ethical considerations **Chapter 4**

Questionnaires are generally self-administered. The respondent completes the questionnaire without having the researcher there with them. They therefore have to be able to read and understand questions, and have the time and the inclination to reply. This will depend to some extent upon the way the questionnaire is designed – which will be examined shortly – but there are other issues that affect it too. Clearly, if someone cannot read, or speaks poor English, a written questionnaire in English is not useful no matter how willing the respondents are. If material is highly personal or commercially sensitive, people may be understandably unwilling to give an honest answer, and there are ethical implications in asking such questions.

When you can write questions which are self-explanatory...

With a self-administered questionnaire there is no opportunity for people who are completing the questionnaire to check what you meant by a particular question. The questions must therefore be clear and unambiguous. If different interpretations are possible, you will not know what question the answer actually refers to. A good balance between open and closed questions is often desirable.

> Questionnaires are a useful means of data-gathering provided that the questionnaire is carefully and skilfully designed.

PRODUCING QUESTIONNAIRES

It is far from easy to produce a good questionnaire. You will have to put substantial effort into ensuring that your questionnaire gives you useful information. A badly designed questionnaire will at best allow you to gather inappropriate and irrelevant information, at worst will mean that you gather no information at all, or information that is misleading. There are two key elements to successful questionnaire design. The first is the nature and the type of questions that you must ask in order to gather the data you need – the content. The second is the overall framework within which those questions are presented – the design.

Content + Structure = Well-designed questionnaire

MAPPING THE INFORMATION YOU NEED

Having decided that a questionnaire is the best way for you to gather the information you need, there are some general ground rules about the process of design. You must be systematic in the ways in which you undertake this process. Even though the temptation is to jump straight in to writing the questions, you must take a step back and really think about the information that you need. It is a bit like baking a cake – you have to know what you want to come out of the oven before you can decide what should go in!

So what information do you need? A good place to start is with your research question/purpose and your research objectives. With these always at the forefront of your mind, ask yourself what you have to find out in order to be able to answer them. To give you an idea of how this mapping process works, here are Ellie's notes.

RESEARCH CASE

Ellie's notes

Research question/purpose: How can we improve customer satisfaction levels at Chez Nous?

Sub-questions:

· *Who are our current customers?*

· *What factors influence their overall satisfaction?*
· *How satisfied are the customers with each of these factors?*
· *What could be done to improve customer satisfaction?*

OK - so where do I start? I need to know who our current customers are so that I can see what satisfies or doesn't satisfy any particular group. So what information must I get?

· Gender
· Age
· Salary (I need to be careful not to frighten people off with this one!)
· Whether they live locally.

Also, their dining habits would be useful, so:

· Do they dine here alone, with their friends, their family? Do they bring children? Do they dine in the week or at weekends? Do they dine here in the day or at night?

OK - I think that is all I need to know about the customers, but I am not sure if I should ask this first or not. I will think about that later.

Next I need to know what we do that results in satisfaction or dissatisfaction. When I think about this, for the information to be really useful it has to follow the stages involved in dining here, so if I 'walk through' the process, this should help me spot the points at which people may be happy or unhappy with their experiences. The process maps out like this:

1st - Booking
2nd - Reception
3rd - Décor/environment

4th - Menu/drinks list
5th - Food quality
6th - Service
7th - Perhaps their overall satisfaction would be useful?

Identifying these points means that I can get customers to rate how satisfied they are with each. So far so good - but this will only tell me whether they are satisfied or not satisfied: it won't give me an understanding of why. Maybe what I should do is provide a space for people to add their comments if they feel it necessary. That way, if there are things that are really important to them but which I have missed off the list, they can add them.

Now for the tricky one . . .

What can be done to improve satisfaction against each of these factors? If I have lots of issues above, I must think about whether I want them to give me an answer to each of them. I suppose if the research is to be useful, the answer has to be Yes. But . . . I haven't got a set of clearly defined answers here for them to select from. I have some closed questions and some comments, so I may have to allow them to make their own suggestions. Perhaps I should just ask for one key improvement in each area and make a note that they don't have to fill them all in, just those that are important to them. Still not sure, but will put it together and see what happens when I pilot this.

Considering each of your research objectives and thinking in real and practical terms about the data you want to collect helps you form the central spine of the questionnaire – the skeleton on which you can build the actual questions. Once this skeleton is mapped out you can think about what questions will enable you to get the information. There are a few basic rules regarding *good questions* (language and good question structures) and *good response structures*.

To draw your attention to what can go wrong when designing a questionnaire I have produced the case of Jasper. Jasper is a fictitious character whose work represents many (but not all) of the problems encountered in questionnaires, concentrated (unusually) into one questionnaire.

ACTIVITY

Imagine that you are one of the supermarket customers and have been given the questionnaire below. As you complete it, note down any difficulties, uncertainties or issues that you experience. Jot down your ideas about how you could improve upon the questions. Subsequent discussions will draw upon both the questionnaire and the notes you have made.

Jasper's Questionnaire

Name: ....

Salary: ....

Tick the following, as appropriate:

1 Age

   ☐ 20–30 ☐ 31–35 ☐ 36–53 ☐ 54–61 ☐ 62–80

2 Income (in £thousands)

   ☐ a) 1–5   ☐ b) 5–10   ☐ c) 10–15
   ☐ d) 15–20   ☐ d) 20–25   ☐ e) 25–30
   ☐ f) 30–35   ☐ g) 35–40   ☐ h) 40–45
   ☐ i) 45–50   ☐ j) 50–55   ☐ k) 55–60
   ☐ l) 60–65   ☐ m) 65–70   ☐ n) 70–75
   ☐ o) 75+

3 Do you think that loyalty is a strategic imperative for companies vying for position in the global competitive paradigm of C21?

   ☐ Yes   ☐ Definitely yes   ☐ No

4 Please rate these
   (1 = Absolutely true; 2 = Very strongly agree; 3 = Strongly agree; 4 = Agree; 5 = Agree a little; 6 = Neutral; 7 = Disagree a little; 8 = Disagree; 9 = Disagree strongly; 10 = Disagree very strongly; 11 = Absolutely false)

	1	2	3	4	5	6	7	8	9	10	11
It is easy to park at the store	☐	☐	☐	☐	☐	☐	☐	☐	☐	☐	☐
There are always enough trolleys available	☐	☐	☐	☐	☐	☐	☐	☐	☐	☐	☐
The trolleys are in good working order	☐	☐	☐	☐	☐	☐	☐	☐	☐	☐	☐

5 What do you think about mobile phones?

6 Do you think our stores are well laid out, well stocked and easy to park at?

   ☐ Yes   ☐ No

7 Please rate us

		1	2	3	4	5	6		
Amicable	◊	☐	☐	☐	☐	☐	☐	◊	Hostile
Smart	◊	☐	☐	☐	☐	☐	☐	◊	Not smart
Fast	◊	☐	☐	☐	☐	☐	☐	◊	Slow
Attentive	◊	☐	☐	☐	☐	☐	☐	◊	Lackadaisical

8 How often do you buy the following?

    a) bread ....

    b) toiletries ....

    c) household goods ....

    d) luxury goods ....

9 Our IPM is currently averaging at 36IPM: is this

    a) too fast?

    b) too slow?

    c) just right?

  What could we do to make this better?

10 Rank these statements in the order in which you agree with them:

    a) This shop is best because of the prices

    b) This shop is best because of the location

    c) This shop is best because of the quality

    d) This shop is best because of the product range

11 Is there anything that infuriates you?

12 Divide the following into a pie chart that ranks the relative importance of the above features to you:

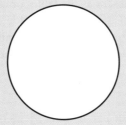

  Explain why.

13 Do you consider yourself loyal?

  If you do, why?

  If you don't, go on to Question 14

14 Why?

15 Have you never been to other supermarkets?

16 Is there anything you think you might like to add that might help us to help you become a loyal customer of ours or at least to increase the level of your loyalty to us in the future?

Thankyou, merci beaucoup, danke, gracias.

Jasper

Jasper works part-time in his local supermarket, and for his degree project he has decided to look at customer loyalty. He plans to sample 20% of the supermarket's customers in a 24-hour period to ask them about loyalty. He wants to find out whether or not the customers perceive themselves as being loyal customers. For those who do consider themselves to be loyal he plans to find out why, and for those who do not consider themselves loyal he plans to find out what the supermarket can do to make them into loyal customers. To support his research he has designed a questionnaire.

Jasper's research question has been clearly articulated – he is looking at the issue of issue of customer loyalty. Yet despite this clarity, the questionnaire that he has produced seems to be covering a whole range of issues. Some of them are clearly connected to loyalty, others it is not possible to be so sure about. With questionnaires you have one chance to gather the data you require. You must therefore make sure that you ask every question that you need to ask, and that every question you ask is relevant to your inquiry.

> Make sure you ask the questions you need to ask, and don't ask things that are unnecessary – no matter how interesting you may think them.

TYPES OF QUESTION

Stakeholder interests
Chapter 4

Questions can be divided into two main types: *open* questions and *closed* questions. In practice many people tend to use a mixture of the two to try to achieve a balance. Open questions alone may give you very many explanations, but the data gathered can be difficult to analyse, and hard to present as the tables or charts your client may expect. Closed questions may be easier to analyse and provide quantitative data but seldom explain the reasoning behind the figures. Managers usually want more information on the 'how' and 'why' before they set about devising a solution to a problem.

OPEN QUESTIONS

Open questions ask respondents for perceptions, views or explanations. They have to be clearly expressed in such a way that people can identify the key themes and develop their own answers. Care should be taken when using words such as 'what' or 'why' because these might imply that you are blaming the respondent. Below is an illustration of how this can happen.

RESEARCH STORY: HOUSE OF HORRORS

The problem with teaching

A Master's-level research proposal intended to look at staff turnover rates in the teaching profession using the following questions:

1   What made you unhappy about staying in the teaching profession?

2   What personal efforts did you make to resolve these difficulties?

3   Did you discuss your concerns with your family? If so, why?

Did you spot some of the potential problems here? The respondent filling in this questionnaire might reasonably feel it is being suggested that the problems are caused by their 'unhappiness' rather than by particular issues with the teaching profession. The second question almost implies that they should have been able to sort things out. Presented with such questions, a respondent might justifiably decide not to bother answering them at all.

> **Open questions must be clearly articulated, logically sequenced and worded so that they do not imply blame or fault on the part of the respondent.**

Look back at the notes you made on Jasper's questionnaire. How did you respond to his Question 5? Perhaps your first response was 'What do you mean by this?' Or maybe you said, 'They're a good thing,' or 'They're a bad thing.' Others might have said, 'I hate it when people talk loudly on them on trains,' or 'People should be prosecuted for using them while driving.' What about Question 11? I had much less difficulty in coming up with an answer (but maybe I am just naturally grumpy). Top of the (very long) list was people driving too close to the back of my car, and people who put empty milk bottles back in the fridge. However, how will knowing this help Jasper establish whether or not I am a loyal customer? There is also the issue of using emotive language here. What does he mean by 'infuriate'? The problem with these questions is that the list of potential answers is endless – they use vague or emotive language *and they don't seem to address the research question*.

THE USE OF LANGUAGE IN QUESTIONS

There are some straightforward and commonsense rules about the use of language on a questionnaire, all directed towards making sure that the questions are understandable:

- be precise and concise
- use simple language
- avoid jargon
- avoid ambiguity
- avoid double-barrelled questions
- avoid negatives.

Be precise and concise

Questions should say exactly what you want them to say, in as few words as possible. Words that are surplus to requirements mean that people take longer to read the question, and can also cause confusion. Look at Jasper's Question 16 and think about how you could reword this into something more succinct. You could probably come up with an equally meaningful question using half as many words.

Use simple language and sentences

Language should be simple and understandable. There are two things guaranteed to put people off completing your questionnaire. One is 'talking down to' respondents, the other is using language that people do not understand. For example, if you are sending your questions to Senior Finance Officers, it would be perfectly reasonable to use terms like 'internal rate of return', 'working capital' and 'pre-tax profits'. In fact if you were to spend time trying to translate these terms into everyday language, they might think you were implying that they would not understand the 'professional' language. Conversely, the use of technical terms and unnecessarily long words is unlikely to impress, and just makes the questions harder to understand.

Consider Jasper's Question 3. If you have studied business, you have at least some chance of understanding what Jasper is asking, but his respondents are supermarket customers. Few will understand what it means. They are unlikely to be able to answer the question honestly or accurately, and may feel stupid!

Avoid jargon, abbreviations and acronyms

Abbreviations and acronyms are problematic on questionnaires. Unless you are certain that every respondent will know exactly what they mean, they should be avoided. If you do need to use them (because the term is going to come up time and time again in the questionnaire), you should explain the meaning the first time it is used, preferably in the introductory text (which we will look at shortly). So, for example, you might say 'In this questionnaire I shall be asking you to think about the practice of human resource management (HRM) in your organisation.'

In Question 9, Jasper is assuming that everyone knows what an IPM is, when actually very few people will know. ('IPM' stands for 'items per minute': it is the speed at which checkout operators scan items going through the till.) What will happen here is that people may either tick a box regardless of the accuracy of the answer (after all, they have three answers to choose from and nobody is going to know that they don't understand the question) or miss the answer out altogether. Either is problematic in that the response undermines Jasper's ability to answer his research question accurately.

Avoid ambiguity

You should avoid using convoluted questions or ambiguous questions. Convoluted questions tend to be those that try to include too much about context and not enough about focus. The example below is from a questionnaire seeking to evaluate employee attitudes to organisational communication. By the time the respondents have got to the end of the question, they may well have forgotten what was at the beginning!

Ambiguity is created when a question is written in such a way that the words might mean more than one thing. Look at Jasper's Question 8. What are 'household goods'? Are these cleaning items? Soft furnishings? Paint and paint brushes? Because they could mean anything, respondents will put their own interpretation on 'household goods'. If each of your respondents interprets your words differently, you will not obtain accurate information.

RESEARCH ILLUSTRATION

A question of communication

Q Thinking about internal communication (and not external communication), and communication which flows between the departments and inside the departments, do you agree that the organisation does a good job in communicating between departments regarding changes or decisions that affect people in those departments?

A Yes ☐   No ☐

Avoid double-barrelled questions

This is a very common mistake in questionnaire design. A double-barrelled question is one that asks more than one question but gives the respondent only one option for the reply. In Question 6, Jasper asks people to rate whether the stores are 'well laid out, well stocked and easy to park at', but only give one yes/no response box. What happens if the store is well laid out but the parking is poor?

Avoid negatives

Try to avoid using negatives. Jasper's Question 15 shows why these are problematic. What does this mean? How are you supposed to answer this, and who is really going to spend time and effort working it out?

> **The use of language in constructing open questions is crucial. It guides the respondents to provide you with the information that you need.**

QUALITATIVE DATA FROM QUESTIONNAIRES

An alternative way of gathering open information is to ask people to elaborate on their responses to structured questions. You can do this in either of two ways – with open adjuncts or with open 'Other' categories.

Open adjuncts

Sometimes you will want to find out why someone has ranked or rated something in a particular way. These additional open questions attached to a structured question are referred to as open adjuncts. They usually appear at the bottom of a rating scale and either simply ask 'Why?' or they ask the respondent to explain. To illustrate:

RESEARCH ILLUSTRATION

An open adjunct

Please rate the following:

	Very satisfied	Satisfied	Neutral	Dissatisfied	Very dissatisfied
The current menu	☐	☐	☐	☐	☐

Please explain the reason behind your rating...

....

....

....

Here the researcher will have quantitative data to indicate just how many people are happy or unhappy with the menu, and qualitative data to explain the reasons behind the figures.

Although Jasper's Question 12 is seeking clarification of the response to the (vague) first part of the question, respondents are unlikely to be able to help. Question 13 is better in this respect, although problematic in other ways.

Open 'Other' categories

Open 'Other' categories are used when you cannot include all the possible responses that the respondents might want to give, but have a reasonable idea of what the main responses are likely to be. By including the words 'Other – please specify' at the end of the list of responses, you invite the respondent to add their particular response to the list if it is not already included. For example:

RESEARCH ILLUSTRATION

Open 'Other' categories

Why did you choose to book your holiday with us? Please tick all that are relevant.

1   The brochure gave us a good impression   ☐

2   The price was competitive   ☐

3   The hotel offered all the facilities you were looking for   ☐

4   The insurance was included in the price of the hotel   ☐

5   We have travelled with you before   ☐

6   Other – please specify: ....
            You are the only company that flies from my local airport.
    ....

    ....

The potential usefulness of this category was clear in a piece of research I did some time ago. I included an 'Other' section at the end of a list of motives behind the implementation of total quality management (TQM). I had derived the list from the literature and, to be honest, added the 'Other' category as an afterthought – a sort of 'just in case'. When the responses came back, the vast majority of respondents had written the same issue in the 'Other' category, a motive which came from the political influences on the organisations and which I could not have got from the academic literature. This completely reframed the issues that I was looking at, in a much more realistic and useful way.

Adding open adjuncts or open 'Other' categories helps you to elicit explanations or gather a wider set of responses that is more reflective of the views of the respondents.

CLOSED QUESTIONS

Closed questions are also known as *forced choice questions*. They present the question and a limited range of responses from which to choose. Closed questions are useful for obtaining comparative data (eg how many people agree, how many people disagree), for obtaining statistical data (eg 20% of respondents were aged between 25 and 35) or for getting people to rank their preferences (eg respondents preferred toast to cereal for breakfast), and can be presented in a number of ways:

- yes/no questions
- category choice questions
- Likert scales
- differential scales
- rank orders.

YES/NO QUESTIONS

These are the simplest form of closed question. The respondent simply notes their agreement or disagreement. Such questions can be used to obtain a single response (Yes or No) or to get a response which then requires elaboration (if Yes, please explain why). However, they can also be used as *filtering questions* and as *streaming questions*.

A *filtering question* helps you to make sure that the people whom you are asking questions to are actually able to respond. There would be little point in asking people who do not drive whether they prefer a six- or seven-speed gearbox! Filtering questions are of use when you are not able to clearly define your target sample/population beforehand and you may recognise these as being commonly used by people doing market research questionnaires in the street.

A *streaming* question allows you to ask two different sets of questions in parallel. The yes/no categories direct people to the set of questions relevant to them. Referring back to our previous example, if Gary were to stop people in the street to ask about restaurant choice, he might usefully start by asking if people ever dined out. There would be little point in asking them to fill in the rest of the questionnaire if the answer was No. Gary might also use yes/no questions as streamlining questions. Below is an illustration of how this might work.

RESEARCH ILLUSTRATION

Filtering and streaming questions

1 Do you dine out at restaurants? *[Gary is using this as a filtering question]*

   Yes ☐   No ☐

2 Do you dine at Chez Nous?
     Yes: please go to Question 3
     No: please go to Question 5

3 How often do you dine at Chez Nous? *[Gary is using this as a streaming question]*

   Occasionally ☐   Every week ☐   Every two weeks ☐   Once a month ☐

4 Please rate the following:

	Very satisfied	Satisfied	Neutral	Dissatisfied	Very dissatisfied
Accessibility of the restaurant	☐	☐	☐	☐	☐
Internal environment	☐	☐	☐	☐	☐
The menu choices	☐	☐	☐	☐	☐
The quality of the food	☐	☐	☐	☐	☐

Now please go to Question 7

5 Which local restaurants do you dine at?

The Fresh Fish Restaurant ☐　　The Italian Job ☐　　Americana ☐

Le Bistro ☐　　The Golden Triangle ☐

Other – please specify:..

6 What do you think would make you want to dine at Chez Nous?

....

....

....

7 What are the key features you look for when choosing a restaurant? Please tick all that are relevant.

Easy access, good parking/public transport links	☐
Nice décor	☐
Friendly staff	☐
Knowledgeable staff	☐
Good choice of dishes	☐
Good wine list	☐

Gary has successfully used yes/no questions both for filtering his respondents (Question 1) and for streaming the respondents (Question 2). By the time we reach Question 7, both groups of respondents (those who do dine at Chez Nous and those that don't) have now been brought back together again, allowing Gary to find out from both groups what people think makes for an enjoyable (and therefore hopefully repeatable) restaurant experience.

> Yes/no questions can be used to filter out inappropriate respondents and to direct respondents to the appropriate sections within the questionnaire.

CATEGORY CHOICE QUESTIONS

These questions are often used to collect demographic data about the respondents. For example:

In what age-group will you be on 1 September 2011?

☐　below 20

☐ 20–30

☐ 31–41

☐ 42–52

☐ 53–63

☐ 64–74

☐ 75+

These questions provide people with a clearly defined set of responses from which they can choose. To make the answers meaningful, there has to be a reasonable number of categories and they must be comprehensive. The rationale behind batching groups together is that it helps you to produce a more useful analysis. This is undermined if, as in Jasper's Question 2, you produce too many potential responses. Try to keep response categories to seven or fewer. Jasper has also overlapped response categories. In his Question 2, respondents will struggle to know where to tick if their salary happens to be £5,000, £10,000 or £15,000, etc. All of these (and many more) numbers appear in more than one response box. Lastly, to create meaningful data, the response categories must be of equal size. In Jasper's Question 1, although the difference in size might not be immediately apparent, this will have a significant impact on the analysis of the data. If more people tick the third age-group, it may well be because that category is three times larger than the second age-group, comprising a spread of 18 years as compared with five.

> **Category choice should contain no more than seven categories which are comprehensive, of equal size, and mutually exclusive.**

LIKERT SCALES

Likert scales are named after the psychologist Rensis Likert who first used the scales in the 1930s to describe attitudes. Likert scales provide people with a range of responses from which they can choose. Although some people prefer to use an even number of categories to force a positive or negative response, these are often arranged in a series of uneven numbers to allow for an equal number of positive and negative responses and a neutral or 'don't know' category in the middle. For example:

	Strongly agree	Agree	Don't know	Disagree	Strongly disagree
The food here is of good quality	☐	☐	☐	☐	☐

The response categories usually have five or seven options. Any more than seven and it becomes increasingly difficult for the respondent to decide which category they fall into. Jasper's Question 4 illustrates the point. How would you distinguish between 'absolutely true' and 'very strongly agree'? And it takes so much time to go through each of the 11 categories that I personally would be tempted to either give up or just tick anything. This idea of just ticking anything is one of the reasons for varying the types of questions used when constructing a questionnaire. It prevents people from adopting this *central tendency bias* in which they tick the middle box without having to think about their responses.

> Likert scales should have an odd number of response categories to allow for a neutral reply, and should be used intermittently to prevent central tendency bias from distorting the data.

DIFFERENTIAL SCALES

Differential scales present two opposing views on an issue with a continuum between. The continuum might be numerical – for example, numbered from 1 to 6 or from 1 to 10 – or it might simply be a line along which people plot their agreement with one factor (and therefore disagreement with the other). The latter is most often used in professionally designed questionnaires and read using a magnetic scanner. For example:

Exceptionally

Exceptionally   **good**   **bad**

Please rate the   ☐   ☐   ☐   ☐   ☐   ☐   ☐   ☐   ☐   ☐
quality of service   1   2   3   4   5   6   7   8   9   10
received

Differential scales must have opposing views at opposite ends, because agreement with one denotes disagreement with the other. Problems arise where this is not the case. In Jasper's Question 7, the opposite of 'amicable' is not 'lazy' – what happens if staff are very friendly but fundamentally lazy? And even though I have used the word 'staff' here, Jasper does not actually use that term: he simply says 'rate us'. People may find that they want to ask, 'Who are "us"'? The term could relate to the managers, the people working in the bakery, the warehouse staff, the checkout operators – or all of the above.

Differential scales, like category choice questions, must have a limited number of categories if they are to produce useful results. Six categories are commonly used, occasionally 10. Any more than 10 and you would have to seriously consider how you could meaningfully analyse the data.

Likert and differential scales are *rating* scales. They are used to encourage people to note the extent to which they agree or disagree with a statement. An alternative type of scale is a *ranking* scale. A ranking scale helps you to distinguish the relative merits

RANK ORDERS

Rank orders ask people to prioritise what is important to them. They are presented with a sliding scale which they use to record their priorities according to their own personal criteria. A ranking scale should include a limited range of categories and a key that clearly distinguishes the top of the scale (the most important) and the bottom of the scale (the least important). The advantage of rank orders is that that they allow you as the researcher to see what the respondents like and do not like, and how they judge the relationship between factors.

For example:

On a scale of 1 to 5 – 1 being not very important and 5 being very important – please rank the following in the order of importance to you:

Issues	Ranking
Location of restaurant	
Value for money	
Exceptional-quality food	
Comprehensive wine list	
Outstanding service	

Attention thus far has been focused largely on the ways in which questions should be structured so that you can communicate clearly to your respondents the type of information that you require. Within this the issue of response structures has been mentioned. So important is the issue of response structures that the messages have been extracted from the text to provide key learning points. After all, no matter how good the questions are, if the response structures cannot record the replies reliably, the questions are redundant.

KEY POINTS

- Response categories need to be clearly explained.
- Response categories need to be mutually exclusive.
- Response categories need to be of equal size within each question.
- Avoid using more than seven response options for category choice or differential scales
- If using a Likert scale, offer an odd number of response choices to allow for a neutral response.

Once you have identified suitable questions to elicit the information you need to answer your research question, you must think about the visual design elements of your questionnaire.

VISUAL DESIGN ELEMENTS

A well-designed and well-structured questionnaire engages the respondents and encourages them to answer the questions honestly and accurately. To do these things the questionnaire must be visually appealing and not too long. No matter how attractive the questionnaire is, if it is 26 pages long, you are unlikely to get anyone to fill it in. Two to three pages should normally be sufficient. The questionnaire must ask only those questions specifically relevant to your inquiry and ask them in the most concise way possible.

Brevity assured, there is a need to consider how to make your questionnaire aesthetically pleasing. First you must think about the visual impact – it should convey the right message. The layout, the font you use, the use of image and the use of colour will all depend on the type of people you want to complete your questionnaire.

Each of these designs is likely to have had a different impact on you. Example 1 some of you will have found a little bit condescending. The slightly grandiose style of presentation, the font and the use of language implies that the writer is somewhat 'superior'. The second reflects the type od visual layout you would expect to see. Standard black writing on a white background, 'sensible' Times New Roman font, and words that relay the importance of the research and your contribution to it. The third makes the research sound like something that may or may not be important. The pink background and the 'jovial' style of the font undermine the seriousness of what is being proposed.

ACTIVITY

Below are three pieces of text. Each one technically means the same thing, but each has been produced using different expressive language. Write notes about the impression each piece of text makes, the people you think it might have been produced for and how your manager might react to a document in that format.

Example 1

Introduction and welcome

Your HR department is proud of its on-going commitment to the sharing of best practice between you all, and you may be able to help us here. We are reviewing the current system of performance appraisal and this questionnaire is part of the investigation being carried out.

This questionnaire has been designed to try to identify

· the strengths
· the weaknesses, and
· the opportunities for improvement.

Below are 20 questions, which should take the average employee no more than 20 minutes to complete, so go on and have a go. We cannot help you if you don't help us!

Example 2

Introduction

This research is being carried out as part of the HR department's on-going commitment to the sharing of best practice and your help in completing the following questionnaire would be very much appreciated.

The questionnaire has been designed to try to identify the strengths and the limitations of the current performance appraisal system, and to seek your suggestions for opportunities to improve things.

There are 20 questions, which should take you no more than 20 minutes to complete.

We hope that the research findings will help bring about some real improvements

Example 3

Hi there!

As part of the HR department's on-going commitment to the sharing of best practice, we were thinking we might send around a little questionnaire. What we were thinking of doing is trying to identify the strengths, the weaknesses and the opportunities for improvement of the current system of performance appraisal.

So we have sent you this questionnaire to see if you might like (or even just be willing!!) to help. There are 20 questions, which should take you no more than 20 minutes to complete. If you do it, we might be able to make some suggestions that could make things better.

Whereas managers may expect to see something akin to example 2, ie a formal and professional design with minimal or no use of colour or image, consider whether teenagers would find this quite so appealing. If they are your target then including colour and image may be very important. A good way to frame how you want your questionnaire to look is to think about the respondents and what type of documents they usually read. This will give you a good idea of what formats and layouts and layouts they are familiar with; and if they are familiar with the visual image then they are more likely to help you by completing the questionnaire.

Based on this, think about how you might add interest for the respondents. Judicious use of colour might help you to theme the questionnaire and give a 'professional' feel. However if colour is used inappropriately it can both distract people and undermine the credibility of the questionnaire. The same applies to the use of image. The inclusion of smiley faces might encourage 12-year-olds to complete your questionnaire, but would this have the same effect on a group of bankers?

Guidelines for questionnaire layout

Think about light and shade. The relationship between text and space determines whether the questionnaire looks clear and easily navigable or whether it looks cluttered and crammed.

Be consistent. Use a clear font size (10–12pt). If you embolden or italicise text, do so consistently. Use subheadings carefully. They are good for helping people to navigate through the questionnaire but can also break up the flow.

Stick to tradition. If you are producing the questionnaire in a language that reads from left to right, your questions should read from left to right. Keep that alignment and do not randomly centralise text for no good reason – this simply means extra navigation for the respondent.

Vary the question structures. Using different question structures can help avoid central tendency bias discussed previously and can help to add interest to the questionnaire. However, it also means that the respondent has to familiarise himself/herself with the 'new rules'. If you change the structure every second or third question, he/she will soon get fed up.

Try to theme the questions. Batching questions by themes can help create a logical flow between these themes. (Remember how Ellie mapped out 'the dining experience' as the basis for her question structure.)

Make clear the relevance of each question. The respondent should be able immediately to see why the questions you ask are relevant to your research.

You must think carefully about how to handle questions that might be sensitive. Some of them might be obvious – for example, those seeking personal information. Others might be questions that require the respondent to be critical of something or of someone. Some feel that sensitive or personal questions should be left to the end of the questionnaire because by then people are more relaxed, and having completed the questionnaire they know the type of data that their personal details could be connected to. Others argue that people tend to answer the first section of a questionnaire but often fail to complete the latter sections. If sensitive data are vital to your inquiry (that is, if they form part of the actual research question – for example, 'Are younger employees more concerned about job security than older employees?'), these questions should be at the beginning of the questionnaire.

If sensitive information is vital to your inquiry, the questions should be asked early on. Otherwise, sensitive questions may be better asked towards the end.

MAXIMISING RESPONSE RATES

You need to think about how you can increase the proportion of questionnaire recipients who actually return it. There are a number of ways that you can try to encourage people to fill your questionnaires in. Adopting these approaches is as important as the way in which you put the questionnaire together.

ENVELOPES

If you are using a hard-copy questionnaire, the first thing that your respondents will see is either the envelope or the front sheet of the questionnaire itself. Their first impression must be a good one. Subtly coloured envelopes with handwritten addresses and a postage stamp attract attention far more quickly than do standard white or brown printed and franked envelopes. Although you can get help, writing out names and addresses for more than a small number of questionnaires would be an onerous task. You may have to make compromises. If, for example, your organisation has agreed to pay the postage, you may have to put your questionnaires through their franking machine. Perhaps you could compensate by hand-writing the envelopes or by producing impressive address labels. It is important that your envelope attracts attention that is likely to make people want to respond to your questionnaire.

COVERING LETTER

Whether you are using an envelope or not, the covering letter is *absolutely vital*. The covering letter is the point at which your respondents will make a decision whether or not to complete your questionnaire. The letter has to be professional, informative, engaging, accurate, aesthetic and concise. It need not be a separate letter. If you are handing out questionnaires personally, a précis of the contents of the covering letter on the front page of the questionnaire may be preferable.

If possible, address the letter and the questionnaire to a named respondent. Personalising the letter makes them feel as though they personally are valued. If you do not have the name of an individual, it is for you to decide how to head your letter. Some people feel that 'Dear Sir or Madam' is an appropriate and proper form of address. Others argue that this implies that you don't even know the gender of the respondent. In some cases it may be better using a generic introduction such as 'Please let me introduce myself'. That way you potentially avoid offending people.

Once you have decided on the greeting, there are a number of things that you have to communicate – and communicate quickly. You must establish your credibility and the credibility of your research, and let people know what you wish them to do, as briefly as possible and as quickly as possible in the introduction.

Introduction

A good covering letter lets your reader know:

- who you are

- what the research is about/the importance of the research
- the sponsors of the research (where appropriate)
- assurances of anonymity and confidentiality where necessary
- what the questionnaire involves
- the logistics of the process.

Examples

Dear Dr Smith,

My name is Matthew Henry and I am undertaking a BSc research project considering the role and potential value of knowledge management practices to service sector organisations. Because you are a senior manager in a high-profile service sector organisation, I was hoping that you might help my research by completing the attached questionnaire.

and

Dear Mrs Johnstone,

Please let me introduce myself. I am Ian Dale and I am the technical support consultant for the LardXstrap and Partners Consultancy. I have been commissioned by the managers of your organisation to review the technical services provision. I am told that this is an area in which you have a great deal of expertise, and I was wondering if you would be so kind as to complete the enclosed questionnaire.

The introductions in the above examples do a number of things. They name the specific respondent and demonstrate that the researcher has taken the time to see what this person does or knows, and that he/she understands something about the organisation. They explain why the project is being undertaken (as part of an academic course of study or as part of a consultancy assignment) so that the respondent knows that it is not just another anonymous 'market research' survey. The introduction attracts the attention of the respondent by framing the focus of the research in such a way that it will grab his or her attention. In the first example the recipient is a senior manager in a high-profile service sector organisation and may well therefore be extremely interested in the value of knowledge management practices. In the second example the researcher notes that the research been commissioned by the managers. Lastly, each of the examples outlines exactly what is being asked – to complete a questionnaire. The introduction above has done all that in just four lines!

PRACTICAL CONSIDERATIONS

Once the content and design issues have been addressed and you have optimised your chances of having your questionnaires completed and returned, there is a need to think about some of the practical issues:

- confidentiality
- logistics
- follow-up and coding.

Confidentiality issues

In some cases it may be important to assure potential respondents of anonymity and confidentiality. It is sometimes enough to say that 'Your responses will be treated in confidence', but at other times you might have to give a stronger indication of what this actually means. If so, you may have to say something like 'Your responses will be treated in confidence and will be used only as part of this research project. Your anonymity will be respected and there will be nothing in the results that might connect you or enable others to connect you to the data.'

It is also important to be aware of the implications that this promise has for you as a researcher. If you are doing this research as part of a programme of study, can you guarantee what the University will do with the data/information? To help in this situation, most universities and colleges have a 'confidentiality agreement' which is usually signed on behalf of the university by the registrar or his/her representative. It is useful to find out how this system works as early as possible, because many organisations require you to produce such assurances before they will allow you access to their people.

You must be familiar with the appropriate data protection legislation for the country (countries) that you are operating in. In the UK, the relevant legislation includes the Data Protection Act and the Freedom of Information Act. If you are dealing with children or vulnerable adults, there is additional legislation that you have to be aware of. In most cases your tutor, your mentor, your manager or your supervisor should be able to help here.

Logistics

Logistics must be considered from two perspectives: filling in the questionnaire, and the process for returning the completed document. Both can be considered in the covering letter. You have to tell people about the questionnaire, how many pages it has, how many sections it is in, and how long it will take them to complete it. Be honest and be accurate. If you say that the questionnaire will take 15 minutes, and 25 minutes later they are only halfway through, they will give up. As a general rule people will be put off by questionnaires that take half an hour or more to complete. Between 15 and 20 minutes is a more reasonable length of time. With clear and unambiguous guidelines, specifying a reasonable time requirement, recipients are more likely to decide to complete the questionnaire.

Along with the information about how long the questionnaire should take, you should include contact details for any queries (an email address is usually sufficient), details for returning the questionnaire (even if you have included a return envelope – these can sometimes get lost) and a specific date by which you would like the questionnaire returned – expressed diplomatically! Rather than say '… and you should get this back to me by 12 February at the very latest', use something like 'Your prompt reply would be much appreciated because I would like to start the analysis on 12 February'; or like this: 'If your completed questionnaire could be returned to me by 12 February, I would be extremely grateful.'

One tactic that works quite well is to link the return date to a small 'inducement' – for example, by offering people a précis copy of the results for completing the questionnaire.

Follow-up and coding

To ensure that you get as many completed questionnaires back as possible you may have to send respondents a reminder. In order to do this you have to institute a system of data tracking.

Coding is a good means of keeping track of which questionnaires have been returned and which have not. To track all returns, each questionnaire must be individually coded and the codes traceable to an individual respondent. Noting which people have responded enables you to send polite reminders to those who have not responded.

Coding can also be used as a means of tracking the sub-groups of the sample. This is useful when you wish to analyse your data by groups but do not necessarily need to know who the individuals are within each group. There are a number of ways of doing this. The use of different-coloured paper, different fonts or a minor change in wording in the introduction can all help distinguish particular sub-groups.

RESEARCH STORY

Seniors v juniors

In a piece of research that I was involved in previously, I wished to separate out the responses that the senior managers gave from the responses that the middle managers gave and the responses that the junior managers gave. All three groups were given the same questionnaire, but to distinguish between the groups, in the version for the senior managers the heading on the questionnaire ended with a full stop; in the version for the middle managers the full stop was replaced by a colon; and for the junior managers there was no punctuation mark at all. This allowed me to give out the questionnaires to people personally, and then allow for them all to be collected in together in one batch because I could still distinguish between the three groups by simply looking at the heading.

Having a follow-up strategy is important. For electronic questionnaires the process can be automated. Respondents are sent an email to forewarn them before the questionnaire is sent. They then get the questionnaire with a clearly marked return date, and a week before the questionnaire is due back, a reminder email is sent to those who have not responded. Email reminders can also be used even if the questionnaires that you have sent out are in hard copy. Where it is not possible to email reminders to people, alternative strategies must be devised. If you have sent the questionnaires in your own organisation, it is often possible to use things like general bulletin boards to remind people. This might be an electronic board or it might be simply by posting a notice on a noticeboard. Telephone calls are also a useful way of reminding people to return the questionnaire.

ACTIVITY

Now you have a clear idea of how to design a questionnaire, you can start to put some of the ideas into practice. Think about the research that you are planning to do, or might be able to do in the near future. Go back to your research question and start to design your questionnaire.

Think your way logically through the process and refer to the things that you have read, when necessary, to remind yourself of the key points. You need not design the full questionnaire at this stage – before you do that, you will have to get to grips with the analysis methods later on in this book. What you should do is map out the structure, design a few different types of questions and response formats, write the introduction, and think about the layout and image that it creates.

Once you have drafted your questionnaire, ask a friend or a colleague to pilot the questionnaire so that you get feedback on the strengths and the limitations of the work that you have done. If you can, watch them filling it in, note any hesitations, and answer any queries.

It is important, however, to be realistic here. Remember that people are doing you a favour by spending their time filling in your questionnaire. Remind them by all means, but try not to appear to be pestering them. Give them at least half of the time between the date they got the questionnaire and the date by which you need it back, before you remind them.

RESEARCH STORY

Cultural understandings

A student of mine working for a large multinational company with headquarters in Japan wanted to send electronic questionnaires to her colleagues across a number of different international sites. Although she naturally, out of courtesy, wanted to ask the managers of each of the sites for permission to undertake her research, because the headquarters was based in Japan she had to adopt a different approach. She could only send questionnaires out to her colleagues if she had emailed each person beforehand to ask for their permission to send the questionnaire to them. Failure to do so would have meant that nobody at the Japanese headquarters would have completed the questionnaire, and more importantly, this would have had a damaging effect on her reputation within the organisation.

ELECTRONIC QUESTIONNAIRES

Electronic questionnaires can be significantly cheaper than hard-copy questionnaires. Moreover, they allow you to send pre-survey notice of the questionnaire. In some countries where it would be deemed impertinent to simply send the questionnaire, this is very important.

Electronic questionnaires can be distributed in a number of ways. Table 15.1 gives a comparison of these ways, and the strengths and the issues to be aware of with each.

The advantages of emailing questionnaires are apparent. You can send out large numbers relatively cheaply. You can send pre-questionnaire notification and reminders to those who have not returned their completed questionnaire. Electronic questionnaires allow you to make sure that respondents answer the key questions by stopping them from progressing until they have answered the appropriate questions. And questionnaires in electronic format can be run through a range of analysis software to produce graphs and charts from the quantitative results.

The main disadvantage is that you will be limited in your sample group to those who have access to email or the Internet and then to those who have the technological capabilities to complete the form.

Guidelines for using electronic questionnaires

Restrict the size of the questionnaire so that it does not fill the respondent's in-box. If it does, it will be deleted.
Test the questionnaire with different browsers to ensure compatibility.
Use Rich Text Format (RTF) or Adobe pdf to avoid version compatibility issues.
Do not have a complex format that requires respondents to change pages.
Include the instructions clearly at the beginning.

If you are limiting the number of characters available in a response box, make sure you allow sufficient to answer the question.

If you are using streaming questions, make sure the technology takes the respondents to the correct question.

Consider how you can reassure people of anonymity if they are emailing the response back to you.

Look at proprietary brands such as Survey Monkey, Smart Survey and similar.

Table 15.1 Electronic questionnaire distribution

	Email questionnaires	*Web-based questionnaires*
Send	Designed questionnaire emailed directly to respondent	Email the URL to potential respondents
Return	Respondent can complete and email back, or may wish to print out and send back	Can log on and complete questionnaire in real time. Can download questionnaire to own address, fill in, and send back. Can print out questionnaire and send back in hard copy
Strengths	Can reach a large number of people. Reduced security issues as long as it goes straight to their email address	Allows you more scope for larger questionnaires or more design features/images. Allows access to a large number of people. Does not fill the respondent's in-box or your own in-box
Considerations	Email may get lost in the mass of everyday emails. Not all respondent groups will have access to email. Must include a postal address for those who wish to send hard copy back. Must consider how to deal with multiple returns from a single respondent. Must consider how your in-box will cope with large numbers of returns	People may have problems saving data if filling in the questionnaire in real time – and if they lose it, they are unlikely to start over again. People may not be willing to go searching around the Web to find your questionnaire. People can send more than one response back. Unless you have security-coded access to the website (which may have implications for anonymity), people who are not in your sample may log in and complete the questionnaire

SUMMARY

Questionnaires are an effective way to gather large quantities of information from groups of people, provided they are well-designed and distributed. A poorly designed questionnaire can generate misleading information or even no information at all. Your research purpose and research objectives must determine the content of the questions asked. Questions must be understandable by the audience. The visual presentation of the questionnaire has to appeal to the respondent group and the logistics have to be based on timely processes and systems.

Well-designed and well-executed questionnaires can produce a large quantity of valuable information. They can generate quantitative data to inform managerial decision-making, and also high-quality narrative data suggesting explanations and ideas in support of the figures.

REVIEW QUESTIONS

1. When are questionnaires most useful?

2. What factors must you be aware of when thinking about the content of your questionnaire?

3. What factors must you be aware of when thinking about the design of your questionnaire?

4. What mechanisms can you use to optimise the return rate of your questionnaires?

5. When are questionnaires *not* useful?

EXPLORE FURTHER

Boynton, P. (2004) 'Hands-on guide to questionnaire research. Selecting, designing, and developing your questionnaire', *British Medical Journal*, 5 June: 1372–5

Boynton, P. and Greenhalgh, T. (2004) 'Hands-on guide to questionnaire research. Selecting, designing, and developing your questionnaire', *British Medical Journal*, 29 May: 1312–15

Boynton, P., Wood, G. W. and Greenhalgh, T. (2004) 'Hands-on guide to questionnaire research. Selecting, designing, and developing your questionnaire', *British Medical Journal*, 12 June: 1433–6.

A series of three articles which give a good practical guide to designing and producing questionnaires. Access to supporting electronic materials through the *BMJ* links provided

Dillman, D. A. (2000) *Mail and Internet Surveys: The tailored design method*, 2nd edition. New York: Wiley. A useful book which is particularly strong on the design elements

Leung, Wai-Ching (2001) 'How to design a questionnaire', *Student British Medical Journal*, No.9: 171–216. Available online at http:student.bmj.com/issues/ 01/06/education/187.php [accessed 22 February 2009]. A brief practice-oriented paper which provides some good checklist-type prompts

Saris, W. E. and Gallhofer, I. N. (2007) *Design, Evaluation and Analysis of Questionnaires for Survey Research*. Oxford: Wiley. A more technically oriented book, strong on analysis. Particularly useful for those wishing to use surveys to produce quantitative data

Webb, J. (2000) 'Questionnaires and their design', *Marketing Review*, Vol.1, No.2, Winter: 197–218. Offers a good step-by-step approach to questionnaires. Provides a really useful list of questions that you should ask yourself in order to effectively frame your questionnaire

 Visit www.cipd.co.uk/brm for web links, templates, activities and other useful resources relating to this chapter.

CHAPTER 16

Interviews

INTRODUCTION

Interviews are a familiar and widely used technique, and can provide much richer information than a questionnaire. They are sometimes described as 'a conversation with a specific purpose', but differ from conversations in significant ways, and require different skills. Because they are particularly prone to bias, interviews need careful planning and careful recording in order to generate valid and reliable data.

Interviewing may *seem* an obvious method to use, but the choice must be carefully considered. This chapter will help you evaluate the method's suitability for your particular project. If interviewing, there will be choices to be made. Who will you interview, and how? Will it be individually or in groups? You will have to obtain participants' agreement, and design and manage the interview. You will have to record and analyse the data you gather. How you do all this must depend upon your research purpose and the role of the interviews in achieving it.

For any interview a wide range of skills will be needed. Some aspects of question construction were covered in Chapter 15, but interviews require additional types of question: prompts and probes to gather additional information or clarification, and questions which check understanding and summarise. You also need the skill to steer an interview in productive directions without biasing answers too much. Careful recording and analysis of the interview will help you check for possible bias, and reduce its impact.

LEARNING OUTCOMES

This chapter should enable you to:

- evaluate the advantages and disadvantages of interviews as a source of information at different stages in an investigation

- make appropriate choices about structure and question design

- keep useful and detailed records of both questions and answers when interviewing

- approach potential interviewees in ways that encourage participation and sustain their willingness throughout the interview

- identify and address the ethical issues associated with interviewing

- assess your interviewing skills and plan any necessary development.

INTERVIEWS FOR DIFFERENT PURPOSES

Your purpose in interviewing needs to be clear and kept firmly in mind at every stage. It should determine whom you select to interview and the approach you adopt. As you will see shortly, the same feature can be an advantage or disadvantage depending on your purpose in interviewing. I shall look first at potential purposes that interviews might serve.

 CONSIDER...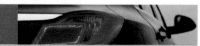

If you propose to use the interview method in the research you are considering, what purpose(s) will your interviews serve?

Purposes can be categorised in different ways. Important factors are the type of information you are seeking and the stage in your investigation at which you are seeking it. Your philosophical preferences will influence both your purpose and the type of interview you will feel comfortable with. Your interviewing choices will depend upon whether you are seeking to check existing information or to generate new information. A number of common interviewing purposes are outlined in Figure 16.1, broadly categorised by the stage in your investigation.

TYPES OF INFORMATION

You have to get your interview to generate information that will provide the strongest possible evidence in your investigation. So when planning your interview it helps to start thinking about how you will use what people say. As with questionnaires, your goal is to keep your interview as short as is consistent with obtaining the evidence you need; your interviewee's time is precious, and so is yours. Thus you must think carefully about what sort of information you are seeking, and how best to obtain it. Some of the information that interviews can usefully elicit is listed below:

- personal information
- 'facts'
- perceptions
- interpretations
- beliefs and assumptions
- values
- feelings
- intentions
- evaluations.

Figure 16.1 Stages and interview purposes

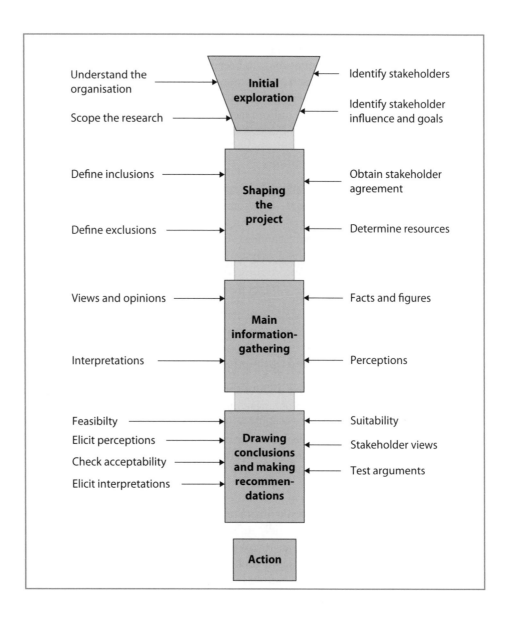

Personal information

Seek personal information (such as age, earnings, length of service) only when it is genuinely needed. If the interviewee agrees, and you can obtain what you need from organisational records, do so, rather than use interview time. In particular, avoid seeking 'sensitive' personal information such as details of pay or health unless vital to your investigation: it may be seen as intrusive and threatening and destroy rapport and trust.

'Facts'

As with personal data, if facts are available from records (complaints, errors, etc) use these. However, it is often useful to check the 'official' data against the perceptions of those involved. In my own research I encountered a bonus scheme that did not operate at all as management believed it did. As an investigator you must be suspicious of 'facts': different people may give you different 'facts'.

Perceptions

Perceptions may be more relevant than fact. The perceived impact of effort on pay may be more important than the actual relationship. Some discrepancies between 'fact' and perception may be because of misperceptions rather than 'factual' errors. Revealing such discrepancies may be highly relevant to your investigation's interpretation of data. Perceptions of others' motivations may be important in understanding aspects of situations and/or reactions to them. Perceptions of causality may be extremely relevant – *why* did or does X happen?

Interpretations

How people make sense of situations may be important. Whereas perceptions tend to be about what something *is*, interpretations concern what it *means*. Weick *et al* (2005) drew attention to the importance of the process of sense-making, and for many business researchers, understanding how individuals or groups interpret the world around them may be a central part in their investigation. For example, a comment such as 'You've got to understand that what this new system is really about is making sure that . . .' might be highly informative.

Because such articulation is, according to Weick, a social process, focus groups (discussed shortly) are particularly useful for eliciting information about interpretations.

Beliefs and assumptions

These drive a lot of thinking (and action) and tend to be invisible. An interview is a good way of surfacing them, and exploring their impact upon behaviour. Provided you have the skills required for the sort of gentle probing involved, you may help the interviewees become aware of their tacit assumptions. Again, focus groups may be particularly helpful, allowing participants to probe each other's assumptions.

Values

Values are qualities (for example *honesty* or *equality*) that are important to people. They often profoundly influence how people understand a situation and/or decide what to do. Again an interview may be the most obvious way to address values, because it allows in-depth probing (provided you have the skills to do it) to elicit things that people may not readily think about or discuss.

Feelings

Emotions are powerful drivers of behaviour. A key factor in many situations will be how stakeholders *feel* about a situation or about a possible future scenario. An interview is the most obvious research method here, although to access feelings the interviewer will probably have to establish a fairly high level of trust, and to tread carefully in asking about feelings. Some may be strong and painful, and it would not be appropriate (or ethical) to venture into such areas without the necessary skills.

Intentions

There may be other potential sources of information about actions, but if you are interested in future intentions, the interview is likely to be the most obvious source. Note, however, that an expressed intention to act does not necessarily indicate that the action will sooner or later take place.

Evaluations

The factors above will contribute to individuals' assessments of current situations or past initiatives. The resulting evaluations may inform diagnosis of any issue, or form a substantial part of data collection for evaluation research. An interview allows you to probe the perceptions, interpretations, values and evidence that result in the evaluation, and to look for positives as well as negatives.

THE ADVANTAGES AND DISADVANTAGES OF INTERVIEWS

Interviews can elicit many types of information, and have potential uses at most stages in your research. But they have disadvantages as well as advantages. In choosing to interview, you need to identify both. If advantages do not clearly outweigh disadvantages, you should consider whether they can be strengthened or disadvantages reduced. Only if the advantages predominate, or can be made to do so, should you choose to interview.

Widespread familiarity with interviewing often leads to the dangerously misguided impression that 'anyone can interview'. Consider the story below. Mary is a full-time student, doing a project on graduate recruitment. She is interested in what it is about recruitment websites that attracts potential recruits, and what it is that would deter them from applying to that organisation. She is interviewing Jane, a fellow student.

This extract, although an extreme case, illustrates at least some of the hazards of interviewing for the inexperienced.

Closed questions
Chapter 15

You may have noted that Mary sounds uncomfortable at the start. She has not introduced herself at all clearly, nor really explained her project. She leaps straight into her first (double-barrelled) question without checking that Jane is clear about the purpose of the interview, and knows what to expect. Introductions to interviews need to cover the same issues as introductions to questionnaires. Predictably, Jane answers only part of the complex question – the closed part.

Mary, perhaps feeling defensive, justifies the question, and starts *giving* information rather than seeking it. This reduces the time available for Jane's replies. Worse, it risks influencing subsequent answers, introducing bias. And if Mary confuses what she is

RESEARCH STORY: HOUSE OF HORRORS

Interviewing about websites

Mary: Um, thanks, Jane. Like I said, I'm doing this project about websites and wanted to ask you about what you thought. Have you looked at any websites for jobs, and what did you think about them?

Jane: Of course I have.

Mary: Well, yes, it's the obvious thing to do, isn't it? But there are loads of them, and I tend to get a bit lost – I don't know which ones to believe!

Jane: I guess they are all trying to make themselves look attractive, like they are the best organisation in the world to work for. You do wonder, don't you? I mean, I can't believe that they all are!

Mary: Well, obviously they can't be. I did a summer job once and the website looked great – really good artwork, and it was so easy to get the application form. But the job turned out to be rubbish.

Jane: Yes, it was the same for me last summer. I chose the job precisely because of the website, but then the job was nothing like I'd expected.

Mary: It makes you wonder if they ever talk to the people who actually work there!

CONSIDER...

Where has Mary gone wrong? How might this interview generate misleading data? What would you have done differently?

saying with what she is hearing, her misperceptions will lead her to conclude wrongly that Jane's opinions agree with hers.

From this point the exchange becomes a conversation, with Mary responding to Jane rather than seeking information from her. She is no longer steering the interview, and indeed they have wandered into discussion irrelevant to her research question. Jane offers her an opportunity to get at least partly back on track with her last comment. Mary could have asked Jane what it was about the website that influenced her choice, but the opportunity is missed.

Interviews require careful preparation and careful steering: they are not simply conversations.

To understand how Mary might have obtained better information from her interview with Jane, it is worth looking at the specific advantages and disadvantages of interviewing as a method. First, though, think about interviewing in the context of your own research.

ACTIVITY

List the potential advantages and disadvantages of interviewing as a research method for the project you are considering. Add to your list as you work through the chapter, and keep the final list in your journal.

POTENTIAL ADVANTAGES OF INTERVIEWS

Interviewing offers advantages of flexibility, interactivity, and informality. These features mean that you steer the interview in directions suggested by responses, can prompt and probe, explore meanings and thus generate rich qualitative information. This may help you understand key elements in a situation and/or interpret other findings. Interviews *appear* valid to clients, so the method is likely to be acceptable. Interviews can also generate quantitative data so that your conclusions may be more credible to clients of a positivist persuasion. Table 16.1 shows the main advantages and disadvantages of interviewing as a research method. These are dealt with in more detail below.

Table 16.1 Advantages and disadvantages of interviews as a research method

INTERVIEWS	
Advantages	**Disadvantages**
Face validity	Not a simple method
Flexibility	Time-consuming
Interactivity	Sample size is smaller
Various types of data obtained	Susceptibility to influence
Richness of information	Lack of comparability
Exploration of meaning	Scope for misinterpretation
Illustrative quotes to record	
Networking opportunities	

Face validity

With sensible questions and a reasonable sample, interview responses are likely to be readily accepted as valid information, thus providing credible support for your arguments. Another advantage is apparent transparency; the method *appears* to be open and its workings clear.

Flexibility

If you adopt a flexible design, you can ask different questions if something interesting emerges. This is particularly important in the exploratory stages of an investigation, when you are not sure what approach to take or perhaps even which issue to address. Think back to Deborah's example of a case where she included an 'Other' category in a questionnaire, and almost everyone suggested an option she had not thought about. It can be really frustrating to discover something like this only when you have collected all your data and start to analyse it. In an interview you can probe for more information there and then, and include an additional question on this topic in all subsequent interviews.

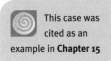
This case was cited as an example in **Chapter 15**

As well as adapting *during* the interview, you can intentionally use different questions for different interviewees where appropriate. For example, Jankowicz (1995) distinguishes some interviews as *key informant interviews*. Suppose you need the finance director's views on elements of strategy and performance measurement, and the marketing director's views on key competitors. In such cases each interview will be a 'one-off'. Although some questions might be common, there would be other specific questions needed for each key informant. Interviews are flexible enough to allow for such tailoring.

Interactivity

Interviews are a social interaction. This allows the interviewee to check his or her understanding of a question, and for you to clarify the matter if necessary. It enables you to ask supplementary questions to clarify or extend answers given, and to explore any unexpected or apparently contradictory answers, and to check your understanding of what they mean. You can also encourage interviewees who seem to be flagging.

Generating both quantitative and qualitative data

Quantitative data can impress clients, meeting their demands for 'facts and figures'. Qualitative data can offer explanations or ideas about the meaning of the numbers. Interviews can be used for either type of data, or indeed a single interview can generate both types.

Generating rich information

If you are using unstructured interviews, you leave interviewees free to express what is important to *them*. This can generate extremely rich and finely textured qualitative information about individuals' perceptions and feelings.

The potential to explore meanings

If you are looking at something from a constructionist perspective – perhaps to discover the meanings attributed to something or how those meanings have been constructed – interviews may be one of your prime methods.

The provision of illustrative quotes

Confirmatory bias **Chapter 2**

This is a double-edged advantage. Carefully selected quotes from interviewees can explain and support points you are making, and render your report far more interesting, compelling, and impressive to a client. But you must be particularly careful to avoid bias. There is a high risk that you will select powerful quotes that support the points you want to make, and ignore quotes that would suggest the point is wrong (perhaps because of confirmatory bias).

Networking opportunities

Chris's project featured in **Chapters 1 and 2**

If your topic is perceived as important, senior people may be willing to be interviewed. If you create a good and professional impression in your dealings with them, it may form the basis of useful future contacts. This was one of the reasons Chris chose to interview key trainers and purchasers of training in his reflection and leadership development project in part because he was hoping to build contacts for future consultancy work. If you are doing research in your own organisation, similar arguments apply, and your increased visibility may help your career.

In practical business research almost every silver lining has its attached cloud, as well as *vice versa*. Interviews are no exception. Indeed, some of the disadvantages listed below may be the reverse side of some of these advantages.

POTENTIAL DISADVANTAGES OF INTERVIEWS

Some of the disadvantages of interviews result from the misperception of 'simplicity' highlighted earlier. Some are the converse of the 'richness' and individuality that can be an advantage of interviewing. The balance of advantage/disadvantage will depend upon your research purpose. Table 16.1 listed the main disadvantages, which are described below.

The method is not 'simple'

Simplicity may be one of the main apparent attractions of this method, but this 'advantage' is usually illusory. Interviewing, and afterwards analysing interview data, takes a high level of skill, particularly for qualitative data. Without these skills your conclusions will not be trustworthy. Necessary skills include establishing and sustaining rapport, asking questions clearly and without influencing answers, steering the interview, listening (far less common a skill than most people imagine) and analysing qualitative information. Focus groups will require additional group facilitation skills.

The time required

Qualitative data
Chapters 18
and 19

Interviews are *extremely* time-consuming for both interviewer and interviewee. Actual time spent interviewing is the tip of a far larger time iceberg. It can take a long time to arrange interviews, travel to them and reschedule if interviewees cannot make appointments. Transcription of the interview record may take several times as long as the interview itself (Jankowicz, 1985, suggests seven times as long, but this may well be an exaggeration). Analysing qualitative data puts huge demands on time. Interviews are *not* a quick or easy main data collection option.

A smaller sample size

The time required for interviewing almost inevitably restricts your sample size. Whether this matters will depend upon your research purpose. If you want to understand how the six directors of an organisation interpret current strategic challenges, a 100% sample might be feasible. If you want to draw conclusions about the workforce as a whole, you would require a bigger sample than you might have time to interview. It is important not to draw wider-reaching conclusions than your sample can support.

Susceptibility to influence

When interviewing, there are many ways in which you can influence the answers you get. Before you start to interview you have decided how the study is to be framed, the information you will seek and the shape of the interview. During the interview there are more subtle influences. Even on the telephone the tone of voice, the language used and the insertion of additional or differently worded questions can all affect replies. Differential use of 'mmm' and 'thank you' may convey approval and disapproval, thus selectively rewarding certain ways of answering.

Scope for influencing face-to-face interviews is far greater because there are also non-verbal cues such as smiles and body posture. The greater your interpersonal skills and the stronger your rapport with your interviewee, the more the interviewee is likely to want to please you. So although establishing rapport is a good thing, it does increase the likelihood of inadvertent bias.

Lack of comparability

Comparability is not a problem with a fully structured interview, but the more flexible the interviews, the less likely they are to produce comparable information. Each interview becomes a different 'tool'. This may not matter at the exploratory stage, but if your ultimate aim is to make explicit comparisons or generalisations, unstructured interviews would be unsuitable as your main method.

Susceptibility to mishearing and misinterpretation

 Confirmatory bias **Chapter 2**

Because of the previous two points and the potential richness of information, it is all too easy for confirmatory bias to operate. You selectively 'hear', and/or selectively record, only what is consistent with what you want to hear. This is a real risk if you are 'trying to prove a point' with your research. If you unconsciously filter the data before you analyse, your conclusions will be misleading. If you select quotes to support a point (as noted above), the scope for bias is greatly magnified. An interviewee who generates pithy and compelling quotes may have a disproportionate influence on your interpretations. If you select quotes for use in your report, they can strongly influence your reader. It is important to be extremely careful to select quotes that are *representative* of the whole sample in content, and 'balanced' in their persuasiveness.

ACTIVITY

Check that you are happy with your extended list of advantages and disadvantages of using interviews in your planned investigation.

The checklist at the end of this chapter will help you to decide whether and when interviews would be an appropriate method for your own investigation.

KEY POINTS

- The flexibility and interactivity of interviews allows you to develop understanding as your research progresses: you are not restricted to exploring those issues identified at the outset.
- Interviews allow you to explore meanings (difficult by other methods) and may generate compelling 'quotes' to illuminate a point.
- However, interviews are usually far more time-consuming than anticipated, and require a high level of skill on the part of the interviewer. Producing a convincing *and* trustworthy account of interview findings is not easy.
- The individual nature of all but the most structured interviews means that caution is required when making comparisons or drawing conclusions from answers.
- Interviewer influence has to be taken into account, and minimised.

DIFFERENT INTERVIEW STRUCTURES

One of the most obvious ways in which interviews differ is in how much structure the interviewer imposes. Unstructured, semi-structured and structured interviews are often treated as if they were three discrete categories, but 'semi-structured' covers a wide range of degrees of structure, and corresponds to an extended part of a continuum rather than a discrete category. It is also possible to mix structures: a single interview may contain some parts that are structured and some that are less so.

STRUCTURED INTERVIEWS

A fully structured interview is basically a questionnaire administered face to face or by telephone, rather than being self-completed. The interviewer sticks to a schedule (specific questions and allowable answer options) and ignores anything else that might be said.

Table 16.2 Advantages and disadvantages of structured interviews as a research method

Structured interviews	
Advantages	**Disadvantages**
Face validity	Lack of flexibility
Reliabilty	Value depends on deciding in advance upon
Generalisability	the questions and the best way to ask them
Ease of analysis	Takes more time than a questionnaire
Low interviewer influence	
Narrower range of interviewer skills required	
May get higher response rates than a questionnaire	

Unlike other interviews, structured interviews are *not* flexible – the design is predetermined. Like a questionnaire, a structured interview can be useful as a means of collecting or checking specific information or where there is a clear research question and it is possible to ask a series of specific questions that will provide answers which will help you to answer that question.

A totally structured interview is equivalent to an administered questionnaire, with the interviewer in control throughout. Because questions are standard and normally offer a specified range of answers, comparisons between different groups of interviewees are possible using statistical techniques.

Structured interviewing requires no knowledge of the topic addressed by the schedule. (I know absolutely nothing about luxury cars, but would be perfectly capable of conducting a highly structured interview about brands and significant features of such cars.) Structured interviews tend also to require fewer interpersonal skills than less structured interviewing, although some training will still be required. Assistants can therefore do some of the interviewing if resources are available.

The disadvantage, of course, is that the information obtained is limited, and predetermined. The lack of flexibility, adaptability and scope to explain means that a pilot is essential to minimise some of this disadvantage. You need to check that questions convey your meaning, and response options cover what the interviewee sees as relevant factors. Once you finalise your schedule there is no further scope for change. If you are testing a specific hypothesis, or have done extensive exploratory work and are confident about the questions you are asking, this may not matter. The ease of analysing answers and making cross-group comparisons may far outweigh any disadvantage.

UNSTRUCTURED INTERVIEWS

In an unstructured interview the interviewer suggests a broad topic but leaves it very much to the interviewee to determine what to say about it. Thus the interviewer has paradoxically both more and less scope for influence than with a structured interview. Less, because the question is less defined and the interviewee has far more scope over the agenda; more, because unstructured interviews tend to be much more like conversations. The interviewer responds, probes and prompts as appropriate. Interviewer influence is thus much less obvious but may be even more powerful. You need a high level of both skill and self-awareness to keep the interview within a frame that is relevant to the investigation, without influencing the answers in your preferred direction.

Table 16.3 Advantages and disadvantages of unstructured interviews as a research method

Unstructured interviews	
Advantages	*Disadvantages*
Flexibility Openness Interviewee is not constrained by the interviewer's pre-existing mindset Ideal for issues when you have few preconceived ideas	Potential for interviewer selectivity and influence Analysis may be difficult Low comparability Low generalisability May lack credibility with readers of a positivist persuasion

The term 'unstructured interview' normally means a clearly labelled 'interview' in which the interviewee is consciously participating in your investigation. But organisation-based projects involve many informal conversations and it may help to think of these as informal unstructured interviews. This will help you to relate what is being said to your purpose, to steer the conversation and to probe when points seem important, and above all to listen with your full attention. It will remind you that you need interpersonal skills to build trust, and a willingness to co-operate in your investigation.

 Informed consent **Chapter 4**

It will also prompt you to think about what you should record from the conversation, and how to record it. Note, however, that this raises ethical issues of honesty and confidentiality. Although informants have agreed to a conversation, they may not feel they have agreed to an interview, so there is a real issue of 'informed consent' (discussed more fully later).

SEMI-STRUCTURED INTERVIEWS

Semi-structured interviews lie somewhere between unstructured and fully structured, and are a widely used practical business research method. The degree of openness and flexibility may vary considerably. The advantages or disadvantages tend to depend upon where on the scale they lie. Sadly, many dissertations claim to use semi-structured interviews when all that is apparent is that a conversation has taken place, ostensibly in connection with the research topic. No further information is given beyond claims that the 'interviews showed' something. To create convincing evidence from semi-structured interviews requires rather more than this.

Table 16.4 Advantages and disadvantages of semi-structured interviews as a research method

Semi-structured interviews
Advantages and disadvantages
Semi-flexibility Semi-openness Some comparability Some generalisability Relatively high face validity Easier to analyse than totally unstructured Harder to analyse than structured

Unless you prepare carefully you risk a 'worst of all worlds' result, with most of the disadvantages and few of the potential advantages. A successful semi-structured interview requires you to keep clear objectives for the interview firmly in mind throughout the interview. You need to listen effectively and be open to the interviewee's way of seeing things. And you need to decide how much structure is needed at any given point in order to meet your objectives. An invaluable aid in this is a well-prepared interview guide.

Interview guides

Although you will not be working to a rigid interview schedule, it makes sense to develop an interview guide for a semi-structured interview. This guide will act as a memory prompt and ensure that you cover all the areas you intend. Having a written guide will free your mind from thinking about what to ask next. This is vital if you are to listen properly to the interviewee. An example extract from such a guide is given below. The full guide appears in a later section.

Interview guide (extract)

Introduce self and purpose of study.
(Hello. I'm — —. Thank you very much for agreeing to take part in this interview. As I said in my email, I'm looking at . . . etc.)

Explain confidentiality. Check any concerns and give any necessary reassurances.

Explain the interview process and likely length of interview. Check that interviewee is happy with the recording method.

Seek background information on qualifications, length of service, etc.

Perceived reasons for recent changes.

(If not already clear) Perceived goals of the changes.

The coverage and detail would depend upon your purpose and the degree of structure that you feel is appropriate. You would normally follow this guide unless, for example, the interviewee seemed uncomfortable with some areas, or anticipated later questions while answering an earlier one. As Bryman (2001) pointed out, it is not the *guide t*hat creates the openness and flexibility of a semi-structured interview, but the open and flexible attitude of the interviewer.

MIXED STRUCTURES

A semi-structured interview, in which the degree of control is intermediate throughout, is not the same as an interview with a mix of structures, some parts of the interview being highly structured, others less so. A mixed structure is a valid approach to interviewing, but interviewees may need help in 'changing gear' at different points. For example, if you have established a pattern of short answers (with multiple-choice or other closed questions), it is good practice to signal that a change is required by saying something like this:

> "Thank you for that. Now I'd like to open up the discussion a bit. I'm interested in what you think are the important aspects of [X] in general, whatever they might be . . .

[Prompt if necessary] For example, what do you think . . . ?"

DESIGNING YOUR INTERVIEW

The discussion thus far suggests that it is crucial to plan and design any interview very carefully. You must design process as well as content, and pay particular attention to the ways in which you ask questions and record answers. Otherwise, you may flounder, as Mary did in the earlier illustration. Your design has to maximise the chance of achieving your purpose, and minimise the chance that things will go wrong.

ACTIVITY

If you plan to interview and have not yet scheduled planning time for your interviews (see Chapter 23) – including time to clarify your purpose for each type of interview you intend to carry out – update your action plan now to include this.

Before going further, let us look at the sorts of things that can go horribly wrong in an interview. The most common are that the interviewee talks too much, too little, or completely off the point. The following, fuller 'hazard list' should help sensitise you to what your interview design should be careful to avoid.

 List of interviewing hazards
  ▲ You are not sure what you wish to get out of the interview.
  ▲ You ask unclear or leading questions.
  ▲ The interviewee misunderstands your question.
  ▲ You misunderstand the interviewee's answer.
  ▲ You fail to hear part of the answer.
  ▲ You haven't a clue what the answer means.
  ▲ The interviewee gives the answer he/she thinks you want.
  ▲ The interviewee feels too uncomfortable or too nervous to give you an honest answer.
  ▲ The interviewee won't say anything.
  ▲ The interviewee won't stop talking.
  ▲ The interviewee drifts off the subject.
  ▲ You run out of time before you have covered half the topics on your guide.
  ▲ You get drawn into a discussion, perhaps because you feel strongly about the subject.
  ▲ You can't read your notes.
  ▲ You misremember what the interviewee said earlier.
  ▲ You can't remember what the interviewee said at all.
  ▲ The technology won't work, or disrupts the interview.
  ▲ The interviewee gets into trouble over what he/she has said.
  ▲ You get into trouble over what you say he/she said.

 Questionnaire design

Chapter 15

Planning and design are crucial to avoid these hazards. Interview design shares many features with questionnaire design, but with additional features. Your design has to include introduction and reassurance for your interviewee, building and sustaining rapport and trust, and appropriate closure. Your questions must seem logical to the interviewee, and easy to understand, and must generate sufficiently full and understandable answers. The next section looks at the areas you must consider when designing your interview in order to avoid the many potential hazards and pitfalls of this method.

DESIGN ELEMENTS

Everything you do – deciding on interviewees, on areas to address, and on the way you formulate questions and steer and probe – has to contribute to achieving your research purpose. Your design decisions will have to relate to all the factors shown listed below:

- the interviewee(s)
- managing expectations
- social flow
- coverage: topics to address
- use of language
- content flow
- recording the answers
- any follow-up.

Issues such as sampling and questionnaires are dealt with in more detail elsewhere.

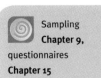

Sampling **Chapter 9,** questionnaires **Chapter 15**

Managing expectations

Interviewees' expectations will influence how they respond to the interview itself and the extent to which you can gather appropriate information. Creating and managing expectations starts before the interview, at the point of your very first contact, and continues until your last contact with the interviewee. You therefore need to think about how you will convey the purpose of your study, the role of the interview within it, why the interviewee has been selected and what will be required of them, and what you will offer in return. What and how you communicate will help you to create realistic expectations that you are able to meet.

Social flow

Interviewees need to feel comfortable in the interview situation if they are to be open and honest in their answers. You can create such flow by your initial welcome, and by asking unchallenging questions until they feel at ease. If you need to address more challenging issues, wait until the interviewee appears comfortable and settled in the interview situation. Even then it may be helpful to say that you know this may be a difficult question, and to offer the interviewee the choice of not answering, while explaining why it would be helpful if they did. Closure, with thanks and reassurance, is part of the flow, and you need to design for this as well.

Coverage

What areas is it appropriate to cover in an interview in this context with this interviewee? Which areas might be sensitive? Are these essential? How far will you determine the areas to be covered in advance, and how much scope will you allow the interviewee to influence coverage? Questions need to seem relevant to your purpose, and not feel intrusive.

Language

You must think about how to phrase your questions in ways that will help the interviewee to relate to you, thus building trust. Seek to be professional but clear, and to use language your interviewee will understand and be comfortable with. Jargon is likely to create barriers rather than break them down. Remember that language can be a major source of misinterpretation and misunderstanding. The same word can have very different meanings for different people.

RESEARCH STORY

'Critical' engagement

A current project of mine aims to increase the extent to which MBA students 'critically engage' with their studies. Early focus group discussions showed that 'critical' had very different meanings for different people, even within a fairly narrow section of society. I shall over-generalise only slightly. Academic colleagues of a sociological persuasion saw me as talking about an extremely important aspect of study – the ability to build on insights from people like Derrida and Foucault, and critique the social context and the power structures within it which created the phenomena we were addressing in our courses. Non-sociologically inclined academics thought I was talking about the very real need for students to learn to question what they read, its

relevance, and the evidence and logic upon which it was constructed. Some students thought that it was really good that they were being encouraged to be critical of some of the poor management practices to which they were subjected. I won't go into the different interpretations of 'engagement'! One colleague accused me of failing to consider students' professional practice. For me this is so central to the idea of engagement that I had not thought it needed to be said! It slowly became clear to me that although everyone agreed that the issue of critical engagement was absolutely vital in management education, each was agreeing to something different.

Content flow

As with questionnaires, your interviewee will be more comfortable if questions seem to flow logically. Your interview guide should follow what *you* see as a logical structure. However, one of the advantages of a flexible approach to interviewing is that you can adjust the order of questions. If your interviewee seems to see a different logic, you may have to depart from your own 'obvious' flow and follow theirs. This does not negate the importance of thinking about content flow.

Recording answers

This has to be considered at the design stage, and is dealt with in more detail shortly. If you plan a mixed structure, how many questions do you want to pre-code? How many do you want to be able to 'code on the spot'? Will you be able to make an audio-recording?

KEY POINTS

- You need to think very carefully about your objectives in interviewing, and about the best form of interview to achieve those objectives.
- You need to think equally carefully about how you form your questions, and about the many ways in which the researcher can influence the outcome of the interview.
- You will need to draw upon a sound understanding of what counts as data and evidence [see Chapter 9] and upon the question design issues discussed in the previous chapter as there are many issues that are common to both questionnaires and interviews.

QUESTION TYPES

The previous chapter explained the difference between open and closed questions, and the use of filters, and outlined the requirements for a 'good' question. Because similar principles apply to interview questions, you should now go back and read the relevant sections of Chapter 15. The same points apply.

> **Questions need to be clear, unambiguous, address a single point, and not 'lead' to a biased answer.**

Filtering and streaming questions **Chapter 15**

Closed questions

Structured interviews are based on closed questions. The data they gather is limited to a set range of responses. However, closed questions are also used in mixed-format interviews. Here they can gather specific responses or can act as filtering or streaming questions. Where they are used as part of a mixed-structure interview, you may want to vary the format frequently so that respondents do not become too set in a monosyllabic answer mode.

Open questions

Open questions are used in all but structured interviews. They present the interviewee with a theme from which he/she develops his/her own answers. The interviewer has little influence on those answers but can encourage the interviewee to elaborate by the use of *probes*, *prompts*, *tests of understanding* and *summaries*.

Probes

Sometimes an interviewee may mention briefly something that is really relevant to your research. Probing is a way of getting them to say more on this. You can do it without using words – simply remaining silent (or saying 'Mmmm?' on a rising tone) may be enough to indicate that you would like to hear more.

Sometimes you can 'reflect' what the person just said, perhaps rephrasing it slightly, and perhaps using the intonation of a question, and then wait. This often elicits further comment.

> Interviewee: 'Morale after the changes was really low.'

> Interviewer: 'So you noticed that morale was low?'

Sometimes you may wish to ask a specific follow-on question, such as:

> 'What makes you rate the marketing project as so successful?'

> 'What aspects of the situation do you think the management failed to understand?'

> 'So what methods did you actually use?'

> 'How did you and your colleagues reach that decision?'

> 'Why was that such a problem?'

> 'That's really interesting. Can you tell me a little more about it?'

Sometimes you may want to probe because there seems to you to be an inconsistency between two different things that an interviewee has said. Then reflecting both and asking how they fit together may be helpful.

'My understanding was that [X]. Is that not the case ...?'

(Note that you need to assume it is your understanding that is still incomplete, and avoid any impression that you suspect the interviewee of not telling the truth. If you storm in with 'I fail to understand how [X] and [Y] can both be true. Explain that!', you will destroy any rapport and trust between you.)

Prompts

Even in a semi-structured interview you will have an idea of the areas you want the interviewee to address. You may want to see what respondents say unprompted, and then prompt on areas that have not arisen spontaneously.

If you have a long list of prompts, you may choose to write them on a card and hand it to the interviewee. You might then ask something like:

> "Could you tell me whether any of the things written on this card played a part in the decision?"

Subsequent questions can then focus on the things that the interviewee identifies as relevant.

When using prompts it is important to use the same prompts with everyone, and to distinguish between unprompted and prompted answers. Often the unprompted answers will reflect the aspects that are regarded as most relevant and important by the interviewee, and will be least influenced by your 'framing' of the situation.

Tests of understanding or accuracy

You may not always understand the full meaning of an answer. Interviewees are talking from their frame of reference and their own assumptions. You are hearing them through your own (possibly very different) frame and assumptions. It is important to test your understanding at regular intervals *and* whenever you are at all puzzled over the interviewee's meaning. If your interviewee is giving you a lot of complicated factual information, you may also need to check the accuracy of what you have grasped with something like:

> "Can I just check that I've understood you fully? Are you saying that [paraphrase of interviewee's statement] is the case?"

Note: it is vital that you do paraphrase. If you merely repeat the interviewee's words, of course they will say that that is what they meant. It is only when you put the point in your own words that differences in meaning will start to become evident. Failure to fully understand or to 'hear' quite what the interviewee is saying is one way in which you can easily bias your data. Such checks are therefore important if you want your data to be valid.

Summarising

'Summarising' refers to a summary of a 'chunk' of the interview, together with a check that it is accurate. (When testing understanding you will be summarising only a particular point.) Summarising can serve several purposes. If you feel someone is starting to ramble, it can be a useful way of closing down that particular topic.

> "I think we've covered a lot of interesting ground here – would you mind if I try to summarise the key points you've made?"

You can then check that this *is* the interviewee's understanding of the ground covered. You might also use the summary as the basis for asking whether there were any further important points they wanted to make, as a way of moving the interview on. If you are relying on notes rather than audio recording, summarising can act as a useful check on the completeness of your notes.

DESIGNING THE SOCIAL DYNAMICS OF AN INTERVIEW

The social dynamics of the interview are so important that it is worth pulling together briefly the points relating to this. You are dependent upon the interviewee's willingness to co-operate and answer fully and honestly. This requires you to establish rapport at the start, and sustain a good relationship with them. They must trust you not to take advantage in any way of their co-operation. You are probably familiar with the stages a group meeting goes through. An interview is similar:

Introducing/explaining
↳ Relaxing/establishing rapport
   ↳ Core information-gathering
     ↳ Cooling
       ↳ Closing
         ↳ Post-closure.

The stages are explained below.

Initial explanation

Settle the interviewee into the situation, explain the purpose of the study, outline the nature and duration of the interview, reassure them of confidentiality and explain how you would like to record answers. (If you wish to make an audio recording, ask their permission to do so.) Explain that there are no right or wrong answers – you are genuinely interested in the interviewee's responses, whatever they are. Invite the interviewee to interrupt you or to ask questions whenever he/she wants clarification.

The relaxing stage

Make the interviewee feel comfortable about answering your questions. Easy but relevant questions help here. As in the previous stage, your own openness and relaxation, and a concern for the interviewee's comfort, will help to relax them. Although building rapport is important at all stages, this is where it is most crucial.

The interview core

Here you gather most of your information. Questions need to appear reasonable and logical, and your attentive listening should show that you value and appreciate the answers. When you prompt or probe, it helps to say that you are doing so because their answer is interesting. Ask any essential sensitive questions as late as possible so that by then the interviewee is relaxed and trusts you. (Avoid any sensitive questions that are not essential.)

The cooling stage

It helps to 'wind down' the interview with some relatively straightforward and positive questions so that any tension is defused and the interviewee leaves feeling good about the experience. This is particularly important if some questions were difficult or sensitive.

The closing stage

Thank the interviewee for their co-operation, and the valuable information they have provided. Ask if they have any questions about the interview, and reassure them again about confidentiality. You may want to let them know what will happen when your research is finished, and/or offer to send a report of your findings.

Post-closure

You will often find that once 'the interview' is over people will relax and start to give you a lot more information. This raises interesting ethical questions over whether or not this information should be recorded. Some researchers run to the cloakroom to make a covert record as soon as the interviewee has left. Others feel it is unethical to use such information at all. If you do wish to use something said outside the designated interview, it would be ethically sound to ask the interviewee if they minded you adding the point to your interview notes.

The specimen interview guide below is an example of how these considerations might be reflected in a semi-structured interview conducted as part of a project on the impact of change.

Note that although there is a question about negative effects, it is towards the end so that it does not influence earlier responses. If this question had been asked earlier, it might have biased all subsequent answers towards the negative.

Specimen interview guide (topic: change evaluation)

Introduce self and purpose of study.
(Hello. I'm — —. Thank you very much for agreeing to take part in this interview. As I said in my email, I'm looking at . . . [details].)

Explain confidentiality. Check any concerns and give any necessary reassurances.

Explain the interview process and likely length of interview. Check that interviewee is happy with the recording method.

[Note: it often helps to script this introduction fully, even if you do not exactly follow the script. It helps you to relax if you know it is there, and know roughly what it says.]

Seek background information on qualifications, length of service, etc.

Perceived reasons for recent changes.

(If not already clear) Perceived goals of the changes.

(If not already clear) What the main problem was with the existing situation.

What was the overall reaction to the initiative?

What did you feel about it?

[Prompt re extent to which goals were achieved, if not already clear.]

[Prompts re information flows, clarity objectives and overall morale, if not mentioned.]

What has been the impact on your own role?

[Prompts re pressures, job satisfaction and achievement of personal objectives, if not already mentioned.]

(If not already mentioned) Are there any changes that seem to have had a negative effect?

If there are: a) what sort of negative effect?
          b) how serious has it been?

What action could management take to ensure that things continue/start to improve?

Are there any other things you feel about the changes that I have not asked about?

Is there anyone else you think I should speak to?

Reassurance re confidentiality and uses to which data will be put.

Offer of copy of report.

Thanks.

TELEPHONE OR OTHER 'REMOTE' INTERVIEWS

The design considerations above apply to all interviews, including telephone interviews (or interviews via Skype or a video link). However, some aspects of remote interviewing are sufficiently distinctive to deserve separate consideration. Most of the following points refer to remote interviews with or without a video link, and in the discussion which follows 'phone' should be taken to include interviews with a video link.

The phone is frequently used for highly structured interviews and/or questionnaire administration. It can generate higher response rates than electronic or paper questionnaires. Although taking more time than a pure questionnaire, a phone interview allows you to vary the structure, and respondents can ask questions if they are unsure of the meaning of a question.

For less structured interviews, phone interviewing offers time and cost savings and allows you to interview people over a wider geographic area. However, the 'reduced social bandwidth' (no body language unless there is a video component) may make it harder to develop rapport and trust, and thus reduce the potential richness of the information. This will be less of a disadvantage if you are working on an internal project and know the interviewees and/or they know you, or know of you. In this case there will already be a basis for trust, and you are likely to be speaking something closer to 'the same language'. If these are people with whom you normally interact by phone (or video conference), this medium may be as good as face-to-face.

In phone interviews you need to pay particular attention to the 'social flow', and to making the interviewee feel at ease. The 'tone' of your introduction and explanation of your study and the interview process is crucial. Show your consideration for the interviewee. Check that they have enough time for your conversation and are comfortable. Check at regular intervals that they are OK, and can hear you easily. If the line becomes difficult, suggest that they hang up, and ring them back. Interviewing over a bad line is seldom worth the effort. For phone interviews it can be particularly helpful to send a list of questions in advance.

Telephone interviews tend to be more tiring for both parties than face-to-face, so if this is your main research method you should aim to keep the interview as short as possible. You will also find it much easier if you have a speaker-phone, leaving you free to read your guide and make notes without dropping the handset. Audio-recording a phone interview can be difficult, so taking notes is important.

You will sound more relaxed if you are sitting comfortably with a speaker-phone, which will help the interviewee to feel more at ease. By the same token, wear clothes that make you feel 'professional'. Even without video your 'comfortable' tracksuit can mean you create a less 'professional' image with your interviewee, while smiling may make the interviewee feel better. Standing up may be surprisingly effective in bringing a telephone interview to a speedier close.

Close a phone interview carefully: it is easy to sound abrupt. You may want to ask more than once whether there is anything else the interviewee would like to add on any of the questions. Without visual cues it is harder to tell whether a silence means someone has really finished or is still thinking, so you may have missed some points during the interview.

If you are a reluctant telephone or Skype interviewer, it will help to practise using both the medium and your schedule or guide. Do some practice interviews with friends or family. This will make you feel much more confident with both the context and the structure, and your confidence will relax your interviewees.

EMAIL INTERVIEWS

Although phone or video interviews may be the obvious 'remote' medium, it is possible to interview asynchronously, using email. Such interviews can be surprisingly effective. Some of my interviews with Chris took place successfully via email. An email interview usually starts with a list of questions akin to a short questionnaire. Once replies are received, follow-up questions can be used to prompt or probe answers which are interesting. With a willing interviewee this method can be surprisingly effective, allowing a great deal of useful information to be elicited via no more than three to five exchanges. If necessary, a follow-up phone interview can be held.

Email interviews have obvious advantages in terms of convenience and expense. No travel is required and there is no need for synchronous availability. They also allow the respondent time to think about answers, and allow you time to think about their replies and where you would like further information or clarification. If your interviewee is not fluent in the language of your questions, they have time to work out what you mean. Your reactions are also less likely to influence responses because your body language is not a factor.

The downside is that your interviewee may not feel as comfortable about seeking clarification as they would face-to-face, and you may not always pick up on misinterpretations or misunderstandings of the intention of your questions. Because of the lack of social rewards you might also need to restrict the scope of your interview.

CAPTURING DATA FROM INTERVIEWS

To minimise bias you must capture and analyse data carefully. Your goal is to produce a trustworthy answer to your research question, and present credible conclusions to your client and others. Interviewing tends to produce 'information overload' for the researcher. It is hard to think about your questions while listening carefully and thinking about what an individual or group is saying. These challenging conditions make it difficult to hear, interpret and retain the information offered by the interviewee, and this gives scope for selectivity and therefore bias.

Your own mindset, and any preconceptions you have, will probably have a major influence. Selective *hearing* is the first potential hazard. Clearly, what you hear, and the interpretation you place upon it, limits what you will retain. But retention itself may be a problem – selective (as well as comprehensive) *forgetting* is highly likely. Attention to how you record your interviews can reduce this source of bias.

Figure 16.2 Forces for and against bias

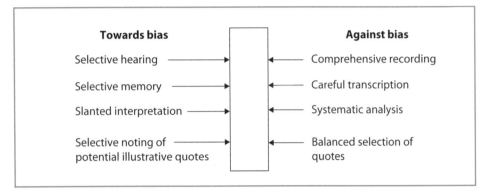

Towards bias		Against bias
Selective hearing	⟶ ⟵	Comprehensive recording
Selective memory	⟶ ⟵	Careful transcription
Slanted interpretation	⟶ ⟵	Systematic analysis
Selective noting of potential illustrative quotes	⟶ ⟵	Balanced selection of quotes

The use to which you intend to put the information will determine the best way to record interviews. Are you seeking to identify as many potential issues as possible, to work out key informants' perspectives, or to draw conclusions about a wider group from the responses of those sampled for interviews? Do you want to analyse the content of interviews or otherwise use them to provide the main evidence for your argued conclusions? Do you want to use specific quotes to make points in a final report, or to draw on the views of particular groups by way of convincing others to agree to proposals? You must have thought about such issues at the planning stage, and part of the reason for this is that they will determine your approach to recording.

Think about how your client is going to respond to your final report. How can you present the results of your interviews or focus groups so that your conclusions appear credible?

HOUSE OF HORRORS RESEARCH STORY

A dearth of information

A senior manager has commissioned three different projects to look at the impact of the introduction of a new information management system on the organisation. This system will record all the information on product design relevant to particular customers. The information includes design modifications made during the 'build' stage, information relevant to delivery and invoicing, and all contacts with customers thereafter (eg set-up help required, complaints and responses, subsequent visits by customer relations teams and potential for future business).

The report on the impact on engineers states that:

> A number of engineers were interviewed. The majority felt that the new system adds to their workload without adding any real benefits. It is therefore concluded that the enhancements offered by the new system have not justified the costs, and I recommend that we revert to the 'old' system in the interests of saving engineers' time ...

CONSIDER...

What questions might you ask if you were the client who received this report?

So little information is given that you might be suspicious of both the validity of the investigation and the researcher's credibility. Is this an example of 'low-rigour' research intended to prove a point? (Perhaps the researcher is an engineer and hates the new system.) How many engineers were interviewed? How were they selected? What questions were asked? How were they answered? Was it just Fred, Tom and Harry, known malcontents, 'interviewed' over their lunchtime chips in the canteen?

Why is the system not adding benefits? How are the engineers using the new system? What is it that takes more time? Why is it that anticipated benefits are not apparent to those interviewed? How big is the 'majority'? A client is unlikely to discard a system which cost nearly £1m to buy, and as much again in terms of training and other changes, on the strength of an 'investigation' that begs so many questions.

This may seem an extreme (even unbelievable) case but in student dissertations this dearth of information is common when reporting on 'research' that uses 'semi-structured interviews' as the approach. As managers students may go on to do equally unimpressive research later in their careers on the basis of their dissertation experience. As consultants they may draw equally far-reaching conclusions (albeit ones that clients *want* to hear) on barely more explicit information. As clients they may be willing to accept these. An evidence-based report offers so much more to both researcher and client if evidence is discussed in more detail.

RESEARCH STORY

A more detailed report

'Seven key customers were selected as the basis for this investigation. They were chosen to represent a range of size of customer organisation, and complexity of orders (see Appendix A for information on the sample). Internal discussions with customer relations teams and the help desk suggested that the likely impacts on customers would be the areas of *xxx*, *yyyy* and *zzzz*. An interview schedule was drafted to allow systematic collection of information from these customers on these issues as well as giving space for customers to raise additional points in relation to the new system. This schedule was piloted with two other customers, and modifications made to two questions that seemed hard to understand, and an additional area added that both these pilot customers felt to be important. The final schedule is shown in Appendix B.

Table 3 summarises each customer's perception in relation to each of these areas. You will see that in most cases there was a high degree of agreement, and answers suggest that while *aaa* and *bbb* are seen as substantial improvements, *ccc* has led to a perceived greater distance between the customer and 'their' relationship manager, and a feeling that it is 'the system' rather than the individual that is controlling things. Marina Pounds, purchasing manager for EMNOCo, neatly summed this up when she said: '........'

The only area of disagreement related to customer support. Here there seemed to be two distinct views, some feeling that the quality of help had been greatly increased, others that it had been substantially reduced. Size seemed to be a factor here, because it was the larger customers who felt dissatisfied. Their comments about reasons for their dissatisfaction help to explain the differences. These are given in full in Appendix C, together with the answers to the same question from the other customers. In summary, it seems that ....'

ACTIVITY

List the ways in which this report is more likely to impress the client – and the implications for recording interview data.

The second example is more convincing in many ways. Firstly, it is clear how the information was gathered, and the reasons for the choice of interviewees. It is difficult to interpret 'findings' without an understanding of how they were found. This makes the point that 'recording' in your research journal starts as soon as you begin to think about your investigation. You must record the thinking, and any preparatory stages, that led to the particular way of approaching your interviewing, and your selection of interviewees. Your record has to be fairly detailed, with entries showing what you did, and with whom, and your associated thinking. You also need a file for 'pre-evidence' – evidence collected during earlier stages that shapes or informs your final research.

Secondly, there is enough information to allow you to decide whether or not to believe the conclusions. You know how many people were interviewed, who said what in summary, and who said what in full where this is important because of the need to understand differences. There is enough information for you to feel confident that the quote is representative, and that the differences have been correctly interpreted.

This section of the report and the clear thinking and systematic approach that is apparent throughout contribute to the researcher's credibility. Your aim in any investigation is to build a strong and convincing case based upon evidence. Being convincing (and making a justified case) when you have a fairly 'mixed bag' of interview responses takes great care. The way you report upon interviews presents major challenges but is an essential part of establishing credibility. Unless you have a reliable record of all the aspects of the evidence that you may need to draw upon, you may not be able to meet the challenge.

RECORDING TO MINIMISE BIAS

Unconscious bias can easily reduce the validity of interview data. To minimise bias you need to record actual questions as well as answers as comprehensively as possible. Audio-recording your interviews will achieve this. The recording is 'evidence' that you can go back to later, if questions emerge after you start to analyse your information. The problem with paper notes is that if you are concentrating on listening attentively, and on sustaining a good relationship with the interviewee, you cannot possibly write down every word you and they say. Selectivity is inevitable.

If the interviewee agrees to recording, make it clear that they can switch it off at any point (although once people feel in control they usually forget that the recorder is there). Trust will be more easily established if you make it clear that the recording is in the interests of accuracy, but it is completely up to them whether the recorder is used.

RESEARCH STORY

The value of audio recording

Jacinta was interested in identifying training needs and interviewing employees about this. She had not arranged access to recording equipment, so was taking paper notes of answers about training needs. After a number of interviews she realised that answers seemed to make more sense in terms of communication problems than training needs. Her training-related notes contained nothing on communication. Although she could add a question on this in future, she had lost a lot of relevant data.

An audio record would have allowed her to go back and reconsider answers from the perspective of communication.

She obtained a recorder for future interviews. While she was transcribing her first recorded interviews she became aware of differences In the way she was framing questions for men and women, reflected on the implications of this, and became a better interviewer as a consequence.

It still helps to make brief notes while you interview, to sustain your concentration, and to jot down issues to probe once the answer is finished. You can also note points to refer back to later in the interview if they may be relevant there as well. Your in-interview notes will also help you to flesh out anything that is unclear on the recording, or act as back-up if the technology fails. You can note the non-verbal elements of an interview such as hesitations, signs of unease, or signs of light dawning as an idea takes shape.

You may find it helpful to print out your guide with space for notes (use 'overflow' sheets for areas that are unexpectedly productive). For an interview where the interviewee clearly follows a different logic from yours, using the guide as the basis for notes will let you see at a glance which areas still have to be covered.

If much of the interview is tightly structured, you will be able to code answers as you go along (and your guide will look like a questionnaire for this part of the interview). For open questions, if you are not recording, you will need either to note answers as verbatim as you can manage, or if you already have established codes, to code as you go. It will usually be important to note whether answers were prompted or unprompted because this *may* indicate the relative importance to the interviewee of these issues. In the light of the difficulties in recording group interactions, supplementary written notes are particularly helpful with focus groups.

Analysis
**Chapters 19
to 22**

Careful recording and systematic analysis is one of your greatest safeguards against bias. If all narrative answers are captured and treated in the same way, there is less scope for you to selectively record or differentially weight answers in accordance with your own views.

SUPPLEMENTING AN AUDIO RECORDING

Thus far the discussion has centred on recording questions and answers, ideally with a machine. But many other elements may be informative. There may be background factors that are relevant – why an interviewee was selected, their willingness or otherwise to take part, and any relevant information that would predispose them to a particular perspective. You must find a way of tying your notes on such factors to your interview notes and transcript.

During the interview you may notice many non-verbal cues – signs of tension at a particular point, other elements of body language, perhaps slight difficulty with certain questions. These may not be apparent in an audio recording, and could usefully be noted as context or as sources of future questioning. In focus groups there may be aspects of the interaction which are not apparent from the words alone. Again it may be helpful to make notes on these to supplement the audio record. Because of the speed with which memory decays, it is important to capture and clarify any such additional notes as quickly as possible after the event.

INTERPERSONAL SKILLS

Interviewing skills are highly transferable, and one of your personal learning aims for your research may be to become better at interviewing or facilitation. You need to treat the interviewee in a way that makes them want to co-operate, while avoiding suggesting answers in any way. The skills that are described below are mainly common to individual and group interviews.

RESPECT AND APPRECIATION

Respecting your interviewees and appreciating interviewees can make a huge difference to the success of your interviews. *Showing* your appreciation will quickly build a rapport with interviewees and develop their trust so that they feel that they can be honest with you.

Guidelines for showing appreciation

- Be open and straightforward about the reasons for your study, for selecting the interviewee, and the process, giving reassurances of confidentiality.
- Smile (even on the phone) and thank people for participating when you first meet them (smiling alters your voice as well as your face). Ask for any questions before you start, and answer them carefully.
- If someone has a problem with a question, respect their difficulty or concern, question until you are sure you have understood their difficulty, and explain until they are happy.
- When introducing a personal question acknowledge that it may seem an intrusion, explain why it will be helpful to have an answer, and reassure the interviewee about confidentiality.
- If the interview is lengthy, it may help to thank the person part-way through for their time and concentration thus far and to reassure them (honestly) as to how few questions are left.
- At the end of the interview express your gratitude for their help, concentration and thoughtfulness. Ask if they have any questions about the interview, and take the time to understand these to their satisfaction.

BEHAVING PROFESSIONALLY

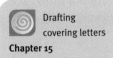

Drafting
covering letters

Chapter 15

Your personal credibility will influence the extent to which people are willing to co-operate in the research, and their willingness to accept your conclusions. Appearing professional in every contact with the interviewee is an important element in gaining trust and co-operation. As well as ensuring that letters are well drafted, your appearance and behaviour need to convey your professionalism. You need to appear confident and courteous during the interview, use appropriate language and be thoughtful in everything you say. You must keep any promises you make, whether over how long the interview will take, over confidentiality or regarding steps you will take after the interview.

LISTENING ATTENTIVELY

Real listening is a surprisingly uncommon skill. It rests upon valuing the speaker and their thoughts and a genuine desire to understand them. Real listening means:

- focusing on the person speaking, rather than upon your own thoughts or upon the next question you want to ask

- trying to see the meaning behind the words, and looking for threads in the answer that could usefully be picked up on

- remembering what people have said so that if it becomes relevant to a later point you can refer back to it

- listening for what they are not saying, so that you can consider prompting if it seems significant.

You have to be listening this intensely while at the same time remaining aware of your purpose in interviewing and of the areas of your interview guide. We rarely listen with this degree of attention in everyday conversation, so you could usefully practise listening. One useful practice method is something I call *extreme listening*.

Find a colleague or friend who is happy to talk about something – ideally, something that is important to them, or even better, something that is important to you. (You might ask them to talk about what they think about your research proposal ...) Set a timer for three minutes, and then just listen while they talk. Really listen, trying to hear what they are saying, and meaning. And the difficult bit – what makes it *extreme* – is that you say nothing. Even if you violently disagree with them, or know what they should do/think/say. If they dry up, you can say 'Is there anything else?', but that is all. This is not a three-minute conversation. It is one person talking and another person listening. Then find another willing 'talker' and repeat ... and repeat ... and repeat. Once you are comfortable with *extreme listening*, you will be a much better interviewer.

STEERING GENTLY BUT FIRMLY

You need to steer the interaction so that the maximum time is spent on issues relevant to your investigation. Prompts, probes and summaries (described earlier) are invaluable tools here. Prompts can steer the interview towards areas of interest to your research. Probes can encourage answers towards greater length or depth. Summaries can curb interviewees who tend to go on for too long, as can asking a few closed questions. Remember to convey to the interviewee that you *value* what has been said, and this is why you would like to shift direction slightly or go into more depth. You should avoid giving the impression that you are not interested in an interviewee's answer, or that they are boring, or that they are giving the 'wrong' answers, or are not fitting some predetermined idea of what they should say. Any of these impressions will destroy co-operation and trust.

Forming apparent links from what is being said to what you want them to talk about may help you redirect an interview that is veering off course. For example:

> "You know – I hadn't considered X before, and I'll clearly have to think about that some more. But what you've said has made me wonder about . . ."

And in terms of bringing an interview to a close, something like this should be effective:

> "You've been so generous of your time, and I'm really grateful, but I promised you I wouldn't take up more than an hour, so I feel we should probably draw it to a close now."

This is far better than a more abrupt ending that suggests that the interviewee is boring you rigid.

ETHICAL ISSUES

 Ethics **Chapter 4**

Ethics in research has already been examined. Here I want only to highlight the ethical issues particularly important when interviewing. These concern honesty, confidentiality and non-abuse of power.

HONESTY

You must be honest about your purpose and process, about the ways in which data will be recorded and about how it will be used. Consider whether 'informed consent' has been given to the use of information obtained outside the defined interview, and to the ethics of surreptitious note-taking. It is better to ask permission to note any points you feel to be relevant from post-interview or informal conversations.

You must also be honest in representing your results, making clear any limitations in your data, and any potential sources of bias. In particular, beware the power of the pithy quote to influence you and your client. It is misleading, and unethical, to use a biased selection of quotes to make a point more strongly than the data supports.

CONFIDENTIALITY

This is easily promised but may be harder to achieve if you are interviewing small numbers of people. A quote might be attributable even if anonymous because of the small sample or another factor. If so, use it only with explicit permission. Go through any reports or records with extreme caution to ensure that all names or other identifiers have been removed. Interview records should be stored extremely securely, away from the organisation in question, and destroyed as soon as the project and any reports or papers derived from it have been completed. If you are going to present highly confidential data in a dissertation, you may have to arrange with your university for restricted availability. Most universities allow this if necessary.

POWER

Informed consent **Chapter 4**

It is important to be aware of the potential power differentials within the research interview situation, and to ensure that they are not exploited. Client power has already been discussed, but note that *you* may be seen as having power derived from your client. Interviewees may feel coerced into taking part, or forced to answer whatever you choose to ask, or to answer in particular ways. You need informed *and willing* consent. It is not ethical to interview anyone taking part against their will, or to ask questions which might be felt as threatening or otherwise disturbing by the interviewee. (If your client wants to 'observe' interviews, this is a recipe for unreliable evidence.)

You may have *expert power* over your client, perhaps derived from your research expertise or knowledge gained from an MBA. If so, you must ensure you do not abuse it. Be careful not to exceed your expertise or exaggerate your claims to expertise. And be equally careful not to make claims that exceed your information and your ability to analyse and interpret it. (Remember the microwave horror story in the previous chapter!)

If you are operating within an organisation that has an ethical code, and/or studying with a university that has a research ethics code, you should obviously make sure that you are thoroughly familiar with the code, and comply with it in every respect.

PRACTICAL CONCERNS

Selecting a sample
Chapter 9

Once you have decided to interview, you need to select an appropriate sample. And once you have selected your sample, you need to think in very practical terms about how to persuade those sampled to take part, and how to ensure that interviews go smoothly.

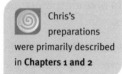

Chris's preparations were primarily described in **Chapters 1 and 2**

OBTAINING AGREEMENT

The clarity and professionalism of your first approach is crucial in gaining agreement to taking part. Your letter or email must include details of the nature, location and duration of the interview. You will remember that Chris sent potential interviewees a short overview of key concepts when seeking their co-operation. This was of potential value to recipients whether or not they agreed to be interviewed. It also served to establish both their trust in Chris's professionalism and expertise in the subject. If they read it (and as busy managers they may not have), it will have further served to create a shared understanding of the ideas about which Chris proposed to interview them.

Inducements to be interviewed raise some ethical issues. It *may* be appropriate to offer a small incentive such as a chance of a meal out or a bottle of wine, a draw to take place once interviews are completed. However, this might be deemed an ethical step too far in some contexts, so you would have to consider it carefully. If your topic is relevant to interviewees, a less contentious incentive might be a copy of your eventual report. For some types of research personal feedback on, for example, managerial strengths and weaknesses, might be possible and more relevant.

LOCATIONS AND TIMINGS

Interviewees are more likely to agree to take part if arrangements are convenient to them, but you must balance this against your own costs in time as well as money. Aim to schedule interviews to minimise travel involved. Timings must be realistic. If it seems 'obvious' to you that if you interview for an hour, you can do eight interviews in a day – think again. Three one-hour interviews would be a normal limit, four the absolute maximum, and then only if they were in the same place and you had the whole of the next day – and perhaps some of the day after – for recovering and transcribing. Interviews are mentally and often emotionally taxing. You have to sustain a high level of constant concentration.

Some interviews will over-run, some interviewees will arrive late. You need to schedule slack time between interviews – otherwise, subsequent interviewees will be kept waiting. You will require time between interviews to eat and drink, walk around, go to the bathroom and generally recover before switching your concentration back to full volume. If you are relying on your own notes, you will need time between interviews to clarify and expand upon them while the interview is fresh in your mind. If you do not do this, it is all too easy for the next interview to drive out all recollection of the previous one, leaving you with notes that might as well be written in hieroglyphics.

If you are keeping an audio record, then ideally you will transcribe one day's interviewing before interviewing again, and remember how long this takes. Leaving it until later has two substantial disadvantages. The job is likely to assume nightmare proportions and cast a black cloud over your entire life. And you may miss out on substantial learning from early interviews.

While transcribing, you can usefully reflect on your interviewing practice, noting where you interrupt, where you let people ramble on, and where it is clear that the interviewee is surprised by something you say, suggesting imperfect understanding between you. You can see if there are times at which an interviewee noticeably relaxed, and perhaps learn from this how to set people at ease at an earlier stage. You can see where something you have said has caused the interviewee to stop answering freely, and think about whether this was necessary and inevitable, or whether you might have avoided it by asking a question differently. Something may 'jump off the tape' at you that you missed in the interview, and you might wish to add a further question or prompt to subsequent interviews in the light of it.

 Checklist to use before interviewing

Have you considered carefully whether interviews are an appropriate means of collecting relevant and valid information?

Have you thought about what information you might seek, and how it might help progress your investigation?

Are there other purposes (eg networking) that you hope your interviews will serve?

Have you thought about which stage(s) of the investigation would be informed by interviews, and the different sorts of information you might seek at each?

Are you seeking key informant interviews and/or survey interviews and/or interviews which may contribute to readiness for future change?

Have you thought carefully about the breadth of conclusions which you are hoping your interview data will inform (eg how far you wish to generalise from your data)?

Have you thought carefully about how many, and whom, to interview, and why?

Have you thought carefully about the degree of structure that would be most useful?

Have you drafted a clear and professional-looking invitation to be interviewed?

Have you considered whether other material could usefully be sent with this?

Have you scripted your initial introduction, reassurances of confidentiality, etc?

Have you thought about how to ask questions in ways that avoid bias?

For a structured interview, have you designed questions in line with the guidance in Chapter 15?

For a semi-structured interview, do you have a clear and logical structure?

Have you piloted any closed questions you will be using?

Have you worked out locations and a timetable for your interviews that is efficient and feasible?

Have you arranged audio recording and other facilities?

Have you developed (or arranged to develop) any relevant skills?

Have you budgeted generous time for pre- and post-interview activities?

Have you thought about the potential ethical implications of the interviews you propose?

As well as a macro-location issue (shall I come to Germany, or are you coming to London in the next month?) there is a micro issue. For an interviewee to feel comfortable, they should be in a place that offers reasonable privacy, is free from interruptions and offers physical comfort (good chair, drink available if required). Your office or the interviewee's may serve. If not, a good hotel lounge allows you to relax in comfortable surroundings with a suitably 'professional' feel, without interruption or breach of privacy, and potentially for the price of two coffees.

SUMMARY

Interviews are an attractive way of eliciting information for many purposes. They have high face validity, can elicit information about interpretations and intentions, and can be used to collect a much wider range of information.

Important choices include sample size and characteristics, and the type of interview to use. A key variable is structure: advantages and disadvantages depend upon this. Choices depend upon the purpose of the investigation, and the role of interviews within it. The less structure you have, the greater the flexibility and interactivity, and the greater the potential for generating extremely rich information and powerful quotes. But a higher skills level is needed both to interview and to analyse responses.

The process is time-consuming and there is a higher risk of interviewer bias. Comparability will be reduced.

Telephone or video interviews may offer economies of time and cost, and allow greater geographical scope. It may, however, be harder to build and sustain trust and interviewees may feel less relaxed.

For both group and individual interviews care is needed in question design, and in ensuring social and content flow. Full (preferably audio) recording of the interview and careful analysis helps reduce interviewer bias. If selecting illustrative quotes, you must ensure that they are representative.

Interviews raise several ethical issues. It is important to ensure that you use only data which is openly and willingly provided, for purposes which you have explained before gathering the data, and that you preserve total confidentiality unless there is a specific agreement with the informant to the contrary.

REVIEW QUESTIONS

1. What purposes may interviews be used for at different stages in an investigation?

2. What sorts of information might an interview generate?

3. What advantages might an interview have over a questionnaire? What disadvantages?

4. What is the difference between a semi-structured interview and one which uses a mix of structures?

5. What is an interview guide, and what purpose does it serve?

6. What aspects of an interview have to be 'designed'?

7. Distinguish between social flow and content flow and say why each is important.

8. Distinguish between a probe and a prompt, and say when each might be appropriate.

9. Why might it be important to distinguish between prompted and unprompted answers?

10. What stages might usefully be considered when planning the social dynamics of an interview?

11. Compare both phone and email interviews with those conducted face to face in terms of advantages and disadvantages, and demands upon the interviewer.

12. Why is it important to consider the potential for bias in the interview, and what factors should you think about if you are seeking to reduce bias?

13. What are the advantages and disadvantages of making an audio recording of your interviews?

14. What ethical issues must you consider if planning to interview?

Explore further

Fontana, T. H. and Frey, J. H. (1996) 'Interviewing – the art of science', in Denzin, N. K. and Lincoln, Y. S. (eds) *Handbook of Qualitative Research*, 6th edition. London: Sage. Shorter but still useful guidance

Kvale, S.and Brinkmann, S. (2009) *InterViews: Learning the craft of qualitative research interviewing*, 2nd edition. Thousand Oaks, CA: Sage Publications. Provides useful and extensive coverage

 Visit www.cipd.co.uk/brm for web links, templates, activities and other useful resources relating to this chapter.

CHAPTER 17

Focus Groups and Workshops

INTRODUCTION

Focus groups have long been popular in market research, but the method is now increasingly popular in other types of investigation. Some authors regard focus groups as simply a form of group interview (Bryman and Bell, 2007), but there are some distinctive differences which ought to be noted. These stem from the interaction which focus groups allow – indeed, encourage – between informants, and the influence which the presence of other informants may have upon what is said. The researcher will need additional skills to facilitate the group, and there will be additional challenges associated with capturing, analysing and interpreting data.

Although focus groups and workshops differ in many ways, there are some similarities, and useful data can also be obtained from workshops. Both provide a context in which the nature of interactions may be examined as well as the content of what is said. And the group context may have similar advantages and disadvantages in terms of the quality of the information generated and the different forms of bias that may result.

The chapter therefore briefly considers the strengths and weaknesses of each approach as an additional data-collection method, the skills that you will need if the data you collect is to be valuable, and the ethical issues that you will have to address if you use this approach.

LEARNING OUTCOMES

This chapter, taken with the preceding one, should enable you to:

- assess the relative advantages and disadvantages of focus groups, workshops and individual interviews for your own research

- plan and facilitate focus groups and workshops in ways that will generate useful information

- capture relevant elements of data from either or both

- address any additional ethical issues posed by the method.

THE RELATIVE ADVANTAGES OF FOCUS GROUPS

Although 'interviewing' is usually thought of in terms of individuals, focus groups are a well-developed technique for eliciting information from groups rather than individuals, and are sometimes described as group interviews, although not all accept this classification. They involve a group holding a discussion that is 'focused' on a particular topic, prompted and facilitated by the researcher. Although you can choose the degree of structure you impose upon a group, unless you run a highly structured group, with a high level of control by yourself, the debate is likely to feel significantly different from an interview. Most of what people say will be prompted not by you but by contributions of those taking part.

> **Focus groups involve a facilitated discussion between members that is 'focused' on a topic or area specified by the researcher.**

Discussions normally last for between one and two hours. In its pure form a focus group is similar to an unstructured or (more normally) semi-structured interview but with the added dimension of interaction between group members. As you will see, the term may refer to an event that seems closer to a workshop than to an interview. Both approaches can generate useful data, as can workshops which make no claim to focus group status.

Focus groups have been used in market research since the 1920s but are now a popular business research method in many more fields than marketing. A good focus group can be synergistic, its members sparking ideas off each other. They can ask other members to explain their view of something, and perhaps change their own perspective in the light of what they hear. The researcher may learn a lot from the differences in how individuals respond to or make sense of a situation. Such differences might not emerge in individual interviews. As with individual interviews, there are both advantages and disadvantages to focus groups, as summarised in Table 17.1.

Table 17.1 Checklist of advantages and disadvantages of focus groups

Focus groups	
Advantages	**Disadvantages**
Different perspectives visible	Recording presents challenges
Observable interactions	Needs facilitation skills
Observable sense-making	Demands transcription
Concerns surface	Individuals may dominate
Helps build commitment	Participants may be inhibited or 'in role'

KEY POINTS

- Focus groups allow the researcher to observe interactions between members as they collectively explore the topic.
- They may enable the articulation of tacit knowledge, and differences between participants may be informative.
- However, strong individuals may bias results, and groups have to be carefully moderated.
- Focus groups require careful recording and analysis, and can be extremely time-consuming.

THE ADVANTAGES OF FOCUS GROUPS

Construction-ism and pragmatism in **Chapter 2**

Focus groups allow the *collective* exploration of issues of interest to the researcher, and thus make both group interactions and individual ways of thinking more visible to an observer. Focus groups may be a good way of surfacing the *differences* in views and assumptions between different players in a situation. If your research question concerns the way people make sense of a situation, group members may challenge others' ideas and assumptions more effectively than you could do as an individual interviewer.

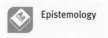

Epistemology

Weick claimed (1995) that management was all about *sense-making* – about the meaning that people actively gave to their experiences. He saw this as an important social process in groups, allowing tacit knowledge to be made more explicit or usable. (You can see the underlying constructionist/pragmatist elements of epistemology.) *Articulation* of this tacit knowledge is at the heart of the sense-making process. Such articulation can be observed in a focus group where the facilitator has encouraged participants to talk through an issue in a way that recognises – and indeed, takes into acount – different perspectives, and finds a way of aligning these so that new understanding can emerge.

> A key benefit of focus groups is that they allow the articulation of tacit knowledge and theories.

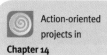

Action-oriented projects in **Chapter 14**

Focus groups can enable you to observe the nature of interaction between staff who normally work closely or loosely together. Aspects of dynamics and differing assumptions and values may become apparent in the ways they interact, as much as in the verbal content of the interaction. Observing the extent to which people agree or disagree with each other can give you insights into conflicts that might not be apparent from individual interviews. (You may have to treat this aspect more as an observational study than as an interview.) However, if you have the necessary facilitation skills, you may be able to explore with the group the reasons for these differences.

In an action-oriented project, a focus group may be a useful way of surfacing concerns that the project will need to address if it is to be successful. A focus group can help you gather a range of relevant perspectives on the issue in a fairly short space of time. It may be a useful way of building group commitment to a project. Focus groups are extremely useful at the diagnostic stage of an investigation because they can be run in an unstructured and open way, allowing the participants to define the territory rather than the researcher. They can, for action-oriented projects, also segue into exploring requirements and constraints for ways forward, or even possible actions to be taken.

THE DISADVANTAGES OF FOCUS GROUPS

Focus groups may seem to offer substantial economies over interviews, allowing you to obtain information from perhaps 10 people in the same time that you could obtain it from one. But there are several obvious snags to the 'efficiency' argument – an hour of a focus group still generates 'one hour's worth' of information.

Complex social dynamics mean that complex skills are needed to facilitate a focus group. You have to energise and guide the group, and if possible note aspects of the interaction (eg reasons for silences) that are not caught on the recording. An assistant to help with this makes it slightly easier, if that is feasible.

Recording can present challenges. The quality of audio recorders is improving, however, and a flat-bed multi-directional microphone (two recording devices with a large group) should enable you to record the discussion clearly, although it may not be possible to identify individuals. But converting the audio 'text' into written documents is notoriously time-consuming, and transcription when there are multiple voices is particularly challenging.

The group context may limit what people are prepared to say: they might volunteer more information in a confidential individual interview. If group members work together, they may not be able to escape from the 'work role' that they have come to play in the group. This may be some way from their authentic self, and is another reason why views expressed in a group may differ from those that would be expressed privately

You may receive a false idea of agreement if the views of one or two dominant individuals prevail. A minority view may look like consensus. If some members have been largely silent, you will not know their views, and so will have little idea of how far the apparent consensus is representative of the group as a whole.

Despite these disadvantages, focus groups do have considerable value, not least as a means of generating observed debate that is itself informative, and as a way for the group to work together creatively on an issue of concern (more of the focus group/workshop divide shortly). It is worth looking at these advantages in greater detail.

RUNNING EFFECTIVE FOCUS GROUPS

Two aspects of the group will have a major impact upon its success. The first is the size and composition of the group. If the group is too big, it will be hard to manage; if too small, interaction may be limited. If the 'wrong' people are there, you may get poor data. The second major factor is how well you facilitate the group.

GROUP COMPOSITION

Size and membership of the group requires careful thought. Whose views are important to you? How will people interact? And how big a group do you want? It is possible to run groups as small as four (this may be necessary if topics are sensitive) or as large as 12. Around six to 10 allows for a good but still manageable discussion. In deciding how many to invite, remember to allow for some invitees to decline and for some to fail to show up, if this is likely in your context. Some 'over-booking' increases your chance of a big enough group.

In market research homogeneous groups are sought. For other purposes you may prefer some heterogeneity. Grouping those who work together gives the opportunity to observe dynamics within the group, which may be relevant. On the other hand, when they are with close colleagues people may be more inhibited and fall back into habitual roles and habitual ways of thinking. It is often recommended that members know each other slightly, or at least share frames of reference, but do not work closely together. Similarly, you may want either to put together people of different levels to allow different perspectives on an issue, or to avoid it because junior staff might feel inhibited. You may also want to combine (or avoid combining) internal and even external customers with some of those serving them.

Normally, you will want participants to have enough in common to have a meaningful discussion but different enough that they do not share too many assumptions which are hard for you to perceive. You do not want a group so diverse that tensions make it hard to manage, yet some unfamiliarity will mean that more things are made explicit in the discussion. This makes it easier for you to understand the issues involved. Your research purpose will determine the ideal group composition.

 A checklist for running focus groups is available at **www.cipd.co.uk/brm**

You must also think about how many groups you need to run. Again this will depend upon your purpose in running groups and on the stage in your investigation. But normally you will need several, not least because of the way in which a single group can be influenced by one or two of the participants.

FACILITATING THE GROUP

Interview design **Chapter 16**

Most of the same design features apply as for interviews. Thus for a semi-structured group you will have to consider social flow as well as content flow, and a discussion guide will be useful. Discussion will be more effective if members understand what is expected of them and why, are happy with the use that will be made of the data, and feel comfortable with each other, with you, and with the arrangements for recording.

> **Points that are selectively recorded and/or from focus groups that are poorly facilitated may be misleading as evidence.**

Part of this 'making comfortable' is ensuring physical comfort. You need a location that is suitable for the size of group, with comfortable chairs. Refreshments at the start can also help. Gathering over tea or coffee and cakes enables group members to talk informally and relax together before the discussion starts.

Social flow

Social flow is important. Introducing members informally over refreshments provides a good beginning. If this is not possible, you will need introductions at the start of the group session: members may feel suspicious of any 'strangers' in the group, and inhibited by them. At the start of the discussion aim to 'settle' the group (as in any interview) with a fairly easy first topic. Consider when in the discussion to introduce more challenging issues if these are important. (This is usually best towards the end, allowing time to resettle the group before the end so that they leave feeling positive about the experience.)

Introducing purpose is particularly important, because members are likely to feel uneasy if your purpose, and what you expect of them, is not made clear. Discussion may not be 'focused' on what you want if they do not understand this. You will also need to explain the focus group process and your role as facilitator.

Your role as facilitator

Your role will be to pose questions to stimulate discussion on your chosen topics. Your aim, once the group is settled, will be to ensure that the discussion:

- is relevant but not too constrained by your own preconceptions of relevance
- provides enough detail and context to be useful (prompts and probes will be important)

- explores feelings as well as facts where they is relevant (note that this requires skill and sensitivity)
- involves all members.

You may have to ask quieter members what they think, and tactfully encourage dominant members to contribute slightly less (a gate-keeping role). You want to make members feel good about their contributions, while moving the discussion on where appropriate so that it covers all the areas of concern to you. Groups can take on a will of their own, so you may have to steer the direction of discussions. Such steering needs to allow the group flexibility to set the agenda, to focus on aspects that *they* see as important, and to explore relevant differences which emerge between group members, while still generating relevant information.

Inviting contributions from quieter members, testing your understanding, summarising discussion at intervals, and prompting and probing will all be important. But maximise your listening and minimise your talking – it is the group's views that are important, rather than your own.

Facilitation skills development

Focus groups depend heavily upon the skills of the facilitator. Facilitation skills are highly transferable and will be useful in many management and consultancy situations. If you are studying business research methods and choosing a dissertation to develop key professional skills, this might be an additional reason for choosing focus groups as a method. The practice will make an important contribution to your learning. You might seek to shadow a more skilled researcher, and perhaps ask them to observe one or two of your early groups and offer feedback.

If you feel you lack the necessary skills and do not have time to develop them, avoid using focus groups as your main research method.

 CONSIDER...

What role might focus groups play in the context of your own research? Note down your thoughts in your research journal.

DISCUSSION AIDS

Sometimes it can be helpful to use visual aids to help people discuss. If you are discussing a product or a procedure, it can be helpful to have an example there. Other aids can be directed towards the discussion itself. A common approach is to use Post-Its to capture points made. These can then be arranged and rearranged according to themes that emerge from the discussion. Post-Its can be put up on a wall near the discussion, with participants standing up when a new one has been written, although this will take them away from the microphones. Alternatively, the discussion can take place around a table onto which Post-Its can be placed (you might want to tape down some flipchart paper first).

When using this approach you need to pay particular attention to pens. The pen tips/ points should be thin enough for people to write a sentence (say) on the size of the Post-Its you are using but thick enough for what is written to be easily legible from the distance at which people will mostly be from the wall or sheet. You may want to use different colours to denote different types of element.

Peterson and Barron (2007), writing on 'How to get focus groups talking', suggest the following sequence:

- generating information (akin to brainstorming)
- checking for understanding of what has been captured
- elaborating when necessary
- sorting, ordering and grouping the Post-Its.

They say that this is an effective way of eliciting opinions. It makes people feel involved, and works towards a shared view of the emerging structure and a sense of shared outcomes.

Malhotra and Birks (2000), writing in the context of market research, suggest that a useful focus group technique is the creation of a 'mood board'. Group members snip words and photos from magazines and create a shared collage which they then jointly scrutinise, questioning what is in as well as what is not in, thus helping to 'creatively reveal ideas' (p162) as they suggest focus groups are intended to do.

Making thinking 'visible' in this way helps avoid repetition because people can see if a point has already been made. Grouping related points together can encourage development of arguments: it is often easier to see the connections between them and any implications. The 'board' also provides a useful supplementary record. Note: if using Post-Its on paper, remember that they come unstuck quite easily. It is best to tape them to the backing paper, or photograph or copy the display before leaving the room.

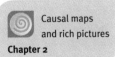

Causal maps and rich pictures
Chapter 2

With some groups it can help to use diagrams. Causal mapping may be useful, or you could construct a shared rich picture in order to surface aspects of a situation, perhaps for subsequent discussion. Rich picturing can also be an excellent icebreaker, helping the group to relax and 'gel'. Drawing such pictures need not take too long. Spending the first 20 minutes drawing a picture could make subsequent discussion far more productive.

As with everything, this approach is not suitable for every group and every topic. It is a very open approach and therefore may be best used early in your investigation. And only use such techniques if participants are happy with them. Unfamiliar techniques, unless very skilfully introduced, can make participants nervous and more inhibited. (Mike, in the story which follows shortly, had planned to use some more creative techniques but could see that his participants were not happy with them.) However, visual techniques can be a useful tool in your toolbag, particularly for the diagnostic stage of a project.

In both these examples of 'making visible', the focus group is starting to sound more like a workshop than a simple group discussion. Since in practical research the distinction between the two may be blurred, a brief discussion of workshops as a means of generating data may be helpful.

KEY POINTS

- Group composition is important: size, familiarity and uniformity of views should be considered.
- As with interviews, social flow is important.
- The facilitator must also encourage free participation, enabling process without influencing content.
- Discussion aids, including diagramming, may be useful for some topics.

WORKSHOPS AS RESEARCH METHOD

You can see from the above that some practitioners clearly use the term 'focus group' more broadly than for a mere group interview. The focus groups discussed by Peterson and Barron (2007) sound more like workshops than interviews. If focus groups can use workshop techniques, can workshops be regarded as a form of focus group? The following story shows some of the classification difficulties.

 CONSIDER...

As you read the following research story consider whether you would describe Mike's group meeting as a workshop or as a focus group. Why would you so classify it, and what are the implications of your classification?

RESEARCH STORY

Team diagnosis

Mike's research was investigating reasons for delays in prototype development. As part of his diagnostic process he arranged a half-day session with team members to explore the causes of problems, using causal mapping as a way of exploring problems, and voting as a way of identifying the perceived relative importance of these causes.

The aims of this meeting were:

- to surface and grow awareness within the team of issues affecting project delivery

- to test the assumptions and output of the initial diagnosis

- to allow different perspectives to form a common picture of issues affecting the team and its projects

- to provide a basis for agreeing on subsequent activity to address the problem.

The team was therefore given a broad remit for the discussion: to explore the root causes of delays to projects.

In reflecting on the success of this exercise Mike concluded that the group session had been successful in achieving these aims. The meeting identified and agreed on a range of root causes for delays. Some of these Mike had been unaware of previously. It is unlikely that these would have been uncovered with a more structured approach.

However, the team drew fairly narrow boundaries around their diagnosis, and did not look at causes beyond their immediate area of project activity. Mike concluded that he would have to run a group with a broader membership to gain insight into these wider influences.

 Action-oriented research

Chapter 14

Mike's group was advertised as a workshop, yet served a similar function to a focus group in that the group discussed the issue and generated useful information for his research. Part of Mike's aim in running this group was to involve and engage those who would have to be involved in any improvements suggested by the research – one advantage of using focus groups in action-oriented research is that they can create a greater sense of involvement than being interviewed as individuals. Resistance to change is usually less if people feel they have helped design the change.

Classifying a meeting as a focus group would normally imply that the activities involved would be limited to discussion, would be primarily for the researcher's benefit, and that the discussion would be recorded, transcribed and analysed. Classifying it as a workshop would imply a benefit for the participants as well as for the researcher, and there would normally be a range of activities. The 'data' would be more likely to be in the form of notes plus outputs (flipchart lists, etc) rather than of a transcription of a recording. Indeed, part of the workshop might involve sub-group working.

Although it is probably safer not to conflate the two, an early diagnostic workshop can be virtually indistinguishable from a focus group, and can generate outputs which can reasonably be treated as data. Many practitioner-researchers carrying out action-oriented research find it useful to use workshops as a means of involving stakeholders in the investigative process, but are unsure whether or how to use the outputs of these workshops as data.

Provided the researcher has considered whether the process might have biased the output, and is reasonably confident that it has not, it seems reasonable to analyse such outputs as you might the outputs of a focus group, applying the same cautions to your interpretations of results. Thus the outputs of a series of workshops with different groups but addressing the same issue could be compared, and/or common elements of all extracted and considered, in the same way as focus group outputs. Conclusions from a single workshop could usefully form part of the data in a multi-method approach.

If you are using workshop 'data' to support your conclusions, you must disclose the number and nature of both participants and workshops, and make clear the extent to which you had influenced the process. Your analytical methods would have to be explained, and the steps you had taken to ensure that the data presented a balanced picture. Selected workshop outputs are as potentially misleading as selected interview quotes.

KEY POINTS

- Focus groups involve a 'focused' moderated (facilitated) discussion between a group of relevant people: they are *not* equivalent to interviewing a number of individuals simultaneously.

- Social dynamics may be hard to handle. Moderating requires facilitation skills, and it may help to have an assistant to take notes.

- Because groups may be influenced by one or two more dominant members, outputs may be misleading. If focus groups are your main method, you may have to run a number of groups to enable you to be confident about your conclusions.

- The group's social dynamics may themselves be informative. Group composition requires considerable thought, and you will need a high level of facilitation skills.

- Focus groups are particularly helpful at the exploratory and framing stages of an investigation, in inquiries where you are seeking to understand how people make sense of issues, or in action-oriented projects.

- It is important to budget sufficient time (far more than you think) for preparation, transcription and analysis.

ASSESSING DATA FROM FOCUS GROUPS AND WORKSHOPS

It is important to be aware of the potential impact of social pressures on the contributions of those participating in a group situation. It was noted earlier that some members and their views might dominate, and that you might have to bring in less dominant members. Although you can ensure that they make a contribution by doing this, you must make a judgement on the validity of the resulting statement. To what extent was it influenced either by the dominant view (especially if it was expressed by someone senior to the reluctant contributor) or by the nature of your own intervention?

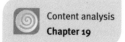

Content analysis
Chapter 19

There are no rules by which you can make this judgement – and indeed, no set way of analysing focus group discussions. It would depend partly on the stage at which you are using the method. If it is an early stage, you might merely want to note all the points that emerged, with a view to a subsequent systematic exploration. You might want to ask the group to provide their own summary of key points or perspectives. Or (perhaps later in your study) you might wish to content analyse the transcript. But whatever approach you adopt, it is important to be aware of possible influences upon what is actually said, and aware that these might stem from the context.

ETHICAL CONSIDERATIONS

You need to be aware of all the relevant ethical issues raised in the previous chapter. These relate to honesty, confidentiality and power. However, in a group context there are additional aspects to consider.

Concerns relating to openness and honesty are similar, but because focus groups may be unfamiliar to participants you may have to pay more attention to explaining the process beforehand and making clear who else will be participating. This is particularly important when other participants are colleagues and/or potential competitors. Because you will almost certainly need to make an audio recording, this point must be made clear when seeking informed consent. As with interview recordings and transcripts, your focus group records have to be kept securely and destroyed as soon as you no longer need them.

There may be a particular issue with workshops where data collection is only a part of your purpose in holding the workshop. Your research aim needs to be explicitly understood by those taking part, and you must have clear agreement to the subsequent use of any workshop outputs for research purposes.

Confidentiality is slightly more complicated when participants are reliant not only on your observation of confidentiality but on that of fellow participants. You will need the firm agreement of all participants to treating everything said within the group as confidential, but you cannot personally guarantee that they will observe this. You will therefore have to be very careful about introducing potentially sensitive topics. Some may be unsuited to discussion in groups with a particular membership.

Power has additional dimensions when colleagues are assembled, and you need to be aware of the power relationships between participants and avoid putting any of them in uncomfortable or difficult positions because of them. It would be unethical, for example, to ask a group to discuss the quality of management if it contained some members who were managers and some who were managed by them.

The ethics of honesty extend to drawing trustworthy conclusions. If you are relatively unfamiliar with the focus group approach, have any doubts about your facilitation skills, or find the systematic analysis of qualitative data challenging, you must be careful about the strength of the conclusions you draw from the groups you run.

SUMMARY

Focus groups add a group social dynamic which individual interviews lack. This may provide useful and relevant additional data. Group membership can also provide a sense of involvement which may reduce subsequent resistance to change.

However, they can be more time-consuming than they appear at first sight, and require skilled facilitation. Systematic analysis of focus group data to inform other than tentative conclusions may take considerable time and skill.

Workshops can generate similar information to focus groups if run in a similar way: the distinction may be blurred in practice. If the workshop has another explicit purpose, it is important to be open and honest about your research agenda.

Additional ethical issues associated with focus groups derive from their unfamiliarity, the difficulty of ensuring confidentiality from all participants, power relationships within the group, and the difficulty of analysing the data generated.

REVIEW QUESTIONS

1. Why is a focus group not simply an efficient way of getting data from 10 people while devoting only one session of your own time to the exercise?

2. What are the advantages and disadvantages of capturing the group discussion on an audio recording?

3. What additional data can focus groups generate compared to individual interviews?

4. What skills does a researcher need in order to use focus groups as a research method?

5. What factors might influence the nature of the contributions participants make in a group context?

6. What are the potential advantages and disadvantages of these influences?

7. What features of focus groups and workshops raise ethical issues for the researcher?

EXPLORE FURTHER

Barbour, R. S. and Kitzinger, J. (1999) *Developing Focus Groups: Politics, theory and practice*. London: Sage. Offers a range of useful ideas

Fern, E. F. (2001) *Advanced Focus Group Research*. Thousand Oaks, CA: Sage Publications. Offers much the same, with particular reference to research

Kitzinger, J. (1994) 'The methodology of focus groups: the importance of interaction between the research participants', *Sociology of Health and Illness*, Vol.16, No.1: 103–21. Gives an interesting discussion of reasons for using focus groups in a non-management context, and a good 'feel' for the sorts of issues you may encounter in running a group

 Visit www.cipd.co.uk/brm for web links, templates, activities and other useful resources relating to this chapter.

PART 4

DATA ANALYSIS

CHAPTER 18

Grounded Theory

INTRODUCTION

Grounded Theory is an inductive approach to research, based on the belief that data should drive theory, rather than the reverse. It relies fully on qualitative data, and generates 'theory' in the form of concepts which 'explain' the ways participants view situations. We have 'classified' the approach as an analytical rather than a data-collection method, although in practice it is both. Its inclusion here rather than earlier is because analysis is integral to the approach, as opposed to something that takes place once data is collected. This on-going approach to analysis is a characteristic aspect of Grounded Theory, and is particularly challenging for the business researcher.

The arguments for a fully inductive approach are compelling if your issue relates to individuals' interpretations of their context: it would be unwise to use your own conceptual frameworks as a starting point for such research. Many dissertations claim to use a Grounded Theory approach but apparently see it as an excuse for either not considering existing literature sufficiently or for giving little thought to data-collection methods. Likewise, the approach is often cited when what is actually being used is a simply content coding as a means of analysis. Neither of these is appropriate. A fully Grounded Theory approach is rigorous, demanding and time-consuming. It is unlikely that it would be feasible within the constraints of a commercial consultancy or a Master's dissertation. And unless it is done in a rigorous way, the value of any findings may be slight.

This chapter is included for several reasons. Firstly, the ideas are interesting and may cause you to question some of your assumptions about research. Secondly, if you are to make well-judged use of Grounded Theory research done by others, you have to understand the strengths and limitations of their method. Finally, it is intended to deter you from trying to use it yourself for short-term practical projects, or to use it as an excuse for not thinking sufficiently about your research methods. Using elements of Grounded Theory in a random and uninformed way without understanding the underlying philosophy will reduce Grounded Theory to no more than a system of coding. This destroys the integrity of the approach.

Grounded Theory is based upon a constructionist philosophical view, and entails a flexible, emergent approach which may not seem credible to those with differing philosophical preferences and expectations of what 'research' should entail. There is also a debate to be resolved as to the extent to which you can free yourself from theory in order to be truly inductive, and a further debate as to the nature and value of the 'theory' generated by this approach. This chapter explores the rationale for Grounded Theory, outlines the stages involved, and then considers their strengths and limitations.

LEARNING OUTCOMES

This chapter should enable you to:

• identify the elements of a Grounded Theory approach and their underlying philosophy

• assess the strengths and limitations of any business research using a Grounded Theory approach

• re-evaluate your proposed research from a Grounded Theory perspective, and amend it if appropriate.

UNDERSTANDING GROUNDED THEORY

Grounded theory was devised by Glaser and Strauss in 1967, and presented a radical challenge to prevailing (positivist) ways of thinking about research. Now it is widely used in academic social research, although still the subject of controversy. At least three types of Grounded Theory have emerged from the on-going debate. Following their original work, Glaser and Strauss have each taken up different positions. Strauss, with Corbin (1990), produced a new variant of Grounded Theory. Glaser (1998) offered a critique of their new approach and added new elements. In a useful account of this chequered history of Grounded Theory, Dey (2004, p80) describes the history of the theory thus:

> "Like parents outgrown by their children, its authors have suffered the indignity of being 'corrected' by their offspring. And sadly, what started out as a most productive partnership between Glaser and Strauss ended in something akin to an acrimonious divorce."

In their original text, *The Discovery of Grounded Theory*, Glaser and Strauss (1967) suggested that much so-called 'qualitative' research was not truly qualitative, merely less structured than quantitative research. They argued that research output depends on the research process, and that both qualitative and quantitative research processes were fundamentally the same. The traditional research process is:

Stage 1: Review the literature

⌐→ Stage 2: Define and refine the research question

Stage 3: Construct the research methodology

Stage 4: Collect data and analyse, drawing on literature

Stage 5: Draw conclusions.

You will note the close similarity between these stages and conventional dissertation chapter headings. Note too that this represents the 'academic' literature-driven research process. Here, reviewing the literature leads to defining and refining the research purpose or the research question. Research methods are chosen, which in turn direct the sampling method, the data gathered and the means of analysis.

This is the same *process* that this book has been taking you through! Although this process is still the most frequently used approach to business research, Glaser and Strauss thought that the theories or results produced by such an approach were fundamentally narrowed – they were confined by the literature which then directed researchers to use specific means of analysis which in turn produce specific results. You will remember that theory serves as a lens to focus elements of a situation. However, like a lens it enables you to view from a very particular perspective, which limits what you see.

RESEARCH ILLUSTRATION

The research lens

If your business research is trying to sort out the problem of a lack of leadership, using the traditional approach you might start by reading the literature on leadership. You would frame your research questions in the light of your reading, and so on through the traditional research process. Glaser and Strauss would argue that the problems that you will uncover will relate only to those problems that you have looked for. If, for example, you have taken the theme of Kotter's (1990) five dimensions of leadership (direction, alignment, relationships, personal qualities and outcomes) as the basis for your research, the results you come up with will be problems (or not) related to – you've guessed it – direction, alignment, relationships, personal qualities and outcomes!

Grounded Theory suggests that what is uncovered through research relates only to those features that have been selected. If your goal is to test existing theory, this does not matter. If theory provides a useful lens, again this may not matter. But it is important to remember that it may matter, particularly if existing theory provides an inadequate frame for your particular issue. Elsewhere (Price, 2006) I have elaborated on this point that as business researchers, we edit our research by:

- the framing of our research question: the words that we use when we structure the research purpose or questions – What we ask and the ways in which we ask it has an effect on the methods we choose and ultimately on the answers we get.

- the research methods we choose: the ways in which we gather data – The way in which we phrase and ask questions is important. This is not just about the issue of 'leading' questions (you will have read about these previously) but involves the tone, the voice and the mannerisms we use.

- the analytical methods we use: the ways in which we analyse the data – We impose specific frames onto the data and these become the lenses through which we find our results. As in the illustration of the Kotter (1990) model above, if we look for specific things, those are what we shall find.

 Open questions **Chapters 15 and 16**

Grounded Theory is an attempt to break out of the constraining effects of this 'framing' of an investigation by taking an inductive approach by which results are derived purely from the context of the research (Glaser and Strauss, 1967). Grounded Theory researchers ask open questions which are not based on theories and models from the literature. They analyse the responses to these using categories *suggested by the data*, rather the literature. The next section explores the implications of this approach.

STARTING WITH YOUR QUESTION

Like much practical business research, Grounded Theory starts with the perception of an *issue* worthy of further investigation: this issue arises from the context rather than from the literature. There is no literature review to begin with (or *a priori* as it is often described in literature), as you would expect with other methods. From a Grounded Theory perspective, the literature will start to create conceptual frameworks which will inevitably influence your research question, your data collection and your interpretation of the data. In Grounded Theory your research must be driven by the issue and the context.

You are obviously going to need *some* general understanding of your issue, and will never have a totally open mind. You already have an armoury of tacit and formal theory. Researchers need sufficient background knowledge of the theories and concepts to allow them to combine this knowledge with the research context. This loose coupling between knowledge and ideas helps to guide the developing inquiry.

 Literature review **Chapters 7 and 11**

However, McCallin (2003, p206) notes that this lack of an *a priori* literature review often 'causes tension for new researchers' who like to feel properly prepared before they start to gather their primary data. This tension is understandable; in a short-term project you are unlikely to have more than one opportunity to gather your primary data and must get it right first time. It causes tension, too, within programmes which require an initial literature review as part of the research proposal. Many people suggest that if you are planning to use Grounded Theory, it is useful to find a mentor, a tutor or a supervisor who is familiar with or has used Grounded Theory themselves.

In Grounded Theory you start with a general sense of the issue, rather than a clear definition of a problem. This may seem counter-intuitive; it is certainly counter to some of the approaches you will have considered earlier. Even a case study approach to research requires a clearer sense of what it is you are trying to achieve. Here, however, your research purpose or question must be very general rather than specific. What you are trying to do is to create a *theme* that will allow you to find out what is actually happening in that situation, rather than directing people to what you think they should be looking for.

> A Grounded Theory approach is driven by a general theme rather than a specific and focused research question.

STAKEHOLDERS' EXPECTATIONS

Identifying the various stakeholders
Chapters 2 and 4

In business research, projects typically have more than one group of stakeholders. Even if your research is part of an academic programme of study, this (usually) takes place within an organisation, requires you to gather data from people, and often needs the approval of the university, of the organisation's managers or of ethical committees. Stakeholder expectations pose a major challenge to a Grounded Theory approach. Managers, ethics committees and supervisors often want a clear understanding of your research purpose and proposed methods. A Grounded Theory approach does not allow this. Instead, it deliberately starts from an 'unframed' and vague view of the issue, developing the ideas, the questions and the sample as the research progresses. If you use the literature, it will be as part of your data, not to frame your research. Business research undertaken in the Grounded Theory tradition involves an emergent research strategy. Although this may seem to stakeholders to be simply ill-thought-through, it is essential that it is not.

THE GROUNDED THEORY PROCESS

The first step in the Grounded Theory process involves framing your inquiry in terms of genuinely seeking to discover the views and concerns of those involved (McCallin, 2003). Rather than being driven by models or theories, your research question asks 'How do others see it?' 'Meaning, action and interaction are central to Grounded Theory' (Giske and Artinian, 2007, p68) – however, this does not mean that the aim is to produce a simple description. The aim of a Grounded Theory approach is to generate concepts and theories rather than describe actions: it is 'conceptual, not inter-actional' (*ibid*). In order to generate concepts and theories, Grounded Theory adopts a very particular approach based on theoretical sampling, constant comparison and data saturation (Figure 18.1).

Figure 18.1 The Grounded Theory process

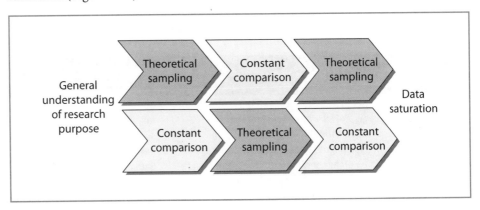

COLLECTING AND ANALYSING DATA

The inductive nature of Grounded Theory means that both sample definition and data collection are very different from what they would be if your research was aimed at testing or developing existing theory, or even using theory to structure the issue or its context in order to make sense of it and pose significant questions. The sequence is different too: analysis and data collection take place in parallel rather than sequentially.

Many forms of data are potentially useful within the approach, although relatively unstructured interviews are most commonly included. You can also use transcripts from field notes, from conversations, from focus groups, or from observations or diaries, and secondary data such as newspaper or journal articles, historical documents or literature (Strauss and Corbin, 1990), or multi-media data such as DVDs or videos, film clips or audio recordings. Whichever source of data you are planning to use, the underlying principle is the same: narratives form the basis from which you identify the core issues and concerns of the participants. These issues then become part of the constant comparisons which feed the development of codes (which we discuss shortly) and direct the sample chosen.

Theoretical sampling

As with most features of Grounded Theory, the approach to sampling is emergent. The process is known as 'theoretical sampling'. Glaser and Strauss (1967, p45) suggest a

> "process of data collection for generating theory whereby the analyst jointly collects, codes and analyses his data and then decides what data to collect next and where to find them."

The way the sampling evolves depends on the inferences and the themes that the researcher takes from the data he or she is collecting and has already collected. This might seem similar to a snowballing or a convenience sampling strategy, but it differs because it is in effect not a strategy at all: there is no prescriptive plan of action. Rather than being a purposeful means of ensuring that you have sufficient data, and rather than the researcher deciding ahead of time what constitutes sufficient data, theoretical sampling is a truly emergent approach in which the decision about which people to speak to next is premised on the themes and the inferences the researcher takes from the previous data collection. Inductively, the researcher draws provisional conceptualisations and theories from the data and uses these to determine the next stage of data-gathering. Likewise, where the data-collection process stops is not determined by a prescribed number of responses or by having completed a set number of interviews – rather, the data collection stops when the process of constant comparison ceases to generate any new concepts or theories.

RESEARCH ILLUSTRATION

If your research project was to consider the problems of organisational change within your organisation, you might start your data-gathering interviews in a number of different places. You could start by interviewing someone from the bottom of the organisation to see how they understand, perceive and make sense of organisational change. Alternatively, you might start at the top of the organisation, trying to find out how managers perceive, describe and explain change. At the point of data-gathering you would start to derive concepts and theories from the use of language. People might talk about fear or about uncertainty; they might speak about excitement or about having to acquire new skills. These issues are coded as you collect the data and then used to help you decide where you gather the next data from. In this example it may be that talk about developing new skills leads you to speak to someone in the Training and Development department, or talk of fear and uncertainty may lead you speak to someone in Occupational Health. The key impetus behind your choice of who to interview next is the data and the coded themes and concepts gathered from the previous interviewee(s).

> **Theoretical sampling is an emergent process of data collection, driven by the theories and concepts that the researcher derives from the data he or she collects.**

Theoretical sampling means that the sense of direction, the navigational map, should emerge from the data. The following research story shows how this can work in practice.

RESEARCH STORY

Chan Wai's toys

Chan Wai works in a toy manufacturing company based in Hong Kong. His chosen theme is some idea of seeing how marketing works in Company AJP. Chan Wai is interested in seeing which themes are generated by people within the organisation – which issues are of relevance to them – rather than focusing on a specific evaluation of some component of marketing. Because he is supported by his university supervisor and is not constrained by time, he has opted for a Grounded Theory approach. He needs now to think about sampling. Chan Wai's first thought is to interview the marketing manager who is responsible for designing, launching and managing any marketing campaigns run by the company. Chan Wai does an unstructured in-depth face-to-face interview with the marketing manager and in the course of the interview his attention is drawn to a number of themes that seem to relate to the responsiveness of the sales teams. In line with the notion of theoretical sampling, Chan Wai decides that the next people to be interviewed will be two members of the sales team. The interviews are arranged and using the concept of constant comparison, the issue of responsiveness is brought up in the interviews. However, what emerges from the sales staff is an issue of communication between all the parties involved. In the light of this Chan Wai decides that the next people he will interview will be people from the production side – those who actually manufacture the products.

The illustration in the Research Story above shows how Chan Wai has allowed his sample to emerge from the data he has gathered from the people he has interviewed. This idea of theoretical sampling lies at the heart of a traditional approach to Grounded Theory. Chan Wai used unstructured in-depth face-to-face interviews as a means of data-gathering, although he could also have supplemented this with secondary data gathered from the organisation's intranet or from internal reports.

Constant comparison

Constant comparison is of crucial importance at every stage of a Grounded Theory approach (Tesch, 1990). It is the means through which you as researcher determine the next step in the sampling process – it is the means by which you categorise and code the themes which emerge, the means by which you connect them to theories and concepts, and the means by which you derive trustworthy research findings.

Constant comparison is based on the skills of the researcher recognising issues which emerge from the narrative, classifying or categorising these into themes, and then drawing out connections between the themes. It is an on-going process until the point of saturation is reached. So data from the first interview is coded and classified, and the next interview takes place. The researcher's understanding of the emergent themes, the phenomena that are revealed, is then compared with the emergent themes from the previous interview. The process is at the same time contemporaneous and retrospective (Figure 18.2).

This process of constant comparison continues until the data reaches the point of data saturation.

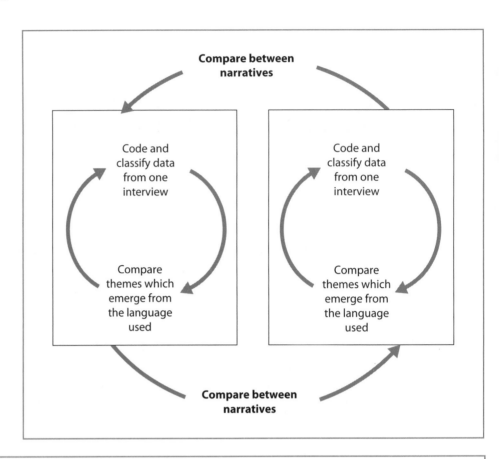

Constant comparison is the process through which themes are derived, coded and classified by comparison within an interview (or data source) and comparison between interviews (or data sources).

Data saturation

Saturation of data is the point at which the data being gathered, coded and compared is no longer generating new theories and concepts. It is the point at which the key themes being extracted from the narratives are simply replicating the themes that have been previously identified. Because the on-going analysis of data is a key part of a Grounded Theory approach, the point at which you are unable to determine any new themes, the point at which each of the categories is sufficiently populated to enable a robust and trustworthy discussion and the point at which you can inductively generate reliable connections to theories and concepts, is the point at which the data-gathering stops.

Saturation of data is the point at which no new concepts emerge from the data-coding process.

A key theme that has emerged from this understanding of a Grounded Theory approach is the practice of coding. The coding system used is the means by which you translate the narrative data collected to a series of concepts, codes and categories from which you can derive theory.

THE CODING PROCESS

Constant comparison is used for 'generating and plausibly suggesting (but not provisionally testing) many categories, properties and hypotheses about general problems' (Glaser and Strauss, 1967, p104). In practice this means that you have to read and reread the data to draw from the text the key areas of concern. In order to do this, the data is subjected to a series of actions which may be described as

- codes
- concepts
- categories
- theory.

OPEN CODING

The coding process is central to analysing data within a Grounded Theory approach. Open coding is the initial stage in the analysis (see below) and is the point at which you start to draw out and then label the key issues within the data. But codes are not simply labels – they are *classifications* which communicate the meaning or inference the researcher has drawn from the language used by the participants. It is the process by which you undertake 'a detailed inspection of the data' (Dey, 2004, p84).

Coding is highly time-consuming (Allan, 2003). It requires a word-by-word line-by-line detailed reading of the data. You have to ask yourself 'What is happening here, and what shorthand can be used to best characterise this?' 'Shorthand' here implies the use of concise description – no more than five words at most – that accurately conveys the concerns of the participants. A popular format to use for coding is margin notes and memos (Bryman and Bell, 2008). The illustration below shows part of Chan Wai's data and coding. In using this approach a wide margin is drawn at the side of the narrative, which gives you space into which you can annotate the text with the codes (the brief descriptions) as you read through the text.

The coding process involves constant comparison between the text being coded and previously considered text and codes to see how the coder's current view of

RESEARCH ILLUSTRATION

Extract from a transcipt of the interview with Miss Cheung, Marketing Manager

Notes

Chan Wai: How well do you think marketing at Company AJP works?

Miss Cheung: I think it works reasonably well, really. Well, the products usually get to the right places in the right quantities by the right time, so that is good. That's not to say that things can't be improved on. In fact, in the case of a recent product launch there were very, very many things we could have improved on *[laughs]*. I think the main issue was knowing where we were up to, getting people to tell us what they were doing, tell us when they had done the things that we had asked them to do, and tell us when they couldn't do the things we asked them to do. This last point was a real problem – especially for my team. You can't launch a new product if you don't know how well or otherwise the sales team are doing in generating orders. This is the goal, the end point, and if we don't know where that is, then we can't work out how to get there. Sales just didn't seem to realise this. Half the time when we asked them what the confirmed order status was, they would simply say 'It is too early to tell.' For goodness sake! 'It is too early to tell' – what does that mean? I'll tell you what my team thought it meant. They thought it meant that they were too busy playing golf or having fun at one of their numerous team-building days out – that's what we thought it meant. It meant 'Sorry, we don't know what we are doing but there is actually nobody there to do the work at the moment.'

But to be honest, this was a very tricky situation for me to deal with. As the Marketing Manager in charge of the launch project, I should be able to tell the sales team what to do, to make sure that every part of the system, every cog in the wheel, is working together. But because of the way the organisation is structured I have no authority over sales. I cannot tell them what they should be doing, even if the success of the project is under threat because of them. No, I can do nothing except stand in front of the senior management team and take the blame for failure. Not that it did fail – it didn't. As I said before, it all worked out OK in the end, but there were some tricky moments, and I couldn't imagine the sales manager putting his hand up and saying to the senior managers, 'Excuse me, I think you'll find that this failure was actually my fault.' To be honest, he'd probably still be playing golf *[laughs]*.

I'd hate you to think that I am just moaning, but this was a real problem – and it wasn't just a problem for me. Mr Fung, the production manager, was almost at his wits' end trying to calculate the amount of raw materials to order, trying to work out the production schedule and then trying to staff the department to meet that schedule when he had no idea how much stock to produce. He did ask me on a number of occasions to try to act as a sort of go-between, to liaise between him and the sales manager to help him get just some idea of what he should be doing to prepare for production. To be fair, I think I could have been more helpful here, you know. I probably could have made more of an effort to act as go-between, to help him sort the problems out – but in my own defence I have to say that when you feel that it is all going wrong and it is your head on the chopping-block, your priority is to look after your own team, to protect them from whatever accusations and blame may be going around. I suppose I was a bit too busy looking after my own team to be worried about his team and whether or not he was able to get on with his work.

Success

Lack of information

Communication
Poor relationships
Working together

Problems with sales

Lack of authority

No control over sales

Problems for other departments

Success

Managing the project
Problems for production
Problems for his team

Guilty: not been helpful

Defensive

Looking after her team

Not managing the project

Memo

There seem to be problems in deciding who should be managing the project. Three departments each apparently doing their own thing. Would help to speak to each of them and see what they think the issues are.

Possible divide being created between sales and everyone else. Would be useful to see if production recognise this and what sales think has happened here.

the text is informed by what they did previously. Glaser and Strauss (1967, p106) say:

> "While coding an incident for a category, compare it with the previous incidents in the same and different groups coded in the same category."

By doing this the researcher is starting to create insights into the categories that will be the output of the next stage of coding.

Accurate documentation of the processes that the researcher goes through is necessary to allow well-reasoned conclusions, grounded in the context of the research, to be drawn. Keeping a *help memo* is a useful part of the documentation process. This is a format in which you make notes of your ideas and thinking in relation to the codes. Memos are important, especially when you have a number of transcripts to code. They help you to recall what you were thinking as you coded the document, and how these codes relate to text either earlier in the document or in the analysis of previous documents. There are two ways of keeping the memos. The first uses memos as footnotes on the same page as the narrative, as Chan Wai did. This makes it easier to work between the text, the codes and the memo. The alternative is to keep memos as separate documents which you can then print off as individual sheets; this is often useful for the next stage of coding.

Open coding is the first step towards drawing out the main concerns of the participants. The next stage in the coding process is the point at which the researcher starts to draw these themes together. The aim here is to produce 'concepts' (Allan, 2003). Concepts are the higher-level groups of issues created by pulling together issues that are related, and these groups are created by using a process called axial coding (Saunders *et al*, 2007).

AXIAL CODING

Axial coding (see above) requires you to read and re-read the codes derived from your initial reading of the data. The aim is to look for relationships between the codes, for areas that are connected, for concerns that seem to be linked. These groups are drawn together under new headings as the researcher starts to condense the important issues drawn from the wider text that they started with. So far the research has gone from reading the text and creating codes for the concerns that people express in it, to drawing together those codes which are similar, connected or related in some way. In axial coding there may be numerous concepts created –

the number of them will be reflective of the breadth of concerns expressed by the participants.

If we look at how Chan Wai has done this, we can see that having undertaken the selective coding, he now has to start to draw out some of the main themes from the codes included here. This is the first iteration of axial coding in which the codes selected thus far are grouped and labelled under main headings.

Code	Concept
Success *appears important, so this should be a concept*	Success
Lack of information Communication issues	Communication
Poor relationships Problems with sales Problems with other departments	Conflict
Managing the project Problem for his team Lack of authority No control over sales Problems for production	Ability to manage
Working together Looking after her team Guilty Defensive	Emotional impact

Having gone through the first stage of axial coding and having produced a list of *concepts* from the codes, Chan Wai now has to go through a second iteration of axial coding to draw the themes more tightly together. By drawing these themes together Chan Wai will be able to produce the *categories* that will be used as the basis from which to produce theory. It is important to remember that this process is not one of simply reading the previous list and deriving new groupings from it. A key element is this idea of *constant comparison* – that in producing the list of categories Chan Wai will refer back to the original transcripts and the codes produced from those as well as referring to the list of concepts. This process helps to ensure that the new categories produced are grounded in the issue raised by the participants rather than being simply a product of Chan Wai's imagination!

However, to produce meaningful results, to produce 'theory' from the analysis, there is a need to draw these issues together still further. Here you are looking to identify a more limited number of groups, known as *categories*. These categories (see below) represent the most important features drawn from the data. They pull together the concepts created from the first process of axial coding, identifying the major and most significant issues drawn from the data.

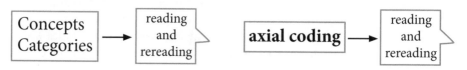

If we again draw on the example of Chan Wai to see how he has translated concepts into categories:

Concept	Category
Success – Important, but only brief comments	
Communication – A major factor possibly related to a misunderstanding of who should be communicating with whom	**Poor communications** **Lack of clear lines of responsibility**
Conflict – A result of a lack of understanding about who should be doing what, and who is in charge	**Lack of clear lines of responsibility**
Ability to manage – A major theme with lots of components, that must be taken forwards	**Managerial power and responsibility**
Emotional impact – The responses of the Marketing Manager to the problems and issues raised; *interesting, but may not answer the research question*	

What we can see from Chan Wai's production of the categories is that lots of the main issues grouped as concepts have been condensed into the hub of the problem, the central point from which each of these issues has emanated. Again, in devising these categories it has been important for Chan Wai to refer back to the transcript and to the previous codes. In the example that we have used here, the researcher is using only the categories devised from this particular extract from just one transcript. In reality, what would happen here is that this point would pull together the categories from across all the transcripts and all the codes derived from each. This means that the researcher would have many more than five concepts feeding into the categories. This is important as a key indicator that the researcher is ready to move on to the next stage, when the categories are saturated. Saturation occurs when all the codes and the concepts have been considered and everything that could be placed in a category has been placed in a category, no more categories are needed, and there is nothing else that must be included.

If, however, the constant comparison that has been key to Chan Wai's analysis reveals the need for more information, more data, Chan Wai would have to sample further.

Axial coding can be seen as a filter which acts on two levels. At the first level it is a process by which the *codes* devised initially are grouped into *concepts*. At the next level it is the means by which the concepts are drawn together to identify the *categories*. The last stage of the analysis process is the stage known as *selective coding*. This is the point at which you identify one of or the most important issues, which will form the basis of your theory or your results.

SELECTIVE CODING

Selective coding (see above) requires a judgement on your part as to which of the categories that you have identified from the data should contribute to the 'theory' or the results. You have to identify and engage with the themes that connect the categories and that therefore represent the themes which underlie the issues raised. This is the point at which you draw together the categories and the relationships between them to produce an explanation of events. In business research terms, this is the point at which you produce the results.

Next, then, is the final stage in Chan Wai's Grounded Theory analysis, the point at which the theories or the main themes are used to draw the conclusions. Here, Chan Wai is using the categories from which to build the arguments and discussions aimed at answering the research question. This is the point at which the research produces 'an explanatory theory' (Saunders *et al*, 2008, p510).

Category	Theory/Results
Poor communications are a constant theme and are related to the issue of the lack of clear lines of responsibility. Nobody knows who should be communicating with whom, when and why.	**Clarity of objectives, roles and responsibilities**
Lack of clear lines of responsibility crops us again, with the consequence that conflict occurs. There are indications here of a 'blame culture'.	**Organisational culture and interdepartmental relationships**
Nobody seems to be taking control of the situation here, seeing where things are and are not working, deciding what should be done, and how.	**Managerial power and responsibility**

In producing his results Chan Wai can now build his discussions around the theories he has extrapolated from his data. The process of coding has allowed him to condense a large amount of narrative text into the issues that are salient to the people involved. In presenting his research findings he can discuss the themes and illustrate the points he is making by using direct quotes from the people involved. This adds face validity to his results.

This is also the point at which Chan Wai should engage with the literature on the subjects. By now there is little danger that the literature will provoke a particular set of results; the results have already been produced. Instead, the literature is used to inform those results, to see where what he has found is similar to the results of other research or where his results differ – to see where the literature helps him comment more widely on the issues raised from the organisation, and where theories and concepts can throw light on the results he has produced.

THE STRENGTHS AND LIMITATIONS OF A GROUNDED THEORY APPROACH

A Grounded Theory approach presents a useful and probably unfamiliar way of addressing problems where it is important to understand the sense that participants make of a situation, or the issues that concern them. It produces results that are derived purely from the context of the research, rather than results which are a tripartite hybrid generated by an uneasy alliance forced between the literature, the method and the context. But despite the empirical benefits of this approach, there are a number of important costs and limitations that you must consider before adopting the approach.

THE LIMITATIONS OF GROUNDED THEORY

The first difficulty is that Grounded Theory is very time-consuming – you are unlikely to have the time for the in-depth analysis on which it relies within a normal dissertation project.

The second difficulty is the extreme flexibility over sample and data collection methods involved. It is impossible to propose a specific method and time-scale at the proposal stage, and academic and other stakeholders, including ethics committees, may be unwilling to accept a fully flexible proposal. Project management is also difficult if you have a fixed end point but lack a reasonably detailed plan for getting there.

Grounded Theory uses qualitative data, and involves no attempt to quantify it. Some stakeholders in business research may want to see facts and figures rather than pure explanations.

There is an argument that even if you are not using formally explicit theory you will be drawing upon tacit theory in all your research choices, and therefore valiant as is the attempt at a truly inductive approach it can never be more than an ideal.

There are also questions asked about the nature of the 'theory' that Grounded Theory produces. If it is no more than the researcher's attempt at collapsing concepts used into a framework of concepts that the researcher finds a satisfying representation of what informants said, how does the value of this framework compare with the value of frameworks derived through other means? Your answer to this will depend upon your philosophical perspective on knowledge and the role of theory.

DRAWING ON THE STRENGTHS OF GROUNDED THEORY

It may not be feasible to use a Grounded Theory approach within the constraints of most practical business research assignments. And it was argued earlier that to use parts of the approach in an unthinking way, and without the necessary rigour, was likely to destroy the integrity of the approach and seriously diminish the value of any results.

So what can you usefully take from an understanding of Grounded Theory? I would argue that it raises questions that any business researcher could usefully ask of their own research:

- Are my findings as rich as they might be, or are my own preconceptions limiting what I am finding?
- To what extent do my conclusions reflect the thoughts, ideas and perceptions of the participants rather than my own?
- Is my data-collection method flexible enough for me to be able to direct my data-gathering in line with what I am finding in my research?
- To what extent can I focus my efforts by gathering 'just enough' data for maximum information?

SUMMARY

Grounded Theory offers an inductive approach to research which contrasts with most of the other approaches in common use. It is a fundamentally qualitative approach directed towards the collection of rich data. This is then condensed into the salient issues by undertaking a series of coding activities.

Since it makes no attempt to reduce qualitative data to quantitative, it does not produce the 'facts and figures' often expected in business research. Because the process is emergent, it is difficult to anticipate when you will have sufficient data. Scheduling and planning your research can be difficult, and you will not be able to define your sample in advance.

The approach often generates vast quantities of data. Coding is a continuing, time-consuming and conceptually demanding process.

Despite these problems the approach asks questions and offers ideas which may be valuable in other approaches to research. Theoretical sampling may be useful during the exploratory stage of a project, to ensure that the issues which are important to participants are included. The sequential approach to coding may enable you to produce concepts and categories against which to code qualitatative data gathered through more structured means. The idea of data saturation may inform a decision on when to stop collecting data.

Using these elements as part of a robust research strategy is not a problem as long as you are able to explain why these elements have been chosen, and do not imply that by using these elements what you are using is Grounded Theory.

REVIEW QUESTIONS

1. What features distinguish a Grounded Theory approach to research from more traditional qualitative research approaches?

2. What do you understand by the term 'theoretical sampling', and what does it entail?

3. What do you understand by the term 'constant comparison', and what does it entail?

4. What are the strengths of a Grounded Theory approach?

5. What are the limitations of a Grounded Theory approach?

EXPLORE FURTHER

Boeije, H. (2002) 'A purposeful approach to the constant comparative method in the analysis of qualitative interviews', *Quality and Quantity*, Vol.36: 391–409. An interesting paper which uses a practical example to guide readers through the use of constant comparison in qualitative research

Giske, T. and Artinian, B. (2007) 'A personal experience of working with classical Grounded Theory. From beginner to experienced Grounded Theorist', *International Journal of Qualitative Methods*, Vol.6, No.4: 67–80. A practical article that describes the journey through which the researcher goes in trying to familiarise himself/herself with the use of a Grounded Theory approach

Glaser, B. G. (1998) *Doing Grounded Theory: Issues and discussions.* Mill Valley, CA: Sociology Press. In this book Glaser discusses the original notion of Grounded Theory and the various iterations of the approach that have emerged

Glaser, B. G. and Strauss, A. L. (1967) *The Discovery of Grounded Theory: Strategies for qualitative research.* New York: Aldine de Gruyter. The original text which launched Grounded Theory as a research approach

Locke, K. (2001) *Grounded Theory in Management Research.* London: Sage. A very useful and accessible all-round textbook which talks you through the practice and the theory of Grounded Theory

Strauss, A. L. and Corbin, J. (1990) *Basics of Qualitative Research: Grounded Theory procedures and techniques.* Thousand Oaks, CA: Sage Publications. In this second major iteration of the Grounded Theory approach, Strauss and Corbin discuss the changes they feel are necessary to the original approach and the practice of Grounded Theory

Suddaby, R. (2006) 'From the editors: what Grounded Theory is not', *Academy of Management Journal*, Vol.49, No.4: 633–42. A really useful article which, although presented in an academic journal, is of particular use to practical business researchers who want to understand what a Grounded Theory approach actually entails

 Visit www.cipd.co.uk/brm for web links, templates, activities and other useful resources relating to this chapter.

CHAPTER 19

Content Analysis

INTRODUCTION

Qualitative data (involving words rather than numbers) is a potentially rich source of information. It gives insights into what people think, what people perceive and the opinions that people hold about a whole range of issues. Despite this, qualitative data has been referred to as 'an attractive nuisance' (Miles, 1979, p590), and even when collected, it remains troublesome. Analysis is more of a craft than the application of a set of rules that can be learned (Seale *et al*, 2007), so the skills of qualitative analysis cannot be 'transmitted simply by explicit instruction' (Hammersley, 2004; p551). Rather, they must be acquired and then practised. But acquiring these skills is necessary if you wish to get the best results from your business research. Most business research projects seek information from people – their understandings can give insights that quantitative data alone could not possibly reveal. Qualitative data can be gathered by using interviews, questionnaires and/or focus groups. Qualitative data can also be gathered from secondary sources: company reports, minutes of meetings, marketing or promotional literature or internal communications.

The previous chapter on Grounded Theory described an inductive and qualitative approach to data collection and analysis, aimed at producing a set of concepts. It was suggested that it was a difficult research strategy and one that was not acceptable to all the potential stakeholders in small-scale business research projects. Content analysis offers an approach to textual data that is both less demanding and more likely to meet with stakeholder approval.

Like Grounded Theory, content analysis relies on coding. However, the codes are predetermined rather than being derived from the data. This makes the whole process more predictable and the results can be perceived as more 'scientific' than those produced by a Grounded Theory approach. Yet this process is not prescribed – it is as much an art as it is a science – and this chapter will provide some basic guidelines that should help you to draw trustworthy research findings and conclusions from narrative data on interview transcripts, from text on questionnaires or from secondary sources.

UNDERSTANDING CONTENT ANALYSIS

Interviewing
Chapter 16

Earlier it was suggested that researcher bias may influence both what you perceive when collecting data and how you interpret the data you capture. It is very easy to draw impressionistic conclusions that simply reinforce your own views. If you simply select 'quotes' to support your position, there is a serious risk that you will mislead those whom the research is intended to inform. It was suggested that if you are interviewing, an audio recording and full transcription will reduce the selectivity of perception. Content analysis is designed to reduce the selectivity of interpretation.

Content analysis is described as an objective method which identifies, in relation to a specific context, the prevalence of key themes or issues. It is a systematic process which enables the business researcher to draw well-reasoned conclusions from the frequency and the nature of the themes identified. We should explore this issue of objectivity a little further.

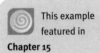

This example featured in
Chapter 15

Although many definitions include this term (Berelson, 1952; Holsti, 1969), the extent to which content analysis can be described as objective is dependent on the nature of the content analysis. Where the researcher simply counts up the number of times the word is used, or runs the data through a computer system which does this on the researcher's behalf, some objectivity is assured. The word is either there or it is not there. Think back to our previous example of the restaurant: if the majority of respondents commented that the plate on which the food was served was cold, then little 'interpretation' would be necessary – the results would simply relay the 'fact' that 80% of respondents commented that the plate was cold. However, if they frequently mentioned the word 'quality', unless you know the context in which they use the word, the information is of little use (eg 80% of the respondents mentioned the word 'quality'). There would have to be some form of analysis which looked at the context within which the word 'quality' was used.

 CONSIDER...

Using the restaurant example above, if you had been presented with the 'fact' that 80% of customers used the word 'quality', what additional information or explanations would you want in order to make that data useful?

Your answers may differ slightly from those listed below but you have probably identified similar types of issues. The types of things that I would like to be told are:

- Was the issue of quality raised as a *good* thing?

- Was the issue of quality raised as a *bad* thing?

- Did it relate to the quality of the service?

- Did it relate to the quality of the food?

- Did it relate to value for money?

- Was the quality consistent (consistently good or consistently bad)?

I would also like to know in what other ways 'issues' surrounding quality were raised. People might not have used the word directly but comments such as 'The food was sensational' or 'The staff were inefficient' both imply that there is an issue related to 'quality'.

Here some further consideration is required to determine the context within which the word is used so that the data can be converted into meaningful information.

Content analysis, then, is often thought of as a quantitative as well as a qualitative method of analysis. In its simplest form it means looking at a piece of text and seeing how many times certain terms or words are used, or how often certain themes are raised. So how is this information useful? Knowing how often specific themes or issues are mentioned can be an important way of gauging their importance to the customers. In the restaurant survey, you may find that one person out of a sample of 250 people would like to see all the walls painted purple, whereas 150 people all commented on the food being served on cold plates. Some idea of the frequency with which issues are spontaneously raised by people can be an important consideration. However, content analysis in terms of simply counting up the number of times certain words or terms are used may not be sufficient on its own to help you answer your research question. You may have to support these 'frequency counts' with explanations or discussions. Because of this, there are a number of different 'levels' of content analysis to help you draw meaningful information from the data you have.

Before choosing to use content analysis it is important to be aware of its limitations. These relate to the extent to which your chosen categories limit the informational content of the analysis, and the need to be aware that your conclusions should not go beyond the sample of text that you analyse.

When thinking about the use of content analysis, you must be aware that the value of your analysis will depend upon the coding categories that you choose to use. These must be

- clear

- appropriate, and

- comprehensive.

They must be clear in that the terms used must not be easily confused or conflated with others. They must be appropriate in that they must relate specifically to the core focus of your research. And they must be comprehensive in that they must relate to all the important factors in your research.

Although content analysis can be applied to a wide range of texts, the research findings relate only to the context of your particular research. Just as you would sample informants carefully in order to be able to draw conclusions about the population in which you were interested, so too conclusions drawn from other forms of text have to be limited to the population from which the text is sampled. Texts from one organisation's communications would allow you to draw conclusions relating to that organisation. A sample of newspaper articles would allow conclusions relating to the particular section of the media sampled and the time period within which the sample was located.

KEY POINTS

- Content analysis is a means of analysing qualitative data.
- Content codes are derived before the data is collected.
- Content analysis can identify the frequency with which words and terms are used.
- Content analysis can identify the context within which words and terms are used.
- The quality of the research findings will be directly affected by the quality of the coding.
- The results of content analysis are not generalisable to the wider population.

WHEN TO USE CONTENT ANALYSIS

Content analysis is useful when the research purpose or question is best answered by analysing the data gathered in a thematic way. As with all research analysis methods the key starting point is the research question and the research objectives. For content analysis to be successful, these must be specific and sufficiently focused for you to be able to extract from them the key themes to be searched for in the text. Provided that the research purpose/question and objectives clearly map out what you are intending to do, recognising and coding the themes is 'relatively' easy. Where the research purpose/question is vague or is too wide, identifying and coding the themes becomes much more problematic.

ACTIVITY

Read both of the cases below and see how easy or difficult you think it would be for the researchers mentioned to identify key words or themes from the texts that they have.

Meena and organisational change
For her business research Meena is planning to evaluate how successful a recent department-wide change process ('the realignment project') was in her organisation. Meena's research question is:

> Evaluating organisational change: How effective was the realignment project managed in MyX Company?

In order to answer this question Meena has set the following sub-questions:

1 In terms of Kotter's eight-stage framework, what were the strengths of the approaches used?
2 In terms of Kotter's eight-stage framework, what were the weaknesses of the approaches used?
3 What suggestions for improvement would people make?

Meena plans to use a semi-structured interview in which she will ask people to talk her through their experiences of the change process and identify what worked and what did not work. Although the interview questions start at the beginning of the change and finish at the end, she is not planning to use the Kotter framework as part of the question structure.

Would it be relatively easy or relatively difficult for Meena to identify (and then code) a series of themes, and why?

Verity and new business start-ups

Verity works for a local borough council and so for her dissertation wanted to choose a topic that would meet the need of an academic piece of work while at the same time being of value to her organisation. Accordingly, she decided on the following research question:

> What would encourage successful local entrepreneurs to invest in innovative business start-ups in an area of high socio-economic deprivation?

For her primary data-gathering she has used open interviews which consisted of her asking the initial question and then allowing the respondents (successful local entrepreneurs and elected members of the council) to develop their answers in whichever way they felt most appropriate.

Would it be relatively easy or relatively difficult for Verity to identify (and then code) a series of themes, and why?

You may have come up with some slightly different perspectives, but my own thinking is that because Meena is using a definite framework against which to judge the success of otherwise of the change process that has taken place, she is probably in a good position to consider using content analysis. To do this she could take each of the dimensions of the Kotter model and identify key words from this framework.

The eight stages listed by Kotter (1995, p58) in his model are:

1 Establish a sense of urgency.

2 Form a powerful guiding coalition.

3 Create a vision.

4 Communicate the vision.

5 Empower others to act on the vision.

6 Plan to create short-term wins.

7 Consolidate improvements and produce more change.

8 Institutionalise the new approaches.

Words like 'teamwork' and 'leadership' would be easy to recognise, but what about the slightly more complex themes? For example, people are unlikely to use expressions like 'empower others to act'. Instead, Meena might have to think about how people might use other terms or phrases to mean the same thing. She may well look for terms like 'being involved', 'taking responsibility' and 'making decisions'. However, Meena probably has sufficient focus to suggest that content analysis may be really useful in helping her to answer her research question.

Verity has a rather more open format to her data-gathering. Rather than setting people a range of questions or directing them across themes, she is allowing the respondents to develop their answers in whichever way is most suited to them. This will mean that she will be able to find out how the respondents frame the answers to the question, rather than providing them with a framework within which they can answer. So would content analysis be appropriate here? Well, the answer would have to be No. The main problem is looking for the categories, the themes that she could codify and then look for in the text. Because the research question is so wide and there is no structure to the ways in which people could answer the question, it may be almost impossible to pick out a set of relevant themes that she could then search the text for. In this case content analysis would not be a good idea.

Although the examples above both use primary data, the same issues apply when analysing secondary data. Content analysis is only useful where you have a clear idea of the themes you are looking for and when these themes are likely to be clearly recognisable from the data that you have. Content analysis can be used only where the themes you have identified lend themselves to a coherent coding system. The aim of the analysis is to enable you to answer your research question. If your data analysis is fragmented and disjointed, the information that you produce will be likewise. Any research findings produced will lack the coherence necessary to help you to produce robust and well-reasoned conclusions.

Lastly, content analysis requires you to devise a specific set of coding rules to apply to the data you have gathered. It is important therefore that all the data gathered is amenable to these rules. This is especially important where you are analysing data from both primary and secondary sources, or data gathered by more than one data-collection method. To draw reasoned comparisons, you will have to apply the same set of coding rules to each data set.

If you are thinking about using content analysis on secondary data, it is worth also thinking about the format in which you have access to that data. Where you have access to electronic copies, you have the option to use one of the many computerised analysis systems. This often means that you have scope to analyse a much greater quantity of data than you would be able to by doing the analysis manually. However, where you have data in hard copy only, you will have to think about how this impacts on your ability to undertake the analysis.

> **Content analysis is useful where your research question and/or your research objectives are sufficiently structured to allow you to identify the themes you have to look for in the text.**

THE CODING PROCESS

Research question
Chapter 8

The analysis process starts with two questions about the documents you are going to use:

- which documents will you use to derive the codes for your analysis from?
- which documents will you use for the basis of your analysis?

Secondary-data-only research Chapter 12, mixed-methods research Chapter 13

Those of you who are using primary data for your business research will have previously used a range of academic and professional literature as the basis for developing and refining your research purpose/question. The key themes derived from this literature are used to inform the structure of the data-gathering process and the questions you ask, as well as being used to derive the codes that you can use to analyse that data. Your analysis will use the primary data that you have gathered, the transcripts from interviews, the open comments that people have included on your questionnaires, or the written-up field notes that you have taken from your interviews or observations. However, those of you who are undertaking research using the analysis of secondary data (either as a piece of research using secondary data only or as part of a case study or mixed-methods approach) may not have such a 'self-contained' data set. If you are using secondary data, the quantity of data available to you may well be vast.

SELECTING DOCUMENTS

Think back to the example of Constantinos in Chapter 6. He is doing his dissertation based purely on secondary data, and his Google search on the term 'corporate social responsibility' came up with over 8 million hits – and that was just one part of the wider literature. Constantinos may take some time to complete his dissertation if he is planning to use all of this! Where using secondary data, either as the only data gathered or as part of a wider data set involving primary data as well, there is a need to frame exactly what you will use. Constantinos had to select a specific sample of the literature. And to do this there must be some selection criteria, a rubric that clearly distinguishes which literature will be used. Constantinos may decide that because he is looking at present-day manifestations of CSR, he will limit his search to academic articles published in the last 12 months. He may decide that because academic articles and case studies written by the organisations themselves are motivated by different factors, he will take half of his sample from organisational reports and half from academic journals. There are many different ways in which he could choose to select his sample (Bryman and Bell, 2007, note how the ways in which the media 'characterise' specific events has been used previously). The important issue is that a robust sampling strategy is selected.

> Because content analysis is limited to the context of the text that you are reviewing, you must have a robust and well-reasoned sampling strategy.

DECIDING ON YOUR FOCUS OF ANALYSIS

This is possibly the most crucial stage of your content analysis. It is the stage at which you are using your understanding of the literature, of the context of your business research and of your research question to decide which aspects of the narrative you will focus your analysis on. There are three aspects that you must consider: *words*, *themes* and *dispositions*.

- words – Can you identify the key words that you will then search for in the text?
- themes – Can you identify the themes that may relate to the words, even if the words themselves are not used?
- dispositions – Can you identify how people react to the words and themes?

Of the aspects mentioned, the identification of words is the most straightforward. Drawing on your understanding of both literature and context, specific words can be identified and used to create a clear, appropriate and comprehensive set of codes. However, as was evident previously in the restaurant example, sometimes words in isolation from context can be meaningless. (Remember the problems with the word 'quality'.) It may be that issues of quality are raised without actually using the word – instead, people use such expressions as 'good food', 'excellent service' or 'miserable staff'. Identifying and coding themes allows you to draw meaning from the wider implications of the words used. Considering dispositions enables you to recognise the ways in which people use the words. Again referring to the restaurant example, simply counting how many times the word 'quality' is used conveys little meaningful understanding of what is meant by it. Identifying dispositions, how people react to the words and themes, whether they use them positively or negatively, enables you to gather a greater depth of understanding and of meaningful information.

These aspects, when extracted from the narrative text, become the basis for constructing a *content coding manual*. A content coding manual is a central reference document in which you record the key words and themes, the codes used to record them, and the associated dispositions. It starts life as a template for your research but as you undertake your analyses becomes the central point at which your preliminary research findings are documented. Table 19.1 shows you what a content coding manual looks like.

Table 19.1 Template for a content coding manual

This table template is available at **www.cipd.co.uk/brm**

No.	Word/Theme	Code	Features	Disposition
1		1	i ii iii iv	a) positive b) negative c) neutral
2		2	i ii iii iv	a) positive b) negative c) neutral
3		3	i ii iii iv	a) positive b) negative c) neutral
4				
5				
6				

PRODUCING A CODING MANUAL

In producing a coding manual you are trying to map out the key words or themes that you have derived from the text, and then translating them into the alternative words or expressions that people might use to communicate that same information. The purpose of this coding is to extract the salient issues from the narrative so that you can look at the wider data and identify the relative importance of issues, see how people characterise these issues and see what insights and understandings you can gain from the ways in which these issues are considered. What becomes apparent here is the crucial need to identify and code the correct issues. Coding requires a thorough engagement with the data, and an understanding of the literature which informs your research purpose/question and clearly thought-through research objectives. Through this engagement you have to produce a comprehensive set of codes, each of which is mutually exclusive. Even then, coding is not without its difficulties. There will have to be a local judgement call over how many codes are included, how you judge relative importance (is it by the number of people who raise an issue, the vehemence with which the issue is raised, or the seniority of the respondent?) and to what extent you derive the codes from the primary data rather than the secondary data.

Even where the codes selected are clear and precise, there can be problems. You have to consider the extent to which reducing the wider data to a limited number of specific items undermines the richness of that data. Likewise, you have to consider how your own approach to coding and the codes that you select might be seen to privilege a particular view which could compromise the idea of objectivity mentioned previously.

Once you have decided on the key words and coded them into the content coding manual, you must consider the alternative ways in which these words or themes might be articulated. The 'Features' column is where you should list the different ways of expressing the key words or themes. These too must be coded. What you can see emerging from this is a hierarchy of coding, in which the word or theme is the first code, the way in which it is expressed is the second code, and the third code is that of disposition. Disposition gives you information regarding how people felt about the word or theme – whether it was a good thing or a bad thing or was well managed or poorly managed.

PILOTING THE CODING SYSTEM

Before embarking on large-scale data collection and analysis, it is important to pilot your coding system. The following checklist of questions and procedures together amounts to a summary of the piloting process (adapted from Woike, 2007):

- what is the research purpose/research question? Does it lend itself to being broken down into words, themes and dispositions?
- does breaking the research focus down into words, themes and dispositions enable you to produce any meaningful data?
- what sources of data will provide the best material for you, and are they accessible?
- what are the units of analysis, and how will they be coded?
- produce a content coding manual and clarify the means of analysis.
- obtain pilot data and test the coding manual and means of analysis.
- check that the data and information produced allow you to answer your research question.

By obtaining a small quantity of 'representative' data (ie the same style, quality and format as the wider data that you plan to gather) and running through the process of analysis, you can see the ways in which the codes you have chosen are more or less appropriate, the ways in which the themes accurately (or inaccurately) reflect those emerging from the data, and areas where there is scope to develop a more comprehensive set of categories.

It is often quite difficult to get to grips with how mapping the content works in practice, so as an example mapped out below is what might be a useful approach based on the story of Meena introduced previously.

What is evident in the illustration below is that having mapped out the key words based on Kotter's framework, Meena has translated these into alternative ways in which these issues might be mentioned or raised by the respondent group.

Before you are able to undertake the analysis itself, you must have piloted the processes. You have to make sure that the themes you have identified are themes that occur in the transcripts. If you have derived some of the themes from the transcripts, this will not be a problem. However, if you have derived some or all of the themes from secondary data, you must make sure that they are reflected in your primary data. You should also

RESEARCH ILLUSTRATION

Meena's case

The first thing that Meena must do is to map out the table into which she will note the words and the themes that she will look for. A key point here is that she is looking for how well the change was managed by using the Kotter framework as the basis for her analysis. Her interviews allowed people to talk through their experiences of change from beginning to end, and she now has to draw from the content of those interviews the areas where people connect to the themes of the Kotter model.

Meena's first mapping of terms might look something like this:

No.	Word/Theme	Code	Features	Disposition
1	Drivers for change	1	i opportunity/opportunities ii problem(s) iii more efficient iv more effective v developing people	a) positive b) negative c) neutral
2	Leadership	2	i leadership (team) ii management (team) iii driven by iv idea/brainchild	a) positive b) negative c) neutral
3	Vision	3	i sense of direction ii know where we're going iii goals iv objectives	a) positive b) negative c) neutral
4	Communication	4	i aware(ness) ii understand(ing) iii roles/responsibilities iv support(ing/ive)	a) positive b) negative c) neutral
5	Empowerment	5	i responsible/responsibility ii authority iii autonomy iv decision-making v problem-solving	a) positive b) negative c) neutral
6	Quick wins	6	i results ii success(es) iii achievement(s)	a) positive b) negative c) neutral
7	More change	7	i next step(s)/stage(s) ii next level iii further improvements iv momentum v keep the ball rolling	a) positive b) negative c) neutral
8	Institutionalise the new systems	8	i way in which we work ii what we do now iii the norm	a) positive b) negative c) neutral

ensure that your 'Features' are an accurate representation of the terms and phrases that the participants in your research use in common parlance. Make sure that you have not missed out specific turns of phrase that are important. This is especially important if you are undertaking your business research as part of a consultancy project. It may be that the everyday language of the organisation is not one that you are particularly well up in – they may use unique phrases with which you are not familiar – and so it is worthwhile checking that you have made allowances for the terms and expressions that may be specific to that organisation.

> Coding must accurately reflect the key themes. Pilot your first ideas and refine them as necessary.

THE ANALYTICAL PROCESS

The analysis itself involves the careful reading of each of the texts to identify where the themes occur and how they are dealt with (the disposition). There are a number of ways to document the analysis. The first is by annotating each text in turn, the second is by using a thematic review.

ANNOTATING TEXTS

Examples of this kind of presentation are available at **www.cipd. co.uk/brm**

Reading each text in turn, carefully line by line, allows you to code the relevant areas as you go along. This is a useful approach for a number of reasons. It allows you to get a comprehensive feel for the entire text, the ways in which words are used, and the sentiments which underpin those words. It enables you to see how frequently the same person returns to particular themes and the ways in which they build arguments and justify their opinions. Also, because you map the codes as you read, there is the opportunity to annotate the text as well as map the issues into the content coding manual. As you review the analysis to write up the results, you can revisit the transcript to remind yourself of the context of the comments, and this makes it easier to see where you can find specific quotations that you can use to support the arguments you present and increase the face validity of your research findings.

THEMATIC REVIEW

Examples of this kind of presentation are available at **www.cipd. co.uk/brm**

A thematic review is a process by which you take each of the key words or themes identified in the content coding manual and search for manifestations of them in each of the texts. Rather than reading each text from beginning to end, you simply skim through the narrative of each to identify particular themes in turn. These can be annotated on the main texts themselves but can also be collated separately to produce a batch of references to a particular theme. This is extremely useful when you come to map out the arguments that you wish to make in discussing your research findings because each batch can be used as the basis for a particular part of your discussions.

DRAWING CONCLUSIONS FROM CONTENT ANALYSIS

Content analysis is unusual in producing both quantitative and qualitative research findings. Quantitative data is produced by identifying the frequency with which specific words or terms are used. Qualitative data is produced by drawing meaning and explanations from the themes and dispositions. In drawing conclusions from these findings there is a need to consider not only the nature of the conclusions drawn from each type of data, but also the relationship between them. Quantitative findings produced from the incidence of the use of particular words and themes are usually a good place to open a discussion. They can draw the reader's attention to the relative importance of issues; usually the more often the terms are used, the more important they are to the respondent. However, there is a need to be aware of the ways in which the questions you ask can provoke the use of particular terms and therefore increase the frequency with which they appear in the text. If as a researcher your questions are dominated explicitly or implicitly by a particular theme, then it will come as no surprise that the theme is mentioned frequently by the respondents. If you ask 10 out of 15 questions on the subject of leadership and the respondents mention leadership twice as often as other themes, is this an indication that leadership is important to them, or that leadership is important to you?

Quantitative data can be used to set the scene for more in-depth discussions drawing on the use of qualitative data. While it may be useful to know that a particular theme is of importance to a particular group of people, it is of equal importance to understand why this is the case. By drawing on the research findings that relate to disposition, you should be able to construct reasoned discussions that reveal how you make sense of the information you have generated. Using examples from the coding manual and quotations from the text allows you to suggest why issues might be of importance to people. It gives you the opportunity to proffer potential explanations for the research findings generated and allows you to discuss the insights and the understanding created by engaging with the qualitative data.

THE STRENGTHS AND LIMITATIONS OF CONTENT ANALYSIS

The strengths of content analysis are that it:

- enables you to generate a wealth of quantitative and qualitative data that can be used to create rich insights and understandings
- offers a clear and replicable research strategy which, once coded, may be used by one researcher on numerous occasions or a number of researchers simultaneously
- allows you to undertake a robust piece of research on purely secondary data and has the potential to be repeated as part of longitudinal studies.

The limitations of content analysis are that it:

- is completely dependent on the accuracy of the coding – where the coding is inaccurate or incomplete, the integrity of the research is compromised
- is completely dependent on the quality of the data being analysed, whether primary data or secondary data – where the data collection is skewed (as in the example of leadership given previously) or incomplete, again the integrity of the research is compromised.
- can be accused of being neither one thing nor the other. It does not produce the detailed inferential statistics that can be produced from more formal quantitative analyses, neither does it produce the same level of richness that is generated from more qualitative means of analysis.

SUMMARY

Content analysis is a method for deriving quantitative and qualitative data from text. The most basic form of content analysis counts the frequency of occurrence of particular terms or words. This is useful when specific and predictable themes can be identified within your narrative data, but its usefulness will depend upon your skill in selecting appropriate themes or words to tally. The themes and words that you select must be comprehensive, mutually exclusive and clear.

Because structure is necessary in content analysis, the research question and objectives must be such that unambiguous boundaries for analysis can be set.

This basic approach is likely to be of limited relevance to business research, so a more sophisticated analysis may be required which also looks at the context within which those words are used. This addresses, at least in part, the criticism that content analysis reduces rich qualitative data to ticks in boxes and a few structured clarifications (see, for example, Saunders *et al*, 2007). However, where both quantitative and qualitative aspects are attended to, content analysis proffers a useful means of screening narrative data to produce well-reasoned research findings.

REVIEW QUESTIONS

1. For content coding analysis to be successful, the codes must be clear, appropriate and comprehensive. What do you understand by each of these terms, and why are they important?

2. How might the production of both qualitative and quantitative research findings be useful to you as a researcher?

3. Why is it important to pilot your coding manual and means of analysis?

4. What are the strengths and limitations of content analysis?

EXPLORE FURTHER

Gibbs, G. R. (2002) *Qualitative Data Analysis: Explorations with NVivo*. Buckingham: Open University Press. This book considers the different ways in which content analysis might be used and looks at how NVivo can be used to support the analysis process in each of them

Krippendorff, K. and Block, M. A. (2008) *The Content Analysis Reader*. Massachusetts: Sage Publications. A comprehensive consideration of content analysis from the history of content analysis, through the process of analysis, to the types of coding

Neuendorf, K. A. (2002) *The Content Analysis Guidebook*. Thousand Oaks, CA: Sage Publications. A good breadth of consideration and written in a style which would make this accessible to practical business researchers as well as to an academic audience

Woike, B. (2007) 'Content coding of open-ended responses', in Robins, R. W., Fraley, R. C. and Kreuger, R. F. (eds) *Handbook of Research Methods in Personality Psychology*. New York: Guildford Press; pp292–307. A useful chapter which walks through the process of coding qualitative data

 Visit www.cipd.co.uk/brm for web links, templates, activities and other useful resources relating to this chapter.

CHAPTER 20

Representing Quantitative Data

INTRODUCTION

Research is all about collecting relevant data and turning the data into evidence to support an argument. In many business research projects some at least of this data will be in the form of numbers. You have to interpret and communicate the meaning of this numerical data to your client and others. Any misinterpretation of your data may seriously mislead your client or others. Any correct interpretation will be wasted if you cannot convey it to your client.

The aim of this chapter and the next is to help you to turn the numbers your research generates into something that you and your audience genuinely understand and can use. They aim to enable you to make justified claims on the basis of the data, extracting from them their full potential as evidence, and no more. If you fail to understand what numbers mean, and what you can and cannot legitimately do with them, and consequently make stronger claims than your data justify, your conclusions will be untrustworthy, your client may be misled, and your reputation may be put seriously at risk.

Few people 'read' numbers easily. Faced with large tables of numbers, their brains tend to disconnect. If at least some of your data is in the form of numbers, you will have to think carefully about how you can summarise or describe the data in a way that makes it easier for you to 'grasp' and think about, and to begin to see any patterns, and to communicate those patterns and their significance to your client. This is the territory of descriptive statistics, and the focus of this chapter.

The second essential stage is to work out just how meaningful these patterns are. Are any apparent differences or relationships purely the result of chance? There are many different methods for testing the (statistical) significance of such findings, and these will be the focus of the next chapter.

If you love working with numbers, neither interpreting nor communicating your findings will be problematic – you will really enjoy using a variety of techniques to extract their full meaning. But if you are nervous about anything remotely numerical, you may be tempted to feed the numbers into a spreadsheet (such as Excel) or statistical package (such as SPSS) and feel grateful that it turns out impressive graphs and statistical values.

The ease with which different 'summaries' of the data and derivative statistics can be calculated, and the highly professional presentation which even a programme like Excel can achieve, is impressive. But this ease and seeming professionalism is potentially a hazard for researchers who do not have a 'feel' for the numbers. It is very easy to assume that because the output *looks* good it *is* good, and to question it no further. Non-numerate clients may be so impressed by the graphs, tables and statistical tests your software achieves that they accept without question the conclusions you draw from them. But unless appropriate numbers were input and appropriate operations carried out on these numbers, the 'impressive' output can be seriously misleading. This raises ethical issues. It could be argued that if you do not fully understand what you are doing with your quantitative data, it is unethical to present them as if you do.

These two chapters will not make you an expert statistician – or even a competent one. The hope is that they will enable you to represent and draw appropriate conclusions from simple sets of data, and be extremely cautious about doing anything else. For more sophisticated analysis you will need access to statistical expertise beyond the scope of this book.

LEARNING OUTCOMES

This chapter should enable you to:

- understand some of the properties of quantitative data which will influence how you represent them

- select appropriate numbers to communicate

- represent 'average', 'range' and 'distribution' of a set of numbers in an appropriate form

- supplement this with a suitable visual format where appropriate

- describe the data verbally in a way that does not claim more than the numbers warrant.

DIFFERENT FORMS OF DATA

To avoid presenting impressive but misleading findings you need to understand the nature of the numbers you are dealing with. Not all numbers mean the same. Earlier, we distinguished between qualitative data and quantitative data. But there are different sorts of quantitative data, depending on what the 'numbers' signify. There are different sorts of numbers, with different 'meanings'. You can put whatever numbers you like into a spreadsheet or statistical program, and the computer will do whatever you instruct it to. However, unless you understand the sort of numbers you are dealing with, and what it is appropriate to do with them, your computer output may be seriously misleading. This is not a case of 'GIGO' (garbage in, garbage out) but of perfectly good numbers – in their way – being turned into garbage by inappropriate processing. This is somewhat analogous to putting your finest silks and woollens through the 90-degree wash cycle. A common cause of 'untrustworthy' conclusions is failure to realise legitimate and illegitimate ways of dealing with particular sets of numbers.

NOMINAL OR CATEGORICAL DATA

Numbers in maths are easy: $1 + 2 = 3$, $2 \times 2 = 4$, etc. But in business research they are more complicated. Sometimes numbers mean nothing more than a coding category. A survey of car ownership might code Ford as 1, Fiat as 2, Peugeot as 3, Seat as 4, and so on. In these cases the numbers are no more than a name or label for a category. It would be meaningless to say that a Ford and Fiat added up to a Peugeot. When numbers have no more meaning than an arbitrary label for a category you cannot treat them in any sense as numbers. Some of your data will still be quantitative – the number of Fiat drivers will be meaningful – but you need to be careful that you do not inadvertently treat your category numbers as if they too were subject to quantitative analysis.

> **You cannot perform mathematical operations on nominal data.**

ORDINAL DATA

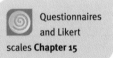

Questionnaires and Likert scales **Chapter 15**

In ordinal data, as you might expect, the numbers indicate an ordering. The categories in the examples above could appear in any order. You might as easily have labelled Fiat as 1 and Ford as 2, or allocated the numbers in a variety of different ways. But often categories can be ordered, if nothing else. Suppose you are using a questionnaire with Likert scales such as the following:

Please rate the following:

	Very satisfied	**Satisfied**	**Neutral**	**Dissatisfied**	**Very Dissatisfied**
The current menu					

If you gave a score of 5 to Very satisfied, 4 to Satisfied, 3 to Neutral, 2 to Dissatisfied and 1 to Very dissatisfied, the numbers would have some meaning. You could reasonably say that a score of 5 indicated a greater level of satisfaction than a score of 4, which itself indicated more satisfaction than a 3, and so on. You could not, however, really say that two 'Dissatisfied' scores equated to one 'Satisfied' score, or that someone with a 4 was twice as satisfied as someone with a 2. (Questionnaire scores are normally added up to give an overall score on precisely this basis, which raises interesting questions about the nature of the total score so derived . . .)

Where the numbers reliably indicate order, but no more, your data is referred to, sensibly enough, as *ordinal data*. Some writers regard both nominal and ordinal data as categorical, since you are effectively dealing with categories even in examples such as the scale above. Others would, cautiously, add or average scores on a series of Likert scales to provide an indication at least of comparisons between different groups.

INTERVAL DATA

In order to be able to add or subtract scores from each other in a way that makes sense, the intervals between different numbers have to be meaningful. Thus it makes sense to say that 25°C is 10 degrees hotter than 15°C, and that 50°C is 10 degrees hotter than 40°C. '10 degrees hotter' means the same in each case. For a specified object you would have to apply the same amount of heat energy to raise its temperature from 15°C to 25°C as to raise it from 40°C to 50°C, assuming no thawing or boiling was involved. So if you have interval data, you can add and subtract. However, you could not meaningfully say that 50°C was twice as hot as 25°C. The intervals are the same, but there is no clear zero to which they relate. 0°C is in that sense arbitrary. Water may be an important substance, and its freezing point important for a number of human reasons, but a large number of other points could have been chosen as 'zero', including that on the Fahrenheit scale.

RATIO DATA

To multiply or divide numbers the scale has to have a 'real' zero. If you are counting the number of employees, or the number of Fiat or Ford drivers, or your numbers represent money, then you have a meaningful zero and can not only add and subtract but can multiply and divide. It makes sense to say that a company with 2,000 staff has twice as many employees as one with 1,000 staff, or that a profit of $3 million is half as big as one of $6 million, or that 20% of the cars bought in a certain locality are Fiats. But unless you have ratio data, you need to think carefully about what you can and cannot do to summarise or otherwise represent your findings.

> **You can add, subtract, multiply or divide ratio data.**

CONTINUOUS OR DISCRETE VARIABLES

Another distinction between forms of numerical data is whether the scale is continuous or discrete. On the whole, things which you have to *measure* – such as length – are continuous. A piece of string might be any length. You could say a particular piece was 24 cm long or 24.0001 cm depending on the accuracy of your measures. And the next piece you measured might be 24.0002 cm as far as you could tell . . . There is no limit on the value the length might take beyond that imposed by your ability to measure. This is very different from things you can count. If 24 people apply for a job, it is 24. You might have 25 or 35 or any other whole number of applicants, but not 25.5, any more than you can actually have 2.4 children. Data based on counts are discrete data.

WAYS OF SUMMARISING DATA NUMERICALLY

Imagine that you are investigating an invoicing problem. There is a problem because a number of customers have yet to be invoiced, and many of those who have received invoices have queried the payment requested. You have conducted an audit of a sample of 500 invoices, looking at the time interval between order completion and invoice despatch, and the accuracy of the amount invoiced. To be accurate, the order quantity, unit price and discount must be entered correctly, and the value invoiced correctly as calculated from these figures. The quantity must match that on the purchase order, the unit price must match the price list that was current at the time of the order, and the discount must be that agreed with the customer's relationship manager at the time of ordering. You find that for 150 of the 500 invoices you audit, the original purchase order is not on file.

CONSIDER...

Which elements of this data would help you to understand the 'invoicing problem'? How might you present the data you have been given in order to make the 'message' it contains as clear as possible? What further information might help you understand the problem?

One useful piece of further information might be the time taken to invoice the customer. Time from order completion to payment represents a zero-interest loan to the customer. This money either has to be borrowed (at a non-zero interest rate) or would otherwise be available for investment or deposit (at a non-zero interest rate), so payments outstanding are 'costing' the company a substantial amount. Although time to invoice is not a 'measure' of time to pay, it will be related to it: few customers will pay *before* being invoiced. It is therefore worth thinking about how data on time to invoice might be usefully summarised.

'AVERAGES': MEANS, MODES AND MEDIANS

If you presented your client with a list of 500 numbers, ranging from 1 day to 3 months and 13 days, it would be very hard to make sense of the numbers. You could make it a little easier by turning all the times into days, so that they could be compared more easily, but 500 numbers are hard to make sense of. We are used, however, to understanding 'averages'. If you told your client that it was taking on average 25 days to invoice customers, and that this represented 25 days of 'free' credit, this would be evidence that the 'invoicing problem' was worth investigating.

Calculating the average is easy. You add all the values in your sample (assume the total in this case was 12,500 days) and divide by the number (here 500) of values that you added. This gives you the average. It is a really useful 'statistic' because everyone knows what an 'average' is, and can understand what it means. The average is often referred to as the *mean*, or more correctly the *arithmetic mean*. In order for averaging to make sense, you require interval or ratio data.

The **average** or **(arithmetic) mean** of a set of measurements is the total of all the measurements divided by the number of measurements taken.

Since this is such an easy way of summarising a set of figures, why might you need any other ways of doing it? One reason might be that the measures are *ordinal* rather than *interval* data. You will remember that it only made sense to add measures if the intervals between numbers were the same. If your numbers represented points on an ordinal rather than interval scale, it would be inappropriate to add them. The other reason might be that the numbers have a strange *distribution*. Distributions become really important when you try to work out the statistical significance of differences between sets of numbers, so there will be more about them in the next chapter. For now, imagine that instead of looking at 500 invoices you are doing a small pilot study and looking at 10.

It is often helpful to play with a small quantity of your early data to see the sorts of questions it raises and those that it answers. You may find that a simple change in the way you are recording your data might make it easier to answer some of these questions, or that you are not recording something that would help you make a great deal more sense of the data which you are collecting. Interpreting data from a pilot study can suggest improvements in methods.

Imagine that in this small pilot sample the number of days taken to generate the invoice was: 1, 15, 147, 14, 18, 14, 15, 15, 17, and 15.

Looking at these numbers it seems typically to take around 15 days to raise an invoice. On one occasion it was much faster, on another occasion very much longer indeed – apparently all the paperwork went missing for some reason and the client did not query the absence of an invoice until the accountant asked about it at year end.

If you average these figures, you get 27 days. Is this a reasonable 'average' of the time to send an invoice? Mathematically, it is accurate. But does it convey a fair picture? This is a difficult question to answer: it will depend partly on what you plan to do with the average, and partly on the nature of the sample. If the paperwork goes missing roughly every tenth order, it might be fair. If this is the only time in the company's history it has happened, the 'average' would be misleading. There will be more in the next chapter on sampling error, but meanwhile it is an indication of why 'averaging' numbers with one wildly different value may be misleading, and why other ways of showing the central point in the distribution may be more useful. The two other widely used measures of central tendency are the mode and the median.

Look at the distribution above. You have four occasions when it took 15 days to despatch an invoice, two where it took 14 days, and only one occasion for each of the other values. Another way of summarising a set of figures is to take the value which occurs most often. This is called the *mode*. The mode of the 10 values above is 15. If it occurs most often, there is some sense in seeing it as the most 'typical' value in a data set, and therefore a good summary figure. It makes sense to talk of the mode of a set of ordinal data as well as of interval ratio data.

 The **mode** of a set of numbers is the number that occurs most frequently in the set.

For the 10 figures given above, the mode would be a reasonable way of describing a 'typical' invoicing time. But suppose there were two sorts of invoices – the very simple ones and the more complicated. The very simple can be dealt with very quickly, the others normally take about 15 days. In the sample above there was only one 'easy' one, but suppose you had happened to sample three easy ones, and the harder ones were more varied. The times in your sample were therefore 1, 1, 1, 12, 14, 15, 15, 16, 19, and 147.

The mean would be 25 – not all that different from that of the original set of numbers. But the mode instead of being 15 would be 1. How representative would this be of the sample as a whole?

I have ordered the set of numbers above in ascending size order. This makes it easy to see that there is another possible 'middle' or central value – that which occurs in the middle of the list when the values are ordered according to size. This value is called the *median* value. If there had been 11 numbers in the ordered list, the middle number would be the sixth (with five lower and five higher). Here there are 10 numbers, so the 'middle' is the average of the two middle numbers – in this case the fifth and the sixth. These are 14 and 15, so the median value of the numbers above is the average of 14 and 15, or 14.5.

The median value makes sense for ordinal and interval data, as well as ratio. It gives some weight to 'outlying' or extreme values, but this weight is according to how many of them there are, rather than their absolute value.

 The **median** of a set of numbers is the number that occurs at the middle point of the list (or the average of the two middle numbers) when the list is ordered by size.

You can see that the most useful indicator of the central point in a set of data depends upon both the nature of that data set and what you want to do with it. If you are using Excel to analyse your data, you can automatically generate the mean, median and/or mode of the data you enter into the spreadsheet. You should now know which you want to use.

RANGE

Measures of central tendency such as mean or mode offer one way of summarising a set of figures. Another way of providing a snapshot focuses not on the centre of the distribution but on its extent. The distance between the largest and smallest value is the *range*. It can be useful to know what range figures are likely to fall within. If you are designing a car seat, for example, or a kitchen worktop, it is helpful to know the tallest and the shortest person for whom you are likely to have to design. But as with the sets of numbers above, you may have a problem with rare and outlying figures. Very occasionally you will encounter a person as short as 90 cm or as tall as 2.4 m. If you are a car designer you could, in theory, design a seat sufficiently adjustable to accommodate both. But this would be extremely expensive. Rather than describing the full range of a set of numbers, it is common to describe it in terms of some proportion. A common one is the *inter-quartile range*. The idea of a quartile is an extension of that of the median. The mid-point between the lowest figure and the median is the first quartile, the mid-point between the median and the highest number is the third quartile. The inter-quartile range is the distance between these two quartiles. You can see that half of the values in the set of numbers will lie within this inter-quartile range. It is therefore a useful way of summarising one aspect of your set of numbers.

For practical design purposes this would be too restrictive. While it would be unreasonable to expect a kitchen or car seat designer to suit every possible purchaser, it would be somewhat restrictive to suit only half of them. Designers therefore often design for 'the 95th percentile'. You can probably work out what this means. If you took a large and representative sample of the population for whom you were designing and ordered your sample by size, and identified the smallest 1% of numbers, the first percentile would be the value of the biggest of these. And if you counted back from the biggest values until you had passed 5% of your measures, you would have reached the 95th percentile. Traditionally, ergonomists have designed to satisfy this middle 90% of people.

CONSIDER...

Go back to the 'time to invoice' example. Would the average (or median or mode) and range (or inter-quartile range) provide an adequate summary of your findings, and sufficient evidence upon which to base decisions?

It is likely that although these figures would be useful, they would be only a beginning. You might be able to make an argument that times and variability were such that it looked as if there might be substantial scope for improvement and estimate credit days saved if the mean were reduced by a certain amount. But this would be only a start. What additional questions might you want to use your data to answer? (Remember, time was only part of your data.)

An immediate additional question is whether there might be a relationship between the time and the value of the invoice. The time to invoice is not in itself significant. It is relevant information, but has to be interpreted in the light of other data to become more meaningful. Its impact upon the size of 'free' credit the company is offering is what matters. You could assess this by multiplying the average time by the average value of the invoice. (Both are ratio measures, so this is legitimate, provided the sample on which the averages are derived is reasonably representative.) But in the last example I suggested that more valuable invoices might take longer to process. If this were the case, multiplying the averages might underestimate the value of the free credit provided.

Look at a possible sample of invoice values and time taken to prepare them (Table 20.1). You can see that smaller invoices are associated with shorter preparation time.

A simple way of estimating what invoicing delays were costing you per year might be to work out the average delay per invoice and multiply by the average value of an invoice, and then multiply this average by the number of invoices generated in a year. Assuming (for simplicity's sake) you generated 1,000 invoices per year, multiplying average value by average time (from the table above) would give an estimation for $days of credit offered of 181,478. (You would then have to multiply this by current interest rates to estimate the value of this provision.) On the face of it, this seems perfectly reasonable.

But the final column shows the value of each entry, totals these, and this generates a very different average. This would suggest an annual $day cost of 399,100. This is significantly higher.

Table 20.1 Example of invoice values and the time taken to prepare them

Invoice number	Invoice value ($,000)	Number of days taken to invoice	Value × days (,000)
A771823	2.3	5	11.5
A786321	0.6	1	0.6
B330331	1.2	3	3.6
B707779	12.7	14	17.8
B710446	18.1	14	253.4
B900913	16.7	15	250.5
C004003	20.9	15	313.5
C117089	47.1	63	2,967.3
C704442	12.2	13	158.6
D123067	1.2	1	1.2
E556771	6.4	2	12.8
Total	124.3	146	3,991.2
Average	12.43	14.6	399.1

CONSIDER...

Which figure is 'right', and why? Might there be a better figure altogether to use?

Neither is absolutely 'right'. Your ten values are a sample, and they may be atypical of all the invoices generated during the year in question. You would have to know how they had been sampled to judge this, and even with the most careful sampling 'randomness' can occasionally mean that your sample differs significantly from the population as a whole. But there are good reasons for placing more confidence in the figure of 399, 100 than that of 181, 478.

The first figure would be a reasonable estimate if the delay and value were unrelated. But if there *is* a relationship, you lose a lot of information by working with separate averages. Multiplying two large figures gives a much larger figure. (Think of the way in which squares of numbers increase: 1, 4, 9, 16, 25, 36, etc.) The average of 1 to 6 is 3.5. The square of this is 12.25. The sum of the squares of 1 to 6 – ie of 1, 4, 9, … 36 – is 91, so the average value of x^2 is 15.2, already larger. The discrepancy would increase the more numbers you took. Try working it out for the numbers up to 10, if you want to check this for yourself. Play with some lists like this if you want to get a better feel for why multiplying averages might provide a poorer estimate than the average of each multiplied value.

However, neither might be the 'best' figure for estimating 'cost of the invoicing problem'. Time to pay will be longer when there is an error in the invoice. So where an invoice is queried, the time between delivery and despatch of a correct invoice would be a more useful figure upon which to base estimates of the cost of 'the problem'.

This example is intended to make you aware of just how careful you must be in drawing conclusions from even seemingly simple numbers. It is also a reminder that when you summarise numbers you are losing information.

KEY POINTS

- It can be helpful to 'summarise' a set of numbers by some indication of its central point and the extent to which numbers are spread around it.
- The most useful indicators to use will depend upon the nature of the numbers themselves and their distribution.
- In summarising a set of numbers, you lose information, and must be aware of the implications of this.

Suppose that you have established that further analysis is needed. The real question is not how much credit is currently being 'given' as a result of the invoicing system, but how much it could be reduced, and how. To address these questions you need data on the causes of errors and on reasons for time variability. Presumably, invoicing will always take some time, so the question is not how long it takes but how much less time it could take.

Let us assume that your preliminary work (discussions with stakeholders, review of customer queries, analysis of what was required in order to invoice correctly) had generated the following possible error categories (codes shown in brackets):

Item omitted (1)

Item duplicated (2)

Incorrect unit price (3)

Incorrect quantity (4)

Incorrect discount factor (5)

Incorrect customer address (6)

You can only count errors in those invoices (350/500) for which a purchase order is on file. For every invoice in which you find an error you enter your data into a table such as Table 20.2, using 1 to indicate a particular error was present, and showing the value of the invoice in the final column.

This table when complete contains over 200 rows – more than half of the invoices sampled contained errors when compared with the purchase order. But the table by itself is not particularly informative.

A number of obvious 'summary' statistics spring to mind, such as mean values for time and value or each error type, and total number of errors. What further meaning might you extract? Consider the full 500 values obtained in the audit for time taken to invoice. You could usefully summarise the information in terms of a number for the mean (or median or mode, if you preferred, although these are ratio data, so the mean would be justified, and with a sample this big, outlying values might have less of an impact). You might wish to supplement them with a figure for the range or inter-quartile range. But would these mere numbers have much impact upon your client? Many people might find a graphical representation carried more impact, allowing them to 'see' what was happening in a way that neither the raw numbers nor the summary statistics allowed.

Table 20.2 Example of incidence of error categories related to time and value

Invoice	Error 1	Error 2	Error 3	Error 4	Error 5	Error 6	Error sum	Time (days)	Value ($ooo)
A11763	1		1				2	31	257
A22491								19	377
A788665								5	48
A788788	1		1	1			3	15	221
A664121								5	35
B000542								72	379
B001823		1	1				2	14	100
B013567								16	60
B015621			1				1	55	279

CONSIDER...

If you were trying to understand 'the invoicing problem', what might you do with these numbers to make them seem more meaningful? What other numbers might you require?

GRAPHICAL REPRESENTATIONS

Summary statistics such as the mean or inter-quartile range can convey something useful about an array of numbers, but you lose a lot of information in the process. If you show the numbers in graphic form, you can convey quite a lot of information to most people, and any patterns in your results may be far easier to see.

You will find that experimenting with different ways of showing your numbers in 'pictures' can help you get a feel for what you are finding, and perhaps suggest analyses that you had not considered. When you come to report on your research, graphs can carry a lot of information, but will also increase the 'perceived value' of your product – an important consideration if you are hoping for further business from your client. Fortunately, even a basic spreadsheet will transform numbers into bar charts, pie charts or graphs; a statistical package such as SPSS will offer a wider range of options; and there are specialist graphics packages which allow for output of a higher visual quality. However, you have to know the purposes, advantages and disadvantages of different ways of presenting data if you are to 'tell the story' in the numbers as clearly as possible.

BOX (AND WHISKER) PLOTS

One neat way of conveying information about median, range and inter-quartile range at a glance is to use a box plot or 'box and whisker representation' (the label varies).

The box covers the inter-quartile range. It is divided vertically at the median, and has a 'whisker' extending the full range (or sometimes to the 10th and 90th percentile). If you wish, you can add an *x* to indicate the mean. Figure 20.1 shows three examples.

Figure 20.1 Examples of a box and whisker plot

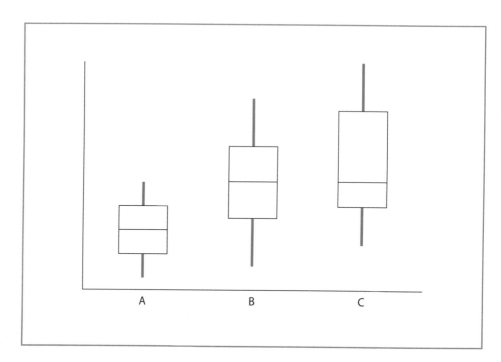

Figure 20.1 Examples of a box and whisker plot

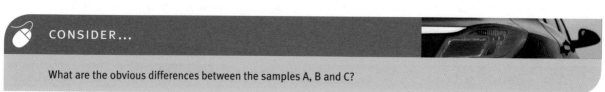

What are the obvious differences between the samples A, B and C?

You can see that the values in A are closely concentrated around the median, and seem to be fairly symmetrical in their distribution. The values in B are less concentrated, but still look symmetrical, albeit around a higher median value. Those in C have a similar median to B but are still more spread out and are clearly not symmetrical.

PIE CHARTS

You may be interested in the proportions of different categories in a sample. One popular way of showing proportions is a pie chart. The whole pie represents the sample. The slices show how much of the pie is made up of different categories. Figure 20.2 is an example.

You will note that although this gives an instant picture of the sort of breakdown, you have to refer to a key to see what each colour represents, and if you wanted an accurate figure you would have to look at the numbers themselves (shown beneath the chart). A pie chart gives a good impression of relative proportions, provided that there are not too any slices. Up to six is easy to read – much more becomes difficult. Very thin slices are also difficult to read. But the eye is not good at estimating the absolute size of a slice, so if this is important, a different form of chart would be better. Despite these limitations, pie charts are popular because of their attractive appearance and visual impact, and if care is taken to use them only for what they are good at, they can improve the presentation of your data.

Figure 20.2 Pie chart of respondents' length of service in their current jobs

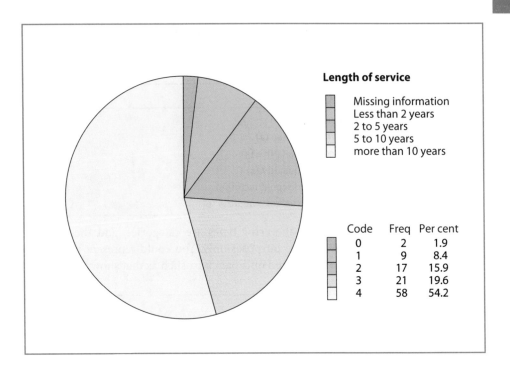

Length of service

Missing information
Less than 2 years
2 to 5 years
5 to 10 years
more than 10 years

Code	Freq	Per cent
0	2	1.9
1	9	8.4
2	17	15.9
3	21	19.6
4	58	54.2

BAR CHARTS AND HISTOGRAMS

Another easy form of graph to understand is the bar chart – a variant of a pie chart that represents the whole not as a circle but as a bar, with different colours or shading to represent the proportions of each category within the circle. If you wish to compare the composition of different categories in different sets of data, it is easier to do this with a series of bars than with a series of circles. Figure 20.3 shows an example.

Figure 20.3 Proportion of new and repeat sales for three products

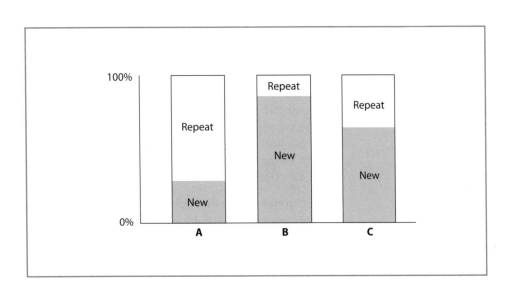

In 'percentage' bar charts such as that in Fig 20.3 the vertical scale always shows percentages, and the top of the scale – the length of all the bars – is 100%. The bars will be discrete, and will have to be clearly identified.

Many bar charts, however, will have other figures on the vertical (y) axis. Suppose that you were working with the invoicing problem above. In your pre-training sample you found:

Error categories	Number of errors
Item omitted (1)	75
Item duplicated (2)	60
Incorrect unit price (3)	42
Incorrect quantity (4)	38
Incorrect discount factor (5)	17
Incorrect customer address (6)	57

Note that the error types are categories, and the number allocated to each is for convenience purposes only. You could represent the frequency with which different errors occurred on a bar chart such as that shown in Figure 20.4.

Figure 20.4 Bar chart showing distribution of different error types

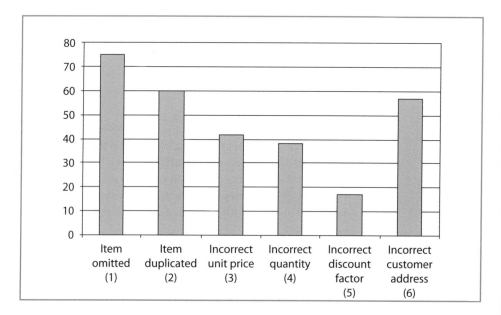

In Figure 20.4 (originally produced in Excel) the bars are shown as separate. This is good practice when drawing bar charts – the diagram is clearer and it makes it harder to assume (wrongly) that the categories are in any sense part of a 'scale'. Figure 20.5 shows a similar-looking chart, this time of the distribution of answers to a questionnaire item asking respondents to give an overall evaluation of a leadership programme they had experienced.

You will perceive that in this case the categories are not arbitrary. A score of 7 means something more than a score of 6, although you could argue whether the difference between scores of, say, 5 and 6 was the same as that between 9 and 10: this might be better treated as an ordinal scale. There is one exception to this ordinal scale that is potentially misleading. You will note that the statistical program used the code 'missing information' as zero. This is a nominal code, different in nature from the ordinal scores represented by the other bars. One potential disadvantage of this is that the eye interprets it in the same way, making the central point of the distribution appear more 'positive' than in fact it is.

Figure 20.5 Percentage distribution of responses to a question on the evaluation of a leadership programme

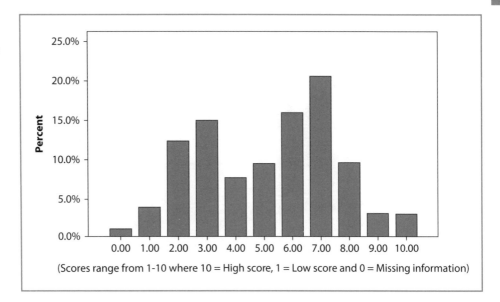

(Scores range from 1-10 where 10 = High score, 1 = Low score and 0 = Missing information)

Despite this disadvantage you can see that the numbers 'speak' more clearly as a bar chart than they do as Table 20.3 below.

Table 20.3 The figures from which the bar chart Figure 20.5 was drawn

Score	Frequency	Percent	Valid percent	Cumulative percent
0	1	0.9	0.9	0.9
1	4	3.7	3.7	4.7
2	13	12.1	12.1	16.8
3	16	15.0	15.0	31.8
4	8	7.5	7.5	39.3
5	10	9.3	9.3	48.6
6	17	15.9	15.9	64.5
7	22	20.6	20.6	85.0
8	10	9.3	9.3	94.4
9	3	2.8	2.8	97.2
10	3	2.8	2.8	100.0
Total	107	100.0	100.0	

You can also see that whereas a pie chart allows you to 'see' the proportion of the whole represented by any category, a bar chart makes it much easier to compare each category with the others.

Often you will have data where it makes sense to join the bars. If you are plotting frequencies using categories that are contiguous, a chart in which the bars are drawn without spaces between them give the best representation. This specific form of a bar chart is called a *histogram*.

Imagine that you are looking at the time to prepare invoices. All invoices are prepared within 20 working days. You decide to count the numbers of invoices taking less than 2 days to prepare, 2–3 days, 4–5 days, 6–7 days and so on, up to 18–19 days. You then show the frequencies you observe for each category of preparation time. Figure 20.6 shows what you might find.

Figure 20.6 Histogram showing the distribution of times taken to prepare invoices

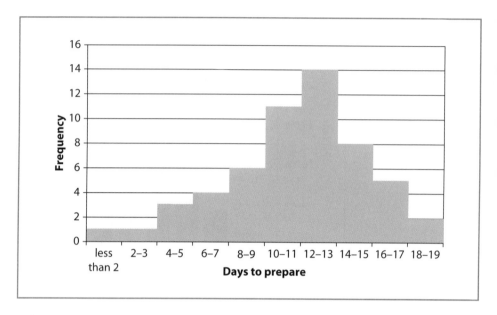

When drawing any form of bar chart you should normally start your vertical scale at zero. Variation in bar height will appear disproportionately large otherwise. There are several points you must remember when drawing a histogram. Firstly, you have to think carefully about the categories you use. Too few categories and the information conveyed may be reduced too far. Too many (and this will depend in part on how many observations you have) and patterns may be lost. Categories must be clearly defined. You could not, for example, have 1–2 days, 2–3 days, etc, because there would be ambiguity about classifying all your 2s. Categories must cover the full scale. It would be misleading to show only 1–2, 5–6, 7–8, just because you had no observations between 2 and 5. Your scale would still have to include all the possible categories in order to be complete.

It is normally best to use equal-sized categories. This makes the 'meaning' of the histogram clearest. If you do want to include broader categories, perhaps because there are few observations at the ends of your scale, you would need to take care to make sure that the *area* of the bar had the same meaning as the area of other bars. So if you had combined all frequencies of 6 or less in the example above, thus creating a category three times the breadth of the other categories, you would have to divide the number of observations in this category by 3 so that the (fat) bar shown was as tall as the *average* of the heights that would have been shown in the three separate categories. Otherwise it would look as if there were more 'low' times than was the case.

Because a bar chart can be used in so many ways it is important to label your scales and categories clearly so that the meaning of the bars is plain. You also need a key to explain any colour coding used to distinguish bars or parts thereof. The significance, if any, of the order in which the bars are shown also has to be immediately obvious to the reader. As with any diagram, you need display a clear title explaining what the diagram is and, if possible, indicating what the reader is intended to make of it. The title 'Error rates' would for instance be much less help to the reader than the title 'Frequency of different error types before and after training'. Over-lengthy figure titles look untidy and lose their impact, so you require almost a poet's skill in choosing the minimum number of words to convey the important message of the diagram. Try to start from the viewpoint of the reader when deciding what information is likely to be needed to give the diagram maximum impact.

KEY POINTS

- Pie charts give a clear impression of proportions, if there are not too many 'slices'.

- Percentage bar charts may give a slightly less clear impression of proportions but allow easier comparison between different sets of data.

- Bar charts allow easy comparison of actual values in different categories of data. Bars are normally best separated.

- Histograms show the frequency of occurrence of values along a scale. The scale has to include all possible values, and if bars are of different width, the height must be adjusted accordingly.

- Bars on a histogram can usefully be shown without spaces between.

- Clear labelling of axes, a key showing any colour or other coding, and an informative title are essential if your diagram is to carry information to your reader.

GRAPHS AND SCATTER PLOTS

You will remember graphs from school, and will be familiar with them from publications such as *The Economist*. A graph consists of a series of dots, each representing a pair of values, joined by a line. (A scatter plot is the dots without the line.) Research often involves looking at relationships between variables, either by measuring them as they already exist or by deliberately changing one variable and measuring its impact upon something else. The thing you changed (called the *independent variable*) was often called *x*, and the thing that it affected (the *dependent variable*) was called *y*. Traditionally in plotting a graph the *y* axis is the vertical one, and the *x* axis is the horizontal one ('*x* is a-cross').

Suppose you wanted to look at how production cost varies with volume produced. For any volume (*n*) of production you can calculate costs using the simple formula:

Total costs = Fixed costs + Variable costs

And variable costs will be unit cost of production × number of units produced.

To take a ridiculously simple example, your fixed costs (FC) might be €200 and your variable costs (VC) €2 per unit. You can plot these on a graph as shown in Figure 20.7.

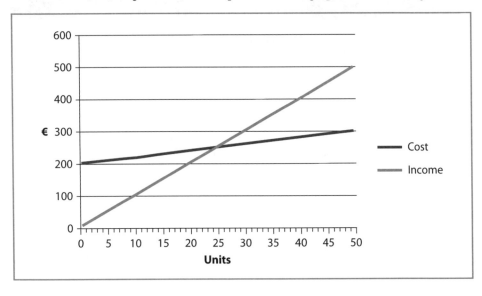

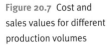
Figure 20.7 Cost and sales values for different production volumes

Now assume that you plan to sell your product at €10 per unit. You can also plot the value of sales (VS) against number sold. The point at which these two lines cross is your break-even point. You can see from the graph where this occurs. You could also work it out mathematically. It will be the n for which VS = Total costs.

VS is $10n$, so this gives you the equation:

$$10n = 200 + 2n, \qquad \text{or } 8n = 200, \qquad \text{or } n = 25$$

This was easy, but for more complicated simultaneous equations a graph can sometimes be the easiest way of reaching a solution.

In practical research it is more likely that you would want to look at trends or to plot your observations from a natural or designed 'experiment'.

Part of your diagnosis of a situation might involve looking at whether things are changing over time, and if they are, in what direction. Have sales of different products been going up or going down? How have profit margins on these different product lines been changing? Graphs offer the clearest way of showing any trends. You can go further than this and make rudimentary forecasts by assuming that any trends will be continued.

Suppose that you have the following figures for percentage profit margins for three products (A, B and C) over the last eight quarters (Q1–Q8).

	Q1	Q2	Q3	Q4	Q5	Q6	Q7	Q8
A	12	12	10	11	10	10	7	8
B	50	53	56	60	66	65	69	67
C	20	16	17	10	21	18	13	11

By plotting figures such as these over time, as shown in Figure 20.8, you can often see any trends and make tentative predictions.

 CONSIDER...

What do you think the likely profit magins will be over the next four quarters? How confident would you be in your forecasts?

It would be tempting fate to forecast the next year on the basis of only two years' data, although a reasonable guess might suggest figures somewhere between 10 and 6 for the next two quarters for Product A and between 66 and 70 for Product B. It would be seriously unwise to make any guesses at all about C, because there is so much variability in the figures. The next chapter looks at possible ways of showing trends that might allow you to make better guesses – and to know how much confidence to place in your estimates.

Figure 20.8 shows existing data. But you may wish to create data by changing things and seeing what effect it had. Suppose you feel that you might be able to increase the

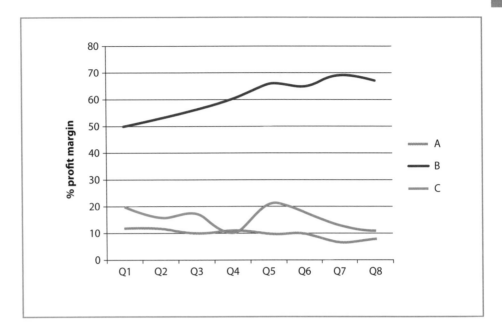

running speed of a machine but are worried about a potential increase in error rates. You decide to run the machine at different speeds, sample some of the output, and look at the error rate in your sample. Assuming everything else was constant, any change in error rates could reasonably be attributed to machine speed.

Suppose (and these data are intended to make a point rather than be realistic) you got the following results:

Day	1	2	3	4	5	6	7	8	9	10
Speed	30	65	40	75	45	60	55	35	70	50
Errors	6	18	3	12	8	11	10	5	15	9

Remember, the variable you are deliberately altering – the independent variable – is traditionally represented on the horizontal or *x* axis, and the thing you were observing or dependent variable – in this case the error rates – on the *y* axis. For each day you find the point on the grid which corresponded to the speed and error rate observed as shown in Figure 20.9.

 ACTIVITY

Replot the data using speed as your *x* axis and error rate as the *y* axis. What would be your reaction to this (and to Figure 20.9) as evidence that increasing operating speed created errors?

You should of course be cautious about any conclusions drawn from such a limited set of data. Your next reaction might have been that although on the whole error rates go up with speed, the relationship is far from perfect, and you might therefore wonder whether it really existed or was due to sampling error. (The next chapter will explain that the greater the variability in the population, and the smaller the sample, the less you can rely on the sample to be representative.) If you were going to make firm recommendations about speed, you might want to gather more data. You could repeat the exercise with a larger sample, or perhaps extend the period so that you had data from more days for each running speed. If you were working with one machine and one operator, who might be more or less healthy and/or hungover on different days, this would be a good idea.

Figure 20.9 Error rates and operating speeds over 10 days

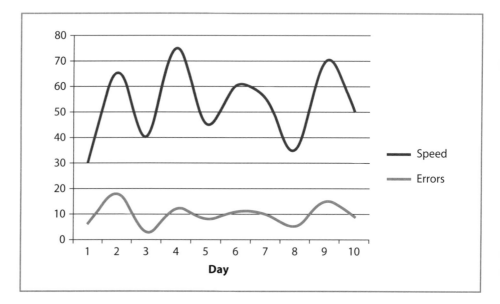

If you did obtain a number of different samples for each speed, how might you show the results? Two options are immediately possible. You might work out the average error rate at each speed and plot this average for each speed. Or you might plot all the values at each speed as a *scatter plot*. Figure 20.10 shows an example. You can see that it is messier than a plot of the averages, but contains more information. The tidy plot would not show you how much variability there was in your data, and the next chapter will make it clear that this variability is an important factor in deciding upon the significance of your findings.

Figure 20.10 Scatter plot showing error rates at different operating speeds

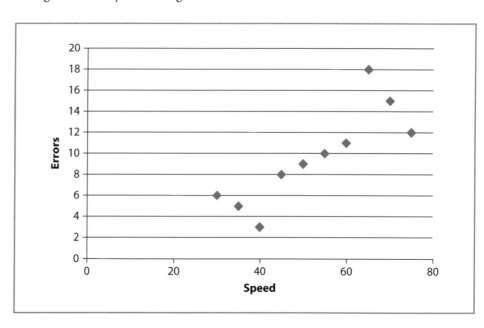

When drawing graphs you need to be careful of several things if they are to tell as clear a story as possible. Firstly, as with all graphics, you need a clear title and clear labelling (of axes, lines and any coding used). Secondly, you need to think carefully about the scale you use. Your aim is to convey a message clearly but without misleading.

> **All graphs need a clear descriptive title and clearly labelled axes. You must also insert a key to any symbols used.**

Choice of scale is important. Although it is not always necessary to start your axes at zero, you must make it very clear if you have not done this. It is possible to choose axes in ways that magnify differences unreasonably. Suppose you wanted to show how your department's error rate had decreased since you took over. Error rates for the year you have been there have averaged 20.2% For the previous two years they were 20.5% and 20.6%. If you started your scale at 20, you could draw a graph suggesting your arrival had produced a dramatic decrease. But this would probably be misleading. If you failed to show the values of the y scale, it would definitely be misleading. In most circumstances 20.2% would still be a worryingly high error rate. However, it might be that small variations like this have huge implications, and in this case simply presenting a graph with the y axis starting at zero could minimise any significance of the apparent change: the line would appear to be almost flat.

SUMMARY

Numbers may be used to represent different aspects of data. What the numbers mean will depend upon their relationship to each other, and this will limit what you can sensibly do with the numbers. You need to know whether they represent positions on an ordinal, interval or ratio scale, or are arbitrary.

Sets of numbers do not 'speak clearly' to most people. It may help to summarise key aspects of the numbers such as the mid-value or the extent of the variation. Simple summaries of the 'centre' of the set are the mode (the commonest number), the median (the middle largest number) and the arithmetic mean or average number. Simple summaries of elements of the dispersion of the numbers are the range (spread from largest to smallest) or the inter-quartile range (the spread encompassing the middle half of the numbers when ordered by size). Summarising in this way, while helpful, loses a lot of the potential information in the numbers; it is important to be aware of this when drawing conclusions from summary measures.

Graphical representations can allow a similar ease of understanding while retaining all or most of the information. They are easy to produce from Excel or a similar package but you have to choose appropriate charts for your purpose. Pie charts or percentage bar charts are good for showing relative proportions of a whole. Bar charts are good at showing how values vary from group to group. Bars are normally best separated. Histograms, in which bars are better joined, can be used to plot frequencies of values. Graphs or scatter plots can be used to show how one value varies or is related to another.

When presenting data graphically it is important to be careful to choose scales that convey the information clearly and without misleading.

Review questions

1. What is the main point of trying to find ways of representing your quantitative data other than as mere sets of numbers?

2. What is the advantage of summarising your numbers in some way, and what is the price you pay for this?

3. What do you most need to avoid?

4. What different types of data should you distinguish, and why is the distinction important?

5. What are the main ways of describing the 'centre' of a set of data, and what are the relative advantages and disadvantages of each?

6. What information does a box and whisker plot communicate?

7. When might a percentage bar chart be preferable to a pie chart?

8. What is a histogram?

9. When would you want to have spaces between the bars on a chart, and when would you want bars to adjoin, and why?

10. Why is it important to consider the scale you use on a graph?

11. What should you include in any graph you use in a report?

Explore further

Morris, C. (2008) *Quantitative Approaches in Business Studies*, 7th edition. Harlow: Pearson Education. Gives more detailed information on representing numbers, and on doing it in Excel

http://www.ted.com/index.php/talks/hans_rosling_shows_the_best_stats_you_ve_ever_seen.html for a fascinating (and entertaining) lecture given by Hans Rosling in 2006 showing how graphs can be used to tell the story in the numbers. The context is global health, but the messages about representing data are universally applicable

http://www.statcan.gc.ca/edu/power-pouvoir/ch12/5214889-eng.htm for further information on box plots

 Visit www.cipd.co.uk/brm for web links, templates, activities and other useful resources relating to this chapter.

CHAPTER 21

Inferential Statistical Analysis

INTRODUCTION

If you summarise your numerical data and present them in ways that make it easy for readers to 'see' what they mean, you will already have achieved a lot in terms of making sense of your findings. But it is easy to draw misleading conclusions from beautifully presented data. The problem is chance. Seemingly obvious messages in your data may have resulted purely from chance variation. To know how much faith to place in the conclusions you draw from 'obvious' features in your data, you have to be able to estimate the likelihood that such patterns would emerge by chance alone. The branch of mathematics called inferential statistics is designed to enable you to do this.

Practical business research frequently involves drawing conclusions from one or more relatively small samples about a larger population. You may want to estimate features of that larger population, or to test a more general hypothesis on the basis of your samples. Thus you may be hoping to estimate or look for differences between groups, or look for associations between variables. In order to know how much confidence to place upon any conclusions you draw, you need statistics. Statistical tests are designed to help you estimate both the size of an effect and its likelihood of arising by chance.

Some of the statistical tests that have been devised are relatively simple to apply using nothing more than a calculator and the relevant statistical tables. Slightly more complex ones are also easy using Excel or similar spreadsheet software because the functions are built in. For more sophisticated techniques, use a specialist statistical package such as SPSS or Minitab (although learning the package may take a little while). Thanks to IT it is now relatively easy to carry out complex analyses of your data. Unfortunately, such analyses can produce credible but highly *untrustworthy* conclusions unless you understand what you are doing. A common flaw in dissertations is the inappropriate use of statistical tests.

This chapter cannot make you an expert in statistics. What it aims to do instead is to introduce some of the key concepts involved.

In introducing those key concepts, this chapter should help you understand what a statistical test is actually doing, and therefore enable you to choose and use statistics appropriately, where you have the ability, and to know when to seek further help. This should ensure that you avoid going beyond your level of statistical competence: it is highly inadvisable, and arguably unethical, to use statistical tests unless you understand what you are doing.

The chapter therefore discusses the ideas of probability and statistical significance, and links these to ideas about populations from which you are sampling. This will help you to understand, and correctly interpret, the statistical significance levels which your tests will provide. It explains the difference between parametric and non-parametric tests and when to use each, and briefly describes the common parametric tests for association and difference. The chi-squared test is used as an exemplar of how statistical testing works, and sources are suggested for more sophisticated tests should you want them.

LEARNING OUTCOMES

This chapter should enable you to:

- define *probability* and appreciate its importance when interpreting quantitative data

- correctly interpret a *statistical significance* level, and assess its role in hypothesis-testing

- appreciate the meaning and significance of *distribution*, and of the *normal distribution*, and calculate the variance and standard deviation of a set of values

- identify the issues involved in testing for differences between samples, and choose an appropriate test for the significance of such differences

- assess the issues involved in testing for associations and causal links, and choose appropriate statistics to estimate the size of associations and test their significance

- find a line to fit sequenced data if this is appropriate to your research

- use statistical tests appropriately to draw trustworthy conclusions from your statistical analysis.

PROBABILITY AND STATISTICAL SIGNIFICANCE

Odd things happen by chance, probably more often than you imagine. You might think it a weird coincidence if you find someone at a party who shares your birthday. You might find it equally weird if you pulled 10 odd socks out of the drawer before you found a pair (assuming you have 10 or more pairs of socks in the drawer, and are selecting without looking). Your quantitative data may throw up similarly striking results. The sock phenomenon is not impossible: very occasionally it would happen. You need to know whether the patterns you see in your results just happen to represent a similar 'freak' occurrence. Tests of statistical significance tell you how confident you can feel that they are not due simply to chance. To understand quite what statistical significance means, you first need to understand the idea of probability.

PROBABILITY

Probability theory applies in any situation where the outcome is uncertain, but where a particular outcome will occur in a fixed proportion of the time in the long run. Here, an outcome is one possible result of the experiment or trial. The outcomes need not necessarily be *equally* likely, but just one of them will occur. In the case of the socks, a trial might consist of taking one sock from the drawer; each individual sock represents an outcome. An event is any combination of outcomes in which you are interested.

'Probability' in this chapter is very close to its everyday meaning: the chance or likelihood of a particular event occurring, or the proportion of times it will occur in a long series of trials. It is expressed as a fraction from 0 to 1. A probability close to zero means that the event is incredibly unlikely to occur; 0 means that it is impossible. A probability of 1 means an outcome is certain; near 1 that it is very, very likely. If you consider the probabilities of *all* the possible outcomes you could get, they must add up to 1 – after all, if these *are* all the possibilities, you are certain to get one of them. In the case of the socks, consider the simpler case of four pairs of socks in the drawer. Each sock is thus an outcome with a probability of ⅛. If four of the socks are red, then drawing a red sock is an event with probability ⅘ = ½. If the other four are black, there is similarly a probability of ½ that you will get a black sock. There is a probability of ½ + ½ (ie it is certain) that you will get either a red sock or a black sock.

We are fairly poor at guessing at probabilities unaided, and it is customary to use methods to help. Think back to the earlier sock and party 'improbability' exercises. Depending upon the number of people at the party (or the number of unpaired pairs of socks in your drawer) neither outcome might be all that improbable.

 CONSIDER...

Imagine that you have four (different) pairs of socks loose in your drawer. You pull out one sock at a time. How many times in a hundred do you think you would have to pull out five socks before you had a pair?

There are 23 people at the party. How likely do you think it is that two of them will share a birthday?

If you gamble, you will be familiar with thinking about probabilities, and probably worked out the answers easily. If not, it may help to explain how these probabilities can be calculated. In each case it involves working out how many sorts of results would be this extreme, and multiplying the probabilities of the different events which must happen to produce the outcome you are interested in.

If you play board games which involve throwing dice, you are presumably happy with the idea that if the dice are fair, each face has an equal chance of landing upwards, so you have a one in six chance of throwing any single number. If you throw two dice there are 36 different possible 'results' or outcomes, and only one of these is a double six, so your chance of throwing a double six is $\frac{1}{36}$ (the number you get when you multiply the probability of throwing a six first time by the probability of throwing it the second time).

In the case of the four pairs of socks, how many possible choices will not result in a pairing until the fifth sock emerges? And how many choices are there altogether? You have eight ways of choosing your first sock, six ways of choosing a second that does not match it, four ways of choosing a third, and two ways of choosing a fourth odd sock – ie $8 \times 6 \times 4 \times 2 = 384$.

If you were simply choosing eight socks without caring whether they match or not, you can choose the first in eight ways, the second in seven ways, etc. This works out at 1,680 different ways. So the probability is 0.23. (If you want to work out the probability of choosing 10 odd socks when you have 20 different pairs in your drawer, use the same logic. You should find that the answer is around 0.005, or half a per cent – ie it would still happen once in 200 times. So, weird it might be, but far from impossible.)

ACTIVITY

If you do *not* pull out four socks before finding a pair, you must have found a pair on the second, third or fourth sock. Work out the probability of each of these 'events' and add them to the probability of getting no matches. These are all the possibilities. Check that the probabilities add to 1.

For the slightly more complicated party, you approach this by finding the probability that no one shares a birthday with anyone else. The probability that at least two people share will be 1 minus the probability that no one shares. Select two people. There is a $\frac{1}{365}$ chance that the second one has the same birthday as the first, and a $\frac{364}{365}$ chance that it is different. (We are assuming no one has a birthday on 29 February in a leap year.) The third person will have $\frac{363}{365}$ chance of having a different birthday from either of the first two, the fourth a $\frac{362}{365}$ chance, and so on. If you keep going until you hit the last person in the room, they will have a $\frac{343}{365}$ chance of having a birthday different from all the others. For no one to share a birthday, each must have been different, so you multiply all these probabilities together: $\frac{364}{365} \times \frac{363}{365} \times \frac{362}{365} \times \ldots \times \frac{343}{365}$. You should find that there is a roughly even chance that two people in the room will share a birthday.

Another thing that often surprises people is the likelihood of two of the six numbers in the UK National Lottery being consecutive. Again there is a roughly even chance of this. Yet fewer people will pick consecutive numbers, so if they do come up you will probably have to share the prize with fewer people. A good strategy is therefore to pick some of the numbers at least (if not all) as consecutive. That is, of course, if you think it is worth investing in something where your chance of winning is something like 1 in 17 million.

As a final test of your grasp of the concept of probability, imagine that you have won a prize on a game show and are shown three doors. Behind one of the doors is a car, behind the other two are goats. (I assume that you want the car rather than a goat.)

You choose a door. The host Monty Hall (who knows where the car is) opens another door and shows you a goat. He asks if you want to change your choice to the other unopened door.

CONSIDER...

Should you stick with your original choice, or change to the other door?

The common mistake is to assume that when one door is open, it is equally likely that the car is behind either of the other two doors, so you might as well stick with your original choice. In fact, you double your odds of getting a car by switching. Imagine that you play the game many times. About one-third of the time you will choose the door with the car behind it; then clearly you win if you stick. The other two-thirds of the time, the car is not behind your door (this fact does not change when Monty Hall opens a door), and it is not behind the open door, so it must be behind the remaining door, and you win if you switch.

These are simple examples, where the probabilities of specific events are known. But you probably still had to think twice about how to work out the probabilities of combinations of events, and may have been surprised by what they actually were. Deciding what your research results mean may be rather more difficult. And yet if your conclusions are to be trustworthy it is important both that you recognise the import of your findings and that you do not overstate their significance. The area of statistical testing provides ways of doing this.

STATISTICS AND HYPOTHESES

It is all very well thinking about socks and dice and birthdays as a means to understanding probability, but you have to go beyond this and think about why you want to use statistical tests in practical business research.

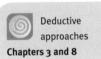
Deductive approaches
Chapters 3 and 8

A key use is for hypothesis-testing. You will remember that in a deductive approach you derive hypotheses and then collect data to enable you to test them. The full procedure is outlined below. This reinforces the point made in Chapter 9 that you must think about analysis at the data-planning stage. It also shows what you have to be able to do to use statistics effectively, appropriately and ethically to test hypotheses.

The steps in hypothesis-testing are:

- Formulate your null and alternative hypotheses, H_0 and H_1.
- Decide on an appropriate statistical technique and test statistic.
- Decide on the level of significance you want (more on this shortly).
- Work out the test statistic and use tables to see whether it reaches the significance level you specified.
- Decide whether or not to reject the null hypothesis.
- Relate this decision to your research question, and draw conclusions.

Thus you might have a null hypothesis similar to one of the following:

The training programme has not improved individuals' performance.

Marketing spend has not increased sales.

There is no association between selection test score and subsequent performance.

There is no association between employee commitment and customer satisfaction.

The change initiative has had no impact upon employee satisfaction or unit cost of service provision.

You want to decide whether or not your results are consistent with the null hypothesis. What is the likelihood that if the null hypothesis is true, you would get results such as yours purely by chance? A note of caution is in order here. These hypotheses relate to things which are far more complicated than socks and dice and birthdays. This is why you need something far more complicated than the sorts of calculations outlined above. Statistics provide this.

Before thinking about different statistical tests that will help you answer this question, it is important to understand the ideas on which they are based. The idea of statistical significance is perhaps the most basic of these.

STATISTICAL SIGNIFICANCE

When your data shows an association between two variables, or a difference between two groups, you want to know whether this is just a chance happening. Statistical tests will tell you how likely it is that your result is due to chance. If you read academic research papers which collect and analyse quantitative data in order to test hypotheses, you will find p values quoted for different results. These will usually be small, such as $p < 0.05$, or $p < 0.01$, or even $p < 0.001$. This indicates a probability (p) less than the figure stated that a difference (or association) this big or bigger could arise by chance alone. Thus $p < 0.05$ indicates a probability of less than one in 20, $p < 0.001$ means less than one in a thousand.

Many journals will accept papers where results are significant at the 5% level. Yet you will find many papers where whole arrays of figures are presented, only some of which are significant. You might want to consider what proportion reach this significance level, given the likelihood that $\frac{1}{20}$ will be that 'significant' purely by chance! You might also consider the implications of accepting 5% as the threshold when any results 'less significant' will not have been submitted for publication. Remember: 1 in 20 experiments will reach this level by chance!

RESEARCH ILLUSTRATION

Suppose that you want to assess the impact of a training intervention on error rates in invoices generated. You measure error rates in the month after the course for the trainees and for a comparable group who have not yet gone on the course. (If you knew the error rates before the trainees went on the course, you might have chosen this as the basis for comparison, or if you knew the overall error rates you might have compared ex-trainees with the whole population of invoice staff.) Suppose the control group made an average of 20 errors each, while the ex-trainees made on average only 18 errors. A statistical test suggests that the difference between these two sets of figures is 'significantly' different, with a $p < 0.05$.

Does this finding prove that the training was effective?

This result means that *if both samples were drawn from the same population* you would get a result like this less than one in 20 times. If training had no impact, the trainees *would* be part of the same population – ie their rates would be indistinguishable from those who had not gone on the course. If you had found a *p* greater than 0.05 you might be unconvinced that the training had had any impact. But most people might be prepared to accept that once in 20 is a reasonable cut-off, and therefore be willing to accept that the training has probably had an impact in this case. Note, however, that it has not been proved to be effective. It could still have been a chance finding, even though this is moderately unlikely: things this unlikely still happen, albeit only 5% of the time. And note that this only says that the result is unlikely – not that it is commercially significant. Depending on the cost of the training you might or might not feel that the error reduction was worth the cost of the training.

A *p* value of 0.05 or less is usually referred to as *statistically significant*. If the *p* value is smaller – say, $p < 0.01$ – you can feel more confident that the populations sampled were genuinely different. A difference this big would arise only once in 100 times by chance alone. The size of the *p* denotes the *level of significance*. Less, in this case, is more.

If you expressed your research question(s) in terms of testing a null hypothesis, you can see that a *p* value tells you how confident you can be in rejecting this. If you had formulated a null hypothesis

H_0: Training has no effect upon error rates

and found a difference significant at the $p < 0.05$ level, this would be reasonable grounds for rejecting the null hypothesis. In rejecting it, you are arguing that your results support your alternative hypothesis, that training *does* have an effect.

There are a number of things to be careful about when making such inferences.

Statistics don't prove anything

You will encounter claims that 'you can prove anything with statistics'. As suggested above, the reverse is true. Even a very high level of statistical significance does not *prove* that an effect was not due to chance. Unlikely things, by definition, occasionally happen. A statistically significant result does not *disprove* your null hypothesis. It merely tells you how likely or unlikely it is to be true. And your conclusions will always have a chance of being wrong if they depend only upon statistical significance. Because of the probabilistic nature of statistical testing, two types of 'error' or faulty conclusions are possible. Table 21.1 shows them.

Table 21.1 Types of error

	Null hypothesis true	Null hypothesis false
Reject null hypothesis	Type I error	Correct decision
Accept null hypothesis	Correct decision	Type II error

Traditionally, the probability of a Type I error is referred to as alpha (α), and the probability of a Type II error is referred to as beta (β). Since your H_0 relates to the absence of a difference or other effect, a Type I error means that you are wrongly identifying a significant effect, and a Type II error that you are failing to identity a real difference. If you reject a null hypothesis on the grounds that $p < 0.01$, then α is 0.01 – ie you have a 0.01 chance of making a Type I error.

The power of a statistical test is defined in terms of its likelihood of producing Type II errors – that is of failing to identify a 'real' effect as statistically significant: in other words, a false negative.

> **The power of a statistical test is $1 - \beta$, ie the probability of a correct rejection of a false null hypothesis.**

If you want to publish your results in an academic journal, you may wish to use the highest-powered test you can, because many journals do not publish research unless results are 'significant'. In a practical context the bigger danger may be false positives, leading to investment in something that is not in fact effective.

A brief introduction to Greek

Mathematicians use Greek letters a lot (you will already be familiar with this from using π (pi) at school. Because certain Greek letters are traditionally used for certain things in statistics, and you will find them used in a range of online resources, this chapter follows the normal convention. But for those who are not familiar with the Greek alphabet, here is the code that will be used in this chapter and which you will find used in many of the Web resources.

Greek letter	Lower-case form	Upper-case form	Use in this chapter
alpha	α		Probability of a Type I error
beta	β		Probability of a Type II error
mu	μ		The mean value of a variable in a population
rho	ρ		Pearson's correlation coefficient (often referred to as just 'the correlation')
sigma	σ		The standard deviation of a variable in a population
sigma		Σ	The sum of a number of values
chi	χ		The chi-squared test is a widely applicable non-parametric test

Statistical significance is precisely – and only – that

A p value does not indicate the *size* of an effect, nor indeed anything else that might contribute to its significance in business terms. A statistical significance level merely indicates how likely it is that a difference or relationship is due to chance variation. A very small difference between two samples could be highly statistically significant if your samples were large enough, although the commercial or other significance of the difference might be negligible. You may therefore also need to find reliable estimates of the size of a difference or association and/or its impact if you want to judge signifi-cance in other than statistical terms. For this reason you should always talk about *statistical significance*, rather than merely significance, if it is statistical significance that you mean.

Statistical significance will depend upon the size and variability of your sample(s)

Imagine you measured the error rates of five staff before and after a training programme. If the average error rate before was 20, and afterwards it was 15, the statistical signifi-cance of this effect would be greater if all were making 19–21 errors before and 14–16 after than if the range of scores ranged from 10 to 30 before and 5 to 25 after. In either case, if you had a similar spread with 100 staff rather than five, you would feel more confident that the difference was 'real', and indeed, the statistical significance of the difference would be greater.

The nature of your hypothesis affects significance levels

Some predictions are directional. Compare the two possible null hypotheses in the training case:

H_0: Training has no effect upon error rates

H_0: Training does not reduce error rates

CONSIDER...

What is the difference between these two hypotheses?

In the first case both an increase and a decrease in error rates would cause you to reject the null hypothesis, whereas in the second case only a *reduction* in error rate would cause you to reject it. A directional hypothesis allows something called 'one-tailed hypothesis testing' – this will be discussed shortly. For now, remember that direction-ality of a hypothesis is important.

KEY POINTS

- Probability refers to the likelihood of an event and can range from 0 to 1.
- Statistics do not 'prove' anything: you should be careful not to make such claims in your research.
- Statistical significance levels indicate the likelihood that a difference or association at least as big as the one observed would arise purely by chance.
- Statistical tests can generate Type I errors, where you wrongly identify an effect, and Type II errors, where you fail to identify one that exists.

DISTRIBUTIONS AND THEIR IMPORTANCE

We have already noted that the *distribution* of the variable you are interested in will affect the statistical significance of any differences or associations you observe. In

Histograms
Chapter 19

the invoicing example you could feel more confident about the difference in means when all rates were close to the mean than when they were scattered more widely. You will remember that you could show distributions using histograms. For a small sample the histogram will have clear 'steps', but where you have a very large sample, and very narrow categories your histogram will look much smoother. The bigger the sample and the narrower the categories, the more closely the histogram will resemble a smooth curve.

The normal curve

There is information on how a great many variables are distributed in nature. For people, you can find curves showing weight, height, IQ, blood pressure and so on for adult men or women in different countries, or for people in different age groups. You could find distributions of rainfall, or biomass, or temperature, or other distributions of frequencies relating to the natural world. In less natural contexts you might find distributions of errors in products or processes in an organisation. When you look at the distribution of many variables where you have very large samples, one 'shape' of curve occurs so often that it is called the *normal* curve (or sometimes the bell curve, because of its shape).

Figure 21.1 gives examples of normal curves.

Figure 21.1 Two examples of normal curves

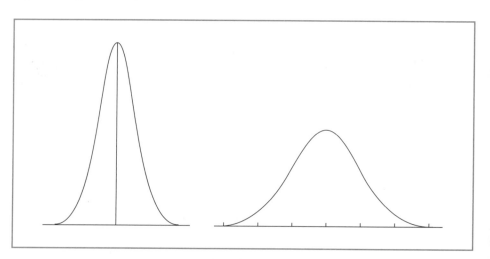

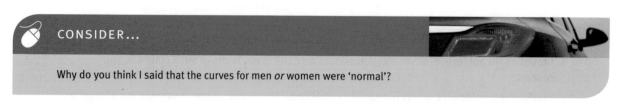

CONSIDER...

Why do you think I said that the curves for men *or* women were 'normal'?

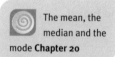
The mean, the
median and the
mode **Chapter 20**

You can see that for the curves in Figure 21.1 the mean, median and mode all fall at the same point. But think about heights for men and heights for women. Men tend to be taller. The mean height for men would therefore be to the right of the mean height for women. So if you drew one curve for both men and women you might well find that it had two peaks with a small dip in between – ie that it had two modes, or was *bimodal*.

Whenever you have the sum of a lot of small independent differences, you get a normal curve (because of something called the central limit theorem). Because it is so common, many statistical tests are based upon the properties of this normal curve. You can use these tests whenever it is reasonable to assume that the variable in which you are interested is normally distributed in the population from which your sample is drawn. Such statistical tests are called *parametric* tests: more about these shortly. There are a number of other distributions related to the normal curve which statisticians have studied (you will shortly encounter the chi-squared and t distributions) which form the basis for tests you can use with smaller samples or those that are not normally distributed. First, though, it is important to see why distributions have anything to do with statistical significance, and to look in particular at the normal curve in more detail.

In the previous chapter we talked about the *range* of a distribution, and defined the inter-quartile range as the range within which half the values in a sample lay. We went further and looked at percentiles. But these figures were ways of describing characteristics of an observed sample. They were 'real' in the sense of describing a specific aspect of a specific set of numbers. They carried some information, but some was lost.

The normal curve is a *theoretical curve*, the curve that you would expect to get if you had infinitely many measurements. Note that although the ends seem to hit zero, there is a vanishingly small gap between these and the *x* axis, reflecting an infinitesimally small (theoretical) probability of very extreme values. Obviously, in reality there may be limits: no matter how many nine-year-olds you measure you will never get one smaller or larger than certain values because the design of the human body would render this unsustainable. But because the discrepancy between real and theoretical distribution is so tiny, the curve is still a good fit.

Defining features of a normal curve

Two things are needed to identify a particular normal curve. The first thing is its central point – ie the *mean*, μ, of the population which the curve describes. If you measured 12-year-olds, the average height (if the curve is symmetrical this will be the point at which the curve peaks) will be greater than that for nine-year-olds. The second defining feature is the degree of variability around this mean. You might find that there was greater variability in your sample of 12-year-olds than among the nine-year-olds, because some of the older children had experienced the growth spurt associated with puberty while others had not. If so, the peak of the curve would be lower, and the spread wider, more like the second curve in Figure 21.1.

You may remember the instruction to average the height of bars in a histogram when amalgamating categories so as not to mislead the eye. This is because the area under any part of a histogram represents the number of observations falling within that range. The same is true of the area under a normal curve. If you draw a vertical line through the curve at any point, the area under the curve to the left of the line represents the number of observations equal to or less than the value of *x* where the vertical line hits the *x* axis.

And this is the root of the connection between the distribution and significance-testing. For a normal curve you can specify the equivalent of quartiles and percentiles in a real set of observations – that is, points above or below which a certain proportion of the sample can be expected to lie. These points are identified in terms of something called a *standard deviation*, which measures the variation about the mean. There is a simple formula for calculating this.

> **A normal curve is defined by two parameters: its mean and its standard deviation.**

There are infinitely many normal curves, but they all have effectively the same shape. By playing with the scales of the axes you can reduce them all to a singe 'standard' curve. This standard curve has a mean of 0 and a standard deviation of 1. Once you know the standard deviation and the mean of your curve you can 'standardise' it by expressing your 'x units' in standard deviations. You can then use tables for the standard normal curve to look up the probabilities that a value will fall a specified number of standard deviations from the mean.

CALCULATING A STANDARD DEVIATION

The standard deviation of a set of numbers is an indication of how much variability there is in the set. Excel will do the calculation for you, but if you know what the program is doing, it will help you understand what it is and what it means.

The standard deviation of a set of numbers is worked out from the distance between each number and the average or mean value of the set. Look at the following sets of numbers:

> Set A: 1 3 4 4 5 5 6 6 7 9
>
> Set B: 3 4 4 4 5 5 6 6 6 7

Both sets of numbers have an average value of 5, but the second set of numbers is much more tightly clustered about the mean than is the first. You could just subtract each number that is not the mean from the mean, but if you then added them you would get zero because the pluses and minuses would cancel each other out. It would be fairly simple just to ignore the minus signs and add all the numbers, and this would give you a measure of variation called the *mean absolute deviation*.

However, a (mathematically) more tractable way of turning negatives into positives is to square the differences because multiplying two negative values results in a positive value. (Imagine I 'took away' your overdraft twice – I would be *giving* you twice that much money . . .) Adding these squares would give you a positive figure that would increase as the variability in the numbers increased. The average of this sum of squares is called the *variance*. However, the variance is in different units from the measures because it is a square. So although you will find references to variance, its square root is more frequently used. This alternative measure of variability about a mean is called the *standard deviation*.

> **The standard deviation indicates the variability of observations about the mean.**

To work out the standard deviation of a set of observations you must:

- find the mean or average value of the set of observations
- work out the extent to which each number in the set deviates from this mean
- multiply each of these numbers by itself
- add these squares together, and divide by the number of observations
- take the square root of this.

The variance and standard deviations of a sample can be expressed (if you like equations) as the following formulas:

$$\text{variance: } s^2 = \frac{\sum_{i=1}^{n} (x_i - \bar{x})^2}{n}$$

$$\text{standard deviation } s = \sqrt{\frac{\sum_{i=1}^{n} (x_i - \bar{x})^2}{n}}$$

Thus for the numbers in Sets A and B above, the calculation would be as shown in Table 21.2. The value for the standard deviation appears at the end, shown as s.

(The calculation is shown to give you a feel for how it works. Excel or any statistical package will calculate this function for you, as well of course as calculating the mean value.)

Table 21.2 Calculations for variance and standard deviation of two samples (s_a, s_b)

Set A

x	x − mean	(x − mean)²
1	−4	16
3	−2	4
4	−1	1
4	−1	1
5	0	0
5	0	0
6	1	1
6	1	1
7	2	4
9	4	16
$\Sigma x = 50$		$\Sigma (x-\bar{x})^2 = 44$
$\bar{x} = 5$		
variance		4.4
s_a		2.10

Set B

x	x − mean	(x − mean)²
3	−2	4
4	−1	1
4	−1	1
4	−1	1
5	0	0
5	0	0
6	1	1
6	1	1
6	1	1
7	2	4
$\Sigma x = 50$		$\Sigma (x-\bar{x})^2 = 14$
$\bar{x} = 5$		
variance		1.4
s_b		1.18

It may be easier to work out the squares of each x and find the average of these squares, subtract from this the square of the mean value of x, and then take the square root of what is left. This will give you the same value as the 'averaging the differences' approach in the worked example above.

This alternative formula is:

$$s = \sqrt{\frac{\sum x^2}{n} - \bar{x}^2}$$

Work out the standard deviations for the above samples to check that this gives the same answer.

ESTIMATING POPULATION VALUES

Once you know the mean and standard deviation of a sample, you can use statistics based on the normal curve to make inferences about the population from which it is drawn. The mean and standard deviation of a sample are *actual values* which you can calculate. But you will often be interested in the mean or standard deviation of the population from which the sample was drawn. These you will have to *estimate* from the values in your sample. To make clear which you are talking about it is normal to call the actual mean value of your sample 'm' and the estimated mean value of the population by the Greek equivalent, mu (μ). Similarly, s indicated the sample standard deviation, but the Greek sigma (σ) is used to indicate the estimated population standard deviation.

The mean value of your sample is your best estimate for the mean value in the population (although you may want to indicate a range within which you are reasonably confident – say, 95% likely – that the actual population mean lies: more on this shortly). However, the variability of the larger population is likely to be slightly larger than that of your sample, so s does not provide the best estimate of σ. A better estimate of the standard deviation of the population divides by n – 1 rather than n to compensate for this.

Thus the best estimates for the population are:

$$\mu = m = \frac{\Sigma x}{n}$$

$$\sigma^2 = \frac{\Sigma(x - \bar{x})^2}{n - 1} \qquad \sigma = \sqrt{\frac{\Sigma(x - \bar{x})^2}{n - 1}}$$

You will remember that a normal curve was defined in terms of the mean/median/mode of the curve – the 'x' value of the highest point – and the fatness of the curve. The standard deviation is an indication of 'fatness'. The greater the standard deviation, the shorter and fatter the curve. For any set of normally distributed numbers the standard deviation allows you to identify key points on the x axis similar to percentiles or quartiles in a sample. Approximately 68% of the area under the normal curve lies between $-1\ \sigma$ and $+1\ \sigma$ of the mean. More usefully, approximately 95% of the area lies between $-2\ \sigma$ and $+2\ \sigma$, and approximately 99% lies between $-2.5\ \sigma$ and $+2.5\ \sigma$. (The more accurate figures are *1.96 σ* rather than 2, and *2.58 σ* rather than 2.5: you will see these figures appearing in calculations shortly.)

So you would have a probability of approximately 5% or 0.05 of obtaining a value more than 2 standard deviations from the mean, and approximately 1% or 0.01 of obtaining a value more than approximately 2.5 σ from the mean, and a probability of approximately 0.0027 of obtaining a value greater than 3 standard deviations from the mean. The importance of these figures lies in the concept of statistical significance.

5% of the area under a normal curve lies more than approximately 2 σ from the mean.

1% of the area under a normal curve lies more than approximately 2.5 σ from the mean.

The 'Six Sigma' title of a widely used statistically based approach to process improvement refers to this use of sigma. The lower case is significant. Pretty well all of the area under the curve lies within 6 σ of the mean. If your distribution is so tall and thin that this span is within the allowable range for your product or process – ie a 'fault' would occur in the area beyond 6 σ – you would have no more than three to four defects per million 'opportunities' for a defect. The argument is that if this were the case, you would not have a quality problem.

ONE TAIL OR TWO?

Figure 21.2 shows why the one-tailed or two-tailed distinction mentioned earlier is important. If you had decided on the null hypothesis that training made no difference, a higher or lower error rate might lead you to reject this hypothesis. So areas under the curve at both ends would be relevant. If your null hypothesis was that training does not reduce error rates, the area at only one end is relevant.

Thus a given difference would have half the probability of arising by chance on a one-tailed test as a two-tailed – ie it would be twice as significant, statistically speaking. In the one-tailed case, a smaller reduction in errors would lead you to reject the null hypothesis than it would take for a two-tailed test. Remember: with a normal curve, *approximately 95% of the area lies between –2 σ and +2 σ.* Thus if the difference was 2 σ it would be significant at the 5% level for a two-tailed test, and at the 2.5% level for a one-tailed test. (Tables of statistical significance are calculated using the real points for 95% and 99% rather than these approximations.)

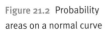
Figure 21.2 Probability areas on a normal curve

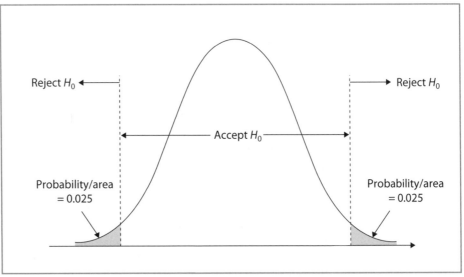

Source: Bee, F. and Bee, R. (2005) *Managing Information and Statistics*, CIPD; Fig. 17.1. Reproduced by permission

STATISTICS FOR ESTIMATING POPULATION VALUES

The idea of a distribution of values is really important when you are seeking to estimate aspects of a larger population from a sample. This is a common aspect of market research. Such estimates commonly relate to the sorts of things you were showing graphically in the last chapter: proportions, average values and variability of whatever you are looking at in the population in which you are interested. Although it is easy to show these for your *sample*, it is more of a problem to estimate with a specified confidence level the likely values in the *population* you sampled.

Suppose you asked 10 people in a Glasgow café their preferences between butter and a new margarine. Only two of them preferred the butter. You could (just about) then say that 80% of your sample preferred the margarine (although arguably this would imply a rather larger sample than you actually had). You could *not* say that 80% of Glaswegians prefer margarine, and it would be even less justifiable to draw conclusions about Scots in general. Even if you had carefully sampled a representative 100 Scots and 80 of them preferred margarine to butter, you could still not say with any confidence that 80% of Scots prefer margarine.

You might have more confidence that the population figure was around 80% in the second case because your sample was larger and selected at random. But even then the figure might be much lower or higher, depending on how 'unlucky' you were in your sample. (Remember the odd socks – you could theoretically have picked the only 80 people in the country to like margarine, although the chance of this would be vanishingly small.) However, the larger your sample, the more confident you can be of your estimates concerning the population from which the sample is drawn.

SAMPLING ERROR

You can see that it would be helpful to know how good your sample is: that is, how much difference there is likely to be between your sample and the population from which it is drawn. This is referred to as the *sampling error*.

 Sampling error is the difference between the (unknown) population value (that you are estimating) and the sample statistic (that you are using as the basis for your estimate).

Part of this might be due to bias: if you have adopted 'convenience sampling', then none of this is relevant to you. We are talking here about a properly randomly selected sample. (You will, of course, if planning to use statistical tests to help you draw conclusions about a wider population, have sampled in a 'proper' random fashion.) Here we are talking about error due to chance rather than bias.

If it is really important that your estimates are within a particular confidence level – for example, if you are planning substantial investment on the basis of your estimated values – you would need to take a repeated number of samples. This would allow you to calculate an average mean and standard deviation for your samples, from which you could estimate a confidence interval for your estimate. The process is based upon the central limit theorem in statistics referred to earlier, which states that for simple random samples of size n drawn from a population with mean and standard deviation μ and σ, the sample mean m will approach a normal distribution with the same mean as the population (μ) and a standard deviation (s) of $\sigma/\sqrt{n}$. (Your estimate of σ gets more accurate in proportion to $\sqrt{n}$.)

This enables us to say that you have a 95% chance that the true value of μ will lie in the interval from $m - 2.58\ \sigma$ to $m + 2.58\ \sigma$.

Because you do not know σ, you estimate it from your sample standard deviation s, and your confidence interval is from $m - 2.5s$ to $m + 2.5s$. (There is a subtlety here. You really need a confidence interval for σ as well. This is taken care of by the *t* test, shortly to be introduced.)

Alternatively,

$$\mu = \frac{\pm\,1.96s}{\sqrt{n}} \quad \text{with a 95\% probability.}$$

You can use this approach provided – and this is important – that

- the samples are sized 30 or more (unless you are pretty sure the value you are estimating is normally distributed in the population)
- you have simple (ie not stratified) random samples
- your population is big enough for removing your sample not noticeably to affect what is left.

For much practical research it will not be feasible to select multiple samples, but you might still want to give an indication of likely error. A simpler statistic estimates sampling error from a single sample. This is the standard error of the mean or proportion.

Standard error of the mean (SE_m) is calculated as follows:

$$SE_m = \frac{s}{\sqrt{n}}$$

where s is standard deviation of the sample.

The standard error is the distance within which we can be 95% sure that the population mean or proportion lies.

Software such as SPSS will calculate standard errors as a routine function, or there are websites which will perform the calculations for you.

In the Glasgow margarine survey the researcher was looking at proportions of the population. You can use the same approach as you would for a mean value if you simply score 1 for one answer (say, butter) and 0 for the alternative. The mean value will then represent the proportion saying (here) butter.

You can, if you prefer, use a similar but slightly different equation to estimate population proportions directly from the average proportion (p) found in your samples. Thus you can be 95% confident that the population proportion level lies within the range

$$\bar{p} \pm 1.96 \sqrt{\frac{\bar{p}(1-\bar{p})}{n}}$$

And in the case of a single sample,

$$SE_p = \sqrt{\frac{p(1-p)}{n}} \quad \text{multiply the fraction by 100 to express it as a percentage.}$$

WORKING OUT THE SAMPLE SIZE YOU NEED

Chapter 9 said that it was extremely difficult to say how big a sample you need. You can perhaps begin to see why. It depends upon what you want to do with your estimate, how important it is to get the estimate right, and what you already know about the situation. (Whatever you work out will then have to be scaled up to allow for the expected proportion of non-responses.)

If you are seeking to estimate a particular value with a particular confidence interval, you can see that you might work out a size of sample that would let you do this for a particular expected variance. The steps you would have to follow are:

- Decide how much precision you want – how broad a band you are happy for your estimate to lie within (call the maximum permissible difference between the sample mean and the population mean D).
- Decide on the level of confidence you want in your specified range.
- Work out the z value that this implies (z is the number of standard deviations the edge of your limit is away from the mean).
- Estimate the standard deviation of the population (either from known information or from a pilot study).
- Calculate the sample size from the formula for the standard error given above, by rearranging the formulae.

Thus if it is the mean value you are estimating, the sample size you need will be given by:

$$N = \frac{\sigma^2 z}{D^2}$$ (for a 95% level of confidence, z would be 1.96)

If you are interested in a proportion, the formula you need is:

$$N = \frac{p(1 - p)z^2}{D^2}$$

I hope that this convinces you that determining sample size requires more thought (and understanding) than is evident in the following two examples of 'discussion' of proposed sample size taken from dissertation proposals.

CONSIDER...

As you read the following illustration consider why these examples qualify for the 'House of Horrors' heading.

RESEARCH ILLUSTRATION: HOUSE OF HORRORS

Don't say it if you don't understand it!

Chander was going to look at the Indian automobile industry, choosing car manufacturers 'at random' in order to investigate how customer relationship marketing (CRM) wins customer loyalty in India's automobile industry. His null hypothesis was that the two are unrelated, and he proposed using a questionnaire and interviews with people working in marketing, asking about their approach to CRM and the impact they thought it had on customer loyalty. In his dissertation proposal Chander said only:

> 'Sample size:
> A probability sample will be selected using statistics method where SE = 1.96sqrt (variability/n) at 95% confidence level (Saunders et al, 2003).'

Ming's proposal was for a study of the impact on customer awareness of the marketing mix used by an electrical goods manufacturer in China. She said the following:

'Sample size:
A pilot study will be conducted by taking 20 samples and the sample size of 100 consumers will be determined using the following formula with confidence level 95%.

P is probability of customer awareness; Q is probability unaware; E = error at 0.05%.

Sample size needed is therefore

$$\frac{1.96 \times 2 \times 0.85 \times 0.15}{0.05 \times 2}$$

= 200 approx.

The method used will be non-probability convenience sampling, and sample size will be 100.'

Chander does not specify what he means by 'variability': there are many different items in his proposed questionnaire and he does not propose to pilot it. Nor does his literature search refer to any attempt at 'measuring' CRM which might allow him to guess at a figure. In fact, he is looking for an association rather than to make an estimate, so it is unclear that even if he proposed to find some means of estimating the variability of something it would be an appropriate determinant of sample size in his case. Because he would need a sample of 30 or more to justify this sort of 'estimation' and the size of the Indian automobile industry is not hugely greater than this, he would also violate the condition that the population must be large enough that the population is unaffected by the 'removal' of the sample. (I shall not begin to discuss the other reservations you might have had about his proposed methodology.)

Several aspects of Ming's comments are equally puzzling. She seems to have a clearer idea about what is needed to use the formula, and since she is looking to determine a proportion, and is doing a pilot that would enable her to estimate variance from her sample, she could subsequently estimate the size of sample she will need. (She has not done it yet, though, and nowhere in the proposal does she justify the values for P and Q (Q is $1 - P$) that she has chosen to use.)

Yet in advance of the pilot, and before she has actually done the calculation (even with these unexplained numbers), she has decided she needs a sample of 100. The fact that her own calculation seems to suggest a sample of 200 does nothing to change her mind. But more worryingly, she then says that she is going to use a convenience sample. 'Convenience sampling' is not at all suited to hypothesis-testing – indeed, Malhotra and Birks (2000) point out that it is theoretically indefensible to generalise to any population from a convenience sample, since such a sample is not representative of any definable population.

The first and most powerful question is therefore why she is doing a calculation at all, if her mind is made up, and she is not in any case going to use a probability sample. If she were going to use a probability sample, the second question would be why she is doing it now when she could do it so much better after the pilot. The third question would concern her reasons for using 85:15 as her proportions. And the final question would be about where the rest of her equation comes from. A '2' simply appears on both top and bottom, and these cancel each other out. And why is D^2 taken to be 0.05? Some explanation might have helped.

These two examples may be horror stories in the depth of ignorance they reveal, but are far from atypical of what students write in dissertation proposals. I hope that they have served to alert you to the many pitfalls of 'quoting' text on statistics without understanding what it is about. I also hope this chapter will enable you to understand enough to avoid such errors, but it is always a good idea to find a tame statistician to advise you if you do not feel you fully understand what you are doing.

CHOOSING A STATISTICAL TEST

In practical business research you are most likely to use statistical techniques in one or more of the following contexts:

- drawing conclusions about a population from a sample drawn from that population (*examples*: market research, attitude survey)

- testing the significance of differences between groups (groups may be independent samples or matched ones such as before-and-after measurements for the same individuals) (*examples*: performance before and after training, difference in error rates with different procedures)

- estimating the strength of a relationship between two variables (*examples*: the relationship between selection test results and subsequent job performance, the relationship between absence levels and stress levels)

- testing the statistical significance of such a relationship

- describing the relationship between two variables in terms of an equation (*example*: finding an equation to predict the impact of elements of the marketing mix on sales).

Estimating, and using z statistics for this has already been introduced, although only a parametric approach. In choosing a suitable statistical test for other purposes you must first decide which of the above categories applies. What are you testing for, and are you interested in the size of an effect/difference/association and/or its statistical significance? There are different approaches to both questions. To complicate matters further, the appropriate test will depend on the number of variables you are dealing with, and their nature. How big are your samples? Is your data interval or ratio data, or neither? Are your variables likely to be distributed normally? It is important to understand the importance of each of these aspects of your data in determining the appropriate test.

> **The appropriate statistical test will depend upon the question you are asking, the nature of your variables, and the size of your sample.**

PARAMETRIC OR NON-PARAMETRIC TESTS

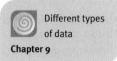
Different types of data
Chapter 9

Whether or not you have interval or ratio data is an important determinant of the appropriate test. As already indicated, statistical tests fall into two categories, referred to as parametric and non-parametric.

Parametric statistics are the more powerful – that is, they are more likely to detect a difference that exists, without risking an increase in the number of Type II errors.

But your measures use an interval scale (or, a ratio scale). Then they assume that you are dealing with a normal distribution, or something approximating to it. They also assume that the samples you are dealing with have similar variance, and that they were randomly selected. If these conditions are not met, parametric statistics will be misleading. (The interval scale is an essential condition: the others might be flexed slightly without the test becoming totally invalid.)

CONSIDER...

If you use a Likert scale such as:

	Strongly disagree 1	Disagree 2	Neutral 3	Agree 4	Strongly agree 5
People here are committed to the organisation's vision					

and score responses as indicated above the boxes, would you be justified in using parametric statistics on scores?

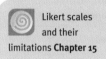

Likert scales and their limitations **Chapter 15**

You will frequently see such scores added to provide an overall score, and parametric statistics used on the resulting totals. However, this is questionable. This is ordinal data – you cannot say that the difference between 'Strongly disagree' and 'Disagree' is the same as that between, say, 'Neutral' and 'Agree'. Strictly, then, scores should not be added. It would be more appropriate to use median scores than an average. And you should use non-parametric statistics on your results.

> **Parametric tests can be used only with interval or ratio data that can be expected to be normally distributed.**

Non-parametric statistics do not make assumptions about scale or distribution, so if your data does not meet the conditions for parametric tests you should use the corresponding non-parametric test. These tests are less powerful – ie you do not make Type II errors – but this is at the expense of possible Type I errors (failing to detect an effect when one exists).

PAIRED OR UNPAIRED RESULTS

Another consideration when you are testing for differences is whether your observations are paired. For example, if you want to test a hypothesis about the impact of training on error rates, you might do it in a number of ways. Assume you have 200 operatives and 20 are going on the first training course.

- You could compare the number of errors made by the 20 in the month after training with the known error rates for the entire department of 200 over the last year.

- You could compare the number of errors made by the group of 20 in the month after the course with the error rates in that month made by a comparable group who had not been trained.

- You could compare the number of errors made by each of the 20 in the month before training and the month after training.

- You could compare the error rates made by each of the 20 in the month after training with error rates of a matched group (for each of the 20 you would identify another operative with the same length of service, working on the same machine, etc).

The 'month' is arbitrary, chosen merely as an example. You might choose any period at some point after the course. But you can see that in the first two cases you would be comparing group scores, whereas in the second two cases you could match up the before-and-after scores so that for each 'before' there was a specific 'after'. This additional information allows you to use a more powerful test.

Table 21.3 shows which tests are appropriate for which purpose and sort of data. Those that are shown in bold you should be able to perform on the strength of this chapter. The others will require further support.

Table 21.3 Choosing an appropriate Parametric or non-parametric test

Purpose	Parametric test	Non-parametric test
To test for differences: one sample	**t test** **z test**	**Chi-squared** Kolmogorov-Smirnov
To test for differences: two independent samples	**Indpendent t test** **z test**	**Chi-squared** Kolmogorov-Smirnov Mann-Whitney U
To test for differences: two paired samples	**Paired t test**	**Chi-squared** Wilcoxon matched pairs signed rank
To test for association between two variables	**Chi-squared** One-way analysis of variance	**Chi-squared**
To assess the strength of such an association	**Pearson's rho (correlation coefficient)**	**Spearman rank correlation**
To predict one variable from another	**Regression line**	
To look at relationships between more than two variables.	Multivariate analysis of variance	

If you possibly can, however, talk to a statistician before selecting a test – and do so at the data-planning stage.

STATISTICS FOR DIFFERENCES

Many research questions relate to differences. Do parents of small children take more days off than those without small children? Are there fewer errors after training than before, and if so, how many fewer? Is someone with this personality type more effective than people with other types in a particular role? Does one approach to customers generate fewer complaints than another? Does a new procedure for logging information centrally increase the proportion of activities logged, and if so, by how much?

Questions can boil down to:

- Is a sample different from a known population?
- Are two samples different from each other?
- What is the best estimate of the difference in either case?

One question about difference relates to estimating from a sample. Suppose you know the mean of a population and want to know if the sample you have ended up with is significantly different from the population. Imagine that you are concerned with length of service. You have sampled at random, and had a fairly low response rate. HR can give you information on length of service for all employees. You want to know if the 60 people who sent back your questionnaires are typical in this respect of the workforce as a whole.

CHI-SQUARED GOODNESS OF FIT

One of the most popular statistical tests in dissertations is the chi-squared (χ^2) test of goodness of fit. When you have n random variables, each with a normal distribution, the sum of squares of those variables has a chi-squared distribution. Table 21.3 shows just how many contexts you can use it in. Despite its relationship to the normal distribution, it can be used when a non-parametric test is called for because it makes no assumptions about the distribution of your sample or the population from which it is drawn. It looks at the 'fit' between what you observe and what you expected. It can be used to see whether there is a difference between two distributions, or by extension, whether there is an association between two variables. You can use a χ^2 whenever you have a set of categories and you assign individuals/observations to one and only one of these categories. Thus it is one of the few statistical tests you can use with categorical data. The χ^2 that you calculate is derived from the difference between what you observe and what you would expect.

Thus in my absenteeism study I might have wanted to see whether there was a 'day of the week' effect. If I took the last 500 days of absence and noted what day of the week each fell upon (some spells might cover several days), I would expect 100 to have been on each day of the week, if day of the week had no effect. In fact I observed something rather different:

	Mon	Tue	Wed	Thur	Fri
Expected absence	100	100	100	100	100
Observed absence	130	80	70	70	150

To calculate the χ^2 statistic you work out the square of the difference for each category, divide each by the expected value, and sum them.

The equation is written

$$\chi^2 = \sum_{i=1}^{n} \frac{(o_i - e_i)^2}{e_i}$$

(in which 'o' is observed and 'e' is expected and you have n catagories).

To use this formula in respect of the absenteeism study, you might draw a table thus:

Table 21.4 Example of working out chi squared in relation to figures above

	Mon	Tue	Wed	Thur	Fri
Expected absence	100	100	100	100	100
Observed absence	130	80	70	70	150
$o_i - e_i$	30	−20	−30	−30	50
$(o_i - e_i)^2$	900	400	900	900	2,500
$\dfrac{(o_i - e_i)^2}{e_i}$	9	4	9	9	25
(sum of final row)	\multicolumn{5}{c}{$\chi^2 = 56$}

To interpret this, you need two more things. The χ^2 distribution depends on the number of *degrees of freedom* you have, so you have to work this out before you can consult a χ^2 table. A simple χ^2 table is shown as Table 21.5. Of course, this is unnecessary if you are using a statistical package that will do all this for you.

Table 21.5 Selected values of χ^2

Degrees of freedom	$p = 0.05$	$p = 0.01$	$p = 0.001$
1	3.84	6.64	10.83
2	5.99	9.21	13.82
3	7.82	11.35	16.27
4	9.49	13.28	18.47
5	11.07	15.09	20.52
6	12.59	16.81	22.46
7	14.07	18.48	24.32
8	15.51	20.09	26.13
9	16.92	21.67	27.88
10	18.31	23.21	29.59
11	19.68	24.73	31.26
12	21.03	26.22	32.91
13	22.36	27.69	34.53
14	23.69	29.14	36.12
15	25.00	30.58	37.70

More extended tables are available if you Google 'chi squared', or see for example, http://www.unc.edu/~farkouh/usefull/chi.html .

If you instruct Excel to work out a CHITEST, it will calculate chi-squared and look up the probability of it for you, returning simply the probability.

But you need to know how many degrees of freedom you have if you are going to do the calculation and look up the tables yourself. Imagine you have five categories, like my weekdays. All your observations must fit into one or another of these categories. Once you have logged all the Monday-to-Thursday absences you have no choice about where to log the remainder. If the absence was not on Monday-to-Thursday, it had to be on a Friday. The number of degrees of freedom is therefore one less than the number of categories you have. So in the absenteeism case there are 4 degrees of freedom. (More generally, if you were working out a χ^2 with several rows and several columns, the same argument would apply to the rows and the columns, and your number of degrees of freedom would be (number of rows – 1) $\times$ (number of columns – 1).

> **The number of degrees of freedom for a χ^2 is: (number of rows – 1) x (number of columns – 1)**

The bigger the difference between your observed and your expected values, the bigger will thus be your χ^2. If you look up 4 degrees of freedom on Table 21.5, you will note that the χ^2 for 4df is 18.47 at the $p = 0.001$ level, and my value is substantially bigger than that. So I can be very confident indeed that there is an association between the day of the week and the absence rate. By establishing a difference between the two distributions you are also establishing an association between the nature of the distribution and the factor which distinguished your 'observeds' from your 'expecteds'.

Thus if you wanted to see whether an advertising campaign addressing two of your product lines had had an impact, you could look at sales for these two products before and after the campaign and work out the χ^2 value. In this case the first set of sales figures would become your 'expected', because your null hypothesis would be that the campaign had had no effect. Your sales figures after the campaign would be the 'observed' values. (In fact, it would not matter which was which because the χ^2 only looks at the difference, and the differences are squared, so the sign is irrelevant.) You would have 1 degree of freedom in this case.

Now you can perhaps understand the popularity of the χ^2 test. You can use it to test whether there is a difference between two groups. You can use it to test whether something has had an effect. You can even use it to test whether the questionnaires you got back are significantly different on age, or gender, or anything HR can tell you about the workforce as a whole and which you asked about on the questionnaire. If you have a low response rate, this can be useful.

And as well as serving a number of purposes, the χ^2 is amazingly easy to calculate. You can use it when one of your variables is nothing more than a set of categories, and you do not need to know anything about the population from which the sample is drawn (unless you are using it to test for representativeness).

STUDENT'S *t* DISTRIBUTION

The price of all these benefits is that because the χ^2 makes so few assumptions it is not particularly powerful. It may discount an effect that a more powerful test would deem statistically significant. So if you have interval data and can make fairly strenuous assumptions about the normality of your distribution (and the distribution of differences), you can use tests derived directly from the normal curve (a *z* test) or use the Student's *t* statistic. 'Student' was the pseudonym of W. S. Gosset who explored the *t* distribution on which the statistic is based. The pseudonym was necessary because his employer (Guinness) did not allow its employees to publish. To derive probabilities directly from the normal curve, you must have a fairly large sample and know the standard deviation of the population. The *t* distribution is similar to a normal curve, but you can use it when you want to estimate the population variance from your sample. It works better than the normal distribution if your sample size is less than 30.

As Table 21.3 showed, t tests have several uses. You can use them when you want to draw conclusions about a single sample, for two independent samples, and for cases where you have paired values. Again, Excel will do it for you.

One-sample t test

This enables you to test the null hypothesis that the mean of your sample is not significantly different from the mean of a known population.

$$t = \frac{\text{sample mean} - \text{population mean } (\mu)}{\text{estimated standard error of mean (derived from sample)}}$$

You will remember that the standard error of the mean was

$$SE_m = \frac{s}{\sqrt{n}}$$

As with the chi-squared test, you need to know how many degrees of freedom you have before looking up the t statistic. In the one-sample situation, if your sample size is n, the t statistic will have $n - 1$ degrees of freedom. Table 21.6 shows selected values of t for different degrees of freedom suited to a one-tailed test. (If you need a two-tailed test, look up the column for half the probability you would need for the one-tailed test.) For a fuller table consult a statistics book or use an online table.

Two independent samples t test

The t statistic for the difference between two means is derived from the obtained difference between means divided by the difference expected by chance. This is *not* zero, but the standard error of the difference!

Working out the difference between the means of the two samples is easy. The standard error of the difference can be estimated by dividing the difference between means by the standard deviation of the two samples combined (ie all observations treated as if they were a single sample), and dividing by the combined sample size minus 2. This is because you are estimating the variance of the population, rather than calculating it for the sample, and you will remember that a slightly smaller denominator is used to allow for the likelihood that the sample variance is an underestimate.

Note that if the variance of the two samples looks different, you should not use a t test.

Matched pairs t test

To calculate this statistic you find the difference, D, between each pair of values, and calculate its mean and variance. If there is no difference you would expect D to be 0.

The variance will be the sum of the squares of the differences divided by n where there are n pairs. The standard deviation of D will be the square root of this. The t statistic will have $n - 1$ degrees of freedom.

Thus:

$$t_{n-1} = \frac{\overline{D}}{S_D / \sqrt{n}}$$

where $\overline{D}$ is the average difference, and $S_D = \sqrt{\frac{\sum D^2}{n} - \overline{D}^2}$.

The following table shows selected values of the upper tail area of the *t* distribution for selected degrees of freedom. A larger value of *t* than that shown for the appropriate degrees of freedom (df) indicates statistical significance at the level for that column.

Table 21.6 Selected values of *t*, upper tail

Degrees of freedom	90%	95%	97.5%	99.5%
1	3.08	6.31	12.71	63.66
2	1.89	2.92	4.30	9.92
3	1.64	2.35	3.18	5.84
4	1.53	2.13	2.78	4.60
5	1.48	2.02	2.57	4.03
10	1.37	1.81	2.22	3.17
30	1.31	1.70	2.04	2.75
100	1.29	1.66	1.98	2.63
∞	1.28	1.64	1.96	2.58

STATISTICS FOR ASSOCIATIONS

Many research questions concern *relationships* between variables. Are error rates related to experience? Does pay influence job satisfaction? Is training spend related to retention? Does job satisfaction influence absence levels? Does satisfaction with a leadership programme depend on the seniority of the person in question and/or on their level of education? Do more intelligent people get promoted more quickly? Are happy people absent less often?

You can get a visual impression of whether two variables are related by plotting your observations on a scatter plot. Imagine that you had six employees, and their error rates and length of service were as shown below.

	Employee A	Employee B	Employee C	Employee D	Employee E	Employee F
Years employed	0.6	1.0	1.5	2	2	3
Average error rates	27	21	22	18	15	10

ACTIVITY

Plot these points to see whether they 'speak' clearly.

You will note that although the points are vaguely in a line, they are not exactly so. It would be rash to draw conclusions from six observations. This was used merely as a reminder on plotting if you needed it.

CONSIDER...

Look at the four more realistic scatter diagrams c) to f) in Figure 21.3. How would you describe the likely relationships between *x* and *y* in each case?

Figure 21.3
a)–f) Different associations

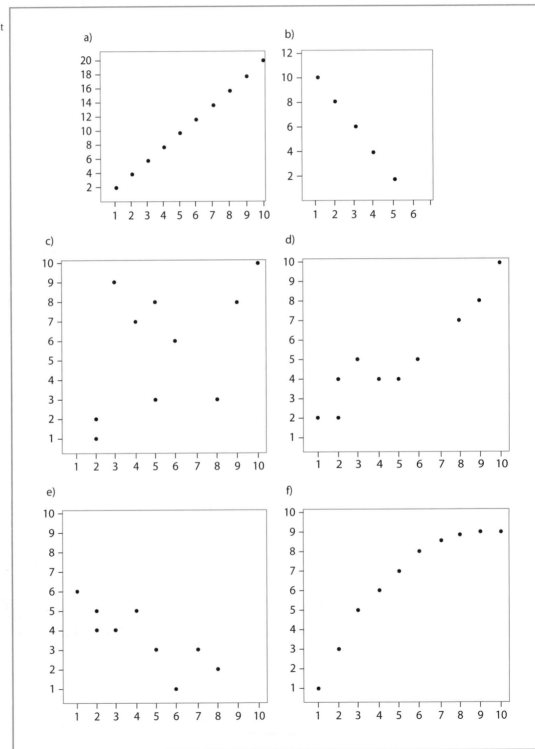

Figure 21.3 shows plots for different larger sets of observations where the numbers do lie on a perfect line. Observations like a) and b) would be highly unlikely in most research. In a) every unit of increase in x is associated with two units of increase in y. In b) every unit increase in x is associated with two units' decrease in y. In a) the variables are perfectly and positively correlated. In b) they are perfectly and negatively correlated. Real-life data is seldom so tidy. You are more likely to get results closer to those in c)–f).

My interpretation of these figures would be that in c) there is no real evidence of any association at all; in d) there seems to be quite a strong positive relationship between the two (as one increases so does the other); in e) there seems to be a rather weaker negative relationship (the higher one variable, the lower the other); whereas in f) there seems to be a very strong relationship, but instead of a straight linear relationship between them, if you drew a line best representing the data, it would be curved.

From now on I shall consider only *linear* correlations – those in which a straight line best fits the data. The variables in a) are strongly positively correlated, and in d) they are less strongly correlated. If you were interested in these variables, there are three things you might want to find out more about:

- Is there a relationship at all, or is the apparent association merely a chance feature of your data?
- If there is a relationship, how strong is it?
- If you know the value of one variable, can you predict the value of the second?

If you are interested in the relationship between two variables, it is always best to start with a scatter plot. This enables you to see at a glance whether there is any point in further examining any apparent relationship. If there seems to be a line but it is curved, you will have to draw the curve that best fits the dots by eye. If there seems to be a straight linear relationship, you can think about measuring the strength of the relationship between the variables.

The scatter plot may throw up curious points that do not seem to fit the pattern of the rest. These are sometimes called *outliers*, and it may be worth checking your original data to see if there is any explanation why they should be so different.

MEASURES OF CORRELATION

Although you can get a 'feel' for the degree of association between the variables, this is not very satisfactory. The impression depends upon the scale you are using, and our eyes are not very good at judging such things in any case.

One way of testing whether there is an association is to use the χ^2 test. You could reduce each of your variables to a set of broad categories (say, low, medium, and high) and then proceed as you did earlier. But if you have ordinal or ratio numbers, this would be discarding a great deal of information, and the test would therefore be crude/less powerful. It would also tell you neither the direction of the relationship nor how closely it approximated to a straight line.

Ideally, your measure will be positive for a positive relationship, negative for a negative one, and 0 when there is no correlation at all. The measure should not depend on the units you are using for your variables, and it would be nice if a perfect correlation were 1.

To get rid of the unit problem you shift the axes of your plot so that they cross (ie the origin of the graph is) in the middle of the scatter plot. This point will can be defined as the average value of x, $\bar{x}$ and the average value of y, $\bar{y}$.

All points are then expressed in terms of their relationship to this new origin. Figure 21.4 shows how the earlier sets of Figure 21.3 c), d) and e) look with this shift of origin.

Figure 21.4 c)–e) Shifted origins

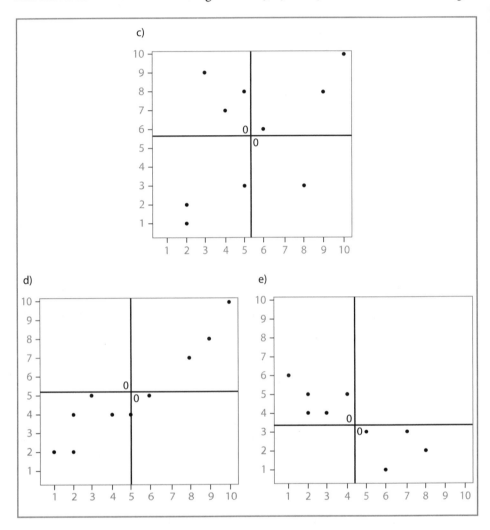

In relation to these new axes each point x_i, y_i will become $x_i - \bar{x}$, $y_i - \bar{y}$. Looking at Figure 21.4 you can see that if you multiplied all the new x values by their new y value and added them up, the total would be positive for d) and negative for e), and for c) would be pretty near 0.

Unfortunately, the size of the sum will depend on the number of observations. You can easily take care of that by dividing by the number of variations. This gives you a value called the *covariance* of x and y.

$$\text{Covariance } (x, y) = \frac{\Sigma(x - \bar{x})(y - \bar{y})}{n}$$

(where the sum is for all n pairs of values). If you have the software to work this out, fine. If you want to do it by hand, an alternative way of expressing the covariance makes the calculations easier. This is:

Covariance $(x, y) = \dfrac{\Sigma xy}{n} - \bar{x}\bar{y}$ where there are n observations.

Note that there is a parallel here with the variance of a single variable, which was:

Variance of $x = \dfrac{\Sigma(x - \bar{x})(x - \bar{x})}{n}$ ie its covariance with itself.

Note also that variance can be written in a way which makes calculations easier:

Variance of $x = \dfrac{\Sigma x^2}{n} - \bar{x}^2$

Standard deviation $= \sqrt{\dfrac{\Sigma x^2}{n} - \bar{x}^2}$

The size of the covariance still depends on the size of the numbers you are using, so the next stage is to get rid of this effect. To do this, we divide the covariance by the product of the separate standard deviations (ie the square roots of the variances) of x and y.

The resulting figure has all the requirements for a measure of association, and is called *Pearson's product moment correlation* (often simply referred to as ρ, r, or 'the correlation coefficient').

This can be written as:

$r = \dfrac{\Sigma(x - \bar{x})(y - \bar{y})}{\sqrt{\Sigma(x - \bar{x})^2 \, \Sigma(y - \bar{y})^2}}$ (for all pairs i = 1 to n)

If you divide top and bottom by $n - 1$, the expression is reduced to:

$r = \dfrac{\text{covariance of } x \text{ and } y}{s_x s_y}$

Table 21.7 Correlation between the figures of Sets A and B from Table 21.2

x, y	x −mean	$(x - \text{mean})^2$	$y -$ mean	$(y - \text{mean})^2$	xy
1, 3	−4	16	−2	4	3
3, 4	−2	4	−1	1	12
4, 4	−1	1	−1	1	16
4, 4	−1	1	−1	1	16
5, 5	0	0	0	0	25
5, 5	0	0	0	0	25
6, 6	1	1	1	1	36
6, 6	1	1	1	1	36
7, 6	2	4	1	1	42
9, 7	4	16	2	4	63
$\Sigma x = 50$		= 44	$\Sigma y = 50$	= 14	$\Sigma xy = 274$
$\bar{x} = 5$			$\bar{y} = 5$		$(\bar{x}\bar{y}) = 27.4$
	variance	4.4	variance	1.4	
	S_A	2.10	S_B	1.18	

The following illustration shows how you might work out such a correlation for a simple set of data. Take the two sets of figures Set A and Set B shown in Table 20.2, in which we have already worked out the means and standard deviations of both these samples. We called each x before, but if they are now to be taken as indicating single data points, call the variable in Set B y instead of x.

So the denominator of r will be 2.1×1.18, which is 2.47.

What about the figure above the line? This was $\frac{\sum xy}{n} - \bar{x}\bar{y}$

$\frac{\sum xy}{n} = 27.4, \bar{x}\bar{y} = 25$

So $r = \frac{2.4}{2.47}$

$\quad = 0.97$

This is a very high correlation indeed, suggesting that almost all the variance is shared. Which is what you would expect from the data.

Excel will work out both COVAR (covariance) and CORREL (correlation).

There are two things to note here. Although it seemed reasonable to think that the length of service 'caused' the reduction in error rates, the correlation coefficient does not tell you whether or not this is the case. As has been repeatedly stressed:

Correlation does not mean causation.

There might be many reasons why A and B might be correlated. A might indeed cause, or be one of the causes of, B. But equally, B might cause A, or C might be related to both A and B.

Some research into mobile phones made the news not long ago. If I remember it correctly, a significant correlation was found between mobile phone use and both binge drinking and physical fitness. It would be unreasonable to think that using a phone drove you to drink, and despite the hazards of drunken dialling, neither is the reverse all that likely. And how would either square with high levels of fitness? The 'C' in this case is age. Mobile phone use is highest in the age group that is both fitness-conscious and prone to 'having a good time'.

Spearman's rank correlation

The second point to note is that Pearson's rho only works for interval or ratio data. Often in practical business research your data will not meet this requirement. Fortunately, there is an alternative for ordinal data: the Spearman's rank correlation. Provided you can order your data, you can work this out. Suppose you had 10 graduate recruits and you had ranked their communication skills at interview so that 1 indicated the recruit deemed best, 10 the person deemed worst. You want to see whether performance at interview is related to performance at the end of the training course, where again they are ranked, this time by the trainers, on their communication skills. To find the rank correlation you rank the pairs of observations according to one of the variables – in the example below they are ordered by interview ranking. Then you work out the difference between the two ranks and square it, as in the example below, adding these squares.

Table 21.8 The correlation of ordinal data

Student	Interview ranking	End-of-training ranking	d	d²
Angela	1	3	−2	4
Bonita	2	5	−3	9
Charlie	3	2	1	1
Devon	4	1	3	9
Ellie	5	4	1	1
Farouk	6	6	0	0
Gautham	7	8	−1	1
Henri	8	10	−2	4
Isobella	9	7	2	4
Jung	10	9	1	1
			$\Sigma d^2 =$	34

The formula for Spearman's rank correlation is:

$$r_{rank} = 1 - \frac{6\Sigma d^2}{n(n^2 - 1)} \quad \text{where } n \text{ is the number of pairs.}$$

Thus in this example:

$$r_{rank} = 1 - \frac{6 \times 34}{10 \times 99} \qquad = 1 - 0.21 \qquad = 0.79$$

The ease of calculating a rank correlation should not lead you to use it in preference to Pearson's r if you have a choice. It is a less accurate figure, and may over-estimate the actual correlation.

How much shared variation?

What does a correlation coefficient tell you? It indicates how much shared variance there is between the two variables – how much of the variance in the dependant variable is accounted for by the independent variable.

$$r^2 = \frac{\text{explained}}{\text{total variation}} = \frac{\text{total variation} - \text{error}}{\text{total variation}}$$

That is, r^2 measures the proportion of one variable 'explained' by another (but note the caution about causality above). Because it is symmetrical, r^2 is as much an 'explanation' of the variation in x in terms of y, as it is of the variation in y in terms of x.

But note that the statistic we calculated was r, not r^2. Thus to find the shared variance from the correlation coefficient you have to square r. And since the figure is always a fraction, and a fraction of a fraction is less than you started with, this can be surprisingly small. You might feel impressed if your psychometric test correlated 0.4 with subsequent performance (and indeed, this would be a respectable correlation to obtain from a test). But this would mean that only 0.16 of actual performance variation was associated with test score variation. This might or might not be commercially significant.

LINES OF BEST FIT

If you have data such as you have been using to establish correlations, you might also want to make predictions. Suppose you had plotted advertising spend against sales, and had found they were correlated. This is reassuring, but if you are a marketing manager wanting to make a bid for further advertising, it would be useful to be able to predict the impact of a particular increase in advertising budget on future sales. Likewise, if you want to make recommendations on the basis of correlations found in your research, you might be thinking along similar lines (but always with the 'correlation is not causation' caution at the back of your mind).

The line best fitting your data would provide a simple basis for prediction. So what counts as a good fit? One that goes near to the most points? If we wanted to estimate y from x, then it would be the line which minimised y's distances from the line – ie the vertical distance from point to line. If we were interested in predicting x, we should have to minimise the horizontal distance. Provided you make sure that you 'fix' x and predict y, you can concentrate on the vertical distances, and look for what is called the *regression equation of y on x*.

The term 'regression' comes from genetics. It is well known that if you plot characteristics (such as height) of children against those of their parents, the children seem to be less extreme than their parents – this is called 'regression towards the mean'. This seems counter-intuitive, because it would seem to suggest that variation in the population would reduce in each successive generation. What is less well known, except to statisticians, is that this is a statistical artefact. If you were to plot height of parent against height of child, you would get a similar regression towards the mean, only this time it would be the parents' height that was less extreme than the children's. This provides further evidence of the need for caution in interpreting statistics.

You could find the regression line by drawing a series of lines and measuring the distances of points from each, shifting the line until it was the best you could get. Or you could, much more quickly, calculate the formula for the line, using the correlation coefficient. To do this you work, as so often, with squares of distances, to avoid the problem of some being negative, some positive.

The equation is:

$$y - \bar{y} = \frac{rs_y(x - \bar{x})}{s_x}$$

– that is, the least-squares regression line of y on x is Pearson's r times the standard deviation of y times $(x - x)$ divided by standard deviation of x.

You have already worked out the standard deviations to get the correlation, so it is fairly trivial to arrive at the regression equation. Or (of course) Excel will do it for you. It will also forecast an unknown data value based on existing values. Thus you could predict the value of any *y* from *x*, using the line, allowing you to predict the effect of a specified marketing spend, say, on sales. You can also use Excel to extrapolate from the line to give a number of future values. Thus if you had 12 months' sales data you could use the TREND function to estimate, say, the next three months' sales.

Note that this is worth doing only if the correlation is fairly high. If it is not, any predictions from the line could be highly inaccurate. And it is only worth doing if relevant conditions are relatively constant. Extrapolating from pre-credit-crunch data to post-credit-crunch, say, might also be inaccurate.

The discussion thus far should have convinced you that statistics is a fairly complicated area. The appropriate statistical test can tell you a lot about the degree of confidence you can place in any associations or differences that you find, but it is not a magic bullet. Chance variations may still cause you to make Type I or Type II errors in dealing with your null hypothesis. However, you can avoid some at least of the errors by following the guidelines below.

Guidelines for using statistical tests

Choose a sample adequate for your purpose.
Choose an appropriate statistical test for your sample size and the nature of your data.
Only use a one-tailed test if your hypothesis is genuinely one-directional – ie the direction was incorporated into your hypothesis before you started collecting your data.
Check that any computer output makes sense (it is easy to make data entry errors).
Report your results in a way that does not mislead your reader by suggesting proof or drawing conclusions in any other way that the data does not justify.

SUMMARY

Statistical tests allow you to work out how likely it is that associations or differences that you have observed were the result of chance alone. Different tests are appropriate for different purposes and different sorts of data. It is important to choose an appropriate one.

No matter how appropriate your test there will still be a chance of making both Type I and Type II errors (falsely rejecting or accepting the null hypothesis). However, the choice of the most appropriate test can reduce these probabilities.

It is important to remember that establishing the statistical significance of an association or difference does not establish its practical or commercial significance. The size of the effect will also be important, as will the implications of the effect for the business.

REVIEW QUESTIONS

1. When would you find tests of statistical significance useful, and when would they be totally inappropriate?

2. Why is it important to understand the idea of probability if you are using statistics?

3. You want to assess the impact of a new selection process on staff retention in an organisation after 12 months. What might your null hypothesis be?

4. You have read a paper which looked at correlations between 10 different factors in a selection process (a variety of test and interview scores) and five different job performance measures 12 months after induction for each of 500 candidates recruited. Two of the correlations were significant at the 0.05 level. One of these was the correlation between IQ and supervisor rating of problem-solving skills. Problem-solving is important in the job. Would this be sufficient grounds for recommending that selection is simplified to include only IQ tests?

5. When would you be justified in choosing a one-tailed test of statistical significance?

6. What is the value of knowing the standard deviation of a distribution of observed measures?

7. What questions might you usefully ask before you can decide how big a sample you need?

8. What does it mean to say that parametric tests are more powerful than non-parametric tests, and why does this *not* mean that they should always be used in preference to non-parametric tests?

9. Why is there a trade-off between Type I and Type II errors, and what might cause you to prefer to risk one rather than the other?

10. What statistical tests are commonly used to assess the significance of a difference between two samples?

11. Which statistical test might be deemed the most versatile in practical business research? When would it *not* be appropriate?

12. There is highly significant correlation between the number of training days staff have successfully completed and job performance. Are there any reasons why this correlation might *not* demonstrate the impact of training on performance?

13. Why is it unethical to use statistics without understanding them?

EXPLORE FURTHER

Bee, F. and Bee, R. (2005) *Managing Information and Statistics*, 2nd edition. London: CIPD

Blutman, K. and Aitken, P. G.(2007) *Excel 2007 Formulas and Functions for Dummies*. Indianapolis, IN: Wiley. For those who plan to use Excel and are having difficulty

Burns, R. B. and Burns, R. A. (2009) *Business Research Methods and Statistics Using SPSS*. London: Sage. Useful if you have access to SPSS

Cameron, S. (2008) *The MBA Handbook*, 6th edition. Harlow: FT/Prentice Hall. For help with basic numeracy if some of the equations in this chapter had you puzzled

Morris, C. (2008) *Quantitative Approaches in Business Studies*, 7th edition. Harlow: FT/Prentice Hall (see last chapter)

Online tutorials that could usefully supplement this chapter include the following [all accessed 5 January 2009]:

http://faculty.vassar.edu/lowry/webtext.html gives an extensive and clear description of concepts in inferential statistics with worked examples, and has a 'calculator' for working out key statistics

http://www.wadsworth.com/psychology_d/templates/student_resources/workshops/stat_workshp/chose_stat/chose_stat_04.html for a free workshop on choosing appropriate statistical tests

http://www.qub.ac.uk/directorates/media/Media,52086,en.doc for clear explanations of Excel statistical functions

http://www.cs.uiowa.edu/~jcryer/JSMTalk2001.pdf for an interesting though possibly dated critique of Excel statistical functions

http://phoenix.phys.clemson.edu/tutorials/excel/regression.html for linear regression

http://phoenix.phys.clemson.edu/tutorials/excel/stats.html for means, medians, modes and standard deviations

http://www.robertniles.com/stats/stdev.shtml for similar information

http://home.ubalt.edu/ntsbarsh/excel/excel.htm#rtesthypo for comprehensive and comprehensible tutorial advice on using Excel for testing statistical significance

http://www.enumerys.com/linreg.htm for a clear description of linear regression in a marketing context

http://mathworld.wolfram.com/Studentst-Distribution.html for a description of the *t*-distribution

http://www.speedlinetechnologies.com/docs/Six-Sigma.pdf for a discussion from a practical perspective of confidence intervals and sigma in the context of circuit board production

http://www.itl.nist.gov/div898/handbook/eda/section3/eda3672.html for online tables

 Visit www.cipd.co.uk/brm for web links, templates, activities and other useful resources relating to this chapter.

CHAPTER 22

Drawing Valid Conclusions

INTRODUCTION

Business research projects are undertaken for a purpose, usually to address an organisational problem or opportunity, to meet the requirements of an academic programme of study, or both. The conclusions that you draw are the point at which you demonstrate that you have achieved what you set out to achieve. Valid conclusions are a clear indication to your stakeholders that you have met their expectations.

The credibility of a business research project is established by the effectiveness with which you answer the research questions. This effectiveness is not judged by your ability to prove or disprove a particular hypothesis or by your ability to confirm what you and/or your stakeholders intuitively thought was the case all along. Instead, the credibility of the research is dependent on your presenting a robust and coherent set of conclusions which articulate genuinely and clearly the results derived from the research; and do so in a way that is persuasive.

Conclusions are important because they distil the very essence of the business research. They are the means by which many people will judge the credibility of the business research and *de facto* of you as the researcher. The conclusions are the point at which you demonstrate a sound understanding of the key issues, an informed approach to the subject, a robust research method and valid research findings. The conclusions to any business research project are the point at which the reader's attention is brought back to the original focus – namely, the research questions being addressed. They attract attention to the research and persuade people of the value of the work that has been done.

This chapter starts by discussing why robust conclusions are such an important part of your business research report. It then walks through a logical process designed to help you to make sure that the conclusions that you present are a fair and trustworthy reflection of your research and that they meet the demands of possibly disparate stakeholder groups. The chapter then presents the mistakes that people often make in writing their conclusions, as an indication of what you are trying to avoid.

LEARNING OUTCOMES

This chapter should enable you to:

- appreciate what valid conclusions are and why they are an important part of business research

- familiarise yourself with the process required to help you to produce valid conclusions

- recognise the key errors made in writing research conclusions and be able to avoid them in your own practice.

CHARACTERISING CONCLUSIONS

Your conclusions are the culmination of your business research. They are the point at which the *important* findings of the business research are presented to the reader in a genuine, credible and persuasive manner. Your arguments are explained and the implications explored. Explaining is important. The conclusions that you present to your audience will have been synthesised from a wide range of sources. They will have been framed by your research purpose and research questions and must clearly and obviously demonstrate that you have met your objectives. They will have drawn on secondary data from the literature and/or organisational publications and must show, implicitly or explicitly, that they have been informed by this literature. They are shaped by the research context and must demonstrate that you are sensitive to the nuances of the research situation. And they will be premised on the research findings and must draw on the evidence produced in order to present a convincing argument.

Producing valid conclusions is therefore quite complex. The ways in which all these factors interact and the extent to which they are important has to be explained to the reader rather than simply described. In order to produce an explanation, it is important to build coherent arguments, and in thinking about these arguments it is important to be absolutely clear about the specific points that you wish to make. You must ensure that any claims you make in the conclusions are supported by appropriate and accurate evidence, and that the arguments that you present build on each other to develop into a specific and well-reasoned story.

It is important to note also that conclusions should be drawn only from the *important* findings. Your readers do not want to be re-presented with the entire set of research findings yet again. Instead, they want a succinct consideration of only those factors that are salient to them and to the research itself. This idea of focusing on only the *important* factors requires you to make an informed judgement on which of the research findings are important.

> **Conclusions should explain the most important research findings clearly to the readers.**

Strange though it may seem, it often helps to clarify your thinking about what conclusions are by considering what they are *not*. Conclusions are not:

- a repetition of all the research findings. They must be much more succinct and focus on the key issues

- a brief summary of the findings (Bryman and Bell, 2008). Although the research findings will be the necessary foundation for the conclusions, they must be explained and discussed. Description is not sufficient

- an overview of the entire research process- Very little of the research process should be included in the conclusions. If your audience is concerned about this, they can simply go to the main body of the report where you will have considered it more thoroughly

- an opportunity for the researcher to offer the reader unsolicited opinions or their own unjustified views about the problems or about the findings. The conclusions should present only those issues which are derived directly from the research

- an opportunity for the researcher to present the reader with a synopsis of the research findings that they *wish* they had produced.

WRITING VALID RESEARCH CONCLUSIONS

There is a great temptation for business researchers when writing research conclusions to simply narrate the processes they have been through – that is, to present a précis version of the entire research process. After all, you will have spent considerable time and effort devising and undertaking the research, analysing the data and producing the research findings, so this should be relatively easy to do. The reason that this approach is problematic is that it does not produce a set of robust conclusions. Instead, what emerges from such a process is a chronology of the researcher's experiences. Not only does this fail to prioritise or explain the research findings, but the conclusions produced often lack any sense of structure or of logic that would enable the reader to realise the implications of the findings.

The best way to avoid this scenario is for business researchers to be as methodical as possible when writing their conclusions. A methodical process that researchers might find a useful approach to writing valid conclusions is itemised below.

- revisit the research purpose/question
- gather together all the data
- consider the audience
- draft the conclusions
- review, and recognise the limitations
- close the conclusions.

REVISIT THE RESEARCH PURPOSE/QUESTION

In writing valid conclusions, the best place to start is with your initial research purpose/question. What was the research specifically trying to achieve? What research objectives did you set? Use the key points from the research question to devise an outline framework for your conclusions. Breaking the research question down into component parts can help you to ensure that the conclusions that you present are focused on what your research was trying to achieve.

ACTIVITY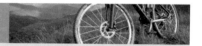

The research purpose as devised by Toby in Chapter 8 was:

> An investigation into what the sales staff of XYZ Company understand by the vision of the company, and how well they think this vision motivates them to do a better job.

Try breaking this research purpose down into component parts to see what issues you think Toby should use as sections to structure his conclusions.

Your answers probably include many of the issues here. Essentially, Toby should probably emphasise in his conclusions that his research was focusing on the sales staff of the organisation. It is important to remind the audience that the results were derived from a very particular group and are unlikely to apply to everybody who works in the organisation. He may or may not mention the company itself – this would depend on who the business research was being presented to. If it was part of an academic programme of study (which it was), he may wish to *briefly* mention the nature of the company to remind the marker of the context of the research. In this particular example Toby also wanted to present the results to his line manager, and accordingly wrote two conclusions – one that communicated those issues important to an academic piece of work, and one that placed an emphasis on those issues most important to his line manager.

> If you are writing reports for different stakeholders, you may have to alter the way you present your conclusions to meet their unique needs.

Next it would be useful for Toby to remind the reader of the vision of the company, and it would probably be helpful to also mention briefly why the vision was created. That way the reader can immediately understand why this piece of research is useful to the organisation – ie the research is trying to determine whether or not the vision is achieving what it is supposed to achieve. Additionally, a key point to mention here would be that the research focused on sales staff who are based *remotely*, and the vision is accordingly seen as an important way of connecting them to the company.

Then, having set the context, Toby could go on to discuss the results of his research. In the main body of his project report Toby considers all the results, highlighting the factors that are important as well as those that are not important. However, within his conclusions he must focus in on only the most important factors from his results. In presenting this discussion there has to be a clearly mapped-out argument (we will look at argument-mapping shortly) which leads to the key points that Toby wishes to present. Again, an understanding of who the report is being written for will help him to make that decision. It is important to note that the research findings, as they appear in the conclusions, will also explain the implications of these findings and indicate why these issues are important.

> **Start with your top-level research question or purpose as the foundation of your conclusions, and then build your conclusions up from there.**

GATHER TOGETHER ALL THE DATA

The second stage is the point at which you start to build on the foundation provided by the research purpose or research question. Before you start writing you should gather together all the information you are likely to need. It is important to cross-check what you are saying with this data because any errors – even if they are only errors of transcription – will undermine the whole research project. Make sure that you check everything, that the numbers add up, that the spellings are correct. Even check the way in which you have transcribed the research question – this must be exactly the same in the conclusions as it was at the beginning of the project: any minor alteration in wording immediately undermines the credibility of the conclusions. Although this sounds basic it is a common mistake which can have quite dire consequences.

For example, if Toby were to start his conclusions with:

> *"This research project set out to answer the question 'What do the sales staff of XYZ Company think about the vision of the company, and how well do they think this motivates them to do a better job?'"*

readers who had read the beginning of his report would quickly notice that the original question actually asked what the sales staff *understand by* the vision of the company, yet the conclusions seem to be telling us that the questions asked what they *think about* the vision. The two are not the same, and the credibility of the research and the researcher are immediately compromised.

This is such an easy mistake to make. Simply changing 'analyse' to 'assess' or to 'evaluate' not only alters the meaning but it makes the research and the researcher look unreliable. After all, if the reader cannot rely on them to simply transfer the research question from the front to the back of the report, how sure can they be that the rest of the data is reliable?

Revisiting all the necessary data also acts as a sort of 'reality check' to make sure that the conclusions drawn are realistic, genuine and clearly derived from the data. At this point a final check is made on the data to ensure that it is valid, reliable and complete.

> **Transfer the research question and any context information verbatim, and always check the wording.**

CONSIDER THE AUDIENCE

The ways in which you write the conclusions and the stories that the conclusions have to tell should be focused on the audience with whom you are trying to communicate. Reports for your manager may have to focus on issues of practical concern. Consultancy reports may have to draw out the key points from the brief, whereas academic research projects may draw on the limitations of method to suggest future areas of investigation. Knowing the audience also enables you to write using the appropriate language – technical language where the audience expects and understands it, and a more vernacular approach where it better communicates with the readers. The need to communicate with potentially disparate groups of stakeholders effectively means that it may be useful to ask yourself the following questions when thinking about your conclusions:

Questions to ask about your audience

Whom am I writing these conclusions for?

What questions do these people want answering?

Which aspects of the research findings is it most important for me to communicate to them?

Why are these issues important?

Do I have the data to support the contention that these issues are important?

How could I best communicate these issues?

Which aspects could be left as part of the research findings section?

Write in a style and language that is appropriate to the reader. Your aim is to communicate, not baffle.

DRAFT THE CONCLUSIONS

In order to draft your conclusions you have to consider not simply what you want to communicate to the reader but also how you justify treating these issues as important. The conclusions should briefly describe the research findings but then develop arguments that explore and discuss the findings.

Mapping your argument

An argument is generally thought of as one or more assumptions (also known as claims or premises) which lead to a conclusion. For an argument to be valid the assumptions must be supported by evidence and the evidence presented should unambiguously lead to the conclusions. A good argument then has a clear logic which propels the reader to drawing the same conclusions as the writer.

In drafting your arguments you should start with the assumptions, claims or premises. Refer back to the research purpose/question to see which areas you should be attending to. For each of the themes that you identify you should draw together your research findings and see how they can be turned into well-reasoned conclusions. It is important to consider two levels of coherence here: coherence within each of the arguments, and coherence between each of the arguments. Within each argument assumptions, claims or premises should be supported by reliable evidence and should logically lead the reader to drawing the conclusion that you have presented. Between each argument there must be a flow of narrative or discussion that connects the theme from the previous argument to the next argument. In this way the reader can easily follow the discussions.

Part of these discussions should explain the reasons these issues are important. The reasons you present must be as trustworthy and as reliable as the data itself, and not simply a post-hoc intuitive justification on your part. A good point to remember here is that the conclusions should not contain any new information – everything that appears in the conclusions should have appeared previously in the research project.

We return to Toby's research project to see a good example and a poor example of justifying conclusions.

CONSIDER...

Toby discovered that the vision of the organisation, rather than motivate the remote sales staff, irritated and frustrated them. The main problem, it appeared, was that the vision focused on driving for market success; the message it communicated to sales staff was that all the company valued was results. This 'exclusive' focus on the market created in the sales staff a sense that as people they were not really valued, just a means to producing profit. The company evidently did not understand how important it is to keep nurturing relationships with customers even if that does not always result in immediate sales, so time and effort spent maintaining good relationships with customers was thought by managers to be 'non-productive' time.

A poor way to communicate these findings might be:

Interviews with the sales staff demonstrated their frustration with the company vision. A significant number of people said that they thought the vision placed too much emphasis on the market and on success, and that they felt undervalued because of it. This issue is important for the organisation to consider because it may lead to increased staff turnover and I think that some of the regions may already be understaffed. Also, my experience of the organisation's recruitment and selection process is such that although all staff have to work a three-months notice period, the time it took to recruit my last member of staff was just over six months, and the rest of the team were not happy about having to cover.

Why might you think that the above conclusions might be poorly expressed?

You have probably recognised many of the issues here but it is useful to compare notes. The conclusions seem to start well enough by communicating the research findings based on the evidence from the data. However, although there has been a good attempt to justify the issue as important, Toby then starts to throw in many issues not raised previously. The whole drift into recruitment and selection – which he then backs up with his own personal opinion rather than with reliable facts – undermines the credibility of the data which is genuinely factual.

So why are these conclusions better? The start of the conclusion remains the same – however, as Toby gets on to the issue of the implications for staff turnover, instead of regaling the readers with his own experiences he uses a brief reference to the literature to support his claim and then backs this up again with evidence derived from his research findings. What he has produced here is a much more reliable and persuasive conclusion.

By constantly referring back to the data, you can ensure that you retain the integrity of this data as it is transferred into the conclusions. A good habit to get into is to check what you have written – that is, draft your conclusions and then reread this draft to

Toby's good conclusions

A better way to communicate these findings might be:

Interviews with the sales staff demonstrated their frustration with the company vision. A significant number of people said that they thought the vision placed too much emphasis on the market and on success, and that they felt undervalued because of it. This issue is important for the organisation to consider because, according to Cameron and Price (2008), where staff share a sense of being undervalued it may lead to increased staff turnover. Of the people interviewed, 65% confirmed that they had thought about leaving the company in the last 12 months, and of those, 35% are still actively looking for another job.

identify every claim that is made. Once these have been identified, you should ask yourself where the evidence is to support each claim. Where there is no evidence to support any one claim, you have a choice: you can remove the claim from the conclusions, you can find and add the evidence, or you can make it clear that what you are presenting is conjecture – your own opinion of the issues (Figure 22.1).

REVIEW, AND RECOGNISE THE LIMITATIONS

All business research is limited by time, by access issues, by resources and by the skills of the researcher. However, where there have been serious limitations – so serious that they may be seen to challenge the veracity of the result – it is important to surface them in the conclusions and explain how your research findings and conclusions have

Figure 22.1 Checking your conclusions

This figure is available at
www.cipd.co.uk/brm

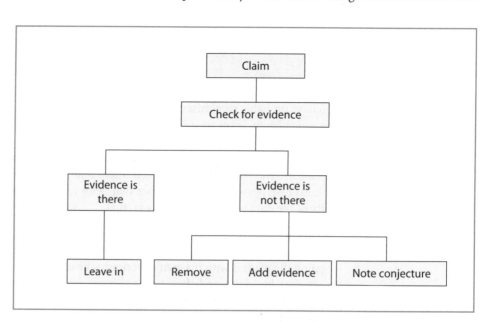

Identify every claim made in the conclusions and ask yourself where the evidence is to support each claim.

taken account of these limitations. To draw once more on Toby's poor conclusion above: it might have been more credible had he noted that although there was potentially a problem with turnover, and that this had implications for the organisation's recruitment and selection processes, it was outside the scope of his research to consider such implications in any depth. Limitations may relate to the size of the sample and the ways in which it influences the generalisability of the results. They may relate to the inability to access certain types of data, or they may relate to the constraints of the time-frame. Although the conclusions should not be a 'confessional' list of everything that the research could not do, it is important to raise any issues that are likely to be raised otherwise by the people reading the conclusions.

> **Explain how you have taken account of the limitations of the research that are salient to the reader.**

CLOSE THE CONCLUSIONS

The ways in which you draw your conclusions to an end will depend largely on the audience for whom you are writing and the messages you want to communicate.

It is important to consider the final impact your conclusions will have on the reader. As you close your conclusions you may wish to remind the reader of the single most important feature of the research findings. In the case of Toby's research, the discovery that the company vision makes people want to leave the organisation may be the key point that he wants to emphasise. This may be especially important where the business research project is undertaken as a piece of consultancy in relation to which you are almost obliged to make sure that the reader knows that you have fulfilled the brief you were given, and that you have discovered some issues that are particularly important to the organisation.

Where the research has been undertaken as part of an academic programme of study, it would be usual to expect the conclusions to consider the limitations of the research methods used. This may or may not be the case for consultancy assignments or for work-based research projects. However, if the consultant is seeking future assignment within the company, it may be useful to point out to the audience the potential value of extending the study, developing it in a different area, or addressing it in a more focused way by further investigating one of the themes that emerged from the research.

Considering the lessons learned is also a useful way to close your conclusions. This draws on the generic implications of the research findings. It summarises the general themes from the research that have been considered in more detail earlier on in the conclusions themselves. Using Toby's case once again as an example, he may wish to end his conclusions with the following:

> "This research project has demonstrated the importance of having a company vision that communicates not only the purpose of the business and the commercial aspirations but also the ways in which the company values the people who work within it."

> **Ensure that the final message that you leave is appropriate to the needs of the specific audience.**

The process of writing valid conclusions is a logical one in which you have to think clearly about the demands of the different stakeholders. This means that for business research projects where stakeholder demands differ, it may be necessary for you to produce two (or possibly even more) sets of conclusions, particularly if a work-based project is also being used as the research element of an academic programme of study.

KEY POINTS

- Think about your audience and their expectations of your research.
- Build your conclusions from a focus on the research question or purpose.
- Communicate the key points succinctly and in ways that the audience will understand.
- Support all claims with evidence.
- Identify and account for any limitations in the research.

MISTAKES MADE IN CONCLUSIONS

Conclusions are effectively the finale to any business research project, and must therefore accurately and reliably reflect the motives for and the results of the research. However, there are a number of problems which frequently occur when producing robust research conclusions.

OVER-INTERPRETATION OF THE DATA

Chapter 9 alluded to some of the problems that commonly arise when trying to draw valid conclusions, not only from qualitative data and information but also from quantitative data and information. To be credible, conclusions must draw only on the data and the information that you actually have, and that you have actually presented earlier in your project report. It is also important to recognise the limitations of your data and information. For example, using discourse analysis allows you to present your own interpretation of the data, but you cannot assume either that it is correct or that your interpretation is an accurate reflection of what the respondent was thinking. You can only justify your claims with well-reasoned argument.

UNDER-INTERPRETATION OF THE DATA

This is a frequent error in business research conducted as part of an academic programme of study, often because of imposed word limits. Researchers spend a great deal of time on the discussions of the research findings and then leave very little scope for their conclusions. The conclusions they produce are less useful than their findings would have allowed. This is problematic in an academic piece of work, but it is even more problematic if the research is then given to the organisation. People are likely to judge the credibility of the research and of the researcher by the conclusions drawn. Where these are too brief, weak, or not supported by evidence, the reader may choose not to bother to read the rest of the report.

INCONSISTENT ARGUMENTS AND EXPLANATIONS

Conclusions that are presented in a partisan way fail to anticipate the arguments that might be raised by the readers. If there are alternative explanations, they should be alluded to and, if necessary, a brief rationale for dismissing these views should be presented. This point also draws on the issue of recognising the limitations of the research, and although it may be inappropriate to surface every little limitation in the conclusions, where issues are likely to be raised by the audience, these must be addressed.

BROAD GENERALISATIONS FROM NARROW DATA

Where the research has been based on a statistical calculation of representativeness, and where the generalisations are being made to the relevant wider population, the process of generalisation is supported by the data. However, often in practical business research constraints of time, of resources and the lack of the necessary skill sets mean that many projects are able to offer only local-level solutions. Where the data set is narrow and pertains to one particular group only, your conclusions should reflect this. To use a well-known analogy, it would be foolish to conclude that birds do not fly simply because the research only looked at ostriches.

CONCLUSIONS COMMUNICATE DESIRED RATHER THAN ACTUAL FINDINGS

You invest considerable time and effort into producing your business research, and are likely to start the process of research with some instincts or some intuitive ideas of what the research findings are likely to be. It can therefore be quite a shock sometimes when you find that your instincts or your intuitions were wrong. Perhaps the actual problem was not what you had anticipated; perhaps the solution that you had hoped to suggest was inappropriate; perhaps the research findings show that *you* were complicit in the problem. Regardless of what you had hoped for, and how similar to or different from what you actually found it is, the conclusions must present a genuine reflection of the research.

CONCLUSIONS SKEWED BY PARTIAL EVIDENCE

This can be a problem where you have a vested interest in presenting a particular set of results, or where there is pressure from stakeholders for you to produce a particular set of results. Aside from the ethical issues that are brought into consideration here, it is problematic to present conclusions which reflect only a part of the research findings. As soon as people begin to engage with the entire report, it will become apparent that what has been presented is a particular view of the world which is not a genuine reflection of the research that has taken place. The credibility of the research and of the researcher is compromised.

KEY POINTS

- Conclusions should emphasise the key findings only.
- They should draw on the actual research findings.
- Opinion should be kept to a minimum, and where included be supported by well-reasoned argument.
- Claims supported by evidence should be used to create coherent and persuasive arguments.

THE CHARACTERISTICS OF GOOD CONCLUSIONS

Your conclusions must present your stakeholders with an unambiguous, focused and robust response to the research questions set. In order to do this, there are a number of criteria you should check. Good conclusions are:

- focused
- valid
- substantial
- convincing
- coherent
- informed.

SUMMARY

The conclusions to your business research project are often the first thing that your readers will turn to. Based on the quality of the conclusions you present, they will make a decision about the credibility of your research, the credibility of you as a researcher, and about whether or not they will read the entire report. These reasons make it imperative that time and effort is put in to crafting a robust set of well-reasoned conclusions.

Using a framework that ties your conclusions to the research question is a good starting place. It prevents you from drifting away from the core themes. Using a logical structure through which you surface the assumptions and premises and seek evidence to support them allows you to map out a coherent set of arguments and ensures that they are backed up by evidence. And by drafting and reviewing the conclusions, making sure that any limitations have been taken into account and accounted for, you ensure that what you present is a fair and trustworthy representation of the salient features of your business research.

REVIEW QUESTIONS

1. Why is it important to present readers with valid, well-reasoned conclusions?

2. What should your conclusions include?

3. Identify three of the problems that can commonly arise when producing valid conclusions.

4. What are the characteristics of good conclusions?

 Visit www.cipd.co.uk/brm for web links, templates, activities and other useful resources relating to this chapter.

PART 5

ESSENTIAL RESEARCH SKILLS

CHAPTER 23

Managing the Project

INTRODUCTION

Poor management of the project is one of the greatest threats to research success. Failing to complete a dissertation is the commonest cause of failure to qualify on many MBA programmes, and this is a consequence of poor project management. Real-life projects often fail to deliver what stakeholders expect, and poor project management is again a common cause. Good project management is an important research skill, and a highly transferable one. A research project shares many characteristics with other management projects, so it is worth using tools and techniques of project management to make sure that you are most likely to achieve your research goals.

Project management techniques have been developed to cope with one-off, finite projects trying to achieve objectives within the constraints of the situation and in the face of risks posed by the environment. They rest upon clear definition of objectives, careful analysis and scheduling of the tasks involved, and on-going monitoring of progress against the plan. Research projects have much in common with other projects, and have to cope with similar uncertainties. They too are constrained by the context, by budget and resource limitations, and are subject to the influence of variations in their context. Things happen and circumstances change and these changes may seriously impact upon the research or sometimes threaten its continuation.

This chapter looks at how clear project definition, detailed task and resource analysis and careful scheduling can increase your chances of producing a successful research project, and how on-going monitoring will enable you to respond promptly to any threats to completion. It provides a useful complement to your work in Chapter 11 on developing a research proposal, because it will help you to check the feasibility of what you propose, and to produce the project plan that is likely to form part of your proposal.

LEARNING OUTCOMES

This chapter should enable you to:

• identify the key characteristics of projects and the management challenges they pose

• define the scope for your project, identifying what is 'in-scope' and what is 'out-of-scope'

• develop a project plan that takes into account the potential risks and contingencies you may face, and acts as a useful tool for managing progress

• follow the plan, adapting it where necessary to ensure successful completion.

ELEMENTS OF PROJECT MANAGEMENT

Slack *et al* (1998, p589) define a project as

> "a set of activities which has a defined start point and a defined end state, pursues a defined goal and uses a defined set of resources."

Research projects evidently fit this definition. They have a clearly identifiable beginning and a specific end point. Good business research is premised on achieving a clearly defined goal and has to attain it within the boundaries of limited resources. If the nature of a business research project so clearly maps on to this more general understanding of what constitutes a 'project', then the tools and techniques of generic project management may be a useful way of co-ordinating research activities to produce the desired results.

Using tried and tested project planning and management techniques can greatly increase the quality of your research and your chances of achieving your purpose. If you are already familiar with project management techniques, you will not need to read this chapter – you merely need to remember to use them! If you are not familiar with project management techniques, this chapter will introduce you to some of the basics.

Project management comprises three key elements:

• the scope of the project

• the time-scale for the project

• the resources required for the project.

The scope of the project maps out what the project is intended to achieve. It defines the research purpose or research objectives and makes a clear distinction between what is 'in-scope' and what is 'out-of-scope'.

The time-scale for the project maps out what has to be achieved by when. The starting point for any time-frame is normally the time by which the project must be finished.

From here you can calculate back to where the starting point is and determine the crucial deadlines that must be hit.

The resources required for the project are important not only because they are necessary to help you produce your research, but because you may also need to factor in time to access these resources.

Projects are finite exercises which have a clear start and clear finish. However, describing them in this way gives the impression that they are somewhat isolated from the day-to-day activities of the organisation – and they are not. Projects take place within the wider *environmental and organisational context*, and because of this they are subject to the *risks and opportunities* presented by this context. Not only does this mean that circumstances beyond your control may have an impact on your ability to successfully complete your project, but it also means that the circumstances surrounding your project may be in a constant state of flux. Key, then, is the idea that a project plan must be a dynamic rather than a static document. Nonetheless, ideally it comprises four specific stages:

1 Clearly define the project objectives

2 Analyse the tasks

3 Devise your project plan

4 Monitor the plan and adapt it as necessary.

1 CLEARLY DEFINE THE PROJECT OBJECTIVES

Project management is an analytical approach that depends on clarity to enable you to map out what you have to do to convert your ideas for research into a practical plan. Everything rests on establishing *clarity* over what is involved, on having a clear definition of your project.

Until your objectives are totally clear you cannot *analyse* the work into discrete tasks. But this is perhaps easier said than done. Because projects require you to juggle the demands of the research against resource, organisational and environmental constraints, and because you have to define a feasible project, and one that is not subject to too many risks, there will be a lot of exploration and looping before and after you reach this point of clarity.

2 ANALYSE THE TASKS

Once you are reasonably clear about *what* you are trying to achieve, and have a rough idea of the resources available and the likely constraints, you can think about *how* to achieve it. What tasks will you have to carry out to complete the project? Project management techniques involve a fairly fine level of analysis. 'Collect data' would not be enough. Having identified the tasks that will achieve the objectives, there is further information needed before you can *schedule* these tasks. You must *estimate* the time they will take, which is never easy, and is particularly difficult if your project is taking you into unfamiliar ground. You must *identify interdependencies* between activities and schedule tasks to ensure that when A needs to be completed before B starts, your schedule allows for it. You must similarly *analyse the resources* you will need, and plan to have them in place by the time they are required.

The stakeholder engagement plan featured in **Chapter 4**

An important further element in this analysis-of-tasks stage is to think about risks to success, and your stakeholder engagement plan will help you here. By identifying any *significant risks*, you can plan to minimise their impact, and allow a contingency for the unexpected.

KEY POINTS

Once you have set the objectives for the project, you must think about how you can achieve them. Analysis of the tasks requires you to consider:

- **what you want to achieve**
- **how you want to achieve it**
- **what the schedule of activities might look like**
- **the time-frames involved for each activity**
- **the interdependencies between activities**
- **the need for resourcing activities**
- **the means and methods of accessing these resources.**

Once you have considered all of these issues, you are then ready to move on to devising your project plan.

3 DEVISE YOUR PROJECT PLAN; 4 MONITOR AND ADAPT AS NECESSARY

Your final plan should take all these aspects into consideration and outline a sequence of activities that will enable you to meet the final deadline. The plan should incorporate 'milestones' – key points at which key tasks should be complete. These will enable you to check that you are on schedule, and take corrective action if necessary.

Hazard warning

Flexibility is key here. There is a balance to be struck between the need for your project plan to be robust enough to make sure that you hit key milestones at the appropriate time, and for it to be adaptable enough to allow you to change your plan of action should organisational or environmental circumstances dictate.

PROJECT DEFINITION

The first principle of good project management is *clarity* and this has to apply first of all to your *purpose*. You and your stakeholders must agree on what it is that you are trying to achieve. If you are doing research for a dissertation, this clarity and agreement must be tripartite and include aggreement by your supervisor as well as agreement from your organisation. Equally importantly, it must be clear what you are *not* trying to do. Determining the *scope* of any project is an important step. In addition to defining your objectives and scope – often phrased in terms of 'deliverables' – you need clarity over time-scales. *When* will you deliver them? Your definition also has to make clear the resources that will be required and who will provide them.

These three aspects –

- deliverables
- time-scales
- resources

– will define your project and help you to think clearly about the demands made, the constraints within which you have to work and the choices that these leave you with (Stewart, 1984). The demands placed upon your project are the things that you and or others want your business research to achieve. Unless you are clear about the objective, you cannot identify the tasks involved in achieving the objective. Unless you are clear about time-scales, you cannot schedule tasks in a way that will ensure your meeting deadlines. And unless you and your client are clear about resources, you cannot ensure that those that you must have will be available.

Likewise, projects are almost always carried out within *constraints*. Clarity over objectives, time-scales and resources will serve to clarify constraints. Without this clarity you may be unaware of some of the limitations on resources, and risk undertaking something that is not feasible. By paying attention to the deliverables, the resources and the time-scales, you can clarify the choices that are available to you.

Effective project management is dependent on a clear identification of the demands, constraints and choices that you face as a researcher.

Chapter 11 emphasised the importance of clarity in your research proposal for your supervisor, and Chapter 24 emphasises the need for your client to commit in writing to a detailed project specification outlining what will be delivered, and by when. The written agreement covering all these aspects of the project protects you against subsequent changes of mind (or personnel) or 'mis-rememberings' over what would be delivered, involved and/or provided.

DEFINITION INVOLVES LOOPING

Reaching this degree of clarity is necessarily an iterative process. You will normally need a detailed exploration stage before you start. You will have to understand the risks posed by the environment. If some of the necessary activities depend upon the co-operation of a stakeholder hostile to your project, or involve a department under threat of closure, you might want to rethink your project. If those involved are expecting to be tied up at some future point on activity connected with an anticipated but as yet uncertain merger, you might want to schedule their involvement earlier rather than later, plan activities that do not involve them or redefine your project. You might want to explore and define, discuss with stakeholders, explore more, redefine, etc, a number of times before you reach a working definition.

Looping does not end there. Until you take this working definition and start to analyse the tasks required to 'deliver' the project, you cannot feel confident that the project defined is feasible within your own limitations and other constraints. So once you start analysing the tasks required in more detail, and thinking about how long they will take and the potential risks associated with them, you may have to further redefine your project in order to reach a definition that both satisfies your stakeholders and is feasible within the constraints operating.

The following research story demonstrates one student's thinking about her project at an early planning stage. You may find this set of questions useful in your own context.

RESEARCH STORY

Theatrical expenditure

Cerys works in the finance office of the OscarX Theatre Company, checking and approving invoices from actors and theatre staff recruited on short-term contracts. She wants to carry out a project that will contribute to a more accurate and efficient process, with better control over costs.

Having progressed her thinking to the point of defining her project, she used a series of questions to check that her definition was adequate.

1 Is the research objective sufficiently clear?

The project is trying to identify current weaknesses and suggest improvements to the system of invoice reconciliation so that it is more accurate and gives the finance department more accurate and timely financial information that will ultimately improve financial control. I think this is clear enough as an objective.

2 What are the boundaries of the research? What is 'in scope' and what is 'out'?

I need to be very careful to retain a focus on the issue of reconciling invoices. I can make suggestions about new processes and systems but must be aware that the introduction of new systems for contracting is outside the remit of this research. I must also be aware that I should not be drifting into the issues of pay rates. The main thing I may have to think about is how to point out that where money leaves the business faster, we may need it to come into the business faster. I will have not produced any 'evidence' for this from my research but may have to recognise that as one of the weaknesses of any recommendations I make.

3 Is the time-scale/delivery date clearly specified?

My line manager wants me to have finished the report by the end of December 2010. That means that she can try to work with the necessary people in the other departments and have any new systems introduced in the new financial year starting in April. I cannot start the project until after the end of this financial year so I am looking to start properly in June 2010.

4 What tasks will be involved?

The starting place will be finding out about the current systems for reconciling invoices. Finding out what people think works and what people think doesn't work. This must be informed by the literature, and having read some of the accountancy and finance literature and professional accounting journals, I am building up a picture of what is thought to be best practice. The finish is a bit more tricky. I have to be quite clear that the finish is the point at which I make suggestions for improvements to the system and point out the other factors that the company may wish to consider. I must try not to get embroiled in detailed discussions about these issues because they are outside my remit and I will have no evidence to back up what I am saying.

5 What resources will I need?

It would be really useful if the Director could email everyone and say how useful and potentially important my project is. That way people may be more willing to take part than if I just ask them to. Apart from this, there are no significant resource commitments needed – other than loads of my time, that is!

6 What interdependencies must I take into account/may influence the ability to keep to time? Where is the project dependent on other people (providing data, allowing access, responding to questionnaires, etc)?

I will have to allow time to go through the Director's PA to ask him, and then allow time for him to produce the email. (Perhaps I could draft this for him to speed things up?) I also have to allow time for the interviews, fitting in around people's commitments. I need time between interviews to allow me to transcribe the tapes. And I must finish the interviews well before I start writing my dissertation, because analysis is likely to take me a long time.

You can see that by surfacing key issues in the project remit, Cerys was starting to become aware of some of the constraints that she faced in undertaking her research project. Cerys does not refer to the literature here, but before agreeing your project definition you would normally have done substantial reading. This will help you to think more clearly about the data you are going to collect and how best to collect it. For a dissertation you will have to be sure – before confirming your definition – that there is sufficient relevant literature, and that your research is informed by it.

Research purposes and deliverables

Does your over-arching research question or research purpose definition equate to the project's 'deliverable'? Defining your research purpose or over-arching question is a key part of defining your project. It clarifies what *you* (and any research supervisor) are seeking as the output from the research. It is important to keep the research purpose firmly in mind. As you become exposed to more and more data, more and more information, there is a temptation to broaden the focus of the research. In some cases this 'project creep' results in the focus becoming so wide that it is simply no longer a feasible piece of business research. A clearly defined research purpose, and planning and monitoring activities that ensure that activities are directed towards achieving this purpose, is an important element in maintaining control of the project.

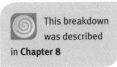

This breakdown was described in **Chapter 8**

You saw earlier that you could usefully break down your overall research purpose (or question) into a set of subordinate research objectives (or questions). Some of them – for example, an interim report on one aspect of an issue, or an early analysis of financial or marketing trends – might be valuable in their own right as well as feeding into subsequent analysis. These sub-parts of the project will be useful as units for planning, and their completion may serve as milestones on your journey.

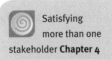

Satisfying more than one stakeholder **Chapter 4**

For practical research you may have other deliverables. Your client may be seeking a different sort of report from your research supervisor, and may require interim reports or additional ones addressing issues that are not part of your key research focus. In defining your project it is important to identify and gain clear agreement to any variants in deliverables to different stakeholders. Your planning and monitoring will have to apply to *all* deliverables if your research is to satisfy all the key stakeholders.

TASK AND RESOURCE ANALYSIS

An important part of keeping a project under control is to carry out a *work breakdown analysis*, which allows you to split the whole into more manageable parts. You need a sufficiently detailed analysis of the tasks involved to allow you to estimate how long each will take, and work out the resources that will be required for each. So the first step in this analysis is to identify all the tasks.

 ACTIVITY

Imagine that the purpose of your research, like the project described in Chapter 3, is to assess the impact of executive coaching on performance. You are a full-time student, so you have to find a willing 'client' organisation. You intend to look at 'before' and 'after' performance measures for a group receiving coaching and another group not being coached, and to interview those coached to explore what they perceived as its impact. Coaching will be done by five qualified executive coaches who are associated with your business school.

List the tasks that might be required, and estimate the time each might take.

Your list will not necessarily be like the one below, but there are several clear sets of tasks. Some had to do with finding suitable 'subjects' – identifying a suitable organisation, and a 'client' to sponsor the research, identifying suitable subjects and obtaining their consent. Some had to do with design of the study – deciding how many 'subjects' are needed, how they will be identified, how a control group will be identified, and how performance will be measured, constructing an interview schedule. Some will be logistical – arranging testing for both groups, arranging coaching sessions, and interviews. Some will concern the production of deliverables. An organisation will usually agree to host research if it can see a useful output of the research. For example, this project might enable the researcher to write a report highlighting some of the management development needs and issues that would be of more value to the client than any conclusions on coaching. Some tasks will relate to 'client management' during the project.

This example is more complicated than would be likely for a dissertation (although many initial proposals are of a similar complexity, and scaled down only after forcefully expressed advice from the tutor). But it serves to highlight many of the aspects that are likely to be problematic in scheduling. Let us take one set of tasks – those related to the logistics of arranging the coaching. This might involve:

- agreeing with the client who will be offered coaching, in how many sessions and over what time-frame
- ascertaining coaches' availability within this frame
- agreeing with the client how line managers will be informed/involved and staff informed of the study
- offering coaching sessions to selected staff (with further information and the informed consent form)
- liaising with the client to identify suitable dates and times for coaching
- ascertaining the availability of those to be coached

- arranging the timetable for coaching
- confirming the schedule with coaches and those to be coached
- arranging the contracts for coaches
- checking that a suitable office has been booked for sessions
- writing a 'welcome letter' to coachees a week in advance of the first session.

You can see that there are resources that have to be arranged and co-ordinated. You need the right number of willing coaches, and they must be available at the same time as the coachees. There must be somewhere suitable for the coaching to take place. If you had explored the 'measure performance' set of activities, there would have been other resources required, and other things to get organised.

PROJECT PLANNING

Thus far you have been working out what must be done. Now you move on to planning when and how you are going to do it. This involves:

- estimating how long you will need to complete the different activities
- identifying dependencies between activities and other constraints
- analysing the risks that might mean it takes longer
- and constructing a plan that will act as your route map through the project, and your 'speedometer' to ensure that you are travelling sufficiently quickly towards your goal.

TIME ESTIMATION

Once you have identified all the tasks you will have to carry out, and the resources you will need in order to carry them out, you can start to work out how long each task will take, and therefore how long you will need to complete the project. Some task times may have to be 'guesstimates' – a sort of best guess based on your own previous experience and/or advice from others. However, if you have never done similar activities before, and nor have those you can ask for advice, you will have to make educated guesses based upon your most similar experience.

A good rule of thumb in estimating task time is 'Think of a number and double it'. In other words, you are far more likely to under-estimate than to over-estimate. Tasks involving others are particularly likely to take longer than you imagine. Not only does co-ordinating diaries take time but 'your' research may be a much lower priority for them than it is for you, so work they have undertaken to carry out may take longer to complete than you expect.

It is at this stage that some serious looping may take place. If the tasks you wish to carry out look like taking more time than you can commit to the project, you will have to loop back and redefine your project as something more manageable.

If you are relying heavily on estimates, you should monitor your progress regularly against the project plan. If early estimates are way out, you may have to revise your plan or even redefine your objectives.

IDENTIFYING DEPENDENCIES AND CONSTRAINTS

Having worked out a realistic (ie pessimistic) set of times for tasks, you must then think about the relationship between the tasks. This involves determining the order in which you are going to tackle the tasks. Some aspects of your project can only happen when other things have been completed. If you think back to the example used previously, it would not be possible to effectively schedule coaching sessions before the people running these sessions (the coaches) had been contacted and their availability checked. Likewise, it would be poor practice to offer these people contracts of employment before someone had made sure that the managers of the organisation were prepared to resource this. For some activities there is a clear order in which things have to happen. For others there is the opportunity to run two activities together or in parallel. A useful tool to help you map out these relationships is a critical path analysis (CPA).

CPA allows you to walk through the process of your research and map out which things must be done in which order. It is usual to start this process by arranging the activities in a table (see Table 23.1).

Table 23.1 Critical path analysis in respect of the activity 'Arrange interviews with trainers'

Task	Description	Time (days)	Order	Parallel to	Involves
Arrange interviews with trainers					
1	Obtain suggestions from supervisor	3	1st	Task 2	Supervisor
2	Obtain contacts from training manager	1	1st/2nd	Task 1	Training manager
3	Devise written information/ invitation pack	10	2nd/3rd		
4	Telephone all those suggested to invite to take part.	15	4th – start after Task 3 has ended	Task 5	Coaches
5	Devise interview proforma	15	4th	Task 4	
6	Send written invitation	2	5th – start after Task 5 has ended		

Once you have done this for all activities, you can start to map them out. Project management software makes it easy to take durations and interdependencies into account. Otherwise you can use Post-Its or a simple Excel spreadsheet to sequence activities that can be done in parallel, and identify those that have to wait for other activities or resources, or that because of other constraints cannot start until a particular point in time.

You must take a range of constraints into account when scheduling the tasks you have identified, including the necessity of finishing some before others can be started. A key resource constraint will be your time, so you must ensure that you do not over-commit yourself in any period by scheduling too many parallel activities at that time. Other necessary resources may be available only at certain times or there may be a lag between requesting them and obtaining them. There may be external constraints too. For example, you will find it very difficult to arrange interviews with accountants during the financial year end.

Once you have identified the dependencies, you can determine the minimum duration of the project by identifying the critical path through the activities. A very basic mapping example is given in Figure 23.1.

Figure 23.1 Critical path analysis from which to gauge minimum duration

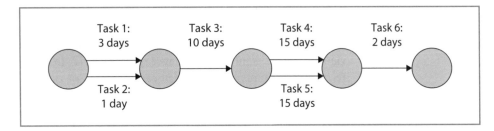

The critical path is the sequence of activities that cannot be done in parallel, and through the longest-lasting one of each set that can. This is the shortest time in which the project can be completed. Activities on this path are critical because unless you have built in some slack time, delay to any one of them will mean that the project is not completed on schedule. If completing your project on time requires you to complete every activity on the critical path within your (optimistic) time estimate, you must reconsider your project. Business research has too many uncertainties for this to be likely to work.

Milestones

A key element in project planning is the idea of a *milestone*. This is a point at which an important part of the project should have been completed, or a key criterion met. At such points it is possible to check that a project is on schedule, and if relevant, not over-running on costs. For a dissertation, obvious milestones are submission (or agreement) of a project proposal, ethical approval, and the completion of a substantial section such as the literature review. Other typical research milestones might be design of a questionnaire, the completion of a pilot study, or completion of your preliminary diagnosis.

ANALYSING RISKS

Risk assessment is an important stage. It allows you to try to anticipate the types of problems that may occur at the various stages throughout your business research project. Anticipating risks is of particular importance when your research has to be completed within a particular time-frame. Obviously, it is not possible to anticipate all possible problems, nor indeed is it possible to anticipate the risks with any degree of certainty or accuracy. However, by thinking through the possible problems and the possible solutions beforehand, you are more prepared for whatever eventualities may occur. A systematised approach to this is to brainstorm the risks, the things that could go wrong, along each activity on the process flowchart or on a Gantt chart (see below). Once each risk is identified, it is for you to make a judgement on the best form of action. Such actions may involve:

Eliminating the risk by taking action to ensure that the threat does not materialise. One threat to Cerys's theatre project was the risk that people might not respond to her questions. This could be almost eliminated by persuading the Director to mandate people to answer her questions, although this might have introduced the risk of less than fully honest answers. A risk to the coaching evaluation project might be the non-availability of coaches. This might be eliminated by contracting them before you started, albeit at the risk of having to pay them if you could not identify suitable coaching clients who were available during the contracted time.

Mitigating the risk by taking action to reduce the severity of the threatened event or to lessen the ramifications should the threatened event take place. Cerys wanted to talk to departmental managers. She might have mitigated the risk that they would be too busy by obtaining agreement to interview assistant managers as well, and interviewing the assistant if the manager refused. A risk to recorded interview data is that recording equipment will fail. You can mitigate this risk by taking some notes during the interview. Another risk with interviews is that transcribing the data might take longer than you think. A way of dealing with this is to budget some time for over-run or to have identified someone willing to help you if necessary.

There is a strong risk that you will become ill, or have to deal with some sort of crisis, during the project. You might take steps to reduce the risk of ill-health, for example, by not over-committing yourself, avoiding anyone with flu, and taking exercise and Vitamin C. But there will still be a significant risk that at some point you will be unable to work on your research for some reason. You can mitigate this risk by planning to complete your work well in advance of the deadline. This will allow you to let the plan slip by a week or two if contingencies make it necessary.

Transferring the risk to someone else or some other project. This means that someone else takes the risk. Cerys might have agreed to do the project only if her sponsor obtained the potential interviewees' agreement to take part. If the sponsor then did not involve the interviewees, it would have been the sponsor that failed, not Cerys. However, although this would absolve Cerys from the risk of being blamed for any shortfall, it might not reduce – indeed, might increase – the risks to the success of the project.

Accepting the risk if you cannot or are unwilling to do anything about it, and feel that it is acceptable.

Rejecting the project if you feel that the inevitable risk is too high, and you cannot be sufficiently confident of completing in time or of doing sufficiently good research. It is far better to loop back at this stage and redefine your project than to decide to be optimistic.

CONSTRUCTING A PROJECT PLAN

Everything you have done thus far is to enable you to produce your key project management 'tool', your project plan. This serves several purposes. It enables you to check that the project is 'do-able' within the allowed time-scale – ie that unless you are extremely unlucky the necessary tasks are capable of being completed within the required time-frame. It acts as a route map to activity, showing you what has to be done at any point in time. And it allows you to check that you are on schedule. Without a clear plan it is quite likely that you will get well into the project only to realise that it is impossible to complete it by the deadline.

'Failing to plan is planning to fail.'

A standard format for project planning is the Gantt chart. This was devised by Henry Gantt (cited in Buchanan and Huczynski, 2004) as a means of scheduling. It provides a simple visual prompt that shows where the project should be at any one point in time, which activities should have been completed by when, and which activities have yet to be completed as long as progress is line with the schedule (Slack *et al*, 1998). Figure 23.2 shows Cerys's Gantt chart.

Figure 23.2 Cerys's Gantt chart

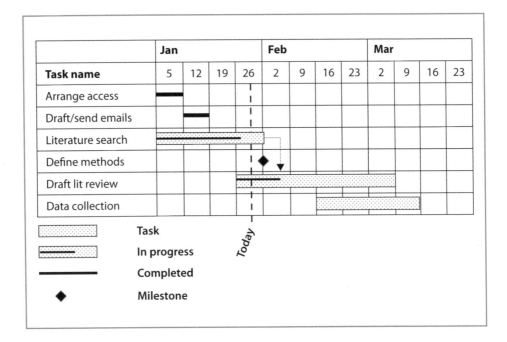

A Gantt chart gives you a clear overall view of where you should be at any point in time. So what can we read from Cerys's chart? We can see that her literature search is running a little behind schedule. The slippage is not huge but she must be aware of it to make sure that it gets no worse. On the other hand she appears to be slightly ahead of schedule in drafting her literature review. From a brief look at her Gantt chart Cerys may well decide to slow down slightly on the writing of the literature review and use the time to catch up with her literature search.

Gantt charts may look rather different, depending on the software you use, but will contain the same elements in some shape or form. They are commonly used for large projects.

CONSIDER...

If most business research is best seen as a process of messy looping, what might be the disadvantage of a Gantt chart like Figure 23.2?

You may remember from Chapter 1 that there is a high risk that with a linear approach to research you will miss out on some of the 'looping' processes which allow you to develop and then refine your ideas. This might be a serious problem if you draw such a chart too early, because you will then be committed to a process of research that is ill-thought-through. For many projects there must be some sort of compromise, creating a project plan which allows you to move efficiently through the things that you need to do while retaining sufficient flexibility to allow you to make changes and adaptations as necessary.

The Gantt chart is not the only approach to mapping your project and you may prefer a simpler approach such as the examples extracted from research plans shown in Table 23.2 and 23.3.

Table 23.2 Part of a plan of activities for a project on a marketing issue

Activity	Due start	Due end
D SDC Team motivation		
D1 Complete appraisals (to verify team motivation)	3/11	24/11
D2 Agree PRP proposals	3/11	14/11
D3 Focus on intrinsic motivation via involvement in project planning process	1/12	15/12
D4 Review level of team motivation	5/1	2/3
E Improve project planning process		
E1 Meet with suppliers to review options for projects	3/11	8/12
E2 Prepare for internal planning review	1/12	15/12
E3 Share project options with key field partners	8/12	15/12
E4 Review feedback and start new projects	5/1	26/1
F Improve communication within the team		
F1 Run problem-solving activity on project processes	1/12	15/12
F2 Write up process guidelines	5/1	23/2

Note that in the second chart the researcher has used traffic-light colours to indicate progress against the plan.

Your choice of how you represent your project plan is dependent on a number of factors. Partly this is a matter of practicalities – do you have access to project management software which makes it easy to draw charts such as those in Figure 23.2? Partly it is personal choice. If you are a highly visual person, you may prefer a map such as the CPA considered previously (Figure 23.1); if you are not, you may prefer a more tabular plan. Or of course you may prefer to use both – a visual version for at-a-glance progress assessment, a more detailed table of activities for daily reference.

Task	Who	Implementation date	Comments
Preliminary analysis			
Cross-shift brainstorming session	Cross-shift	2 May ●	
Meeting to discuss outcomes and agree preliminary analysis	M, S, J & I	5 May ●	
Data collection	Ops, TOs	9 May to 25 May ●	

Task	Who	Implementation date	Comments
Define			
Data matrix kick-off meeting	Project team	9 June ●	
Preparation of project charter	Project team	12 June ●	
Introduction to data matrix session	Project engineers	14 July ●	
BBZ introductory training session for team	IB	22 July ●	
Measure			
Collect and compare samples of good and poor performing cartons and inserts	Shift team		
Shift engineer training on taking screen shots	J	23 July ●	
Set up engineering logs to capture further issues	MM, N, A & K	29 July ●	
Perform further two-week data-collection exercise	All shifts	to 1 Aug ○	Not required
Analyse			
Analyse data from engineering logs	M	30 Aug ●	Ill
Analyse differences on die cuts for low/high/number rejected part numbers	M, S, H	23 Aug ●	Ill
XUZ supplier visit to check set-up of lines	J	30 July ●	
Engineering to send samples of good and bad carton to XUZ Germany	B	30 July ●	
Receive feedback from XUZ re sample and visit from 23 May	J/B	8 Aug ●	
Assess recent improvement in cameras and vision software for L-line	Project engineers	5 Sep & on-going ○	Need data analysis to start
Start devlpmt trials with different-sized data matrix on cartons		28 Aug ●	
Develpmt trials based on best result of prev. trials	M & shift team		
Perform engineering study: Functionality	Project team and supply chain	9 Oct ●	
Start change process on carton/insert specifications	Project engineers	9 Oct ●	
	M & supply chain & regulatory team	Nov ○	Cannot finalise change process until analysis complete, and delay here starting to put these activities at risk
Implement upgrade of software/vision system, if appropriate			
	S & regulatory & agile teams	Nov ○	

Table 23.3 Part of a plan of activities for a project on a manufacturing issue

PROJECT CONTROL

Control is vital because business research projects are planned under conditions of uncertainty and within a dynamic and rapidly changing context. When circumstances change, you have to change to adapt. Just as earlier stages formed a part of project planning, project planning is a core part of project control. Without a plan, control is impossible, and things can go badly wrong. With a plan they still can, although they will do so much less often.

Control of the project requires you to be adaptable, which can sometimes be difficult. If you have invested considerable time and effort in your project plan, it can be very difficult to abandon it and draw up a new plan when circumstances change. However, you still have to keep control of your project when circumstances change, and four things are important if you wish to do so:

- frequent reference to your project definition document to ensure that you have not drifted out of scope

- regular checking of progress against plan. A good habit to get into is to check the status of your project at least once a week

- the use of milestones to reinforce the importance of keeping on schedule

- rapid replanning to get back on track if you start to deviate, or a negotiated redefinition of the project's objectives if this looks impossible.

KEY POINTS

- Your research project should be managed in the same way that you manage any project at work.
- A project plan will help you to map out the things you have to do and the critical path to achieving your required outcomes.
- Project plans are guidelines and you must allow yourself some degree of freedom to reorder the activities.
- Project plans should build in contingencies – so that you know what to do if . . .
- Project plans need updating.

SUMMARY

Throughout this book we have emphasised the messiness of research. For all practical business research you will be dealing with complex issues and contexts. Because poor management is a common cause of research failure, project management is a key research skill.

Project management starts with clear project definition. The complexities mean that you will have to iterate or loop before you can agree a firm project definition. Once you have defined your project you can increase your chances of successfully managing the project by thinking analytically about the tasks that will be required, the time they will take and the resources you will need to complete your project.

Once activities and constraints are identified, you can begin to schedule your activities. You will have to devise a schedule in which all necessary prior tasks are completed before those depending on them begin, and in which you can complete the critical path before the deadline, without making impossible demands upon your own or others' time.

The schedule you devise will act as a guide to action and as a standard against which to assess progress and identify when corrective action is required. Some corrective action is inevitable given the risks and uncertainties of business research and its context.

REVIEW QUESTIONS

1. What are the main elements needed for successful project management?

2. List some of the key factors you have to consider when drawing up a project plan.

3. What purpose do milestones serve?

4. When might a project plan be unhelpful?

EXPLORE FURTHER

Meredith, J. and Mantel, S. (2001) *Project Management: A managerial approach*, 4th edition. London: John Wiley & Sons. A good general textbook on project management which introduces many of the standard tools and techniques that can be transferred to the context of a business research project

Polonsky, M. and Waller, D. (2005) *Designing and Managing a Research Project: A business student's guide*. Thousand Oaks, CA: Sage Publications. Written specifically for business research projects, this is an easy-to-read book which breaks the research project into three sections: planning, execution and feedback

Sharpe, J., Peters, J. and Howard, K. (2002) *The Management of a Student Research Project*, 3rd edition. Aldershot: Gower. Again focused on the management of business research projects, this book uses the issues of research field, purpose, approach, and the nature of the research to help frame the best way to manage the project

http://managementhelp.org/plan_dec/project/project.htm for useful basic guidance on project management and links to many other sources of information

 Visit www.cipd.co.uk/brm for web links, templates, activities and other useful resources relating to this chapter.

CHAPTER 24

Managing Client Relationships

INTRODUCTION

Most practical business research carried out by practising managers or consultants is done for a client, and some business students have the opportunity to study a Consultancy module. Most managers act as internal or external consultants at some point in their career, and building and sustaining a good relationship with a client is a key skill. If you are doing research as a consultant, your client will typically have identified an issue, and will have the influence and resources to commission an assignment to help address it.

As an external consultant, your client will normally be the person who hired you. If you are a student doing an in-company project, the manager who is sponsoring the project will be a client-equivalent. For a project in your own organisation your client might be your own boss, or you might be acting as internal consultant to another senior manager. Sometimes you will be your own 'client'.

A dual research/consultancy agenda may create conflicts if your client perceives you purely as a consultant (see Chapter 2), and conflicts require compromises. Resolving such conflicts will require a firm and open relationship with your client, a further reason why managing this relationship is so important. This chapter will give a brief overview of the issues to be addressed, and the skills you will need to build and sustain a constructive working relationship with your client(s) and to minimise conflicts without compromising the value of your research findings.

The chapter thus covers initial discussions about the project, on-going communications and the need for openness and honesty throughout, and how to conclude the relationship in a positive way. Many of the points will be useful for any consultancy work, and may help you handle relationships with other key stakeholders.

LEARNING OUTCOMES

This chapter should enable you to:

- establish a good working relationship at the start of the project

- recognise the potential for differences in perspective between client and researcher, and the need to be open about them

- appreciate the importance of having a clear agreement about expectations on both sides

- identify emerging differences of opinion and address them constructively

- assess when and how to conclude the relationship in a way that increases the opportunities for future projects.

CLIENT RELATIONSHIPS: THE IMPORTANCE AND THE CHALLENGE

If you are new to business research it is easy to worry about the content of the research so much that you forget about the context. It is important to avoid this trap. Your client is likely to be the most important aspect of the research context, and a poor relationship with a client can seriously threaten the success of your research. Your client normally 'owns' the problem situation, and has the greatest interest in investigating it. Clients usually have a great deal of other influence on your research. They are usually the gatekeepers for information and other necessary resources, and can influence others to co-operate (willingly or otherwise) in your investigation. They can help you find ways of working around unexpected hazards so that the research can still continue. They can themselves be one of the greatest hazards, terminating a project if they become uneasy about the way it is going or what you may find. This power to influence – for good or bad – is one extremely important reason to pay attention to your relationship with your client. Some of the client's potential influences on your research are listed below.

The client

- is a key informant
- influences other informants
- determines the research topic
- approves methods and scope
- approves resources
- approves access to information
- approves report for other audiences
- provides on-going support and legitimation
- approves any redirections.

Your client may be one of your key informants. Many of your interactions with your client will be data-gathering interviews, and need to be captured and analysed overtly, rather than covertly, because otherwise there will be ethical issues. Your project is intended to meet client requirements, so you have to know what those requirements are. Their view of the issue is the starting point for the investigation, and the end point must be their satisfaction. If the looping process has moved the focus of the investigation, the client's perception of what is required needs to have moved in line with your own. Remaining sensitive to, and respecting, the client's perspective, and communicating openly with them throughout the project will protect you from inadvertently moving on without them.

A third, more personal, reason is that you may well work as a consultant for at least some of your career. If so, much of your income will depend upon your clients' happiness with the work you do for them. And this will depend upon the quality of your relationship itself, as well as upon the quality of the results of the projects for which you are hired. Relationship-building skills thus influence not only the success of any individual project but also the likelihood of further business from existing clients, and new business when they recommend you to others.

The challenge lies in building and sustaining an open and constructive relationship with someone who may be more experienced and more powerful than you are, who may have very strong views about the conduct of the project, and indeed may have strong preferences about the results to be obtained. Your expertise is likely to be in how to carry out an investigative project, rather than in running the client's business. The challenge is to build trust and respect in what you *can* contribute without seeking to impress by claiming more expertise than you possess. It involves being able to hold robust debates when your views and the client's conflict, without giving way on points which you consider essential to the validity of your investigation, despite any power differential between you. And it involves being sensitive to the client's personal and business needs and respecting them. To meet the challenge you will require well-developed interpersonal sensitivities and skills.

KEY POINTS

- Clients are key stakeholders in many projects, and learning to work with clients is a key consultancy skill.
- It is important to recognise and appreciate the validity of the client's perspective, without losing sight of the value of your own.
- Building an open and constructive relationship is key to this.

RELATIONSHIPS AT DIFFERENT STAGES IN A CONSULTANCY PROJECT

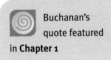
Buchanan's quote featured in **Chapter 1**

Buchanan et al (1988) talked of the research process in terms of getting in, getting on, getting out and getting back. Client relationships are important at all these stages.

- Getting in involves building enough trust in your ability to be of use for the client to be prepared to start working with you.
- Getting on is about sustaining a relationship as the project continues, thus ensuring continued resources and acceptance of your eventual recommendations.

- Getting out is often forgotten, but the nature of your 'exit' is extremely important in ensuring that the client is confident and competent to continue the project without you. It is also important that you both feel that the relationship has been a productive one, with learning on both sides.

Thinking in terms of three stages is a good start, but it may help to break the process down even further. Because a great many consultancy projects are based upon some sort of information-gathering, and all involve a client, the consultancy literature is a rich source of frameworks for thinking about relationships. The 'Seven Cs' framework suggested by Cope (2003) as a starting place, shown in Table 24.1, seems commendable. This is a client-oriented approach that acknowledges the importance of recognising this key stakeholder perspective.

Table 24.1 Aspects of client relationship tasking

Stage	*Your main aims:*
Client	Define the client's views, perceptions and goal for the situation and agree with them what value you will deliver and what value the client will offer in return. *Key tasks* – Establish your credibility, understand the client and the nature of their perception of the problem, and build trust and rapport.
Clarify	Explore the problem in more detail, and the system(s) and people involved, and the potential risks. *Key tasks* – Build a shared understanding of what is going on, of what the client is seeking as an outcome of the project, and agree access to the information and resources that might be involved in both investigation and solution.
Create	Creatively generate options, and evaluate them against identified success criteria. *Key tasks* – Ensure that the client is happy with the way you are proceeding, and with the criteria you are using. Check that the option selected is acceptable.
Change	Identify the drivers and resisters of change, and the resources available. *Key tasks* – Ensure that you and the client have a clear idea of what you are up against in implementing change, and are agreed on how to approach it.
Confirm	Decide on the qualitative and quantitative measures of effectiveness, and apply them. *Key tasks* – Assure yourself that change has taken place as intended and ensure that the client is happy with the impact of the change.
Continue	Decide how long the change is intended to last, and identify resources needed to support the change. *Key tasks* – Ensure that the client is aware of, and committed to supporting, continuing actions to make sure that change is sustained.
Close	End the engagement with client, establishing the added value and the learning gained, and exploring any future opportunities. *Key tasks* – Explore with the client what can be learned from this project, establish the potential for additional related work, and leave the client feeling that the collaboration has been successful, and a learning experience for them, and something they would wish to repeat if an opportunity became available.

Source: adapted from Cope, M. (2003) *The Seven Cs of Consulting*. FT/Prentice Hall

Although the model appears to be linear, Cope explicitly makes the point that there will always be a need for constant iteration both within the cycle and around the whole seven stages. Each of the stages shown can be undertaken independently, jointly, or indeed in parallel with each other. This is much more consistent with the approach to research that we have been suggesting throughout the book. Cope suggests that when you first meet a client you undertake a rapid mapping of the issue and method. A quick pass through the entire cycle with the client in 10 to 15 minutes helps give the client an idea of how you will be working. (This would only be appropriate if you were an experienced consultant.)

Table 24.1 shows the main aim for each of Cope's stages, and associated key 'relationship' tasks.

The important message from Table 24.1 is that the relationship requires attention at *all* stages of the consultancy process.

 ACTIVITY

Cope was writing about consultancy in general. Note in your journal any modifications you might want to make to this list of 'C's to highlight any aspects of particular interest to you in your own project.

For an action-oriented project all these stages are important. For an exploratory project aimed at increased understanding, 'Continue' would not be necessary, and you might or might not need 'Create', 'Change' and 'Confirm'. There are, however, some important additional stages that you may have to go through, largely driven by the complexities of diagnosing organisational issues. The following case example, provided by an HR consultant, shows the importance of such diagnosis, even when the client has already determined 'the problem'.

RESEARCH STORY

New recruitment technology assignment

A large UK company had reorganised its HR function, streamlining structures and processes in the interests of cost-efficiency. But internal 'customers' were complaining, in particular about recruitment inefficiencies. They brought in a consultant to identify, select and implement new recruitment technology to resolve the problem.

When they realised that the 'diagnosis' on which this decision had been taken rested solely on the views of HR managers, the consultants obtained agreement to additional diagnosis, seeking views from operational managers around the organisation. As a result of this diagnosis, two very different projects emerged. One looked at how to attract recruits with key technology skills, and the other at teamworking and joint management within the

HR function. Together these projects addressed the underlying problems that had prompted the complaints. The new technology system, which would have cost a six-figure sum, would have done nothing to improve the situation because it was based upon an incorrect understanding of what the problem really was.

To achieve this redefinition of the problem the consultants had to convince the clients that their diagnosis must be checked before proceeding to implement their projected 'solution' – not always an easy task.

Story contributed by Philip Vernon, HR Consultant (personal communication)

Examples such as this suggest that you need to build a relationship that allows you to question the client's diagnosis before committing to an agreement to particular action. But first you need to be sure that the person you are dealing with actually is a real client. Thus the 'client' stage may require an additional prior step.

CLIENT – IDENTIFY THE CLIENT

The first additional stage is to verify that the client is the real one: you may be working with an 'apparent' client rather than the genuine article. A past colleague with extensive international consultancy experience suggests the following questions:

- who *knows* about the problem/issue?
- who *cares* about it enough to do something about it?
- who *can do* something about it?

If the answer to each of these questions is someone other than your apparent client, you are likely to run into difficulty at some point in the project, and/or your recommendations may not be accepted, no matter how sound they are. It is therefore worth seeking the 'real' client and obtaining their support, or redefining the project to be something for which your contact really *is* the client.

Key relationship tasks at this stage would be establishing enough trust to ask questions about the client's interests and responsibilities, to gain honest answers and to talk through the implications if the client turns out to be apparent rather than real.

CLARIFY (i) – REACH INITIAL AGREEMENT

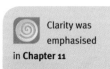
Clarity was emphasised in **Chapter 11**

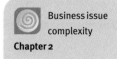
Business issue complexity **Chapter 2**

'Clarify' can be further subdivided. The need for clarity has already been strongly emphasised. 'Clarifying' is frequently the most important stage in practical business research, and because of the complexities of most business issues you are likely to have to do some looping at this point. It is fairly optimistic to think that you can reach a final agreement without more clarification. At this early stage *you* may be unclear about the nature of the issue. Your *client*, although knowing and caring about it, may have misperceived either the problem or the type of (re)solution required. You may have to reach a preliminary agreement to carry out initial explorations, with a view to formulating a more formal agreement at a later stage. This initial agreement must be built on an open discussion of the issues.

Key relationship tasks at this stage would include reassuring your client that your uncertainty was a result of your *understanding* of organisational issues rather than your ignorance of them. You might have to persuade the client that things were potentially more complex than at first sight, and obtain agreement to a preliminary investigation before finalising the consultancy brief.

CLARIFY (ii) – JOINT DIAGNOSIS

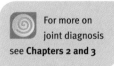
For more on joint diagnosis see **Chapters 2 and 3**

This is another part of the 'Clarify' stage, and may have started while reaching the initial agreement, as you questioned the client about the issues concerned. (The chapter on interviewing is highly relevant because all your dealings with your client are potentially key informant interviews, as well as many other things.)

The key point of this first diagnostic stage is to establish the nature of the issue(s) concerning the client, drawing on relevant evidence – which should normally be more

Interviews and interviewing is covered in **Chapter 16**

than the client's views of the matter. Although their views are important, you would generally wish to check that there was a real issue to be investigated, and that evidence was available which might cast light upon it. You would want to consider how such evidence might be collected and interpreted in ways that would cast useful light upon the issue. If you could not see how, you might risk finding yourself in the role of public relations officer rather than researcher.

Key relationship tasks at this stage would include sustaining your client's trust in your approach and ways of thinking, and starting to build relationships with potential informants and perhaps other stakeholders in the project you are beginning to envisage. Your views may start to diverge from your client's at this point if the issue begins to seem different from the one originally perceived. If so, you will have to develop your relationship with the client to a level that allows open expression of reasoned disagreement, and frank debate about the reasons for disagreeing.

CLARIFY (iii) – AGREEING YOUR BRIEF

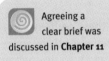
Agreeing a clear brief was discussed in **Chapter 11**

You should agree a final brief only when you are satisfied that you know and understand enough about the issues and the situation to be comfortable that you can deliver on what is proposed. No matter how good a relationship you feel you have built with your client, a written agreement is essential. Memories are unreliable, verbal communication may not have been as clear as you think, or your client may move on during the life of the project. The brief will be extremely useful if so. It may strengthen your case for continued resources, and protect you against claims that you have not delivered what was 'agreed'.

> **An agreed written brief is essential, specifying objectives, activities, resources and completion dates.**

To achieve this, the agreement must specify the objectives of the project, the resources that will be provided by the client, your proposed activities (ideally with a plan showing milestones as well as final completion dates, and specifying any necessary meetings with the client if access may prove a problem). Cope (2003) also highlights the need to look beyond the investigation to possible solutions and identify resources available for any solution.

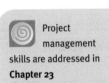
Project management skills are addressed in **Chapter 23**

It is good project management to specify not only what is within the remit but also what is out of scope. Certainly, this should have been discussed in an open way, but it may be useful to include it also in the written agreement.

KEY POINTS

- Your client is a key provider of resources, and of information, and may be more powerful than you.
- It is important to build an honest relationship, and sustain it throughout the project. The consultancy literature is a good source of ideas here.
- Discussion must be frank and open, and if you have doubts about your remit, it is important to express them.
- A written agreement is important, once you have a sufficiently clear understanding of the issue to have a reasonable idea of what research is required.

BUILDING A GOOD RELATIONSHIP

Why does building the relationship take energy and attention? You might feel that you get on well with people in general, so why is a specific process of building a relationship with your client so important? Some of the issues that sometimes work against a good relationship with your client are:

- power differences
- perspective differences
- knowledge differences
- experience differences
- status differences
- different objectives.

I shall consider their general implications before looking at the interpersonal skills you will need.

To build a strong and positive relationship with a client when these influences are operating you need to know your strengths, be clear about your own objectives, appreciate your client's perspective and objectives, and keep your client involved throughout the project.

KNOWING YOUR STRENGTHS

The influences listed above suggest that researcher–client relationships may be subject to a wide range of potential difficulties. Consultants are often hired for their expertise. If you are a relatively inexperienced quasi-consultant, there may be a significant power difference between you. This may make you reluctant to question what your client says. You have to remember that as a researcher your key expertise lies in *asking questions* that will enable you to generate useful answers. The research story above made this point. If you accept the client's answers at the outset, you risk adding little value other than an extra pair of hands.

For more about this power difference see **Chapter 4**

> You need to recognise what you can offer a client, know your limitations, and be open and honest with the client about both.

Your first task is therefore to think carefully about what you can offer. You have a stock of concepts and frameworks that will help you make sense of complex issues, by highlighting possible factors and likely relationships between them. You have time and energy and a desire to find out. You understand the research process, and the importance of not leaping to premature 'solutions'. You also have a different perspective from the client. Although this may sometimes be a source of difficulty, it can also be one of your greatest strengths. You will be able to ask questions that may not occur to your client, surfacing some of their tacit assumptions thus allowing them to be questioned. You may be able to see potentially relevant aspects of the situation that are being ignored. You may be able to see what might be used as evidence to enrich the data already collected and allow triangulation. If you feel you have little to offer, you may not recognise your strengths. It may help to do a 'stock-take' of all you know and can do, and your other strengths. Colleagues may be willing to give feedback.

Your credibility depends upon your awareness of both your strengths *and* your limitations, and as a researcher or consultant your personal credibility is your greatest asset. If you claim greater competence than you possess, you risk being seen as unprofessional. No client will be willing to collaborate in research unless they believe that you will act in a professional and competent fashion throughout. If at any point they start to doubt your professionalism and competence, they may withdraw their co-operation.

BEING CLEAR ABOUT YOUR OWN OBJECTIVES

Because of the potential conflict between objectives for consultancy and research, it is vital to be totally clear about objectives for the *research*. You are also a key stakeholder in this. In 'normal' consultancy the client's objectives are paramount. Although you might choose projects offering opportunities to develop yourself as a consultant, the client's requirements will be the key driver. Where you have separate and explicit research objectives, there is more scope for conflict, and your project has to meet both your own and your client's needs.

Clarity about your own objectives is a prerequisite for open and constructive discussions about the potential of possible projects to satisfy client and research needs. It is here that the power differential is a potential problem. A forceful client with clear objectives of their own may find it relatively easy to convince you to accept their view and requirements. If you are aware of this risk, you may be better able to guard against it. And is vital that you do find a workable compromise if you are seeking to write a dissertation to complete a qualification. The brief you agree with your client has to give you scope for research that will be acceptable to your institution. Part of your clarity about your own objectives relates to knowing which are essential, and which could be flexed if necessary.

> Clarity about your research objectives will enable you to discuss how these can be achieved while still meeting the client's needs for the project.

APPRECIATING CLIENT PERSPECTIVE AND OBJECTIVES

Much of the value you can add to a consultancy research project comes from your *different* perspective. The client may be unaware of the extent to which the particular 'sense' they have made of the situation (eg 'It is a problem with the recruitment technology' in the case example above) is limiting their perceived options. This value comes not because your perspective is *right*, but because it is *different*. Exploring the differences may help both you and the client to overcome some at least of the limitations resulting from your perspectives and ways of thinking.

The first task is to establish what the client's perspectives and objectives are. (This is part of Cope's 'Client' stage.) Careful listening will be necessary, as well as questioning skills. A productive exploration of any differences requires that you communicate to your client the importance of having this discussion. This may require some assertiveness on your part (see below), and a willingness to say what you honestly think and feel, rather than what the client wants to hear. It also requires that you respect the client's view as valid, albeit open to question, and that you establish an explicit shared goal of ensuring that the eventual project meets *both* your requirements in so far as is possible.

Some conflicts may be inevitable. These may include conflicts between client wants and your perception of their *needs* (for example, if you feel they have misdiagnosed a situation). This sort of conflict may be addressed by means of discussion and possible further diagnosis. Other conflicts may be between what the client needs (this may be a quick PR report) and what you need in order to meet your dissertation supervisor's requirements. In these cases you will need to *negotiate* a mutually acceptable project which allows you both to satisfy enough of your needs for you each to stand to benefit from the relationship.

KEEPING YOUR CLIENT INVOLVED

Clients may have a greater or lesser interest in the research process. Some may be very happy to have no contact between the agreement of your brief and the presentation of your final report. Clients tend to be busy people, and the point of using a consultant to investigate an issue is to save their time. Provided that resources continue to be made available and your final report is accepted, this may be an ideal relationship. However, there may be a number of benefits for both of you from some interim contact.

Clearly, you do not want to be 'micro-managed' in your research, and continually answerable to your client. This could seriously interfere with the relative objectivity that may be a substantial part of your contribution. But meeting your client at significant points during the project may allow you to:

- build a relationship that may be of future value
- sustain your motivation to keep on target
- learn, and your client to learn, from the project as it progresses
- check the feasibility of options you are considering
- obtain agreement to any deviations from your original brief
- develop the client's sense of 'ownership' of the project and its findings, and hence ...
- establish a stronger commitment to implementing any recommendations.

Of these, the last three points are particularly *and* generally important. The importance of the others may depend upon the specific context.

ACTIVITY

For the project you are planning, note the potential benefits likely to be of greatest importance. List the steps you will take to encourage your client to meet with you.

RELATIONSHIP-BUILDING SKILLS

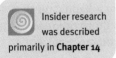

Insider research was described primarily in **Chapter 14**

If your research is within your own organisation, your client may have formed opinions about you even before the project is suggested – this is one of the problems with insider research. You will not necessarily know what any prejudices are, but could usefully be alert to hints in the first conversation (eg references to 'ivory tower academics' or insistence on 'a practical approach' suggesting an assumption that it will not be).

If your client had no pre-opinions, opinions will start to form from your first contact. Your relationship with your client is crucial to the success of your research. Chapters 15 and 16 stressed the importance of creating a good first impression when seeking informants for a survey, and you should follow the guidance given there. But while each informant is important to your study, your client is supremely so. Impression-formation is therefore even more crucial.

Appearances are important, so whatever your client sees of or from you has to be carefully considered. What you wear, what you say, how you say (and spell) it, and even the paper you use will matter. From your first contact (whether it is by phone or letter or email) you must be thinking about how your client is likely to react to you, and consider how you can come across as professional, prepared, informed and competent. Your aim is to convince your client that you can help in addressing whatever issue is of concern. If you can also convince the client that there will be personal learning, stimulation, even enjoyment to be gained from the collaboration, you will go far. But this will probably take several meetings!

> **It is important to create a good first impression with a client.**

Once you have created a good enough initial impression to establish the potential for a project with a client, you must establish a rapport with them. The power difference can be a barrier here, so remind yourself at regular intervals of your genuine potential value to the client. It helps to be sensitive to your client's preferred ways of communicating and 'match' them. This will tend to happen naturally once you are in rapport, but consciously using a similar way of expressing yourself to them in the early stages can accelerate this process, helping them to feel that you 'talk their language' and are therefore 'their sort of person'.

ESTABLISHING RAPPORT

Three of the main ways of starting to build rapport involve matching posture, matching language and matching perceptual frame. *Postural matching* is extremely common. Take a look at friends in a bar or other social situation. You will often find that their postures are mirror images of each other. One may have right leg crossed over left, the other *vice versa*. Or both may have their hands clasped behind their heads, or their heads resting on their (mirrored) elbows. This postural mirroring is a natural consequence of being in tune with someone. Once you have consciously observed it in friends, you will become aware of how often you do it yourself. It is a short step from that to 'nudging' your posture towards that of a client in early meetings. This will speed up the comfort you feel together and therefore the natural mirroring that will occur.

Language matching is suggested by practitioners of neuro-linguistic programming or NLP (see, for example, Andreas and Faulkner, 1996). They point out that people seem to have a preferred sensory mode, and that this can be identified from their use of terms such as 'I see what you mean' and 'I get the picture', or 'I hear what you are saying' and 'That sounds right', or 'I feel we may have a problem', or 'I've got a handle on that'. If you pick up on whether your client is using primarily visual, auditory or kinaesthetic language, and do likewise, you will establish a rapport between you more quickly.

Perceptual frame matching is perhaps more subtle. Cope (2003) suggests that people use different filters to view the world, and identifies three common filtering differences. The first concerns *magnitude* – do we look at the detail or the big picture? The second concerns what he calls *periodicity* – and relates to preferred time perspective. Do we tend to look backward, focusing on causes, or stay firmly in the present, or look forwards to what is likely to happen? The third difference relates to what he calls a *holistic* filter. Do we think in terms of heart (emotions), head (logic) or hand (the pragmatics of a situation)? Again, noticing and then operating within a client's preferred perceptual frame will ease communication and more rapidly establish a rapport.

BUILDING TRUST

Rapport is an important first step in establishing trust but not enough in itself. Trust depends upon the belief that the other person can and will behave not only in accordance with any written agreement between you, but in accordance with the informal psychological contract you establish. Block (2000) stresses the importance of authenticity within the relationship, which is an essential contributor to trust. He says that unless you are being authentic (which includes an element of openness) and 'put into words what you are experiencing with a client as you work' (p27), you are unlikely to build client commitment.

Cope (2003) put forward another useful mnemonic here, suggesting that the elements of trust are:

> *Truthfulness* – by both parties
>
> *Responsiveness* – on the part of the consultant to the client's needs
>
> *Uniformity* or consistency or predictability of behaviour
>
> *Safeness* (or security) – for the client within the relationship
>
> *Trained* – ie the consultant must be competent and sufficiently expert.

The acronym may seem a little stretched, but the points are all important, and the list is an excellent starting point, reflecting elements of Block's authenticity as well as the need for professionalism and expertise already referred to.

From your first conversation, your client's impression of you will be largely shaped by the quality of your shared discussions. You will need listening and questioning skills, as in interviewing. But because your client is so important to you, you will also need to be highly sensitive to their feelings and reactions. This will require 'listening' to much more than the words used.

Thus in addition to a high level of active listening skills you will need the interpersonal sensitivity and empathy which Goleman (1998) suggested were key components of 'Emotional Intelligence'. You need to be alert to and able to interpret signs of unease, or raised emotional tone, relating them to the preceding conversation.

Listening starts with focusing on the client, and concentrating upon what they are saying – and how they are saying it – rather than upon what you will ask next. If you practised *extreme listening* in preparation for interviewing, it will stand you in good stead here. Indeed, you may wish to treat client meetings like a semi-structured interview, preparing a list of topics you wish to cover and questions you would like answered. As when interviewing, try to say as little as is necessary to steer your client in the direction of giving useful information. Clients may not be happy with being recorded, so you will have to pay attention to capturing what they say in a way that is acceptable.

'Extreme listening'
Chapter 16

You will remember how useful jointly drawing a diagram can be when you are trying to come to a shared understanding of a situation. Techniques such as rich picturing or devising causal diagrams may both help the quality of your discussion and provide a useful record, so it may be worth experimenting with this if your client is willing.

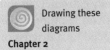
Drawing these diagrams
Chapter 2

EXPRESSING FEELINGS HONESTLY AND OPENLY

Block (2000) saw the open expression of your feelings about the project to the client as essential to building client commitment. It is important to address anything that makes you uneasy as soon as you realise that there is cause for concern: it may be much harder to discuss it, or do anything about it, later on. You may need to 'loop', and the longer you leave this, the more of your client's resources you may have committed to a wrong track. So freely saying what you honestly think and feel does much more than establish trust through authenticity, important though that is.

Freely does not mean carelessly. First, you need a degree of self–awareness – another element in emotional intelligence (and, indeed, many other lists of leadership qualities). Feelings are important indicators that something requires attention, even if it has yet to come over your conscious horizon. But if feelings take over, you are likely to lose the ability to think clearly, and will risk arousing unhelpful emotions in others. Thus it would not help your relationship with your client to get angry about something like non-provision of promised resources and start shouting. It might have far more effect to say something like, 'I'm starting to feel very uneasy about the difficulty I'm having in getting X. As I see it, it may well threaten the success of this project, and I think it might be useful if we could talk about the reasons for the difficulty.'

You will have noticed that your perceptions, perspectives and objectives may all differ from those of your client. On some issues it may be sensible for the client's view to prevail. But other conflicts may concern things which, in your view, threaten to compromise the integrity of your research, preventing you from producing trust-worthy results. On these issues you will need to express your reasons for disagreement firmly and clearly.

GIVING REASONS FOR DISAGREEMENT

Reasons are important. The art of constructive disagreement is to focus on the *point*, not the person, and say why it does not seem right to you. As when interviewing, it is useful to check your understanding. So before disagreeing, check that you have correctly understood the point by expressing it in different words. If you *have* understood the client, it is possible that your disagreement rests on evidence, logic, underlying assumptions or inconsistency with other points. By making clear what feels wrong to you, you open up the possibility of exploring the source of the disagreement. It may be that you have different information, or are making different and perhaps less reasonable assumptions. But it may also be that you have seen a problem in an argument that must be addressed. If you treat the disagreement as a source of shared

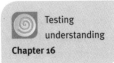
Testing understanding
Chapter 16

learning, you are likely to have a constructive debate. If you disagree with your *client*, rather than the point made (eg 'You are totally wrong!'), you are likely to become involved in a highly destructive escalation of attack and defence, and destroy any relationship you may have developed.

SUMMARISING

You will remember that in an interview summarising was potentially extremely useful. It is equally useful in more general conversations with a client. If you 'capture' agreements as you progress by summarising and noting them, it can speed up a discussion considerably and create confidence in your grasp of matters. Be wary of 'agreeing' before all the relevant information has been established, and any disagreements fully addressed. If you ignore an area in which you do not agree, you can be sure the disagreement will surface more destructively at some later point. Summarising disagreements is as useful as summarising agreements. It may be that you cannot resolve a disagreement during the meeting. If so, rather than ignoring it, you may wish to agree to differ, summarise the nature of the difference and note it for later resolution.

USING ACCESSIBLE LANGUAGE

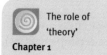
The role of 'theory'
Chapter 1

An important part of what you bring to the relationship is your repertoire of concepts, constructs and frameworks – aka 'theory' – derived from the academic literature. However, you may need to exercise caution in using it with your client or others in the organisation. Some of the 'theory' may be derived from consultancy work and well known, or at least easily accessible. But some may seem like off-putting jargon if used in the original terms and expressions, may fail to communicate, and may seriously impair your relationship with your client.

A key skill is 'translating' the ideas into language that will be comfortable for your client. They may have an MBA and be perfectly happy with it. But if not, consider the likely impact of any framework you want to use. Slight changes in how the key ideas are expressed may make the framework much more accessible to those without an academic background. The main thing is to be clear in your own mind what part of the framework is helpful to your investigation, and why, and then choose the way of expressing it that is most likely to 'speak' to your client.

REFLECTING ON LEARNING

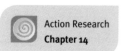
Action Research
Chapter 14

Clients often use consultants in order to learn from their expertise. Your project may enable you to develop some expertise – as it did for Chris in his reflection and leadership development project – or you may already be expert in your research topic. Even if this is not the case, the experience of the project may have substantial learning potential not only for you but for your client. The value of reflection is one of the lessons to be learned from Action Research, and is addressed further in the next chapter.

If you feel sufficiently confident in your own reflective skills, you are more likely to be able to reflect with your client on lessons learned. (Some consultants I know make this shared reflection, and its learning potential for the client, one of their key selling points.) Even if you do not reflect jointly during the project, a shared concluding review of factors that helped and hindered success, and of learning points for any future project, can be a useful exercise. Indeed, it is a central part of Cope's (2003) 'Close' stage, or the 'getting out' that Buchanan referred to.

SUMMARY

This chapter has argued that if your research is done for a client, building a good relationship with that client will be crucial to success. It is also a useful transferable skill. The power differential between you may sometimes make it difficult, but building rapport and trust and sustaining them throughout your relationship will be important.

You need to agree a clear brief with your (real) client once you have done sufficient diagnosis to be confident that the proposed project, revised if necessary, is viable. This can prevent subsequent disagreements. If your research is intended for a dissertation, the scope of this brief also needs to allow you to meet academic requirements.

Your relationship with your client needs to be characterized by authenticity, openness, trust and professionalism, supported by a clear and explicit agreement about what the project does and does not entail, and where possible by on-going contact during the project.

You are more likely to be successful if you discuss openly how to meet both your own and your client's objectives, respect the differences in your perspectives, express your feelings about the progress of the project openly, disagree constructively and apply a high level of listening and other interpersonal skills. Collaborative reflection during, and essentially at the end of, the project will greatly increase the learning potential for both parties.

REVIEW QUESTIONS

1. What are the key reasons why a researcher needs a good relationship with a client?

2. Why is building and sustaining a good relationship with a client a key consultancy skill?

3. What are Cope's Seven Cs, and how relevant are they to a researcher carrying out action-oriented research for a client?

4. Why might you wish to challenge a brief from your client?

5. Why is it important to know who your client is, and how might you find out?

6. Why is it important to have an accurate view of both your strengths and your limitations in the particular research context?

7. Why is rapport important?

8. Three forms of 'matching' can help with rapport-building. What are they?

9. What, according to Cope, are the elements of TRUST?

10. Why might you wish to disagree with a client, and what will help you do it constructively?

11. How might reflection be of value to a client?

Explore further

Block, P. (2000) *Flawless Consulting*, 2nd edition. Chichester: John Wiley. An extremely clear and useful description of many of the issues involved in working with clients

Cope, M. (2003) *The Seven Cs of Consulting*, 2nd edition. Harlow: FT/Prentice Hall. This is easy to read and provides some simple frameworks you may find useful, even if the effort after the memorable acronym is sometimes a bit laboured

http://www.managementconsultingnews.com/interviews/block_interview.php for an interview with Peter Block on authentic consulting

http://www.managementconsultingnews.com/interviews/cope_interview.php foran interview with Mick Cope. This is perhaps more overtly a 'sales' interview, but may still be interesting

 Visit www.cipd.co.uk/brm for web links, templates, activities and other useful resources relating to this chapter.

CHAPTER 25

Learning and Reflection

INTRODUCTION

A research project offers opportunities for learning on many levels. Your report, and particularly the conclusions you present in it, will contribute to learning for a range of stakeholders, including you, the researcher. But much of your learning will be incidental to research findings and will come from the activities which the research entails. This chapter looks at how you can maximise your learning from the experience as a whole. To do this you need to identify and think about learning opportunities from the outset, and choose an appropriate topic.

You then need to continue to focus on your own learning throughout the project, making choices that will create optimal conditions for learning. This involves a dual process: you must both plan research activities with learning in mind, and reflect regularly on your experiences. It will be important to capture your reflections and insights, and to identify any implications for future learning. Because this focus needs to be there throughout your research, I hope you have followed the suggestion to read this chapter while working through Part 1.

You should already have started noting down your thoughts. These may be thoughts about your research project, your activities to do with your research, and other relevant points. It was suggested that you do it in a research journal. Terminology varies, but there is an important distinction between a *research* journal, which ought to capture *all* your project activity, and a *learning* journal or log. The chapter explores the difference and suggests formats for each.

Reflection is a key element in professional learning, and a core element in some approaches to research. Thus it is both highly relevant to your research and a valuable skill in your role as a professional manager or consultant. This chapter discusses the role of reflection in professional learning, and ways in which you can improve the quality of your own reflection. It will also help you to write a 'reflections' section in a dissertation, if you are required to do this.

ACTION PLANNING FOR LEARNING

Chapter 23 on project management should have convinced you that 'to fail to plan is to plan to fail'. It is easy to become immersed in the size and complexity of the task of managing a substantial research project, and to forget that the most significant benefit that it offers for your future career may be personal learning. You have to think about two types of learning: the learning you need in order to carry out your project, and the learning that will help your career, and that the project may provide. Both must be planned.

Learning normally refers to some long-term improvement in your knowledge, way of thinking or behaviour as a result of *experience* and *feedback*. Without feedback you might do the same thing a thousand times without improving.

RESEARCH ILLUSTRATION

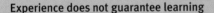

Experience does not guarantee learning

A new MBA student became really angry with me when I failed his first assignment. He particularly resented my teaching comments which drew his attention to a number of weaknesses in his report-writing. 'But I'm a consultant,' he raged. 'I write reports for a living.' Some time later he apologised. He had complained to his wife about his dreadful tutor. She, a partner in the consultancy, asked him quietly why he thought she always rewrote his reports! Perhaps if she had given him feedback rather sooner she could have saved herself a lot of work. Perhaps her marriage was more important (although they subsequently separated). Years later, he sent me some flowers. He had just gained a PhD, having successfully completed his MBA meanwhile. The card with the flowers said that without that early feedback he would never have gained either qualification.

When planning your learning it is therefore important to consider not just how you will gain particular experience or practice, but also how you will get the feedback that helps you to learn. This feedback is important during learning. Some may be apparent from the task itself, but sometimes you will have to seek feedback from others. You also need to know when your learning is sufficient. Thinking about success criteria will help you plan the learning and know when it has been achieved.

Planning for learning is like any planning. You decide what you want to learn, why, how and when, and then record it. A common format for an action plan is shown in Table 25.1

What do I want to learn?	What will I do to achieve this?	What resources and support will I need?	What will be my success criteria?	Target dates for review and completion
How to run focus group	Read about method. Volunteer to act as recorder at one of X's groups.	Suitable book. X's agreement. Time for briefing. Time for group. Time for debrief.	Understand the process. Feel I know what to do to make the group effective.	End Sept.
How to use SPSS to analyse results	Sign up for course. Practise.	Copy of software. Agreement to fund course.	Confident and reasonably speedy analysis of questionnaire data.	Course by end Jan. Starting to use with data Feb onwards.
How to write up literature review in academic style	Look at review section in good past dissertations. Write draft and obtain feedback.	Supervisor (S) to suggest ones to look at. S's (or other academic's) agreement to give feedback.	See what it should look like. Understand what I am doing right and what changes I need to make.	End March. End April.

Table 25.1 Example of a learning action plan

A template for this action plan/table is available at **www.cipd.co.uk/brm**

It is probably useful to keep a plan like this for each major learning area. It provides an overview of your learning and enables you to see progress at a glance when you revisit your action. You should revisit it at regular intervals. This allows you to check progress against your target dates, and adapt as necessary. Visible progress can sustain flagging motivation. You will need to add new learning plans as you become aware of learning needs or opportunities you did not appreciate at the beginning. You will also need to check that the planning process itself is working for you. If it is not, you may have to draw up a different type of plan, or seek help in monitoring progress.

 ACTIVITY

Use the format suggested in Table 25.1 to capture three or four key things you have already decided that you need to learn in order to do good research, and to plan how to approach them. File your notes in your learning journal, together with a reflection on how useful you find the format.

Table 25.1 shows relatively simple learning aims. You may have more complex ones, or aims requiring a series of activities. It may be helpful to devote a separate page to any aim that requires more than one or two activities. This will allow room for sufficient detail. For example, if you were working on assertiveness, or networking skills, you might want to set yourself a series of challenges in these areas, and seek feedback from a range of different sources, not all of them work- or university-based. You could have a master sheet showing all these aims to remind yourself of the overall picture.

Because of the likely changes to your learning action plan it makes sense to keep it on your computer. However, because plans are not easy to follow on a screen you may also find it convenient to print a copy (probably in landscape format) and keep it on your desk or in your main paper file. If you like a tangible record, this will make it more likely that you will revisit it at suitable intervals.

KEY POINTS

- Research projects vary in the learning opportunities they offer: it is important to consider this aspect when choosing a project.
- You will learn more if you actively plan your learning.
- This involves identifying what you need to learn, how you can best learn it, and when, and then monitoring progress against target dates.

THE ROLE OF REFLECTION IN LEARNING

Reflection is a process of observation, mental replay and questioning. Dissertation structures often include a reflective section. This is because reflection is widely accepted as an essential component in professional learning. You will remember that one of the stories used most frequently in this book relates to Chris's project on the role of reflection in leadership development, prompted by a book by Avolio (2005). The book argued that truly authentic leaders were distinguished by their ability to reflect effectively on both their successes and their failures. Avolio suggested that this ability was a key to the development of higher forms of leadership. If this claim is justified, a research project offers the opportunity to develop as a leader.

Interest in the role of reflection in learning is not new. Dewey (1910) was one of the first to emphasise the importance of reflection. He suggested that mostly we act out of habit, without thinking. It is only when some 'disturbance' occurs, and this habitual way behaving surfaces or poses some problem, that we start to think about it. He saw this reflection as an active and careful process (see Figure 25.1) of

- consideration, prompted by the disturbance
- intellectualisation and definition of the problem
- looking into the situation and forming a working hypothesis
- reasoning
- testing the hypothesis in action
- generating a solution *or* generating an idea.

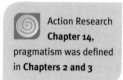

Action Research
Chapter 14,
pragmatism was defined
in **Chapters 2 and 3**

Reijo Miettinen (2000) gives a more detailed discussion of Dewey's approach. As with Lewin's later (1957) but closely related Action Research cycle, this could be taken as a model for any research process. Perhaps that is not surprising if research is a process of learning from observation. Dewey was a pragmatist. Reflection for him was prompted by a problem and directed towards action. Dewey paid careful consideration to the role of tacit and explicit theories in our observations. According to Miettinen (p63):

Tacit theory
Chapter 1

"Dewey considers that one of the purposes of reflection is to be conscious of the layers of cultures weaved in the observations. They can be prejudices and carriers of the circumstances of past time, therefore being an obstacle for sensible action in the present circumstances. Once made visible and critically

Figure 25.1 Dewey's view of reflection in learning

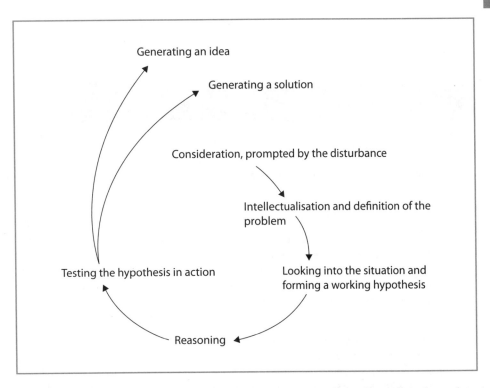

transformed by reflection, they can turn into means of enriching thought and action."

It is this surfacing of ways of thinking and questioning them that lies at the heart of reflection, and which links back to points made earlier about having to avoid being locked into perceptions based on tacit assumptions and theory. Reflection provides a means of escape from a potentially limiting mindset.

You may be more familiar with Kolb *et al*'s (1984) 'experiential learning cycle' – a description of learning as a four-stage cycle of concrete experience, observation and reflection, forming abstract concepts, and planning and testing. This model is is widely used in adult education. Kolb was influenced by both Dewey and Lewin – indeed, he sometimes described his cycle as a Lewinian model. (Miettinen argues powerfully that it is not.) For Kolb, since learning will happen only if you pass through the whole cycle, without reflection there is no experiential learning.

> **Reflection involves considering how your ways of thinking and your action have contributed to a situation.**

REFLECTION IN PROFESSIONAL PRACTICE

Another key influence was Schön (1983), who was particularly interested in the role of reflection in professional learning. The idea of the *reflective practitioner* is now widespread within many professions including management. Reflection is seen as an essential part of the on-going development of a professional's practice. Schön suggested a useful distinction between reflection-*in*-action, and reflection-*on*-action. Reflection-in-action was a sort of 'on your feet' thinking, a 'Hang on, what's going on here?' question that might lead to instant learning. Reflection-on-action was more measured, a conscious attempt to locate a recent experience within a context of other experiences, to ask why we acted as we did, and to explore the thinking involved. You may have to demonstrate such reflective practice as a condition of membership of a professional institute. Even if not, it can make you far more effective as a manager or consultant (or leader).

RESEARCH STORY

Mike's reflection on reflecting . . .

Mike's reflection included the following:

I have found both reflection-on- and in-action very helpful in several ways.

Simply writing a narrative of my reflections on key points has helped me sort out a seemingly complex tangle of issues into something clearer and manageable. It can also bring vague thoughts and understanding together into something more concrete.

This doesn't require me to collect large amounts of data to generate useful learning. As an engineer who is used to assuming that nothing useful can result without analysing lots of data, this has been something of a revelation.

Reviewing my learning points over several months has helped me to see common themes and threads of issues, and to realise just how much progress I have made. This has been quite motivating. Asking 'Now what?' means that the reflection leads to new ideas or further questions, so the effort seems never to be wasted.

I have changed the way I reflect as the project has progressed. I used to have a large A4 notebook in which I captured my reflection: now I use an A6 one. It is much more portable – I can make a quick note of any reflection-in-action on the spot. And in meetings, I no longer write copious notes. Because the smaller notebook means I take only key notes, it forces me to listen.

Reflection, as Dewey suggested, can usefully take place whenever you are surprised or feel uneasy. Both feelings suggest that existing ways of thinking may not fit the situation. For example, stakeholders may react to something you say quite differently from the way you expect. Perhaps you have misread their intentions or have not communicated well. Reflection-in-action may allow you to quickly redirect what you are saying. Your initial exploration of an issue may uncover much that does not fit your pre-existing view of the problem. Reflection on the nature of the inconsistencies and subsequent redefinition of the issue may prompt different lines of questioning or investigation. It may also, as Dewey suggested for the reflective process, generate blinding insights. Such 'light-bulb' or 'Aha!' moments are some of the greatest rewards reflection can offer.

KEY POINTS

- Reflection is a process of stopping and thinking, not just about what is happening and what you are doing, but about how you are thinking about it.
- Reflection can take place during and after action.
- It can be prompted by a feeling of surprise or unease, by completion of a learning event, or be regularly scheduled.
- It enables you to learn from experience to address specific problems and to develop better ways of thinking.

EFFECTIVE REFLECTION

The tacit – and, indeed, explicit – theory that prompted your selection of research topic is likely to be challenged both by your further reading and by your interactions, by stakeholders and informants. Reflection-in-action can protect you from habits that are unhelpful in the research context. So when something 'feels' slightly wrong, stop and ask yourself *why*. What about it feels wrong, what you were assuming, and why might this not be right? Such reflection helps you do better research, by helping your learning *during* research. Practising such reflection will help you become better at reflecting.

> **Reflection is both a skilled behaviour and a habit.**

There are no short cuts to effective reflection. It is a *skill* that has to be developed, and a *habit* that has to be established. Once you realise how powerfully your tacit theory shapes your perception and action, you will see why reflection is so important. You will start to question on a regular basis both your interpretations of situations, and the actions you take in the light of these interpretations. You will be more sensitive to small discrepancies between your expectations and your experience, to that moment of surprise or puzzlement. And you will immediately start an action replay, 'looking' at what might have been going on, and at different ways of making sense of what happened. When you realise that alternative ways of seeing it might be more enlightening, you will take note of them, and the different actions that they suggest.

Reflection-in-action is brief and happens when the moment arises. But it is worth scheduling time for reflection-on-action. You may prefer to do this regularly. Some managers find that 15 minutes of reflection at both the start and the end of the working day allows them to work far more effectively, and to continue learning from their work experiences. You might want to schedule 30 minutes or more each week to review your research-related learning and progress. Others prefer to reflect on learning at the end of each session of project-related work, and at the end of any day during which they have noted reflections-in-action. It is important to find the method that suits you best and then *use* it. After a while you will realise how much it amplifies your learning and will be keen to reflect. Until then, a little discipline may be required.

Questioning of assumptions and ways of thinking is easier for some than for others. It depends on whether you are naturally prone to reflection. One manager who found it difficult complained that it was like being trapped in a mirrored room: he saw endless reflections of his own thoughts. How *can* you escape from your own thinking? The ideas you encounter in your reading provide one route to escape, provided you engage with them sufficiently to test them actively against your own views and experience.

Collaborative reflection is another invaluable tool, and can take you far further than solitary reflection. The Action Research story in Chapter 14 is one example: collaborative reflection is core to most Action Research.

> **Effective reflection mixes reflection in- and on-action, and individual and group reflection.**

The following questions may help you to reflect more effectively. The first few relate to a simple evaluation, the remainder to reflection prompted by surprise or other emotional reaction.

Useful questions for reflection

How did that go?
What was happening there?
How did I feel about it?
What might I have done differently?
What can I learn from this?
What didn't 'fit'?
Why was I surprised?
What was I expecting?
What was I thinking?
How did that affect how I acted?
How might I have thought differently?
What impact might that have had?

Alternatively, you might like to incorporate these questions into a series of more detailed reflective prompts, as shown below.

 Structured reflective prompts

Description of the experience
  What factors were involved?
  What prompted me to reflect?
Reflection on aims and impacts
  What was I trying to achieve?
  What was the impact on myself and others?
  What are my feelings about the experience?
  How might others be feeling?
Identifying what influenced me
  What internal factors were affecting me?
  What external influences were there?
  What information was I using?
How things might have been different
  What different actions were possible?
  What different judgements might have been made?
  What might have been the impacts of these alternatives?
Learning from this experience
  What can I learn from my feelings?
  What are the implications for my learning objectives?
  What will change as a result?
Input from others
  What can I learn from comments from my manager/mentor?
  What can I learn from comments from colleagues?

REFLECTION OR 'PROFLECTION'?

If you are a practising manager, you may feel that 'reflection' sounds altogether too contemplative and leisurely for the busy and fragmented life that you lead. However, reflection-in-action is very quick and action-oriented. It enables you imediately to act differently if necessary. It is a looking back with a view to moving forward.

There are hints to a longer-term proactivity in the questions above, too. 'What can I learn?' to a pragmatist tends to mean 'How can I think and act differently?' And the questions above are directed towards change. You will also remember that reflection was integral to Action Research, and thus followed by action. If the language of reflection is unattractive to you, try thinking of *proflection*, or some other future-oriented word, to reinforce the fact that in reflecting you are looking back with a view to going forwards.

ACTIVITY

Print out either the 'Useful questions for reflection' or the 'Structured reflective prompts' from the website, and keep them with you at work or during group discussions on a course. Use one or the other (or both) to reflect on an experience and 'proflect' on implications for the future. Log your thoughts in your journal, together with further reflection on the usefulness of reflecting.

CAPTURING LEARNING BY REFLECTION

It is easy to have a fleeting insight: you notice or understand something, but then forget it as you become engrossed in other problems. Capturing your reflections is therefore important. You may remember how Mike found a small notebook an invaluable tool for reflection-in-action. He later referred to his 'instant' reflections as part of his reflection-on-action, and captured this more measured reflection in a section of his research journal dedicated to reflection.

NARRATIVE APPROACHES

There are several approaches to this more extended reflective writing. Some are narrative, some highly structured, some a mix of both. A narrative approach is easy and straightforward: you simply write down the results of your reflections. This approach is sometimes called keeping a *learning journal* or *learning diary*. The mere act of writing ideas down will make you less likely to forget them. But it can also be useful to revisit your reflections (as Mike noted), and a simple journal account over a long period does not make for easy reference. Key points may be hard to distinguish from the rest.

The following illustration shows just how simple a learning journal entry may be. This is a quick capturing of 'instant reflection'. Later more measured reflection might include consideration of other possible communication needs or past shortfalls.

RESEARCH ILLUSTRATION

Learning journal, quick entry
27 March

'Bob looked really shocked when I told him I'd spoken to Mary and Carmel about my project. This surprised me because they were the obvious people to identify suitable interviewees. Then I realised that because Bob had been away for two weeks, and busy since he got back, I'd moved my thinking on a long way without updating him. And since Mary and Carmel report to him, I should have first told him how my thoughts had developed, and then got him to agree my talking to them. He hasn't actually approved my doing this project yet. Realised just how easy it is to forget to manage 'stakeholder engagement'! Bob is one of my most important stakeholders. I need to remember to think about what things will look like from his perspective, and ensure that I keep in regular contact with him.'

The next Research illustration includes another example, also related to stakeholders, and captures an 'Aha!' moment. It is these shifts in how you look at things that are the most rewarding aspect of reflection. Dewey (1916, p22) described the ideas that problem-directed reflection can generate as a by-product that is potentially more valuable than the solution – a 'gift of the gods'. Moon (1999) talked of reflection as 'cognitive house-keeping'. Continuing this metaphor, these insights can feel as if you have produced a rearrangement of your cognitive furniture, revealing aspects of the room that you did not realise were there!

Because it is sometimes hard to get the flavour of reflection if you are not used to it, the Research illustration that follows captures two insights and is very shortly afterwards succeeded by another illustration.

RESEARCH ILLUSTRATION

Journal entries noting insights

23 May

I had been finding it difficult to identify my market, given the variety of skills and experience I have, when I had a 'light-bulb' moment from the client feedback - it is exactly that breadth of knowledge, skills and experience that is my competitive advantage.

26 May

I have been really struggling with the idea of having to consider my stakeholders. I thought that because I was a 'sole' trader I could do what I want and take all the necessary decisions myself. Thinking about who my stakeholders might possibly be, I suddenly realised that a lot of people had power over the success or otherwise of my project. I was going to have to approach past colleagues and clients, and perhaps even potential clients, if I wanted a valid evaluation of my consultancy's strengths and weaknesses. It is their perceptions that matter, not mine. And there were other people who could influence my success - my supervisor, others in my learning set, even my family. I suddenly realised that I needed to think about how I engaged with them all.

The second entry above captures insight prompted by problems. Another prompt to such reflection might be reflection on something that went fairly well, as in the following final example.

Several examples have been presented here because it is easy to read about reflection without quite knowing what is meant, and individual reflection tends to be invisible. But you should see from each of the examples some or all of the reflective process in action.

MORE STRUCTURED REFLECTION

It is possible to think of a continuum of structured approaches to capturing learning with a shifting balance from recording 'facts' to recording thoughts. At the most 'factual' end is a simple *learning log* which captures learning from specific 'learning events'. You could log learning from reading an academic paper, for example, or from attending a short training course or working your way through an online tutorial. A common format is shown in Table 25.2, with sample entries.

A format like this works well with a learning action plan, and could form a structure for the 'review' in the plan's final column. The headings form useful prompts to reflection

RESEARCH ILLUSTRATION

Reflective evaluation of the workshops

'Setting up the workshop programme to enable colleagues to work together on issues to do with knowledge management was the first time I had ever done anything like this on my own. One of my personal learning objectives was to develop my own leadership skills during the project. I needed to evaluate the workshop programme in terms of its effectiveness in generating understanding of our current knowledge management issues, but I also wanted to get useful feedback on my role as a leader. I could have used feedback questionnaires, but decided that interviews might produce richer information. This was scary! I often interview others about them, but it is much harder to interview them about me.

When I started thinking about leadership I began by looking at the characteristics of leaders such as Shackleton (Morrell and Capparell, 2001), Churchill and Hitler (Roberts, 2003), as well as business leaders. Key characteristics seemed to be optimism, and self-belief. Goleman (1998) states that 'emotional competence made the crucial difference between mediocre leaders and the best' (pp33-4) and suggests that this emotional competence is made up of self-awareness, self-regulation, motivation, empathy and social skills.

So as well as asking about the task aspects of the workshop I tried to focus on what people had felt during the workshops, and how my behaviours had affected this. However, it was still a fairly stressful experience. In the end I was really glad I did it that way. I learned far more about how I am perceived by others, about how my intentions are sometimes misinterpreted and about quite small things that I could do differently to be more effective. I don't think I would have got this information from a questionnaire. It was only when I used follow-up probe questions that much of this emerged. Some of it was a bit painful, but it has been a profound learning experience. I shall do a number of things differently in future as a result!'

Date	Event	Purpose	What did I learn?	How will I use this?
25 May	Worked my way through the online argument-mapping tutorial	Seemed a potentially useful approach to both critical review and drafting my dissertation	Hadn't realised how complex arguments can get, and the need to separate claims, and argue each from evidence	Propose to analyse the next paper I read in this way to help me be more critical, and to map what I have already drafted on lit review to test my logic
27 May	Read Miettinen paper	To clarify ideas about reflection and test mapping technique	Philosophers are clever! Gave up on mapping as too many arguments. Got much better understanding of Dewey and Kolb, though	Be more proactive – and more confident about 'reflection-in-action', so will do more of this from now on

Table 25.2 Sample extract from a learning log

Table 25.3 Alternative template for a learning log

Date	Event	Outcome	Learning	Reference/ Key words	Actions	Free thoughts

Templates are available at **www.cipd.co.uk/brm**

on the event. This format tends to be used for planned 'reflection-on-action'. Table 25.3 provides an even more structured alternative format.

KEY POINTS

- **Reflective writing can be structured in a variety of ways or unstructured.**
- **A learning log tends to be a structured capture of learning from specific events.**
- **A learning journal tends to capture your reflection in a less structured way, and entries may relate to issues as well as events.**
- **If you keep quick reflective notes 'in-action', it may be useful to incorporate them into a more structured reflection when you have time.**
- **Your reflective writing can usefully form one section of your research journal.**

Thus far the chapter has considered reflection to be a key element in professional practice, enabling learning from experience as your career develops. Research is a form of professional practice, and offers a wealth of learning opportunities. It is important to take full advantage of them. Establishing a habit of reflective practice will enable you to do so, as well as to develop a key professional skill. If you are doing research for a dissertation, you may be required to include a reflective element in your dissertation. The requirements for this may be slightly different from the requirement for reflective writing for personal use.

ACTIVITY

Plan a week in the near future when you will focus on reflection-in-action. Note it in your diary. During the week, carry a small notebook or other recording device, and make a point of jotting down points that strike you at work or during your course. At the end of the week, review these reflections, trying to draw out additional learning points, and any learning plans. Capture these in your learning journal, organising this to allow for future structured and unstructured reflective writing.

THE REFLECTIONS SECTION OF A DISSERTATION

There are two distinct possible purposes for including reflections in a dissertation. If your university believes in the importance of a 'reflective practitioner' approach, they may require you to demonstrate your reflective skills as part of demonstrating professional competence. If they do, the sort of writing described above may act as evidence of this, and all you will need in your dissertation is an overview of why reflection was important to your learning, how you went about reflecting, some particularly striking results of your reflection, and a reference to an appendix containing edited highlights of your journal and/or learning log which demonstrate particularly well the points you have made in your main report.

Sometimes, however, the focus is less on reflection and cognitive shifts, and more on practical lessons learned about research. If this is the case, you will be able to demonstrate learning by saying what, with the benefit of hindsight, you would have done differently.

Whatever your university's preferred approach, they will *not* be looking for a restatement of your conclusions section. The focus will be on lessons learned from going through the research process, rather than lessons learned from the data. And in most cases a personal account will be required, so you can use 'I' to narrate your learning process.

These questions are available at **www.cipd.co.uk/brm**

Key questions to ask yourself when thinking about writing your reflections section might usefully include:

- What went according to plan, and what did I learn from it?
- What did not go as expected, and what did I learn from that?
- What adjustments did I make to the research as a consequence, and why?
- What with hindsight might I have done better, and how?
- What are the implications of the above for the conclusions I have drawn?
- What skills have I used in this project? Which of these did I have to develop?
- What is the most powerful learning I shall take away from the experience?
- What will I do differently in future as a result of the experience?

As well as providing evidence of your learning, a good reflective section can enable you to remedy shortcomings of your research. This requires you to recognise the shortcomings and discuss them openly without trying to conceal or to justify poor practice. An examiner is unlikely to pass a dissertation with a major flaw in the approach if the student seems unaware of its shortcomings. They might just pass the dissertation if there was a clear discussion of the shortcomings, the reasons for their presence, the implications for the conclusions, and the lessons learned.

The following illustration is an example of reflection on learning from the research experience, and of an adaptive approach to the research, presumably as a result of reflecting on the problem of low response rates.

Learning about how you think about organisational issues and your own professional practice will have a major impact on your future career. Learning about how to do better research will help you base your future practice on valid evidence. Both are important, and a regular habit of reflection can contribute to each. Whether or not you are required to submit such an account for your dissertation, a reflective account of your learning during the project can be invaluable. It will show how your thought patterns have shifted, how your assumptions have been challenged, and how new ways of thinking have emerged. Reviewing this account at intervals will strengthen your motivation and reinforce your learning. It will help you change the glasses through which you view the world, and this can have a profound effect on your future career.

RESEARCH ILLUSTRATION

If I knew then . . .

'It is disappointing that the results on the relationship between reported stress levels and absence were not statistically significant: I did not appreciate the importance of sample size in a study such as this, nor had I anticipated the low response rate. I had assumed that since I was sending the questionnaire to colleagues, they would all return it.'

'However, I had always intended to do some follow-up interviews to discuss the questionnaire findings, and managed to increase the number when I started having difficulty getting the questionnaires back. So although I did not, as hoped, establish that there was a significant correlation between the two factors, the analysis of interviewee comments on stressors at work identified a number of factors that we are not currently considering relevant to the problem.'

This allowed me to recommend some changes that could be made in the next few months that would be likely to reduce stress levels in the most affected sections, even though I had failed to demonstrate a significant stress–absenteeism link.

'On reflection it would probably have been more useful to focus on qualitative information from the outset. Establishing a significant correlation would still have left unresolved the question of what to do about stress. I propose now to monitor absenteeism levels in those sections which accept the recommendations, in order to assess the impact on absenteeism.'

SUMMARY

Reflection is deemed by many to be an essential element in learning from experience. It involves an interrogative process of considering events and experiences and the thinking that contributed to them.

Many professions regard reflective practice as an essential part of professionalism. It allows on-going learning. You may have to demonstrate your reflective practice to your professional institute, and to include a reflective section in a dissertation.

Even if not required, a habit of regular reflection will greatly enhance your personal learning from your research. Individual reflection will be helpful, but collaborative reflection may be even more productive.

Different forms and formats are possible for reflective writing. It is important to pick approaches that you are comfortable with and persist with the practice until the insights and learning generated form such a powerful reward that it becomes habit.

Your learning journal can represent an important element in your research journal.

Review questions

1. Why does experience not guarantee experiential learning? What else is needed?

2. What is the role of reflection in learning, and in learning from research in particular?

3. What does successful reflection require beyond the necessary skill?

4. What might serve to prompt reflection?

5. Why did Schön distinguish between reflection-in- and on-action?

6. What sorts of questions might you ask when reflecting?

7. What worries about reflection might prompt its description as 'proflection'?

8. What might influence your choice between structured and unstructured reflective writing?

9   What might distinguish a good 'reflections' section in a dissertation from a less good one?

10. What has been the main benefit from your reflections in response to 'Consider ...' and Activity prompts thus far?

Explore further

Miettinen, R. (2000) 'The concept of experiential learning and John Dewey' s theory of reflective thought and action', *International Journal of Lifelong Education*, Vol.19, No.1: 54–72. Also available online at http://pdfserve. informaworld.com/598596__713815823.pdf . Provides an extensive and challenging discussion of reflection, learning and pragmatists and empiricists and Kolb and a whole lot else relevant to research and learning. Not an easy read for non-philosophers, but not an impossible one. Regard it as going to the brain gym

Moon, J. (2000) *Reflection in Learning and Professional Development*. London: Kogan Page

Schön, D. (1983) *The Reflective Practitioner. How professionals think in action*. London: Temple Smith. An influential book that examines professional knowledge, professional contexts and reflection-in-action. Describes the move from technical rationality to reflection-in-action and examines the process involved in various instances of professional judgement

http://www.infed.org/thinkers/et-schon.htm for an overview of Schön's work on reflection and on 'theory-in-use'

http://www.ericdigests.org/2000-3/thought.htm for an overview of some of Dewey's thinking

 Visit www.cipd.co.uk/brm for web links, templates, activities and other useful resources relating to this chapter.

CHAPTER 26

Writing About Research

INTRODUCTION

No matter how well thought through or how well executed a business research project is, its impact depends upon how successfully it is communicated. One of the key ways in which you will communicate your research will be in writing. You may have to present an interim report on your work to your client, your manager or your supervisor, and of course you will also have to present a final report to these people. Likewise, you may in addition have to make presentations of your findings to other stakeholders to gain their acceptance of whatever you are recommending, and their commitment to any future action.

Communicating business research is difficult because there are often different audiences, each of whom uses a slightly different language. It may be necessary for you to translate the language of research methods into something that your audience will better understand, or it may be important to present the same information to different groups in slightly different ways. Despite the need to use different ways of presenting your research, it is important to retain the integrity of your work and the validity of the research findings.

Aspects of communication have been addressed at many points in this book, from initial discussions with stakeholders to writing a clear proposal for your project, questioning informants and perhaps checking interpretations of results with them. Where communication challenges have been dealt with previously, they will be revisited only briefly. This chapter will act as a general resource to support the more specific points made in earlier chapters. Looking at the different ways in which you will be required to communicate during your project will sensitise you to the importance of paying attention to it, and show that your dissertation is merely a continuation of activities you have probably been practising at intervals throughout your research.

The issues of trustworthiness and sound argument are crucial and must be dealt with in detail. Trustworthiness concerns the importance of *honest* communication, and a subset of this is the importance of avoiding accusations of *plagiarism* or intellectual theft. Another has to do with the justifiability of the claims you are making. These issues are vital to any communication, not just to a dissertation. Plagiarism can and does occur, and both forms of dishonesty can damage your professional reputation. The second crucial point concerns *sound argument*. Making unwarranted claims through faulty argument or misunderstanding of your data leads to an untrustworthy communication as surely as does deliberate misrepresentation, and has similar potential for damaging your reputation.

This chapter will help you write a good dissertation. But in common with the approach adopted throughout, it locates this within a consideration of the wider issues impacting upon the success of research in general. Thus it starts with a review of the total communication 'territory' to give a more unified view, looks at the basic principles that will underpin all successful communication of your research, and then addresses in more detail key communications including writing a final report for a client, and writing a successful dissertation.

LEARNING OUTCOMES

This chapter should enable you to:

- appreciate the importance of communicating your research intentions and findings at key points in your project

- clarify your aims in communicating at different stages and to different audiences

- use your understanding of communication principles to achieve these aims and, where appropriate, to:

- write a dissertation that will maximise the marks obtained for the research you have done

- write a report for those who commissioned your research.

THE IMPORTANCE OF ON-GOING CLEAR COMMUNICATION

Practical research in and around organisations is about increasing understanding so that this understanding can inform decisions and actions. It is about your understanding and other people's understanding. You will usually have to develop your understanding through dialogue with others, and consideration of the information they provide. You may also be aiming to shift other people's understanding of an issue or situation so that they see the need for action and the value of what you propose.

Lastly, stakeholders who will be involved in subsequent action will require a shared understanding of the situation, and similar ways of interpreting it, if they are to act coherently.

Clear communication with key stakeholders throughout your project will help develop this shared understanding, as well as ensuring that you have the information you need. You must communicate with others from the outset, sharing your initial ideas for project areas with a supervisor and/or discussing goals and constraints with a potential client. You might usefully talk about your ideas with other managers or researchers to help clarify your thinking. You will probably need several discussions with any client before writing your proposal to ensure that your proposed project will be acceptable to both of you. You may have to submit a separate proposal to an academic supervisor. You will usually have to communicate with those who are providing resources and/or information throughout the project to ensure their continued support.

When you have finished your investigation you will have to present a report to your client, and perhaps a shorter report to those who provided information, if you promised this. You may have to write a dissertation. There may be potential for gaining further recognition for your research (or yourself) by presenting it at a conference and/or publishing an article based on your work in an in-house or external professional journal. Although the need to communicate regularly with your stakeholders is obvious, in practice it is all too easy to become so involved in actually doing your research that you lose sight of others' communication requirements. This is problematic because poor communication can be costly.

If you do not convince potential clients or potential key informants of your credibility and the value of what you are doing, they may withdraw their support. Poor communication can lead to reduced co-operation and the withdrawal of resources. Failure to communicate clearly with interviewees may reduce the quality of the information they provide. Failure to communicate effectively with key stakeholders may mean that they are less supportive of your work. And failure to present your findings in a convincing way may mean that your work is ignored and/or you fail your dissertation.

Communication is important because it is the means by which you accurately convey the research findings to the appropriate stakeholders in an efficient and effective manner.

KEY ELEMENTS IN SUCCESSFUL COMMUNICATION

Communication often fails to achieve its aims. If you are aware of the possible reasons behind such failure, you may be able to take steps to avoid the hazards.

CONSIDER...

Think of one or two instances of successful and unsuccessful communication directed towards you, and list the main factors which seemed to distinguish those that were successful.

My most recent failures of communication have all stemmed from failing to realise just how far apart my own thoughts and knowledge-base were from the assumptions, knowledge and ways of thinking of those with whom I was trying to communicate. Things that seemed so obvious to me that I didn't even consider saying them, were not at all obvious to those with whom I was trying to communicate. Indeed, they were starting from such a different 'place' that what I said was interpreted quite differently from the way I had intended.

Your experience is of course different from mine, but you probably came up with some or all of the following when you thought about the more *successful* instances of communication:

- The communicator had a clear aim in communicating.
- The message was presented in a way that captured your attention and interest.
- The communicator made you want to know what they had to say because it seemed to be clearly relevant to your own concerns.
- The message was easy to follow – you did not have to spend ages working out what was meant.
- Diagrams or other visual aids were used to help you understand what was meant.
- You believed what was being said because it was clear that it was derived from relevant and adequate evidence.
- Clear and compelling logic and arguments were used to reach conclusions from the evidence.
- The conclusions made you want to do something (or think some more about it, or change or stop what you were doing).
- Overall, you trusted in the competence of the person communicating in relation to the topic, and in their intentions to communicate honestly.

These points apply equally to *all* communication – from explaining what you are interested in investigating through to submitting a final report and/or other publication. You may find the list above useful as a checklist for any communication. Overall, the requirements can be summarised briefly as:

Good communication requires
– clarity concerning your own aims
– understanding the concerns and ways of thinking of your audience
– the preparation of an appropriate communication
– the avoidance of any form of misrepresentation or untrustworthy message.

This sounds easy and obvious, but the practice is more difficult. You must be sure about what you want to communicate. You may have to develop new skills or to draft and redraft numerous versions of your work until you produce one that you and your stakeholders are happy with. Time pressures or feelings of inadequacy may tempt some researchers to misrepresent their findings, or take other short cuts. You may feel that your research has not achieved what you or your client had hoped for, or it just is not impressive enough. You may doubt your writing skills and feel that you will produce something better if you use words chosen by others who are better than you. Or you might just feel that it is quicker/easier to submit someone else's work than labour over your own.

Any of these reasons might lead you to misrepresent what you have found, or to misrepresent the authorship of what you write. Both are ethically unacceptable, and can cost you your reputation and/or the qualification your research is intended to deserve. It is also possible to produce a misleading account of research through incompetence, whether in analysis or reasoning.

THE MISREPRESENTATION OF FINDINGS

It can be difficult to judge what counts as misrepresentation. Some departure from complete honesty may be necessary. Buchanan *et al* (1988, p54) suggest that:

> "research accounts in academic journals depart considerably from the research practices of their authors. They offer instead a 'reconstructed logic' (Silverman, 1985, p4) which brings the illusion of order to what is usually a messy and untidy business."

Dissertations and project reports are similar in that they are a post-hoc construction rather than a blow-by-blow 'diary' account of everything you did. But where is the 'ethical line' between creating an 'illusion' and misrepresentation? Or, indeed, is there a line at all? Does it matter what you write as long as you achieve your aims?

CONSIDER...

Which, if any, of the following would you find ethically unacceptable, and why?

a) Leaving out your earlier 'looping' and blind alleys, and merely reporting on thinking and activities that contribute to your eventual research design and/or findings

b) Creating a retrospective justification for selection of your case organisation and/or informants when in fact the rationale was convenience or opportunity

c) Drawing upon others' research findings consistent with your own while omitting any mention of findings which directly contradict your own

d) Selecting quotes from interviewees to support your conclusions, while not quoting from those who made points which are inconsistent with your arguments

e) Drawing 'conclusions' from data which you know to be inadequate without discussing the cautions required in accepting these conclusions

f) Selecting data and statistics that create the result which your client wants from the research

g) Modifying your data so that it is 'tidier' and the messages clearer.

You will remember from Chapter 4 that ethics is a slippery topic, a mix of explicit professional standards and implicit personal preferences. However, despite professional, personal and cultural differences, it is absolutely essential that you are truthful about your research findings. The behaviour in g) would be universally unacceptable. The whole world of research would lose its value if 'results' were fiction.

But is selectivity untruthfulness? It depends upon whether it alters the 'message'. So the selectivity in a) allows you to convey a clearer message without reducing its trustworthiness. This sort of selectivity helps, rather than hinders.

The way to judge the trustworthiness of your research findings is to ask yourself if the way in which you communicate your findings leads to a misrepresentation of what was actually found, or misrepresents the implications of these findings. In the exercise above, points from c) onwards do, and most professional or academic ethics committees and most professional researchers would have concerns that the substantive message would, as a result, be misleading. Selectivity which distorts the conclusions from research, or leads others to place more reliance upon them than is warranted, constitutes misrepresentation and is unacceptable. Deliberate falsification of data in the interests of more acceptable results would be even worse. Remember, your credibility as a researcher depends upon others trusting your findings, so any immediate gain from presenting your results in a misleading way is likely to be short-lived.

THE MISREPRESENTATION OF SOURCES: PLAGIARISM

Taking credit for other people's work by using it as if it were your own is intellectual dishonesty. It is called plagiarism. If you have ever submitted work for assessment, you will probably have been warned against plagiarism. But as with misrepresentation of findings, there are lines to be drawn. There are cultural differences in attitude to 'recycling' other people's ideas. And the situation is complicated by the prevalence of undetected 'copying' in schools and undergraduate study. Plagiarism is particularly prevalent in dissertations, perhaps because both feelings of inadequacy and time pressures tend to be acute. However, it is increasingly likely to be detected, and penalties can be severe.

> **Plagiarism occurs whenever you claim work done by others as your own. It is dishonest and may cost you your reputation and/or qualification.**

There are two aspects to this dishonesty: depriving others of credit due to them, and taking undeserved credit yourself – thus gaining marks under false pretences. Sometimes plagiarism is accidental. Chapter 6 warned you that when taking notes on what you read you must make absolutely clear any direct quotations. If your notes do not do this and you later include these notes in your report, you will be accidentally plagiarising the person who actually wrote those words. This is plagiarism by carelessness.

Sometimes plagiarism occurs because the researcher does not understand the importance of avoiding plagiarism, and feels perhaps that others' words are better than his or her own and therefore to be preferred. Sometimes students, not knowing how to write about something, paraphrase someone else's work – thus taking their ideas and thinking, if not their exact words. Either is a form of plagiarism by ignorance.

Sometimes, alas, plagiarism is a deliberate form of 'intellectual theft'. Students may copy past students' work. Researchers may 'steal' others' results. (I know two people whose PhD supervisors 'stole' their findings, publishing them as their own.) Or researchers may 'borrow' words from obscure publications or websites to save time or energy, or generate text of a higher quality than they know themselves to be capable of. In all these cases, this is plagiarism as intellectual theft.

All categories of plagiarism will lay you open to severe criticism if found out. Academic honesty is one of the basic foundations upon which universities rest, and academics are particularly severe on plagiarism. Their careers rest upon their research and their professional reputation, and plagiarism puts these at direct or indirect risk. If you are found to have plagiarised part of your dissertation, you may be asked to leave the programme without a qualification. If an academic is found to have deliberately plagiarised, his or her career may be at risk. But 'media experts' and other authors have also found that it has seriously damaged their status. (You may remember the case of the media psychiatrist Raj Persaud a few years back, and the Blair government's 'dodgy dossier' that was used to justify the invasion of Iraq.)

Some people undoubtedly plagiarise without being caught. But this is much harder than you may think. Sophisticated software exists to catch out students who copy either from each other or from published sources. Markers are very good at spotting changes in style. Reviewers have sophisticated websearch tools to hand. Even if you do not have ethical concerns about plagiarism (and most would consider it highly unethical), it is highly risky, and to be avoided on pragmatic grounds alone.

 Guidelines for avoiding plagiarism:
- Clearly attribute any ideas you are using to their originators (even if you are rephrasing them).
- Clearly attribute any evidence or arguments you are using to their original sources.
- Show clearly where you are quoting directly from something by using italics and/or quotation marks, and give the full reference, including the page number on which the quotation occurs, immediately after the quoted text, or the URL of the relevant website, together with the date you accessed it.
- Where you are paraphrasing rather than quoting directly, or 'combining' material from a range of sources, acknowledge the original sources (in the text at the appropriate time, as well as in your list of references).
- Paraphrasing means that you have substantially reworded what the original author(s) said. It does not mean simply replacing random words.
- Ensure that what you write is significantly your own, and reflects your own thoughts and reasoning. Even if you are using entirely secondary sources, you can interpret them, and reason about them in your own way, building on the (attributed) work of others.
- Do not copy from other students and be careful about whom you allow access to your work.

The following guidelines will help you avoid charges of plagiarism in almost all cases. They apply to all material you use, whether printed, on the Internet or produced by fellow students or other colleagues.

As with any simplified rules, you may sometimes wonder quite how they apply to your particular case. There are judgements to be made between what can reasonably be assumed to be common knowledge and what is an idea to be attributed. Follow the guiding principle of honestly acknowledging the contributions of others to your own work. Your attributions, far from losing you credit, will gain it – for knowing the origins of 'received' ideas or having successfully found useful new ones.

KEY POINTS

- It is vital that all communications about your research are trustworthy and do not mislead.
- Any selectivity in your reporting that threatens the trustworthiness of your results is to be avoided.
- The purpose of research is to generate new ideas and understanding. Plagiarism consists of passing others' work (writing or thinking) off as your own.
- Check what system/format of referencing is required by your institution and make sure you conform to it.
- Misleading communications may cost you your qualification and/or reputation.

REFERENCING

Academic integrity requires you to reference all work that is not your own, and there are a number of systems of referencing (Harvard, Chicago, American Psychological Association, etc) to help you to do it effectively. You should check with your institution or with the journal – if you are producing an academic or professional paper – which system of referencing they advise you to use. Because the Harvard system appears to be the one mostly commonly used, it is this system that is used later here to demonstrate how to reference. First, it may be advantageous to familiarise yourself with some of the terminology of referencing (Table 26.1). This often helps by giving you a 'shorthand' that can be used in the text.

Table 26.1 Some elements of referencing terminology

Term	Meaning
Et al	In full, *et alii*, meaning 'and others'. This is used in the text to indicate where the referenced source has more than two authors – for example: 'Saunders *et al* assert that . . .' The full list of all the contributing authors should appear in the references at the end of the report.
Ibid	In full, *ibidem*, meaning 'in the same place (as the immediately preceding citation, including the page number)'. For example: 'Locke notes that although grounded theory categories are "standalone" (2001, p39), this characteristic creates "some ambiguity" (*ibid*).'
Op cit	In full, *opere citato*, meaning 'in the work cited' – that is, the same as the preceding reference to this author. This is distinct from *ibid* because it allows for other references to used in between. For example, if you cite Locke (2001) on page 2 of your project report, and then again on page 30, as long as you are referring to the same work it is sufficient to put *op cit*.
Cf	In full, 'confer', but better thought of as meaning 'compare (with)'. For example: 'Johnson (2009) says that quantitative methods are the only valid form of business research (*cf* Bryman and Bell, 2008; Saunders *et al*, 2007).'
[sic]	Literally, 'so' or 'thus'. It is used to denote that an error appearing in the original has been recognised but left in rather than altered. It may be an error of meaning – for example: 'Johnson (2009, p2) states "most nurses depend on their husband's salaries" [*sic*]. One of the many problems here is the false assumption that most nurses have husbands.' – or simply of defective spelling or grammar.

THE HARVARD REFERENCING SYSTEM

The Harvard system of referencing is premised on an accurate account of all sources being given in the main body of the report. Subsequently, there is a comprehensive list of these at the back of the report. Some institutions require two lists: one list of references – the sources that you have used explicitly in your research, and one bibliography – a list of sources that have been used generically to advise your thinking. The format of both is the same. The references should be arranged in alphabetical and then chronological order (if you have two papers by the same author, the earlier one is referenced first). We will look first at referencing in the main body of the report before considering how to reference properly in the references/bibliography.

Referencing in the body of the report

Direct quotations

Wherever quotations are used, text taken verbatim from external sources must be clearly indicated in the text. The reader should be in no doubt whatsoever that the words that you have presented are the words of another person. Quotations should be referenced thus:

> Cameron claims that 'giving feedback is a skill' (2005, p169).

or

> Cameron (2005) claims that 'giving feedback is a skill' (p169).

The 'in text' reference should include the surname of the author, the year and the page number. The full reference to the book by Cameron will be included in the references/ bibliography at the back of the book.

Citing the ideas of others

Where you take ideas from another author but translate them into your own words, you still have to acknowledge the original author. However, because you are paraphrasing their ideas, you need not include the page number as part of the in-text reference. For example:

> Cameron (2005) argues that giving feedback is not easy – it is a skill that has to be acquired.

It is vital to note that paraphrasing requires that you completely reword what the original authors said. You are representing their ideas with *your* words.

Citing citations

Where you wish to use citations made by other authors you must acknowledge that the work you are citing has been taken from an intermediary source. For example:

> Smith (1998) draws on Gusdorf's (1980) assertion that autobiography is 'a sort of posthumous propaganda for posterity' (p188).

Referencing at the end of the report

Referencing at the end of the report – ie in the reference list or the bibliography – requires what are known as full bibliographical references.

Books

Single authored book:

> Surname, initial. (year) *Title*. Place of publication: Publisher.

> eg Locke, K. (2001) *Grounded Theory in Management Research*. London: Sage.

Single authored book – subsequent edition:

> Surname, initial. (year) *Title*, edition. Place of publication: Publisher.

> eg Cameron, S. (2005) *The MBA Handbook: Skills for mastering management*, 5th edition. Harlow: Prentice Hall.

Multiple authored book:

Surname(s) and initial(s) (in the order in which they appear) (year) *Title*. Place of publication: Publisher.

eg Glaser, B. and Strauss, A. (1967) *The Discovery of Grounded Theory: Strategies for qualitative research*. New York: De Gruyter.

Multiple authored book – subsequent edition:

Surname(s) and initial(s) (in the order in which they appear) (year) *Title*, edition. Place of publication: Publisher.

eg Saunders, M., Lewis, P. and Thornhill, A. (2007) *Research Methods for Business Students*, 4th edition. Harlow: FT/Prentice Hall.

Edited book:

Surname, initial. (ed.) (year) *Title*. Place of publication: Publisher.

eg Price, D. (ed.) (2008) *The Principles and Practice of Change*. Basingstoke: Palgrave Macmillan.

Chapter or paper in an edited book:

Surname, initial. (year) 'Title of chapter', in Surname/initials of editors (eds) *Title of Book*. Place of publication: Publisher; page numbers.

eg Smith, L. (1998) 'Biographical method', in Denzin, N. and Lincoln, Y. (eds) *Strategies of Qualitative Inquiry*. Thousand Oaks, CA: Sage Publications; pp184–224.

Journals

Single authored paper:
Surname, initial. (year) 'Title of paper', *Title of journal*, Volume, Issue: page numbers.

eg Doyle, M. (2002) 'Selecting managers for transformational change', *Human Resource Management Journal*, Vol.12, No.1: 3–16.

Multiple authored paper:

Surname(s), initial(s) in the order in which they appear (year) 'Title of paper', *Title of journal*, Volume, Issue: page numbers.

eg Oakland, J. and Tanner, S. (2006) 'Quality management in the twenty-first century – implementing successful change', *International Journal of Productivity and Quality Management*, Vol.1, No.1–2: 69–87.

Electronic media

Internet journal:

Surname, initial. (year) 'Title of paper', *Title of journal*, Volume, Issue: page numbers. Available online at: URL [date accessed].

eg Allen, G. (2003) 'A critique of using Grounded Theory as a research method', *Electronic Journal of Business Research Methods*, Vol.2, Issue 1: 1–10. Available online at: http://www.ejbrm.com [accessed 12 December 2008].

Websites:

(Author, if there is one) Title. <u>Complete URL</u> [date accessed].

eg The Prime Minister's Strategy Unit. http://interactive.cabinetoffice.gov.uk/strategy/survivalguide/downloads/stakeholder_engagement.pdf [accessed 15 October 2008].

STARTING YOUR WRITING

Most business research reports follow a fairly standard format. Although there are variations depending on the particular type of audience that they are written for, the structure remains fundamentally the same. The structure of the report is important – it creates a logical sequence through which you can systematically lead your audience, enabling them to follow your lines of argument. In communicating research you are seeking to bring your audience to the same conclusion that you have reached, and therefore sound arguments are important. In communicating your research you should draw on the principles of argument-mapping mentioned in Chapters 8 and 21. You should apply the techniques to your own arguments and make sure that each claim you make is supported by appropriate evidence, and that you have made clear the nature of the links to the question. Above all, do not make claims you are unsure about. If your data suggests that something *might* be related to something else, say just that. Do not assert that there *is* an association, or even worse, that one factor *causes* the other.

In producing your final report, it is sometimes not easy to unearth these well-reasoned arguments from the mounds of papers, computer files and notes that you will have accumulated. By the time that most business researchers come to produce their final report they have already done a substantial amount of writing. However, it will almost always require redrafting and refining. Additionally, you will have to produce new writing for your conclusions and recommendations. The most important thing to do at the writing-up stage is to revisit the project in its entirety. If you assume that texts written earlier are still sufficient and that new texts will simply fit in with them, there is a high risk that your final report will be fragmented and incoherent.

OVERCOMING OBSTACLES

In producing a business research report, it is important to start writing as early as possible. You will have already produced outlines and drafts of various sections, the literature review, the methodology, etc, and are now looking to synthesise these with the newer pieces of writing to produce the 'masterpiece'. All too often people sit down and stare at an empty screen or a blank piece of paper hoping that they will suddenly be struck by divine inspiration. Alas, this seldom happens. Instead, business researchers have to start writing on the assumption that whatever they write, they will revisit and revise at a later date. The two main problems that prevent people from writing are:

Paralysis by analysis

Many people put off writing until they have collected together as much material as possible and have what they think is a relatively complete understanding of what they need to do. This is problematic for a number of reasons. First, this tendency to collect as much material as possible means that it becomes impossible to know where to start. So much data and information can overwhelm you and create this 'paralysis by analysis'. Second, this approach implies that events like reviewing the literature are one-off events, rather than the messy 'looping' which is more reflective of the reality.

Fear of getting it wrong

Putting off writing is often linked to this idea of writing once and once only – of getting it right first time. In practice this is not going to happen. As you continue to write, your ideas develop and refine, and it is therefore almost always necessary to go back to the beginning to make sure that your arguments are still consistent, that there is a coherent flow of debate, and that the ways in which your ideas have developed have not taken you outside the confines of the original brief or research question. A good rule of thumb is – first get it written, then get it right.

MANAGING THE WRITING PROCESS

Although Chapter 23 deals with project management in much more depth, here it is useful to consider how you manage the writing process. There are three sub-processes involved:

- managing your time
- managing your mindset
- managing your attention.

Managing your time

Writing the final project report is not something that you can do in short bursts. It is something that requires extended concentration. This can be managed in a number of ways. Some people prefer to allocate very large chunks of time – a whole week, for example – in which they do nothing but focus on writing the final project report. Others prefer to set aside a few hours every day in which they can work on the report. Yet others manage their time by setting deadlines in which they have to produce a section or a chapter or write a specific number of words. However best you manage your time should be the approach you use, with the caveat that short bursts of time randomly allocated to producing the report are unlikely to be sufficient.

Managing your mindset

It is here that insight into how you study best is of particular value. Knowing your own strengths and limitations is a crucial part of efficiently and effectively producing your report. Think about the circumstances that you find most conducive to study. Some people like background music, others absolute silence. Some people study best in the mornings, other people best in the evenings. Think about what helps and hinders your concentration and play to your strengths. One trick that I find helps me is to make sure I have everything I am ever going to need on the desk in front of me. Otherwise, when I get up to get something I can quite skilfully distract myself away from whatever I am supposed to be doing, and can do so for some considerable time. When everything is there, there is no need to get up and 'seek' distractions.

Managing your attention

Focusing on producing the final report requires your mind to be focused fully on the task in hand. Producing the report requires you to constantly check what you are doing against the research question; it requires you to ensure that your arguments are coherent and consistent. It requires you to ensure that you are speaking in a language that can be understood by the audience, and that you make sure that you have backed up any claims you have made with evidence. These are only a few of the things that will be going on contemporaneously as you produce the report. High levels of concentration are needed, and the best ways to manage these is by allowing short 'down-times' within your time-frame. Generally, where the work being produced requires a reasonable amount of concentration, study periods of 40–50 minutes without a break will suffice. However, where the work requires very high levels of concentration, it may be better to work to 30-minute time periods interspersed with breaks.

As for the breaks, there are two general rules. First, they should not be longer than the study period! Second, you should not do anything that requires an active mental engagement in the break. If you decide to challenge Fermat's last theorem or Einstein's theory of relativity, you will find that it takes you a good 10 minutes when you resume your report-writing to get back into the mindset that you need in order to be able to write. Instead, have a cup of tea or coffee, take the dog for a walk, go for a short stroll – but try not to move from one mindset to another.

PRODUCING YOUR REPORT

There is a fairly standard format to almost all reports, which most people are already familiar with. The beginning of the report introduces the reader to the main themes and subjects. The main body of the report considers what has happened, what investigations have been done and why, and what the findings of those investigations were. The conclusion to the report summarises the whole piece of work in a brief and focused manner. This section looks at the general principles of report-writing and then highlights the ways in which consultancy reports and academic dissertations differ from this core structure.

THE INTRODUCTION

The introduction to any report is the point at which the writer 'grabs' the attention of the reader. The introduction must therefore do a number of things. It must present a genuine view of what the report intends to do, but it has to do so in a way that compels the reader to read on. Introductions must be written in a language appropriate to the audience – they have to set the context for the report: why the report has been written at all. They frame the problem or issue being considered, and they have to explain how that problem or issue will be addressed.

It is important to remember that the introduction should be concise and clear – it should convey, in as few words as possible, the very essence of the report. Accordingly, it is usual to leave the final production of the introduction until after the report is written. This allows the writer to draw on the specific and salient features of the report – an approach which helps avoid the temptation to reproduce the whole report in miniature in the introduction. Where introductions are written at the beginning, it is easy for the writer to lose sight of just how much they are writing. After all, if there is no main body to refer to, there is no clear identification of what should and what should not be included. A good example of this is evident in the House of Horrors story below.

RESEARCH STORY: HOUSE OF HORRORS

Too much (unhelpful) information

Carol's introduction section to her Master's dissertation was 10 pages long (5,000 words!). The word limit for the whole dissertation was only 15,000 words. There is no point in setting out the 10 pages of 'irrelevant' (albeit interesting) information it comprised. Carol had spent a great deal of time gathering information about the company in which she worked. She had searched the Internet, she had got hold of published financial reports, and she had précised internal documents to present a comprehensive view of the company. Unfortunately, this information should really not have been in the report at all. It was not necessary in terms of framing the business research being undertaken, it didn't help the reader make sense of the results, and worst of all, it took up valuable text space that she should have used for the discussion of the research findings and the conclusions. This is a problem which frequently happens when the introduction is excessively long – the conclusions suffer most.

Leaving the writing of the introduction to the end is not without potential problems either. By leaving the writing of the introduction to the end, there can be a temptation to try to use it as a 'catch-all' – a space into which the writer can squeeze in the things that he or she has not otherwise had space to include (or, indeed, is not sure where to put) in the final report.

> **The introduction engages the audience and provides a brief understanding of what they can expect from the report.**

THE MAIN PART OF THE REPORT

The main part (or body) of the report is the point at which the substance of the investigation or the business research project is communicated. The main body of the report has to be seen as the means by which the writer helps the reader to move from the introduction through to the conclusions. It should deliver different pieces of information at specific points to allow the reader to follow the path of the arguments. When writing the main body of your report, you must be clear about where you are, where you are taking the reader, and what the stages are en route.

A good analogy to use is that of a car and fuel.

To get to the end of a journey (the end of your report), a car requires a certain amount of fuel (information). However, it is not possible to put all the fuel in at the beginning of the journey because of the limitations of the fuel tank (or the limitations of people's ability to retain copious amounts of information). Instead, the driver maps out a route which means that the car has enough fuel to get it to the next stage of the journey. In report terms, this ensures that the writer provides the reader with sufficient information to get them to the next significant point in the report.

In an academic piece of work the literature review gives the reader enough information to allow them to understand the academic premise for the work and the methodology section gives them sufficient information to allow them to see the strengths of the research approach. In a consultancy report, the writer presents a well-reasoned diagnosis of the problem (which may be informed by a literature) as the basis for suggesting possible solutions; and in a work-based project, the writer may communicate the usefulness (or validity) of a range of diagnostic tools before using them as part of the analysis of the problem. In each case the reader is given enough information to get the through the next stage of the journey.

The main body of a report can be structured in one of two ways – in an open narrative structure which may use headings and subheadings, or as a numbered report.

Heading and subheading structure

Whether or not you are expected to use headings and subheadings in the main body (do not use 'main body' as a heading – every heading should flag up the content of what is coming next) of your report will depend on the brief that you have been given. Where you have a choice, it is worth remembering that headings and subheadings make the report easier to read. The use of headings indicates to the reader the direction that the report is going in, which means that they do not have to work this out for themselves. Headings are a way of guiding the reader through. Even where the report itself is not expected to contain headings, using them to help you organise your thoughts is invaluable. Using headings in this way allows you to map out the journey, to identify the key points that have to be made at each stage of the journey, and to plan how to move from one point to another.

This idea of moving systemically from one point to another emphasises the need to create a logical flow of argument. Headings and subheadings should be arranged in a logical order and subsequent themes should connect and help to build, argument by argument, the case that you are making. Where people cannot follow your train of thought, or the arguments are random and disconnected, they will soon lose interest in reading what you have to say.

Numbered structure

In many formal business reports, the convention is to structure the report into sections and to have each part of every section numbered sequentially. This makes referring to particular parts of the report far more easy – people can be directed to find point 3.2.6 rather than to find the first sentence of the third paragraph halfway down page 65! The structure of the main body might therefore look something like this:

2.0 First main heading
 2.1 First sub-section (of the first main heading)
 2.2 Second sub-section (of the first main heading)
  2.2.1 First sub-section of the second sub-section (of the first main heading)

3.0 Second main heading
 3.1 First sub-section (of the second main heading)
  3.1.1 First sub-section of the first sub-section (of the second main heading)

To demonstrate how this might look with example section names:

2.0 **Current thinking regarding staff development**
  2.1. Academic perspectives on staff development
  2.2. Professional perspectives on staff development
    2.2.1 *The importance of talent management to contemporary organisations*

3.0 **Investigating staff development**
  3.1 Popular means of analysis
    3.1.1 *Quantitative versus qualitative data*

Whether your report is expected to be in the open narrative style and built around headings and subheadings, or more formally structured using numbered sections, it is crucial that there is a central sense of direction, an understanding that the main body of the report will guide your reader from a very specific starting point to a very particular finishing point. The very clear starting point should make sure that the reader knows what the report is setting out to do, and the finishing point should indicate that they are now at the end of that part of the journey. In progressing between the two, the report should present a series of arguments each of which builds one on the other, each moving the reader a step further forwards, and within these arguments there should be claims supported by evidence and well-reasoned discussion (Figure 26.1).

Figure 26.1 The components of the main body of a report, consistently building on the main theme and moving the reader forwards

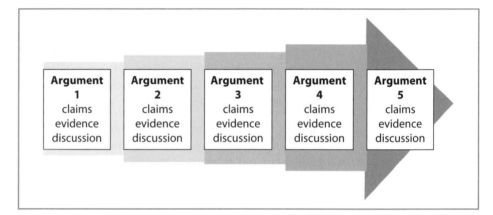

Argument 1	Argument 2	Argument 3	Argument 4	Argument 5
claims	claims	claims	claims	claims
evidence	evidence	evidence	evidence	evidence
discussion	discussion	discussion	discussion	discussion

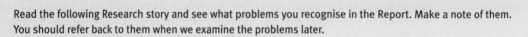

ACTIVITY

Read the following Research story and see what problems you recognise in the Report. Make a note of them. You should refer back to them when we examine the problems later.

There are numerous problems here, and it is sometimes difficult to separate out the issues of structure from the issues of content. However, you may have identified the following problems:

- although there is some sense of identifying the problem at the beginning, there is no clear sense of the journey that the reader will be taken on; likewise, no mention of who commissioned this work or why

- the report lacks any coherent structure. The one thing to be said in favour of this report is that it does follow some sort of chronological sequence, but the flow lacks coherence and the arguments do not seem to build around a main theme. There is a sense that something is happening 'in-between' the assertions made of which the reader is not aware

RESEARCH STORY

Report written for Ms Paragraph by John Smith

1.1 I was asked to look at some problems which had occurred in the Production department. The issue seemed to relate to the ways in which the teapots were being produced. People were not happy at the amount of wastage and sub-standard products being sent out, which they thought might be excessive. I decided to look at this, and after speaking to Peter, it was decided that the best way to sort the issue out would be to map out what happened. This was done, and it was noticed that some of the equipment was not being used all the time.

1.2 Joanne in HR said it would not be possible to pay people double-time for working late on a Saturday evening. They could only have time and a half – but they could have double-time for working Sunday. But Finance pointed out that if we did this it would put the costs up. That would have created even more problems, so that idea was scrapped.

1.3 The second approach was the idea to monitor the work flow and patterns of each of the teams, which was to see what each person and each team actually does. That way some sort of comparisons could be made and decisions about reducing wastage made from there. Each team was asked to monitor what they did every day. This exercise went on for two weeks and showed some interesting results.

1.4 People seemed to work much harder than the productivity figures would suggest. Jobs that Peter and I thought would take about 15 minutes took on average half an hour. When we pulled all the reports together it seemed that everyone was working almost every minute of every day – so it would be difficult to ask them do any more. It was interesting that the blue team and the red team had very similar results, but the red team complained about having to do the exercise.

1.5 They said their jobs would take them even longer if they had to write everything down, and could someone not just come and watch what they did instead?

1.6 I suggest that the remedy for the problems with sub-standard products being produced and excessive wastage is to offer the teams overtime but paid at the normal rate rather than double-time. That way, by increasing production we should be able to find enough good-quality products to meet demand.

1.7 Peter feels that this is a poor solution and would prefer that a proper time-and-motion study be done. That way an alternative solution might be found.

- elaborating on the issue of coherence, there appear to be points in the report when John jumps from one subject to another, and how he has made the connection between the two issues is anybody's guess. For example, to go from the equipment not being used all the time to Joanne in HR saying that people couldn't have double-time on a Saturday is at best a tenuous link and one that can only be assumed by the reader

- although there is some sense of trying to flag up the end of the journey (as a solution) towards the end of the report, John simply points out that Peter is unhappy with the solution he has presented. There is no 'closure' to the report.

You may have noticed many more issues – you may also have noticed how difficult it was to read. The way it is written is not helping you in any way to understand what is being said. So imagine how you would feel if you were the manager who had commissioned this work-based project, and how you would feel if that report was 30 pages long!

The main body of the report is the means by which the reader progresses from the beginning of the report to the end. It needs therefore to communicate the right amount of the right information at the right time.

- The main body of a report should be structured by subheadings whether as paragraphs or in numbered sections.
- These subheadings should map out the arguments which lead the reader through the report.
- The arguments should be supported by evidence.
- The arguments should be connected to each other.

THE CONCLUSION

The conclusion and its impact
Chapter 22

The conclusion to a report is often the last chance for you to make a real impact. It is the point at which you demonstrate that you have achieved exactly what you said you would achieve. The conclusion must be brief and to the point. It should remind the readers what the report set out to do, it should review the key findings in a succinct way, and it should present the author's well-reasoned explanation of those findings. Conclusions should not contain any new information: the only new thing here is the clearly articulated opinions of the writer – and these opinions must be derived from information presented in the report.

> Your conclusions should demonstrate that you have done what you set out to do, and express your informed opinions on the research findings.

ALTERNATIVE REPORT STRUCTURES

Although most report structures are fundamentally the same, there may be demands from the stakeholders in your research to vary the structure in line with their particular requirements.

THE CONSULTANCY REPORT

There are a few areas in which a report written as part of a consultancy brief differs slightly from the standard report structure outlined previously.

Title page

This is the cover of the document. It should contain the title of the document (note that the title must be reflective of the brief given rather than some witty or snazzy title created to try and impress), the name of the person for whom the report has been prepared, and the name of the person by whom the report has been prepared. It is also usual to include the date of the report on the cover.

Executive summary

This is a very short – no more than one page – overview of the entire report. It explains the brief, who commissioned whom to undertake the brief, how the investigations were carried out, the research findings, and the conclusions and the recommendations. Because it takes up no more than one page, this must be written in a very succinct style – but one which gives the reader confidence in the trustworthiness of the results. In consultancy reports it is usual to present the recommendations at the beginning of the report. These may be included in the Executive summary, or in other instances your stakeholders may wish to see a brief Recommendations section at the beginning.

Introduction

In a consultancy report the Introduction usually starts with a consideration of the brief, what it entails, who invited the consultant to take this commission (or a description of the tender process used) and what the objectives of the brief were. Any decisions made at subsequent meetings which pertain to clarifying the brief should also be included here so that as complete a context as possible is presented.

THE ACADEMIC DISSERTATION

An academic dissertation is traditionally divided into more subsections than a business project report or a consultancy report. As such it can be slightly more difficult to retain that sense of coherence and of a logical flow which is necessary to guide the reader through the work. It is important, therefore, when writing an academic dissertation, to consider the connectivity between the sections as well as between the subsections within each section. An academic dissertation usually comprises the following.

Title page

This is the cover of the document. It should, as a minimum, contain the title of the report, the name of the author, the date and the course/module for which the report has been produced. If the dissertation is a major component of the work for which the academic award is to be made, the awarding institution may have a particular set of words that must be included on the title page. These are usually something like

> Dissertation submitted in partial fulfilment [or in part application] for the degree of —.

It is also usual in such circumstances for the institution to require that the cover of the report be in a specific colour.

Acknowledgements

This is the point in the report where you can express your gratitude to the people who have helped you in your work. They may be your colleagues at work, your family and friends, your tutor, your manager or your supervisor. This section should be brief – usually no more than half a page in length.

Contents

The Contents page simply outlines the chapters, the sections and the subsections of the report, giving the number of the page on which each starts. If the report contains illustrations, such as graphs or charts, these should appear on a separate list headed 'Table [or List] of Illustrations'. At the same stage in the report, if you have used a large number of abbreviations and acronyms with which the reader may not be familiar, you should also include (on a separate page) a Glossary of terms. This is usually presented as a table and lists each abbreviation and what it stands for. However – a note of caution here. Even with a Glossary of terms, abbreviations should be kept to a minimum. Many years ago I had a Diploma extended essay (5,000 words) submitted along with a three-page Glossary. Unfortunately, there were so many abbreviations in the text that I could rarely read more than three lines before I had to go back to the glossary. The work took me four times longer than normal to mark and trying to concentrate on the flow of the text was extremely difficult.

Abstract/Executive summary

Depending on the guidelines from the institution, the length of this section can vary from half a page (then usually called an Abstract) to three pages (more often called an Executive summary). An Abstract is a brief outline of the research project in its entirety. It uses a few paragraphs to outline what the research set out to do, how the investigation was conducted, what the research findings were, and the conclusions drawn. Where recommendations have been made, these too should be included. An Abstract is an independent piece of writing that can be read in isolation from the main report and still make sense to the reader. Abstracts (as with the Introduction section) should be written at the end of the research project. An Executive summary is written for a similar purpose but is usually slightly longer. It allows the writer to consider in a little more depth and breadth each of the particular parts of the research project. Again the reader should be able to read it in isolation from the main report and still make complete sense of what the researcher has done.

Introduction

The Introduction lays out more fully the nature of the research project. It sets the context for the project, explains the rationale behind the research and then outlines each of the sections of the report, giving much more in the way of background and information about the project. In scientific-type reports (those of a quantitative or positivist nature), the Introduction should contain the hypotheses to be tested. In more qualitative research, the research questions that have been addressed should be included. The Introduction should convey to the reader why this piece of work is important, and, if the research is based within an organisation, it is usual to present some brief details about that organisation. Note that if it is necessary (ie the research report will not make sense unless the reader understands in detail the nature of the organisation) to include a substantial amount of information about the organisation, it may be prudent to locate this in the Appendices. In academic reports, Introductions are not included in the overall word-count – but check with your institution.

Literature review

The literature review section/chapter should present the reader with an understanding of the academic and professional literatures that have informed the research. Chapter 7 considered the nature of a literature review in detail, but in brief it should synthesise the relevant work in the area and use the understanding and insights generated to inform the research.

Methodology

Methodology sections/chapters tend to be poorly written because researchers fail to appreciate just how crucial they are to an academic report. As a general rule of thumb, the methodology section of the dissertation is of equal importance to the literature review. It is not sufficient to present two paragraphs which basically say 'I am going to use questionnaires'. The research methodology is the point at which you explain your epistemological position, your approach to research, and how it directs method. You must explain how the issue was investigated and the rationale behind the choice of investigation. You should explain the sample size and strategy, how the data was collected and how it was analysed. And you should also recognise the limitations (see Figure 26.2).

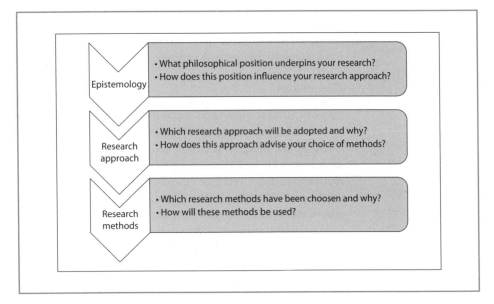

To help your reader follow the ways in which you have developed your approach to research, the methodology section/chapter should start with a higher-level consideration of the epistemological position on which your research is based. Discussing your position allows you to demonstrate how the ways in which you think about research influenced the approaches that you took. The approaches that you used should then be discussed, and from here you can draw out the ways in which these advised the choice of particular methods. Your choice of methods will have to be explained in terms of both why you chose them and how you have actually used them, with specific reference to

- data collection

- data analysis

- sampling strategy.

Your methodology chapter should thus leave the reader in no doubt as to how you gathered the data, how you analysed the data, and from whom the data was gathered. However, it is not sufficient to simply describe this. It is important to demonstrate that you are aware of the limitations of the methods that you have chosen. Your methodology chapter should finish with a brief discussion of the limitations and some understanding of how you have taken account of them.

Results/Research findings

This section/chapter is where you present the information that you have derived from your analysis of the data – where you report the facts that your research has uncovered. It can be done in a number of ways: as open text in which you use your own words to relate the findings to the reader; through the use of charts, graphs and tables which present succinct demonstrations of the facts and figures uncovered by your research; or in the form of quotations derived from the primary data gathered. In practice, most business research projects present data in two if not all three of the formats mentioned.

An important issue to consider when producing the Results section of a business research report is that there is often a need to make well-informed judgements about what information goes in and what information does not. Especially where the size of the final report is limited to a specific number of words, it may be necessary to present only the key findings of the research. Where this is the case, it is important to let the reader know that this is what has happened – otherwise, it might be assumed that you have inadvertently missed sections out.

Discussions

Some institutions like their students to merge the discussion section with the Results section, based on the idea that this is the most economical way of presenting the results – if they are merged, it is not necessary to repeat the findings to contextualise the discussions. Others require a separate discussion section so that it is clear which information is fact derived from the data and which information is informed speculation on the part of the researcher. The discussion section is the part of the report in which you demonstrate how you have interpreted the results and in what ways the results have informed your views and opinions on the subject. Although this section presents the opportunity for you to demonstrate your intellectual ingenuity (or possibly flexibility), it is important that the discussion remains firmly grounded in the results that have been produced. The discussions should synthesise the results with the literature which informed the research and your own well-reasoned thoughts and idea. Claims made should be supported by evidence, decisions made should be based on a balanced debate, and opinions expressed should be cognisant of the limitations of the research.

Conclusions

Chapter 22 looked in more detail at the issue of drawing valid conclusions. The Conclusions section is the point at which the main issues of the report are drawn together. The focus of the research is briefly reiterated and the ways in which the researcher has chosen to answer the research question are presented. As with the discussions, the Conclusions must be grounded in the research that has gone before, they must be focused and specific, and they must relate to the most important aspects of the research. Any claims made should be evidenced, and any limitations in the claims made should be acknowledged.

Recommendations

Not all academic dissertations require you to make recommendations, but you should check with your institution. When making recommendations it is again important to stick to suggesting courses of action that are clearly derived from the preceding research. This is sometimes difficult, especially where the research has been undertaken in an organisation that the researcher knows well. There can be a tendency to conflate the tacit knowledge – the implicit understanding the researcher has about what will work and what won't work – and to make recommendations based on this. The recommendations presented must be suitable – they must be possible to carry out, feasible – there should be sufficient resources for them to be implemented, and they should be acceptable: they should fit with the implicit values that exist within the organisation (Johnson and Scholes, 1993).

References

Some institutions (although a decreasing number, nowadays) require the inclusion of two lists: namely, References and a Bibliography. Where this is the case, the materials used directly in advising the contents of the research report – that is, those specifically cited in the text – should appear in a Reference list. Other materials which have been used indirectly – that is, which provided background ideas – should be included in the Bibliography.

THE CONTENTS OF YOUR REPORT

Regardless of the structure of the business research report, there are a number of content issues that it is vital to get right. Using the car analogy alluded to earlier, it may be fine to stop at regular intervals to refuel, but if you fill the car up with orange juice, you are really not going to get very far. The contents of the report are the fuel – the information, the evidence and the arguments. It is the quality of the contents that drives people forward to continue reading the report.

A report is produced with a specific set of stakeholders in mind and should be tailored to their particular requirements. A report produced for an academic audience is unlikely to be appropriate as a consultancy report or as a report to managers. You must therefore understand what each of the stakeholders is looking for. Knowledge of what is likely to be required in the final report helps inform the research question, it helps frame the research methods that are used, and it can help determine what information is presented and how. If possible, you should ask the client, the manager sponsoring the research and your supervisor what kind of report they expect.

 CONSIDER...

If you are reading this section at the planning stage of your research (as suggested in Chapter 1), as soon as you have a project and a client in mind, think about what you and what your client would like to see in the final report. How do you think they would like it to be presented, how should it be structured, and what are likely to be the key contents?

As you move through the later stages of your research, revisit these questions to see how the data, the information and the evidence you have gathered helps you to refine your ideas.

WHAT ARE YOU TRYING TO COMMUNICATE?

Your over-arching and obvious aim is to convey your findings in a way that makes clear what you have found and why it is significant, thus altering your readers' understanding of an issue and/or influencing decisions and actions on it.

But an equally important aim is to meet your assessors' aims for the dissertation. A key part of what they will be looking for is evidence that you have developed the skills, knowledge and understanding expected of graduates from the programme in question.

Most Master's programmes intend their graduates to leave the programme:

- with a good understanding of the 'standard' management concepts, constructs and frameworks loosely referred to as 'theory'
- with the ability to draw upon this 'theory', as a starting point for making sense of a management-related issue

- with the ability to find additional 'theory' relevant to the issue and draw upon this and the 'taught' concepts in order to identify specific questions that will help address the chosen issue
- with sufficient understanding of ideas and their justifiable sources to do this selectively and judiciously
- with an appreciation of the role of evidence in informing management decisions
- with an understanding of how data can be usefully collected, and the ability to collect reliable and relevant data to help answer the question(s) posed
- with the ability to interpret data to convert it to evidence, and to construct compelling arguments from this evidence and draw conclusions that will inform decisions or actions to address the issue
- with the ability to present the evidence and arguments in a clear and attractive document, following appropriate referencing conventions (usually the Harvard one)
- with the ability to reflect upon the process while it is on-going, and retrospectively to learn from and modify thinking and/or behaviour in the light of this reflection.

> **A successful report is written to meet the needs and demands of the stakeholders.**

KEY FEATURES OF A REPORT

Having established what the stakeholders' requirements of the final report are, there are three key features vital to the success of all reports:

- credibility
- coherence
- clarity.

Credibility

The credibility of a report is demonstrated in the way in which information is presented, and there are a number of basic rules to help writers to ensure that they are presenting information which the audience will view as trustworthy:

- claims should be backed up by evidence. It is not sufficient for the writer to simply assert a point. In order to be able to judge the validity of the point, the audience must be able to see the supporting evidence
- opinions must be justified. Most, if not all, business research reports require that the author includes elements of his or her own opinion. Where opinions are expressed the reader must be confident that they are informed by the literature, the research methods or the research findings, and that the opinions drawn are justified within the context of them
- debates should be balanced. Although readers must see clear and unambiguous themes running through a business research report, it is also important that they see how the author has considered alternative perspectives. It is not sufficient to present a partisan or unilateral view of issues. Contradictory factors must be surfaced and an explanation given about why they are inappropriate or have been dismissed.

Reports should be based on trustworthy data, gathered through appropriate mechanisms. Data gathered through *bona fide* research methods is a good foundation for reports. Conversations undertaken with people in corridors (especially when they are unaware that what they say will be used in the report) or after the tape-recorder has been switched off may raise ethical issues as well as credibility issues.

Coherence

Saunders *et al* (2007) describe this as telling a clear story. To encourage people to believe and trust in the messages that the report is trying to communicate it is important to give people a clear sense of what the report sets out to achieve – to make connections between paragraphs that allow the reader to follow a logical path, and to present the information in such a way that it makes sense to the reader. The issue is encapsulated in a quote from my former supervisor, who once sighed and said 'You quite obviously know exactly how you have got from one paragraph to the next. However, as I am not a mind-reader, I am struggling somewhat.'

Clarity

The aim of a project report is to effectively communicate the research findings and the conclusions drawn from them to a specific audience. To achieve this aim, the report has to be written in such a way that it can be understood. Although this sounds obvious enough, there are ways of writing that can compromise the reader's ability to understand.

Once such way, for example, involves the use of colloquialisms. A colloquialism is a local (or national) turn of phrase that has a specific meaning rather different from its literal meaning.

RESEARCH STORY

Confusing colloquialisms

A well-known colloquialism in the UK when talking about heavy rain is 'coming down in stair-rods'. Many years ago when I was teaching a group of full-time MSc students, a student used this expression in a presentation he was giving. An overseas student asked what was meant by 'coming down in stair-rods' and the presenter explained that it meant 'raining heavily'. The overseas student then asked what stair-rods were, but the presenter (having been born after the time stair-rods had been mostly phased out) had no idea, and so had to find an older student to tell him what stair-rods were and explain it to the overseas student. To cut a very, very long story short, the presentation was interrupted for half an hour, and the conclusion to the issue was that the Greek colloquial equivalent of 'stair-rods' is 'chair legs'!

Colloquialisms obscure meaning. People may interpret them in their literal meaning which makes no sense within the context in which they are being used. The ability to communicate effectively to multicultural audiences is important, and is becoming increasingly so as we move into higher and higher levels of internationalisation, of culturally diverse workforces and of more and more businesses operating globally.

Jargon is also problematic. There is a professional language of management that will be looked at shortly. It uses terms and phrases which have specific meanings and these meanings are recognised by the professional management community. However, jargon is also used in parts of the business community. Expressions such as 'hit the ground running', 'pick the low-hanging fruit' and 'flexecutives' are all terms that have entered into various forms of communication. The use of them is unwise. Like colloquialisms, they are not easily understood by multicultural audiences. To many the meaning of 'pick the low-hanging fruit' is no more or less than you pick the fruit that is hanging lowest down. The question they would ask is 'What has this got to do with the management of organisational change?' Also, many of the terms are not even understood by people for whom English is their first language. To illustrate, I suggest that a good proportion of people reading this will not know what a 'flexecutive' is. Although many will offer an educated guess, that is not what the readers of a business report should be doing. The meaning should be absolutely apparent from a clear use of appropriate language.

RESEARCH STORY

Does anybody understand?

Just over 10 years ago I was teaching on a corporate MBA programme and the group were discussing the use of management jargon. The following is an example of how this can create problems in communicating effectively within an organisation.

A senior manager told of a board meeting of senior executives called to review the progress of an organisation-wide programme of change. After considerable discussion, the conclusion drawn by the board was that the programme ought to be 'ramped'. The message was passed to the meeting of the senior management team and after a long discussion they decided that the responsibility for 'ramping' the programme should be delegated to the middle managers. A meeting of these managers was

duly called and they were instructed to go back to their units and make sure that the programme was ramped. The middle managers went back and called together all their first-line managers, supervisors and team leaders and explained that the directive from the board was that the programme should be ramped. It was only at this stage that one of the supervisors had the courage to ask exactly what 'ramped' meant. Nobody knew. Guesses ranged from 'speeded up', through 'introduced more gradually' to 'given more support and therefore more resources'.

Despite the time it took to communicate this message down through the organisation, very little 'ramping' was actually done.

Incidentally, a 'flexecutive' is a female executive, so called because they are allegedly more able to multitask than their male executive counterparts!

Reports must be credible, coherent and clear.

THE PRESENTATION OF YOUR REPORT

The way a business report is presented communicates a certain impression to the audience. This impression begins with the cover of the report.

TITLE PAGE

In the following examples, the first cover is interesting because it may or may not put people off reading it. There is a title, but what it actually means and how it relates to the contents is unclear. However, the author's name is on the front and the general layout is reasonably smart. The main problem is the failure to say what this 'snappy' title actually means.

CONSIDER...

Look at the following four front covers for a business report.

What conclusions do you draw from your first impressions?

1

*Preparing for tomorrow
today*

A report by
ooo**OOO**ooo

Johnston X Johnston Junior

2

The Sky's
the Limit

3

**Staff Development in
ImproveMentCo.**

**Where we are, and
the way ahead**

A Report compiled by
Johnston X. Johnston Junior

For ImproveMentCo.

December 2009

4

**Consultancy Report which
investigates the current
status of staff development
in ImproveMentCo.,
looking at all levels of staff
and then making
suggestions about how staff
development can be
improved to ensure better
retention of staff**

By
Johnston X. Johnston Junior

The second cover is vague. The reader has no idea what it is about, by whom the report was written, or for whom. Although both words and image have been used, neither really communicates what the report is about.

The third cover quite evidently presents what one would take to be an acceptable report cover. It presents a title that is clearly related to the brief. It says for whom the report has been prepared, by whom, and when. People picking up this report are in no doubt about what they can expect inside.

The fourth cover is intended to make sure that readers know exactly what is in the report. Unfortunately, there is so much on the cover that there is almost no need for them to read the bits inside! The cover must communicate clear messages in a succinct manner.

It has been mentioned previously that the covers (or title page) for academic pieces of work are often required to conform to a particular layout style and format. They usually include a particular set of words that must be used for the course of study involved.

LAYOUT

Where there is a prescribed layout (margin sizes, line-spacing, font size, etc), the writer should stick to it. Where there is no prescribed layout, it is useful to find out what the general conventions are. For example, how are reports normally presented in the organisation, or what have previous consultancy reports looked like? The layout should also be consistent. The same margins, the same font size, the same hierarchy of headings and subheadings should be used all the way through the report. Page numbering is important because it allows people to refer to particular parts of the report much more easily.

Use a suitable font

Choose fonts and font sizes which are in keeping with the tenor of the report. If you are presenting a serious piece of business research, it is appropriate to conform to the use of standard fonts (Arial, Times New Roman, etc). It is also a good plan to use a font with which the audience is familiar – that way they will feel more comfortable with the manner in which the work is presented and can focus their attention on the content. If you are presenting a more 'creative' type of report, it may be preferable to use non-standard fonts to tie in the way the report looks with the ethos of the contents.

Colour and image

Care should be taken when using colour and images in formal reports. Colour can promote or demote the importance of the text. It can also simply distract the reader from the substance of the messages being conveyed. Images, too, can be difficult to incorporate successfully in formal reports. Images should be included in a report only for a specific purpose, not because they look pretty or to break up the text. Every image has to be relevant and reproduced in a way that is congruent with what the report is trying to achieve. Clip art should be used with extreme caution.

Consistency

The formatting, the layout, the use of US or UK spellings, and the use of particular terms must be consistent throughout the report. For example, switching between the words 'organisation', 'business' and/or 'company' creates confusion and makes it difficult for the reader to follow the arguments being made.

Grammar, spellcheck and proofread

It is remarkable that although computer systems now can run grammar and spell-check systems in next to no time at all, some people simply do not bother – even when six months' hard work on pulling together a coherent and persuasive set of research findings may be compromised by the sloppiness of the presentation. Proofreading is important. Many of the mistakes made do not show up on spellcheck systems.

RESEARCH ILLUSTRATION

Proving the need to proof read

To give you an indication of some of the problems, below is a little collection of the typographical errors that I have been presented with over the years:

What was written:

'*In order to make sense of my analysis I am going to writhe around my organisation*'

What should have been written:

'*In order to make sense of my analysis I am going to write around my organisation*'

What was written:

'*The change in management left staff feeling disemboweled*'

What should have been written:

'*The change in management left staff feeling disempowered*'

What was written:

'*Taylorism was created to put an end to soldering*'

What should have been written:

'*Taylorism was created to put an end to soldiering*'

> The final report should have an appropriate layout, and spelling, grammar and format should all be correct, should be consistent and should conform to the demands of the audience.

SUMMARY

If you are reading this chapter at the beginning of you research, you may not have thought specifically about what you want to achieve in communicating your research. Perhaps you see producing the report as being just a ritual requirement – something that just has to be done in the quickest way possible. If so, stop and think about the potential benefits from others' understanding your aims and progress, perhaps becoming more committed to the investigation or to implementing its recommendations, or helping you progress your own thinking.

Producing your project report is an opportunity for you to achieve a number of benefits. Your research findings and your recommendations may be of practical benefit to the organisation, or they may help you to improve the ways in which you do your own job. Your project report enables you to demonstrate your own personal skills and abilities in diagnosing and solving organisational problems and it allows you to show your competence in using research and investigative techniques. It can, however, only do all these things if what you produce is a credible, trustworthy and well-argued report.

To do this you have to think about the journey that you want to take your readers on. You have to map out the starting point, the end point and the key stages in between. Similarly, you have to know the sort of language that will communicate most easily to your audience, and the sorts of arguments they will find easy or harder to follow.

By thinking about what is important to your stakeholders you can tailor your key messages to them, but in doing so must ensure that these messages are still firmly grounded in the research findings that you have generated.

This notion of meeting the demands of the stakeholders is crucial. If you have different groups of stakeholders, do not try to produce one homogeneous report and hope that it will suffice for everyone. Often, it will meet the needs of no one. Be prepared to tailor your reports to the requirements of the stakeholders in order that you can better make sure that you achieve the outcomes that you want from your business research project.

REVIEW QUESTIONS

1. List five key points that make for effective communication.

2. What do you understand by the term 'plagiarism', and why is it crucial to avoid it?

3. What are the main sections of a report, and what should each contain?

4. A report should be credible, coherent and clear. What does this mean, and why are these issues important?

EXPLORE FURTHER

McMillan, K. and Wyers, J. (2007) *How to Write Dissertations and Project Reports*. Harlow: Pearson/Prentice Hall. Good tools and techniques for searching, reading and presenting information

Murray, R. (2002) *How to Write a Thesis*. Buckingham: Open University Press

Murray, R. and Moore, S. (2006) *The Handbook of Academic Writing: A fresh approach*. Buckingham: Open University Press. Rowena Murray has published numerous books related to producing robust academic writing, all of which are extremely useful. These books are really aimed at those studying for a higher degree, but many of the tools and techniques of which she speaks are useful at all levels and for practical business research

Wolcott, H. (2008) *Writing Up Qualitative Research*. Thousand Oaks, CA: Sage Publications. Written in an accessible style, this book helps the practical business researcher to make sense of and present qualitative data in a clear and meaningful way

 Visit www.cipd.co.uk/brm for web links, templates, activities and other useful resources relating to this chapter.

References/Bibliography

Ackoff, R. L. (1971) 'The art and science of mess management', *Interfaces*, Vol.11, No.1: 20–6, reprinted in Mabey, C. and Mayon-White, B. (eds) (1993) *Managing Change*, 2nd edition. London: Paul Chapman, in association with the Open University

Albert, S. and Whetten, D. A. (1985) 'Organizational identity' in Cummings, L. L. and Straw, B. M. (eds) *Research in Organizational Behaviour*. Greenwich, CT: JAI: 263–95

Allen, G. (2003) 'A critique of using Grounded Theory as a research method', *Electronic Journal of Business Research Methods*, Vol.2, Issue 1: 1–10. Available online from http://www.ejbrm.com [accessed 12 December 2008]

Armstrong, P. (2002) 'The politics of management science: an inaugural lecture', *International Journal of Management and Decision-Making*, Vol.3, No.1: 2–18

Asch, S. E. (1963) 'Effects of group pressure upon the modification and distortion of judgements', in Guetzkow, H. (ed.) *Groups, Leadership and Men*. New York: Russell & Russell: 177–90

Atkinson, P. and Hammersley, M. (1998) 'Ethnography and participant observation', in Denzin, N. K. and Lincoln, Y. S. (eds) *Handbook of Qualitative Research*. London: Sage

Avolio, B. J. (2005) *Leadership Development in Balance: Made/Born*. London: LEA

Baker, M. (2000) 'Writing a literature review', *Marketing Review*, Vol.1, No.2, Winter: 219–47

Baker, M. (2001) 'Selecting a research methodology', *Marketing Review*, Vol.1, No.3, Spring: 373–97

Barbour, R. S. and Kitzinger, J. (1999) *Developing Focus Groups: Politics, theory and practice*. London: Sage

Bee, F. and Bee, R. (2005) *Managing Information and Statistics*, 2nd edition. London: CIPD

Beer, M., Eisenstat, R. A. and Spector, B. (1990) 'Why change programmes don't produce change', *Harvard Business Review*, Vol.68, Issue 6: 158–66

Berelson, B. (1952) *Content Analysis in Communication Research*. New York: Free Press

Blaxter, L., Hughes, C. and Tight, M. (2001) *How to Research*, revised 2nd edition. Buckingham: Open University Press

Block, P. (2000) *Flawless Consulting*, 2nd edition. Chichester: John Wiley

Blutman, K. and Aitken, P. G. (2007) Excel 2007 Formulas and Functions for Dummies. Indianapolis, IN: Wiley

Boeije, H. (2002) 'A purposeful approach to the constant comparative method in the analysis of qualitative interviews', *Quality and Quantity*, Vol.36: 391–409

Bourne, L. and Walker, D. (2006) 'Visualising stakeholder influence – two Australian examples', *Project Management Journal*, Vol.37, No.1: 5–21

Boynton, P. (2004) 'Hands-on guide to questionnaire research. Selecting, designing, and developing your questionnaire', *British Medical Journal*, 5 June: 1372–5

Boynton, P. and Greenhalgh, T. (2004) 'Hands-on guide to questionnaire research. Selecting, designing, and developing your questionnaire', *British Medical Journal*, 29 May: 1312–15

Boynton, P., Wood, G. W. and Greenhalgh, T. (2004) 'Hands-on guide to questionnaire research. Selecting, designing, and developing your questionnaire', *British Medical Journal*, 12 June: 1433–6

British Educational Research Association (2004) *Revised Ethical Guidelines for Educational Research.* Available online from www.bera.ac.uk

British Journal of Management (2001) Vol.12, December, Supplement 1

British Psychological Society (2006) *Code of Ethics and Conduct.* http://www.bps.org.uk/downloadfile.cfm?file_uuid=5084a882-1143-dfd0-7e6c-f1938a65c242&ext=pdf

Bruner, J. (1960) *The Process of Education.* Cambridge, MA.: Harvard University Press

Bryman, A. (2001) *Social Research Methods.* Oxford: Oxford University Press

Bryman, A. and Bell, E. (2007) *Business Research Methods*, 2nd edition. Oxford: Oxford University Press

Bryson, J. M. (2003) 'What to do when stakeholders matter: a guide to stakeholder identification and analysis techniques'. Paper presented at the London School of Economics, 10 February 2003

Bryson, J. M., Ackermann, F., Eden, C. and Finn, C. B. (2004) *Visible Thinking.* Chichester: Wiley

Buchanan, D. A and Boddy, D. (1982) 'Advanced technology and the quality of working life: the effects of word processing on video typists', *Journal of Occupational Psychology*, Vol.55, No.1: 1–11

Buchanan, D. and Huczynski, A. (2004) *Organizational Behaviour. An Introductory Text*, 5th edition. Harlow: FT/Prentice Hall

Buchanan, D. A, Boddy, D. and McCalman, J. (1988) 'Getting in, getting on, getting out and getting back', in Bryman, A. (ed.) *Doing Research in Organisations.* London: Routledge

Burns, R. B. and Burns, R. A. (2009) *Business Research Methods and Statistics Using SPSS.* London: Sage

Cameron, S. (2008) *The MBA Handbook*, 6th edition. Harlow: FT/Prentice Hall

Camillus, J. C. (2008) 'Strategy as a wicked problem', *Harvard Business Review*, Vol.28, Issue 5: 98–106

Chad, P. (2001) 'Case research in marketing', *Marketing Review*, Spring: 303–23

Checkland, P. (1981) *Systems Thinking, Systems Practice.* Chichester: John Wiley & Sons

Chryssides, G. and Kaler, J. (1999) *An Introduction to Business Ethics.* London: Thomson Business Press

Churchman, C. W. (1971) *The Design of Inquiring Systems.* New York: John Wiley

Clarkburne, H. and Freeman, M. (2008) 'To plagiarise or not to plagiarise: an online approach to improving honest academic writing', *International Journal of Management Education*, Vol.6, No.3: 21–33

Coghlan, D. (2001) 'Insider Action Research projects: implications for practicing managers', *Management Learning*, Vol.32, No.1: 49–60

Coghlan, D. and Brannick, T. (2001) *Doing Action Research in Your Own Organization*. London: Sage

Cook, S. D. N. and Seely Brown, J. (1999) 'Bridging epistemologies: the generative dance between organizational knowledge and organizational knowing', *Organization Science*, Vol.10, No.4: 381–400

Cooperrider, D. I. and Srivastva, S. (1987) 'Appreciative Inquiry in organisational life', in Pasmore, W. A. and Woodman, R. W. (eds) *Research in Organizational Change and Development* (Vol.1). Greenwich, CT: JAI

Cope, M. (2003) *The Seven Cs of Consulting*, 2nd edition. London: FT/Prentice Hall

Cresswell, J. W. (2007) *Qualitative Inquiry and Research Design: Choosing among five approaches*. Thousand Oaks, CA: Sage Publications

Crotty, M. (1998) *The Foundations of Social Research: Meaning and perspective in the research process*. London: Sage

Daft, R. (2006) *The New Era of Management*, International edition. Mason, OH: Thomson-South Western

Delamont, S. (2004) 'Ethnography and participant observation', in Seale, C., Gobo, G., Gubrium, J. and Silverman, D. (eds) *Qualitative Research Practice*. London: Sage

Deming, W. E. (1960, reprinted 1990) *Sample Design in Business Research*. London: John Wiley

Denzin, N. and Lincoln, Y. (1998) *Strategies of Qualitative Inquiry*. Thousand Oaks, CA: Sage Publications

Denzin, N. A and Lincoln, Y. S. (2000) *Handbook of Qualitative Research*, 2nd edition. Thousand Oaks, CA: Sage Publications

Dewey, J. (1910) *How We Think*. Lexington, MA: DC Heath

Dewey, J. (ed. Boydston, J. A., 1916/1985) *Democracy and Education: the middle works of John Dewey*: Vol.9. Carbondale and Edwardsville: Southern Illinois University Press

Dey, I. (2004) 'Grounded Theory', in Seale, C., Gobo, G., Gubrium, J. and Silverman, D. (eds) *Qualitative Research Practice*. London: Sage: 81–93

Dillman, D. A. (2000) *Mail and Internet Surveys: The tailored design method*, 2nd edition. New York: Wiley

Dixon-Woods, M., Agarwal, S., Jones, D., Young, B. and Sutton, A. (2005) 'Synthesising qualitative and quantitative evidence: a review of possible methods', *Journal of Health Services Research and Policy*, Vol.10, No.1: 45–53

Easterby-Smith, M., Thorpe, R. and Lowe, A. (1991) *Management Research: An introduction*. London: Sage

Eisenhardt, K. M. (1989) 'Building theories from case study research', *Academy of Management Review*, Vol.14, No.4: 532–50

Ellam-Dyson, V. and Palmer, C. (2008) 'The challenges of researching executive coaching', *The Coaching Psychologist*, Vol.4, No.2: 79–84

Elliot, J. (1991) *Action Research for Educational Change*. Buckingham: Open University Press

ESRC (2009) *Research Ethics Framework*. Available online at http://www.esrc.ac.uk/ESRCInfoCentre/Images/ESRC_Re_Ethics_Frame_tcm6-11291.pdf

Fern, E. F. (2001) *Advanced Focus Group Research*. Thousand Oaks, CA: Sage Publications

Fontana, T. H. and Frey, J. H. (1996) 'Interviewing – the art of science', in Denzin, N. K. and Lincoln, Y. S. (eds) *Handbook of Qualitative Research*, 6th edition. London: Sage

Fook, J. (2002) 'Theorising from practice: towards an inclusive approach for social work research', *Qualitative Social Work*, Vol.1, No.1: 79–95

French, J. R. and Raven, B. (1959) 'The bases of social power', in Cartwright, D. (ed.) *Studies in Social Power*. Ann Arbor, MI: University of Michigan Press: 150–67

Gibbs, G. R. (2002) *Qualitative Data Analysis: Explorations with NVivo*. Buckingham: Open University Press

Giske, T. and Artinian, B. (2007) 'A personal experience of working with classical Grounded Theory. From beginner to experienced Grounded Theorist', *International Journal of Qualitative Methods*, Vol.6, No.4: 67–80

Glaser, B. G. (1998) *Doing Grounded Theory: Issues and discussions*. Mill Valley, CA: Sociology Press

Glaser, B. and Strauss, A. (1967) *The Discovery of Grounded Theory: Strategies for qualitative research*. New York: Aldine De Gruyter

Goleman, D. (1999) *Working with Emotional Intelligence*. London: Bloomsbury

Goodwin, J. and O'Connor, H. (2009) 'Contextualising the research process: using interviewer notes in the secondary analysis of qualitative data', *The Qualitative Report*, Vol.11, No.3: 374–93. Available online at http://www.nova.edu.ssss/QR/QR11-2/goodwin.pdf [accessed 9 May 2009]

Gordon, S. (2008) 'Appreciative inquiry coaching', *International Coaching Psychology Review*, Vol.3, No.1: 19–31

Gregory, I. (2003) *Ethics in Research*. London: Continuum International Publishing Group

Hammersley, M. (1996) 'The relationship between qualitative and quantitative research: paradigm loyalty versus methodological eclecticism', in Richardson, J. T. E. (ed.) *Handbook of Research Methods for Psychology and the Social Sciences*. Leicester: BPS Books

Hammersley, M. (2004) 'Teaching qualitative method: craft, profession or bricolage?', in Seale, C., Gobo, G., Gubrium, J. and Silverman, D. (2007) *Qualitative Research Practice*, 2nd edition. London: Sage: 549–60

Hart, C. (2003) *Doing a Literature Review: Releasing the social science imagination*. London: Sage

Hartley, J. (2006) 'Case study research', in Cassell, C. and Symmons, G. (eds) *Essential Guide to Qualitative Methods in Organizational Research*. London: Sage: 323–33

Hassard, J. and Cox, J. W. (1995) 'Triangulation in organizational research: a re-presentation', *Organization*, Vol.21, No.1: 109–33

Heaton, J. (2008) 'Secondary analysis of qualitative data', in Alasuutari, P., Bickman, L. and Brannen, J. (eds) *The Handbook of Social Research Methods*. London: Sage

Herzberg, F. (1966) *Work and the Nature of Man*. Cleveland, OH: World Publishing

Hinds, P. S, Vogel, R. J. and Clarke-Steffen, L. (1997) 'The possibilities and pitfalls of doing a secondary analysis of a qualitative data set', *Qualitative Health Research*, Vol.7, No.3: 408–24

Hodgkinson, G. P., Herriot, P. and Anderson, N. (2001) 'Re-aligning the stakeholders in management research: lessons from industrial, work and organizational psychology', *British Journal of Management*, Vol.12, Special Issue: 41–8

Holsti, O. R. (1969) *Content Analysis for the Social Sciences and Humanities*. Reading, MA: Addison-Wesley

Israel, M. and Hay, I. (2006) *Research Ethics for Social Scientists*. London: Sage

Jankowicz, A. D. (1995) *Business Research Projects*. London: Chapman & Hall

Johnson, A. P. (2007) *A Short Guide to Action Research*, 3rd edition. Boston, MA: Allyn & Bacon

Johnson, G. and Scholes, K. (1993) *Exploring Corporate Strategy*, 3rd edition. Hemel Hempstead: Prentice Hall

Kipling, R. (1902) *Just So Stories*. Full text available online from http://www.boop.org/ jan/ justso/

Kitzinger, J. (1994) 'The methodology of focus groups: the importance of interaction between the research participants', *Sociology of Health and Illness*, Vol.16, No.1: 103–21

Knopf, J. W. (2006) 'Doing a literature review', *Political Science and Politics*, Vol.39: 127–32

Kolb, D. (1976) 'Management and the learning process', *California Management Journal*, Vol.18, No.3: 21–31

Kolb, D. (1984) *Experiential Learning*. Englewood Cliffs, NJ: Prentice Hall

Kosnick, L.-R. D. (2008) 'Refusing to budge: a confirmatory bias in decision-making?', *Mind and Society*, Vol.7, No.2: 193–214

Kotter, J. (1990) *A Force for Change: How leadership differs from management*. New York: Free Press

Krippendorff, K. and Block, M. A. (2008) *The Content Analysis Reader*. Thousand Oaks, CA: Sage Publications

Kumar, R. (1999) *Research Methodology: A step-by-step guide for beginners*. London: Sage

Kvale, S.and Brinkmann, S. (2009) *InterViews: Learning the craft of qualitative research interviewing*, 2nd edition. Thousand Oaks, CA: Sage Publications

Ladkin, D. (2007) 'Action Research', in Seale, S., Gobo, G, Gubrium, J. F. and Silverman, D (eds) *Qualitative Research Practice*. London: Sage: 478–89

Länsisalmi, H., Peiró, J. and Kivimäki, M. (2004) 'Grounded Theory in organizational research', in Cassell, C. and Symon, G. (eds) *The Essential Guide to Qualitative Methods in Organisational Research*. London: Sage; pp242–55

Leung, Wai-Ching (2001) 'How to design a questionnaire', *Student British Medical Journal*, No.9: 171–216. Available online at http:student.bmj.com/issues/ 01/06/education/187.php [accessed 22 February 2009]

Levin-Rozalis, M. (2004) 'Searching for the unknowable: a process of detection – abductive research generated by projective techniques', *International Journal of Qualitative Methods*, Vol.3, No.2, Article 1. Available online from http://www.ualberta.ca/~iiqm/ backissues/3_2/pdf/rozalis.pdf [accessed 7 April 2009]

Lewin, K. (ed. G. W. Lewin, 1948) *Resolving Social Conflicts: Selected papers on group dynamics*. New York: Harper & Row

Lewin, K. (ed. D. Cartwright, 1951) *Field Theory in Social Science: Selected theoretical papers.* New York: Harper & Row

Lewin, K. (ed. G. W. Lewin and G. Allport, 1957) 'Action Research and minority problems', in *Resolving social conflicts. Selected problems in group dynamics.* New York: Harper & Brothers

Locke, K. (2001) *Grounded Theory in Management Research.* London: Sage

Lucas, J. R. (2006) 'The tree in the lonely quad', available online at http://users.ox.ac.uk/~jrlucas/reasreal/treechap.pdf

Malhotra, N. K. and Birks, D. F. (2000) *Marketing Research: An applied approach.* Harlow: FT/Prentice Hall

Marrow, A. J. (1969) *The Practical Theorist.* New York: Basic Books

Marshall, C. and Rossman, G. (2006) *Designing Qualitative Research*, 4th edition. London: Sage

Mason, R. O. and Mitroff, I. I. (1981) *Challenging Strategic Planning Assumptions.* New York: John Wiley

Maylor, H. and Blackmon. K. (2005) *Researching Business and Management.* Basingstoke: Palgrave Macmillan

McCallin, A. M. (2003) 'Designing a Grounded Theory study: some practicalities', *Nursing in Critical Care*, Vol.8, No.5: 203–8

McMillan, K. and Weyers, J. (2007) *How to Write Dissertations and Project Reports.* Harlow: Pearson Prentice Hall

McNiff, J., Whitehead, J. and Lomax, P. (2003) *You and Your Action Research Project.* London: Routledge

Meredith, J. and Mantel, S. (2001) *Project Management: A managerial approach*, 4th edition. London: John Wiley & Sons

Metcalf, M. (undated but post-2006) 'Pragmatic inquiry', available online at http://unisa.edu.au/irg/papers/PRAGMATIC%20INQUIRY%20fin.doc [accessed 8 April 2009]

Miettinen, R. (2000) 'The concept of experiential learning and John Dewey's theory of reflective thought and action', *International Journal of Lifelong Education*, Vol.19, No.1: 54–72. Also available online at http://pdfserve.informaworld.com/ 598596 _ 713815823. pdf

Miles, M. B. (1979) 'Qualitative data as an attractive nuisance: the problem of analysis', *Administrative Science Quarterly*, Vol.24, No.4: 590–601

Miles, M. B. and Huberman, A. M. (1994) *Qualitative Data Analysis: An expanded sourcebook.* Thousand Oaks, CA: Sage Publications

Mitroff, I. I. and Linstone, H. A. (1993) *The Unbounded Mind: Breaking the chains of traditional business thinking.* Oxford: Oxford University Press

Moon, J. A (1999, reprinted 2005) *Reflections in Learning and Professional Development.* London: Routledge

Morgan, D. L. (1998) 'Practical strategies for combining qualitative and quantitative methods: applications for health research', *Qualitative Health Research*, No.8: 362–76

Morris, C. (2008) *Quantitative Approaches in Business Studies*, 7th edition. Harlow: FT/Prentice Hall

Murray, R. (2002) *How to Write a Thesis*. Buckingham: Open University Press

Murray, R. and Moore, S. (2006) *The Handbook of Academic Writing: A fresh approach.* Buckingham: Open University Press

Neuendorf, K. A. (2002) *The Content Analysis Guidebook*. Thousand Oaks, CA: Sage Publications

Pajares, F. (2007) 'The elements of a proposal', available online from http://www.des.emory.edu/mfp/proposal.html [accessed 12 February 2009]

Peirce, C. S. (1878) 'How to make our ideas clear', *Popular Science Monthly*, Vol.12: 286–302

Peirce, C. S. (1955) 'Abduction and induction', in Buchler, J. (ed.) *The Philosophical Writing of Peirce*. New York: Dover Publications: 150–6

Peterson, E. R. and Barron, K. A. (2007) 'How to get focus groups talking: new ideas that will stick', *International Journal of Qualitative Methods*, Vol.6, No.3: 140–3

Polonsky, M. and Waller, D. (2005) *Designing and Managing a Research Project: A business student's guide*. Thousand Oaks, CA: Sage Publications

Porath, C. L. and Erez, A. (2007) 'Does rudeness really matter? The effects of rudeness on task performance and helpfulness', *Academy of Management Journal*, Vol.50, No.5: 1182–98

Price, D. (2006) 'A bi-paradigmatic analysis of organisational culture'. Unpublished Doctoral thesis. University of Leicester

Reason, P. and Bradbury, H. (eds) (2001) *Handbook of Action Research: Participative inquiry and practice*. London: Sage

Reason, P. and McArdle, K. (undated) *Brief Notes on the Theory and Practice of Action Research*. Available online from http://people.bath.ac.uk/mnspwr/Papers/BriefNotesAR.htm [accessed 29 September 2008]

Reed, J. (2007) *Appreciative Inquiry*. London: Sage

Rigby, C.and Dulewicz, V. (2007) 'The role of reflection in leadership development: is there a link between improved reflective practice and improved leadership?' Henley Working Papers

Rittel, H. and Webber, M. (1973) 'Dilemmas in a general theory of planning', *Policy Sciences*, Vol.4: 155–69, reprinted in Cross, N. (ed.)(1984) *Developments in Design Methodology*. Chichester: Wiley

Robson, C. (2002) *Real World Research*, 2nd edition. Oxford: Blackwell

Rodon, J. and Pastor, A. (2007) 'Applying Grounded Theory to study the implementation of an inter-organisational information system', *The Electronic Journal of Business Research Methods*, Vol.5, No.2: 71–82. Available online at www.ejbrm.com

Saris, W. E. and Gallhofer, I. N. (2007) *Design, Evaluation and Analysis of Questionnaires for Survey Research*. Oxford: Wiley

Saunders, M., Lewis, P. and Thornhill, A. (2007) *Research Methods for Business Students*, 4th edition. Harlow: FT/Prentice Hall

Schön, D. (1983) *The Reflective Practitioner. How professionals think in action*. London: Temple Smith

Seale, C., Gobo, G., Gubrium, J. and Silverman, D. (2007) *Qualitative Research Practice*, 2nd edition. London: Sage

Seligman, M. (1991) *Learned Optimism*. New York: Alfred Knopf

Sharpe, J., Peters, J. and Howard, K. (2002) *The Management of a Student Research Project*, 3rd edition. Aldershot: Gower

Silverman, D. (1985) cited by Buchanan, D., Boddy, D. and McCalman, J. (1988) 'Getting in, getting on, getting out and getting back', in Bryman, A. (ed.) *Doing Research in Organisations*. London: Routledge

Silverman, D. (2007) *A Very Short, Fairly Interesting and Reasonably Cheap Book About Qualitative Research*. London: Sage

Slack, N., Chambers, S., Harland, C., Harrison, A. and Johnston, R. (1998) *Operations Management*. Harlow: Prentice Hall

Smith. M. (2001) at http://www.infed.org/thinkers/et-lewin.htm

Sokal, A. D. (1996) 'Transgressing the boundaries: towards a transformative hermeneutics of quantum gravity', *Social Text*, Spring/Summer: 217–52

Soy, S. (1997) *The Case Study as a Research Method*. Available online from http://www.gslis.utexas.edu/~ssoy/usesusers/1391d1b.htm [accessed 30 June 2003]

Stake, R. (1998) 'Case studies' in Denzin, N. and Lincoln, Y. (eds) *Strategies of Qualitative Inquiry*. Thousand Oaks, CA: Sage Publications: 86–109

Starkey, K. and Madan, P. (2001) 'Bridging the relevance gap: aligning stakeholders in the future of management research', *British Journal of Management*, Vol.12, Special Issue: 3–26

Stewart, D. W. and Kamins, M. A. (1993) *Secondary Research: Information Sources and Methods*, 2nd edition. Newbury Park, CA: Sage Publications

Stewart, R. (1982) 'A model for understanding managerial jobs and behaviour', *Academy of Management Review*, Vol.7, No.1: 7–13

Strauss, A. L. and Corbin, J. (1990) *Basics of Qualitative Research: Grounded Theory procedures and techniques*. Thousand Oaks, CA: Sage Publications

Stringer, E. T. (2007) *Action Research: A handbook for practitioners*, 3rd edition. Newbury Park, CA: Sage Publications

Suchman, E. A. (1967) *Evaluative Research Principles in Public Service and Action Programs*. New York: Russell Sage Foundation

Suddaby, R. (2006) 'From the editors: what Grounded Theory is not', *Academy of Management Journal*, Vol.49, No.4: 633–42

Teddlie, C. and Tashakkori, A. (2009) *Foundations of Mixed Method Research: Integrating quantitative and qualitative approaches in the social and behavioral science*s. Thousand Oaks, CA: Sage Publications

Tellis, W. (1997a) 'Introduction to case study', *The Qualitative Report*, Vol.3, No.2, July. Available online at http://www.nova.edu/ssss/QR/QR3-2/tellis1.html [accessed 20 March 2009]

Tellis, W. (1997b) 'Application of a case study methodology', *The Qualitative Report*, Vol.3, No.3, September. Available online at http://www.nova.edu/ssss/ QR/QR3-3/tellis2.html [accessed 20 March 2009]

Tesch, R. (1990) *Qualitative Research. Analysis types and software.* London: Falmer Press

Thorpe, R. and Moscarola, J. (1991) 'Detecting your research strategy', *Management Education and Development*, Vol.22, No.2: 127–33

Wallace, M. and Wray, A. (2006) *Critical Reading and Writing for Postgraduates.* London: Sage

Warfield, J. N., Geschka, H. and Hamilton, R. (1975) *Methods of Idea Management.* Columbus, OH: The Academy for Contemporary Problems

Wattenberg, M. and Viégas, F. B. (2008) 'Emerging graphic tool gets people talking', *Harvard Business Review*, Vol.28, Issue 5: 30–2

Webb, J. (2000) 'Questionnaires and their design', *Marketing Review*, Vol.1, No.2, Winter: 197–218

Weick, K. E. (1995) *Sensemaking* in Organizations. Thousand Oaks, CA: Sage Publications

Weick, K. E. (2001) 'Gapping the relevance bridge: fashions meet fundamentals in management research', *British Journal of Management*, Vol.12, Supplement 1: 71–5

Weick, K. E., Sutcliffe, K. M. and Obstfeld, D. (2005) 'Organizing and the process of sense-making', *Organization Science*, Vol.16, No.4: 409–21

Wenger, E. (1998) *Communities of Practice. Learning, meaning and identity.* New York: Cambridge University Press

Wittgenstein, L. (1997) *Philosophical Investigations.* Padstow, Cornwall: Blackwell

Woike, B. (2007) 'Content coding of open-ended responses', in Robins, R. W., Fraley, R. C. and Kreuger, R. F. (eds) *Handbook of Research Methods in Personality Psychology.* New York: Guildford Press: 292–307

Wolcott, H. (2008) *Writing Up Qualitative Research.* Thousand Oaks, CA: Sage Publications

Yin, R. (1981) 'The case study crisis: some answers', *Administrative Science Quarterly*, Vol.26, March: 58–65

Yin, R. (1994) *Case Study Research. Design and methods,* 2nd edition. Thousand Oaks, CA: Sage Publications

For websites defined not by author but by URL, see lists at the end of individual chapters or visit www.cipd.co.uk/brm

Index